Digital Marketing Fundamentals

Marjolein Visser RM

Berend Sikkenga SMP

Mike Berry

First edition

Noordhoff Uitgevers Groningen/Utrecht

Any comments about this publication or others may be addressed to: Noordhoff Uitgevers bv, Afdeling Hoger Onderwijs, Antwoordnummer 13,9700 VB Groningen, or through 'contact' at www.mijnnoordhoff.nl.

In spite of strenuous attempts it has proved impossible to trace all those who possess copyrights to some of the texts and/or illustrations. Anyone who believes that s/he possesses such copyrights is requested to contact the publisher.

The greatest care has been taken in the realisation of this publication. Author(s), editors nor publisher can be held liable in case any information has been published incompletely or incorrectly. They shall be pleased to receive any adjustments to the contents

0 / 18

ISBN 978-90-01-88712-4
NUR 802

Printed in Canada

Preface

In 2010, when Marjolein Visser and Berend Sikkenga first asked each other whether it wasn't time to write a book about digital marketing that covered the whole marketing process, we could not foresee that this adventure would be such a success. Since then, tens of thousands marketers have read the book and used the basic principles that we then formulated. And we did not anticipate that the success of our book would lead to this international (English language) edition in collaboration with Mike Berry. Mike is an expert in the field of digital marketing with extensive international experience and his valuable input opens the book up to a wider audience. We welcome Mike to the team.

The simple question for a book that covers digital marketing as a whole, has led to an intensive process thatwe have adopted over 8 years and 3 editions. How to create a book that is founded on the core principles of marketing, a solid scientific basis, but also shows the reader how to approach digital marketing in 'real-world' practice? We decided to ask leading specialists in aspects of online marketing to write the book with us. So far, some forty top professionals have contributed to the book. We have consistently followed a process in which for each subject the scientific findings are compared with the experiential knowledge of specialists. This leads to an up-to-date theoretical framework that is directly linked to methods and instruments that have proven their worth in practice. The scientific basis has been strengthened still further over the years. The result turns out to fit well in with the frame of reference of both marketing professionals and academics and lecturers. An even greater compliment is that students experience the book as helpful, easily readable and inspiring. They also appreciate the many examples.

We are very pleased with the contributions of all digital marketing specialists who have contributed to this publication. In addition we thank everyone who has provided us with examples and cases and of course the co-authors of the earlier editions. Without them this book would never have existed. We would like to specially place Tony Williams in the spotlight. It is great to have someone on the team who is not only an excellent translator, but also perfectly at home in the world of digital marketing. In the personal sphere we thank Maureen, Linde, Douwe and Jane: we are grateful for their understanding for all those hours that we spent behind our computer instead of with the people we love. Jasper and Maarten we thank for their supporting work. And, of course, a word of appreciation for our Publisher Bert Deen for his involvement and trust.

We hope to meet all readers soon in the groups for this Book:

- digitalmarketing.noordhoff.nl: the official website including test questions, trainer concepts and PowerPoints
- LinkedIn Lecturers Digital Marketing Fundamentals (linkedin.com/ groups/13568788/): for tips, current events, research results and discussion
- Digital Marketing Fundamentals on Facebook (www.facebook.com/ groups/digital.marketing.fundamentals.book): for recent examples, new insights and information exchange
- Pinterest: for each chapter there is a folder with infographics, statistics and videos (www.pinterest.com/Marjolein Visser)

For educators there is a special Dropbox folder available with additional study material. You can ask access via LinkedIn or Marjolein Visser: info@market-wise.nl.

Marjolein Visser, Berend Sikkenga and Mike Berry

© Noordhoff Uitgevers bv

Contents

© Noordhoff Uitgevers bv

© Noordhoff Uitgevers bv

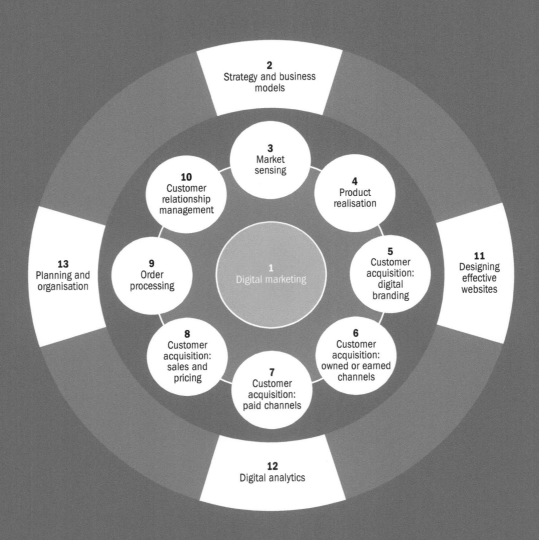

1

Digital Marketing

Author: Marjolein Visser

Over the past decades the framework of marketing has changed dramatically. Internet use has become part of the daily routine for most people. It has radically transformed the behaviour of consumers and business buyers. Knowledge of online consumer behaviour and Digital Marketing are vital to marketers. The modern marketer not only needs to know how Digital Marketing communication works; but also how he or she can make use of the Internet for the purpose of product realisation, market research or distribution. This first chapter will explain what Digital Marketing involves and which basic principles are adhered to in this book. The following chapters will describe the involvement of Digital Marketing within all of the other marketing related business processes. The last chapters of this book describe overarching subjects such as effective websites, digital/web analytics and the planning and organisation of the Digital Marketing process.

After reading this chapter you will be able to:
- explain what Digital Marketing involves
- identify the differences between traditional marketing and Digital Marketing
- name and recognise 'the seven types of websites'
- denote the relationship between the four Ps and the four Cs
- describe the five Digital Marketing-related core business processes

1.1 Definition of Digital Marketing

Kotler and Armstrong (2013) define marketing as follows: 'Marketing is the process by which companies create value for customers and build strong customer relationships in order to capture value from customers in return.' Peter Drucker (1973), a famous management guru, defined the purpose of marketing as follows: 'The aim of marketing is to know and understand the customer so well that the product or service fits him and sells itself'.

According to Kotler, marketing is an integrated process that companies use to create value for customers and to build strong customer relationships in return for a reciprocation of value from their customers. In many instances, products or services are traded for money, but alternative exchanges are also possible. For example, political parties that trade ideological representation of interests for votes or brands that trade interesting/ valuable content for the user's time and attention.

The Internet plays an ever-increasing role within the marketing process. Digital Marketing is a sub-process of marketing. Therefore, we can define Digital Marketing as a process in which organisations and existing or potential customers use the Internet to create value and products as well as interchange them. In this respect we do not discriminate between the various ways that the Internet is accessed and the device on which the Internet is viewed. Whether a computer or a smartphone is used is of importance to the applied technological methods, but not to the marketing principles. Internet marketing, online marketing and e-marketing are all synonyms for Digital Marketing. In this book, we will use 'Digital Marketing'.

Ecommerce

One frequently asked question remains: what is the difference between Digital Marketing, ecommerce and ebusiness? ecommerce refers to selling products or services over the Internet. Customers can complete transactions or submit changes using a website. This book considers ecommerce to be one of the possible options within Digital Marketing. Many organisations do approach their customers over the Internet, but don't sell their products online. In this case it is a question of Digital Marketing communication, an element of Digital Marketing, but not of ecommerce.

Ebusiness

The authors of this book see ebusiness as a way of doing business with the assistance of digital technologies. Ebusiness is a wider concept than Digital Marketing and ecommerce. In ebusiness it's not only about the interaction with markets, but about adequately establishing all of the processes that enable an organisation to make their products or provide their services. It's about the front and the back of the organisation, the parts the customer does not come into contact with (see figure 1.1). Ecommerce is simply defined as 'selling and buying online'.

FIGURE 1.1 Ebusiness encompasses digital processes throughout the entire organisation and is more inclusive than Digital Marketing

1.2 Digital Marketing versus traditional marketing

Digital Marketing is becoming increasingly important. According to research conducted by consultancy firm Deloitte, marketing managers expect to spend two thirds of their media budget online by 2020 (Deloitte, 2017).

As a result of the growing number of possibilities regarding digitalisation and interactivity that the Internet facilitates, a number of marketers' dreams have become reality. When used wisely, the Internet makes marketing more effective: marketing objectives can be met with less effort. Consider the following possibilities:
- Thanks to the Internet, the customer's demands for information are more easily and simply met.
- The Internet allows for the provision of tailor-made information.
- The Internet offers the possibility of gathering large quantities of data about potential customers.
- The effects of marketing communications on the Internet can (in most cases) be easily measured
- A high level of interactivity with customers is possible.

Also, Digital Marketing can be more efficient than traditional marketing. For example:
- It is possible to share large quantities of information with potential customers at low cost.
- The marketing budget can be more purposefully assigned due to the fact that the effects of marketing communications are (in general) more easily measurable.

The Internet has accelerated the transition from mass marketing to one-to-one marketing or individual marketing. The aim of individual marketing is to fully tailor products or marketing efforts to the individual customer.

One-to-one marketing

Individual

Because the Internet allows for the customer's individual data to be saved, communications has become increasingly 'personalised'. The profile of the individual customer is recognised; thus, they receive a 'personalised offer', an individual proposition. That way a travel agency can offer a customer, who is recognised in their database as someone who likes to take his/her children to a theme park, a last-minute deal for Disneyland Paris. Simultaneously, an older couple that enjoy walking are offered a peaceful holiday in the Austrian Alps.

Individual proposition

The Internet makes individualised production easier. On the Internet, you can design T-shirts or greetings cards with a personalised image on them, You can even design your own brooch and have it printed in 3D. Digitised services mean users can seek advice or information at any time: even in the middle of the night you can ask your bank for a statement or pay a bill; the Internet and world wide web are 'always-on' 24/7. Individualised distribution of ordered goods or services is relatively cheap and often highly effective via the Internet. When you book a flight online for instance, you can either print your ticket yourself or access it on your smartphone via the airline's own app. A package from Amazon.com is delivered to your doorstep the following day; you don't have to go to the store for it; moreover, you get helpful messages regarding the status of your order.

Individualised production

The website is at the centre of Digital Marketing. Websites can be classified as follows:

Corporate sites

- *Corporate sites* are aimed at supporting interaction between the organisation and the various stakeholders, like customers, employees, press and shareholders.

Ecommerce sites

Selling sites

- *Ecommerce sites* are online stores or selling sites where products can be viewed and ordered; famous examples are Amazon.com, eBay and Taobao (Alibaba). Ecommerce sites can also be procurement sites of a company or sector, where the purpose is seeking/accepting offers, ie buying, not selling.

Communication sites

- *Communication sites* inform their visitors more about the products or services of the supplier. Besides product descriptions these sites also include functional elements such as lists of stores where the product can be purchased (or 'store finder' tools) and user manuals. An example of this type of site is https://www.apple.com/uk/iphone-x/.

Lead generation sites

- In some cases (especially for Business-to-Business ie B2B marketing) this type of website has the specific purpose of reaching out to potential customers. These are called *lead generation sites*.

Branding sites

- *Branding sites* have the aim to improve brand knowledge and brand perception. These sites are usually very interactive and contain recreational elements such as forums or games intended to make the visitor come back more often. For example, Heineken.com.

Service sites

- *Service sites* not only provide information but are also involved in the production process of the organisation. For instance; online banking, and online newspapers. In these cases the content and functionality is the product.

Portals

- *Portals* present an overview of websites for specific target groups or for particular subjects. In web history, brands like AOL, Yahoo! and msn were early examples.

Content sites

- *Content sites* or publishing sites provide their visitors with information. This could be news, but also other kinds of information that would be interesting for a specific target group or in a specific situation, eg reviews. Consider sites such as huffingtonpost.com or tripadvisor.com

5S-model Chaffey

In his 5S-model Chaffey (2015) states five objectives for Digital Marketing communications activity:

- Sell; increasing sales by accessing new markets or by developing new (online) products.
- Speak; initiatives for better communications with (potential) customers.
- Serve; improving customer service.
- Save; cost reduction through the use of digital media.
- Sizzle; initiatives to support the brand.

1.3 Digital Marketing and the Marketing Mix

Marketing Mix

The 'Marketing Mix' is one of the most frequently used concepts from marketing theory. Originally it represents a sort of formula for marketing activities. The idea is that the marketer should be a kind of chef, mixing the four elements together in order to achieve an offer that caters optimally to the taste of the target audience; a product that aligns with their needs and desires, a price they are willing to pay for that product, a place where they can buy or reserve the product and promotion to stimulate the sales of the

© Noordhoff Uitgevers bv

product. Another analogy is that of the marketer as the 'conductor of the orchestra', bringing in each instrument at the appropriate time and at the appropriate volume. Later, the Marketing Mix's element 'place' gained a broader definition. It's not only about the question of where the customer can buy the product (distribution), but also about the answer to the question of how the product will eventually end up in the consumer's hands.

Today, almost every organisation uses the Internet for customer communications. This could simply be a way of providing information (replacing traditional brochures), but also advertising (online display advertising for example) or sales. The Internet can contribute towards each of the marketing instruments: product, place, price and promotion (the four Ps).

Four Ps

Examples of websites as a **product** are auction sites (eg eBay) and dating sites (eg Tinder, Grindr). Websites as distribution channels (**place**) are those of for example music publishers or publishers of scientific publications. After payment you can download the desired song or article. Airlines are a good example of how the Internet can be deployed as part of the marketing instrument '**price**'.

It is remarkable how the different marketing instruments seem to merge on the Internet and particularly in the case of information-based service businesses and publishers. Banks are a clear example of this: online banking is undeniably part of the production process, but it also replaces the physical bank branch as a distribution channel. Simultaneously the website functions as promotional channel for the various financial products that the bank wants to bring to the attention of their customers.

The four Ps are often denounced as not being viewed from the purchaser's perspective. For this reason, Robert Lauterborn introduced the four Cs model. He states that marketing has developed from a technique for organisations to sell a product (P) into a philosophy to endear themselves to their customers and encourage commitment. The old Ps are predominantly suitable for a manufacturer, the modern Cs are a better fit for a more customer-orientated organisation that view themselves through the eyes of their customers (Lauterborn, 1990).

Therefore, Lauterborn transforms the 4P-model into the 4C-model (see table 1.1).

4C-model

TABLE 1.1 From 4P-model to 4C-model

Four Ps	Four Cs
Product	*Customer solution*: solving the consumer's problem
Price	*Cost to the customer*: price/quality ratio
Place	*Convenience*: accommodating the customer
Promotion	*Communication*: reciprocal communication between an organisation and its customers

Dev and Schultz followed up on this model by translating it into the SIVA-model **S**olution, **I**nformation, **V**alue, **A**ccess (Dev & Schultz, 2005). Both the 4C- and the SIVA-model fit in with the interactivity and customer focus that characterises Internet marketing, but they turned out to be less

SIVA-model

suitable for the structure of this book. After weighing the pros and cons of each of the established models, the format that was chosen was one that matches the core processes related to marketing as described in Philip Kotler's recent books. This way the relationship to general marketing theory is retained.

1.4 Digital Marketing in relation to business processes

The five core processes of a business's marketing are (Kotler & Keller, 2014):

Market sensing process

1 The market sensing process: the process that keeps organisations up-to-date with the market's needs, developments and trends.

Product realisation process

2 The product realisation process: researching and developing new core products and services, extending the market supply and the launch of the product.

Customer acquisition process

3 The customer acquisition process: defining target markets and acquiring new customers.

Order fulfilment process

4 The order fulfilment process: receiving and approving orders, shipping the ordered goods on time and collecting payments. (literally: delivering on your promises).

Customer relationship management

5 The customer relationship management process (CRM): building a deeper understanding, a better relationship and a better offer for individual customers.

Among other things, online market sensing consists of actively following and analysing the website's own visitor behaviour, gathering information from social media and online market research (see Chapter 3). One of online market research's biggest advantages is that results can be quickly collected and immediately accessed.

User generated content (UGC)

Crowdsourcing

With the realisation of a new product, activity concepts such as 'user generated content (UGC)' (Chapter 2) and crowdsourcing (Chapter 4) come into play. Users lay the foundation for new products and product improvements by reviewing products and answering the questions of other users. Crowdsourcing organisations actively encourage the Internet community to get involved and come up with new ideas for products.

Digital/web analytics

Market sensing and digital/web analytics (Chapter 12) play a big part in forecasting how successful new products will be. Immediate feedback from users leads to a more rapid process of quality improvement and product innovation.

Digital Marketing communication

Digital Marketing communication (Chapters 5 to 8) provides a way of generating new customers. Online sales and pricing are important aspects for this. One great advantage that the Internet provides is that the results can be easily measured, which allows quick changes to be made if necessary. This way the organisation can also calculate exactly what the most and least profitable communication activities are.

Order handling is done quickly and efficiently when the website is combined with an effective and efficient payment and distribution system (see Chapter 9). The advantage of using the Internet is that there is minimal time between order, payment and approval of the order ('real-time' transactions). The payment process is therefore more efficient and customer-friendly than in the 'offline' world. If the product is digital, it is even more effective: it can be delivered to the customer immediately after payment: the organisation sends a confirmation email or gives the customer access to a download on a website.

Customer relationship management (CRM) uses a variety of channels such as social media, newsletters, web personalization and email (Chapter 10). In this way, organisations stimulate customer loyalty, allowing them to provide a more personalised service, to make individual offers and to generate higher earnings from existing customers. The main focus is to build customer loyalty. Because data from these customers can be directly included in the database, the results of these efforts are easily measurable, and the time needed to act on customers' activities can be minimised.

Market sensing does not only occur when a product is brought to market, but during all business processes. Using digital/web analytics, valuable information about the target market's behaviour is gathered permanently. Based on that information the processes are being optimised and improvements are made to the range of products/services on offer to the customer. Digital Marketing is a continuous cycle (see figure 1.2).

FIGURE 1.2 Digital Marketing is a continuous cycle

1.5 Development of Digital Marketing

In recent years Digital Marketing has advanced rapidly. We can divide this development into three broad phases: the mass media phase, the Internet phase and the social media phase. Figure 1.3 displays the development of marketing, brands and the role of the various forms of media. In short, figure 1.3 explains that brands and consumers are growing closer together.

FIGURE 1.3 The development of marketing, brands and media

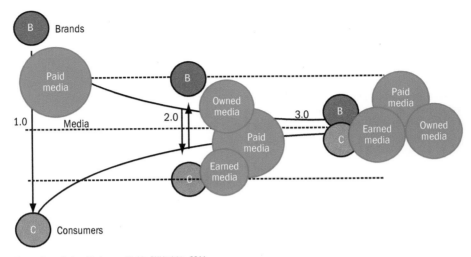

Source: Marco Derksen/Upstream, edited by DVJ Insights, 2011

In figure 1.3 you also see the concepts bought (= paid), owned and earned media. These are collective concepts for types of media:

Paid media
1 Paid media: these are types of media that marketers can buy to create brand awareness (consider online advertising, radio, television and print).

Owned media
2 Owned media: these are types of media that are readily available to marketers themselves and in which they can autonomously decide on the content (for instance websites, apps, email newsletters etc).

Earned media
3 Earned media: these are all types of media that a brand 'earns' thanks to customers or journalists, or bloggers writing about your brand, on social media for instance, or because other organisations refer to your brand on their website.

Mass media phase

Push

Internet phase

Social media phase

Pull

During the first period (the mass media phase) the gap between 'brands' and consumer was the largest; it was mainly the marketer who sent out messages to the consumer, who received them. This is also called 'push'. In the second marketing phase (the Internet phase) there was more interactivity between marketers and consumers and a dialogue started between them. In the last (most recent, current) phase, the social media phase, it goes without saying that consumers are now influencing the brand and therefore are indispensable. Not only is there dialogue, but also a reciprocal influence. In this case there is no 'push' anymore, but 'pull'. The consumer has a say in what the brand entails and the marketer observes the consumer's perception of the brand and will be supportive of this. (You can read more about this in Chapter 4).

1.6 The outline of this book

Chapter 2 covers the strategic aspects of Digital Marketing. The main focus in this chapter will be on determining the relationship between the business model and the online activities.

Chapter 3 discusses the market sensing process; online consumer behaviour, the use of the Internet in marketing and online market research.

In Chapter 4 you can read how Digital Marketing translates itself into the 'product realisation' process.

Chapter 5 covers the first part of the customer acquisition process; online branding.

Chapter 6 covers customer acquisition through owned and earned channels.

In Chapter 7 we will describe the customer acquisition process through paid channels, or in other words: online advertising (display and paid search).

Chapter 8 focuses on online sales and pricing

In Chapter 9 you can read which aspects play a part in the order handling process resulting from online sales of products and services.

FIGURE 1.4 The outline of this book

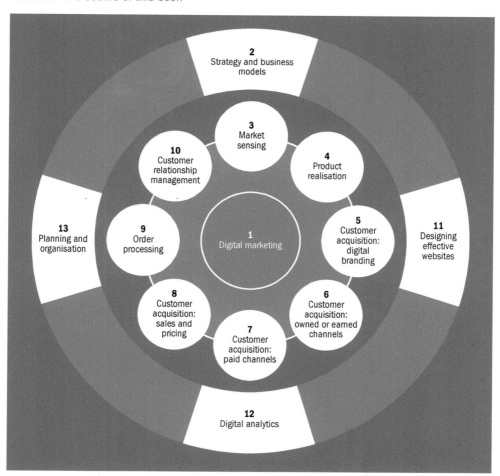

Chapter 10 deals with the customer relationship management (CRM) process.
By this point in the book, all of Kotler's core processes will have been reviewed. Chapters 11, 12 and 13 deal with umbrella topics: designing and building effective websites, digital/web analytics, planning and finally resourcing Digital Marketing within the organisation.
Figure 1.4 concisely displays the outline of the chapters.

This book is structured in the same order that many organisations use to make their marketing decisions. If you're not particularly familiar with marketing and management issues you may choose to read Chapters 3 to 10 first, before you start on Chapter 2. That way you will get a better understanding of the exact contents of the business model and its specific elements and, crucially, why the selection of a business model is so important to every organisation.

Questions and assignments

NOW CHECK YOUR UNDERSTANDING:

1.1 Compare the way that amazon.com sells books to how a bricks-and-mortar bookstore like Barnes & Noble does this.
  a What are the comparisons and differences in the way books are being sold?
  b Describe your idea of how each of the five marketing related processes (see figure 1.2) progress for amazon.com and for Barnes & Noble, the bookseller.
  c How would you characterise both organisations: as Digital Marketing organisations, as traditional marketing organisations or as a mixture of both? Support your answer with evidence.

1.2 **a** In 1.2 seven types of websites are discussed.
    For each of the following websites, specify what category they belong to:
    www.unilever.com
    www.staples.com
    www.independent.co.uk
    web.wechat.com
    www.apple.com
    citymapper.com
    www.airbnb.com
  b Pick one of the above suppliers and construct the Marketing Mix using the four Ps and the four Cs. What do you notice?

1.3

CASE

Digital Marketing at Marriott
By Marjolein Visser

Marriott International uses as much modern technology as possible to respond to the wants and needs of the young, contemporary business traveller, or the so-called Millennial. One of these technologies is the popular mobile check-in and checkout functionality. Members of the loyalty programme, Marriott Rewards, receive a push notification on their smartphone saying that they can check-in after 4 pm. After that they automatically receive a notification as soon as their room is ready.

This kind of prior communication shows that the hotel is prepared for their arrival and creates anticipation of a warm welcome and an enjoyable stay. Their payment details are already saved in their member profile, allowing them to simply walk to the special check-in desk on arrival where their pre-programmed key card will be waiting for them. At the end of their stay guests receive a push notification that tells them mobile checkout is available. If they so choose, the guests will be asked for an email address to send the invoice to, meaning they don't even have to stop at Reception on their way out. (And importantly, this means that Marriott can capture their current email address!).

Also, within the hotel, mobile communication is used to its full potential. Users of the Marriott-app can request a range of services, such as requesting extra towels and pillows or breakfast in bed.

'I am responsible for Marriott.com. My department basically shapes Marriott.com's sales funnel. My team deals with acquisition, conversion and aftersales. We do everything from mobile booking to mobile services. Self-service is a very important topic. In recent years the main focus was primarily on the mobile booking experience. That is quite simple because there are people whose flights have been changed and they have to adjust their hotel reservation. You want to be there for them when that happens. That's why our mobile revenues have increased year after year. But a travel experience encompasses much more than just the online booking.'

The Marriott app can even open your hotel room door

'The mobile experience and the personal interaction between guests and our hotel staff should not be viewed in isolation from one another. When this type of interaction is consistently provided, it changes the whole experience. Our statistics of mobile service requests currently indicate that 86% of the guests that use the functionality choose to chat directly with our hotel staff. That illustrates how much guests appreciate this personal interaction using their mobile devices. Almost nine out of ten guests gave a very high rating and a positive review. We continuously conduct user surveys and research in real-time and we monitor our own web data to identify improvement opportunities. Besides that we use multivariate tests to examine what works best and what it is we should discontinue. This way we can ensure an optimal customer experience.'

-George Corbin, Senior Vice-President Digital at Marriott International

Source: www.emarketer.com and http://computer.financialexpress.com

NOW CHECK YOUR UNDERSTANDING:

a There are seven different categories of websites. To what category does the website Marriott.com belong?

b Make an inventory of how Marriott International uses mobile communications for Digital Marketing. To help you with this, take a look at http://mobileapp.marriott.com/ (N.B. This works on a tablet, laptop or desktop with Windows 10)

c Paragraph 1.2 above explains how Digital Marketing can be more effective and efficient. Which of the seven advantages mentioned would also apply to mobile marketing as used by Marriott? Show evidence for each applicable advantage.

d As part of which of the four Cs does Marriott use mobile marketing?

e Within which of the five marketing-related processes does Marriott use mobile marketing? Give an example for each core process.

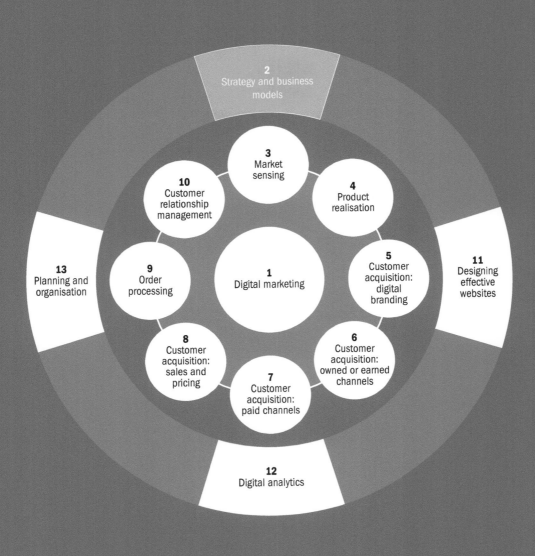

2

Strategy and Business Models

Author: Marjolein Visser

In the previous chapter, five marketing-related, relevant core processes in an organisation were identified:
- market sensing
- product realisation
- customer acquisition
- order handling

and
- customer relationship management (CRM).

These five business processes will be discussed in Chapters 3 to 10. However, before an organisation determines what role Digital Marketing will play in each of these five processes, senior management must establish the organisation and marketing strategy, thereby formulating the management framework for Digital Marketing.

The strategy is closely linked to the business model: the building blocks that the organisation uses to determine the organisation and business processes and to make money. The Internet provides different building blocks from those of the physical, offline world. As a result, new and often surprising business models have emerged in recent years. In this chapter, you will learn various terminology and models associated with strategy and business models. Examples will be used to show how organisations determine business models in practice and adapt to changing circumstances.

In addition, we will look at how an organisation determines what impact digital innovations have on the business model, marketing strategy and on the implementation of marketing activities. If you are still a little unfamiliar with marketing and management and you are finding this chapter difficult, then we recommend reading Chapters 3 to 10 first, after which you can return to this chapter. Hopefully you will then have a better overall understanding.

This chapter will cover:
- the place of Digital Marketing within the organisation's strategy
- the business model
- determining the impact of digital innovations for Digital Marketing

After studying this chapter, you will be able to:
- identify the overall strategic marketing issues within an organisation
- explain how Digital Marketing can have a major impact on corporate strategy
- name the steps in the strategic process and explain them using examples
- define what a business model is and how it relates to an organisation's strategy
- distinguish between online business models in practice
- name examples of 'earning models' that are widely applied online and explain why these models are popular with organisations doing business online
- explain how organisations determine what their business model should look like
- describe the four steps for adapting the business model to external changes
- describe how an organisation determines the effects of digital innovations in Digital Marketing

2.1 Digital Marketing and Strategy

In recent years, digitisation has led to a huge shift in the way organisations implement their marketing strategy, driven mainly by changing consumer media habits. Up until 2010, organisations focused on digital communication primarily through personal computers (desktop and laptop PCs). The rise of mobile Internet (accessed via smartphones and tablets) has led to a huge shift in the way consumers and business users interact with the Internet. The Internet and world wide web (www) is now widely accessible and information is available immediately 'on the go'. Today, it's not only people who are using the internet, also devices like thermostats and cars. This has not led to changes in the way a marketing strategy is established, but the role of Digital Marketing within this strategy is becoming increasingly important. We will first establish what is meant by strategic marketing and then consider the effects of digitisation.

2.1.1 What does strategic marketing mean?

In their book 'Marketing Strategy' Frambach and Nijssen (Frambach & Nijssen, 2017) write:

Strategic marketing

> Strategic marketing deals with the way in which customers can be offered value in a sustainable way, that is, in the perception of those customers, superior and distinctive to the value offered by competitors and potential providers.

An organisation must positively distinguish itself from its competitors in the eyes of the customers. By 'sustainable', Frambach and Nijssen mean that strategy is about establishing long-term goals, making fundamental

© Noordhoff Uitgevers bv

choices about target markets, about the extent to which the organisation approaches the target markets identically or differentiated, the mode of positioning and in a broad sense what is put into the marketing mix. A marketing strategy is usually determined for a period of three to five years (which in practice may be longer than the time the Marketing Director/CMO remains in their job!). The marketing strategy sets the framework for the processes described in this book: from market sensing to customer relationship management (CRM).

2.1.2   Rethinking processes

The way in which the marketing strategy is established has not changed significantly in 'The Digital Age'. Where digitalization has had a major influence in recent years is on the choice of resources and methods used by an organisation to implement the marketing strategy. There is an increasingly broader array of choices. Location-based communications, such as beacons and wearables (devices which you can carry/wear on your body and which collect personal information, such as the number of steps you walk or your heart rate), robots and mobile payment platforms, are examples of new techniques that are being utilised in marketing.

Beacons
Wearables

Beacons are devices that transmit a signal that can be picked up by smartphones. This allows retailers to monitor customers in a store, to advise them and make them appropriate offers

Digitisation has a huge impact on user/customer interaction. For example, a customer's online search behaviour, what products they buy and how they communicate online about these products can be tracked exactly. Intelligent devices connected to the Internet, eg smart thermostats, provide rich data about user preferences and behaviour. This not only provides insight into the customer's purchasing process, but also facilitates very personalised communication.

Digital technology can also be used in an organisation's production or service processes. This can have far-reaching consequences for the way of thinking and working. For this reason, Cruise Company Royal Caribbean equips their ships with state-of-the-art technology, making it possible to monitor guests' behaviour, and to adjust their service accordingly, ie they adopt an increasingly customised approach. Checkout is also no longer a problem: exactly who has booked what activities and what they have consumed is recorded digitally. The customer only needs to authorize the final invoice. Another example is 'Amazon Go' technology (see http://bit.ly/2G5UpFk).

Digitisation also has an effect on prices. Due to openness (transparency) on the Internet, price pressure has increased. All prices, product specifications and ratings are public. So, retailers have 'nowhere to hide'; price comparison ('shopping around') is easier than ever before. Manufacturers or brokers can opt for price leadership and carefully monitor who offers the lowest prices or alternatively focus on service. In some branches, brokers are becoming obsolete, as consumers are no longer willing to pay for the 'added value' they offer. Examples of distribution channels currently in difficulty are travel agencies and bookstores. Also, due to the influence of digitisation, we see reverse vertical integration. For example, travel company TUI merged with TUI hotels and TUI cruises in 2012, making it possible to offer the end-customer hotels and cruises that are not for sale anywhere else. An additional advantage is that all fees for intermediary channels remain in their own pocket. Price transparency may also lead to changes in the service concept (brokers, notaries) or to new services. An example of this is 'First Direct', an innovative UK telephone and online bank (part of HSBC) aimed at 'making life easier' for its customers.

First Direct offers a full range of banking services but has no branches. It offers its customers: 'Banking just the way you like it. Talk to real people 24/7, or go online, on your mobile or on your tablet. We're here whenever and wherever you need us'.

Vertical integration

First Direct uses its website to explain who they are and what they stand for

Rapid developments make it necessary to test the marketing strategy very regularly for future sustainability.

⬤2.2 Marketing Strategy

The marketing strategy takes shape by answering the following questions:
1 What does the organisation want to achieve?
2 What is the current and future situation in the market? What are the opportunities and what are the threats?
3 What are the possibilities and competencies of the organisation in the technical, financial and organisational fields? What are their strong points and what are their weaknesses?
4 What conclusions can be drawn from looking at these strengths and weaknesses in relation to the opportunities and threats? What should the organisation do to ensure lasting success in the future?
5 How can the organisation best segment the market and what choices does the organisation make regarding target markets and positioning?
6 What does the organisation need to change in order to achieve this? Broadly speaking, what will the new marketing mix look like?
7 What needs to happen in technical, financial and organisational terms to achieve this?

Figure 2.1 shows schematically the steps of formulating a marketing strategy.

FIGURE 2.1 Formulating a Marketing Strategy

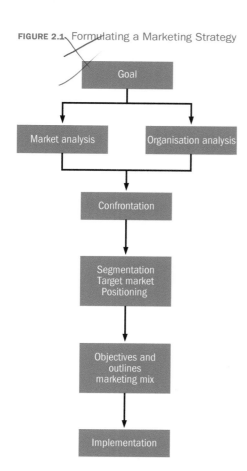

The starting point for describing the marketing strategy are the marketing goals that an organisation strives for over the next three to five years. These are general goals, such as a larger share of the market, introducing new products or approaching new markets. These goals are based on the mission and vision of the organisation and expressed in the organisational strategy. The mission describes the organisation's 'raison d'être' and the vision is the shared concept for the future that has been formulated by the organisation's management.

Mission
Vision

An important basis for the marketing strategy is the current market situation (competition and potential customers) and expected future developments. If you want to look at the role of Digital Marketing within the marketing strategy, then the technological developments are especially relevant, combined with the socio-cultural consequences of these developments. For example, the rise of social media has led to a completely different way of communicating within society. Today, people are available 24/7 and there are no real obstacles to contacting someone living on the other side of the globe. For instance, an organisation may ask what further 'robotization' will mean for the market. How will consumers react, how far along is the competition and what will they do in the future? Would it for instance be possible to replace face-to-face sales staff with robots? That could certainly be useful: by providing them with information from the customer database, robots can offer customers personalised help, they know exactly what a customer has bought before, they can advise them about matching products, they know the prices, can rapidly calculate/adjust prices, can tell exactly what the composition of products is and so on. Will customers appreciate that? Or would a flesh-and-blood human sell more? Is robotization an opportunity or a threat to the sector the organisation is in? These are big questions, and they're not going away.

There are, of course, many uncertainties. The future cannot be fully predicted. You can already find robots at airports and in hotels, but on on what scale will robots be introduced? Will the economy benefit, causing individuals and businesses to have more disposable income, or will there be a recession? And will this lead to further digitisation or not? Furthermore, what are the competitors doing: will they opt for digitisation or personal service? Due to the large degree of uncertainty, strategists often work on the basis of scenarios. A scenario describes a possible future and is based on assumptions and suppositions about developments that are relevant to the market. These should not be 'finger-in-the-air' guesses; each scenario should be supported by solid research.

Scenario

An example of an organisation that often makes use of scenarios is Siemens (see photo). They often conduct as many as 100 interviews with a variety of experts before establishing a scenario.

Image from one of Siemens' scenarios for 2035. A young professor in the field of Health Sciences from Nigeria buys a tailor-made suit made in Hamburg. Throughout the process, he observes the creation of his suit in this era of global networks

If management has an accurate vision for the future, it should be looking at the resources and competencies. Is the organisation, for example, knowledgeable about robotics at home? Is there enough money to develop and introduce systems? If the answer is 'no,' maybe that technology is best left to others and a more personal approach may be a better option. Examining the consequences of the organisation's strengths and weaknesses in relation to expected market developments, opportunities and threats is called a confrontation analysis. The entire process of cataloguing the opportunities and threats in the market, determining the strengths and weaknesses and performing the confrontation analysis is called a SWOT analysis. SWOT stands for 'Strengths, Weaknesses, Opportunities, Threats'.

Confrontation analysis

SWOT analysis

When all developments and opportunities have been analysed, the organisation will determine the way to segment the market, decide which target markets are most attractive and how the brand will be positioned in the coming years. These are general assumptions, although in this instance it is very relevant whether the organisation sees Digital Marketing as the core of the marketing process or if they see the Internet as no more than one of many communication and distribution channels. An online bank like First Direct has a completely different target group and a completely different positioning from that of a traditional bank. First Direct positions itself as a bank that allows you to deal with your money in a cleverer way, your personal advantage being the central point. Positioning is influencing the way a product is perceived by a target market according to several key attributes. The goal is to create a distinctive place in the mind of the consumer in comparison to competing products.

After the basic choices for the next three to five years have been made, they are translated into goals for the following years. Preferably as **SMART** (Specific, Measurable, Acceptable, Realistic, Time-bound) as possible. In addition, the consequences that these choices have for the five marketing-related business processes and/or the marketing mix are formulated in broad terms. Subsequently, the marketers that are responsible for each of these processes are given a framework and guidelines within which they can operate. It is therefore clear what role Digital Marketing has within the organisation's marketing activities. The strategy is then further refined in subsequent marketing plans and the ensuing annual planning. In these plans, the measures are clearly integrated into the activities related to the marketing mix and into the marketing-related business processes, thus clarifying exactly what is expected of the (digital) marketers.

2.3 The business model

Business model Every organisation has a business model. A description of how the company creates value for customers and is then compensated in the form of revenue is always present. Sometimes explicitly, sometimes implicitly. The business model is a way to coherently consolidate the various factors that influence the way an organisation operationalises its strategy. It is a description of how the strategic goals must be realised in a profitable, sustainable way. When looking at a business model, we must examine not only the strategy, but also how it is translated: the way in which the organisation and business processes must be arranged.

In this section we look at the elements of a business model. We will see that the model consists of building blocks and we will discuss these components. After designing the building blocks, the organization does a final check, executes the business model and innovates when necessary. Finally, in this section, we briefly deal with the role of Digital Marketing in the business model.

2.3.1 Formats for the business model
A business model can have different formats, ranging from simple to very complicated. All of them will contain the following elements:

Value proposition
Earnings model
Key resources
Core processes

- The value proposition for the customer: what problem does the organisation solve for the customer?
- The earnings model: which revenue sources does the organisation have, what are the most significant costs and how will the organisation make a profit?
- The key resources: what knowledge, individuals, technology, products, facilities, and tools enable the organisation to create the value proposition for the customer?
- The core processes: which processes enable the organisation to deliver value successfully to the customer and to achieve a competitive advantage?

© Noordhoff Uitgevers bv

FIGURE 2.2 Fixed elements of a business model

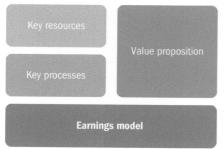

2

EXAMPLE 2.1

Ryanair has a unique earnings model

Airline Ryanair is an organisation with a unique earnings model. In 1991 the (then failing) Ryanair brought in Michael O'Leary to get the company out of the red. He opted for a radical innovation to their business model. Business model innovation is a redefinition of existing markets, customers, and value proposition in an innovative way so that the rules of the game change and you can get ahead of the competition.

The value proposition of Ryanair became, very simply, 'fly cheaply'. Although O'Leary's earnings model for Ryanair was partially based on Southwest Airlines, it was unique in its implementation. In addition to the income from passenger fares, there is also money to be made from baggage check-in, airport check-in, priority boarding, on-board food and drinks, advertising inside and outside of the plane, arrangements with car rental providers, hotels and travel insurance and subsidies from regions who want to attract Ryanair to their (small, local) airports. Expenditure wise, everything has

Anyone who flies with Ryanair knows that there are no exceptions

been done to minimise the cost of marketing, fuel, maintenance, airports and cleaning. By building in ample margins in their timetabling, Ryanair aircraft are rarely late, which limits complaints and costs. Ryanair maximises the occupancy per flight by offering extremely low fares where necessary, in order to generate as much income as possible, including subsidies. The key resources are obtained at the lowest possible price, while the processes are standardised to a large degree. Customers are encouraged to be as self-sufficient as possible, using Internet/web/mobile technology to do many things themselves such as online booking, check-in and managing boarding passes. There are no exceptions and any extra help from Ryanair employees must be paid for. Interestingly, it can be argued that such an extreme 'no-frills' attitude is today out-of-step with the times and indeed Ryanair has recently made an effort to be 'nicer' to its customers.

Business model innovations

Developments in Internet-related technology have led to many business model innovations. The way in which producers, brokers and customers approach each other and how they are able to interact has changed significantly. For instance, the switch to a digital distribution channel is a significant one for most organisations. Sometimes it even results in a completely different strategy, method and organisational structure.

One example of a successful innovative business model is (taxi) ride hailing company Uber, which started in San Francisco in 2010. Uber provides an app-based taxi service. In the application, users can request 'an Uber' as well as monitor how long it will take for the car to arrive. The app allows the customer to review/rate the driver, so bad drivers are automatically flagged up. Payments are also made via the app itself. The rates are much lower than those of normal taxis. This has led to major unrest in the taxi industry and resulted in a ban in several countries and cities. Uber is a classic example of Digital disruption. In many such cases existing providers are threatened and will, naturally, attempt to defend their business.

Uber: an alternative business model for taxi transport

2.3.2   Building blocks of the business model

Within the business world, the business model canvas by Osterwalder and Pigneur (2009) is a popular framework for understanding business models.

Business model canvas

The model has nine components or building blocks:
1 customer segments
2 value proposition
3 channels
4 customer relationships
5 income sources
6 key means
7 key activities
8 key partners
9 cost structure

Figure 2.3 will show you how to fill in each of these building blocks.

FIGURE 2.3 The Business Canvas Model

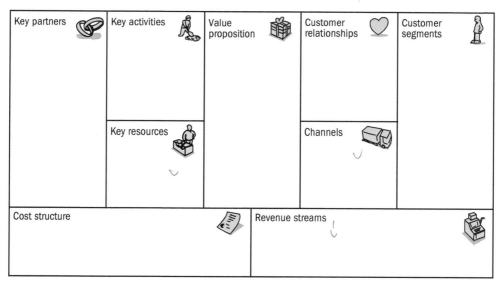

Source: Osterwalder, Pigneur et al., 2009

1 Customer segments

An organisation serves one or more customer segments. The core questions for this building block are:
- For whom do we create value?
- What are our main market segments?

This question is answered within the marketing strategy.

Customers belong to different segments if:
- their needs require a separate offer
- they must be reached via different distribution channels
- they have a different type of relationship with the provider
- their profitability differs greatly
- they are willing to pay extra for various aspects of the offer (Osterwalder & Pigneur, 2009)

The last point, for example, could be applicable to wealthy people who are willing to pay for tailor-made and extra service, while the 'average' customer is willing to spend money on more speed or increased convenience. In terms of Digital Marketing, it is relevant to know the extent to which customer segments are discoverable online and whether they find doing business online advantageous. Indeed, certain segments may be particularly digital/mobile-savvy, whereas others may still prefer paperbased communications.

2 Value proposition

An organisation wants to solve customer issues and fulfil customer needs through a value proposition: an attractive offer to the customer. Osterwalder and Pigneur state that the value proposition consists of a mix of elements that match the needs of the segment. Values can be quantitative, such as price or speed of service, or qualitative, such as design or customer experience. The value proposition closely matches the chosen positioning.

Questions that must be considered when completing this building block are:
- What value do we offer to the customer?
- What customer problems do we help to solve?
- What customer needs do we satisfy?
- What collection of products and services do we offer to each of the customer segments? (Osterwalder & Pigneur, 2009)

To determine the role of Digital Marketing within the value proposition, it is relevant whether the core of the value proposition is a physical product, a human service or a data-based product. Following on from that, the value proposition can be wholly or partly digitally realised in the 'product realisation process'. One example is eLearning, where course material can be accessed online and tests can be marked automatically.

EXAMPLE 2.2

The value proposition of BlaBlaCar

An example of a value proposition made possible by the Internet is BlaBlaCar, founded in France in 2006. The idea behind BlaBlaCar is that you share your car with others, enjoying a pleasant chat along the way. You only need to fill in your date of travel, place of departure and your destination on their website or in their app and you will get a list of drivers who are heading in the same direction. Alternatively, you can offer a place to a passenger in your own car. The value proposition is cheaper transport by sharing a car journey. The whole business model relies on digital technology.

© Noordhoff Uitgevers bv

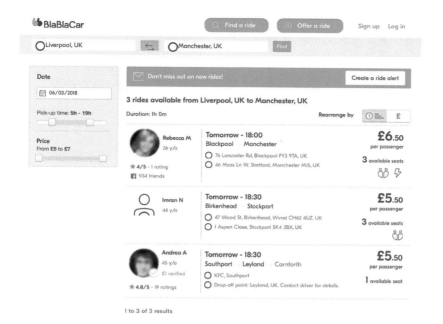

Get a ride on BlaBlaCar

---

3 Channels

Value propositions are delivered to customers via communications, distribution and sales channels. Through these channels, customers must be made aware of the products and services that the organisation offers; they must be helped in evaluating the value proposition and must be able to purchase products and services. They must also receive the value proposition and be provided with after-sales service (Osterwalder & Pigneur, 2009).

The core questions for this building block are:
- Through which channels do our customers from each segment wish to be approached?
- How do we do that now?
- How are our channels integrated?
- Which channel works best?
- Which channels are most efficient?
- How do we integrate them with customer habits and behaviours?

Communication with (potential) customers can be done using the Internet (eg via desktop pc, laptop, tablet or smartphone) without any technical problems. Distribution is more complicated. The best-known form of distribution is physical trading. The manufacturer makes a product and sells to a store where the customer can then compare and buy said product. The advantage is that customers can compare and evaluate products easily and that sellers can persuade the potential customer to buy the product or provide them with additional information. Disadvantages are the cost of distribution and the need for a large amount of widely dispersed stock. This

Bricks-and-mortar

system is called 'bricks-and-mortar' (physical sales through retail and brokerage) as a counterpart to 'clicks' (online sales).

As mentioned above, the intermediary ('middle-man') can sometimes be circumvented through the Internet. This is especially advantageous for products and services for which tastes, smells and feelings are less important. Cost savings can be a big advantage for the business. Not only is stockholding limited (in terms of the products themselves), but also the cost of stock held by a broker has disappeared.

EXAMPLE 2.3

Alibaba Group

Not all products can be distributed entirely digitally. Alibaba Group Holding Limited is a Chinese multinational ecommerce, retail, Internet, AI and technology conglomerate founded in 1999 that provides consumer-to-consumer, business-to-consumer and business-to-business sales services via websites, as well as electronic payment services, shopping search engines and data-centric cloud computing services. It is one of the top 10 most valuable and biggest companies in the world. In January 2018, Alibaba became the second Asian company to break the US$500 billion valuation mark, after Tencent. It is the world's largest and most valuable retailer, with operations in over 200 countries and 550 million monthly active mobile users across its platforms. Its online sales and profits exceed all US retailers (including Walmart, Amazon and eBay) combined. It orchestrated China's Singles' Day, creating the world's biggest online and offline shopping day, with its own sales reaching over US$25.4 billion on 11 November 2017.

The key point here is the cost savings from the reduction of stockholding by brokers and retailers.

----

4 Customer Relationships

There are many different ways that a company can manage its relationships with its customers: from 100% manual to fully automated. Osterwalder and Pigneur (2009) identify several different possibilities for maintaining customer relationships:
1 a personal point of contact such as a representative
2 co-creation
3 communities
4 personal assistance
5 self-service
6 automated service

1 A personal point of contact

Personal representative

A personal representative is specifically bound to a customer and maintains a long-term relationship with him or her. For example, many people visit the same hairdresser each time or use a fixed tax consultant. In business services, this representative is often called a (key) account manager

2 Co-creation

Co-creation is a strategy wherein business processes are realised in *collaboration* with customers. This can be applied to a variety of processes, such as product development, user generated content, service and customer service.

Co-creation

One example of this is from global coffee shop chain, Starbucks. Since launch, the My Starbucks Idea community has generated more than 300 implemented innovations and more than 150,000 ideas from customers and members, which have included benefits such as free wi-fi at Starbucks and the introduction of 'skinny' drinks. This innovative program was based on ideas taken from an online crowdsourcing platform. In fact, only one in 500 users' submitted ideas were ultimately selected for implementation. The number of implemented ideas increased significantly at the early stage of the platform. At the mature stage, even though an increasing number of ideas are submitted, the percentage of implemented ideas was relatively small. There were three categories of ideas – product, experience, and involvement. The likelihood of an idea to be implemented largely depends on votes received by and points earned on that idea.

Co-creation will be discussed in more detail in Chapter 4.

3 Communities

Organisations can offer the opportunity for customers to enter into a partnership through an online community so that they can share knowledge and experiences with each other and with the organisation. An example of this is the T-Mobile forum, where T-Mobile customers can ask questions or initiate discussions and respond to each other. Social media and communities will be discussed in more detail in Chapter 10.

Community

4 Personal assistance

Personal Assistance means direct contact with employees during or after sales in stores, through call centres, by email or using an online 'Live Chat' function. In these instances, there is no 'fixed' representative.

Personal Assistance

5 Self-service

In the case of self-service, there is direct contact with the customer, enabling them to acquire the necessary information and services. One example is self-scanning in supermarkets, another is the case of rail companies where customers can search for departure times independently and then print their own tickets or save them on their smartphone.

Self-service

6 Automated services

Automated Services are a form of self-service that make use of automated processes. For instance, an online airline ticket provider, where the customer can indicate their destination and travel dates and the system then lists the various possibilities. The booking is then concluded without the need for human intervention and the customer will automatically receive their eticket in their email inbox or app.

Automated Services

2

Digitising the business process of obtaining a driver's license

In many countries today, the process of obtaining a driver's licence has been largely moved online. In the past, the process was rather time-consuming, involving a lot of paperwork. Forms had to be completed manually. The driving test had to be requested by the driving instructor well in advance which was then confirmed in writing in the form of a 'call-up' letter. Sometimes the date was an unpleasant surprise, for example because you were on vacation. You would then have had to apply again and pay again. After taking the test/ written examination, you were immediately told if you were successful, but the administrative processing required more time. You could not receive your driver's licence right away.

In recent years, the business process has been largely digitised. Now the processing of reservations, payment, examinations and results is done digitally and communicated directly to the customer. The examiners use their smartphones to send the results of the test directly to the central office for processing. Successful candidates can pick up their driving license from the town hall using their ID. Any who have failed, can immediately make a reservation and pay for a new test online. The process generally runs smoothly and fewer mistakes are made. Note that the driving test centre value proposition, ie the testing of driving proficiency, has not changed significantly. However, now that a large part of the customer relationship is conducted directly via automated services, customers receive a better experience – ie more value than before.

Organisations that focus on one-off sales or offer products with a very low price are often transaction-oriented. Many organisations however, are looking to build a long-term relationship. You can find more about customer relationship management in Chapter 7.

Questions that organisations must ask before making a decision regarding this building block are (Osterwalder & Pigneur, 2009):
- What type of relationship do each of our customer segments expect us to enter into?
- What type of relationships do we already have? What impact does this have on costs?
- How are customer relations integrated with the rest of our business model?

5 The revenue streams

According to Osterwalder and Pigneur, the building block 'Revenue Streams' represents the money that an organisation generates from each of the customer segments. After deducting the expenses from these revenue streams, the remainder will be profit. Needless to say, some segments are inherently more profitable than others.

Questions that organisations must ask are (Osterwalder & Pigneur, 2009):
- What value are our customers actually willing to pay for?
- What do they currently pay for?

- How do they pay at the moment? How would they like to pay?
- How much does every revenue stream contribute to the total turnover?

Such questions are closely linked to pricing strategy. In recent years, many online companies have struggled with the question of what customers are willing to pay for, ie what represents real value to them. Whereas in the past organisations could ask consumers to pay for (say) news, travel information, music or software, the free availability of these things on the Internet made it difficult to conceive of a definite earnings model. This has led to many organisations deciding to also provide their valuable content free of charge and earn money through, for example, advertising revenue. More recently, a change has become apparent. Companies with content sites are increasingly putting their best content (their most valuable information) behind what is called a 'paywall'. Only after payment will visitors to the website gain full access. The websites and apps belonging to newspapers are a good example of this. Indeed, it would appear that unless publishers can make this model work, their very existence is threatened. This issue is currently causing a shakeout in the publishing industry, to name but one of many.

In addition to direct payment per unit (product, hour, MB), the following ways to generate revenue are widely prevalent on the Internet (Houtgraaf & Bekkers, Business Models, 2013):
1 subscription model
2 bait and hook model
3 entry or freemium model
4 ad model
5 auction model
6 brokerage model
7 sale of user data
8 yield management

1 Subscription Model

Subscriptions are much more common online than elsewhere, especially for information-based services. For example, you can subscribe to Software as a Service (SaaS), to a music service like Spotify or (very traditionally) news from a newspaper. For the organisation, the subscription format is attractive because it provides a continuous source of income. It does demand efficient administrative processes including, registration, data security, and customer service. Moreover, if paid by bank direct debit, the option to cancel lies with the customer and inertia tends to favour the provider.

Subscriptions

Software as a Service (SaaS)

2 Bait and hook model

The bait and hook model is also known as the Gillette or razor and blade model, as it was invented by Gillette. You may know it from printers and the associated ink cartridges. This model is widely used online, for example for games, software and apps. The basic product ('bait') is placed on the market very cheaply. The profits come from extensions or add-ons, such as important functionalities or nicer themes. Those paid parts you call the 'hook'.

Bait and hook model

© Noordhoff Uitgevers bv

3 Entry or Freemium Model

Entry model
Freemium model
The entry model or freemium model implies that the use of an online service is partially free. Often this is a simple version of the service and/or a version containing ads. The idea is that customers who make use of the basic version of the service will be convinced of the quality and then go on to purchase the more comprehensive or advertisement-free version (ie effectively to 'trade-up') eg free wallpapers for your tablet, where the act of downloading gives the vendor permission to send you advertisements. Massively multiplayer online role-playing games (MMORPGs) like World of Warcraft often use a freemium model that allow you to play the first levels for free after which you may be 'hooked'. Also, some online/mobile games are free for the basic game, but any extensions or virtual items that make the game more fun must be purchased.

Spotify uses an entry-level ('Freemium') model to let people try the service. To avoid the ads and gain some extra functionality, users must pay a monthly subscription.

To generate income, it is possible for website owners to combine the different options mentioned here.

4 Ad Model

Ad model
Many websites and apps earn money by displaying ads. This is similar to a traditional print magazine. In the very first phase of the web, the method of billing was copied from newspapers and magazines. You paid per 1000 'impressions' (more accurately, 'displays') (CPM = Cost Per Mille). Because everything that's happening on a website is measurable, this billing model has in some cases been replaced by Pay-Per-Click (PPC), and later sometimes even by payment per realised request or actual sale (CPL = Cost per Lead or CPS = Cost per Sale). This means that an organisation only pays if the advertisement actually delivers results. However much online display is aimed at awareness and attitude change rather than lead generation, in which case the CPM model is still valid.

5 Auction Model

Auction Model
At an auction, supply and demand for a specific type of product are brought together at a specific moment and in a specific place to determine the price. It is a mechanism where, in theory, the provider receives the maximum return, in exchange for their product or service and the buyer pays only what they are willing to pay. In the past, an auction meant that a great number of suppliers and a large, well-known group of users had to be brought together. Think of auction houses such as Sotheby's, Christie's or a traditional cattle market. The limitations in time, space, and supply and demand have been eliminated with the arrival of online auctions such as eBay. These organisations gather providers and buyers together on a web platform. The organisation not only provides the website and online tools, but most importantly, has a reliable system for managing payments (Houtgraaf & Bekkers, 2013). Of course, this can only replace a physical auction if the quality of the products can be established objectively and can be effectively and persuasively displayed online. For highly valuable products, the old-fashioned auction may continue to exist. Usually, an auction's organiser will earn their fee by storing transactions. The provider charges a fee for each transaction and/or makes money indirectly through, for example, ads.

eBay uses the auction model

6 Brokerage Model

In the brokerage model, supply and demand are also brought together, but additionally, the broker also brings extra information and expertise to the table. The added value of the broker is in organising and facilitating the transaction as well as contributing their relevant expertise. In many cases, they contribute added value by including ratings or reviews from previous users/buyers. Examples are www.haart.co.uk which is a (real) estate agent, selling houses direct to the public and comparethemarket.com, an online insurance comparison site. Both get paid a commission from the seller when a sale is made. Some companies using the brokerage model are affiliate marketers earning commissions on referral business.

Brokerage Model

Information brokers facilitate the distribution of data and a referral to the supplier. These providers earn their money by providing organisations with data about the web search and purchasing behaviour of users. An example is www.momondo.com, an originally Danish company which gives its website users information on flight tickets, hotel rooms or car hire deals. They show the available prices and let the user choose the offer they prefer. One click and you're taken directly to the chosen site where the booking is completed.

What is striking when looking at these models is that the value proposition often cannot be seen in isolation to the revenue model. Moreover, online providers often combine multiple revenue streams.

7 Sale of user data

Some providers focus on collecting and selling data derived from the users of their website or app. For example, they offer their target audience an attractive service, create a contest or ask them to fill in a questionnaire. To be eligible for access, a prize or compensation, participants must not only fill in their details but also authorise its use by third parties. The user can read this in the terms and conditions, although in practice, many people accept these without reading them. The organisation sells the data or makes it available indirectly to third parties who then use it for marketing communications or market research (see example 2.5).

Sale of user data

Although most organisations ensure that they remain within the boundaries of the law, not every user sees this earnings model as being very desirable. Organisations such as Google and Facebook get a lot of negative feedback from consumers about this.

We should also bear in mind the privacy and data protection implications of this activity. Many consumers all over the world are concerned about who can access their personal data and how brand owners are collecting, storing and exploiting it. Privacy laws (eg the EU regulation GDPR) seeks to provide additional protection for consumers. Key concepts are 'informed consent' and 'permission'. Read more about this in Chapter 13.

EXAMPLE 2.5

LinkedIn analyses data from 467 million professionals

The profiles of the over 467 million LinkedIn users contain a huge amount of information regarding the user's job titles and experience, training and education, vacancies, contacts and so on. A sub-division of LinkedIn is LinkedIn Universities, which is initially aimed at US students. Based on data from these students and professionals, LinkedIn has identified what the most promising degree courses are for students: the courses where most of its graduates find an attractive job within their field of work, preferably in a company with a good reputation. LinkedIn has published the results on their website. This demonstrates the enormous possibilities that LinkedIn's database has to offer.

LinkedIn does not sell individual data, but it does offer recruiters, jobseekers and traders, in return for a paid subscription, the opportunity to make contact with people who might be of interest to them. For example, LinkedIn has a service called Sales Navigator, through which B2B Sales Professionals are given the opportunity to search and gain access to a company's decision-makers. This is of course controversial, as many users may not like being 'sold to' on LinkedIn.

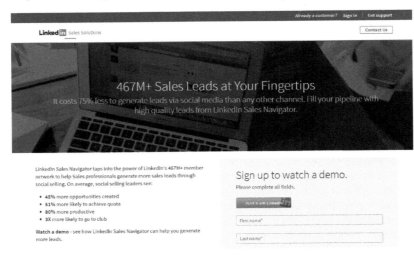

LinkedIn shows you what you can do with their users' data

© Noordhoff Uitgevers bv

8 Yield management

Yield management is widely used in the travel industry, for example for selling airline tickets and hotel rooms. Prices are constantly changing, depending on fluctuating demand, available capacity (rooms, seats), and how much time remains to sell the product or service. This is a way of optimizing the occupancy rate by means of pricing. An organization operating in this way needs advanced algorithms. This method can be used effectively in a digital environment, because all data is available in real time and many 'instant' calculations can be made. Yield management is more a method to fix prices, than an earning model. More methods for online pricing can be found in Chapter 8.

Yield management

6 Key resources

In order to achieve a competitive advantage, an organisation needs to make sure their value proposition is more attractive than the competition's and build a solid relationship with its key target customer segments. In order to ensure this, the organisation will need specific resources. What these are varies according to the business model (Osterwalder & Pigneur, 2009). Key resources may be physical, financial, intellectual or human in nature. For example, an offline (bricks-and-mortar) supermarket must have a suitable location (with a big enough car park), a hospital must have specialist doctors, nurses, a practical building and good medical equipment, while a peanut butter manufacturer will need access to quality raw materials, a good recipe and an efficient production line.

Questions that should be posed by an organisation when putting this essential 'building block' in place are (Osterwalder & Pigneur, 2009):
- What resources are the key to our value proposition?
- What resources are needed for our distribution channels?
- What resources are needed for building and maintaining customer relations?
- What resources are needed to generate our revenue?

For ecommerce, it is desirable that an organisation can provide real-time information to (potential) customers, to its own management and also to its partners in the value chain. Subsequently and on this basis, the customer must receive the right product, at the right time, via the correct channel. The organisation must be able to facilitate and complete online transactions, for both customers and suppliers. It is also important to be able to provide relevant personalised information before, during and after producing and delivering the product. The products or services must be distributed to the customer effectively and efficiently.

7 Key activities

The 'key activities' building block describes the most important steps the organisation needs to take to create the value proposition, to reach their customer segments cost-effectively, to build customer relationships and to generate revenue.

Questions that should be raised when completing this building block are (Osterwalder & Pigneur, 2009):
- What key activities are needed for our value proposition?
- What key activities are necessary for our distribution channels?
- What key activities are necessary for our customer relationships?
- What key activities are needed to realise revenue streams?

As an example: Apple produces electronic devices and software. A clothing store like H&M produces fashionable clothes at 'reasonable' prices and presents them attractively in their stores (offline and online).

Key activities within organisations that focus heavily on Digital Marketing are often related to online product realisation, Digital Marketing communications, online sales, digital CRM, order handling and the generation, analysis and interpretation of data.

8 Key partners

Key partners are the organisations that the company chooses to work with, to optimise their business model, reduce risk, or to obtain resources from. These are not simple supplier relationships, but essential partners. Some examples are partners from the distribution network, the suppliers of raw materials and services, the media partners that provide the product communications and also strategic alliances.

As an example, Walmart has a partnership with Rakuten, one of Japan's leading ecommerce companies, to provide products and services including an online grocery service in Japan, and the sale of ereaders, audiobooks and ebooks in the U.S., via Rakuten's subsidiary Kobo.

The questions that must be raised with regard to this building block in the business model are (Osterwalder & Pigneur, 2009):
- Who are our core suppliers and partners?
- What key resources do we purchase from partners?
- What key activities do partners carry out?

The key question is:
- What can we do ourselves and what should we outsource (Osterwalder & Pigneur, 2009)?

9 Cost structure

Each of the elements within the business model comes at a price. If the organisation has decided to opt for cost leadership (generally implying low price), the costs should be kept as low as possible. An organisation that chooses a differentiation strategy and distinguishes itself from the competition by delivering *superior value* will be faced with higher costs. In all cases, costs, given the circumstances, must be minimised so that the price/value ratio for the customer is as attractive as possible.

Questions that should be raised when completing this building block are (Osterwalder & Pigneur, 2009):
- What are the most important costs inherent to our business model?
- Which key resources are the most expensive?
- Which key activities are the most expensive?

The organisation must determine whether the fixed costs are relatively high or low and which activities and resources contribute the most cost. Of course, what the variable costs are and what their sources are is also looked into. In addition, it remains to be seen whether there is a financial advantage to be had by increasing scale and/or optimizing cooperation between departments or with external partners. By utilising Digital

Marketing, there are frequently significant financial advantages available, compared with 'traditional' (offline) marketing.

2.3.3 Check, execute and innovate the business model

Once all building blocks have been put in place, you will need to review the business model as a whole again. You will review:

- The business model itself: is it consistent, distinctive, and efficient and does it provide sufficient earning opportunity?
- The organisation's competencies: are the necessary knowledge, resources, systems and skills available or can they be acquired?
- The potential reactions of competitors: are you strong enough to ward them off? (If it's a new launch, are you prepared for the incumbents to fight back?)
- Future resilience: can you respond to changes and growth by adapting your business models accordingly without encountering any major problems?

EXAMPLE 2.6

The business model of a credit card organisation

Credit card companies provide data-based services. This means they are highly dependent on technology. They provide services to various parties: shops, consumers and banks. Most credit card companies do not issue cards themselves but do so through banks or large organisations. Examples include Starbucks Visa Card and John Lewis and Waitrose MasterCard.

Figure 2.4 shows how the process unfolds when someone uses a credit card to pay. When a cardholder pays with a credit card; a payment request will be made to the bank which the retailer has appointed to deal with its credit card payments. They will then contact the credit card issuer via the credit card company's network. The issuing authority indicates whether there is sufficient balance to pay by credit card. The issuer sends the cardholder a monthly bill. The actual process contains more data streams, among other things for the payments between parties internally. A credit card company also offers more services than purely the authorisation, eg insurance.

FIGURE 2.4 Simplified Process Payment with Credit Card

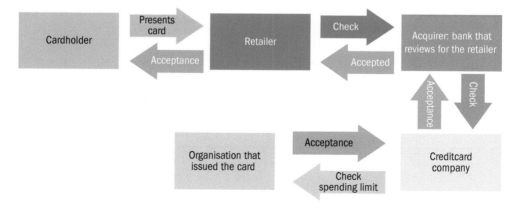

The various parties earn money by charging a 'merchant fee' to the retailer. The credit card company receives revenue from the service to banks, and also from the authorisation and remuneration if the cardholder comes from another country.

In order to fill in the value proposition, the credit card company has a processing centre. Most credit card companies have several of these centres, all of which are connected. Managing these payment networks so that they provide an efficient and reliable 24/7 service to banks, retailers and cardholders is a core activity.

Cardholders are a profit booster for the credit card company. The greater the number of cardholders, the greater the need for card acceptance by retailers and the more attractive is the card for the issuing agencies, thus increasing again the number of cardholders. Figure 2.5 shows the business model as conveyed by the Business Model Canvas from Osterwalder and Pigneur. This is a business model that generally applies to all credit card companies. In reality, every organisation will strive for a business model that offers a competitive advantage.

FIGURE 2.5 Business model of a credit card company

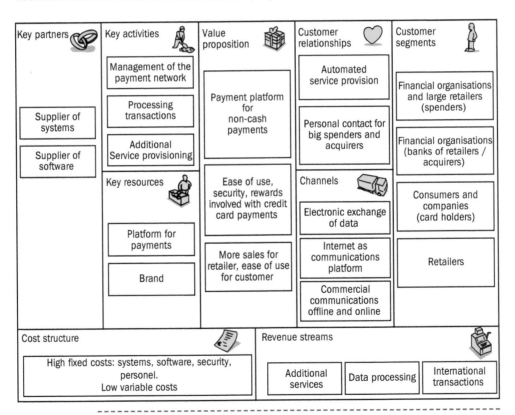

After completing the Business Model Canvas, the model must be adapted to reality and then adjusted according to 'real-world' factors. In doing so, Houtgraaf and Bekkers' (2013) method is useful. They use a slightly different layout of the business model from that of Osterwalder. However, keeping the Osterwalder model in mind, you can easily recognise the elements in their model. An important difference is that Houtgraaf and Bekkers (2013) distinguish between three layers of the business model: the strategy, the connection (architecture) and the organisation (see figure 2.6). With it they indicate that, once the broad strokes have been established, the business model has to be adapted to fit into the organisational structure, people, systems, processes and cost structure so that the value proposition can be realised.

FIGURE 2.6 Houtgraaf and Bekkers' model

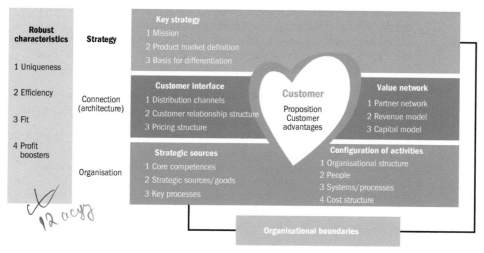

Source: Houtgraaf & Bekkers, 2013

Robust characteristics can be found on the side of this figure. Houtgraaf and Bekkers (2013) highlight four features that strengthen the structure and thus, importantly, the business model's (and the business's) chance of success:
- Uniqueness: The degree to which the business model is unique and distinctive in terms of customer groups and its ability to earn money.   *Uniqueness*
- Efficiency: The extent to which the business model is an efficient whole, so that the added value exceeds the cost.
- Fit: The internal consistency of the components of the business model, the extent to which they work in a coherent way towards a single end result.   *Fit*
- Profit boosters: The possibilities for strengthening and enhancing the organisation's goals in the long-run. For example, outsourcing competitors, a lock-in of customers or mutually enhancing scale and focus benefits.   *Profit boosters*

Houtgraaf and Bekkers (2013) provide the following four systematic steps that bring structure to your quest for improvements and can ensure that any new or customised business model is a balanced one:

Step 1   Describe your current business model in detail. Describe how all components are currently put together.

Step 2   Describe the changes in the world around us in relation to the components in your current business model. Also indicate where you think the (potential) weak points/components are.

Step 3   Examine any possible adjustments. Hopefully there will be a variety of possibilities or scenarios. Analyse the pros and cons of these scenarios and select the best.

Step 4   Keeping in mind future stability, such as consistency, do another run through of your model. When doing so, try to figure out how competitors might respond.

When going through this process, it is important to ensure the participation of people from several different disciplines. Finance Directors (CFOs), for example, have different priorities from people working in production, marketers and IT managers. This type of planning ensures attention is given to all relevant factors ie justice is done to all relevant aspects. Moreover, the advantage is that there will be wide support throughout the organisation

2.3.4   Role of Digital Marketing in the business model

Digital Marketing is a way to shape an organisation's marketing activities: using the Internet or Internet-related technology. Choosing Digital Marketing has important consequences for the business model. The value proposition can change, especially within service organisations: for example, there is a world of difference between a training organisation that offers traditional classes in a classroom setting, and one that provides online classes only. This also means choosing a target audience is digitally 'savvy', ie they know exactly how to use digital channels and are comfortable learning in this way.

The communication/sales channel also looks different: either only online or a mix of digital and traditional channels could be present. Of course, variants are possible, such as communicating through mobile or social media. The customer relationships can be formed through co-creation, communities and/or automated services. In addition, communication with the customer actually consists of sending data back and forth, but in such a way that communication with the customer is personalised as much as possible. Ironically, although the customer is 'anonymous', a lot is actually known about them. But in this case, in aggregated form, by systems and not by people about individuals.

EXAMPLE 2.7

Ocado has no stores

Ocado is a British online grocery retailer. Unlike its main competitors, it has no physical stores and fulfils all home deliveries from its warehouses. In the UK, Ocado's products include own-label groceries from the Waitrose supermarket chain as well as their own Ocado brand, and also a selection of branded groceries and household products, including flowers, toys and magazines. Ocado partners with Carrefour and Amazon Alexa. Ocado is a 'learning' company; it knows a lot about its customers and offers them products it believes they will want, delivered in a way that suits them.

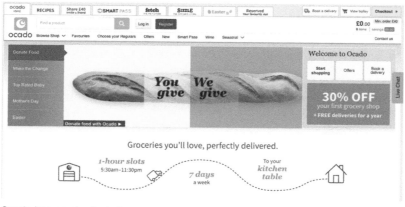

Ocado has no physical stores

For the earnings model, several of the options as mentioned in paragraph 2.3.5 are possible. When an organisation chooses Digital Marketing, this will usually also be one of their key activities. Important resources or key resources are then the website and/or app and the underlying systems, the CRM system and the customer data. This can be a significant part of the fixed expenses. In the case of pure-play ecommerce retailer (ie with no bricks and mortar outlets) the website is the store and is therefore crucially important.

2.4 Determining the Impact of Digital Marketing on New Internet Technology

In the event of the emergence of a new Internet technology, the effects on an existing business can be seen on four levels:
1 the business model
2 the marketing strategy
3 the marketing instruments
4 the marketing operation

To illustrate this, we can look to the past, to the first emergence of the Mobile Internet. It becomes attractive for an organisation to deploy mobile technology if it leads to more sales, reduced costs and/or increased customer satisfaction. The benefits of accessing the web on a smartphone compared to via a desktop PC are:
- Ubiquity (omnipresence): Data can be sent and received anywhere and at any time.   *Ubiquity*
- Context Sensitivity: The content of messages can be customised to the time, location, individual, and anything else that is measurable by the smartphone's sensors.

- Identification: The owner can be identified, and his/her movements can be tracked.

Command and Control functions

- Command and Control functions: The smartphone can be remotely operated via sensors/chips and so on (Pousttchi, Selk & Turowski, 2002).

2.4.1 Impact on the business model

Sometimes the benefits of a new Internet technology are so significant that an organisation is compelled to completely change their business model to ensure survival. For over a hundred years, Kodak dominated the photography market (via its cameras and film products), but the company was completely overtaken by competitors when the digital camera became popular. Ironically, it was Kodak who invented this camera. They failed to sufficiently realise that their business was not about 'printing photographs' (or even selling film) but rather about 'capturing and preserving memories'. Kodak eventually switched their focus to the image processing market for the entertainment industry, commercial printing and the packaging industry. The rise of the mobile Internet provided them with a new opportunity to take advantage of the brand awareness that Kodak already possessed in the consumer market. Crucially however, the organisation did not adapt its business model, leaving room for new parties such as Instagram to fill the void. Instagram was bought by Facebook for $1 billion in 2012, at the time having just 13 employees. Kodak, meanwhile, reduced their total employee headcount from 140,000 at the peak of their success, to just over 8,000 in 2014.

2.4.2 Consequences for the Marketing Strategy

The emergence of a new (Internet) technology can completely destabilise an organisation's marketing strategy. It can affect the organisation's target markets, the solutions or products that the organisation offers, and even its competitive positioning.

Figure 2.7 shows the business definition of a language institute that helps people to communicate in foreign languages. They position themselves as reliable and stable, with more than 50 years of experience. The figure is based on the model for defining businesses according to Abell (Abell, 1980). Before the language institute was able to use the web, its management focused on three target groups: government, teachers and businesses. For these groups, they provided classical language courses and translated documents. The emergence of the web made it possible for this organisation to expand their target markets to include the private market (direct to end users). For this market, they set up an eLearning course, accessible on the PC. The interaction with the other groups remains personal. The Mobile Internet made it possible for real-time audiences to help translate wherever they are. The organisation then developed a paid app for individuals and teachers. Here you can see how the possibilities of new Internet technologies have changed the marketing strategy: a market segment has been added and its needs are filled in by the language institute in a different way. This has led to new products: the eLearning language course for individuals and the translation app.

FIGURE 2.7 The business definition of a language institute

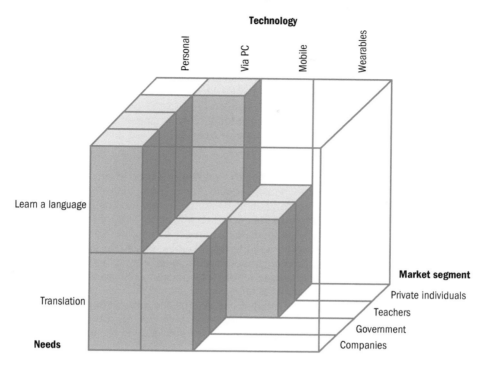

The language institute should also look at what the rising popularity of wearables means for their marketing strategy. Wearables are devices that are worn rather than carried eg smartwatches, fitness monitors, headsets etc. It may also be useful to develop an advanced translation app, possibly including voice operation and sound. That way, business travellers are also an attractive market. Perhaps the positioning should also be adjusted. It is possible that these innovations may not be sufficiently consistent with their positioning as a stable, reliable, over 50-year-old language institute.

Changing the marketing strategy also changes the business model. They cannot be seen as separate from each other. The choices affect market segments, channels, customer relationships, core processes, core business, the earnings model and the cost structure.

2.4.3 Consequences for the marketing instruments
The emergence of a new Internet technology doesn't always have far-reaching consequences for the marketing strategy and business model. Sometimes, it only leads to changes in the way in which the marketing tools are arranged.

Some examples:
- *Product:* Lay's (Walker's) Crisps involves consumers in the development of new flavours of crisps.
- *Distribution:* Brabantia sells its household items in a number of large online stores.
- *Price:* Dutch Airline KLM's online prices are not only geared to making sure their aircraft are fully booked and to accommodate the development in demand, but are also customised to suit the online behaviour of the customer.
- *Promotion:* Red Bull communicates through offline advertising and events, as well as through its own website, the Red Bull app and on social media.

2.4.4 Consequences for the marketing operation

Often, using Internet technology results in marketing activities that are simply cheaper and which get better results. Here are some examples:
- UK Department store John Lewis uses a special Twitter account (twitter.com/jlcustser) to seek feedback and resolve customer service issues. They combine this with their market research data to develop a fuller understanding of their customers' wants, needs and preferences. Customers are encouraged to follow twitter.com/johnlewisretail for news, views and useful content.
- Wearables technology made it possible for the popular Runkeeper Fitness App to make use of a heart-rate sensor in earphones that allows it to adjust the music accordingly. This adds value to the product for Runkeeper users.
- Starbucks' regular customers can pay via a mobile app for Android or iOS. This makes the payment process more efficient.
- Booking.com, the hotel booking website, collects and analyses the online search and booking behaviour of its customers, both in their app and on their website. This makes it possible to personalise offers to customers' tailored to their situation and place of residence.

2.4.5 Setting priorities

A new Internet technology often offers many possibilities for additional competitive advantage, but an organisation only has a limited amount of resources and time. Therefore, it is vitally important to set priorities. First of all, the organisation must estimate the impact of the new technology on its own sector. For example, the rise of robots may have little impact on the online book industry (except perhaps in the warehouse), but significantly more in the hospitality industry. In addition, senior management will have to look at how significant the necessary changes will be in order to adapt to the new situation. If the impact on the sector is small and the required change in the organisation is relatively minimal, then optimising the organisation's operational marketing will usually suffice. However, if the impact of the new technology to the sector is high, such as the original introduction of digital photography, and the organisation must make a major change, it may be necessary to innovate the business model radically. Figure 2.8 contains an overview of the necessary measures.

© Noordhoff Uitgevers bv

FIGURE 2.8 Technological Impact / Change Matrix

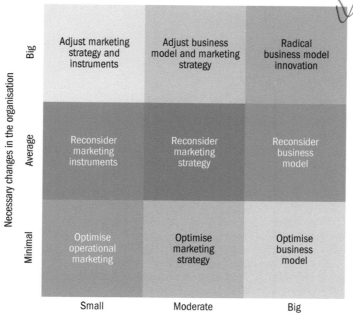

The final priorities depend not only on the need for change, but also on the expected revenue and expenses. For each improvement, the expected return on investment (ROI) is calculated.

Questions and assignments

NOW CHECK YOUR UNDERSTANDING:

2.1   BT (formerly British Telecom) provides consumers with fixed-line, mobile, broadband, subscription TV and IT services. It has operations in 180 countries.
a   What general strategic issues will BT's marketing strategy have to provide an answer for?
b   How should BT determine what role Digital Marketing should take within the marketing strategy?

2.2   Go to: www.thinkwithgoogle.com.
a   What are the top ten internet-related technological and social trends that you can find there?
b   Choose a chain of fashion stores that appeals to you. How could an organisation capitalise on these trends using Digital Marketing?
c   Would the marketing strategy of these fashion stores need to change? Please substantiate your answer.
d   According to which four steps should this retail chain determine how much their business model needs to be innovated?

2.3   The Ritz-Carlton is a chain of luxury hotels with a rich tradition (it is now owned by Marriott International). The Hotel's mission is to 'provide guests with genuine care and comfort, the most refined personal service and facilities and a warm, relaxed, refined ambiance'. The Ritz-Carlton 'stimulates the senses, fosters wellbeing and fulfils even the unspoken wishes and needs of its guests'.
a   Explain why the mission and objectives of an organisation are of great importance to the chosen business model.
b   Who do you think the target audience of Ritz-Carlton hotels is?
c   On what characteristics do you think Ritz-Carlton has based its positioning?
d   When you look at the mission and positioning of the Ritz-Carlton, what role do you think 'digital' plays in their business model?

2.4   WhatsApp is a cross-platform application for mobile messaging, allowing for the free exchange of messages. It is available for smartphones with various operating systems in many countries. WhatsApp users can send each other an unlimited number of images, video and audio messages. When originally launched, WhatsApp was free for the first year. After that, users paid a fixed, yearly fee for usage of the app. Indicate what you think the following building blocks were for WhatsApp:
a   Value proposition
b   Customer relationships

© Noordhoff Uitgevers bv

c   Revenue sources
d   Key resources

N.B. WhatsApp subsequently dropped the subscription charge, making the service completely free to users and relying on revenues from partners/ brand owners.

2.5   Look at the list of earnings models in paragraph 2.3.2 'The revenue streams'. Find a new example for each of these earnings models. Why do you think these organisations chose this earnings model?

2.6   Below is the business model for 'Fit and Fun'. Fit and Fun's mission is to ensure that overweight people adopt a more active lifestyle, moving more and engaging more consciously with diet. In figure 2.9 you can see the business model Canvas, as filled in by Fit and Fun.

a   What improvements would you make to this business model Canvas?
b   Explain, for each component, what role online marketing could play.
c   How should 'Fit and Fun' determine the impact of new wearables on online marketing?

FIGURE 2.9 Business model of Fit and Fun

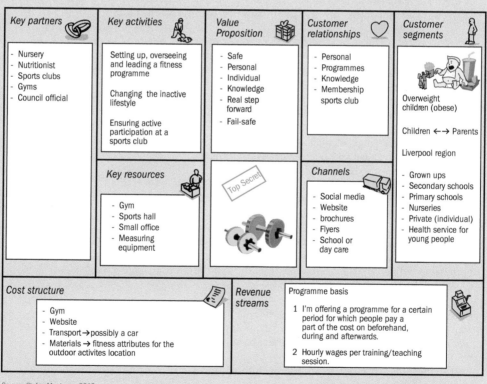

Source: Stefan Maatman, 2012

2.7

Cleartrip
By Mike Berry

Cleartrip is an online travel agent headquartered in Mumbai, India. It provides an online booking service for flights and train tickets, hotel reservations, and domestic and international holiday packages. Cleartrip was founded by Stuart Crighton and Hrush Bhatt in 2006.

Cleartrip's website is intended to help travellers to: 'Book cheap airline tickets and get amazing discounts to your favourite destinations around the world'. Cleartrip claims to be 'Your most trusted partners for booking Domestic & International flights, Hotels, Holiday packages & Local activities with 24/7 customer support'. Users can access Cleartrip through its mobile app for Android and iPhone and also on desktop/laptop PC by visiting www.cleartrip.com.

Cleartrip gives its customers special offers on hotels and flights and provides holiday packages at discounted prices. Cleartrip also provides a detailed travel guide for many cities and hill stations across India via its Activities section. There is a list of the best restaurants and places of interest at each destination plus in many cases special discounts for Cleartrip customers with these partners.

Cleartrip seeks to replace the traditional high street travel agent by taking care of all its customers' travel needs all at the touch of a mouse/finger. However, it increasingly finds itself competing with other online players, even as its customers become increasingly demanding.

The stated mission of Cleartrip is to make travel easier and cheaper for its users. Cleartrip allows users to book flight and train tickets and also provides hotel room booking services, often at discounted rates, all from one convenient website, providing seamless travel booking for its customers.

Cheap Flights: Cleartrip enables flight ticket bookings for both domestic and international travel. Users can compare ticket prices for all airlines in a single window and book the best-priced, most convenient ticket to meet their travel needs.

Train tickets: Cleartrip has partnered with Indian Railways (IRCTC) so that its users can book train tickets easily. It provides a hassle-free super-convenient ticket booking experience. Users can also cancel/amend their bookings through the Cleartrip website.

Hotel Bookings: Users can book hotels in almost all Indian cities through the website. Cleartrip offers competitive prices for hotels across India and also features useful user reviews and ratings for each hotel.

Very simply, Cleartrip makes its money from commissions earned from its partners/suppliers, for introducing business to them. It earns a margin of 15-20% from its hotel business and a margin of 5-6% from flights and train bookings.

Cleartrip allows users to compare ticket prices for all airlines in a single window

Average ticket value for Indian bookings is between 8,000-9,000 rupees while for international bookings it is between 24,000-25,000 rupees. Cleartrip handles around 2,000-5,000 transactions per day in flight and hotel bookings.

To put these figures in perspective, the total Indian online travel market is approximately 30,000 transactions per day, so that Cleartrip's market share is currently around 10%; ie it still has plenty of room for further growth in India.

Throughout its history, Cleartrip has always invested significant budgets in its marketing communications with a series of TV commercials and extensive social media campaigns. As a result, Cleartrip has become a well-known brand among Indian travellers, and a respected name in the online travel industry. Cleartrip spends an annual budget of approximately 1.5 million USD every year on marketing.

To monitor customer satisfaction, Cleartrip uses various social media platforms to gather feedback and improve its offerings, to provide troubleshooting and to deliver customer service.

There are several other Indian travel websites but Cleartrip's key competitors include MakeMyTrip and Goibibo. MakeMyTrip is the biggest player in the market with 25% market share of online bookings in India. In the hotel booking market, Cleartrip competes with giants like OYO Rooms.

Overall it is clear that travellers in India are growing more web-savvy and consequently more demanding. Internet penetration in South Asia has now reached 36% but is clearly much higher amongst upmarket frequent travellers. Cleartrip has been highly successful and has won many awards for its marketing. However, to continue its impressive growth, it must focus on delivering a superior customer experience, while keeping an eye on its powerful competitors.

Source: www.whizsky.com/2017/09/case-study-cleartrip-business-model-marketing-competition-indian-travel-sites-market

NOW CHECK YOUR UNDERSTANDING:

a Describe Cleartrip's business model.
b What explains the success of Cleartrip so far? How much does digital marketing drive its overall corporate strategy?
c What new digital technologies should Cleartrip take into account in the future?
d What do you estimate the impact of these changing technologies to be on the travel sector in India? Globally? Please substantiate your answer.
e Do you think Cleartrip needs to make small, medium or big changes to adapt to the changing market conditions? Which of the four steps (see 2.3.3 by Houtgraaf and Bekkers) should they take? What consequences does this have for their business model, marketing strategy, marketing tools and operational marketing?
f If you were CMO of Cleartrip, what improvements would you make to their marketing strategy, in line with digital innovations? Apply clear criteria and substantiate your answer with relevant arguments.

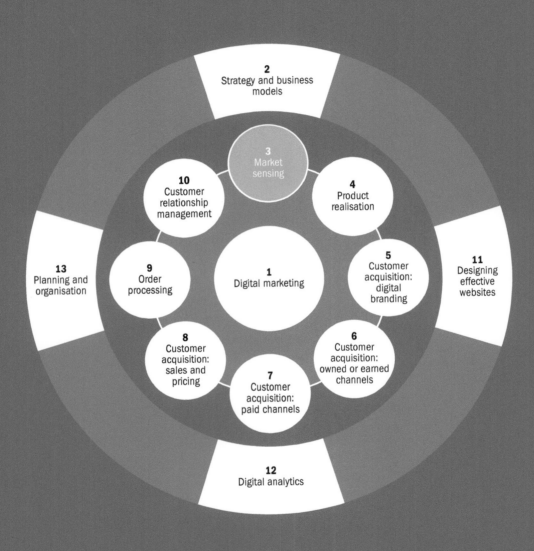

3

Market Sensing

Authors: Marjolein Visser (3.1 to 3.6 and 3.9), Lucas Hulsebos (3.7) and Frank van Delft (3.8)

The previous chapter describes how organisations come up with a Digital Marketing strategy and business model. In order to make the right choices, it is necessary to understand the expected behaviour of future customers. This is done by market sensing, ie getting a sense of what is happening in the market. The 'market sensing process' is the process whereby the organisation makes sure that it is continuously up to date with the needs, developments and trends in the market. Only when an organisation knows the market intimately, can it offer products online that will be successful now and in the future.

This chapter will cover:
- global Internet usage
- buying online
- use of social media
- relevant trends for Digital Marketing
- a model for online consumer behaviour
- the Digital Marketing funnel
- online market research
- data analysis and customer insights
- social media monitoring

After studying this chapter, you will be able to:
- describe the growth of Internet usage
- identify the main reasons why people buy online, show the different risks that consumers experience when shopping online and translate them into real-world examples
- indicate what motivates people to participate in the various levels and forms of interaction with social media
- indicate how the main trends in digitalisation affect Digital Marketing
- describe the different phases in the consumer purchasing process, indicate what role the web plays in each phase and what factors play a decisive role in each of these phases
- name the elements of the Digital Marketing funnel and indicate what the core success factors are for each phase

- name the main offline and online market research channels, indicate what the pros and cons of each channel are and describe the various research forms that can be applied online
- identify which online and offline research forms are appropriate for measuring the effectiveness of Digital Marketing
- explain how data and analytics can be used to formulate customer insights
- indicate how social media monitoring can be employed

3.1 Internet usage

The rise of the Internet and specifically the worldwide web (www) as a medium for communication has dramatically changed the purchasing behaviour of consumers in recent decades. All competitors are collected in one place and consumers can consider many alternatives within a limited time. An offer in a store can be compared to the offers on Internet within a few minutes. This means that consumers are often very well informed and therefore are in a very strong bargaining position. It's important that marketers get to know their potential customers well so that they can respond to their needs and wishes. In this section you will find more information about the growth of Internet usage, digital lifestyles and the influence of the Internet on the buying behaviour of today's digital consumer.

3.1.1 The state of the Internet

British physicist Sir Tim Berners-Lee invented the web in the early 1990s while he was working at CERN; his idea was to build a network of connected computers based on the internet and using the common standard language HTML so that information could be shared effortlessly and globally between users via a 'World Wide Web' (www). Today, according to We Are Social (2018) there are now more than 4 billion people around the world using the internet (see figure 3.1).

FIGURE 3.1 Global Internet statistics

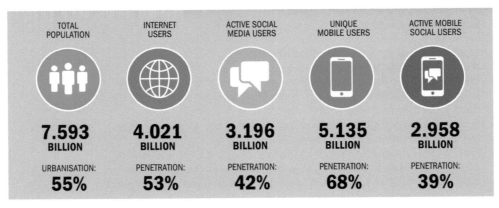

TOTAL POPULATION	INTERNET USERS	ACTIVE SOCIAL MEDIA USERS	UNIQUE MOBILE USERS	ACTIVE MOBILE SOCIAL USERS
7.593 BILLION	4.021 BILLION	3.196 BILLION	5.135 BILLION	2.958 BILLION
URBANISATION: 55%	PENETRATION: 53%	PENETRATION: 42%	PENETRATION: 68%	PENETRATION: 39%

Source: We Are Social/Hootsuite, 2018

Here are some key findings from We Are Social/Hootsuite (2018):
- The number of social media users is 3.196 billion.
- The number of mobile phone users is 5.135 billion.
- More than two-thirds of the world's population now has a mobile, with most people now using a smartphone.
- Almost 1 million people started using social media for the first time every day in 2017 – that's equivalent to more than *11 new users every second*.
- The global number of people using social media has grown by 13% 2017-2018, with Central and Southern Asia recording the fastest gains (up 90% and 33% respectively).
- Saudi Arabia has posted the fastest individual country growth rate across major economies at 32%, but India is only just behind, with 31% annual growth in social media users.
- Worldwide, the number of people using ecommerce platforms to buy consumer goods (eg fashion, food, electronics, and toys) grew by 8%, with almost 1.8 billion people around the world now buying online.
- Roughly 45% of all internet users now use ecommerce sites, but penetration varies considerably between countries.

Meanwhile the Mary Meeker Report (2017) summarizes the current picture:
- Global smartphone growth is slowing: Smartphone shipments grew 3% year over year last year, versus 10% the year before. Note this refers to growth in sales; usership is still growing fast by consumers and marketers.
- Voice is beginning to replace typing in online queries. 20% of mobile queries were made via voice, while accuracy (ie correct understanding of voice queries) is now about 95%.
- In 10 years, Netflix went from 0 to more than 30% of home entertainment revenue in the U.S.. This is happening while TV viewership continues to decline.
- China has seen huge growth in mobile services and payments and services.
- Internet growth is slowing globally, but not in India, the fastest growing large economy. The number of internet users in India grew more than 28% year on year. The figure is still only 27% online penetration, so lots of room for internet usership to grow in India. Mobile internet usage is growing as the cost of bandwidth declines.

3.1.2   Digital Lifestyles

TNS conducted a worldwide survey of Internet usage in 2010. Based on this study, they identified six digital lifestyles. Below you will find these lifestyles listed and explained according to typical statements that exemplify each lifestyle separately:

1 Influencers: 'The Internet is an integral part of my life. I am young and a frequent mobile Internet user and can access it anywhere. I am a blogger, a passionate social networker with many online friends. I'm also a big online shopper, even on my mobile phone. I want to make sure that as many people as possible hear my online voice.'   **Influencers**

2 Communicators: 'I just love talking and expressing myself, whether face to face, on a landline, on mobile or social networking sites, instant messaging, or just by email. I want to express myself in the online world in a way that cannot be done offline. I'm a clever smartphone user and I connect online to my mobile, at home, at work or at school.'   **Communicators**

Knowledge Seekers

3 Knowledge Seekers: 'I use the Internet to acquire knowledge and information and to learn about the world. I'm not very interested in social networks, but I want to listen to the opinions of like-minded people, especially to help me decide on what products to buy. I am very interested in the latest things.'

Networkers

4 Networkers: 'The Internet is important for me to create and maintain relationships. I have a busy life professionally as well as when it comes to managing my private life. I use things like social networks to keep in touch with people for whom I otherwise would not have enough time. I'm a big home user of the Internet and I'm very open to communicating with brands and promotional actions. I'm not really the kind of person who gives advice online.'

Aspirers

5 Aspirers: 'I'm looking to create a personal space for myself online. I have little Internet experience and although I do connect to the Internet via my mobile phone, I do so mostly from home. I do not do much online at the moment, but I am desperately looking forward to doing more, especially with a mobile device.'

Functionals

6 Functionals: 'The Internet is a functional tool; I do not want to express myself online. I email, check news, sports and weather, but I also go shopping online. I'm really not interested in novelties (such as social networks) and I'm concerned about data privacy and security. I'm older and have been using the Internet for a long time.'

The three groups that buy the most online are the influencers, the communicators and the knowledge-seekers.

3.2 Buying on the Internet

Mary Meeker (2017) explains how USA parcel traffic is expanding rapidly as consumers become increasingly comfortable with ecommerce (see figure 3.2).

FIGURE 3.2 USA parcel growth is accelerating

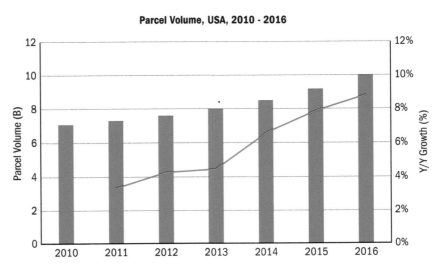

Source: Kleiner Perkins, 2017

© Noordhoff Uitgevers bv

Marketing Land refers to the Mary Meeker report in providing some insights into current online shopping trends (most examples are USA-based but indicate trends that are affecting all countries):
- a withering brick-and-mortar landscape as Amazon/ecommerce grows
- Walmart is sprinting to catch up online
- the new retail is mobile-informed
- location-driven advertising is becoming more targeted and accountable

What are the reasons people do/do not buy online? What causes a channel switch? What obstacles are there for Internet purchases? What determines whether someone shops on the Internet? We will now elaborate on these questions.

3.2.1   Reasons for and against buying online
Ecommerce is growing rapidly as people become increasingly confident that goods will be delivered and their personal information kept safe. Other major factors (Marvin, 2017) are ease of use (customer experience, especially on mobile) and convenience (delivery to your home or office at a time that suits you).

Against this, there are some types of shopping where consumers still enjoy the bricks and mortar shopping experience eg fresh fruit and vegetables and fashion, which can be a social experience, enjoyed with friends. BBC Bitesize (2017) explains:

'Nearly everything available on the high street or in shopping centres can also be found online. For example, supermarkets offer home delivery of goods ordered through their website.

Digital downloads are now common too. Items previously sold on physical media (CDs, DVDs, books) can instead be downloaded directly to a customer's computer or handheld device.

The process for buying goods online commonly involves:
- browsing through the online catalogue
- adding items to the virtual basket
- visiting a virtual checkout
- choosing payment and delivery method
- order confirmation
- shipping confirmation (via email or SMS)

Advantages:
- Convenience: shop from any computer with an Internet connection any time while avoiding the need to travel, pay for parking, queue in-store etc.
- Greater variety: more shops online than any highstreet or shopping centre.
- Cheaper goods: increased competition between retailers (for some on a global scale) brings down prices.
- Accessibility: those with a disability that limits their mobility can choose to have goods delivered.
- Comparability: using the Internet it's easy to research products or services very thoroughly, comparing prices and product details in order to get the best deal.

Disadvantages:
- security concerns surrounding payment by credit card over the Internet
- not being able to physically inspect the goods before purchase
- goods getting damaged during transport
- goods not arriving in time or at all
- concerns over what information retailers are storing about customers, eg buying habits.'

3.2.2   Channel switch

Doing research online does not always lead to a purchase. While the Internet appears to be the most widely used research channel for people who want to buy a product, the physical store is still a key place for product investigation for many people. However, there are big differences per product type. Online, people focus on products that can be viewed or compared digitally, such as travel, computer software and technical products, although this aspect of tangibility is becoming less important. The main reasons for online orientation and subsequent purchasing in a store (channel switch) are:
- the product cannot be seen, felt or altered online
- the store has an attractive price/offer
- you can take the product home directly
- there is personal contact
- there are no shipping costs

The main reasons to research in a store and then order online are:
- the price is lower online
- the purchase is easier because it can be done from home
- the product is not available in the store
- there is less choice due to a smaller range of products
- it is immediately clear whether the product is in stock
- opening hours are too limited
- buying in the store costs more time

There is also a growing trend for people to switch channels according to what suits them at a particular point in time eg research in store then buy online (often via mobile), click and collect (ie buy online and then visit a store). There is also the growing phenomenon of 'showrooming' where the retail outlet is simply used to select a product which the consumer then buys online, often at a cheaper price. This is a serious threat to many traditional retailers.

3.2.3   Obstacles for buying on the Internet

Forsythe and Shi already researched what risks people worry about when buying over the Internet. They distinguished four types of risk (Forsythe & Shi, 2003):
1 financial risk
2 functional risk
3 psychological risk
4 time-saving risk

As time has passed, these threats have receded, and online commerce has grown.

1 Financial risk

By financial risk, Forsythe and Shi mean the risk that the customer might lose money, including misuse of credit card information.
For people who rarely or never buy online, financial risk is the main obstacle. The lower the financial risk that the Internet user experiences, the more often they will buy online, and the more they will spend.

The use of trustworthy payment methods, but also, for example, a good image and affiliation with a recognised industry organisation, can help reduce the fear of financial loss for the website visitor. Many online retailers therefore allow for a post-pay billing option, but at an additional cost. In addition, Apple Pay and Google Pay for Android are growing in importance.

Financial risk

2 Functional risk

Functional risk of the product is the loss that occurs if a supplier or product does not do what the customer expects it to (ie 'deliver' in every sense). Products purchased on the Internet are intangible (at the time of order). The consumer cannot sense, feel, smell or try these products and thus depends on a correct representation of the product itself and the technical data. When shopping online, the likelihood of choosing a product that does not meet expectations is greater than when making an offline purchase. The functional risk of the product is seen as being very high by people who do not shop online often. Reviews and feedback by other users are decisive for reducing risk perception. Again, as time has passed, and online retail experiences have been generally positive, more and more of us are confident to shop online.

Functional risk

3 Psychological risk

According to Forsythe and Shi, psychological risk concerns the disappointment, frustration or shame that will be felt if personal information regarding the customer should become visible to others online. An example is the feeling of having no control over the access that others have to personal information that they might discover when performing a search query on the Internet.
Older Internet users and people with little Internet experience are often afraid of these psychological risks. Their main trepidations are regarding security and privacy. The older they are, the more they worry. It is therefore important for brand owners not only to comply strictly with the relevant privacy laws, but to also include a privacy statement prominently on the website, to state the terms and conditions, including the customer's right to exchange and return and to explicitly state what any personal information is used for. Naturally these factors will be more relevant in countries where internet usage is still growing rapidly so that many older consumers are going online for the first time (including India, Africa and China).

Psychological risk

4 Time-consuming risk

Time-consuming risk refers to time lost and inconvenience experienced searching the web, during the order process or as a result of late delivery. Irritation experienced as a result of a slow working or inaccessible website also falls under this risk (colloquially described as 'hassle' or 'aggravation').

Time-consuming risk

The older you are, the lower you estimate the time-consuming risk of online purchases. It has been observed that young people see few risks in buying online but score relatively highly on this ('aggravation') point. The less time-consuming risk the Internet user anticipates, the more often they will browse the Internet for the purpose of making a purchase. How readily the website can be found, as well as its performance are of importance, but particularly the ability to guarantee delivery times.

People who spend very little time shopping online perceive there to be many more risks than people who shop online frequently. For ecommerce retailers, It is important to remove as many of these risk perceptions as possible when planning a Digital Marketing programme.

3.2.4 What determines whether someone shops on the Internet?

It is important for marketers to know how their customers feel about using the Internet and online shopping. It makes no sense to invest time and money in promoting online sales to audiences who anticipate too many risks or who are simply predisposed to physical shopping. It is wiser to invest in groups (segments) where the chances of success are higher.

Lim (2015) suggested the factors which determine whether an individual shops online or not. He claims that it is dependent upon their attitude towards online shopping, determined by the following factors:
- The value they expect from online shopping: do they expect to save money, have access to an extensive range of products and experience less 'hassle' when compared to offline shopping?
- The expected ease of use: do they expect ecommerce websites to be easy to use so that they are able to find what they are looking for?
- Experience: is it faster than offline shopping, does it lead to better purchasing decisions, is it easier?
- Social factors: do they worry about what others say about online shopping, do they tend to buy online products and go to ecommerce sites that have been recommended by friends on social media?
- Entertainment gratification: do they have fun shopping online? do they find it difficult and unpleasant?
- Internet irritation: do they find the web disorganised and irritating, for example, because of too many ads?
- Emotional state: does online shopping lead to satisfaction and happiness? is it very stimulating?

Entertainment gratification

Someone may be positively inclined to online shopping, but their expectations still need to be met: the actual experience must be a good one, so a foundation of trust is created. Only then will someone become a habitual online shopper.

It is wise to investigate customer attitudes regarding online shopping. If there are many people in your target audience (eg a particular age group or geographical region) who are not comfortable using the Internet, it is wise to adjust the policy accordingly. Even if it's only a small group, it would be pertinent to find out how to educate and motivate these people to help them engage with your online services.

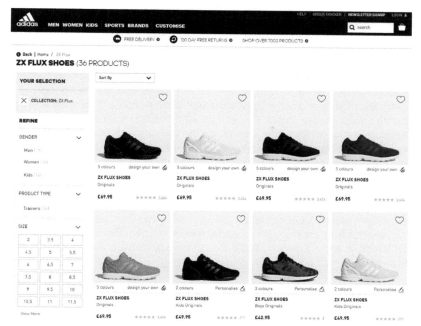

An example of entertainment gratification. Many people enjoy designing custom shoes at Adidas

3.3 Use of social media

The role of social media when communicating with key target audiences (both business to consumer B2C and business to business B2B) continues to increase. It is therefore important for organisations to continue to work towards social business: this phase means that communication through social media is fully integrated into the thinking behind the business as well as into the day-to-day practice.

As an online marketer, it is important to know what drives the consumer to use social media, in order to respond to their needs. The use by marketers of social media - as well as other media - should be active and goal-driven, based on the needs of the user. Because 'social media users' is a very broad concept and the motivations for using social media can vary depending on the user's activity, we will firstly define three different types of social media user. Next we will discuss six types of motivations that lead to using social media. Finally, we will determine what motivates each different type of user.

3.3.1   Three types of users

Muntinga, Moorman and Smit (2011) argue that the activities of social media users can be classified into three types of brand-related activities based on increasing activity: consuming, contributing and creating. 'Consuming' requires the least amount of activity from the user and includes, for example, viewing brand-related photos or videos or reading about product experiences, without contributing or creating any content. Users of the 'contributing' type respond to, for example, articles, photos or videos, or contribute to discussions or wikis.

Social media

Social business

Consuming

Contributing

Creating | Users of the 'creating' type are active producers (creators) of brand-related content, such as photos, videos, reviews, or articles.

3.3.2 Six types of motivations

Marketers' use of social media should be active and goal-driven and based on user needs (Dainton & Zelley, 2005). This statement stems from a theory that focuses on why individuals use certain media. The Uses and Gratifications Theory states that you as an individual have a free will and therefore make choices about which media you use and when you use them. The choices and decisions you make as an individual are based on personal needs and values that you wish to fulfil. McQuail (1987) has defined four general motivations for why individuals access media and thus perform brand-related activities: for Entertainment, for Information, Personal Identity and lastly for Integration and Social interaction. Based on a literature study, Muntinga et al. (2011) added two motivations to the original four that are relevant to social media, namely Reward and Self-fulfilment. In the diagram in Table 3.1, these six motivations are briefly described.

Uses and Gratifications Theory

TABLE 3.1 Motivations that are relevant to social media

Motivation	Description and examples
Entertainment	For relaxation, enjoyment, escaping reality or 'killing time', watching videos on YouTube or participating in a social game on Facebook
Information	Seeing what's happening in your immediate vicinity by reading status updates on Facebook/ Instagram, seeking out opinions and stories, increasing your knowledge by viewing pages on Wikipedia or videos on YouTube or reading reviews on a product before purchasing it to decrease risk.
Personal Identity	For self-expression, gaining recognition and self-confidence, presenting yourself to the world by posting home-made videos or photos online to YouTube or Instagram or by updating your LinkedIn profile with your most recent experiences
Integration and Social Interaction	For social interaction on a social network like Facebook, seeking and giving support and advice on, for example, a forum, identifying with others by joining a LinkedIn Group and participating in social media because others do – to 'hang out with people like me'
Reward	Consuming, contributing to or creating brand-related information because you expect to get something in return in the future
Self-fulfilment	Using social media to exercise influence or power on others, ie by writing their own blog

Research from Whiting and Williams (2013) shows that social media also provides topics for discussion for many users and allows them to keep an eye on what others are involved in. Social media participation also influences the 'offline' lives of the users.

3.3.3 Users have different motivations

Research from Muntinga et al. (2011) shows that the defined user types - people who consume, who contribute and who create - all have different motivations for performing these brand-related activities. Next, we will discuss some of these motivations.

Motivations for consuming brand-related information

Users who consume are driven mainly by information-related motivations. Within information-related motivations there are four sub-motivations, namely observing, acquiring knowledge, acquiring information in order to

Information-related motivations

make a purchase and gaining inspiration. Within the information-related motivations, observing is by far the biggest motivation for consumers to engage in brand-related activities. For example, social media users observe other people's opinions about a brand or note which news articles are currently relevant to their brand. In addition to the information-related motivations, entertainment also appears to be an important motivation for consuming brand-related information. Users of social media consume brand-related information to relax, kill time or for entertainment. (and to stop being bored, to be amused/distracted, to relax). Finally, motivational reward also plays a role in why users consume brand-related information, although this motivation is only slightly present (Muntinga et al., 2011). In B2B marketing, target customers may consume content in order to deepen their knowledge, to do their jobs better or to advance their career.

Brand-related
information

Reading reviews from other consumers before going on a city trip is an example of consuming brand-related information to reduce the risk of making a bad purchase decision

The information-related motivations for consuming brand-related information are consistent with the online consumer behaviour model discussed in section 3.5. In that model, *seeking information* is referred to as one of the six stages of the purchase process.

Motivations for contributing to brand-related information

Users who contribute, primarily engage in brand-related activities as a result of integration and social interaction motives, with social interaction being seen as the main sub-motivation for the use of social media. Social

Social
interaction

media users, for example, contribute to discussions surrounding a brand and thus engage in dialogue with other individuals who are interested in the brand. In addition to social interaction, entertainment is also a motivation for contributing to brand-related information; despite the fact that entertainment as a motivation is most present when consuming brand-related information, this motivation also plays a role in contributing to this information (Muntinga, 2011).

An example of contributing to brand-related information. On Twitter, humour and entertainment form the cornerstone of Taco Bell's presence, and the motivation behind why consumers contribute to this brand-related information by responding or sharing with friends will also be entertainment.

Motivations for consuming brand-related information
Personal identity is seen as the motivation behind creating brand-related information. Users of social media express themselves, for example, by making it known that they feel a connection to a particular brand. On Facebook you can become a fan of a particular brand and you can also follow brands on Pinterest, Instagram and Twitter.
As is the case in consuming and contributing to brand-related information, entertainment is also a motivator in the creation of brand-related information. This motivation is most relevant when consuming brand-related information. Nevertheless, the creation of brand-related information is also driven to a certain extent by the desire to pass the time, relax or entertain yourself (Muntinga et al., 2011, see Table 3.2).

This example of creating brand-related information after a positive brand experience is in itself a positive experience, but consumers will also share negative brand experiences on social media

TABLE 3.2 Types of social media users and the motivations these users have for brand-related activities

User type	Types of motivations
Consumption	• *Information (observing,* knowledge, information before making a purchase and inspiration) • *Entertainment (relaxing,* killing time and for fun) • Reward
Contributing	• *Integration and social interaction (social interaction,* helping and social identity) • Entertainment (relaxing, killing time and for fun)
Creating	• *Personal Identity (self-expression, self-confidence and self-presentation)* • Entertainment (relaxing, killing time and for fun)

Note: italicised motivations are motivations that are most present.

3.4 Relevant trends in Digital Marketing

The main trends in Digital Marketing are:
- augmented and virtual reality (AR and VR)
- further development of social media and networks
- Internet of things (IoT)
- Artificial Intelligence (AI) and advanced machine learning (ML)
- conversational systems (Chatbots)
- digitisation of services
- 3D printing
- blockchain
- big data, augmented information and the increasing importance of data security

The world wide web has always been a very innovative environment. For online marketers, this means that it is necessary to constantly keep their knowledge up-to-date and to successfully differentiate between important and minor innovations. What is a trend and what is just hype? For example, augmented reality was seen as hype for a long time whereas it is now rapidly becoming part of marketing communications. Meanwhile, platforms and applications have proliferated. No wonder some (especially older) marketers find it all rather overwhelming!

3.4.1   Augmented and virtual reality
Virtual reality (VR) depicts reality in a digital world. An example of this is online games. In the future, VR is likely to be used for market sensing and customer acquisition. For example, you can already create life-like product prototypes and investigate what people think of them. Or you can show people your product in virtual reality, so they have a better idea of what they can buy. Additionally, you can choose whether to use animations (or real images. For example, the international hotel chain Best Western has made 360 degree videos of their hotels in the United States.

Augmented reality (AR) is the fusion of the physical with the virtual world. An application puts a 'virtual layer' on the real world. Some possible implementations of this are: information about landmarks and sights, background information on paintings, the nearest mailbox and the nearest

Virtual reality

Augmented reality

Best Western Plus Casino Royale 360 VR

Best Western shows hotels in virtual reality

Virtual changing rooms

shop where they sell a particular brand. Websites also employ augmented reality, for example in virtual changing rooms, where you can project clothes onto a picture of yourself or mix and match them with each other.

Google Glass was an early example of augmented reality although consumers' reaction to the concept was mixed. This type of technology is expected to develop even further and offers interesting opportunities for sales promotion for creative online marketers.

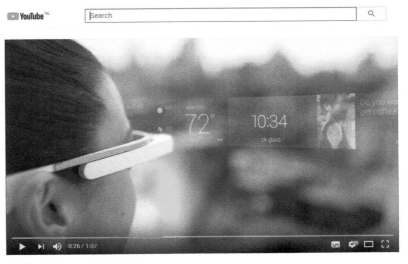

Google Glass How-to: Getting Started

Google Glass was an early example of augmented reality

In mixed reality, the real world and virtual world are running consecutively in real-time. For example, you communicate with a virtual image of a colleague or you operate a virtual keyboard with 'real' results.

Mixed reality

For the online marketer, VR and AR mean new opportunities for market sensing, product realisation, customer acquisition and customer relationship management. As always, however, we must be careful not to be dazzled by the latest 'shiny new thing' and to maintain our perspective; these are emergent technologies and consumer adoption will be patchy. Marketers should adopt a 'test and learn' approach at this early stage.

3.4.2   Further development of social media and networks

Social networks are an unmissable part of modern life. They have changed forever the way we communicate with family, friends, and people that share similar interests. Major social networks such as Facebook are developing further by using new technologies that allow them to do things such as displaying highly personalized content. There is also more and more data integration: eg what people do on Instagram affects what they see on Facebook. When people want to share something, they can do it via Facebook or Instagram, but also directly, via Messenger or WhatsApp. In addition, there are an increasing number of smaller networks for people with specific lifestyles and information needs. (N.B. Facebook Inc. owns all four of these brands).

Social networks

Data integration

Social media houses a huge amount of information. This is also called 'wisdom of the crowds'. The best-selling book, The Wisdom of Crowds (James Surowiecki, 2004) deals with the aggregation of information within groups of people, resulting in decisions that, he argues, are often better than could have been made by any single member of the group.
The methods for finding and analysing this information are becoming more and more advanced. Consumers as well as companies will continue to make more use of it.
Social media are increasingly being used to mobilise and activate people for commercial and non-commercial purposes, such as providing information or gathering news. Social selling, ie making sales using social media, is becoming commonplace.

Wisdom of the crowds

Social selling

Accessing social media is becoming increasingly easy. In recent years, social has gone mobile and new platforms have flourished which are messaging apps ie mobile only (eg WhatsApp, Snapchat, WeChat). Due to the fact that in the future all kinds of devices (mobile and/or wearable) will be connected to the Internet, we will be able to use Social Media almost anywhere and at any time. Typing of texts will increasingly be replaced by dictation (Voice is the new 'Killer App'). Social media will increasingly become part of our 'self'.
For the online marketer, this means that social media will become increasingly important, especially within market sensing, customer acquisition and CRM.

3.4.3   Internet of things (IoT)

The number of mobile applications is growing by the day. Apps are becoming better and better at using sensors. Think of recognition of music, speech, patterns, image, motion, light, temperature and speed. This means

Wearables

that the amount of useful applications is increasing rapidly. The number of devices, 'things', that access or use the Internet, is also increasing rapidly. Below you can see, for example, a forecast for sales of wearables, body-portable devices with an Internet connection (see figure 3.3).

FIGURE 3.3 The number of connected devices increases rapidly

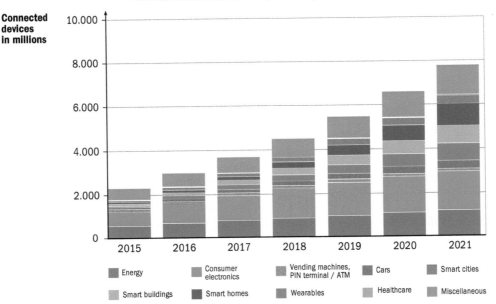

Source: Statista, 2017

Beacons

Internet of things

Wearables and shared touchscreens make Web access and social communication even easier. Beacons, small devices in stores and airports, for example, capture signals from smartphones and wearables that are nearby and respond to them. For example, they are able to send personalised promotional offers to customers in a supermarket, using Bluetooth Beacon technology. Increasingly, all kinds of devices are connected to the Internet, such as the thermostat, lighting and security of a home. Through the Internet, those devices can exchange data with each other and with their owner. For example, the heating (or air conditioning) can be set to the correct temperature a quarter of an hour before the owner arrives home, the coffee machine will warm up and the lights will come on the moment they have parked their car or opened their front door. In principle, any devices with Internet access can communicate with each other. This is what we call the 'Internet of things', or IoT. For the online marketer, this means countless new opportunities within, for example, market sensing, product realisation, customer acquisition and customer relationship management. IoT (also known as 'Your intelligent home') will generate huge amounts of data, raising many ethical/privacy issues.

3.4.4   Advanced machine learning and conversational systems

Artificial intelligence (AI) is something that computer scientists have long been aiming to create. Advanced machine learning (ML) is related to this and allows computers to learn. Based on the results of data analyses, the software can acquire knowledge without explicit programming. The computer, as it were, programs itself. Digital systems can then understand, predict and independently understand things.

Artificial intelligence

Advanced machine learning

Machine learning is increasingly combined with conversational systems. These are systems that can communicate through language. This is done by natural language processing, whereby the system understands spoken language. For example, the systems work with voice recognition or by analysing and understanding written text. Applications include smart digital assistants and driverless cars. Examples of smart assistants (Chatbots) are Alexa from Amazon, Siri by Apple, Cortana by Microsoft and Google Now.

Conversational systems

Natural language processing

Smart digital assistants

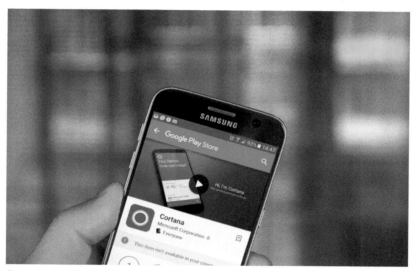

Cortana, Microsoft's smart digital assistant

Machine learning lets marketers build complicated models and algorithms that allow you to make predictions, called predictive analytics. For example, you can predict how customers respond to commercial activities or to what extent a product will sell successfully. The extent to which organisations are able to turn data into insights about what motivates customers and translate this into their strategy will become more and more important for their competitive position. The combination of technology that makes it possible to do this is also called an insights engine. An insights engine can understand natural language, extract all relevant data from the systems, and not only provide what is directly requested, but also other relevant insights.

Predictive analytics

Insights engine

Virtual customer
assistants

Intelligent apps

Chatbots

For example, machine learning is already being used for virtual customer assistants (VCAs) that can communicate with customers in the context of customer service. This type of software is also called intelligent apps. In practice, VCAs are often called chatbots. Consider also smart assistants for consumers eg Alexa, Siri and Cortana.

Advanced machine learning and conversational systems are becoming increasingly important in all digital business processes: market sensing, product realisation, customer acquisition, order handling and CRM.

3.4.5 Digitisation of Services

The trend towards digitising of services has been underway for years. Customer service employees have been replaced by interactive information on websites and virtual assistants. Bank employees have seen their work shrink (and in some cases their jobs disappear) as a result of online and mobile banking and digital advisory services. These developments will continue to evolve, with one next step likely to be robotisation.

Robotisation

A robot is actually a computer that is able to move around. And like any computer it can connect to the Internet. There it can access information that helps it perform its tasks. It can be remotely controlled, and it can upload data to the Internet. Sensors can be built into a robot, which can do more than people are able to do. For example, think of infrared light or heat. The possible uses are endless. There are already robots that drive people around landmarks, a cruise company that uses robots as bartenders and the Thai government uses a robot to test and approve the quality of food. Deep question answering software will enable computers or robots in the future to combine a range of knowledge and answer the most diverse questions. Watson, IBM's supercomputer, is an example of this. For the online marketer, this is opening up opportunities for product

Deep question
answering
software

Connie speaks to customers at a Hilton Hotel. The robot is connected to IBM's Watson system

© Noordhoff Uitgevers bv

realisation, order handling and customer service, although the use of a 'sales robot' is of course also conceivable and indeed already being tested. In Chapter 4, you can read more about this emerging technology and how product managers design and realise products with the help of online channels.

3.4.6   3D Printing

Although this technology has existed for quite some time, 3D printing has really taken off only recently. This has to do with the increasingly accessibility and decreasing cost of 3D printers and the necessary materials. Using a 3D printer, you can build your own three-dimensional objects by 'spraying' the material onto itself, layer upon layer. Now that there are many thousands of 3D hubs, the technology is also accessible to consumers and hobbyists.

3D printer

3D printing can quickly build prototypes in, for example, plastic. You can also print entire products or parts, such as a precisely fitting ring. In the future, companies will increasingly focus on 'produce-to-demand', the rapid production of small numbers of (customised) products, rather than the mass production techniques of the 19th and 20th centuries. In the future, imagine ordering a 3D design and printing it yourself at home or at a local printing facility.

For the online marketer, 3D printing may lead to new possibilities in the product design and production process, but also, for example, in order handling (no need for shipping) and customer service: a replacement component could simply be 3D printed.

3.4.7   Blockchain

Blockchain is the technical system behind the peer-to-peer online payment system bitcoin but it is a broader concept than that. It is based on a technique whereby a combination of algorithms and cryptography causes multiple computers to come to the same result independently.

Blockchain
Bitcoin

Using blockchain, it is possible to register (immutably) what someone owns as well as register any changes in value or ownership. Think of certified diamonds, certified art, contracts and warranty certificates. There is no need for a central body that keeps a registry and rights can be passed from one owner to another with ease.

For the online marketer, this means new opportunities, within fields such as order handling and customer relationship management (CRM).

3.4.8   Big data and the increasing importance of data security

As a result of the large amount of activity on and surrounding the Internet, a huge amount of data is available. Some of this is real-time data, data available for use at the moment it is collected. For example, consider the directions you receive based on your GPS location. For a company, saving these directions is not interesting, but your GPS location may be. This will then be saved. For example, Google looks at your daily commute to and from work. They are subsequently able to communicate with you on your smartphone, in real-time, how long this journey will take you. The collective name for this type of data is big data. Storing it is getting cheaper, computers are becoming more powerful and new analytics tools are available

Real-time data

Big data

that can interpret these large amounts of data. Based on this, companies can optimise their marketing, improve their service, and create new products and services.

This not only requires fast systems, that can access the required data very quickly, but also advanced algorithms and smart marketing analysts, also called 'data scientists'. Because huge amounts of, often very sensitive, information is collected, excellent data protection and well secure systems for accessing it are an absolute requirement. Marketers should keep in mind that some of their customers will not give permission for the storing of personal information that is used for marketing purposes. In section 3.8 we will further elaborate on big data and customer insights.

Data scientists

3.5 Model for online consumer behaviour

Anyone who purchases a product or service goes through the following stages of the purchasing process: acknowledgement of needs, seeking information, evaluation of alternatives, purchase and result (Engel, Blackwell & Miniard, 1990). In online shopping there are two decisions: the choice of the product to be purchased and the choice of the online store. Therefore, an additional step in the model shown below (figure 3.4) is included: the channel selection. After some online orientation, consumers can purchase the product in an online store, physical store, or through another sales channel (for example, by phone).

FIGURE 3.4 Model Consumer Behaviour

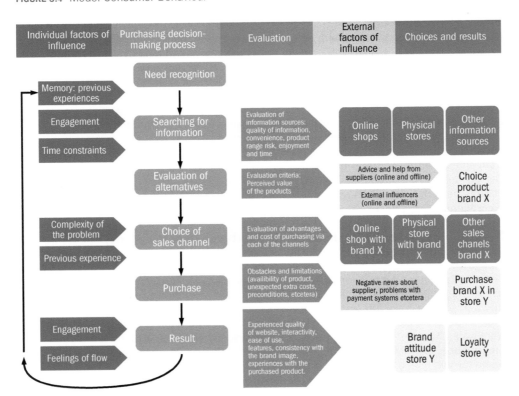

Source: © Marjolein Visser RM

We will discuss the six phases of the online purchase process:

Online purchase
process

1 acknowledgement of needs
2 seeking information
3 evaluation of alternatives
4 choice of sales channel
5 purchase
6 result

3.5.1   Acknowledgement of needs

The consumer becomes aware that their current situation can be improved
before deciding to buy a product or service. They might feel hungry, thirsty
or suddenly feel like going away for a weekend abroad. This awareness can
be caused by actually missing something in the current situation (eg the
toothpaste has run out) or because the consumer has aspirations for the
future (a fitter body or romantic dinner with his or her partner). This
moment of dissatisfaction could arise whilst using the Internet but could
just as well happen at a different time.

On the Internet, consumers are free to choose their own path. When they
are in a physical store, high street or mall, they are more or less constrained
by the layout. As a result, they experience limitations in distance and time.
On the Internet, the user is exposed to a variety of products within a short
space of time. However, this does not always lead to more impulse buys.

Once people are used to Internet shopping, they respond to 'temptations'
online in about the same way as they do offline (Amos, Holmes & Keneson,
2014). For example, marketers use audience-targeted ads, newsletters,
promotional offers, and rankings of the most viewed or purchased products.
The smartphone is becoming increasingly important: over 40% of purchases
are inspired whilst using a smartphone (Consumerbarometer.com, 2017).

3.5.2   Seeking Information

The consumer seeks out which products or services meet their wishes as
best as possible. They collect and process information. In the previous
chapter we learned that seeking information is one of the most important
activities on the Internet.

The search process can be split into two different classifications: 'internal
search' and 'external search.' Before a consumer seeks information, they
will first try and recall what they already know about the product category
or product. The extent to which an Internet user will then actively go looking
for this information on the Internet, depends on what they assume the
benefits will be. If they have experience in buying a particular product, are
satisfied and do not feel like they are at risk, they will seek out little
information. They are displaying what is called routine purchasing
behaviour and they will base their decision on one or a few simple features
of the product or the provider. If the Internet user wants to buy something
that they have experience with, but still consider to be a risk, they will
consider alternative brands or providers. They already have a reasonable
idea of the evaluation criteria to apply, know about relevant websites and
are therefore performing a very limited search. An example of this is
sourcing a new car insurance contract. When the consumer wants to
purchase a product they have little experience with, they will search

Routine
purchasing
behaviour

extensively. Products such as far-away (long-haul) holidays, mortgages, cars and pensions fall in this category for many people.

Search extensively

When consumers search extensively, the process consists of two phases (Payne et al., 1993):
1 screening of possible alternatives by looking for products that match the preferences in different ways
2 searching for more detailed information about the alternatives that were found

Involvement

The extent to which people are motivated to actually search for detailed information and the depth of their search depends on the extent of their involvement in the purchase decision. Mittal and Lee (1989) define this as 'the extent of interest and the importance that a customer attaches to a careful purchase decision'.

When people decide to search online, the next question is: where do they do it:
• using a search engine
• via a website, such as a content website or an online retailer
• via other online channels, such as social media

Although the search engine's role is decreasing, more than half of millennials (people born between 1980 and 2000) use a search engine if they want to find something out about a product. Over a quarter go straight to a brand website (Consumerbarometer.com, 2017).

Consumers select an information source based on (Vroomen, 2006):
• the information provided
• ease
• the range of products that are presented
• perceived risks
• the enjoyment of using the channel

Decision-making paradox

In theory, the search process via the Internet is faster than when people physically go shopping. In practice, this sometimes disappoints. The Internet contains a huge amount of information and alternatives. The more alternatives the consumer is considering, the better the quality of their decision. But on the other hand, scrutinising all possibilities takes a lot of time. Tamaki (2005) calls this the 'decision-making paradox'.
As a website better enables consumers to combine a high-quality evaluation of many alternatives with speed, it gives consumers more value. This may mean that the tendency of the consumer to look elsewhere decreases. Appreciation of a website leads to lower price sensitivity and increasingly higher-ticket purchases (Teo & Yeong, 2003).

3.5.3 Evaluating alternatives

Evaluation criteria

In order to be able to decide which product or service best satisfies their wishes and needs, the consumer must determine evaluation criteria. Only once the consumer has determined what matters to them, are they able to weigh up the possibilities and determine what is, in their opinion, the best product. By evaluating the different alternatives, the consumer aims to achieve the choice of product that offers them the greatest value. This perceived value is a combination of all the benefits that the consumer will receive when purchasing the product, offset by the size of their investment. In setting evaluation criteria, consumers will be inspired by both online and offline sources of information: eg product descriptions, tests, blogs and posts on social networks.

Perceived value

For marketers it is important to find out what the relevant evaluation criteria are for their target groups. Some market segments are particularly inclined to decide based on pricing, others are more focused on, for example, quality or brand personality. In order to assist the consumer in setting evaluation criteria and evaluating alternatives, there are several options, such as the inclusion of decision support systems on the website, product reviews, user reviews, and independent testing. This will be discussed in greater detail in Chapters 4 and 8.

While providers' websites play an important role in the information seeking process, consumers tend to attach value to the opinion of independent third parties. Websites containing reviews, blogs and other social media play an important role in this phase. This happens both directly because consumers consider the views of others in their decision making, and indirectly, because people experience a renewed feeling of involvement with the brand or product (Wang, Yu & Wei, 2012). Individual customer ratings greatly influence a person's attitude towards a product, more so than general satisfaction scores (Ziegele & Weber, 2015).

3.5.4 Choice of sales channel

If the consumer has found the product that best suits their needs, they either buy the product through the channel where they found it or elsewhere. That may be in the physical counterpart to the website where they found the product or through another online or offline provider. During the purchase phase, the range of products, perceived risk and after-sales service of the (online or offline) store are the most important criteria for the consumer (Vroomen, 2006). There are also indications that the decision to purchase via the Internet or in a physical store is related to the complexity of the purchasing problem for the consumer as well as their experience with that type of product. The choice of channel is highly personal and situational.

Consumers choose between online and offline stores based on their perceived value. Consumers evaluate the possible time savings, a wider range choice, delivery and other factors against money, time and risk. If the consumer feels that they get the 'best' value on a website, they are less likely to look for alternatives (Anderson & Srinavasan, 2003). The quality of the website is decisive for the amount of sales.

When the consumer chooses a physical store, it's not always the counterpart to the online provider they did their orientation on. The number of people that use one website to search for information, but who then make the actual purchase from a different provider (so-called free riders) is high.

Free riders

Many website visitors are 'free riders'

Consumers exhibit complex behaviour when choosing a channel. They sometimes visit a large number of channels for product information and to evaluate products. They do this mainly because they find it easy, because they want the freedom to buy when and where they want and because they want to compare prices. Free riding is especially common with products that consumers don't buy very often and that are relatively expensive, such as electronics, furniture and appliances (Heitz-Spahn, 2013). Even if the customer ends up buying somewhere else, an appealing website leads to a positive attitude towards the brand and to a stronger bond. There are three ways to minimise free riding:

Channel integration

1 channel integration allowing customers to use the online and offline stores simultaneously (for example, returning goods that were purchased online in a physical store or phoning up to request information about a product on the website)
2 uniformity of the messages sent to consumers online and offline
3 stimulating parallel offline and online shopping visits (Teerling, 2007)

Omnichannel strategy

An omnichannel strategy, whereby customer experience moves seamlessly between online and offline channels, offers some protection, but preventing free riding entirely is impossible.

3.5.5 Purchase

The intent to purchase is not always converted into an actual purchase. Payment issues, or an item not being in stock, are some of the many reasons why a purchase might not be followed through on. Research has shown that even the addition of items to the online shopping cart does not automatically lead to a purchase. This is due to the following reasons:

- Consumers do not use the shopping cart as it was intended, but as a way of temporarily storing alternative options or as a wish lists.

- Consumers use the shopping cart to find out what the total price will be, including administrative costs, shipping, etc. Or to respond to a promotional offer and keep the products 'on hold' in their shopping cart while looking for even cheaper alternatives.
- Consumers have the intention of making a purchase but encounter obstacles such as payment difficulties (Kukar-Kinney & Close, 2010).

This underlines the importance of an efficient order and payment procedure, the option of a separate 'wish list' and the ability to hold products in the shopping cart for a longer period of time or to be able to otherwise retrieve the cart after having left the website.
If the consumer encounters too many obstacles, they will find a different sales channel or abandon the purchase completely.

Consumers do not use shopping carts for their intended purpose

3.5.6   Result

In the evaluation phase, the customer will again weigh the pros and cons of buying from the supplier's website. The result of this consideration will leave them more satisfied or less so. Very satisfied customers are usually loyal customers who return to the online store.
Srinivasan, Anderson and Ponnavolu (2002) investigated the many factors that promote 'e-loyalty'.

E-loyalty

They came to the following eight Cs (8C model):
1 customisation
2 contact interactivity
3 cultivation
4 care ·
5 community
6 choice

8C model

7 convenience
8 character

Customisation

1 Customisation

Customisation is the extent to which an e-retailer tailors the products, services and the environment within which the transactions take place to the individual customer. By customising, the likelihood that people will find something they want to buy is increased and the impression is given that there is a broad range of choice. It leads to a better match between customer and product and transactions are more efficient. This is done by for example automatically reading customer data, but also because people are not forced to compare dozens or hundreds of alternatives.

Contact interactivity

2 Contact Interactivity

Contact interactivity is the 'dynamic character of the online retailer's engagement with their customers on the website'. This can be done by the presence of customer support tools website and by facilitating mutual communication between company and customers. Interactivity makes the search process easier: customers have less to remember. This leads to an increase in the perceived value of the website. In addition, interactivity allows a lot more information to be presented to the customer. This increases the customer's sense of control and freedom of choice. Srinivasan et al. (2002), for example, use the example of looking for a book. In a physical bookstore, you can only read the flap texts, whilst online you can also read reviews by others or get recommendations for similar books. The online retailer is able to build up knowledge about the tastes and preferences of their customers through interactive communication, thereby increasing the quality of their recommendations. This allows them to offer more value to the customer.

Cultivation

3 Cultivation

Cultivation is the extent to which an online retailer offers relevant information and encourages customers to expand the breadth and depth of their purchases over time. For example, by using newsletters to proactively provide information to customers, the customer can be encouraged to buy more products and allows for cross-selling. On eBay, advertisers can distribute 'package inserts' included in the parcel delivered to the customer, sent by various sellers. As an advertiser, you can specify which target audience your inserts will reach (eg, female buyers in the 'Baby & Kids' section).

Care

4 Care

Care is the attention an online retailer gives to all interactive activities before and after the purchase, which are intended to facilitate the transaction and strengthen the long-term relationship with the customer '(Srinivasan, Anderson & Ponnavolu, 2002). For instance, the care that the provider takes to try to prevent anything from going wrong and their response if that accidentally happens anyway. Are complaints resolved quickly and prudently? Another component of care is informing customers about the availability of products adequately and in a timely manner.

Community

5 Community

A branded community is an online social unit that consists of existing and potential customers and is coordinated and maintained by the online retailer. Within this online community, customers can exchange opinions

© Noordhoff Uitgevers bv

and information. This can be done, for example, on a forum or by posting reviews. You can read more about this in section 10.5.

6 Choice

Online retailers are able to offer their customers a broad and deep range of products, increasing their options (choice). There is no definite restriction on product availability and floor space because the online retailer is not required to physically exhibit their goods. Additionally, in some cases, the original manufacturer or a fellow retailer can even take care of shipping. A wide range of products allows the website visitor greater convenience and time saving. The online retailer with the most extensive range will often be the dominant player in an industry and can count on many loyal customers.

Choice

7 Convenience

Convenience is the extent to which the customer feels that the website is simple, intuitive and user-friendly. This includes the accessibility of information and the simplicity of the transaction process. In many cases, the customer uses the quality of the website to gauge the extent to which they are dealing with a good, reliable supplier. Moreover, according to Srinivisan et al. (2002), customers don't make as many mistakes on an easy-to-use website, which automatically leads to greater customer satisfaction.

Convenience

8 Character

Character, or the individuality of a website, is the brand image that the online retailer tries to convey to the site visitor by using, for example, text, style, images, colours, logos and slogans or themes on the website. The character of the website underlines the brand personality of the online retailer. If this brand personality appeals to the visitor and they experience a bond with the brand, this will lead to greater loyalty and more visits. Research (from Wang, Pallister & Foxall, 2006) shows that the degree of involvement that the site visitor feels to the product they are looking for is of great importance to their sense of loyalty. The more important the decision is to the consumer, the greater the probability that satisfaction will lead to loyalty to the website and the more they connected they will feel to the online retailer's brand. This means that the probability that they will buy a product again on the relevant website is increased. Website visitors with a strong sense of involvement have a lower risk perception than people for whom the decision is less important. People who feel less involvement with the product they want to buy usually search on a limited number of websites of well-known brands and estimate the risks to be higher.

Character

Another important point for evaluating the value of the website is the extent to which the visitor experiences what is called flow. Flow is the extent to which a person is fully absorbed in what they are doing. Flow gives the site visitor a sense of control over their experience on the website and that leads to an enjoyable feeling and taking pleasure in the visit. This results in a positive attitude towards the online provider and a greater likelihood of a repeat visit (Sicilia & Ruiz, 2007).

Flow

In recent decades, research has shown that the impact websites have on brand awareness is influenced by:
- factors related to the individual: involvement, interactivity they experience and the feelings of being in the flow

Flow is the extent to which a site visitor is fully absorbed in what they are doing

- factors related to the website: the actual interactivity of the website, the usability of the website, the features on the site and the extent to which the website is aligned with the brand image

Likeability

The factors related to the website both affect the extent to which visitors appreciate the website (likeability) as well as brand attitude.
Although marketers cannot directly influence the factors that relate to the individual, they can take them into account when constructing their websites and actively respond to them. This means that they must know the characteristics, wishes and needs of the website's users. Marketers can control the factors that relate to the website: they can maximise interaction and user-friendliness, provide lots of features and stimulate their use, and ensure a good match between the brand's desired image and the website's personality (Voorveld, Neijens & Smit, 2009).
In this way, the online marketer can directly affect the website-related factors. As described in Chapter 2, the enterprise strategy, including branding policy, should be an important starting point when putting together a Digital Marketing plan and the resulting communication tools.

3.6 Digital Marketing Funnel

As mentioned in 3.5, the steps of needs acknowledgement, information seeking, evaluation of alternatives, choice of sales channel, actual purchase and satisfaction with the result, can be translated into the objectives of the online marketer. A useful tool to help you with this is

The Digital Marketing funnel

The Digital Marketing funnel
1 Visit
2 Captivate

3 Decide
4 Order
5 Pay
6 Bind

The Digital Marketing funnel is a channel of goals (see figure 3.5). The idea is that the online marketer leads, step by step, as many visitors as possible through The Digital Marketing funnel. Example 3.1 illustrates what The Digital Marketing funnel for a shopping site might look like.

EXAMPLE 3.1

The Digital Marketing Funnel

Out of the 100,000 visitors to a website, 75% will look beyond the homepage, 25% will immediately leave. Out of the 75,000 visitors who view more than one page, 60% use the site search tool to find products. These are people who are in the process of deciding whether to buy a product. Of these 45,000 who are still deciding, 33.3% (15,000 visitors) will order a product on the website by clicking on the order button. 90% of these orders ultimately pass the payment process, resulting in 13,500 sales. Of these customers, 50% are returning customers, with whom a bond has been established. These customers have their own account and, should they so choose, receive a newsletter. The other half are new customers.

FIGURE 3.5 Digital Marketing Funnel completed

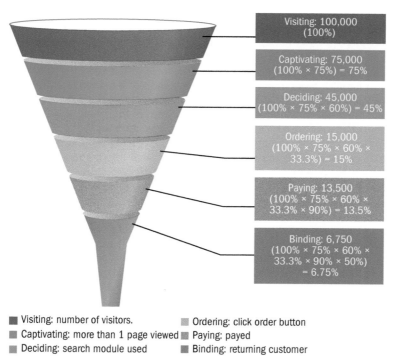

Visiting: 100,000
(100%)

Captivating: 75,000
(100% × 75%) = 75%

Deciding: 45,000
(100% × 75% × 60%) = 45%

Ordering: 15,000
(100% × 75% × 60% × 33.3%) = 15%

Paying: 13,500
(100% × 75% × 60% × 33.3% × 90%) = 13.5%

Binding: 6,750
(100% × 75% × 60% × 33.3% × 90% × 50%) = 6.75%

■ Visiting: number of visitors.   ▨ Ordering: click order button
■ Captivating: more than 1 page viewed ■ Paying: payed
▨ Deciding: search module used   ■ Binding: returning customer

Source: Visser & Sikkenga, 2012

We will further elaborate on the The Digital Marketing Funnel below:

1 Visit

The first goal of the online marketer is to ensure that people with the (possible) intention to buy, visit their online communications or sales channel. This could be a website, an app, but also a social media channel that is aimed at sales. The critical success factors (CSFs) in this phase are brand awareness, brand image, discoverability of the website or app and promise (proposition). The most important instruments for encouraging a visit are the Marketing Communications Programme (Chapters 5 to 7) in combination with the use of social media. At this stage, it is important to measure how many visitors have found their way to the website, whether or not they belong to the intended target audience, through which communication channels they found the website, and, for each communication channel, how much each visitor has cost. This kind of data enables communication efforts to be optimised. In Chapter 12 you will find more information about 'digital analytics', the analysis of these results.

2 Captivating

The second objective is to ensure that visitors are so captivated (=engaged=interested=motivated) by what they find on the website, in the app or on the social sales channel, that they want to find out more about what is on offer. As you can read in section 3.5, the core success factors in this captivate phase are the information (in-depth, current) that the sales channel offers, the range of products on offer, how easy it is to search and navigate, the feeling of security and, not least: the enjoyment that visitors experience and the feelings they experience. At this stage it is important to take note of the amount of time spent by each visitor on the individual online communication channel, eg how many pages they view, which pages are most popular, how the visitor moves from one page to another (navigation) and at which point they finally leave the channel (exit page). Also, the so-called 'bounce rate' is important: the percentage of visitors that click away from the site having visited only one page. With the help of this type of data, the online sales channel can be optimised, and the marketing communications mix can be adjusted, for example, to create a better match between the expectations of the visitors and what they actually encounter. The most important tool for engaging visitors is the online sales channel (eg the website) itself. For more information on building effective websites and apps, see Chapter 11.

3 Deciding

The third goal is to ensure that the visitors compare and evaluate products in order to come to the decision to buy. Core success factors are: adequate product information (in line with consumer search criteria), a variety of products that are readily available, advice that supports the visitor in their decision, product reviews, and clear prices. The most important tools here are the search and advice module and the catalogue, the list of available products and the associated information. Examples of relevant measurements are: use of the search module, applied search criteria, use of product information and price information. Using these measurements, the content of the website can be modified, and modules can be optimised. More information on online sales and prices can be found in Chapter 8.

4 Ordering

The fourth goal is to ensure that the visitor actually buys the chosen product via the online sales channel and does not go to a different provider. Core success factors at this stage are: trusting the provider, the order convenience, the pricing in relation to the competition and responsiveness (responding actively and adequately to potential questions). The order module and the on- and offline answers to questions are decisive tools. In this phase, actual orders are measured: ie requests and reservations, ordered products, realised prices and turnover.

Order convenience

Order module

5 Paying

The fifth goal is to persuade the visitor to complete the payment process so that actual sales are realised. Ease of payment and trust are the core success factors here. The payment module is the relevant tool. What can, for example, be measured are the number and value of transactions. The User Experience (UX) of the checkout page is crucial here. More information about payment can be found in Chapter 9.

Payment module

6 Binding

The sixth goal is to 'bind' or 'stick' the buyer to the organisation to encourage repeat purchases. Core success factors in this phase are: the experiences the buyer has concerning the purchased product, the quality perception of the online sales channel and the extent to which the buyer feels a bond with the brand. Relevant processes at this stage are order handling and customer service (Chapter 9) and customer relationship management (Chapter 10). Customer Service provision and delivery are also key. Important measuring points are the number of returning visitors, repeat purchases and customer satisfaction.

Bind

The information regarding The Digital Marketing Funnel as described above, is shown in Table 3.3.

Using The Digital Marketing funnel allows an online marketer to make calculations, eg of how many ecommerce site visitors are needed to generate a particular amount of sales. Let's say the conversion rate (number of buyers/number of visitors) is 13.5%. If the aim is to achieve 27,000 buyers in the coming period instead of 13,500, you will have to attract 200,000 visitors to the website.

The main purpose of using the funnel is to find out which processes can be optimised and what effect it will have on sales. For example, for a shopping site the ecommerce manager can test whether a change in the search process will lead to more orders. Suppose that by selecting criteria that better match the visitor's wishes, the percentage orders increases from 33% to 40%. This would lead to a conversion rate of (100% × 75% × 60% × 40% × 90%) = 16.2%. That means 20% more sales (16,200 orders). A shopping site ecommerce manager can then compare the result of investing in the search engine with optimising the payment process and other options for improvement. In the end, you should of course choose the improvement that yields the best return on the investment (ROI). Of course, every business is unique and organisations must determine the steps for their own Digital Marketing funnel based on the main goals of their own Digital Marketing programme. The funnel must be custom-made.

TABLE 3.3 The Digital Marketing funnel

	Visit 100%	Captivate %	Decide %	Order %	Payment %	Bind %
Core success factors	Brand awareness Brand image Discoverability Proposition	Information Range of products Ease of use Safety Enjoyment/flow	Product information Range of products Advice Evaluations Price information	Trust Order convenience Pricing Responsiveness	Ease of payment Trust	Experiences with the purchased product Quality experience regarding the sales channel Brand binding
Core processes and instruments	Marketing Communication Social Media	Website App	Catalogue Search and advice module	Order module Answering questions	Payment module	Order handling Customer service CRM
Examples of measurements	Number of visitors Characteristics of visitors Origin of visitors Cost per visitor	Time on site Page views Most visited pages Paths followed Bounce ratio	Use of the search module Search criteria Use of the product information Use of the price information	Number of ordered products Realised prices Turnover Requests/reservations	Quantity and value of the realised transactions	Return visitor Repeat purchases Client satisfaction

3.7 Online Market Research

Owing to the increasing number of web users, consumer behaviour has changed significantly. For various departments within businesses, market research has had to clarify what the buying process now looks like.
In this section we will take a moment to discuss how the Internet influences that process and how digital technology is changing the field of market research. First, we will focus on using the Internet for research purposes. Next, we will look at the development of marketing, showing how market research has evolved and what the definition and purpose of market research is. Then we will discuss the advantages of various methods of online market research. We will briefly look into market research in social media. Finally, the techniques that are used in online research will be reviewed.

3.7.1   Using the Internet for research

Long before the Internet, market research was a field that sought to provide insights into consumer behaviour. However, market research has fundamentally changed with the arrival and development of the Internet. The Internet can be used in two ways to conduct research, namely:
1 The Internet can be used for asking people questions.
2 The Internet is used for registering/observing/recording behaviour.

1 The Internet is used for asking people questions
In order to collect data, surveys are conducted by telephone, in person (face-to-face) and online. In recent years online research has become the most widely used form of research. In addition to the obvious efficiency benefits (it is often faster and cheaper), how accessible people are is also becoming increasingly important. Participating in research on the Internet often means that you can participate at whatever time and place suits you best. Other forms of data collection do not have this benefit.

2 Internet is used for registering behaviour
Everything that happens on the Internet can be recorded. Which websites people visit, what they comment on, what social networks are used and how many tweets are sent. The gathering of this data is being used to better explain people's behaviour with increasing frequency. This evolution to 'big data' is the most important development within research and, in some cases, it seems likely that it will replace traditional surveys.

The digitisation of research has meant that both of these two approaches to using the Internet for research are often being used simultaneously. This is caused by recent developments in the field of research, consisting of three phases, which we will now briefly discuss.

3.7.2   Marketing: the evolution from mass research into social media research

In order to fully understand what research has to offer marketers, it is important to take a moment to consider how marketing, research and market research are developing. In Chapter 1 you were able to read that this development can be divided into three phases: the mass media phase, the Internet phase and the social media phase. Although this book focuses on Digital Marketing and this section on online research, it is useful to briefly review how market research has evolved and what the definition and purpose of market research is.

Social media research

Evolution of Market Research

The greatest distance between 'brands' and 'consumers' can be found in the mass media phase where it is primarily the marketer who is sending messages to the consumer (one-way transmission=broadcasting). The Internet phase creates room for a dialogue between consumer and brand. In the social media phase there is not only a dialogue but also mutual influence. The marketer *observes* how the consumer experiences the brand. That's also exactly what occurs with the research. Research is increasingly becoming a *dialogue* between consumer and brand (ie customer panels) and observational techniques are frequently used.

For the research industry, the Internet itself has of course created a myriad of new possibilities. However, we have reached a point where, if we stick to conventional ways of data collection, we might end up negating the power of the Internet.

Definition and purpose of market research

The definition of market research is (Kooiker et al., 2011):

Market research

> Market research is the objective and systematic gathering of information about certain markets or customers for the purpose of obtaining insights and making informed decisions.

Quantitative research

Cross section

The purpose of quantitative research is to make statements about a population based on a large cross-section. When it's not possible that everyone in the population participates in the research, a cross-section of the population is selected and used for this purpose. This is also called a *random sample*. The most commonly employed methods for this are:
- online survey
- telephone survey
- written survey
- face-to-face survey

Online market research

The sharp decline in response to telephone, written and face-to-face surveys and the rapid penetration of the web in many countries has prompted the revolutionary upsurge of online market research. In many countries, almost all quantitative research is now being carried out online. Face-to-face surveys are only used for qualitative research.

3.7.3 Advantages of online market research

The rapid advancement of online market research is also due to the large number of benefits, which can be summarised as follows:
- *Cost*: compared with telephone surveys, the costs are significantly lower, since call centre agents are no longer required and telephone charges no longer apply.
- *Speed*: thanks to the density of households with an Internet connection, research agencies are able to approach large groups in a very short time frame.
- *Moment of participation*: respondents are no longer called at home, during dinner time or whilst watching the evening news, but they can accept the invitation to participate at whatever moment suits them best. As a result, there are often more people willing to participate.
- *Enrichment of database*: it is possible to follow respondents for a longer period of time and to respond to previous answers (more frequent

participation). Answers that are given online are recorded in a database, which means agencies can gather more information about respondents. This means that future surveys won't need to include as many questions. Online surveys are also able to read other data from a respondent's computer, provided that permission is given. Acquiring permission is an important change. Strict rules have been put in place for this.

- *Processing*: because a direct link can be made, answers can quickly be processed and analysed.
- *Illustrative* material: the use of graphics, videos, illustrations etc. mean that much more can potentially be achieved with these kind of surveys.

To draw in more participants, surveys are becoming more appealing. Many features and techniques that are also used in games are being applied for this purpose, such as the possibility of winning prizes and other game-like properties to answering the questions (this is also called gamification). Images, videos and fun ways to answer the questions, such as card sorting, sliding scroll bars, showing what others have answered and progress bars to show you how far along you are in the survey are being used. Such engagement techniques increase participation and engagement which provides more useful results. Gaining the cooperation of the respondents has become the most important challenge, as people are become increasingly critical and suspicious ('What's in it for me?').

Gamification

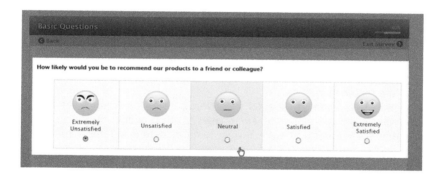

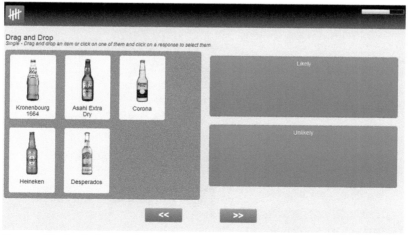

Survey with simple 'buttons' to make answering more appealing

3.7.4 Methods of online research

Online research can be carried out in the following ways:

Website surveys 1 *Website* surveys: these are online surveys where the invitation to participate is linked to the website being visited. Think of an invitation in a banner or pop-up or via a component of the website. Banners are often used to invite people to participate. (eg '*Could you please spare 5 minutes to help us improve our service?*')

Email surveys 2 *Email surveys*: many surveys are sent via email, sometimes with a survey in the attachment, but usually with a URL or link that can be clicked, linking to the online survey. The biggest difference compared to a website survey, is that these types of surveys depend on a database (ie a list of email addresses) in order to get access to respondents.

Website surveys are in fact an essential tool for every site owner, as the users' click behaviour alone is often insufficient. For instance, one retailer was under the impression, based on his web analytics, that the site he managed was an enormous success; lots of visitors that frequently clicked on many different components. A simple survey linked to each visit revealed a remarkable conclusion: 85% of all visitors visited the website simply to check the opening hours. However, these were not listed on the site. For the brand, the result of the website visit was therefore a negative one. By linking a simple survey to each visit, this problem could have been identified far earlier and the site improved. This example highlights the danger of making invalid deductions in analytics.

Regarding the second form of online survey (sent by email), companies have the following options:

Online access panels • *Online access panels*: research agencies, but also panel agencies can create online environments (see image) of which people can become members in order to then be invited to participate in an online survey.

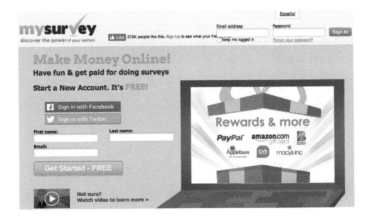

Example of a panel agency

- *Customer* databases: many companies register customer information and can also send out online surveys accordingly.
- *Customer* panels: some companies create their own online customer environments where customers are asked to participate in surveys periodically (with or without help from research agencies).
- *Marketing* databases: many are compiled for use in email marketing or affiliate marketing as well as for market research.

Customer databases

Customer panels

Marketing databases

The research software industry has not stood still and has developed software for conducting online research. In fact, with just a few clicks, it has become possible for anyone to conduct online market research. A widely used example is Survey Monkey (see image), a DIY tool that allows any organisation to carry out online research quickly and easily using email. The big disadvantage of these DIY packages, however, is that the surveys are very simple and the quality of the insights obtained is often lower.

SurveyMonkey·   How it Works   Products ▾   Examples ▾   Resources ▾   Plans & Pricing   LOG IN   SIGN UP

Are my customers actually satisfied?

The world's #1 survey software. 16 million questions answered daily.

PRO SIGN UP   SIGN UP FREE

⌄

Survey Monkey makes it easy to conduct research

Conducting research involves more than copy-pasting a Word survey onto the Internet. Surveys increasingly often churn out repetitions of the same questions. Large-scale validation research (a validation check investigates whether what was intended to be measured was actually done correctly) has shown that a brand's rating can decrease by 25% if the techniques and methods it uses are too repetitive (Hulsebos, 2009). It often comes down, not to the length of a survey, but to the number of times the exact same question is asked. People find that annoying and end up feeling irritated. Variation in the techniques that are used can combat any resultant boredom.

3.7.5   Market research in the social media phase

Companies with carefully constructed, strong brands are aware that all their efforts could be nullified in a very short space of time. And, if they are able to, it should also be possible to use social media to work for the brand's benefit. This requires a new type of marketing, and therefore research, that has at its core the close relationship with the consumer. Brands must enter into dialogue with the customer. Customers can collaborate with brands in formulating new plans, new products and new advertising campaigns.

Market research has clearly changed. There is talk of moving from **active** to **passive** measurements. In other words: from sending out (online) surveys to respondents and asking for their participation to following/observing the (online) behaviour of consumers. Social media are a rich source of data on decision-making and buying behaviour and can give an accurate representation of the 'sentiment' surrounding a brand.
Market research today has become a combination of research and analysis. Digitisation has made significant quantities of consumer data readily available. By analysing this first, an accurate picture arises of how consumers behave regarding brands and of their attitudes to them.

3.7.6   Some notes on online research

As is the case for other forms of research, online research also has a number of disadvantages. The most important two are summarised below:

- *Representation*: it is very important to check whether the group you intend to research is actually accessible via the Internet. In developed internet countries this is no longer a problem, but if you wish to conduct research internationally, there are countries where the penetration of the Internet is not so widespread, and you might be unable to reach all groups in society.
- *Quality*: due to the sheer number of businesses and possible areas of research possibilities, we are increasingly seeing more 'bad' research. Inadequate questioning and too much repetition can significantly reduce data quality (Garbage In → Garbage Out!).

Despite all the benefits of online market research, the old principles of good market research remain unchanged and any research project should meet the following important requirements:

Population
- Population: about what group do you want to make statements? It is important to determine in advance which group you wish to research.

Sampling
- Sampling: how is the sample (group of people) that participates in a survey compiled and from which source? It is important to establish characteristics that determine the representation; ie how will you select the sample to ensure it is truly representative of the underlying population (universe).

Validity
- Validity: is the technique that you apply, able to measure what you need to measure? In other words, are you not using a thermometer to measure shoe size? Much research that is carried out lacks validity.

Reliability
Accuracy
- Reliability and accuracy: how reliable and accurate are the results? In order to be reliable, you must ensure that the result of whatever you measure would remain largely unchanged when measured again amongst a group of people of the same composition. An example for clarification: the statement 'in autumn it will be between 15 and 20 degrees Celsius' is a reliable statement, but not a very accurate one.

Size of cross-section
- Size of cross-section: was the group large enough in order to ensure representation? Formulas can be applied to calculate and determine the optimum cross-sectional size.

Several procedures have been established to determine the quality. The ISO standard is important here. Professional Market Research agencies adhere to the agreements and rules stipulated within it. In addition, ESOMAR has developed several rules for ensuring the quality of panels. By answering 26 questions, it can be determined whether the panels are of sufficient quality.

3.7.7 Techniques in online market research

The Internet phase is primarily characterised by a revolution in technology, both for Digital Marketing and for the way in which Digital Marketing activities are evaluated. This goes hand-in-hand with the development and increasingly frequent application of indirect research techniques that are used online, which rely more on analytics than on research. Organisations use search engine analyses, chat sessions, and forum and click-through analysis to learn more about the online and offline behaviour of consumers. Companies such as Facebook, Google and Microsoft also use their own data and do all sorts of experiments to monitor consumer responses to banners, search results, and website formats, usually without the consumer being aware of it (albeit perfectly legally). This includes analysing media habits such as watching TV and listening to radio via the web. Streaming data can be very accurately analysed, and they keep track of the time you spend watching or listening, to which stations, when you switch channels, to which channel you switch etc.

Research techniques

We will discuss the following techniques below:
1 eyetracking
2 mousetracking
3 online focus groups
4 online communities
5 online website measurement
6 pixel technology
7 blogs and social media analyses
8 mobile research
9 neuroscience

1 Eyetracking
Eyetracking is a technique that uses a special camera that captures the movements of the eyes. A major advantage of this technique is that it objectively (so without asking the individual) tracks what they are looking at. One of the disadvantages of this technique is the relatively high cost: although the cost of this technology has decreased considerably, agencies still need to invite (recruit) respondents, which increases expenses. This technique is used for many purposes (packaging, advertising), but in the context of Digital Marketing (especially for website usability), mostly for banner visibility and search engine behaviour. Eyetracking results are often displayed visually in so-called heatmaps or mountain views. This technique can be especially valuable when assessing the online user experience (UX) eg of a new website or mobile app. Can the customer easily understand what they need to do/click to achieve their objectives on that visit?

Eyetracking

Heat maps
Mountain views

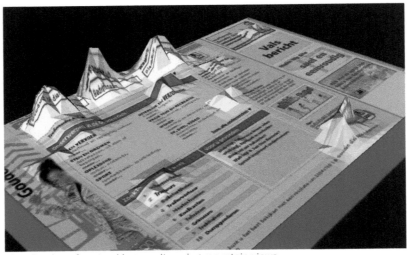

Visualisation of eyetracking results using mountain views

2 Mousetracking

Mousetracking

Mousetracking seems very similar to eyetracking in many respects, but is more quantitative in nature, ie many people can participate online. The premise being that there is a relationship between eye and mouse movements. Research has shown that the accuracy of these techniques is increasingly comparable to 'laboratory standard' eyetracking research. However, it is important that people are well-informed before participating and that rules for validation have been put in place for the analysis of the data.

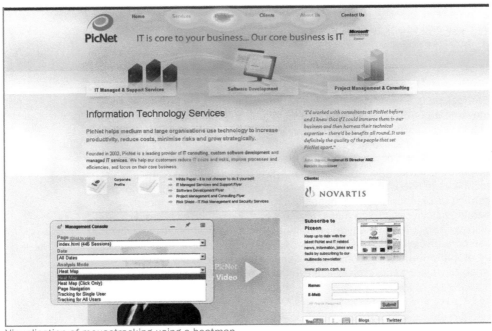

Visualisation of mousetracking using a heatmap

3 Online Focus Groups

The online focus group is based on the traditional focus group, a qualitative research form, in which a limited group of people come together in order to explore awareness, understanding and attitudes relating to a category, to a brand or to specific marketing communications under the supervision of a group leader or interviewer. This technique is suitable for many different purposes but is often used in the web development stage. A great advantage is that it has no borders and is therefore internationally feasible. One thing that is often considered to be a disadvantage, is that it is limited in registering non-verbal communication: posture or facial expressions could of course prove to be useful responses to research of this nature!

Online focus group

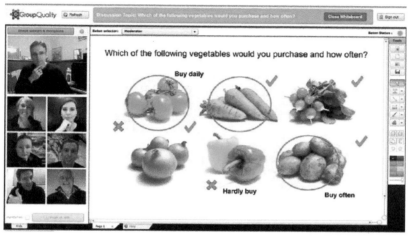

Online focus group

4 Online Communities

Many organisations develop online communities: online groups that mainly allow customers to participate in research over a period of time. An online community can be deployed for various evaluations: for example, new slogans, new online advertising campaigns or new email marketing campaigns can be submitted to them first and tested for comprehension.

Online communities

5 Online Website Measurement

Online website measurement is a technique that makes it possible to use the browser to capture the website visit of online panellists (for example, using cookie registration that places a piece of software on the user's PC). Research agencies first request permission from their panellists to do so. Thus, at target audience level, you will gain insight into who visits which websites. This technique is especially interesting for advertisers as it can analyse the effects of online as well as offline advertising on website visits. Advantage: it is a purely passive measuring instrument, ie the software records online behaviour, which means that the researcher is not required to appeal to the respondent's memory. The disadvantage is that in many cases you cannot be certain who is using the computer, and many providers of this technology also experience problems applying it to multiple devices (eg smartphones).

Online website measurement

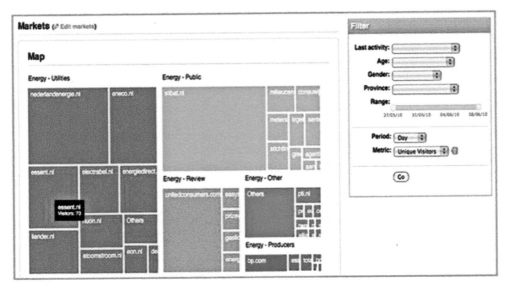

Example of an analysis that shows what websites belonging to energy companies a certain target group have visited

6 Pixel Technique

Pixel technique
Pixel

The pixel technique is best described as a piece of code that is placed in an online banner. This pixel then 'recognises' panel members who arrive on a website where the relevant banner is currently being shown (served). This is also a passive form of measurement: without the panellists being asked anything, the code, or the pixel, registers the visitor. This is an immediate advantage. The disadvantage of this technique is that people increasingly use more than one device and it is not always clear on which device they are presented with the banner. Cookie deletion is also something that is occurring more and more often. Ad blockers may prevent display of the banners. For these reasons, this technique is becoming less reliable.

7 Analysis of Social Media and Blogs:

Blogs and social media analyses

Many more companies are becoming active on social media. Even if they themselves are not, their customers may be. Hence, in a very short space of time, many new agencies have popped up that focus on analysing the massive amount of social media data. Well-known techniques for doing this are the sentiment analyses that allow companies to see how positively or negatively their company, brand and/or product is appearing in social media online sentiment. This growing technique is known as Social Media Monitoring or Analysis.

Sentiment analyses

Online sentiment

8 Mobile research

Mobile research

A feature of the mobile phone, and thus of mobile research, is that it is a device that almost everyone, in many countries, carries on them on a permanent basis. An additional phenomenon is that the number of people who are using the mobile web is also increasing. That combination means that mobile marketing is very interesting for a lot of companies. It follows that it is interesting for researchers too. The main advantage of mobile research, is that you can reach consumers at any time of day. In addition to the fact that people often prefer to fill in surveys on their mobile phone, there are also more apps that have been developed for research purposes. In doing so, it is important that the other features of the phone are used, such as the GPS registration. This means, for example, that if you have attended an event, you can receive a survey to evaluate this event immediately afterwards.

9 Neuroscience
In the eternal quest for the holy grail of research, it was ultimately the human brain that was the researcher's missing link. Although research and science have uncovered to a wide extent how marketing works and how it doesn't, the brain still remained, for a long time, a kind of 'black box'. We have observed that the human subconscious drives consumers to make decisions that do not fit the online orientation models or older purchase models such as AIDA (Attention, Interest, Desire, Action). Since the beginning of this century, we have seen the emergence of neurotechnology, no longer confined to the universities for purely scientific research, but now applied in the field of marketing. How our brain reacts to marketing stimuli is now becoming clearer. It is also important to know in which part of the brain this happens, because the location of our brain activity determines whether we store something short term or long term. To do this, an MRI scanner is used. This is a developing field of study.

Neuroscience

AIDA

Using a webcam: facial coding
As the webcam is increasingly a standard piece of equipment in people's homes, it is more frequently being used for research. It is mainly used to measure people's emotions by looking at their facial expressions. This is especially used to measure the impact of TV commercials. However, the inaccuracy of the observations still makes the information difficult to apply (see also facial scanning in section 11.2).

Online research has given the marketer many new insights into what does and does not work in both offline and Digital Marketing.

The Internet provides researchers with the ability to observe and interpret behaviour but has also made data collection a whole lot easier. It remains important however, that research is carried out in the correct manner. To do this, it is not enough to simply post a survey online. You must take into account not only how Internet works, but how people use it.

3.8 Big data and customer insights

In the previous section on online market research, you read about how to collect online data while actively involving people. In addition to this active form, it is also possible to collect data from people in a passive way. This means that people themselves do not provide active cooperation by answering questions or giving opinions or scores. The online marketer can use data that people generate by signing in, by clicking, searching, or purchasing products or services. This type of data forms the basis for

Digital Marketing communication (see sections 5, 6 and 7) and customer relationship management or CRM (see Chapter 10).

In this section we will examine the complexity of this new and growing data stream and talk about what steps you as a marketer can take to convert (big) data into value. First, you must extract information from that data by using data science and then you must use analytics to gain insight into that information. Finally, we will discuss where and how to apply data analysis.

3.8.1 (Big) data

The growing number of online interactions between organisation and customer is generating a tsunami of data! A few decades ago, the key question was: 'where do I get the information from', whereas today it is: 'how can I get the best information from all that data'? Consider, for example, the data that people generate in email traffic, website visits, whilst using apps, on social media, and by turning on their location recognition services (GPS). In section 10.1 you will find more information about the different types of customer data and data sources.

In addition to this 'man-made data' there is also a 'device-generated data stream.' Examples include: communication between smartphone and thermostat, television, lighting and beacons, as well as data that cars produce from the moment the car is started until it stops (for example: technical information, distances and fuel consumption). The data stream from these sources will increase exponentially in the coming years. Not only more expensive products like cars and TVs will produce this data, but also shoes, clothes and food. Here we are referring to The Internet of Things (IoT). And of course, any new or improved products in the robotics field will also produce data.

Big data

Especially due to the increase of data produced by devices, 'big data' is something we encounter with increasing frequency. When to consider it 'big data' is quite arbitrary. A bit like the difference between lots of money and even more money! To describe big data, three factors are used (the three Vs, see figure 3.6): the amount of data (Volume), the speed (Velocity) with which the data is retrieved and sent, and the diversity of the data (Variety). By the latter, we mean the variety of data sources and data types: structured (for example, the number of clicks counted, or the amount spent) and unstructured (for example, portions of text on social media).

Three Vs

The complexity of big data lies not so much in the data storage, but in quickly processing large quantities in a short space of time (ultimately being described as 'real time'). To do this, distributed processing (or distributed computing) in the cloud is used. Distributed processing uses a program that runs on multiple computers, communicating with each other in order to achieve a common end goal. The world wide web itself is an example of distributed processing. The power of many computers is thus combined. In addition to quick processing, combining data from many sources and different data types is also difficult.

Distributed processing

The use of artificial intelligence (AI) and machine learning (ML) enables us to carry out these processes faster and more efficiently. As you will read in section 3.4, computers can today be programmed in such a way that enables them to develop some code that was not explicitly in the program

FIGURE 3.6 The 3 Vs of big data

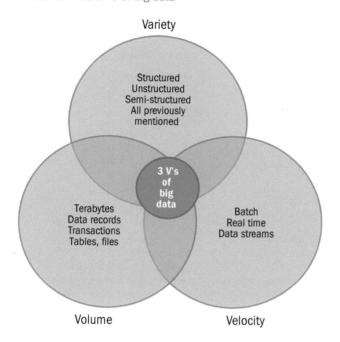

to begin with; by some definitions, they are *learning* and becoming more intelligent. ⟩ *yxceum cue*

3.8.2 Using data science to gain customer insight

Simply gathering all of this data (with or without the informed and active participation of people) is not the ultimate goal, it's about converting it into valuable insights. The first step is to change data into information: show what has happened so that people can understand the meaning of the data. To achieve this, analysts use management reports and dashboards and adopt a 'test and learn' approach (see Chapter 12).

Of course, looking back to the past can be useful, but it does not necessarily tell us what we need to do in the future. Fortunately, we are able to not only describe *what* has happened (descriptive) but also *why* it has happened (diagnostic). We can also predict what is likely to happen in the future (predictive) and why (prescriptive). These last two activities in particular contribute to the development of (customer) insights. You can read more about these types of analyses in section 3.8.3.

Data science is the field where the application of scientific methods, processes and systems are used to extract information and insights from data. It is currently one of the fastest growing fields in the word of business and technology. McKinsey has predicted a shortage of nearly 200,000 data scientists and 1.5 million managers and analysts who know how to make effective decisions concerning big data results, by 2018, in the USA alone. The requirement is for professionals who can combine the results of data analysis with vision and creativity to create customer

Data science

Customer
insight
management
insights that lead to concrete actions that result in additional value for the customer as well as for the organisation (see figure 3.7). This is what we call customer insight management (Van Delft & Van de perre, 2015).

FIGURE 3.7 Data science leads to concrete actions

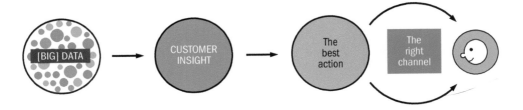

3.8.3 Types of analyses

After translating the *data* into *information*, the second step is to gain *insights* from this information. For this purpose, data scientists use analytical techniques developed in recent decades that are based on mathematics, statistics and computer science. There are many different analytical techniques available. You can read more about some common techniques in this section. We will ask the following questions:

- Are the analyses descriptive (what) or explanatory (why)?
- Do the results relate to past, present or future?

Table 3.4 lists the four categories of analytical techniques that are created by combining these classifications. Within each category, we have named and described the most common techniques briefly. The descriptions of these techniques are partly derived from Verhoef, Kooge and Walk (2016).

TABLE 3.4 Classification of types of data analysis

	Descriptive	**Explanatory**
Past/present	1 Descriptive (what happened?)	2 Diagnostic (why did it happen?)
Future	3 Predictive (what will happen?)	4 Prescriptive (why will it happen?)

1 Descriptive analytics

Descriptive analytics aims to provide insight into what has occurred. We will discuss some commonly occurring uses:

- *Reporting*
There are many tools available for summarising data and creating dashboards. Often it is the display of a business's most important performance indicators (Key Performance Indicators = KPIs) such as sales, turnover, customer satisfaction and customer value. More about reporting the results of Digital Marketing can be found in Chapter 12.

- *Profiling* (customer profiling)
When reaching out to customers digitally, we often use groups of customers that 'look alike'. Each 'persona' represents a discrete 'segment', enabling us to better tailor the online product realisation and

Descriptive
analytics

Reporting

Profiling

communication to those groups. You can read more about this in section 10.2.

- *Web analytics*
  By improving our understanding of customer behaviour on websites and in online stores, we can increase site/store performance. Chapters 11 and 12 will explore this in detail.

Web analytics

- *Social listening*
  Social listening is about measuring brand associations and sentiment by analysing social media messages. The essence of social listening is to monitor social media for information about a business or an organisation. This is discussed in more detail in the next section. The use of the 'word cloud' in the context of social listening (see image) is an example of how we can organise unstructured information (words in an online publication). It is not only a matter of counting words, but also about learning to ignore/down-weight words that are less useful to us. For example, the word 'car' on its own might not have much value for a car manufacturer, but the combination of the words 'electric' and 'car' may be relevant.

Social listening

Social listening is based on unstructured information. In this case, a 'word cloud' containing words about Nike on Twitter.

- *Social network analyses*
  Because of social networks (Facebook, LinkedIn, WeChat etc.), the intensity of customer-to-consumer connections has exploded. As a result, analyses on the extent of their influence have become very popular. Additionally, it isn't only about the number of contacts that an influencer has, but also about how far that contact is removed from them and the extent to which they communicate with one another. Also, 'influencing power' plays a role. Of all customers who are positive about a brand, it is more effective to focus efforts those customers that have a high impact factor (customer influence value = CIV).

Social network analyses

Influencer

Customer influence value

2 Diagnostic analytics

The purpose of diagnostic analytics (explanatory analyses) is to understand *why* consumers behaved as they did in order to benefit from these insights into the future. We will be discussing some of the most important techniques:

Diagnostic analytics

- *Migration analyses*
  The essence of migration analyses is to get an idea of the evolution of (online) behaviour, product use and customer value by individual customers. Even though, for example, turnover and the total number of customers may be steady, it may be beneficial to attract or repel (discourage) individual customers since certain customers spend a lot more and others less. By recognising patterns in customer acquisition,

Migration analyses

growth and reduction, marketers can influence customers who are at similar points in the buying cycle. For example, customers of a shopping site who, according to the results of a migration analysis, have characteristics that predict they will grow into a 'top customer' can be enticed with personal invitations, loyalty program status, or a special customer card.

- *Customer segmentation*

Customer segmentation

Cluster analysis

Customer segmentation is about creating groups of customers who have similar behaviour/needs together so that there is a clear distinction between the behaviours of those in different groups. In order to achieve this, cluster analysis can be used. As with customer profiling, the goal is to use Digital Marketing instruments to serve each segment optimally. Customer profiling is based on one or more variables (such as digital lifestyle), selected by the organisation as a starting point. Statistical segmentation analysis allows many different segmentation variables to be included, and statistical algorithms determine which variables are most impactful and which groups are ultimately relevant to a particular approach. For example, airlines may find that an app is most attractive to a number of specific customer segments, such as business travellers who fly frequently.

- *Basket analysis*

Basket analysis

Basket analysis is the comparison of customer shopping carts to better understand which products are purchased most often in combination with each other in order to further stimulate this. This method is used by online retailers like Amazon for recommending alternatives or similar products to customers who are buying eg a book or music CD.

- *Attribute analyses*

Attribute analyses

Attribute analyses determine the contributions of specific components (attributes) to the total value of the product or service. For instance, suppose a shopping site is usually given a customer satisfaction score of 8 by its visitors. In the last month, this score has decreased. What is the cause of this and what action should be taken? A customer satisfaction survey also revealed scores on a (large) number of the site's attributes (such as the range of products, prices, the search module and the payment module). By analysing the influence of the underlying attributes on the total score, you can get a clear picture of which attributes are more important than others. In the example of the shopping site, the site search tool proved to be an important feature of customer's overall experience of the site.

- *Customer journey analyses*

Customer journey analyses

Customer journey analyses help the analyst to gain a better understanding of the routes that customers take throughout the customer cycle (from problem recognition through purchase to loyalty) and the effect of the various points of contact between customer and organisation (touchpoints) on those routes. These analyses strongly resemble the attribute analyses described above. Here we want to know the exact contact moment, the channel and the proposition, that contributed to the result in order to better understand what is working - ie why customers buy. You can find examples of this in section 4.4.

3 Predictive analytics

Predictive analytics

The purpose of predictive analytics is predicting individual customers' future behaviour in order for online marketers to be able to act on these predictions and increase customer value. The following are commonly used analytical techniques:

- *Customer lifetime value analyses* (CLV)

  The purpose of customer lifetime value analyses (CLV) is to calculate total customer value, considering all revenues, past and future. By determining the CLV per customer, it becomes clear which actions could prove to be useful for certain clients. CLV is a good indicator of the 'breakeven' expenditure to acquire and retain an individual customer. You can read more about this in section 10.1.

  Customer life time value analyses

- *Churn reduction modelling*

  Churn is when customers leave. (Consider a service with an annual membership fee/renewal date eg subscription or annual insurance policy). An analysis aimed at churn reduction can predict which customers are at greatest risk of leaving. By continuing to investigate the effect of a (large) number of variables on whether or not customers choose to leave, data scientists can determine a set of calculation rules (a model) that may predict who does and who doesn't choose to remain a customer within a certain time frame. With special actions aimed at these customers, the online marketer can then motivate them to remain a customer for longer (increasing their CLV).

  Churn reduction modelling

- *Attribute modelling*

  Attribution analysis seeks answers to the question: 'why did they buy?' By using it, a data scientist can determine how marketing and communication budgets can best be distributed across online and offline contact points based on the predicted effect of the different points of contact on the conversion (sales) of individual customers. This analytical technique is the next step on from attribute analysis and customer journey analyses. For example, the probability of conversion for young people may be greatest if they first saw a video on YouTube before visiting and then buying something in a shopping site, while mothers with teenage children may more often buy something if they have seen a display ad on Facebook beforehand. By understanding these factors, the digital marketer can then deliberately distribute his/her budget to these contact channels and, of course, ensure that these communication messages are tailored to the different target groups.

  Attribute modelling

- *Integrated big data models*

  Integrated big data models are a combination of predictive techniques used on data sets from different sources to ultimately achieve an integrated prediction of consumer (buying) behaviour. The strength of this is to achieve better, more accurate forecasts. Imagine if we could use a customer's previous buying behaviour to accurately predict their future buying behaviour. By linking this information to web data (site visit, product search), and social media data it can help us achieve a much better more precise ROI from our marketing communications.

  Integrated big data models

4 Prescriptive analytics

Prescriptive analytics lead to proposed actions. The purpose of these analytical techniques is not only to make predictions but also to recommend one or more marketing communication activities based on those predictions. An example: we can not only predict that a specific customer will leave (churn), but we are also able to indicate which propositions (offers) are the most likely to prevent this from happening. This relatively new form of analysis is quite complex and not yet common

Prescriptive analytics

practice for most companies, but that is changing rapidly. (Hence the increasing demand for skilled data scientists).

We consider the following to fall under this category of analysis:

Dynamic targeting

- *Dynamic targeting*

  Dynamic targeting means that communication messages and offers are modified based on customer profiles, behaviour, location, and most recent interactions. In addition, the results of the customer's latest responses are analysed in a continuous process, and on that basis marketers can customise the product/service offering and the communication about them. Because all of these processes lead to many variants, which employees are simply unable to keep track of, a new technique known as *marketing automation* is gaining increasing traction in many organisations. Read more about marketing automation in sections 6.6 and 10.1.

Recommender/ personalisation systems

- *Recommender/personalisation systems*

  Recommender/personalisation systems ensure that the individual customer receives specific offers of the most relevant products to maximise conversion rate. The system analyses the buying and interaction behaviour of the customer and generates these highly targeted offers. Online retailers in particular are increasingly making use of these systems. For example, think of Amazon.com recommending books to you based on books you've ordered before, but also on the books you're viewing and also on data about thousands of other customers whom it judges to be 'people like you'.

3.8.4 Areas for applying data science and customer insight management

As explained above, data analyses can be applied to almost all components of Digital Marketing (see figure 3.8). The main areas of application are:

- Innovation and optimisation of business models, products and services (the product design and development process). This is actually the 'usual territory' where (research) data and customer insight has been used for decades.
- Innovation and optimisation of the channels used in customer acquisition, CRM and order processing. Organisations spend a lot of energy analysing customer journeys to better ensure sales, communication and distribution channels are in line with one another, and improve customer value for those channels.
- Innovation and optimisation of the dialogue with the target group during the customer acquisition process and CRM process (campaign and content). Marketing communication is increasingly tailored to the specific wishes and behaviour of customers. This directly contributes to a higher customer value for the customer as well as the organisation and reduces the problem of bothering customers with unnecessary information.

In order to apply the above in practice, an increasing range of data, systems, models and (automation) processes are necessary (see figure 3.8). And of course, people with the right competencies to work with them. In practice, online marketers often begin working with larger customer segments which gradually become more defined until eventually coming down to the level of the individual customer. Again, the key is finding and accessing the right data-savvy people (either on the payroll or as consultants/agencies) who can make sense of the new 'big' data and extract the necessary actionable insights to drive better marketing.

FIGURE 3.8 Areas for applying customer insights & predictive marketing

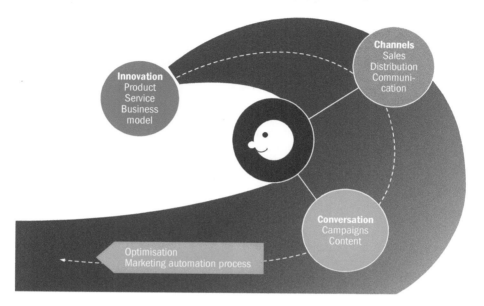

3.9 Social media monitoring

Organisations rightly cherish their customer relationships, seek to understand customer needs, and create customer experiences that lead to repeat purchases and maximise CLV. Communication through social media can play a significant role in this and it all begins with listening to what customers and others say about your brand, product or service.

Social media monitoring: is structurally mapping and analysing messages and conversations about a particular subject and/or brand on social media. This includes information about how often a brand is mentioned, whether the sentiment is positive or negative, and what specific issues are being addressed. Social media monitoring uses analytical programs that can understand not only text, but also images and videos (so-called social media monitoring tools. The simplest way of monitoring what is said about a brand (or about yourself) is to search on the social media platform itself. For an example of this, take a look at www.twitter.com/search. The online marketer is not just interested in the counts alone. They also want the organisation to be able to respond to negative signals, for example, if a customer experiences a problem with a product. Equally, positive signals can be followed up with a 'Thank-you'. The key thing is to understand the trends; what is changing? Is sentiment becoming more positive, more negative or remaining 'flat'?

Social media monitoring

Social media monitoring tools

© Noordhoff Uitgevers bv

There are several software providers that make it possible to understand trends and respond to signals (see, for example, www.brandwatch.com/blog/top-10-free-social-media-monitoring-tools for an overview of free tools).

The outcomes of social media monitoring can be used for:
- adjustments to the product realisation process if it appears that the customer's preferences and needs have changed, or they are not satisfied by the product/its attributes
- to improve (online) brand reputation by adequately responding to negative signals and amplifying positive signals
- adjustments to the Digital Marketing communication based on signals from the target audience or trends within the target audience
- improving the order handling process based on negative signals and requests for help
- getting to know customers better, understanding influences and responding to questions and comments from customers
- recognition of purchase and 'defection' signals from individual customers so that they can be addressed immediately

Social media monitoring helps organisations maintain a constant feedback loop. This helps the customer, both at the individual level, and at strategic level to constantly improve on the basis of insights ('big loop') given by customers. You can read more about this in Chapter 10. For an explanation on how to use social media monitoring to improve online customer service, please read section 9.4. How to measure core performance indicators surrounding social media, such as social mentions and sentiment, can be found in 12.2.

Questions and assignments

NOW CHECK YOUR UNDERSTANDING:

3.1   Conduct an audit of your School/University's (or company's) online presence.

a What do you think people's most important activity on the Internet is currently? Does your own behaviour match that of the 'average' person in your country?
Check the statistics for your country here:
https://www.slideshare.net/wearesocial/2018-digital-yearbook-86862930

b What digital lifestyle do you think most closely resembles your own? Does the lifestyle you have chosen match your online shopping behaviour?

c Which of the risks that consumers experience in online shopping are most recognisable to you? Give a concrete example of every risk. How could web shop owners remove this risk perception?

d To what level do you participate in social media? What are your motives? Compare these motives with the motives in section 3.3. What is your conclusion?

e Think of a recent online purchase you have made. Compare the process that you followed with the online consumer behaviour model in section 3.5. What are your conclusions?

3.2   Now let's consider the global online shopping site Asos.com
Here is a review of the site: http://bit.ly/2pkOstO

a Do you agree with the reviewer?

b What would you like to add to this based on the 8C model (see section 3.5.6)?
Support your answer.

c What role does flow play in a consumer's loyalty to a website?

d How would you measure flow?

e How could Asos improve the customer experience on their site?

3.3   Go to the leading US ecommerce retail sites websites: amazon.com and qvc.com.

a Indicate which of the two providers scores better, as measured against these core success factors of The Digital Marketing Funnel:
- visit
- captivate
- decide
- ordering
- paying
- binding (repeat visit)

Explain the reasons for your answer.

b What would you recommend to both providers based on the trends described in section 3.4?

3.4 You have been appointed Marketing Manager at sports clothing brand O'Neill.com. You will be given permission from the management to spend a significant amount of money on market research regarding their Digital Marketing efforts.

a What are the three most important points you would like to investigate?

b What type of research do you believe should be conducted?
Support your answer with arguments from section 3.7. Weigh up all the different possibilities regarding the use of offline and online channels as well as between the various research techniques that can be used online.

c You also have a number of data scientists (web analysts) in your team What assignment/s would you give them? For which Digital Marketing issues would you like to receive customer insights and what data and analytics should be used to glean these insights?

d What would you monitor using social media monitoring?

e What actions might you take as a result of the above learnings?

3.5

CASE

The rise of the power shopper
By Marjolein Visser

A consumer survey by UPS revealed that online shoppers in the US are most concerned with the ability to be flexible in their online purchases. Today's shopper is a so-called 'flex shopper': someone who easily switches between channels and devices when comparing and buying products.

This consumer research is part of a global survey of emerging trends in online shopping. It has also been conducted in Asia, Brazil, Mexico and Europe. A few of the main findings:

- Around half of all purchases are made in a store. There is however, a clear tendency towards more online shopping.
- Almost 40% of purchases are an 'omnichannel purchase', where the information retrieval process and the procurement process are spread across different channels (see figure 3.9).
- The smartphone was already important for product searching, but it is becoming more and more important for to the purchase as well. This stems from the fact that retailer's apps are enabling an ever-improving customer experience.
- Third party markets, such as Amazon, eBay and Asos.com, play an important role in the ecommerce industry. Lower prices or discounts on delivery are two reasons for choosing a marketplace as opposed to doing business with a retailer directly.

FIGURE 3.9 Global consumer research on trends in online shopping

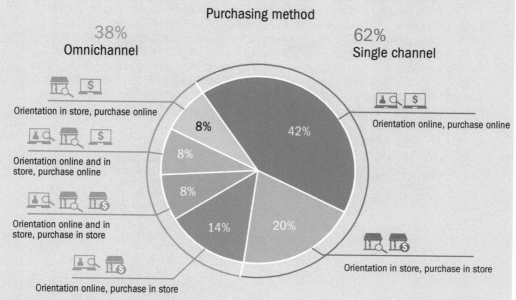

Source: UPS. 2016

Complete information is essential

In addition to convenience and flexibility in ordering and delivery, detailed product information is becoming increasingly important to the consumer's online research before a store is visited. Product reviews, excellent photos, a good site search tool, promotional actions, and the ability to check whether the product is in stock are the most relevant features of a good online shopping app. Consumers also want to receive alerts and notifications about delivery, promotions, and free or more affordable delivery.

Order fulfilment remains decisive for channel selection

The way in which the online orders are handled remains a decisive factor in consumers' selection of a preferred purchase channel. Consumers appreciate options for alternative delivery locations, such as service desks in shops, provided they have convenient opening hours. Online shoppers say they would rather return products in a store, but in fact, they tend to return items by mail. They do however, see room for improvement when it comes to returning purchases. Pricing is also a factor: consumers prefer free delivery but are willing to pay more for speedier delivery if they need the product quickly.

Technology changes shopping

It is estimated that approx. 30% of consumers are aware of new technologies, such as beacons and in-store messaging. A quarter of them are positive about it, slightly less than half are neutral.

About a third of consumers say their decision-making regarding purchases is influenced by social media, a quarter of respondents have purchased something via social media sites. Being able to make comparisons easily and convenience are the main motivators for shopping via social media.

Taking 'power shoppers' into account

The research shows that an important new market segment has emerged: the power shopper (see figure 3.10). These are experienced online shoppers who are 'digitally savvy' and aware of the nuances of online and omnichannel shopping. They use technology (especially smartphones) more often and in more different ways. They are more satisfied with online shopping, because they have confidence in their ability to use the web and, if necessary, make use of customer service. For example, they also make use of ship-to-store options, where products are delivered to a store. This market segment is socially active and enjoys using new features that make shopping easier. They spend a lot of money and have a lot of online influence.

FIGURE 3.10 Power shoppers are a group that must be taken into account

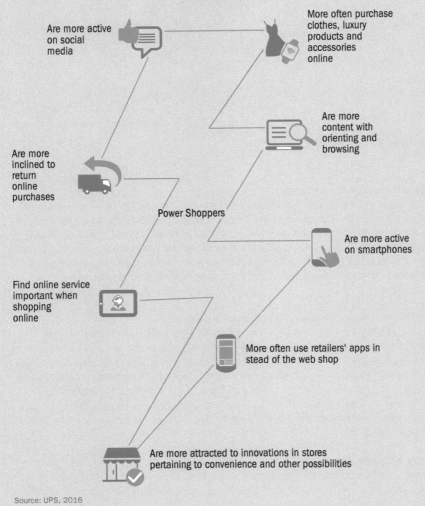

Are more active on social media

More often purchase clothes, luxury products and accessories online

Are more content with orienting and browsing

Are more inclined to return online purchases

Power Shoppers

Are more active on smartphones

Find online service important when shopping online

More often use retailers' apps in stead of the web shop

Are more attracted to innovations in stores pertaining to convenience and other possibilities

Source: UPS, 2016

The consumer research called 'The UPS Pulse of the Online Shopper Study' was conducted in 2016 in the US.

Source: www.pressroom.ups.com

NOW TEST YOUR UNDERSTANDING:

a Does online shopping behaviour in the US differ substantially from other countries? Find recent data online and compare it with the results from the case.

b Which digital lifestyles match power shoppers best?

c This chapter lists the main reasons why people shop online and what risks consumers experience in online shopping. What risks of online shopping will power shoppers experience less frequently than the average online shopper?

d The case mentions that 'technology changes shopping'. What are the main trends in Digital Marketing that are changing shopping? Give one example for each trend.

e The power shopper is active on social media. For various levels of participation in social media, provide an example of behaviour that a power shopper will exhibit more often than the average shopper. What motivates them?

f Section 3.5 above describes the consumer buying process and the role that the Internet plays in each phase. For each phase of the purchase process, indicate how mobile changes the buying process or buying behaviour. In doing so, please take into account the information from the case.

g What can you say about the core success factors for each of the phases of the Digital Marketing funnel based on the research from the case?

h The case does not stipulate how the research into online shopping was conducted. What online research forms do you believe are most suitable for determining emerging trends in online shopping? Compare them all using arguments from 3.7 above.

i What data should an online retailer collect and what analytical methods should they apply to ensure online shoppers experience increasingly levels of customer satisfaction? Support your answer and give examples.

j Should all online retailers use social media monitoring and if so, for what purpose?

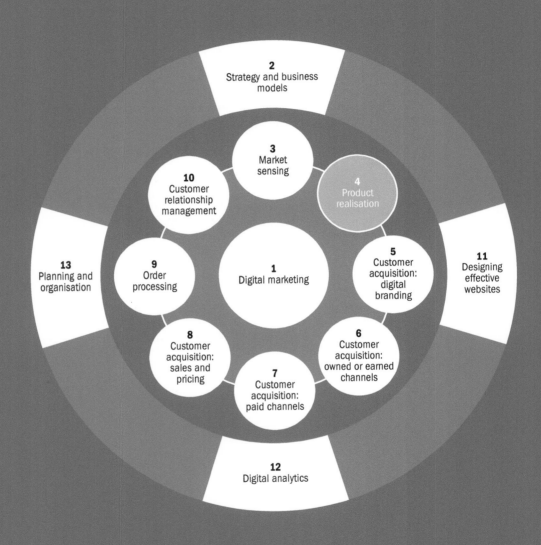

4

Product Realisation

Authors: Marjolein Visser (4.1 to 4.5) and Wout van den Dool (4.3)

The previous chapters describe how senior management determines the organisational and marketing strategy and business model, and how the marketer can identify the wishes and needs of a market (the 'market sensing' process). Once an organisation has used the market sensing process to identify opportunities in the market and (in response to the needs of potential customers) possibilities for adding value, marketers can begin the 'product realisation' process: ie researching and developing new core products and services, building on them to come up with a concrete market offer and making the products or services available to customers. In the Internet Age, the research and development process is facilitated by making use of the Internet and all the possibilities that it has to offer. For the realisation of the product itself, it is important that marketers, together with management, determine which parts of the production process are best performed online and which are not suitable or less suitable for this. In the product improvement phase, the Internet is an important source of information about potential errors or improvements to the product, services and production process. This will all be discussed in this chapter. In the last part of this chapter we will give you some recommendations for the methodical setup of the product realisation process.

This chapter will cover:
- value of and value for the customer
- co-creation
- developing and setting up online products
- product improvement
- methodical product realisation

After studying this chapter, students will be able to:
- demonstrate the role of the Digital Marketer in the product realisation process
- explain what co-creation, crowdsourcing and mass-collaboration involve and how they can play an effective role in the product realisation process

- indicate how online products can be developed and arranged using customer journey mapping, the DNA model and event driven marketing
- understand the implications for front and back office resourcing
- explain which sources and analyses a product manager can use to come up with ideas for product improvement and to determine the priorities for improvement
- specify how product realisation can be set up methodically

4.1 The goal of the product realisation process is customer value

Product realisation process

By the product realisation process, we mean researching and developing new products and services, building on that to come up with a concrete offer for the market and making the products or services available to customers. For example, imagine that you want to come up with a new way of providing airline tickets. You start by generating ideas for your new service. Then, you choose the most promising one and summarise it into a clear proposition. You then 'test-drive' this idea among your target audience and whatever appeals to them most is translated into more concrete resources, such as an information platform and an online booking system. All this is part of product realisation, a task assigned to the product manager within many organisations.

Before the Internet, people bought their products in a store or ordered them by post or telephone ('mail order'). For product information, they relied on print media, such as brochures, or, for example, conversations with sales staff. After purchasing, if there was a problem, they had to look for a paper ('hard-copy') printed instruction manual or call up the manufacturer's customer service. For services, such as financial advice or a doctor's appointment, people relied on personal contact, supplemented by written communication. The ability to communicate and exchange data online has made many things easier for the customer. Organisations have used the capabilities of the Internet to make their product realisation process more effective and efficient. Still however, there are often many things that take place in the offline environment, that could very easily be handled online, and no doubt will be in the coming years. This clearly represents on opportunity for ambitious organisations.

The product realisation process is divided into four phases:
1 develop, evaluate and choose ideas
2 developing products: developing the chosen ideas into a concrete product
3 realising products: making the actual product and then making it available to the customer
4 improvement of products (ongoing)

Customer value

Value to customer

Value to firm

A core concept in the product realisation process is customer value. The idea of customer value has two interpretations: value to customer, often called customer experience (CX) and value for the organisation or value to firm. Value to customer (V2C) is the sum of the benefits a customer receives from choosing a particular offer minus the sacrifices (money, time, energy) that they must make in exchange. Value to firm (V2F) is the total contribution that a customer brings to an organisation over the entire duration of that customer's relationship with the organisation. Usually this is money, but it may also be that the customer writes a lot of positive reviews, introduces friends or colleagues, or volunteers (for example, in a charitable organisation). Customer value is also called customer lifetime value (CLV) (see section 10.1).

In the longer term, it is important that the value of the customer and the customer experience balance each other out. If there is long-term imbalance, then either the customer will not receive enough value and walk away, or the organisation will invest too much value relative to the returns, ie over-service the customers, will lose money and will eventually go out of business. This is shown in figure 4.1.

In addition, both the customer and the supplier naturally endeavour to maximise their respective values. That is a second starting point not only for the product realisation process, but also for other Digital Marketing processes.

FIGURE 4.1 Value of the customer and value for the customer must be in balance

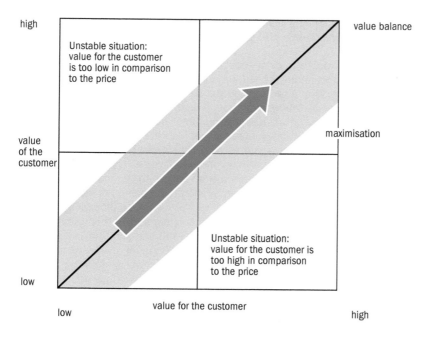

A bad customer experience (particularly if it happens more than once) is a reason for many people to choose a different provider or to switch to an alternative provider. More and more organisations realise that providing a pleasant and consistent customer experience and ideally a 'delightful' one which exceeds expectations, across all contact and sales channels is important for attracting and keeping customers. In practice this can prove to be a difficult task. This is because, in large organisations, many

Customer experience

organisational units and departments are involved in the design of the customer process. Customer contact is fragmented across different departments, environments, work processes and systems. Each department only sees a small piece of the total customer journey and interaction channels are not always in tune with one another. There is also often an 'inside out' way of thinking, which means that the organisation's focus and perspective is internal and not on the customer. As a result, customers often have a bad experience of doing business with such a company and end up coming away feeling disappointed. On the other hand, successful companies take a holistic approach, seeking to gain a 'single view' of the customer, recognising the value of their business to the organisation and rewarding their loyalty which in turn increases CLV.

Customer journey

4.2 Co-creation

The Internet provides many opportunities for interaction with (potential) customers during the product realisation process. This cooperation with the customer is called co-creation. Co-creation is often associated with the first phase of the product realisation process: coming up with ideas for products and services. Techniques such as crowdsourcing and mass collaboration are used. However, co-creation can be used in all stages of the product realisation process. In this section, we will focus on the foundations of co-creation and discuss several different forms.

Co-creation

4.2.1 Foundations of co-creation

In the past, production and consumption were separated: the manufacturer made their products in a factory and the customer bought them in a shop or through another distribution channel. Manufacturers and customers often had little or no contact and the customer had little or no insight into the production process. Nowadays, companies have the opportunity to develop and realise products interactively, in cooperation with the customer and any other collaborative partners. We call this co-creation. The role of production no longer entirely belongs with the manufacturer. They now create value together whereby the process of co-creation itself can also be of value to the customer. If this process is a pleasant experience, they attach more value to the supplier's offer than they would have done had they remained at a distance. Prahalad and Ramaswamy (2004) consider the following to be the 'foundations' of co-creation:

- *Dialogue*: interactivity, profound involvement and willingness to act, both on the part of the customer and the organisation. Both parties must want to learn together and solve problems as equal partners.
- *Access*: the value for the customer lies in the experience, not so much in the possession of the product. The customer must have access to that experience and receive tools from the organisation, such as software, information and access to systems. An example of this is a debt collection agency that allows customers to log in, see how far customer procedures have been advanced and possibly add information or make adjustments to the process. The customer is, in effect, helping to design the product, by tailoring it to their own specifications.
- *Risk* assessment: organisations can no longer operate unilaterally when it comes to decision-making regarding the risks that the consumer is facing. Better information for consumers allows them to make their own risk assessments. Customers are increasingly less likely to accept that

an organisation makes all the decisions for them. This particularly applies in Business-to-Business (B2B) Marketing.
- *Transparency*: in the past, knowledge – and therefore power – was often squarely in the hands of the producer. Thanks to the Internet, information is much more accessible for buyers. It is now even sometimes the case that customers are better informed than the manufacturer's own employee (eg IT, retailing or automotive dealers).

The traditional distribution of roles between an organisation and the customer is no longer the norm. Interaction between customers and organisations leads to innovation, customer participation and better customer service (Dalli & Galvagno, 2014).

4.2.2   Forms of co-creation
There are four forms of co-creation:
1 co-innovation
2 co-production
3 customisation
4 integration

1 Co-innovation
Co-innovation is the development of new products or services in collaboration with (potential) customers. Commonly used methods are mass collaboration and crowdsourcing. Read more about this in section 4.3.

Co-innovation

2 Co-production
Co-production entails that the customer takes over parts of the production process. Examples of co-production include printing tickets for a theatre performance and uploading photos for a photo album. Section 4.5 goes into this in more depth.

Co-production

3 Customisation
Customisation entails that the customer is able to tailor certain parts of a product or service to their own needs or wants. An example is the German online retailer mymuesli, where individual customisation is used: customers can put together their own personal mix of muesli based on their own tastes. This customised muesli is then delivered to them by mail within a few days.

Customisation

Individual customisation

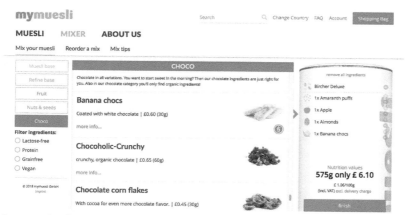

An example of customisation: www.mymuesli.com

4 Integration

Integration
Integration involves gathering several services or products from different providers on one website, so that eventually one end-product is created. An example of this is the compilation of a trip through a travel agency website, where the accommodation, flight and travel insurance are all booked with different providers.

UK-based online travel agent Travelsoon (http://www.travelsoon.com) allows the customer to build their own holiday from individual 'building blocks'; in effect you are building the entire trip like a tour operator does, except it is custom-made for you!

Various forms of co-creation can come together in a process. For example, someone can print their own airline ticket (co-production), select a seat on an airplane other than the one that was automatically assigned to them (customisation) and arrange additional transportation to their hotel (integration). This leads to more value for the customer. A disadvantage of co-creation is that it sometimes leads to inefficiency and therefore to less value for the organisation. The number of products is constantly increasing and if this is not accompanied by highly flexible production processes and/ or being able to discontinue products in a timely manner, this can lead to disarray and lower productivity.

4.3 Product development, mass collaboration and crowdsourcing

Developing and improving products that have an online component requires thorough preparation. Building systems and websites is labour-intensive and can be expensive. Everything is connected and thus co-dependent. Once planned in, changes are not easy to make. Product management in a Digital Marketing environment is a challenging task.

The most important element for successful product development is knowledge of customer wants/needs and experiences. Online, an organisation can communicate with many more people, faster and more interactively than offline. Moreover, blogs, forums, reviews and other social networks provide a rich source of information. In addition, online market research can play an important role in gaining insight into the wishes of a product's potential buyers (see section 3.7). Systematically collecting information via the Internet is a good starting point for new product ideas. The Internet also makes it possible to monitor and measure customer behaviour automatically. This makes it easier and faster to see which products are more, or less, appealing. However, product development necessitates more than just these kinds of basic insights.

Product development
Product development can be divided into five phases (Hauser et al., 1993):
1 generating ideas
2 concept development
3 product design
4 product testing
5 product introduction

Initiatives for product development were previously the responsibility of the research and development (R&D) or New Product Development (NPD) department. Today, more and more companies are moving towards 'customer driven innovation', where the innovation process begins with the customer. During the first two phases, organisations use market research. Qualitative techniques are frequently used, such as focus groups and interviews, but quantitative techniques allow the marketer to test and refine product concepts. After that, methods such as prototyping, product testing, and test marketing are used. However, these traditional methods have many disadvantages:

Customer driven innovation

- It is often one-way traffic: the customer speaks, and the company listens (at best).
- The specific context in which the customer uses the products is not always addressed, thereby leaving out important points for improvement.
- There is no contact with other people from the customer's environment, so social aspects are often excluded.
- The company tends to listen more to its current customers and sometimes only to its biggest customers. This gives a distorted picture of the needs in the market.

Ulwick (2005) concluded, based on a study of more than two hundred studies in more than 70 companies in 25 sectors, that traditional communication methods with customers mostly lead to wastage. He noted that organisations should spend less time listening to customer statements about needs, benefits, specifications and solutions. It is, he claims, more important is to find out which criteria customers use to determine to what extent the tasks and activities they perform have been successfully completed.

The Internet makes it possible to communicate quickly and effectively with customers and others interested in a product or service.
In doing so, two forms of 'co-creation' are used:
1 mass collaboration
2 crowdsourcing

1 Mass collaboration

Mass collaboration is a form of collaboration where large numbers of people work independently on the same project. Wikipedia and open source software such as Linux and Joomla (a free content management system for publishing web content) are examples of products that have been created in this way. Ideas are shared instead of being kept secret and protected with patents and copyright in a 'walled garden'.

Mass collaboration

2 Crowdsourcing

Crowdsourcing means that activities relating to the design, development or production process, that were previously carried out by a company's employees, are performed by people from outside the company. Jeff Howe (2006), one of the first experts in this field, explains the concept as follows:

Crowdsourcing

'Simply defined, crowdsourcing means that a company or institution takes a job that was previously performed by employees and outsources it to an undefined (and generally large) network of people by way of an open invitation. This can take the form of a 'peer-production' (when the task is executed jointly by the group), but the job is often completed by individuals.'

The crowdsourcing network can consist of experts, amateurs or a mix of both. The incentive to participate can be monetary (a reward to be paid in cash), intrinsic (focused on emotional satisfaction) or a mix of both. It can be used to develop goods, services, ideas or to gather information (Howe, 2006). An example of a successful crowdsourcing campaign is example 4.1.

- -

EXAMPLE 4.1

Siemens

Siemens PLM Software organises an ongoing design contest for students, where they are obliged to use Siemens software (see also: http://sieag/2qwu1uj). This motivates students to gain experience with the software and Siemens receives many design ideas in return. The best design is published alongside many business cases in the Siemens PLM Software world calendar.

A winning design for Siemens by American student Jesse Poppin

- -

Many organisations only ask 'The Crowd' for ideas and designs, but some ask customers to develop or improve parts of their product or service. The success of crowd-sourcing lies in the sense of involvement with the product and the ease with which participants can contribute. In addition, openness, transparency and trust are of great importance: participants must know exactly what is happening with their ideas. The organisation's designers need to actively involve them. Although organisations can use crowd-sourcing for publicity (positive PR), the involvement of people from outside in the design and development process must be matched by the organisation being seen to take an interest in the ideas that are introduced. It should not be a 'cheap PR stunt'!

During the creation of a crowdsourcing program, three key issues for the organisation are (Vucovic & Bartolini, 2010):
- incentives
- intellectual property
- information security

Studentcompetitions.com

An interesting example of crowdsourcing is Studentcompetitions.com. The idea is that students are invited to submit entries in over 200 competitions in design, business, engineering and other fields for a chance to win scholarships/ money off course fees at a range of prestigious international schools.

Crowdsourcing website studentcompetitions.com

The incentives or participation stimuli must match the participant's needs and do justice to the required effort. Another point of attention is how many prizes should be available. In addition, it should be taken into account that it is often a very small group of people with a lot of expertise and high productivity that will produce a large part of all winning solutions. The competition will definitely have to be made attractive to this group. It may be important for the organisation to attract participants with different skills: talented people, people with a lot of experience, people with very specific, scarce skills or a mix of these people (Nicolay & Arun, 2009). It is important to avoid there being too many prizes relative to the number of participants, as well as prizes being awarded to solutions that are not valuable to the organisation. On the other hand, more prizes attract more participants. Some organisations who organise crowd sourcing competitions work with mathematical models to calculate the optimal choice of prizes, but many companies decide on the basis of previous experiences and judgment.

Incentives

How to deal with intellectual property rights is an important consideration. Not only should there be proper agreements in place on intellectual property for whoever supplies the concepts or ideas, but it must also be verified that this person has not violated any third-party property rights. When it comes to information security, consideration must be given to the provision of sensitive information without obstructing the participant's ability to develop the best concept or idea (Vucovic & Bartolini, 2010).

Lead user concept

Also, in product development, the lead user concept can be used. A lead user is someone who is ahead of their time. They have needs that others won't develop until further down the line (Von Hippel, 1986). For example, some new online services are first marketed in a so-called beta version. This gives lead users the opportunity to test and comment. The will often make other 'kindred spirits' aware of the new initiative and so the group of users will grow on by itself. Once the initial teething problems have been remedied, the website or app will be accessible to everyone, either for free or at a fee. Many chat services have been introduced in this way.

Crowdfunding

A specific form of crowdsourcing is crowdfunding. Crowdfunding is when an entrepreneur does not go to the bank for a loan but asks 'the crowd' to finance his business or a new product. Each participant then pays a relatively small amount. There are two forms of crowdfunding: the entrepreneur asks for money and offers a share in the future profit in return, or the entrepreneur will ask participants to pre-order the product (Belleflamme, Lambert & Schwienbacher, 2014). Kickstarter.com is a good example of the last option.

4.4 Developing and setting up online products

If an organisation has come up with a good idea for a product, whether through co-creation or not, the product manager must ensure that it is developed into a product that can be effectively used by the customer and made available through a website or app. In this section we will discuss two tools for online product realisation: customer journey mapping and the DNA model. We will also pay close attention to the requirements of the 'front and back office'.

4.4.1 Customer journey mapping

Customer journey

In order to design and produce online products that result in a good customer experience, the entire 'customer journey' must be viewed from the perspective of the customer. With the help of 'customer journey mapping', the customer journey and resulting customer experience can be understood, evaluated and improved.

Customer journey mapping

Customer journey mapping is a technique for optimising customer processes and developing innovative management concepts. It identifies exactly where improvements to the customer contact process are possible in order to achieve an optimal customer experience (CX) across all channels. It also clarifies how and what can be organised more efficiently and with greater synchronicity to give a more joined-up (seamless) customer experience.

Customer journey mapping (CJM) is also a method for visualising the purchase process or service from the customer's perspective (see figure 4.2). It describes the customer's experience during the 'journey' a customer makes during the process of orientation, purchasing and eventual use of a product or service. At all points of contact and every 'touchpoint'. This provides opportunities for improvement across all channels and processes.

Effective customer journey mapping starts from the same place as the customer starts and to understand what they consider a successful outcome. A classic example of this is when Virgin Atlantic re-defined the premium class long-haul travel experience.

FIGURE 4.2 The customer journey map (feeling and service solutions) for Virgin Atlantic Premium Class

Moments of truth	Getting to the airport	Check-in	Comfort until flight	In-flight comfort	Arrival	Getting to destination
Feelings	• Stressful • Complicated • Parking • Lugging	• Long, frustrating lines • Unnecessary (only necessary to the airline)	• Want/need to work • Want/need to relax	• Planes are uncomfortable by nature • Long-time spent in a seat • Boredom	• Unkempt • Unshowered • Clothes a mess	• Traffic • Unfamiliar place
CUSTOMER EXPERIENCE →→→
Service solution	• Transport to airport provided • Driver handles luggage	• "Driver-through" check-in • Airline knows where you are	• Clubhouse with internet access fax, library • Salon, massages beauty • Sound room, driving range skiing machine	• Full sleeper seats • Mood lighting • Gradual dawn • Bar • You decide meals	• Arrival valet • 18 showers • Makeup & shave • Heated floors • Clothes pressed • Hot & cold breakfast	• Chauffered delivery to destination • Comfortable ride door-to-door • Knowledgeable local driver

Source: Mycustomer.com, 2017

It is important to realise that different customer segments are likely to have different customer journeys. Thus, the holiday maker's journey will look very different from the business traveller's customer journey. Someone who is actively shopping (with a deadline) may have a different journey from someone who is 'just browsing'.

Based on the visualisation of the customer journey, also called customer journey mapping, offline and online touchpoints can be recorded, the places where the target group and the organisation meet each other (see figure 4.3). Based on this overview, the marketer can assess whether the most cost-effective solution has been chosen and what adjustments are needed to realise or improve the product or service.

Customer journey mapping

Touchpoints

Customer journey mapping can be applied at several different stages and for a variety of purposes:
• for the organisation and its employees to be able to view Digital Marketing from the perspective of the customer
• identification of market and growth opportunities from the customer's perspective

FIGURE 4.3 The online and offline touchpoints are recorded during the purchase process

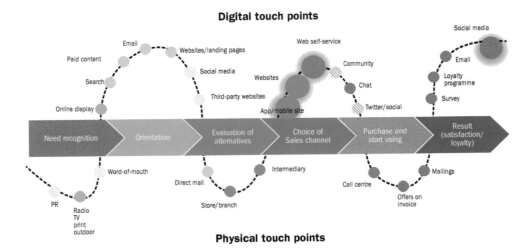

Digital touch points

Physical touch points

- development of innovative operating concepts and new services
- gaining insight into synergy between channels
- development of ideas for products and services that provide the desired customer experience
- helping to identify what organisational changes are needed to facilitate product realisation
- evaluation and improvement of the realised products
- providing direction for and keeping a handle on the process of measuring customer experiences

The customer journey map is an indispensable tool in the designing process of effective websites and apps.
You can read more about this in Chapter 11. Next, let us consider the role of the website relative to the other communication and sales channels (see figure 4.4).

Customer journey mapping is, when used properly, an easy and effective tool for improving customer experience across channels as well as ensuring more efficiency in customer processes.

When customer journey mapping is substantiated by in-depth customer research, the costs can increase significantly. However, this is not always necessary. It is often possible to start pragmatically and relatively cheaply based on already available data. If necessary, assumptions and deductions can be substantiated by customer research at a later stage. Customer journey mapping always starts with the thorough definition of customer groups, which are then followed up with concrete customer descriptions and personas.

To do this, customer knowledge is essential. Without insight into the customer and their close involvement, a reliable customer journey analysis is not possible. An important part of this is the determination of the scope.

FIGURE 4.4 Customer journey across multiple channels

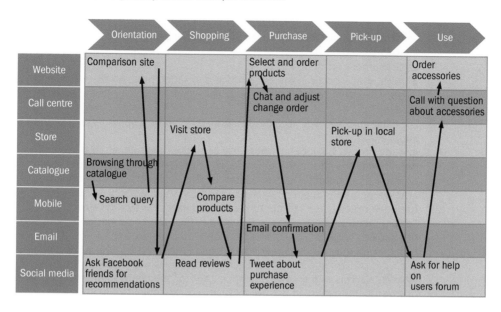

It is wise to determine in advance which part of the total customer needs will be investigated and what products, services, customer processes and channels are relevant.

Many steps in the customer journey can be realised or supported through via online communication media, such as websites and apps. A major advantage of online customer contact is that it allows the marketer to monitor customer behaviour and with the use of advanced algorithms, elicit the most desirable response from the customer. It is possible to deliver bespoke and personalised customer experiences based on customer profiles. This allows an organisation to design and provide products that enhance customer satisfaction, bind the customer to the organisation and increase customer loyalty and of course Customer Lifetime Value (CLV).

4.4.2 The DNA model

As explained in section 4.2, it is important to decide which parts of the product realisation process will be carried out online. Also, as a Digital Marketer, you need to ask yourself what the requirements are for online processes, from the customer as well as external parties. For example, consider legislation and regulations. In doing so the Digital Marketers must try to find a careful balance between user convenience, the organisation's goals and external requirements.

Today, the production process often takes place completely or partly online. An entirely online production process is possible for 'data-based' products, such as ticket sales, financial services and software.

Using De Vries jr. and Dekker's (2011) DNA model, we will look at three examples of service processes that largely take place online: a financial

DNA model

service provider, an online travel agency and an online dating site. The principles that you will learn can also be applied to online services that complement a specific product. We can distinguish three steps:

1 What are the different phases of the process?
2 Who should be present for these phases, the service provider or the consumer? (or both)?
3 What steps occur in the back office and which ones on the website or app (the front office)?

For each step, we will consider the presence of the consumer and of the supplier.

In addition, we will look at where the activities take place. First, some definitions: The 'front office' is the part of the organisation where the provider has contact with the customer. The 'back office' supports the employees and processes in the front office. If an activity takes place in the back office, then the customer has no insight into what exactly is happening. If it takes place in the front office, the customer is able to see the activities. Online, the website or app is considered the front office. Sometimes the choice is made to show a limited part of the back office in the front office (eg a restaurant giving customers a glimpse of the kitchen…). This is because it is important for the client to have some idea of what is happening in the back office. For example, some websites where you can search for cheap airline tickets, run a counter to show how many different options are being calculated. This prevents people from thinking that the search function is 'rigged' and it convinces them of the thoroughness of the search.

The requirements for the front office are strict: the customer bases their quality perception on what they see there. Before we elaborate on the concepts of front office and back office, we will discuss the DNA model.

In Table 4.1 you can see an example of the first step in the DNA model: what are the different phases of the process? We will look at the processes of three different types of organisations: a *financial services provider*, an *online travel agency* and an *online dating site*. The phases are discussed below and examples are given for each phase.

Front office
Back office

TABLE 4.1 Steps in the processes of three online service providers

	Steps	Financial services	Travel Advice	Online dating
1	Support during product selection	Calculations	Selection of holiday packages	Inform/free access
2	The offer	Quote for financial product	Calculating prices and booking	Creating a profile
3	Request/pay	Apply for financial product and confirmation	Book and pay	Pay subscription
4	Inspection	Inspection of account/policies	Information about reserved holiday	Overview of candidates
5	Using the service	Amendment (the transactions themselves are executed in the back office)	Complete digital travel documents (the holiday itself is 'produced' offline)	Selection and digital contact with candidates (the physical meeting happens offline)
6	Termination	Cancellation and distribution	Holiday has been completed (or cancelled)	Unsubscribe

Step 1 Support during product selection

As soon as someone has started the selection process for buying a service or product online, they begin their online search. In principle, this is a customer activity. The aim is to set up this process so that the service provider (brand owner) does not have to be present: the consumer can find information online 24/7. The follow-up question to the DNA model, ie which steps take place in the back office and which on the website or app (in the front office), depends on the type of product or service. We will now illustrate this using examples.

To access a product, the visitor firstly enters some information. This process should be as simple as possible: if the questions are too complex, many consumers will click away (disengage). This data collection process can take place online. The following are the examples of this step for each of the three types of online providers of services and products.

For example, to sign a contract with an *insurance provider (eg take out a life insurance policy)*, the entry consists of data such as age, height, weight, gender, medical history and amount to be insured. In the back office, many actuarial calculation models are then consulted to determine the appropriate premium. The prospective client sees nothing of this process: only the end-result is displayed in the online interface.

first direct

| Personal | Employment | Home | Decision | Options | Submit | Confirmation |

* indicates a required field

Tell us about yourself
Personal details

Title * [Please select ⬍]

First and middle name(s) * [ ]

Surname * [ ]

Please provide in full any other names which you use or have used in the past.

Are you now or have you ever been known by any other * names? e.g. professional or maiden name
 ○ Yes
 ○ No

Gender * [Please select ⬍]

Marital status * [Please select ⬍]

Date of birth * [⬍] [⬍] [YYYY]

Employment status * [Please select ⬍]

Number of dependants * [ ]

Please provide at least one telephone number

Work phone number ❓ [ ][ ] [ext]

Mobile phone number ❓ [ ][ ]

Home phone number ❓ [ ][ ]

Email address * [ ]

Confirm email address * [ ]

We will use these details to keep you updated on the progress of your application

Country of birth * ❓ [Please select ⬍]

Country of permanent residence * ❓ [Please select ⬍]

Data collection by an online financial services provider

For the provision of *a family holiday* (say), the user enters variables such as the destination, date, number of travellers and price range. Based on that, a number of possible holidays are shown. The consumer's requirement could be any one of many things, for example:

- I want to go to a sunny destination on date X.
- I want to go to destination X on any date.
- I want to spend X amount to go to any destination on any date.

Filtering

In order to provide a customer with several attractive travel options, many providers make use of filtering. A visitor determines what their primary goal is and enters it on the website or in the app. This request goes to the back office, and a number of destinations are offered according to availability. For example, out of a 'universe' of 1,000 holidays, some 50 remain after applying the filter 'destination = Greece'. The back office must be aware of whether the accommodation and transportation are still available and what the current price is.

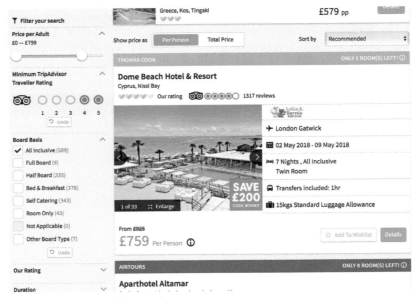

Filtering on travel site Thomas Cook

For a *dating site,* it is crucial in the first phase that an overview of the possibilities is given, without giving too much away or asking too many questions. This means that a visitor, without at first having to sacrifice their anonymity, must be able to see how the website works and what type of people they might meet on the platform. During the presentation of the search results, the new visitor usually receives only a limited amount of information as the dating site wants to entice them into setting up a profile and filling in their personal details. For example, you are usually unable to make contact with any of the selected candidates or the visible profiles if your profile doesn't contain at least your name or photograph.

For many products, comparison sites increasingly play an important role. In order to inform consumers about online products, comparison sites require a real-time product feed (current list of items and related prices and inventory) or a tool for price calculation. Unless they work with affiliate marketing, this often means that these sites access the provider's back office (see paragraph 7.5). The comparison site presents a price with its own 'look and feel', in its own design.

Real-time product feed

This is why those planning to set up an ecommerce operation need to think about what needs to be shown in the front office and arranged in the back office during the first phase of making an online product available to a customer.

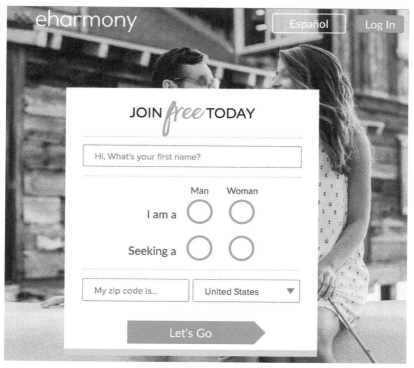

Consumer is enticed into sharing information

Step 2 The offer

If the consumer wants to know what the offer (proposed product/service) is going to cost, this means that the provider must make a definitive calculation (in many cases, an individual, bespoke one). This means that the supplier is obliged to sell the product at a certain price. When the consumer is choosing the product, the online price calculation is an activity where the service provider does not have to be present: the consumer can request prices via the website or app 24/7. The follow-up question from the DNA model: namely what takes place in the back office and what takes place on the website or app (in the front office), will be explained below, using some examples.

To provide a quote or list of prices, data must be entered for the calculation, as well as information such as the customer's name, address and place of residence or the desired date of commencement of the contract. This additional information goes to the back office and is processed there. Sometimes the decision needs to be made whether the consumer will in fact receive an offer at all, such as when taking out a loan (eg 'Sorry – your application is declined on this occasion'). In the background, the additional data is checked. In principle, this process is fully automatic and runs on the basis of confirmatory actions by the consumer.

In this phase, a lot of data is exchanged. Nothing can go wrong here: neither privacy – wise nor procedurally. Unless there is an obvious error, the provider is obligated to follow through with their offer. Fixing errors is often difficult and sometimes impossible. Because personal and confidential data is being sent over the Internet, the online forms must be encrypted. The visitor may recognise that the URL starts with https:// (which for savvy consumers provides some reassurance). The provider must also clearly indicate what happens to the data and provide a strictly secured back office. We will also give some examples for this step.

The procedure surrounding issuing a quote for a *financial product* can be complicated. In addition, someone may be rejected via the website or app for a quote for, for example, a loan or insurance. However, a different process in which provider and consumer meet in person might result in a quote being provided after all. Someone might have registered debts with appropriate authorities (depending on the country) about which they will need to provide clarity. In that case, the back office must arrange for a message to be flagged up to an employee who then schedules an appointment. The person who conducts that appointment must have access to the customer's data to prevent data from being entered multiple times.

In the travel sector, when *booking a trip online*, the customer's product selection is recorded in the back office. Next, additional questions are asked, which allow for a full price calculation, such as the number of guests. Based on this information, a total price is quoted. The customer then fills in the necessary personal information, such as full names and birth dates of all party members. This information must be processed directly in the affiliated back office systems of the relevant travel company. Sometimes this is instantly passed on to the hotel and transportation provider, such as the airline. As a result, there may be a whole chain of providers who capture the booking in real time. The consumer has no insight into this process but is asked to trust that his/her personal data is being safeguarded

Availability

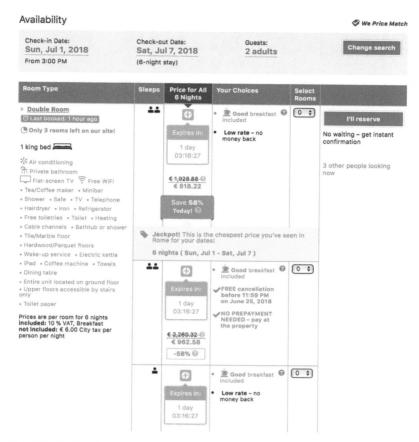

Calculated price of a trip

Dating sites usually operate with a subscription model. To create a profile on the dating site, a comprehensive survey will need to be filled in. Not only personal information, but also the user's preferences regarding a future partner and their own defining characteristics must be filled in. Using this information, the back office can compare profiles. The profiles with the most likelihood of compatibility are then sent to the front office: the customer receives the information and is sometimes shown pictures of candidates that are believed to be most likely to appeal to them. In most cases, the visitor must first fully complete their profile before being required to pay the subscription fee. Only then will their profile be activated.

Creating a profile on a dating site

So, the steps in the offer phase can vary greatly per provider. The quotation process must be considered step by step: online or offline, front office or back office, what generates the most value a) for the customer and b) for the organisation? Something that applies to each type of online product, is that this phase needs to be very carefully set up, with security being at the heart of it.

Step 3 Request and pay
The next steps for finalising the quote differ per supplier and per product. For this process too, it is important to set it up very carefully. Mistakes in this phase often lead to serious problems: people might not receive the service they purchased on time, or at all, or the provider might not receive (timely) payment. As in previous phases, applications and payments are, in principle, a consumer activity. The follow-up question from the DNA model: what takes place in the back office and what takes place on the website or in the app (in the front office), is largely identical for many different online products.

Because applying for a financial product or a non-standardised trip often involves multiple parallel processes, there is ample opportunity for error.

For example, not only must an online form be filled in, but the customer must also have paid. An automated follow-up process ensures that drop-outs are kept to a minimum. The follow-up process can consist of, for example, an email reminder or a call from the call centre. Depending on the drop-out rate, the provider must make the decision whether to automate this process. For example, research conducted by a large holiday home provider shows that about one in ten people who are filling in their booking information will drop-out at some point in this process. A call from the call centre can greatly reduce the number of drop-outs, but of course the cost of this must be considered.

During the process of the request, there are many opportunities for feedback:

- To the visitor: to give the visitor immediate reassurance that their trip has been successfully purchased, that the product is being shipped or is immediately insured, the receipt of an order, ticket or policy number is necessary. Also, the signing of the contract is a good time to give clear feedback about the consumer follow-up process: when can the consumer expect the necessary follow-up activities and documents? Does the customer have any comments about the service he/she has received?

Step 4 Inspection
Once an online product has been purchased, customers receive online access to a secure environment. The inspection itself is a customer activity, providing access to the online environment is, in principle, a fully automated process. In doing so, the security of that access is an important focal point. The organisation must also determine what data is displayed and for how long the customer has access to this personalised information. In the online environment, careful consideration must be given to what the consumer wants to see, and what is subsequently visible. The back office contains all the necessary data, of which only a limited portion is of interest to the consumer. The follow-up question to the DNA model, which steps take place in the back office and which on the website or app (in the front office), depends on the type of product or service. We will now illustrate this using examples.

To give consumers access to *financial products*, a secure environment is used. This certainly applies to online banking. To access online banking, a 'token' is often used. The token looks like a small calculator. Access to the token is obtained via the bank card and/or an access code. In the back-office processes, there are various controls in place to make sure that the correct token is linked to the appropriate customer, bank card and access code.

Travel agencies however don't need to take as stringent security measures as a bank or an insurance company. It is usually possible simply to view the entered data via a website or app and, if necessary, amend it. Also, it is often possible for the reservation to be viewed and additional services to be selected, such as upgrades to a better room or travel insurance. Security often consists of a username and password. The access procedure is done digitally via email: the customer receives confirmation of the creation of their account and, in many cases, is asked to re-confirm.

Sometimes they are sent an automatically generated temporary password with the request to change it as soon as possible. Any changes that are made will usually be confirmed by email.

Past Trips

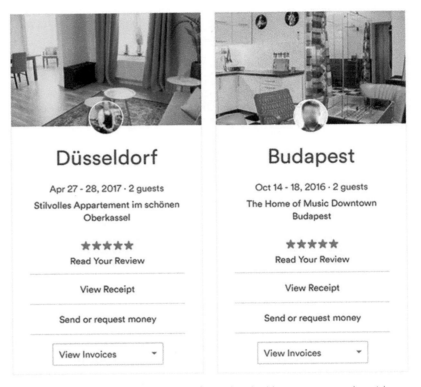

Airbnb provides insight into customer information, in this case your previous trips

Access to an *online dating website* is also usually achieved via a username and password. Once the candidate has logged in, they are able to make changes to their information, change search criteria or even set alerts so that they receive an email if a new candidate signs up that matches their profile. Here too, effective security is necessary, especially given the sensitivity of the information that may be shared.

Mail Online

Home | News | U.S. | Sport | TV&Showbiz | Australia | Femail | Health | Science | Money |

Latest Headlines | *Science* | Pictures | Discounts

Tinder hackers find a major security flaw in the dating app that lets anyone break into your account and expose your private messages using just a phone number

- Experts at Indian computer Security firm Appsecure uncovered the bug
- When you log in with your phone number, it is sent to Facebook's Account Kit
- Appsecure intercepted this data to generate an access token for the account
- Tinder's login system wasn't double checking these tokens to verify the user

Security is also important in a dating site

Step 5 Using the online product

Once the product is purchased and the consumer wants to use the service, it is crucial to support their activities digitally. When it comes to fully online services, using the online product is principally a consumer activity. However, the online product may also facilitate the purchase of a physical product or offline service. Consider the sale of theatre tickets or home delivery of meals. In those instances, the actual service will be used later, in the physical world. The follow-up question to the DNA model, which steps take place in the back office and which on the website or app (in the front office), depends on the type of product or service. Similarly, in this phase, the organisation must determine what must take place in the secure environment and what via the public website. The advantage of a private online environment for the visitors is the limited amount of data that must be entered as this data is already known, so the customer experience (CX) is smoother and better. Below are a few examples of the issues a product manager is concerned with.

Once people have purchased a *financial product* they not only want to have insight into the current state of affairs (such as their balance), they want to be able to report changes of circumstances, report problems or purchase an additional product. However, there are limitations to this. The financial institution has a statutory duty of care and must protect the consumer. For example, if the officially established investment profile shows that someone is a conservative investor, the visitor might not be 'allowed' to buy high-risk shares/stocks or change their investment mix to be able to make high risk investments. A review must take place in the back office. The front office must establish and clearly explain why the consumer cannot (or should not) perform a particular action. The processes surrounding the use of financial services are very complicated and setting up the online environment is a specialist task.

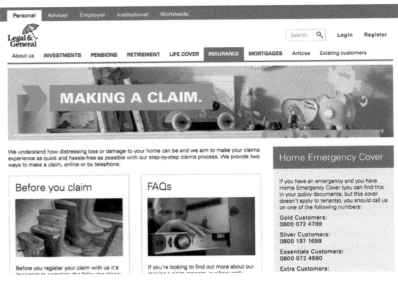

Reporting damages online to Legal and General Insurance

An *online travel agency* has an easier time. Just before the trip takes place, consumers can usually download their travel documents online. These include the tickets, the vouchers for the accommodations and a detailed itinerary. This is actually a summary of the outcomes of the processes that have or may not have been automated in the back office. Many organisations choose a dual approach: vouchers and tickets are sent by email and can also be accessed via the website. Some travel agencies still choose to send the papers completely or partially to the home address by post although this is declining

On an online *dating site*, the online environment facilitates dating: flirting and making contact. The selected profiles are provided in a protected environment. Contact can be made via an online messaging service. The organisation must find the balance between ensuring privacy and ease of use. Are the candidates' personal details, such as the email address and the mobile number visible on the website or app or are they only stored in the back office? At some point, the actual data will progress to a location outside of the dating site; sharing data should then be facilitated. Clearly privacy concerns must be respected at every stage.

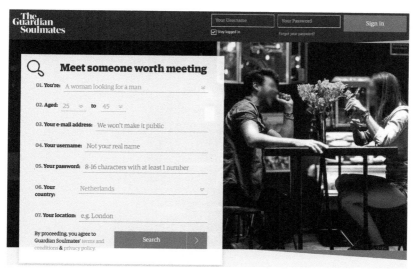

Search for and select candidates on a dating site

Step 6 Termination

Nothing lasts forever and there will come a time when the service is terminated, prematurely or not. The travel advice stops the moment the customer goes on holiday, a subscription to a dating site is terminated if the 'best' candidate has been found and a financial product ends, for example, in case of maturity, death or defection to another provider. The initiative can therefore lie with both the customer and the provider. The follow-up question to the DNA model, which steps take place in the back office and which on the website or app (in the front office), depends on the type of product or service. We will now illustrate this using examples.

Once the service is terminated, the mutual agreement is over. The provider is not required to continue to provide consumers with online access. In some cases, access to the online environment is maintained or the ex-customer will be kept up to date with the latest news by email.

Online environment

For the *financial service provider*, the former customer remains in the back office for a considerable amount of time. The progress of the termination process can often be viewed digitally. Many financial products are purchased for a certain period or expire in case of expiry or death. For many providers, this phase is difficult to automate. In the event that someone dies, and benefits must be paid, they often contact the financial service provider. They usually do not have access to the secure online environment. Other financial products, such as temporary travel insurance, are automatically terminated. In many cases the data is valuable given the opportunity for reactivation/additional sale. In this situation data protection law must be respected (eg in Europe GDPR).

The information displayed in the following frequently asked questions section only covers some of the cover and exclusions in our policies.

For more details of what is and isn't covered, please refer to your policy documents and Terms and Conditions of your policy.

Alternatively please contact us on **03701630657** or **+442920276014** from overseas. Lines are open 8.30am to 6pm Monday to Friday and 9am to 1pm Saturdays. Call charges will vary and we may record and monitor calls. You can also email: **fctlife.enquiries@landg.com**

Contact Us

Whether you're looking for a quote, like to make a claim, or have a query, we're here to help you.

Contact us

Expand All

Can I change the cover I have?	⌄
I've missed a premium. What do I need to do?	⌄
How can I make changes to my payment details?	⌄
How do I cancel my policy?	⌃

We recommend you speak to your financial adviser before cancelling your policy, or contact us to discuss your situation.

We'll require permission from all the owners of the policy, including any trustees, to cancel your policy when you contact us.

Please note that if you originally took out your life cover policy with your mortgage, the policy is not directly connected to any particular mortgage or property and you can continue with the life cover, if you now have no mortgage.

Close ✖

Terminating services

A *holiday* ends when the customer returns home. This is a good time to elicit feedback. A travel agency will often send a few questions regarding customer satisfaction, with the answers then being added to the customer's details in the back office. This process happens automatically. For how long the customer's private environment continues to remain available, is a decision made by the travel agency. Sometimes, the customer or the travel agency cancels the trip prematurely. For the customer, there are often cancellation fees associated with this. Any money that had already been paid towards the holiday, may be returned in the event of a cancellation. Such processes need to be fully mapped: what happens online, what happens offline, what can the customer see? Often a back-office employee will need to cancel the travel arrangements with the travel agency or directly with the airline and the accommodations. In many travel agencies, this process is still predominantly manual.

For a *dating site*, the most logical way of completing a termination of the subscription, is online. Then the process can be automated, and the presence of the provider is not necessary. In practice, it appears that many dating sites make it very difficult to quit. This does not benefit the customer experience and arguably has negative PR implications for the brand.

4.4.3   Front office and back office requirements

If the product manager knows what steps in each of the phases take place in the front office (website or app) and in the back office, they can formulate requirements accordingly. There are some general principles for this. First, we will focus on the requirements that the online front office must meet. Then we will address the requirements for the back office.

Requirements for the online front office

Because the website or app of an online service provider is often the only channel communicating to the consumer, it is essential that the front office inspires confidence for the consumer. In the following sections, we will discuss all the demands made on the communications to gain consumer confidence.

Clear terms and pricing
When choosing a solution, it must be clear which service has been purchased and, at what price, at what time, what starting date and under which conditions. For financial products, there is often a risk perception which must be minimised by clear explanations, eg by frequently asked questions (FAQs).

Range of products and focus products
The involvement and overall knowledge of the visitors is often low with regard to the solutions being offered. This means that attention must be paid during the product display process as to whether the visitor is easily able to recognise the difference between seemingly identical offerings. To emphasise this, focus products can be used. Focus products are solutions that the provider brings to the visitor's attention. On the homepage or page listing an overview of the services, additional attention is given to these products and they are referred to in the call to action. The key is to explain the service clearly to the customer, so they understand not only the features but importantly, can compare the benefits for them.

Wizards
To help the visitor make a choice, intelligent wizards can aid in quickly coming to a solution. The wizard asks a lot of questions, eventually providing a recommendation for a particular solution. Online service providers often program wizards in such a way that they are not dependent on a back office and can be deployed in multiple locations. For example, on a personal theme page or outside of your own domain on a comparison site or in a banner. Often, a wizard refers to a solution or to a calculation aid.

Wizards

Calculation aids
At the moment the visitor has chosen a product but wants to calculate what the trip will cost or what a financial product will deliver, they must be provided with the required information in a simple way. Calculation aids that are connected to the back office can provide the visitor with the necessary insight and help them make a decision, simply by entering a number of variables. In this situation a human customer service operator is in effect replaced by technology. Advances in artificial intelligence (AI) are making this substitution increasingly viable.

Calculation aids

Quality stamps, user reviews, and customer ratings
Visitors who eventually go on to purchase an online service receive confirmation of their choice at every step in the online application form. The following possibilities contribute to a sense of trust:
- Customer ratings can be collected from your own customers, preferably by an organisation other than the organisation who is selling the product
- Authentic reviews or testimonials from other customers about services contribute to transparency. (This reassures customers that they are not making a mistake).
- Solutions that, for example, have been awarded the certification of 'best buy' by consumer organisations, should also be recognisable as such to the visitors.

Customer ratings

User reviews

Successful deployment of quality stamps, user reviews and customer ratings minimise the customer's risk perception (see also Chapter 3). Obtaining reviews from visitors is a process that can be automated.

Confidence in the provider
The feeling that there are other possibilities for getting in touch with the provider gives many buyers the assurance that they can always resort to contact with a real person in a physical location. This also builds reassurance and trust. Elements that can remove uncertainties on the website are:

- address and directions
- quality stamps
- further contact details
- opening hours
- complaints procedure
- ratings and reviews from another 'independent' website
- 'About Us' page with general information about the nature, history and philosophy of the organisation

Mobile communication
Consumers expect service providers to provide access to the data at all times. This means that online services should also be supported on mobile devices, especially smartphones.

Tracking visitor behaviour
Everything that the consumer does in the front office can be tracked. These analyses help improve front office services:

- Digital analytics: to track overall visitor behaviour (in aggregate) and identify trends.
- Visitor behaviour: the behaviour of individual users can be logged in a so-called e-data warehouse. The data from the e-data warehouse serves as input for the CRM system.

E-data warehouse

More information about digital analytics can be found in Chapter 12.

Back-office requirements
Because online service providers get large volumes of visitors, the demands are high:

- They are often held to a 99.95% availability. Server parks are doubled up and if there is a malfunction in one server park, they directly and automatically switch to the other server park.
- The website must be supported by all browsers (Google Chrome, Mozilla Firefox, Microsoft Edge/Internet Explorer, Safari etc) as well as being accessible to visually impaired people. Apps will also need to run properly on all major operating systems.

It seems self-evident that an online provider of services and products knows 'everything' about their visitors, but in practice it takes a lot of effort. Many organisations have gone through mergers in the past or consist of several business units, each with their own back office. These back offices have their own ways of data collection or different data quality. Resolving these logistical issues often requires major investment which may not be realistic within short timescales. Things that reduce perceived trustworthiness of an online service are:

- The total overview (single view of the customer) is incomplete because individuals are listed more than once in multiple databases.
- Information is out-of-date; this is common with address changes that have not been implemented in all systems.
- access is poor and inconsistent: different back office systems with different security and access procedures mean that the customer needs multiple logins.

These types of problems are particularly common when financial service providers have merged.

In the following sections, we will not only discuss the requirements of the back office, but also the challenges of making the online service as customer-friendly as possible.

Altering existing systems
For many online service providers, the partial expansion of the back office is a big challenge for a number of reasons:
- There are no uniform market standards to fall in line with, everyone creates their own system, whereas efficiency and reusability would require a more single-minded methodology.
- Older systems still work with evening and night time processing. As a result, customers cannot see updates until the next working day.
- Peak demand of the back-office system. In the past, the system was used by a limited number of users. This could, for example, lead to slow loading and a poor customer experience.
- The steps that the visitor wants to follow are usually not the same as the steps that an outdated back office demands. The flow in the back office is often geared to purchasing processes that are aided by a human employee. They are used to starting with the personal data and only then working with the product/service data. The consumer wants that exactly the other way around! Levelling out these processes can lead to enormous IT efforts.

Converting existing systems to customer-friendly online services to deliver the optimum customer experience is often a difficult and time-intensive (ie expensive) task.

Presence of the service provider
As described in section 4.4.2, the presence of the service provider in the process is not always necessary. However, even in the Internet age, not all consumers are equally comfortable with buying online. Especially with complex services and products, people want to be able to fall back on personal contact. By offering a fast route to personal contact, this need can be met in the following ways:
- A call centre number is provided.
- Call-me-now feature: the visitor fills in their phone number and the provider calls them back. **Call-me-now feature**
- Reactive chat: the visitor uses a chat button to instantly chat (online) with a specialist. **Reactive chat**
- Proactive chat: when visitors display certain behaviour, a chat window proactively opens up. This can be based on hesitant behaviour, such as **Proactive chat**

the length of time the visitor stays on a page, switching often between pages or visiting the site multiple times in one week.
- A face-to-face appointment is made with an advisor at home, at the office or in the store.

More about online service can be found in section 9.4.

For each step in the DNA model, the need for an analogue touchpoint can be reviewed. When setting up these features, it is crucial that the transition goes smoothly from the visitor's point of view. The chat channel must know what the customer is doing, an online visitor should not end up in the queue of the general call centre and the advisor must know what kind of advice is being sought. The data belonging to unfinished transactions in the front office must already have been processed in the back office so that it is known what the customer was doing at the moment that the process was interrupted. Making sure that all the channels are in tune with one another requires a lot from the provider's automation processes but it is essential deliver a great customer experience.

Stimulating the use of automated services
The business model of an online service provider can often only operate profitably if as much of the service as possible is automated. The customer contact strategy sends consumers to automated channels. This is done by continuously referring the consumer to the online channel during the various steps. The more work that can be taken away from human operators the better, provided this does not detract from the customer experience.

Using event driven marketing to encourage return visitors
Event driven marketing (EDM) is a discipline within marketing, where commercial and communication activities are based on relevant identified changes to a customer's individual needs (Van Bel & Sander, 2005). An example of an event for a bank: via the database it is noticed that a customer was unable to make a payment with their debit card three times in one month because they had exceeded their limit. In such a situation, and depending on eligibility, the customer could be helped by making them an offer for a suitable loan.
The message to be sent to the customer must be available via all channels: as soon as the visitor logs in, the message is brought to their attention. If they make contact with the call centre, the agent must know which offer has been made and refer to it.

Status request via website

Tracking systems

There is some time between the moment of ordering and the actual delivery. To provide insight into this, many providers use tracking systems to indicate where the product is in the production or delivery process and how long it is expected to take. A link with the back office is crucial. This system also means the pressure on the call centre is reduced.

Alerts

Alerts

Visitors can subscribe to alerts. In this way, the consumer shows interest in a particular topic. As soon as anything changes, such as flight times, price changes or the launch of a new service, a short alert is sent by text or email. This form of interest is also an input for the CRM system (see also Chapter 10).

If the product manager, based on the customer journey map and the DNA model, has carefully completed the online product realisation process, the product can be successfully realised and then marketed in collaboration with the automation experts and operational departments.

4.5 Product improvement

After the online product has been introduced and the customers have used the systems for a while, it often appears that there are still some components that do not work optimally. In addition, the preferences of the visitors change, the competition doesn't stand still, and new technologies make it even easier to handle certain elements of the process. Online products are in a continuous improvement cycle. A widely used quality improvement model is the PDCA cycle or Deming cycle (see figure 4.5):

PDCA cycle

- *Plan.* In the first phase, you will plan, as discussed in the previous section: That plan is being executed:
- *Do.* Then check if everything works as intended:
- *Check.* If that is not the case, then you do something about it:
- *Act.* By continuously applying this cycle, you improve the quality. This ensures that a product or service will better meet the needs of customers and be more efficiently realised.

FIGURE 4.5 PDCA cycle

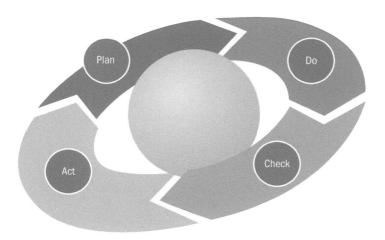

A Product Manager has two kinds of sources for product improvement ideas:
- internal sources: eg insights from product specialists, marketers, customer service and marketing intelligence
- external sources: like customers, visitors, suppliers

We will briefly review these sources and we will look at how to choose from the various ideas for product improvement.

4.5.1 Internal sources of ideas for product improvement

There are more and less structured methods for gathering ideas for optimising the online production process and the services offered. Some unstructured methods include ideation sessions, suggestions for improvements that are made during business meetings and separate input from account managers/ the sales force. In order to continuously respond to the needs of the customers effectively and efficiently, a structured approach is preferred.

Structured methods for collecting data about product quality are:
- customer satisfaction surveys
- reports of comments and complaints that come in to customer service
- overview of frequently asked questions
- periodic meetings with a product improvement team
- analyses of the competitors' sites
- website statistics: where are the bottlenecks in the online process? (see also Chapter 12)
- technological updates: what new technologies are on the market and what can they signify?
- process analyses aimed at preventing and analysing possible errors

Process analysis The DNA model can serve as the foundation for a process analysis. Each phase in the model can be divided into sub-steps, creating a process model. To illustrate this, we have used the fifth step in the DNA model of the online dating site as an example: using the service (see example 4.2). In example 4.2, the third figure shows methods for preventing errors.

Poka yokes These kinds of error prevention measures are also called 'poka yokes'.

EXAMPLE 4.2

Process analysis

Step 5 Use of service: selecting and digitally contacting candidates

The process for this contact could be simplified as shown in the following figure.

FIGURE 1

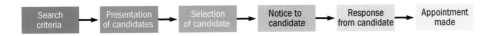

For each step, the product manager can now determine which errors occur on a regular basis. Of course, it is wise to do this for the introduction, but one cannot think of everything in advance. In the figure below, we will discuss some examples of common mistakes.

FIGURE 2

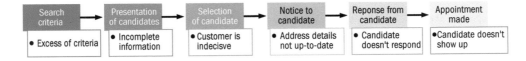

For each error, one can now consider methods to improve this part of the process (see the following figure).

FIGURE 3

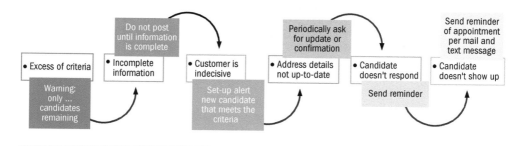

4.5.2   Internal sources of ideas for product improvement

Whether or not they are asked to do so, visitors, customers and suppliers will make suggestions for product improvement. The absence of spontaneous comments does not necessarily mean that the visitors are satisfied. It can also be an expression of lack of interest. Important sources of information are:
- review sites
- websites of consumer organisations and programmes
- magazines and blogs
- social media

There are general review sites, but almost every industry has its own specialist review sites. For example:
- Money Saving Expert, www.moneysupermarket.com
- Review Solicitors, www.reviewsolicitors.co.uk

Organisations can not only learn from what is said about them, but also from positive or negative opinions about the (online) services of their competitors. The same applies to magazines, blogs and other social media.

4.5.3   Choosing from the various ideas for product improvement

One advantage of online products is that you are able to see the result immediately.

If a product manager has ideas for improvements that can be realised quickly and cheaply, they can simply do an A/B test. This involves trying the new approach for a short time or for a limited group of customers and comparing the results with the previous situation. More about this type of test can be found in Chapter 12 on digital analytics.

If the improvements require the product manager to make a large investment, it is a little less easy. They will then have to rely on customer research. One way of getting to the bottom of what aspects of the online and offline services could be improved, is by conducting research into customer satisfaction levels.

It is not only important to know which quality aspects the customers rate highly or less so, but also to what extent quality aspects are *important* for their satisfaction. For example, customers of a travel agency may be less satisfied with the clarity of the invoices they receive by mail, but that this has hardly any impact on their customer satisfaction. In that case, it might be better to choose to improve something that contributes more to satisfaction, customer loyalty and profit. The product manager can then conduct research that provides data for an 'importance performance matrix'. Figure 4.6 shows the results of fictional research into a dating site, which not only looked at customer satisfaction scores, but also at the significance of each of the points to customer loyalty. Points that are important but score badly are priorities for improvement. In the case of the dating site, the product manager will optimise the overview of candidates. Points that score highly and are of importance to loyalty must be monitored. One of this dating site's strong points, is the ease with which the user can create their profile. Falling somewhere in between is the point 'candidate selection'. This point is neither a clear point for improvement, nor a strong point.

Importance performance matrix

FIGURE 4.6 Results of research into customer satisfaction for a dating site

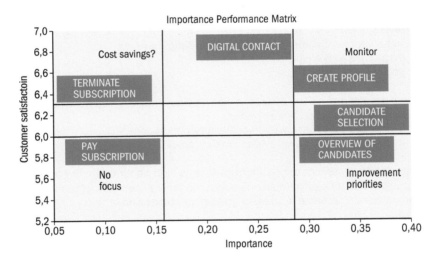

On the left side of the chart in figure 4.6 are points that are less important to customer loyalty. Regarding the way the subscription can be terminated, the users of the dating site are very satisfied. If it costs a lot of money to manage this part of the process, the dating site may consider saving on it. Regarding the payment of subscription fees, users are also not very satisfied, but because this has hardly any effect on loyalty, the product manager can safely ignore this item. The users are most satisfied with the possibilities for digital contact, but unfortunately this quality aspect does not overly affect loyalty.

An importance performance matrix clearly indicates where the priorities should lie, but the image is not yet complete. In the graph you can see that no point scores more than 7.0 on a scale of 1 to 10. That is relatively low.

It is likely that other dating sites score much higher. It is therefore always wise to benchmark research: ie to compare your own scores with those of the main competitors.

Only then does the product manager know if they should be satisfied with their own results.

4.6 Product realisation proceeds methodically

A solid preparation is indispensable in the development and improvement of products with an online component. Building systems and websites is expensive and labour-intensive and often results in significant upheaval within the existing organisation. Once the online components have been developed and connected to other systems, such as the financial system and the reporting system, changes are not easy to make.

The product realisation process always follows a step-by-step approach. Traditionally, many organisations use a 'stage gate process' or similar procedure. The phase-gate process includes the following steps: discovery, scoping, business case, development, testing and validation and start-up (Cooper, 2005). Before the start of each phase, the product manager submits plans to the (senior) management of the organisation, to a steering committee with delegated decision-making power on behalf of the management or to a product owner. They then make a so-called go/no-go decision before each phase: they decide whether or not the product manager and their project team can go through with their plans or not. In the past, many months would sometimes pass between the various go/no-go decisions. Today, many organisations choose 'lean' development. In short, using quick strokes and with constant consultation with the target group a successful online product is developed. You can read more about this in Chapter 13. Table 4.2 illustrates the product realisation process by means of an example: the development of a new online game.

Go/no-go decision

Lean

After the first phase, finding ideas for new products or product improvements, the product manager must consider which ideas are worth expanding on. To this end, the ideas in phase 1 (scoping) are quickly assessed for market opportunities and technical feasibility.

TABLE 4.2 Phases in the product realisation process for a new online game

Phase	Content	Questions
Phase 0 – Discovery	Discover opportunities and generate ideas for new products	What kind of new game should it be? Who is this for?
Phase 1 – Scoping	A quick and inexpensive assessment of the technical advantages and market opportunities	How does the new game fit into our marketing strategy and existing range of products? Does it fit into the present technical environment? Can the employees make it? What are the trends in the game industry? How does the new game fit into this? How big is the market approximately and how many games do we think we can sell?

TABLE 4.2 Phases in the product realisation process for a new online game (continued)

Phase	Content	Questions
Phase 2 - Business case	Analyse technical, marketing and organisational feasibility: product and project definition, project justification and project plan	What are the requirements that the game must meet? What activities are needed to develop the game? What is the duration of the project? What will it cost in terms of money and people? Why is it necessary to develop this game? What happens if we don't do it? What does the development of this game mean: sales, turnover, profits? What will our schedule look like? Who has what responsibility?
Phase 3 – Development	Design and development for the new product, production plan, marketing and business plans and plans for product testing	What will the game actually look like? How do we set up the online and offline process: sign up, playing, support, paying? How will we set up the organisation? Will it be a separate business unit, a separate department? Who is responsible for that? How do we appoint and train the employees? How are we going to test the game? Beta version? For how long? How do we receive and process comments? When and how are we going to make improvements to the game? What do our marketing plans look like?
Phase 4 - Testing and validation	Assessment of the outcome of the development phase	To what extent does the game meet our own requirements? How is the online and offline process going? What could be improved? What are the users excited about, and what less so? What problems are they encountering? Is the game financially successful?
Phase 5 - Start	Market introduction of the product	
Phase 6 – Improve	Improve the customer experience of the product and optimise the value for the organisation.	

Preparations for this review are usually done with a working group or project group responsible for product development. The result is submitted to management. A request for the resources and funds to use one or several ideas and turn them into a business case is then made.

Business case If management gives permission, the product manager or project leader will create a business case in phase 2: the technical, marketing and organisational feasibility of marketing the product will be analysed, and the purpose of the project is described exactly. The business case also includes a project plan and a financial overview.

If management allows the product to be realised on the basis of the business case, phase 3 begins: the actual development of the new or renewed product. Before the organisation releases the new product, management will make another intermediate decision. Does the developed product meet all requirements? Does the company really want to continue with it? If the answer to these questions is yes, the product is tested in phase 4 and management will decide whether a market-wide introduction of the product will make a positive contribution to the success of the organisation. After any potential improvements and a final decision by the management, the product manager will release the new or renewed product to the market in phase 5. This is when the customer acquisition process begins, the subject of Chapters 5 to 8, which is soon followed by the first round of product improvements.

Questions and assignments

NOW CHECK YOUR UNDERSTANDING:

4.1   What responsibilities does a product manager for an organisation that operates online casinos have in the product realisation process?

4.2   What are the four forms of co-creation? Search the web to find a recent example of each of these forms.

4.3   Look at www.studentcompetitions.com
a Which of the competitions do you think best meet the requirements for successful crowdsourcing?
b Indicate how the organisations that organise the competitions can evaluate the submitted ideas.

4.4   A customer journey map illustrates the customer's journey and the corresponding touchpoints and contact moments.
a Look at the example in figure 4.4 and then create a customer journey map for student enrolment at your educational facility (School, College, University).
b What opportunities for improvement do you see?

4.5   Complete the six phases of the DNA model for a supplier of weight-loss programs eg www.weightwatchers.com or www.slimmingworld.com. Which processes can be automated, and which ones cannot?

4.6   Name at least five events that an online insurance company can use to promote the use of automated services.

4.7   What could go wrong when booking an airline ticket? Which 'poka yokes' can you think of to prevent these mistakes?

4.8

BMW's car-share programme in China
By Mike Berry

German global carmaker BMW launched its first permanent car-sharing program in China. BMW has a policy of promoting sustainable urban mobility and car sharing is one of the methods to achieve this. In 2010 BMW had organized an ideas contest called 'Tomorrow's Urban Mobility Services'. Their intention was to find new ideas for mobility services in urban areas. Almost 500 users contributed around 300 ideas that were evaluated and commented on by over 1,000 other users from all over the world and also by a BMW jury.

In 2011 BMW introduced a car-sharing program in Europe under the name DriveNow, in partnership with the Sixt car rental company. DriveNow is not dependent on car hire stations; fixed pick-up and drop-off points are not needed. Customers can find available vehicles online at www.drive-now.com, via a smartphone app or simply at the roadside. Vehicles can be used without advanced reservation. The system is 'keyless': all cars can be locked and unlocked using the app. Over recent years, BMW has built a user base of 1 million+ users for its European DriveNow car-sharing service, an increase from half a million in 2015. BMW has announced that the business is now profitable.

In 2016 the program was introduced in the U.S. under the name ReachNow.

How to use DriveNow

BMW is tapping into a shift in the market globally; customers are valuing the utility of transportation rather than the concept of owning a car. This trend looks likely to increase as driverless cars are introduced in the future.

In recent years Electric Vehicle (EV) sharing has also boomed within China, mainly using fleets of small, low-cost electric cars from local Chinese automakers.

Programs include EVCard run by SAIC and GoFun, (part of the Beijing Shouqi Group leasing company).

For their Chinese Programme, BMW Marketing allocated a fleet of electric i3 models. The program in Chengdu, southwest China, expanded the car maker's ReachNow brand outside of the U.S. It followed a successful pilot program in Beijing.

This was a Marketing Department-driven initiative. BMW's marketers identified changing consumer trends and the audiences most likely to be attracted by a product of this type. BMW Marketing in China tapped into market information, customer data and analytics and also drew on the experience of other BMW marketers around the world to assist with product management and the development of the online product. This was crucial in the product realisation process.

The Chinese government restricts private car sales (in order to combat growing congestion and air pollution) so BMW's initiative in launching its wholly-owned ReachNow service in China was in tune with this policy.

'Growth in the future won't come from building and selling cars but from other services,' says Thiemo Schalk, manager at BMW's Centre of Urban Mobility Competence in Berlin. 'We need to find new solutions not just based on car ownership.'

BMW's Chengdu service used 100 i3s initially. Customers had to park the cars in fixed locations after they finished using the vehicle. This is the same model as in the earlier Beijing pilot programme.

There is an interesting precedent for the new programme which did not escape BMW China marketers. Chinese City-dwellers have become accustomed to accessing shared bicycles without any fixed hire points - this of course delivers maximum customer convenience.

Again, driven by BMW's Marketing Department and in contrast with lower cost local competition, BMW says it is bringing a 'premium' element to car-sharing; ie the vehicles are genuine BMW models reflecting the company's engineering heritage and each with the high build quality for which the BMW brand is world-famous.

In summary, BMW recognises the continuing disruption in its industry including changes in its customer requirements globally. In common with its competitors, BMW is trialling new business models to meet consumers' evolving transportation needs. The charge is being led by BMW marketers.

Sources: www.drive-now.com, www.autoevolution.com, www.press.bmwgroup.com and http://europe. autonews.com/article/20171124/ANE/171129861/bmw-expands-car-sharing-program-to-china

NOW CHECK YOUR UNDERSTANDING:

a What was the role of the Marketing Department in BMW's product realisation process?

b Within the car sharing programme, which of the four forms of co-creation take place? Please support your answer.

c In the ideas contest called 'Tomorrow's Urban Mobility Services' did BMW use crowdsourcing or mass collaboration? Please support your answer.

d Look on www.drive-now.com. What do you think a hirer's customer journey looks like? Map the journey.

e Fill in the DNA model for BMW ReachNow/DriveNow.

f Based on 4.4.3 describe the requirements for the online front office and back office in the context of the online product realisation for ReachNow in China.

g List the errors that might occur in using the app for BMW's car sharing process in China and think of some relevant 'poka yokes' to overcome them.

h To what extent does BMW ReachNow include personal service? Could this ever be replaced by online services, or is this unrealistic?

i In the future BMW wants to add premium elements to the car-sharing programme. Which steps should the product manager take to achieve these product improvements? Use table 4.2 to support you answer.

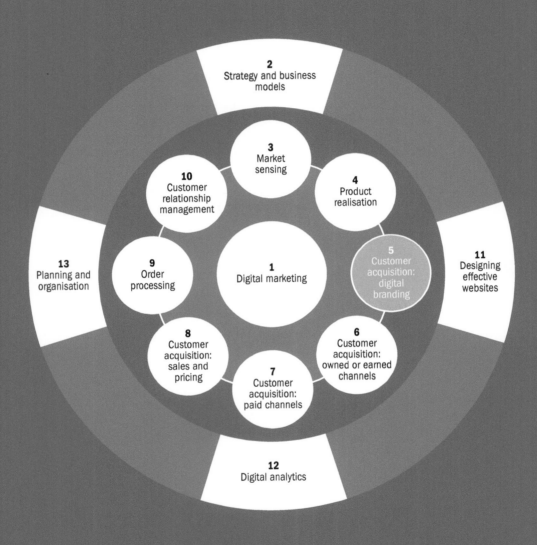

5

Customer acquisition: digital branding

Authors: Marjolein Visser (5.1, 5.2 and 5.4), Martin Kloos (5.3) and Guido van den Anker (5.5)

Previous chapters describe how the marketer can establish a clear idea of what the market's wants and desires are (the market analysis process) and how the Internet can be used to further product development and improvement as well as the creation of processes for the facilitation of the product or service (the product realisation process). Once everything is customer-ready, it is time for the market approach. The customer acquisition process is comprised of defining target markets and acquiring new customers. Customer acquisition consists of four steps: marketing communications to draw attention to the brand and connect to the customer, the sales process for convincing those customers to actually buy the product and finally agreeing on the price of the product. This chapter describes the role of digital marketing communication in brand management. Digital marketing communication for the purpose of connecting to customers will be discussed in Chapters 6 and 7. The sales process and price determination will be covered in Chapter 8.

This chapter covers:
- the basics of digital marketing communication
- the role of digital marketing communication in brand management
- the role of social media in digital branding
- viral marketing, video and games
- content marketing

After reading this chapter you will know how to:
- formulate objectives within and define target markets for each of the four steps of the digital marketing communication funnel, whilst keeping in mind cross media optimisation
- describe how digital marketing communication can be used to increase the value of a brand
- indicate how social media can be deployed within brand management
- describe the success factors for viral marketing and indicate what the role of games can be within digital marketing communication
- explain what content marketing is and describe what a content marketing plan should consist of

5.1 Digital marketing communication: the basics

Marketing communication

In marketing communication, the objectives are commercial: the aim is to acquire customers. An organisation also has communication objectives that are not directly connected to sales. In order for an organisation to function efficiently in society, it is important for the press to have a positive image of the organisation, shareholders to have faith in the company and employees to understand what the brand symbolises and be keen to contribute towards that. It is also crucial that the policymakers rate the organisation highly enough for them to take it into account in the decision-making process. It is down to the corporate communications department or public relations to influence these kinds of stakeholders. This department also uses digital communication methods, but these methods fall outside the remit of this book. Nonetheless, it is important to realise that marketing communications should be in line with the corporate communication objectives. Excellent coordination between these two is necessary.

Corporate communications department

Public relations

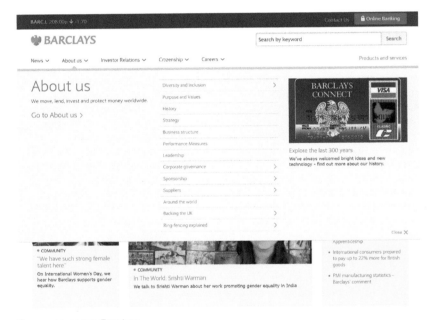

Corporate pages Barclays

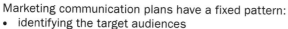

Barclays' website for customer acquisition

The final aim of marketing communications is to sell products, services or ideas to customers of the organisation. Most organisations have both a strategic marketing plan that includes the objectives for the next three to five years as well as a marketing plan for the current period. The marketing communication plan is a derivative of these marketing plans. Some companies have an annual plan; others rely on quarterly plans or programme-based plans. For every marketing activity the brand managers, market managers, product managers and communication managers develop a detailed communications plan in which every step of the acquisition process is addressed. For this they need to seamlessly harmonise both their online as well as offline communication tools.

Marketing communication plan

Marketing communication plans have a fixed pattern:
- identifying the target audiences
- determining the communications objectives
- selecting the communication tools and communication channels
- executing the communications plan
- evaluating and revising
- planning and budgeting

We will discuss these steps in the coming sections.

5.1.1 Identifying target audiences

The marketing plan describes the organisation's most important target markets. Usually these are large groups of people, such as 'families with children living at home'. A communications campaign can be aimed at a much smaller segment, for example 'car owners with children aged 12 to 18'. The groups of people that are addressed as part of a marketing activity are called 'target audiences'.

Target audiences

A marketing activity often has several target audiences. For instance, a digital marketing activity intended to promote the sales of car insurances can be aimed at:

- car owners
- insurance agents that sell car insurances
- organisations that publish online comparisons between different car insurances
- the trade press

Target by data
Target by context
Target by choice

Finding and approaching target audiences for communications can be done in three ways (Merks-Benjaminsen, 2015):

1 by using data on characteristics or behaviour: (target by data)
2 by searching for contextual signals: (target by context)
3 based on individual reactions to brand expressions: (target by choice)

1 Target by data
Using Google AdWords or Facebook you are able to contain the ads you show to a defined target segment. This way, a car insurance provider could focus on a target audience from a specific age range.

2 Target by context

Contextual messages

The digital marketer can look for contextual signals and use them to focus on the target audience's behaviour. For instance, a car insurance provider could look for websites or pages on social media that contain content about getting your driver's licence and place ads there. An example of this would be a pre-roll ad for a YouTube video about taking a driving test.

3 Target by choice
A digital marketer can actively engage in conversation with individuals who have shown an interest in the brand. The digital marketer can make a step by step plan, each step bringing the customer closer to purchasing their product. An insurance company could target young people who have participated in a campaign on Facebook about cars (such as 'like and win' campaigns) and use that network to approach them with a video about their car insurance. If they watch the video to the end, the insurance company can approach them with an offer that relates to the video and lead them to their website to close the deal.

5.1.2 Determining the communications objectives

Communications objectives

We will discuss the digital marketing communication funnel, the long-term and short-term communication objectives and the formulation and determination of these objectives.

The digital marketing communication funnel

Digital marketing communication funnel

The final aim of digital marketing communication is to motivate people to buy a product or service. This will not succeed at once: people go through the process gradually. In Chapter 3 you may have read that the decision-making process consists of the following steps: need identification, information gathering, evaluation of alternatives, selection of the sales channel and evaluation of the final outcome. You will also have learnt about the digital marketing funnel. Central to this is how to incite users of your website or app to make a purchase and consequently return to your website for the purpose of making a repeat purchase in future. In marketing communication, a comparable funnel model is also used. The steps are (see figure 5.1):

- creating awareness of it being interesting to visit an online sales channel (*awareness*)   Awareness
- 'seize' the visitor by convincing them of the attractiveness of visiting the online sales channel (*capture*)   Capture
- motivate the visitor to buy the product (*conversion*)   Conversion
- convince the customer to make a repeat purchase and to endorse the brand (*loyalty*).   Loyalty

The digital marketing funnel's 'visit' phase is split into two steps: creating *awareness* and *capture*, convince. The steps 'enthral' through to 'purchase' are part of *conversion*, whilst the concept of *loyalty* is broader than just 'retain'. The digital marketing funnel confines itself to the act of visiting the website or app, whilst loyalty also covers the endorsement of the brand on, for example, social media.

The more well known the brand is, the stronger the effect of the digital marketing communication is on sales (Pauwels, Demirci, Yildrim & Srinivasan, 2017) and the greater the chance of reaching the conversion phase is.

FIGURE 5.1 The digital marketing communication funnel

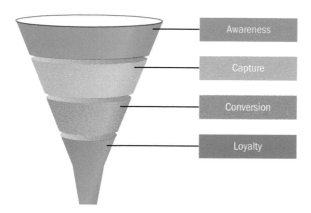

Short-term and long-term objectives
Website visits, app use and conversion – transforming visitors into buyers   Conversion
– are short-term objectives. Besides this, marketers want to positively change people's attitude towards the brand. Giep Franzen (Franzen & Goessens, 1998) defines a brand as 'a network of functional and   Brand
emotional associations between elements in the consumer's memory'.

5

Digital branding   Digital brand communication is called digital branding. That is what the digital marketer will create long-term objectives for.

Coca-Cola: emotional associations; pleasure and freedom, functional association; 'refreshing'

Formulating SMART objectives

In order to be able to monitor the communications objectives well, the digital marketer must formulate objectives as 'SMART' as possible: Specific, Measurable, Assignable, Realistic and Time-related. It is important to be able to precisely measure whether the objectives will be achieved. Measuring digital marketing results, digital analytics or web analytics are covered in Chapter 12. Examples of SMART objectives are:

SMART

- in the coming year, increase the brand awareness within the target segment from 10% to 15%
- in half a year's time, increase the conversion of web shop visits that result in purchases from 0.5% to 0.75%
- generate € 500,000 from web shop earnings in the first quarter
- generate 10,000 extra users for our app in the coming month

SMART objectives always answer the following questions: what do we want to achieve, to what extent and when?

© Noordhoff Uitgevers bv

5

Establishing communication objectives

The best way to formulate communication objectives is to follow the order of the digital marketing communication funnel. For example (see figure 5.2):

- 25% of the target audience is aware of the existence of our web shop (*awareness*)
- 10% of those that are aware of the existence of the web shop actually visit it (*capture*)
- 10% of the visitors purchase an item with an average value of €50 (*conversion*)
- 20% of the buyers endorse the supplier on social media (*loyalty*)

FIGURE 5.2 The digital marketing communication funnel applied

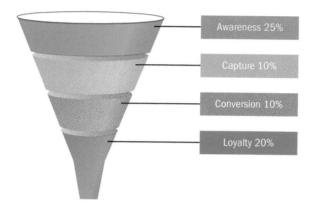

A calculation shows that of a target audience of 100,000 people: 25% x 10% x 10% x 500,000 = 0.25% x 500,000 = 1,250 people buy an item with a value of € 50 and (20% x 1,250 =) 250 people refer to the supplier's website on social media.

When this revenue is not achieved, or when there are less positive reviews than expected, the cause can easily be identified on the basis of the percentages.

How B2B brand SAP analysed the digital marketing communication funnel and applied the learnings as part of an innovative social media strategy in Latin America

In this region, there are 176 million social media users, each on average spending 7.5 hours per month on social networks.

SAP used social media to target key B2B personas across the region, building on learnings from other parts of the business to set the strategy for Latin America.

'It's the community experience of allowing people to share information — great stories and great ideas — to do that internally so they can be smart

about how they deal with their customers. That's really the heart of what we're trying to do with the social strategy.'
– SAP's VP of demand generation Adriel Sanchez

One of the first decisions was to review the number of social accounts across the region; SAP decided to reduce them in order to achieve a more focused communication of key SAP messages.

Today, SAP Latin America operates four Facebook pages, four Twitter feeds and two LinkedIn accounts. The above profiles are split out by language (eg Portuguese and Spanish) rather than by country. SAP's strategy is to provide 20% advertising/promotional material vs. 80% of engaging content for its community. They adopted a three-year plan:
1 building critical mass of users.
2 targeting and fine tuning the messaging
3 turning that critical mass into measurable business results

Having launched the strategy; after the first year SAP Latin America had more than 100,000 fans and followers (an increase of 900%) and they reported a 17% interaction rate across the region, while a follow-up campaign featuring a social app targeting specific buying personas drove more than 12,000 visitors and a 15% engagement rate; both these figures were well in excess of the targets.

Although detailed results are commercially confidential, based on average industry conversion rates, we may estimate that the campaign generated over 500 new customers and total incremental revenue in excess of $5 milion.

This campaign meant that SAP sales teams were able to uncover new opportunities and is now part of a broader longer-term initiative which includes measuring the impact of events and campaigns using social sentiment analysis, which is a growing area within social media marketing.

Source: Moth, 2013

5.1.3 Selecting contact moments and communication messages

Once the digital marketer has determined who they want to communicate with and what their objectives are, they must decide what the most effective moments are for interacting with their target audience. When can they inform them, inspire them and help them with their decision? Throughout the buying process, the digital marketer wants their target audience to be exposed to their products or services at the earliest possible moment. Imagine you work for a travel agency that specialises in long distance holidays, you want to inspire people to choose such an exotic location for their holiday. You could post breath-taking pictures on Instagram that give a good idea of the amazing experiences that a far-away holiday has to offer. This could lead people directly to your website. Google calls this first moment of contact the 'Zero Moment of Truth' (ZMOT), wherein a person's subjective experience of the product is formed that will drive their decision to buy. The 'First Moment of Truth' is when the

Zero Moment of Truth

customer sees the holiday on the website and s able to actually buy it. The 'Second Moment of Truth' is when they actually go on holiday and discover if the trip lives up to their expectations. The 'Ultimate Moment of Truth', coined by Brian Solis (2013), is when the holiday maker shares their experiences. These shared experiences give people who are in the 'Zero Moment of Truth' the impression that the brand is trustworthy. Together, these four moments determine the commercial success of the organisation. At each of these moments, the brand must positively distinguish itself from other brands.

The digital marketer must make an inventory of all the relevant moments of contact and decide what type of information they must provide. Merks-Benjaminsen (2015) distinguishes three types of information, or 'content':

Content
Hero content

1 Hero content: information that makes your brand stand out. For a travel agency this could be the introduction of new destinations, information about a holiday where the guests were extremely satisfied or entertaining communication centred around the brand's values. One example of this is the video 'The DNA journey' by holiday search engine Momondo. In it they try to get people to view other cultures more openly and accepting.

2 Help content: information surrounding the product that must always be kept up to date and available. The marketer uses this to answer any queries from their customers. Also sometimes called hygiene content. For a travel agency an example could be the sharing of practical information regarding the trip, such as the itinerary and the departure times.

Help content

Hygiene content

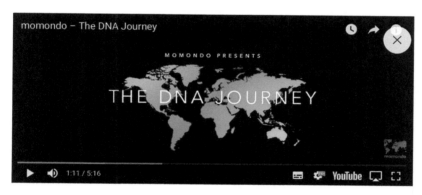

Join the journey

We asked 67 people from all over the world to take a DNA test. It turns out they have much more in common with other nationalities than they thought …

It's easy to think there are more things dividing us than uniting us. But we actually have much more in common with other nationalities than you'd think.

Hero content: video of 'The DNA Journey' from holiday search engine Momondo

5

Hub content

3 Hub content: content that is aligned with the target audience's specific areas of interest. The marketer is able to provide a fresh perspective about the products or influence the way that the service is perceived. A travel agency could share photographs from a previous trip to South Africa with people that have shown an interest in travelling to that destination.

5.1.4 Selecting communication tools and channels

First the marketer determines which communication tools are most suitable for achieving their objective. Then they select the communication channels through which they want to deliver their message. These subjects are covered in this sub-section. We will also cover the merging of different forms of media and introduce the digital communication methods.

Traditional marketing communication tools can also be found online

Floor, Van Raaij & Bouwman (2015), famous researchers in the field of marketing communication, distinguish the following marketing communication tools:

Advertising
- Advertising: paid marketing communication such as advertisements, TV commercials and banners.

Public relations and information
- Public relations and information: regular encouragement of mutual understanding between organisations and the external public such as by sending out press reports and setting up a corporate website.

Sponsorship
- Sponsorship: making a financial or practical contribution to a 'crowd-pleaser', such as an event or a sports team in exchange for brand visibility.

Promotions
- Promotions (sales promotion): special offers to increase sales temporarily, such as discounts or extras.

Direct marketing and dialogue marketing
- Direct marketing and dialogue marketing: direct communications from the manufacturer of a product or service to the end consumer (not through the means of a medium such as a magazine, TV or an agent's website).

Retail communications
- Retail communications: means of communication within shops aimed at increasing sales, such as displays, packaging and the design of the store.

Direct sales
- Direct sales: the salesperson personally communicates with the potential buyer.

Events
- Events.

Communications mix

Video advertising

Every communications tool has its own role within the communications objectives. The combination of instruments that a marketing communications specialist selects to achieve their objectives is called the communications mix.

Almost all of the traditional methods of communications can also take place online, albeit under a different name. Advertisements are found in the form of banners and video advertising. Email is a form of direct marketing communications. Public relations is frequently found in the form of content marketing and other publicity on social media for example. Online, promotions are commonplace: suppliers use emails, discount sites, auction sites, social media etc to draw attention to their offers. Direct sales is becoming increasingly popular online, for example through online chats. The manner in which marketers use the various communications tools online are summarised later in this chapter as well as in the next.

Promotions on discount sites

Communications channels

After the marketer has determined which communications tools are most suitable to achieve his goals, he selects the communications channels or media through which he wants to deliver his message. For online, these are for example third-party websites, apps or email.

The communications mix must take the target group's searching and purchasing behaviour into account, but also the specific characteristics of the selected media as well as the type of content. This is why a lot of digital marketers are very wary of the quality and content of websites where they may place their banner. It makes a huge difference whether a banner for a perfume brand appears on the site of a ladies' glossy magazine or on that of one about erotic lingerie. In technical terms this environment is called 'editorial context'. When the contents and design of an online advertisement are in line with this context, this is called 'native advertising'. 'Native' advertisements have a better conversion than regular ads, because they are consistent with the interests of the visitor.

Editorial context

Native advertising

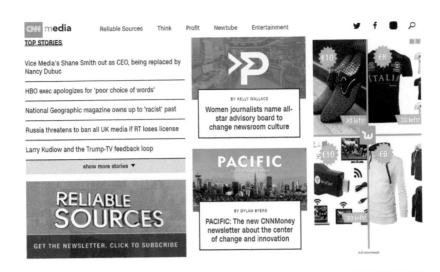

Native advertising on Wish.com

5

Media convergence

Media convergence	In recent years a lot has changed in the way marketers draw attention to their brands. An important development is the uniting or merging of various media (convergence). An example of convergence is the magazine Columbus Magazine. Whereas a magazine used to only appear in 'print', a lot of magazines now also have an online version. Columbus Magazine has an extensive website, on which consumers actively participate. You could question which communication channel is more important at this moment: the glossy magazine or the website. Another example of media
Second screen	convergence is the 'second screen', the use of a tablet or smartphone whilst watching a TV programme. Because of this the media plans of the modern marketing communication specialist are considerably more complicated than they used to be. They include a broad range of media and communications tools which all have their own role in creating brand awareness and brand experience.
Cross media	When online and offline communications are combined, we call it 'cross media'. When selecting the marketing communications tools, it is of importance to pay attention to the specific characteristics of all the various possibilities within offline and online media and to align these in such a way that they complement and reinforce one another, in order for it to result in communicative added value or synergy (Floor, Van Raaij,
Cross-media optimisation	Bouwman, 2015). In cross-media optimisation it's about reinforcing the message by embracing a carefully selected marketing communications
Multimedia brand consistency	mix. The ultimate goal is to achieve multimedia brand consistency: a uniform representation of the brand across the different channels.
Storytelling	To reinforce the integration between the different media, a philosophy and a suitable narrative are applied (storytelling). By way of this story, the consumer is persuaded to switch to another medium. When the story becomes more layered and includes multiple levels, the message is equated with more depth and therefore it becomes more relevant to the user.

© Noordhoff Uitgevers bv

Digital communication methods

Digital communication methods aim to guide the target groups through the process of the first step of the digital marketing communication funnel. These methods aim to increase brand awareness and/or encourage people to visit the provider's own media channels such as the website, apps, social media, the digital brand community and also the physical store. The most important digital marketing communication methods for guiding people to owned sales and communications channels are:

Digital communication methods

- email marketing
- search engine marketing
- display advertising
- affiliate marketing
- link building
- content marketing
- social media marketing
- video, virals and games

The last three methods will be further discussed in this chapter; the remaining methods will be covered in Chapter 6.

In table 5.1 you can find the most important characteristics of the digital marketing communication methods with a score of ++ (very favourable) to - - (highly unfavourable). An example: ++ regarding the capital intensity of Search Engine Optimisation means that it requires little money, which is very favourable for the digital marketer.

TABLE 5.1 Characteristics of digital marketing communications methods

	Short term result: conversion	Long term result: brand communication	Labour intensity	Capital intensity
Email marketing	++	++	+	+
Search engine advertisements	+	+	+	-
Display advertising	+/-	+	+/	- -
Affiliate marketing	+	+/-	-	-
Organic search results (SEO)	+/-	+/-	-	+ +
Link building	+/-	+	- -	+
Content marketing	+/-	++	- -	++
Social media marketing	+/-	++	- -	+
Virals and games	-	++	+/-	- -

5.1.5 Implementing, evaluating and fine-tuning the marketing communications plan

The interactivity on the Internet makes feedback on marketing communication activities quickly apparent. But a happy or an angry customer can also cause spontaneous brand communications to arise. A positive or a negative review can start a wave of publicity on social media or on the website of the brand itself. This necessitates a very proactive attitude: the organisation needs to actively monitor the markets' feedback and be willing to engage in real-time dialogue with customers. Where necessary, this should lead to fine-tuning of the plans (see figure 5.3).

Real-time dialogue

© Noordhoff Uitgevers bv

FIGURE 5.3 Real-time dialogue can lead to changes in the marketing communications plan

A/B test

It is also customary to test marketing communication activities, for example using an A/B test. In this, multiple variations of communications are deployed side by side. For instance, a small number of customers receives an email with heading A and another small number of customers receive the same email with heading B. Then the marketer determines which of the two emails scores best and sends that mail to all of the other customers. They could do the same with banner advertisements; various order buttons, etc. The analysis of and learning from all the digital marketing activities are addressed in Chapter 12 on digital analytics.

5.2 Role of digital marketing communication in brand management

Brand building

Digital marketing communication is playing an increasingly important role in brand building, strengthening the brand, for example by building brand recognition and a good image, creating customer engagement and creating online communities.

CBBE model

The 'Customer Based Brand Equity Model' (CBBE model) by Keller (2013) is one of the most frequently used models for brand communication (see figure 5.4). The model assumes that a brand adds value for the customer: a customer prefers a product or service from a brand that they know and appreciate. The brand value increases as the customer strengthens their bond with the brand. The communication around the brand aims to reach the top of the CBBE pyramid step by step. The model describes six forms of brand equity that are completed in four steps:
1 brand identity: *brand salience*
2 brand meaning: *brand performance* and *brand imagery*
3 brand response: *brand judgements* and *brand feelings*
4 brand relationships: *brand resonance*

FIGURE 5.4 Customer Based Brand Equity Model

Source: Keller, 2013 (edited)

1 Brand identity: brand salience
'Brand salience' refers to the question: 'Who am I, as a brand?' The target segment must be able to identify clearly with the brand. The brand must stand out and it must be clear what associations people should have when communicating about it. Only then can brand knowledge be worked on. Salience or singularity indicates the extent to which consumers are familiar with a brand and will consider it. Is there, for example, spontaneous brand recognition? Brand salience results in brand awareness.

Brand salience

Brand awareness

The creating and sharing of brand stories plays an important role in creating spontaneous brand recognition. Brands can opt for a model in which they tell the brand stories themselves or create them together with consumers. In the first case they do so using paid and owned media and they use online advertisements, for instance, that lead to landing pages on the website. In the case of the latter, they actively interact with their communications target segment via social media. You can read more about this in section 5.3. However, even something as simple as topping the organic search results already contributes to the brand value (Yoo, 2014).

Brand stories

2 Brand meaning: brand performance and brand imagery
If the brand is sufficiently recognised, the digital marketer can work on 'brand performance' and 'brand imagery'. Then the question, 'What are you, as a brand?', is answered. Brand performance reflects the extent to which the brand responds to the needs of the customers. For example, how satisfied are customers with the products or services? This can be highlighted successfully via owned media, but reviews on review sites, in search results and on social networks also play a role in this phase. Brand imagery (or brand metaphors) has to do with the image of the brand, how people think about a brand. With the growth of social media, marketers have decreasing control over the brand image. The brand associations and visual identity that are evoked by online expressions must match the identity of the brand. All online expressions must have the same appearance. An example of a brand that projects a consistent image, is low-cost grocer Lidl.

Brand performance

Brand imagery

Brand metaphors

5

Fanta brings their brand to customers' attention via a pre-roll ad on YouTube

Brand associations

If an organisation adequately substantiates the brand meaning, then this will result in the desired 'brand associations'.

Research by Pauwels, Demirci, Yildirim and Srinivasan (2017) shows that unknown brands can create the most brand value by using a combination of digital and traditional marketing communications. Only brands that already have awareness in their target segment can limit themselves to digital brand communication.

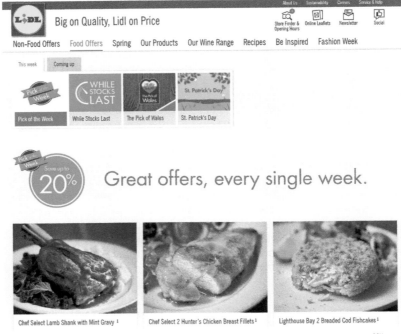

Retail chain Lidl consistently promotes their use of competitive prices both offline and online

3 Brand response: brand judgments and brand feelings
Once the target segment recognises the meaning of a brand, the next step is to influence how potential customers think and feel about a brand. Then the question, 'What do I think of you, as a brand?', is answered. This phase involves rational brand assessments, brand judgments and emotions or brand feelings: warmth, pleasure, tension, safety, social acceptance and self-esteem. In this phase, the brand values of an organisation are filled in. This results, if the digital marketer does their job well, in a positive brand attitude.

Brand judgments

Brand feelings
Brand attitude

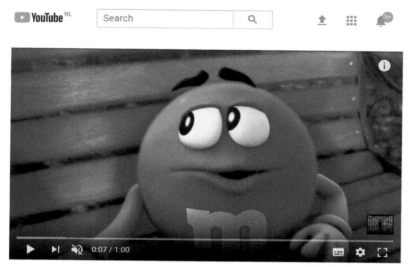

M&Ms evoke 'brand feelings' in this YouTube video for Valentine's Day

4 Brand relationships: brand resonance
If the brand is judged positively, both rationally and emotionally, the marketer can work on brand resonance. Then the question, 'What about you and me together?', is answered. The goal is to ensure that the consumer enters into an enduring relationship with the brand: becoming loyal to the brand, feeling emotionally involved and actively communicating with and about the brand. This creates brand attachment. In this phase, for example, customers can join a brand community and establish themselves as brand ambassadors.

Brand resonance

Brand attachment

Ambassadors

Ultimately, the digital communication around the brand must lead to as much brand activity by customers as possible. These can be purchases, but also reactions on social media or participation in a brand community.

Brand activity

An example of a brand that scores well on 'brand resonance' is www.figleaves.com.
Figleaves.com is a UK-based online female lingerie/swimwear/sportwear retailer established by Daniel Nabarro in 1998 and purchased by N Brown Group in 2010. Figleaves has been attracting customers for a number of years through a strong and consistently implemented traditional as well as

5

digital marketing communication strategy, Figleaves has an easy-to-use website with bright, airy design, high-quality photography and a highly efficient check-out process. Figleaves uses both social media and email marketing to build a relationship with its customers and create a sense of community – a good example of brand resonance.

'Our customers are very important to us, so sending emails based on historic and future purchasing behaviour is crucial to ensure that we communicate relevant, personalised messages to them and continue to deliver the level of service we are proud of through all channels'
– Amanda Clifford, Digital Marketing Manager, Figleaves
(Figarodigital.co.uk, 2017)

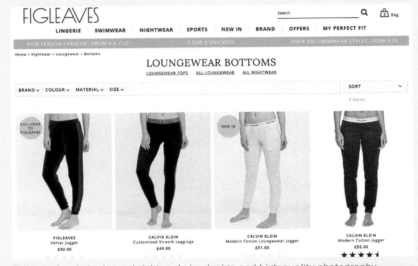

Figleaves' website has a bright and airy design and high-quality photography

In his book *How Brands Grow* (2010), Professor Byron Sharp concludes that in order for a brand to grow, an organisation must ensure a huge growth in 'share of voice', the brand's share of the total communications expenditure. The conversation share is the percentage that a brand spends on advertising in relation to the spending of the total category. The digital marketer needs to do three things to ensure the growth of a brand's conversation share:

Share of voice
Conversation share

1 The marketer must ensure reach among people who do not buy the brand often or at all. This can be done by supporting brand stories on social media with advertising, so that they can reach groups of people who are not yet following the brand on social media.
2 They must stand out by communicating in a consistent and eye-catching way, so that the brand builds recognisable mental patterns in the brains of consumers. This can also be done using advertisements and via social media. Technology makes it possible to tell stories sequentially, so that you can be sure that a consumer has seen all the messages in

a story. Also, more advanced possibilities in the field of (re) targeting make it possible for brands to truly carry consumers through a story.
3 They must have a continuous presence. Research, as mentioned in ie How Brands Grow (2010), has shown that it appears to be beneficial to have a consistent, structural presence and to ensure that you reach a small percentage of your target segment every week.

Three digital marketing communication methods that focus primarily on strengthening brand value and building long-term relationships are social media marketing, viral marketing, video and games and content marketing. You can read more about this in the following paragraphs.

5.3 Role of social media in digital branding

Social media play an increasingly important role in digital branding. Using social branding, digital marketers are able to change the knowledge, attitude and behaviour regarding their brand or organisation. With the increasing use of social media, social media platforms have become indispensable for brands. A number of reasons for this are:

Social branding

- *Range*: social media is used by millions of people. Social media have thus become interesting channels to reach the target segment and to build a relationship with consumers, both through messages and advertisements.
- *Conversations*: brands are frequently discussed on social media, both in a positive and a negative sense. Brands can use these conversations to gain insights, but they can also participate in these conversations, for example by providing a service.
- *Reputation*: social media is an important indicator for society. Many news media regularly quote messages from social media. Also, due to the effect of 'word of mouth', incidents on social media can quickly reach a large audience (see example 5.1 about Zara).

Word of mouth

- *Influence*: it is not only brands that can establish a relationship with consumers via social media. Due to the large reach of social media, there are also many people who have accounts with many followers. These so called 'influencers' can help brands to spread brand communications.

An organisation can profit from this in a number of ways by using social media for a variety of digital branding purposes. These are:
1 *Brand* communication: by developing a direct relationship with consumers, or through advertising. The latter form is dealt with in more detail in section 7.4.
2 *Reputation management*: for instance, by assessing online sentiment, entering into relationships with stakeholders and creating thought leadership (see also section 5.5).
3 *Service*: by identifying and handling questions and complaints from consumers. You can read more about this in section 9.4.

EXAMPLE 5.1

Zara

A huge commotion arose surrounding fashion brand Zara, when one of their Spanish customers published photos on Facebook of skin burns that they got from wearing sandals from Zara. The message spread like wildfire around the world, both on Facebook and on blogs that caught on to the story.

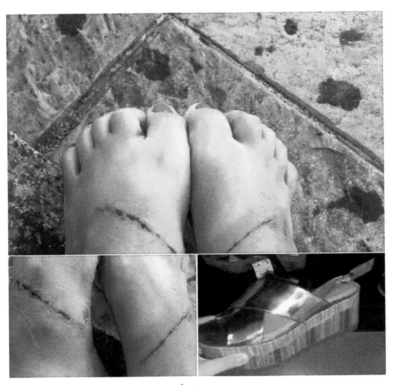

Share

😮😵💀 115

28,912 Shares

Photos of Zara shoes that caused burns spread quickly around the world

----

5.3.1   Social media and brand communication

Brand communication

Brands can use social media for brand communication in four ways:
1 by creating accounts and pages with followers on Facebook, Twitter or Instagram and sharing brand content and conversations
2 by using 'influencers' on social media to communicate about the brand

3 by using consumers to share content about the brand
4 by ensuring that brand communication reaches the right consumers via advertising

Creating accounts and pages with followers

One of the distinctive types of brand communication that has been introduced by social media is the possibility for an organisation to create an account or page. Social networks such as Facebook, Twitter, Instagram and Snapchat make it possible to follow accounts or pages. When you follow such a page or account, you are shown the content that is shared on that page or account. Organisations aim to attract as many followers as possible so that their brand communication reaches a lot of people in a cost-effective way. Coca-Cola and McDonald's have the largest follower bases on Facebook world-wide, with over 100 and 70 million followers respectively. In principle, brands use content to get in touch with these people in a relatively simple way, making social media an attractive channel for brand communication.

The fact that brands can establish a direct relationship with consumers via social media and that their content is communicated relatively easily has led to many brands communicating more regularly. Brands switched from a so-called 'burst strategy', where they use brand communication actively for a few short periods per year, to an 'always-on strategy', where they are continuously active with brand communication. To do this, they often use the 'hero, hub and help' model discussed in subsection 5.1.3 to develop various forms of content that can be shared via social media. A third option is to use a 'drip' strategy. In this strategy, the organisation opts for more spread communication at specific times or after certain actions or events.

Burst strategy

Always-on strategy

Dripping strategy

An example of a brand that has chosen always-on brand communication is drinks company Innocent.

Innocent chooses an 'always-on strategy'

Social media and influencer marketing

There are people who have amassed a lot of followers via social media and hold a lot of influence over these followers. That makes it attractive for brands to use them for brand development. These so-called influentials have a large reach and a lot of influence as they are often seen by their

Influentials

followers as a more reliable source than traditional advertisers. Brands can achieve great success using influencer campaigns.

Zoella, also known as Zoe Elizabeth Sugg (born 28 March 1990) is an English fashion and beauty vlogger, YouTuber, and author. She is best known by her YouTube username Zoella. Her debut novel, *Girl Online*, was released in November 2014 and broke the record for highest first-week sales of a first-time novelist since Nielsen BookScan began compiling such records in 1998. Zoella is one of the most influential Tweeters in the UK.

Zoella's main YouTube channel has over 11.8 million subscribers and over 976 million video views and is the 50th most subscribed channel on the website; her second channel 'MoreZoella' has over 4.6 million subscribers and over 589 million video views. She also has over 8.6 million followers on Twitter and over 11.1 million on Instagram.

My Every Day Autumn Makeup | Zoella

1,890,104 views

A much viewed video of Zoella on YouTube

There are roughly three ways in which a brand can enter into a relationship with an influencer:
1. *Exchange*: the first way is a form of exchange. Influencers share their knowledge and expertise in exchange for visibility. This is particularly interesting for brands who have a large reach of their own.
2. *Incentives*: influencers find it interesting to be the first to be able to talk about new products and services. That is why brands often send products to influencers to use or test. Influencers can then use these products, in the hope that the influencer will communicate with their followers about their experiences with the product or service.
3. *Pay*: influencer marketing is becoming more commercial. It is therefore increasingly accepted that brands pay influencers directly for visibility for their product or service within the influencer network.

© Noordhoff Uitgevers bv

Emilie Tabor and Maddie Raedts link international brands to influencers

One single world-wide campaign for a brand makes little sense, according to Maddie Raedts and Emilie Tabor of IMA. 'Advertising today is human to human.' Their company is on the Forbes 30 under 30 list. They pair up multinationals with social media stars. 'Real people with a story.'

Maddie and Emilie work with 'influencers', people with their own online audience who blog, vlog and post on Instagram, Facebook and Snapchat about what they eat, wear and buy.

Food and fashion, travel and mom bloggers and vloggers are now in the front row. Ahead of the experts, the professionals, the reviewers and the journalists. The KLMs, the Chanels and the Heinekens of this world will want to get involved. So, they enlist the help of the 28-year-old Maddie and Emilie. They have 10,000 influencers from around the world in their network. They know that one single, global campaign for a denim brand hardly makes any sense anymore. Hastily sending jeans to bloggers does not help either. 'In Tokyo the target audience is different to London or New York. We know local influencers there.' Who will like that jacket and jeans, wear it and photograph themselves? Who, under the direction of IMA, will create their own lookbook, photo-shoot or video and become live 'ambassadors' for the brand?

Via IMA, Emilie Tabor and Maddie Raedts pair up international brands with influencers

Yes, that is advertising, and followers know that too. 'Millennials have no problem with this, as long as the brand is a perfect match for the person they identify with.' Maddie: 'It must be sincere.' Emilie: 'Authentic.' This is where their expertise lies. They know exactly whether a blogger has previously written that he thinks it is 'a cool brand'. Just as they also ensure that influencers do not make too many commercial commitments. 'The only influencers who survive are those who stay true to whatever they are passionate about.' Someone who continuously promotes everything, will lose followers.

Source: Koelewijn (2017). Article edited and shortened

Social media and enlisting consumers

The viral nature of social media (about which more can be found in section 5.4) can be used to expand your reach quickly using earned media and word of mouth and has led to an increasing number of brands encouraging consumers to engage in (social media) brand development campaigns. A good example is the 'Share a Coke' campaign by Coca-Cola, where this brand combined a personalised campaign that allowed customers to buy cans and bottles with names on them, combined with the hashtag #ShareaCoke. People who bought a bottle that had their name on it shared photos en masse on social media using this hashtag. This not only delivered an extreme amount of 'earned range', it was also another logical extension of Coca-Cola's brand campaign called 'Share Happiness'.

Earned range

#ShareaCoke: an example of enlisting consumers for a social media campaign

Another way that consumers can be enlisted on social media is the development of communities. Various organisations develop their own communities, where, for example, they give consumers a role in co-creation or providing a service.

As an example, Unilever launched a forum for women in the Benelux countries (Belgium, Netherlands and Luxembourg). Yunomi is a community by women and for women. Every day, users can access relevant content that will help them with every aspect of their daily life: recipes, practical tips, ideas for their holiday (vacation) etc.

As soon as a user has registered on the website, they can join the conversation, reacting to the content, sharing the opinions and even submitting articles, photographs and videos. Members can also collect Nomi's, ie points they can trade for special gifts and exclusive events reserved to the Yunomi community. The Yunomi online magazine is created and managed by Unilever in the Benelux countries; an impressive example of content marketing.

Social media and advertising

In addition to the aforementioned forms that brands can use for digital branding via social media, social media have also developed into more traditional advertising channels. You can read more about social media and advertising in section 7.4.

5.3.2   Social media and reputation management

A second form of digital branding via social media is by using reputation management. Reputation management is systematically influencing what people think and believe regarding the reliability and quality of an organisation or brand by, for example, monitoring what people say online, actively answering questions and taking part in discussions, responding to negative statements, creating content and stimulating sharing. To prevent reputational damage, a great deal of attention is paid to directing public sentiment by creating a positive image and restricting any negativity.

Reputation management

With increasing frequency, organisations actively manage their reputation via social media. Key activities in this are:
1 continuous and active monitoring of stakeholders, conversations and reporting about the organisation and its products and services
2 actively answering questions and participating in discussions
3 developing relationships with stakeholders
4 creating thought leadership yourself by the creation and sharing of content

Following stakeholders, conversations and reporting

The open nature of social media makes it easy for organisations to follow how the brand is discussed on social media. You have already read about social media monitoring in section 3.9.

Actively answering questions and participating in discussions

Answering questions is a form of service, but in the field of reputation management social media can also be used to participate in discussions. For example, brands can share content with a particular hashtag, so that they become part of a broader conversation, or create a theme themselves.

A successful example is the #ALSIceBucketChallenge that was at one time associated with the ALS Association, a foundation that raises awareness about the disease ALS. The hashtag was used en masse to draw attention to this social theme. At the peak of the campaign, more than 2.4 million videos on Facebook were tagged with the hashtag.

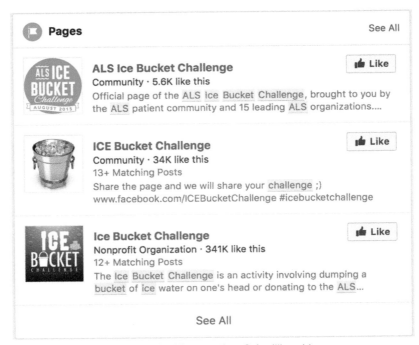

#ALSIceBucketChallenge resulted in more than 2.4 million videos

Developing relationships with stakeholders

Important public opinion leaders such as journalists and professionals are often active on social media. Organisations, often through employees, can develop a direct relationship with such stakeholders via social media, by following them, by sending them messages and by responding to what those stakeholders themselves share on social media.

For example, various financial services companies have their spokespersons actively develop such relationships. This way they are able to get in touch quickly and are promptly informed of what issues are currently important to the stakeholders, they can contribute to the public opinion that the stakeholders (partly) create regarding an organisation.

Establishing thought leadership by creating and sharing content

Thought leadership

'Thought leadership' means that you as an individual or organisation are recognised and seen as an authority in a specific area or for a specific subject (Visser & Sikkenga, 2017). Achieving thought leadership content is a relevant objective for organisations and can assist in attracting and retaining existing and new customers.

Employee advocacy

Thought leadership can be created on the one hand by the brand itself and on the other hand by the employees who work for a brand. We call the latter 'employee advocacy'. The credibility of employees and the value this represents to organisations is becoming increasingly apparent, especially in knowledge-intensive organisations. Activating a large number of employees on social media can thus be an important added value for the brand in creating thought leadership and brand value. Practical examples of Employee Advocacy such as that of L'Oréal who trains all their new

© Noordhoff Uitgevers bv

employees to share positive messages via their social media profiles, show that the reach and impact of the employees' combined networks can be greater than the individual network of the brand itself. You can read more about creating thought leadership using content marketing in section 5.5.

5.3.3   Social media and service

A third way that organisations and brands can use digital branding via social media is by service distribution. It is sometimes said that service is the new marketing. This means that good service and a positive customer experience automatically lead to new customers. Brands can provide services via social media by setting up so-called web care teams. You can read more about this in section 9.4.

Some organisations take service to the next level via social media and use service as a form for brand development. UK Retailer John Lewis provides excellent customer service on an everyday basis mainly due to the way that their staff, or 'Partners', are trained. Having one stand-out customer service moment is great but having stand-out customer service every time a customer deals with a company is even better. John Lewis Partners are recognised for their achievements and they listen to their customers' opinions – eg JL Partners now wear name badges as customers stated that they'd like to remember who had helped them. John Lewis' motto is 'Never Knowingly Undersold' aiming to provide the best quality at an affordable price so that customers always receive the best experience possible. Over recent years John Lewis has worked to implement a similarly high standard of customer service in its online customer touchpoints so that the experience of buying from JL is just as enjoyable via ecommerce (on desktop, tablet or smartphone) as it is in-store. Social Media interactions are a key element of John Lewis's total customer service strategy, creating important extra touchpoints for the brand with its customers.

In this section you have been able to read various ways in which a company can use social media for digital branding. In the next section we will further discuss viral marketing.

5.4 Viral marketing, video and games

The ideal for many organisations would be for brand communications to go 'viral'. There are many misconceptions about what 'viral' entails and how it can happen. For this reason, we will discuss this first. We will also examine the most common form of virals: video. Finally, we will look at what role games play in digital marketing communications.

5.4.1   Viral Marketing

In this section we will cover the spread of virals first. Then you will read about how to encourage the message to be passed along. Finally, we will focus on the concept of a viral marketing campaign.

Viral spread

A viral is not a video or a game. It is a way of distributing digital communication expressions, of which the name is derived from the

Viral

dissemination of infectious diseases. An image or a post on social media can also 'go viral'. For example, April Fool's jokes.

Viral spreading can be compared to an epidemic disease outbreak. There are a number of carriers of the virus who rapidly infect other groups of people in their environment. When carriers of the virus then go to other villages they will then, in turn, infect dozens of other people. This could continue indefinitely. The advantage of viral spreading is that little to no budget is required for buying media. Sometimes companies do buy advertisements (such as YouTube ads). By doing this they hope to jump-start the viral effect. A good concept spreads more or less automatically, and thus provides 'earned reach'. Unfortunately, there can be no guarantees. Media purchases in a magazine or banners on a website allows you to create a more or less stable (predicted) reach. A viral provides no such stability (Hufen, 2015).

Promoting sharing

Research from Ketelaar et al. (2016) showed that people are more likely to share a viral if they have a positive attitude regarding the brand, the advertisement itself and viral advertisements in general. They are also more likely to share something they have received from a friend than if they received it from the brand itself. According to Hufen (2015), whether a message is passed on and for how long, is influenced by the following elements:

1 Complexity of the message (keep it short and simple): define the essence of the brand or message and let this play a decisive role within the concept.
2 The message's impact and 'stickiness' (how impressive is the message): this is mainly determined by the content that is used.
3 The message must offer value (serious value or humour). The recipient must be able to predict whether spreading the message is also valuable.
4 Time and place (context) of the expression of the message: this determines the relevance.
5 The network on which the message is being spread: the personal bonds and level of involvement of the community and its members.
6 The characteristics and the power of the channel that is used: large reach/low reach, static/dynamic, monologue/dialogue).

Complexity of the message (the concept)

A good concept for a viral is based on three elements: an objective, a description of the target audience and the characteristics of the organisation or brand.

The target audience should not only be defined quantitatively (in terms of reach), but also qualitatively. What kind of people are they? What does their world look like and what expectations do they have with regard to our company or brand? A viral aimed at young adults is going to be completely different to a viral aimed at mothers.

Finally, the brand or organisation's defining characteristics should be carefully considered. Ideally, this is recorded in a mission statement or slogan. For example, Philips' 'Innovation & You'; in essence, this is what Philips' brand should be known for. Sometimes the origin of a concept is

Stickiness

not so much the brand, but rather a message. In this case, you must analyse what the essence of that message should be: what is it that needs to be conveyed to the consumer, what should they 'take out' and more importantly: what do we want them to say about it to other people? For example, Momodo's viral from section 5.1.3 – The DNA Journey, was designed to give the message 'travel with an open mind' some emotional gravity. A golden rule in communication is: 'keep it short and simple'.

5.4.2 Video

In the words of Forrester (2012), a well-known Internet research agency: "If a picture is worth a thousand words, then a one-minute video is worth 1.8 million words." Videos lend themselves very well to telling a brand's story. It is less suited to attracting visitors directly to your website or app. What can be done, is to draw people to your sales channel by showing them an advertisement after they have watched your video.

There are several reasons for video being so popular and thus being very suitable as a marketing tool:

Video

- People are naturally drawn to video because there are usually faces to be seen in them.
- Emotions are contagious and, compared to text or static images, video is more suitable for conveying emotions.
- Video is a rich medium that allows for the transmission of a lot of information using both images and sound.
- Video is linear and therefore can tell a story and create an experience. There is a beginning and an end, and it is difficult to switch between different parts of content, which is much more easily done in textual content.

With more than 10 million views, 'The Netherlands welcomes Donald Trump in his own words' from the VPRO programme Zondag met Lubach, is one of the most successful ever Dutch virals. The video was met with a lot of response (http://bit.ly/2pIXUxe)

Viral videos tend to start off with an extremely high number of views, after which the effect slowly wears off. Moreover, extensive research by Tucker (2014) found that there is a strong negative relationship between the amount of times a viral ad is viewed, and its capacity to convince. This means that the effect on sales can even be negative. Viral videos are

Viral videos

often shared because they verge on the extreme. That is exactly what makes them less convincing. Tucker calculated that videos with more than 3 or 4 million views usually don't lead to an increase in sales. What apparently does work, is humour. Funny videos can generate a large number of views and still be convincing. Also, videos that people have commented on appear to be an exception to the rule.

Popularity ration

Juxtaposed to viral videos, are video messages that are not shared quickly, but that are successful in the long term. These can be found using the feature 'related videos'. These can be videos with 'substance' that contribute to thought leadership. An indicator for the popularity of a video in the long term is the popularity ration. The higher this ratio, the longer lasting the effect of the video. A truly viral video will not score highly on this ratio as most of the shares will occur in the first 10 days.

$$\text{Popularity ratio} \ = \ \frac{\text{Number of views in 2}^{nd}\text{ month}}{\text{Number of views in first 10 days}}$$

Within digital marketing communication, video can be used in many different ways, for example:
- as part of a website or on YouTube, such as product demos by GoPro users (http://bit.ly/2FSm75p) and instructional videos by home improvement retailer B&Q (http://bit.ly/2pkeE80)
- as a medium for digital branding
- at a product introduction, such as 'Stroll', a video commercial to introduce Apple AirPods and the iPhone 7+ that was viewed 10 million times on YouTube within the space of 2 months
- as part of other digital marketing communications, such as in display advertisements and on the landing page in email marketing

Pre-roll
- as an advertisement in other videos, like in a pre-roll: an advertisement shown before another video on websites such as YouTube or Vimeo

Branded content
- as branded content on another website, like Harvard Business Review that publishes interviews with authors for the purpose of encouraging people to want to read the original article. An informative example can be found at http://bit.ly/2tUsyDn

Often, the results of a video are remarkably better than from a text or images. Dell for instance received 109% more response using an animation in an email.
Most videos are posted on YouTube, which attracts more than one billion unique visitors every month, regardless of whether they are intended to be viral or not.

5.4.3 Games
Because the gaming industry also brings brands to the attention of consumers, the topic 'games' merits consideration in this chapter as well. We'll first take a look at how games can be used as a digital marketing communication tool. Then we will briefly discuss the unique qualities that games possess.

Games as a digital marketing communication tool

Since the emergence of the gaming industry, games have been used to bring brands to the attention of consumers. The following ways exist to convey a message within a game:

- product placement: presence of a product in the gaming world
- in-game advertising: logos and messages on billboards, bus shelters, etc.
- branded content: scripted events or power-ups sponsored by brands
- visually adapted games: existing games visually adapted to the brand's corporate identity
- advergame: a custom game that fully reflects the brand or organisation's brand values and objectives (Hufen, 2015)

An example of *product placement* is the Diesel add-on in The Sims 4. By installing this add-on, the player can use Diesel clothing and furniture in their 'world'. So the virtual version of the product has a 'real' function within the game.

Games

Product placement

In-game advertising

Branded content

Visually adapted games

Advergame

Another example of product placement: BMW in the PlayStation game Gran Turismo 6

In-game advertising is often used in sports and racing games. Especially within sports games by Electronic Arts, such as the FIFA series, billboards are visible along the pitch or racing track just as they are in real life.

Branded content is often seen in the form of a special car, an avatar that you can unlock, or as animation within a game. Examples are the Red Bull prototype car in Gran Turismo and also Nissan's online competition in this game.

Visually adapted games are existing games such as Angry Birds, Candy Crush or Bejewelled, that are adapted to using the signature colours of a particular brand.

A good example of an *advergame* is illustrated in Example 5.2 with the game Aviation Empire, created by game developer Little Chicken from Amsterdam.

5

5

Advergame Aviation Empire by KLM

Aviation Empire is a game in which the target audience can relive KLM's history. The game is not only fun for children but also for their parents. It is a strategy game and can be played both online and offline (on board of the aeroplane). The aim of the game is to build an as large as possible worldwide empire by increasing turnover and customer satisfaction. This can be done by building more runways, buying more aircrafts and organising more flights, but you will also need to continuously invest in customer facilities to keep them happy.

The game is free to play and is used to reach a new audience; people who have not yet flown with KLM but do like gaming. In addition to the game there is also a comprehensive Facebook page where they engage with users. The game has been downloaded in more than 130 countries by over 550,000 consumers and is continuously being updated with new content. This game is a textbook example of how games can contribute towards brand experience. After all, during the average playing time of 20 minutes (each time the consumer plays the game), a much better story can be told than during a 20 second commercial.

KLM game Aviation Empire

In digital marketing communication, the game will often be used as (part of) the landing page or on social media. In the digital marketing funnel, games especially have a part in the awareness and capture phases. The product is perfectly suited to make people aware of the brand and its values and to then excite and motivate them to strengthen ties with the brand. Thus it can also play a role in the funnel's loyalty phase.

© Noordhoff Uitgevers bv

Unique features of games

Games possess a number of unique features that make them very suitable as a marketing communications tool.

- Games are fun. Consumers are already happy and optimistic as they come into contact with the brand message.
- Games are played voluntarily.
- The game has the consumer's undivided attention. This means the message will be more likely to stick.
- A game is interactive and makes use of multiple senses. This intensifies the experience of the message.

A good game is played for hours, days, weeks or even years, either alone or together. Games such as FarmVille especially, require social interaction between friends and acquaintances in the player's network; this enriches the gameplay and provides a topic for conversation.

A good, digitally-savvy ad agency will be able to recommend an appropriate concept that is rooted in consumer needs and that matches the organisation's unique brand characteristics and their core competences (Hufen, 2015).

5.5 Content marketing

The previous paragraphs have introduced you to all kinds of marketing tools that can help to increase brand value and lay solid foundations for further marketing activities. In this section we will first examine what content marketing is, namely a different way of thinking. After that, we will discuss a step-by-step approach to content marketing.

5.5.1 Content marketing is a different way of thinking

Content marketing is not a separate tool, but an overarching way of thinking. Content marketing is the creation, supply and distribution of content, using a considered mix of online and offline resources in which the content meets a predetermined requirement. This facilitates the creation of new relationships and nurtures and strengthens existing ones, with the direct or indirect aim being to increase profits. The shortened version of this definition is easier to remember: *attracting and retaining customers with relevant information.* You attract customers by creating content that responds to their questions and needs.

Content marketing

Suppose someone uses Google to search for a good book about marketing. They read a review on your blog and end up in your online bookstore. In this review he finds a list of other publications on this topic and links to reviews of this book elsewhere on the web. For him, that is relevant information. The visitor opens some links, checks other online sources, but eventually buys the book in your ecommerce store. Why? You provided this visitor with content that had added value. The customer has a good feeling about your website and feels you are deserving of their purchase. That is what content marketing is all about.

The Content Marketing Institute has as its mission, 'to advance the practice of content marketing, through online education, print, and in-person events'. Its founder is Joe Pulizzi.

An article about content marketing by the website's founder Joe Pulizzi

Social content

Social content is a compound of 'social media' and 'content marketing' and involves sharing content on social media platforms. In practice you will find that this term is sometimes used by marketers in a much broader sense.

Content Marketing is widely used by companies in the business-to-business market but is also increasingly used in consumer marketing. On the one hand it is used as a tool for 'branding', to influence the audience's brand attitude, on the other hand it is used to generate leads.

An example of a company that is very active in digital branding and content marketing is the World-Wide Fund for Nature. The WWF offers fun, low-threshold, positive content via Facebook, Instagram and Twitter and has a live stream on YouTube where you can watch animals.

WWF chooses to be positive on Instagram

Providing content for free works well. Still, many companies are afraid to do so. For example, Consultancy firms may feel that by sharing knowledge for free they will erode their own market. With this knowledge, customers could perhaps solve their own problems and the consultants would become obsolete. In practice however, this seems to be a misplaced fear. Having viewed the content, website visitors will understand what the company does and how knowledgeable they are. Often, larger consultancy firms give away free information regularly. In exchange for this information they ask the website visitors to leave their details, so they can assess whether it's worthwhile to contact them. This is how they generate leads: a **Leads** list of potential customers.

The nice thing about content marketing is that, as a digital marketer, you are communicating with your target audience, without forcing someone to buy something from you. The consumers are in control; they determine what content is of value to them. They will take the initiative to get in touch with an organisation in a way that suits them best. After that, it is up to the digital marketer and/or the sales team to convert site visitors who are not yet customers (leads) into actual customers. This is called lead nurturing. **Lead nurturing**

Where once money was charged for valuable information, it is now increasingly often shared for free. Meanwhile, revenue is generated by selling goods and services. Figure 5.5 illustrates what the new revenue model regarding content looks like today.

FIGURE 5.5 The changing earnings model for content

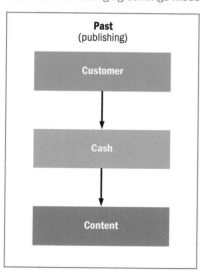
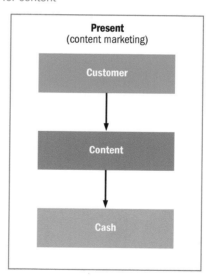

Of course, there are many organisations that do make money from information. Consider market research bureaus or newspapers. They cannot give away everything for free. They often provide a brief impression (or sample) of the available information, for example in an infographic or by displaying the first paragraph of an article. Those who are interested in knowing more will have to pay. The free content is a kind of 'teaser', a way to entice people into buying. In this case, this involves buying the entire research report or downloading the full article. Partially sharing information is also content marketing.

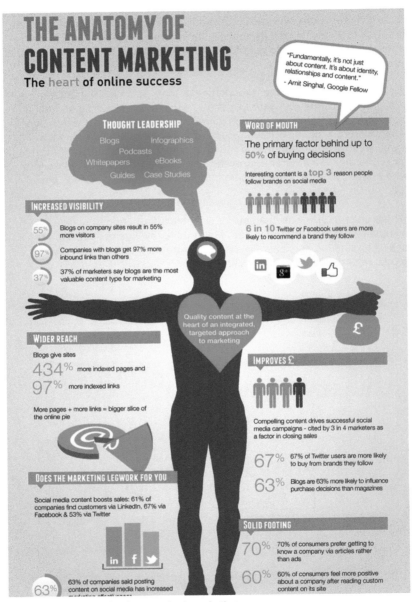

Example of infographic about content marketing

5.5.2   A step-by-step approach to content marketing

Content Marketing is conducted according to the content marketing cycle (see figure 5.6):

Content marketing cycle

1 researching the information needs of your potential customers
2 determining the objectives, themes and approach
3 creating content
4 promoting content
5 measuring and evaluating
6 adjusting

FIGURE 5.6 The content marketing cycle

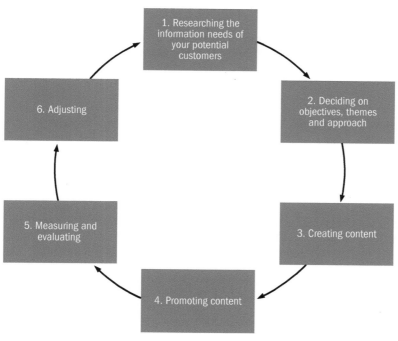

Source: Jeff Bullas, 2014

1 Researching the information needs of your potential customers

Before you begin assembling the content marketing plan, it is important to make a good assessment of the information needs of your potential customers. To assess this, you can; use existing market research, analyse what's being discussed on social media or survey your existing customers on their buying behaviour.

Based on this study, many organisations create 'customer personas'. These are fictional descriptions of their ideal customers, drawn up using existing customers' profiles and behaviour. For more on this, see section 10.2. A customer persona can help you to adapt your content in accordance with the customers' wishes and requirements in terms of knowledge, information needs and 'tone of voice', tailoring the language

Tone of voice

you use to the customer. By formulating customer personas, you are able to identify target audiences and what characterises them.

It is also important to describe the '*customer journey*'. These are the various experiences that a customer has throughout the process of orientation, the purchase of a product or service and when making use of it.
How do they orient themselves? Where do they get their information? What sources do they consult? How is their final decision made? This information is very useful, because if you understand the journey customers make, you are better able to guide them towards your company or brand and retain them in future. More on 'customer journey mapping' can be found in sub section 4.4.1.

Carlijn Postma is the owner of The Post, an agency which specialises in content marketing. She comments:
For a television show, the viewers – the audience – are the most important target. Content marketing is also focused on the audience.

'It is essential for the public to want it. The public decides whether or not they want to be an audience and whether you are relevant. Content marketing means translating everything you do into content in order to get your story up on that stage. This means text, video and sound. Meaning you need to have readers, viewers and listeners. That is your audience. If you aren't relevant, the message isn't delivered. This is why we turn a description of a target segment into a description of an audience. They are essentially different. The essence is: what can we talk about together? Many organisations find this difficult as they can't control it. They are from the '80s, but times have changed. Either people no longer see or no longer hear you and – if you are no longer relevant – they will get rid of you.'

The art of content marketing is to connect to the audience's experience at various times: during working hours, free time, sports or at home in the evenings.

'The audience goes on a journey from the first moment of their need for information until they become a loyal audience. The question is: within what sphere of experience can you as a brand ensure you are relevant to your audience and that they are receptive to your information? That is what you must look for', according to Postma. She was able to define five different spheres of experience, each demanding a different type of content. For instance, 'someone in my environment died recently' might suggest content about funerals. Triggers that arise in this sphere of experience and leave room for content could be: what do I want my funeral to look like? Or: how do you comfort someone that has just lost a loved one? Postma: 'If you create content, you need to make sure that it reaches people's sphere of experience. By explicitly mentioning this, you will know what is relevant.'

Source: Frank.news (2017)

2 Determining the objectives, themes and approach

Successful content marketing begins with creating a content marketing plan. This should include the following components:

- objectives and communications target audiences
- themes that you want to pay attention to
- topics that will be discussed within those themes
- the tools that you will use (ie, a whitepaper or blog)
- channels that you are going to use to draw attention to your content (email, social media, etc.)
- how you plan to encourage the readers of your content to become customers
- a planning or content marketing calendar (content calendar)

Content marketing plan

Content calendar

In addition, there are three key success factors:
1 Seek authority using 'thought leadership'
2 Use 'storytelling'
3 Ensure consistency and continuity

Continuity and consistency is a requirement for actually achieving something with content marketing. If an organisation does not regularly present itself to the target audience or does not consistently profile itself in the same way, then there will be a confusing picture (or none at all) of what the organisation stands for.

In the content plan, the digital marketer must illustrate in detail how their organisation's information will be published via the various online channels as succinctly as possible.

Content plan

3 Creating content

The content itself and the tone of voice must appeal to the target audience. In Chapter 11 you will find many tips on effective digital communications. A basic question is the type of instrument that is used.

Examples of instruments are:
- information on the brand's own website
- blogs
- posts on social media
- infographics
- whitepapers and e-books
- messages and contributions towards discussions on social media
- videos
- visuals (also consider Pinterest and Instagram)
- presentations (eg on SlideShare)
- webinars
- audio, such as podcasts and music

Organisations sometimes create content together with their customers. Consider for example video reports on long-distance travels or book reviews. Co-creation enhances the credibility of the content and underpins the organisation's authority.

Content curation

A simple method of creating content is content curation. Content curation is simply finding and sharing interesting, relevant content. This could be a blog post, a whitepaper, a tweet or an inspirational website. Content curation is most effective if you supply the content that you share together with your own insights, such as your professional opinion, an analysis or an interpretation. This contributes to your thought leadership. Preferably, these findings are then shared via social media.

Content spinning

Content spinning is the re-using of the same content. In this, it is important to not only rewrite this content, but to adapt it to the various formats. An identical message can be delivered in an infographic as well as in a video. Make sure to take your target audience into account, the channel (medium) and the perspective that the content is coming from. If you tailor the content to these factors customers are less likely to get the idea that they are being spammed with identical content. In that case, content spinning could actually be contra-productive.

4 Promoting content

Making online purchases and obtaining information almost always begins with using a search engine like Google. By using the right content in that search engine, you can get your website, product or service to stick in the minds of your potential customers. Google is becoming increasingly better at recognising unique and relevant content. As a digital marketer, search engine optimisation (SEO) can be used to stay one step ahead of the competition. You should also find out what social media platforms are used by your target audience. Consider, for example, Facebook, Twitter, Pinterest and LinkedIn.

Blogging

Blogging is also a good way of marketing content. Google indexes Blog entries. This is very interesting insofaras SEO is concerned, because

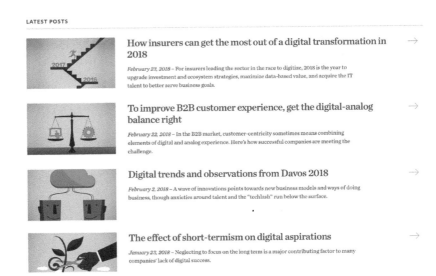

McKinsey's expresses their take on Digital through the means of blogs

Google loves news and regularly updated content on your website. Blogs can also be easily shared on social media. Moreover, blog content remains online permanently. Blogs also contribute towards your thought leadership. Customers can begin to view your ideas and opinions as iconic for an industry or niche. On the website (http://bit.ly/2DBAzwJ), we see 'thought leadership' content from McKinsey (2018). They are effectively giving away valuable content to their key B2B audience and in so doing, positioning themselves as thought leaders.

The different techniques of content promotion are becoming much more advanced. It is possible to draw attention to contextual information. You might consider providing a whitepaper about data security along with news about 'big data'. Location-specific content is also being created (people from London will be shown different videos than people from Manchester) as is target-related content (companies are offered a different whitepaper from governmental organisations). Content is becoming increasingly sophisticated and tailored to its the recipients.

Content promotion

7 Principles of effective content

Effective content meets the following criteria:
1 authentic
2 consistent
3 comprehensible
4 targeted
5 interactive
6 shareable
7 accessible

5 and 6 Measuring, evaluating and adjusting

The results of content marketing are continuously measured. Some of the things you will assess as a digital marketer are:
- Content use: how many people read or see it, how often do they come back, what channels do they use?
- Sharing your content: who shares it, how and when do they do this, what do they share most often?
- The acquired customers: how many leads are generated using which tools and channels, how many leads are converted into customers, how much revenue is generated?
- The effect on the brand: what are the results regarding brand awareness and brand attitude, how often and in what way do people talk about the brand or company?

Based on such data, the digital marketer evaluates the content marketing plan and continually adjusts it where necessary.

Now that you understand the role of digital marketing communication within brand management, you will be able to read about how to contact customers online in the next chapter.

Questions and assignments

NOW CHECK YOUR UNDERSTANDING:

5.1   Here is another example of imaginative Content Marketing. In Australia, Coca-Cola had lost relevance among young Australians and sales were flat. In this now famous campaign, they decided to personalise the Coca-Cola can and bottle!

Coca Cola added the 150 most popular first names to their cans and bottles, changing their biggest piece of advertising real estate. Supporting tactics from traditional to digital platforms rolled out from there: #ShareA-Coke hashtag, apps, an interactive website, outdoor billboards, interactive kiosks in top city centres and more.

Coca-Cola crowdsourced content: Customers contributed digital content for the #ShareACoke campaign. From this first campaign, in Australia alone, Coke earned 12 million media impressions, a 7% increase in young adult consumption and a 4% increase in sales across the category. Coca-Cola has extended the campaign into nearly 60 markets since launch and have continued to add additional tactics. A recent extension to the campaign is that Coke started selling personalized bottles and merchandise.

a What are Coca-Cola's digital marketing target audiences?
b To what phase of the digital marketing funnel do the users who daily visit the website belong?
c If Coca-Cola wanted to make people more aware of the meaning of the brand (brand associations), what do you think would be the most appropriate marketing communication tools? Support your answer.
d What are the issues for Coca-Cola when it communicates both offline and online? How well do they integrate the two?

5.2   Choose a brand that really appeals to you and that you are able to find sufficient information about online. Conduct an audit of how this brand uses digital marketing communication in order to:
a Strengthen their brand identity: brand salience
b Give the brand meaning: brand performance and brand imagery
c Create a response to the brand: brand judgements and brand feelings
d Encourage brand relationships: brand resonance

5.3   As is stated in section 5.3, there are four different ways that a brand can use social media for brand communications. Formulate a recommendation for the educational institution where you are enrolled (or the organisation you work in) regarding the use of social media within brand management, whereby new students/course participants are the target audience.

© Noordhoff Uitgevers bv

5.4 In the Game Gallery on redbull.com (games.redbull.com) there are several different branded games. Red Bull markets 'energy drinks' and links its brand to youth culture, extreme sports and adventure-related sports, ie activities that require a lot of energy. Red Bull is averse to traditional marketing. The organisation uses 'buzz' and word-of-mouth advertising.

a Explain what role games play in Red Bull's brand strategy.

b Does the game Red Bull Racers (see games.redbull.com) involve any of the following?
 • product placement
 • in-game advertising
 • branded content
 • a visually adapted game
 • an advergame
 Support your answer.

c Red Bull regularly records videos with the aim of putting their brand in the spotlight. Today there are several videos to be viewed on the Red Bull channel on YouTube. The videos are very successful as viral marketing expressions. Watch the five most popular videos. How can this success be explained? Support your answer using this book's theory.

5.5 IBM is one of the world's leading companies in the field of information technology. In 2015, IBM introduced the slogan 'Welcome to the Cognitive Era'. To inform as many people about this subject as possible and to get them involved, IBM used content marketing.

a Explain why content marketing is important to an organisation like IBM.

b Perform a search on 'Welcome to the Cognitive Era' and find out what IBM has done with regard to content marketing concerning this theme. Which of the following instruments did IBM use?
 • information on their own website
 • blogs
 • infographics
 • whitepapers and e-books
 • posting and contributing towards discussions on social media
 • videos
 • visuals (also consider Pinterest and Instagram)
 • presentations (eg on SlideShare)
 • webinars
 • audio, such as podcasts and music
 • press releases

c Keeping in mind the success factors of content marketing as described in section 5.5, what is your opinion on the way IBM has used content marketing?

5

5.6

Digital Branding Patagonia
By Marjolein Visser

Patagonia is a US-based globally renowned brand in outdoor sportswear, they consider social responsibility to be of paramount importance. Patagonia's mission is 'to make the best product, without doing unnecessary damage, do business to inspire and implement solutions to the ecological crisis'. Patagonia takes a clear stand against the society of disposability. A well-known example is their campaign on Black Friday in 2011 that included the message that it is best not to buy Patagonia's best-selling product (see the following figure), but to continue to use, repair or recycle an existing jacket.

Campaign 'Don't buy this jacket' in 2011

In 2017, all Patagonia's profits from Black Friday were donated to charitable causes (USD 10 million). The idea came from an internal creative team that was given the necessary freedom from the top to act quickly and effectively. 'There was no time to make the message more noncommittal or to dwell on the approach too long,' says Digital Marketing & Social Media Manager Scott Carington. 'We just did it, and the results were amazing.' Sales were five times higher than usual. Patagonia also has the policy of donating 1% of their turnover or 10% of the profit, whichever is the higher, to groups that are concerned with the environment.

Another example of how Patagonia promotes environmental awareness is the 'Worn Wear' campaign where consumers are encouraged to have their clothes repaired or to sell them on. The additional message is that Patagonia is a socially responsible business, but certainly does not compromise on quality. They also repair sportswear from other brands.

Worn Wear campaign on Instagram

Patagonia's brand story leads to a strong 'brand resonance' in the more luxury focused, socially-conscious consumers that make up Patagonia's target audience. Their average customers are young males, married, well-educated and with a reasonable income. As you can see in table 5.2, for customers in the United States, the information channel with the most coverage are websites. However, magazines, TV, radio and apps are also important for reaching them. Of these five media types, TV has the most relevance for the target segment. Digital branding is important for Patagonia, as part of cross-channel communication.

TABLE 5.2 Media use of Patagonia customers in the United States

	Reach	Popularity	Relevance
Websites	84.46	121.3	147.41
Magazines	50.49	168.84	178.73
TV	33.05	97.57	131.28
Radio	27.40	129.53	152.29
Apps	25.36	25.4	83.18
Newspapers	10.57	180.19	183.40

Source: http://customer-profile.com

Research into relevant websites among Patagonia customers shows that they are particularly interested in websites about the environment and about technology, travel, art, sports, education and culture. Search engines are very important for the reach in this target segment. On Patagonia's blog, The Cleanest Line, you can read stories about the environment, but also other topics about which the brand has a clear opinion, such as how political leaders deal with ecological issues. Patagonia has a large number of social media followers: Instagram has just over 3 million followers, Facebook has more than 1 million and YouTube has nearly 90,000 fans. Patagonia uses social media to direct people to their blogs, not directly to stimulate online sales.

Senior marketing manager Europe Jelle Mul says in an interview with MarketingTribune: 'We want to inform the consumer what we stand for, what we have to offer and what to consider when making purchasing decisions. Our relationship with the media is extremely important to us. We have so much content with no commercial background and the media helps us enormously to communicate this and thus create more awareness among consumers.'

Patagonia has an impressive list of ambassadors (www.patagonia.com/ambassadors), who in turn provide the necessary online publicity. Examples are the legendary surfer and sailor Liz Clark and mountaineer Tommy Caldwell. Millions of people watched his ascent of El Capitan's Dawn Wall in Yosemite National Park, both in a video by Patagonia and in videos by, for example, National Geographic. In this way, Patagonia works at building brand awareness and brand knowledge among athletes who are not yet familiar with them.

Sources: www.investopedia.com,
www.marketingtribune.nl, http://epicprgroup.com and
http://customer-profile.com

a What are Patagonia's digital marketing communication target segments?

b At which stage of the digital marketing communication funnel are the approximately 4 million people who visit the website every month?

c As you were able to read in section 5.3, there are four ways that brands can use social media for brand communication. Which way did Patagonia choose?

d According to the theory, what are the most suitable marketing communication tools in each of these phases? Does Patagonia use these instruments? Do you agree with their approach or do you see points for improvement? Support your answer with the help of the theory.

e Patagonia is strongly committed to content marketing. If you look at the success factors for content marketing in section 5.5, how do you explain their success? Do you also see points for improvement? Please substantiate your answer.

f Make an inventory of how Patagonia uses digital marketing communication in each of the phases of brand building. Indicate what the brand does to:
- to strengthen the brand identity: brand salience
- giving meaning to the brand: brand performance and brand imagery
- create brand response: brand judgments and brand feelings
- encourage brand relationships: brand resonance

g Would games be a good addition to the range of digital marketing communication tools that Patagonia uses for digital branding? Give arguments based on the theory.

h Patagonia regularly creates videos with the aim of drawing attention to their brand. For example, there are several videos on the Patagonia channel on YouTube. Are these videos successful as viral marketing communications? If so, what explains that success? If not, what can Patagonia improve? Base your arguments on the theory from this book.

5

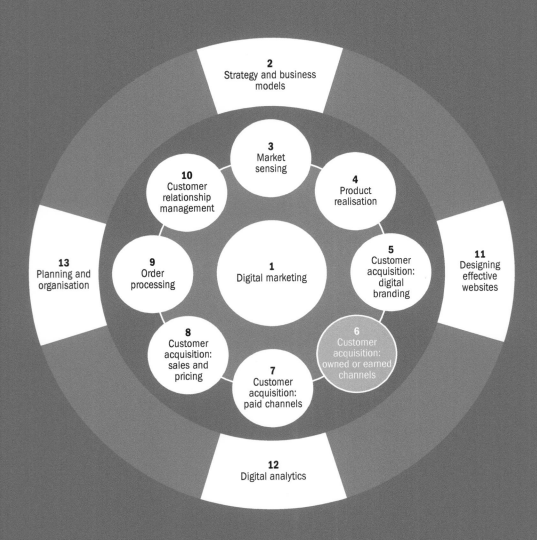

6

Customer Acquisition: recruiting visitors through owned or earned channels

Authors: Marjolein Visser (6.1 and 6.4), Martijn Hoving (6.2), Co van Kempen & Matthijs Jansen (6.3), Martin Kloos (6.5) and Robin van Ommen (6.6)

The previous chapters describe how the marketer acquires a good understanding of the target audience's wants and needs (the market sensing process) and how they can use the Internet for the development and improvement of products as well as for the setting up of processes surrounding the product or the service (the product realisation process). When everything is ready to receive customers, it's time for the market approach. The customer acquisition process consists of defining target markets and recruiting new customers. The recruitment of customers takes place in four steps: marketing communication to bring the brand to attention, marketing communication to connect with the customer, using the sales process to convince customers to buy the product and agreeing on the price of the product. In the previous chapter, you read more about the role of digital marketing communication in brand management. This chapter describes how to use your owned and earned digital marketing communication channels to connect with customers. A digital marketer first ensures that their owned and earned communication channels are in order before implementing paid marketing communications. Paid channels will be discussed in Chapter 7 and the sales process and price determination in Chapter 8.

This chapter will cover:
- recruiting visitors
- search engine marketing
- link-building
- mobile marketing communication
- deployment of owned social media channels
- email marketing

After studying this chapter, you will be able to:
- identify which owned and earned digital marketing communication channels can be used to recruit visitors
- explain the steps in the funnel process for search engine marketing
- explain the role of link-building and content and how to achieve a high positioning within search engines' results pages
- indicate which specific mobile marketing communication techniques can be used in digital marketing communications
- indicate how the digital marketer can successfully deploy owned and earned social media channels and pages for customer acquisition
- formulate objectives for email marketing and show the requirements email marketing needs to meet to be successful

6.1 Recruiting visitors for digital communication and sales channels

As you have read in the previous chapters, the ultimate goal of digital marketing communication is to sell products, services or ideas to customers of the organisation. For each marketing campaign, the market, product and communications managers make a detailed plan that elaborates on all steps in the acquisition process. Online customer acquisition begins with the first step of the digital marketing funnel: motivate the target segment to visit an online sales channel (see figure 6.1).

FIGURE 6.1 'Visit' is the first step of the digital marketing funnel

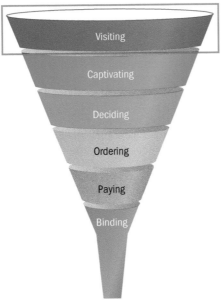

Source: © Marjolein Visser RM

In terms of the digital marketing communications funnel, creating 'awareness' of the existence of the online sales channel as well as 'capture', will lead to visits (see figure 5.1). They can also play a supporting role in 'conversion' and 'loyalty'.

A website or app can function as an online sales channel, but sales can also be made on social media. The buying of products in an app, is called in-app purchasing. Organisations can also sell products on social media. For example, craftsmen and artists sell their work from an account on Etsy. com. The first three steps of the digital marketing communications funnel are then followed on the social media channel: awareness, capture and conversion. Organisations that do not have online sales channels use websites, apps, and social media to interact with their audience and generate leads. The online communication channels convince the visitors to visit the offline sales channels. In this case, it is also important to recruit visitors for the online communication channels.

In-app purchasing

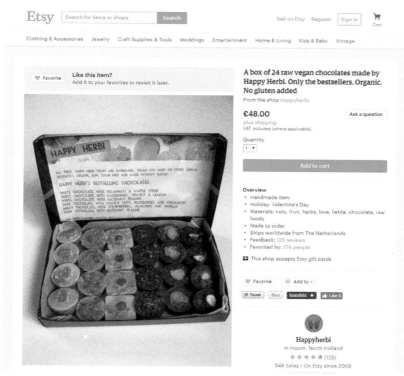

Happyberri globally sells handmade chocolates on Etsy.com

Recruiting visitors for online sales and communication channels can be done via:
- *owned media*, such as email and social media accounts
- *earned media*, such as search engine results, links and third-party social media channels
- *paid media*, such as online advertising (display and paid search) and affiliate marketing

We will focus on the first two possibilities here; lead generation and customer acquisition via paid media are discussed in Chapter 7.

6.2 Search Engine

Recruiting visitors for online communication and sales channels begins with making sure these channels are discoverable. In this section we will discuss the two main forms of search engine marketing (SEO and PPC). After which we will move on to search engine usage and behaviour.

6.2.1 Main types of Search Marketing

Search engines Search engines are as old as the Internet itself and are the most widely used gateway to the vast amount of information found on the Internet today. Here are the global shares of web searches:

TABLE 6.1 Market share of search engines in 2017

Google	91.74%
Bing	2.76%
Yahoo!	1.83%
Baidu (mainly China)	1.39%
YANDEX RU (mainly Russia)	0.58%
Shenma (mobile only; mainly China)	0.45%

Source: Statcounter, 2018

Worldwide, there are more than 167 billion searches on Google per month. Since 2015, more than half of these searches take place on a smartphone (Searchengineland.com, 2015). Searching behaviour has migrated from desktops to smartphones. Search engines are an important part of the digital marketing communications mix.

Search engine marketing The definition of search engine marketing is 'the marketing of products or services via search engines'. It has two main forms:
1 Search Engine Optimisation (SEO)
2 Paid Search (ie Pay-Per-Click, PPC)

Search marketing is a form of 'pull marketing': the prospect enters a search query on Google and are shown an ad or search result, leading them to come into contact with a product or service. Partly since search engine marketing is 'pull marketing', it is a relatively inexpensive and potentially highly effective way of marketing. Although free listing in search engine results seems more attractive than search engine advertising, both forms may be cost-effective. The cost of a visitor 'purchased' through paid search ads is often relatively low (depending on the industry sector). Because the visitor has performed a specific search, they are likely to be interested in what you offer and belong to your target audience. Which form of search engine marketing is best for an organisation, depends on the campaign goals, the current popularity **Page rank** (page rank) of the website and also the available budget.

We will now discuss the two main forms of search marketing and consider the advantages and disadvantages of both forms.

Search Engine Optimisation (SEO).

Search Engine Optimisation is the optimisation of a website for certain searches, so that a page from the website ranks as highly as possible in the natural search engine results. Search Engine Optimisation is also referred to as SEO. There are several factors that influence the position of a search term in the natural (also called organic) search results. Search Engine Optimisation is nothing more than influencing these factors. For example, when building a website, you should already be considering the search terms that the target segment will use. You can also target certain keywords (search queries) in search engines, eg by creating a piece of content that is aimed at that specific search query.

SEO
Search Engine Optimisation

In addition to the content, the authority of a website is of interest to Google. A major factor in this is the number of links from external sites that are made to the site and the relevance of these links. Other influential factors are:

Popularity

- a safe HTTPS connection to your website instead of an insecure HTTP connection
- speed: ie the website's loading time; slow loading has a negative effect
- having a domain name that includes the given search term

Search Engine Optimisation (SEO) is a comprehensive and complex activity which requires up-to-date knowledge of search engines and technology as well as writing and marketing skills. The result is a (hopefully prominent) position (ranking) in the natural (= organic) search results.

Natural or organic search results

6

In addition to text, web pages can also contain other types of information such as videos, images, news items, tweets and blogs. Search engines have developed techniques for these types of information and offer separate search tools for understanding these types of content. We often see videos and images integrated in the search results. On a mobile phone we also see apps in the search results. When 'local searches' (such as 'plumber' or 'mechanic') are performed, you often see a box with contact details for local businesses in the search results. Google Maps will then show the locations of the businesses. Organisations can use Google My Business to arrange this for themselves.

Local searches

Google expands features within Google My Business. Google Posts was introduced in 2017, allowing organisations to post messages directly in Google's search results. Digital marketers can, for example, publish campaigns, news and events. These then appear on the right-hand side of the search engine results page.

In section 7.2, we discuss the popularity (authority) component of Search Engine Optimisation. In Chapter 11 you can read more about building an effective website and practical information about how to optimise the site (ie to do SEO).

Search Marketing: organic (natural) search results outlined in green and paid search engine ads outlined in red

Paid Search or Pay-Per-Click (PPC).

PPC is the placing of ads that are shown if and only if someone types in a specific pre-purchased keyword. On Google, these are called 'Google AdWords PPC ads'.

For each click on an ad, the advertiser pays Google a sum of money which depends on, among other things, the bids from the competition and their own maximum bid (=willingness to pay) on the chosen word. Ads are ranked according to the 'Google Ad Auction'. For example: a popular search phrase is 'car insurance'. The advertiser offers Google €12 per click to (they hope) be at the top of the Google results page. The advertiser only pays when the ad is actually clicked.

Paid Search
Pay-Per-Click
PPC
Google AdWords
PPC ads

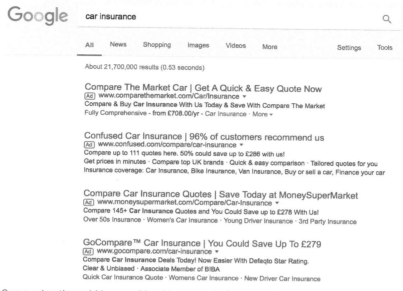

Some advertisers bid a considerable amount of money to be at the top of the results list

The results of PPC are generally easily measurable, especially in ecommerce. Models can be tweaked to work towards a maximum number of conversions at an optimum cost. In section 7.2 we will elaborate on Paid Search advertising.

A good digital marketing communication strategy includes both Search Engine Optimisation and Paid Search Advertising (PPC). It is advisable to begin with PPC, because this quickly establishes which keywords do well (ie attract searches and clicks) and lead to the desired goal (the conversion). This set of keywords can then be used in the Search Engine Optimisation process. Keywords that achieve the best results in Google AdWords in terms of conversion to customers, can then be placed on Web pages, leading to the better rankings in organic results.

Direct Line Insurance Group plc is a UK insurance company. Founded in 1984, as the country's first 'direct' (ie not via an insurance broker) car insurance company, it has since expanded to offer a range of general insurance products online as well as by telephone. Direct Line has learned from AdWords that consumers who want the best insurance provider for their needs, often search for the phrase 'car insurance'. Direct Line has ensured that the company is also easily found organically. However Direct Line also advertises with Google AdWords (PPC), bidding on the most relevant keywords. In this way, Direct Line has achieved the greatest visibility in search results for this keyword, leaving less room for its competitors. More about PPC can be found in section 7.2.

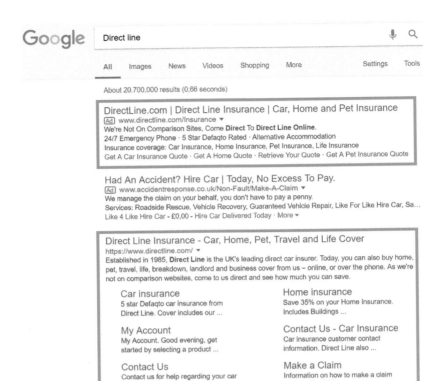

Direct Line is also easily found organically, next to paid search (both outlined in red)

Advantages and disadvantages of SEO and PPC.
The benefits of SEO are:
- You don't have to pay Google for these visitors.
- Increased likelihood of being found often means more traffic.

Disadvantages of SEO are:
- It takes a relatively long time before there are positive results.
- SEO is relatively labour-intensive.
- The % of ads in the search results is increasing, meaning there are fewer organic results on the results page.

Advantages of PPC are:
- It can generate real results rapidly.
- There are clear costs/benefits ie generally easy to evaluate return on investment (ROI).
- There are many possibilities to test, measure and learn.
- There is a lot of freedom customising the ads.

Disadvantages of PPC are:
- You are charged per visitor (per clickthrough to your landing page) even if this leads nowhere.
- Increased competition can increase the price (ie can start a bidding war).
- Once the campaign has ended, traffic disappears!

6.2.2   Search engine use and behaviour

To be easily found, it is important for digital marketers to know what the search behaviour of their audience is. The way people search is changeable. It changes because of experience, but also according to the technology that is available. This is what we will discuss in this paragraph.

Research into search behaviour.

Search engines and search results are as changeable as the weather. This makes thorough research into search engine use a major challenge. There are various scientific studies that give us some insight into search behaviour, search popularity and the effect on brands:

Search behaviour

- People who use common search phrases (keywords) click on fewer search results per query than people who use less popular search phrases. 'Low involvement' products generate fewer clicks per search in comparison to 'high involvement' products. Finally, for the most popular search phrases, the user tends to focus more on organic results instead of paid search engine ads (Jerath et al., 2014). If marketers are selling products or services that people often search for, but in which they have low interest, they should ensure that their website is seen as quickly as possible by their target segment. Their potential customers are not motivated to sustain their search over a long period of time. These brand owners need to have their Search Engine Marketing in perfect order!
- For an online retailer, quality and brand awareness are both factors that drive organic clickthroughs from search results. The more famous the brand and the better the quality in the eyes of the target audience, the more likely they are to click on an organic listing. That is the direct effect. The indirect effect is reflected within the search engines, where high quality websites achieve a better ranking in the search results (Baye et al., 2016).

One trend we see every day is that searchers have less and less patience when searching. The % of searchers who stop searching after the first page is increasing. In addition, searchers are becoming increasingly better at searching and search terms are becoming increasingly more specific (ie longer). While a number of years ago the average number of words in a search query was still between one and two, this has already risen to between two and three, meaning searchers search more specifically. In addition, Google more often tries to provide an answer itself when it comes to Wikipedia-like information. After all, Google is getting better at knowing what context to place a search query in and at understanding the searcher's *intent*.

New technology.

Search behaviour also changes as a result of changes in technology. Conversational search is emerging. This is a combination of voice search (voice-driven queries), digital assistants (like Google Home, Siri and Alexa from Amazon) and artificial intelligence (AI). As a result of this technology, search engines are increasingly more able to understand a series of searches – ie a conversation. Voice-driven searches on smartphones are also increasing. It's important to tailor campaigns and content to better match this new search technique. Research from Moz (2016) indicates that there are five key features of voice-driven commands:

Conversational search

Voice search

Conversation

Voice-driven commands

- the search queries are longer
- they contain a more natural vocabulary

- they are often in question form
- the intention of the search is clearer
- many searches are location-based, allowing the software to respond with more 'quick answers' and 'quick actions'

Now that you know that Search Engine Optimisation is of great importance to the success of your website, you can read more about attracting links in the next section.

6.3 Link-building

Now consider the practice of attracting links from other organisations' websites. We call this practice link-building. This can be done purely to recruit visitors, but as mentioned in the previous paragraph, it can also improve your ranking in search engines' results. In this section we will explain the concepts of link-building and link profiles. The categories that websites can be divided into are also discussed. We will look at the factors that determine the quality of the individual links, as well as what is necessary in terms of preparation for link-building. We will also cover link-building strategies and tools.

6.3.1 What is link-building?

Link-building is the process of identifying and building relevant relationships (links) between websites. Central to this process is the procurement of links and the marketing of 'content' to which linking partners want to refer with the aim of increasing the number of links or optimising existing links.
We will first look at objectives for link-building and then move on to how to begin link-building, in compliance with Google's rules.

Link-building objectives
Link-building should result in higher visitor numbers, improved positions in search engines and contribute to the brand image of a website.
Link-building is mainly used to:
- get more visitors to the website
- improve positions for specific search terms (keywords) in search engines results pages
- give a domain more authority to obtain better results in search engines for more of its web pages
- ensure that website pages are more quickly indexed by search engines
- contribute to the brand image

Starting link-building
To gain better search rankings and an advantage over the competition, it is sensible to start link-building immediately after launching a website. This means systematically working to attract inbound links (also called backlinks) from relevant external websites. One condition is that the site is already functioning correctly on a technical level. This is due to the following reasons:
- Competition for search rankings increases each year.
- The level of knowledge about Search Engine Optimisation and link-building within organisations is increasing.

Link-building

© Noordhoff Uitgevers bv

- Search engines are becoming increasingly stricter and are getting better at detecting 'unnatural' link-building and Search Engine Optimisation. By this, search engine providers mean all digital marketing and web designing activities that fall outside the search engine guidelines. See Google's guidelines. Visit https://support.google.com/webmasters and view the 'Quality Guidelines' section for 'Link Exchanging Programs'. Note: it is not permitted to 'buy' links.

Despite the fact that search engine algorithms like Google, Yahoo! and Bing are not 100% public, search engines do publish guidelines or 'rules' which website owners need to obey.
Examples of Google's rules are:
- Create a website designed for your users, not for search engines. Do not mislead your users.
- Do not try to doctor your search results through a variety of tricks. A good rule of thumb is that you should be able to explain with a clear conscience what you have done regarding competing websites.
- Restrict the number of outbound links on a page.
- Avoid participating in link exchange programs (Zain, 2016).

Between 2012 and 2015, Google introduced several 'Penguin' updates. These updates involved an adjustment to the algorithm, allowing Google to better zoom in on the quality of link profiles. Websites with low quality links were penalised with lower listings in search engines. This caused many companies to lose out on rankings and consequently sales. An example is the website: www.interflora.co.uk (see example 6.1). Nowadays, the update has been integrated and processed real-time into the algorithm, thus allowing Google to detect those in violation, as Interflora were at the time, even faster. These techniques should be avoided, or Digital Marketers risk a Google Penalty (eg demotion in the rankings, or ultimately delisting).

EXAMPLE 6.1

Penalties for a violation

Interflora, a company for ordering and sending flowers, had just *bought* a series of advertorial features (advertisements, paid links) for Valentine's Day 2013 in English newspapers in which they placed a link to the Interflora.co.uk website. In addition, Interflora had a large network of loose domains that linked to one central domain, namely Interflora.co.uk. These two tactics are in violation of Google's guidelines, resulting in Interflora being given a manual penalty by Google. The website was no longer available in Google for about three weeks (for search phrases such as 'send flowers', but also 'Interflora') after which they were slowly returned to a few positions. As a result, Interflora estimated losses of about £2 million revenue per day over those three weeks!

Source: Jongsma, 2013

Example 6.1 is a concrete example of what might happen to a site when you violate a search engine's rules. A website builder must therefore stay up-to-date. But does this mean that Google is against link-building? On the contrary, Google understands that links are needed to promote your website and they have stated the following (source: https://support.google.com/webmasters/answer/66356?hl=en):

'[little 6] The best way to have other sites add high-quality, relevant links to your site is by creating unique, relevant content that can naturally gain popularity in the Internet community. Creating good content is worthwhile: links are usually editorial voices that are voluntarily given. The more useful the content you have, the more likely that someone else finds that content valuable to their readers and so adds a link to that content.'

In summary, Google actually says: good links come about naturally, so adhere to the guidelines and all will be well.

Google's YouTube channel provides interesting videos with information about, among other things, link-building. See: www.youtube.com/user/GoogleWebmasterHelp.

6.3.2 The link profile in website categories

Links are important for bringing your website/web page to people's attention, but they also affect your position in organic search results. How can that be? We will try to explain this using the link profile and the quality of individual links. This says something about what search engines believe they are able to read into the links to a website. After explaining what a healthy link profile contains, we will consider the layers of the link profile, using some visual examples.

A healthy link profile

The total collection of inbound links (backlinks) that a site receives from all other websites is called the site's link profile (see figure 6.2).

Link profile

FIGURE 6.2 The Link Profile

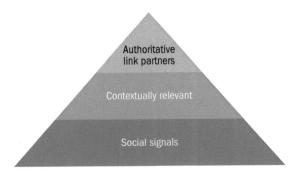

The image of the pyramid illustrates the relationship that roughly indicates which links from which website categories should be present for a 'healthy' and 'natural' link profile. The pyramid is only a fraction of the reality, but it offers a handle for structuring a link profile. Search engines (eg Google) believe links to websites allow them to derive information about the support that exists for the quality of a website.

Search engines have increasingly stricter rules regarding the quantity and quality of links. You can see links as votes that a website receives from other websites. The more qualitative votes a website receives, the higher the position of a site within the organic search results. Because the quantity of links alone does not make a useful contribution to better search results, search engines have looked for other ways to value links to websites. For example, search engines decided to reject links from 'link farms' where you could buy 10,000 links for X amount. Clearly these links didn't imply high quality content.

The pyramid explained

Using examples, we can visualise the layers of the pyramid. This gives you a good idea of the different types of sites that should be represented within the link profile. As an example, we will take an imaginary travel website that wants to score on the search term: 'holiday Chersonissos'. From which sites does this website require inbound links?

Social signals

Social signals contribute to good positions within search engines. Being active and being named on social channels such as: Facebook, Instagram or Twitter is becoming increasingly important. In doing so, the degree of interaction is also important.

Social signals

Twitter: social link partner

Does a 'like' lead to love?

John, Emrich, Gupta and Norton (2017) investigated whether 'likes' on a brand's social media network lead to a better brand image and more sales. Their conclusions were:

- Brand attitudes and purchases are predicted by the strength of positive feelings about a brand, regardless of whether that consumer has liked that brand's posts.
- If consumers see that a friend has liked a brand online, they are less likely to buy it than if that friend told them personally that they appreciate a brand.
- To convert 'Likes' into a positive brand awareness and more sales, a digital marketer needs to do more than simply get consumers to click on the 'Like' button.

Contextually relevant

Contextually relevant

Contextually relevant

When we talk about partners, we mean sites where you can find a lot of information about the same subject or topics that are closely related. This might be a blog about travelling to Greece or an enthusiast who enjoys writing about Chersonissos say. Another example could be the website of a travel agency that specialises in trips to Crete.

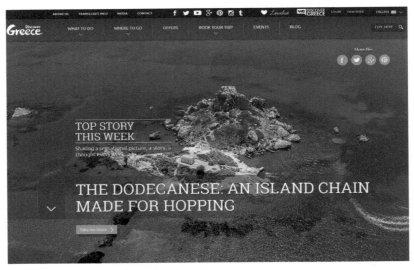

Discovergreece.com contextually relevant

Authoritative link partners

Authoritative link partners

Authoritative link partners

Authoritative partners are parties considered by search engines to be highly reliable and informative. They are recognised nationally and sometimes even internationally as a reliable source of information. The Greek tourism office's website is www.visitgreece.gr. When you receive a

Visitgreece.gr: authoritative link partner

link from such a site, search engines know that your site, in addition to being relevant to 'holiday Chersonissos', is also reliable.

The previous examples are just a few of the many types of websites that exist, but it does give you a concrete picture of the types of websites you need to receive links from in order to rank highly for a given search phrase.

6.3.3   Quality of individual links

In paragraph 6.3.2, we considered suitable link partners within your link profile. In this paragraph we will focus on the factors that determine the quality of individual links.

Search engine algorithms are secret

Link quality is perhaps the most sensitive topic within link-building. Even SEO specialists often have differences of opinion about the factors that influence this. Algorithms are computational rules used by automation programs. Search engine algorithms are well-kept secrets and specialists can only judge them based on their own experience. Also, link-building outcomes are difficult to predict because search engines are sensitive to trends and not all variables are known. The rules are regularly adapted to improve search results. Despite this, there are some specialists who, on the basis of their experience, are able to form theories regarding the quality of links. The following statement comes from 'the godfather of link-building', Eric Ward (2008). He was one of the earliest specialists in this field and was already working on link-building before search engines even existed. Eric Ward says:

> 'A link that is easily accessible and which link builders are unable to assess as either authoritative or relevant is likely to be a bad link because search engines will probably not trust it either. A link thus obtains meaning through the websites that it connects with.'

Despite this theory, it remains difficult to make predictions about the quality of links for a website as they must always be seen in the right context. A website that wants to score highly on certain search phrases should start by examining its competitors' links. The competitor site that scores better on the search phrase 'holiday Chersonissos' has links that the other website does not have, a better profile as regards in types of links or simply more links altogether. It could of course also be that the website is better optimised. Here are some points that, according to most of the specialists, should in any case be met. Keep in mind however, that you should never depend on just one of these factors. You must balance them. This will help you develop a natural link profile. The following list of factors that determine quality is not exhaustive and are for guidance only. Developments are rapid and search engines are constantly updating their guidelines. SEO is an art as well as a science.

Factors that determine quality

Factors that determine quality are:
1 relevance
2 link authority
3 website authority

1 Relevance

Relevance refers to a link that, in essence, covers the subject that it refers to. A link that is posted on a page containing information about holidays in Turkey and that refers to the page: https://www.thomascook.com/holidays/turkey/ is relevant to the topic: 'vacation turkey'. This makes it easy for search engines to determine what the link is about.

2 Link authority

Link authority

Link authority says something about the influence that search engines allow a link to exert on the position of a website for a particular search phrase. When a 'powerful' website links to another website, this increases the value of the second website, ie part of the power of the other website gets passed on. However, not all links can pass on link authority. As discussed in paragraph 6.3.2, it is against Google's guidelines to *buy* links in order to increase your position. If you decide to buy a link because, for example, it can be found on a site that attracts a lot of visitors, then you would not want to be 'punished' by Google. The link should then be provided with a 'no follow' tag. This is a piece of code that is added to the link. Google can see that the link has been purchased and that it should not pass on link authority, ie it should be ignored. The value of such a link is then not in its effect on your position within the Google results, but purely in the *direct* traffic that the link generates to your site. Links should of course also be used for the navigation of visitors from one site to another.

No follow tag

3 Website authority

Website authority

In the correct environment, a link can build authority on search engines as a result of how long it has existed. In practice, this is called link 'ripening'. When a site has held a high position for a particular search phrase for a long time, it becomes an 'authority' in the eyes of a search engine. The reward is thus a sustainable high position. For example, if a website receives links from websites that themselves score well, from government sites or universities, then this site may eventually be seen as an authoritative site.

6.3.4 Preparation for link-building

Link-building can provide additional visitors, brand awareness and even income. The only consideration is whether you can spend sufficient time on it. Perhaps the costs exceed the benefits. In some cases, a Paid Search ad campaign might be a better choice than link-building. For instance, if you don't have enough time to build relationships with link partners.

On the other hand, the profits from a Google AdWords campaign can be so small that you'd rather receive your site visitors organically. Visitors you receive from organic search results do not involve any additional costs. An AdWords campaign requires you to pay per click. Link-building can also be focused on 'prestige' ie vanity and not on a cost-benefit analysis. Companies and individuals sometimes find it important to be in 'pole position'. Important aspects in the preparation for link-building are discussed below.

On-page versus off-page optimisation

On-page optimisation

Off-page optimisation

External optimisation

Within SEO the terminology on-page and off-page optimisation is used. Link-building mainly falls under off-page optimisation (or external optimisation). Together, both elements determine the position of a website within search engine results and therefore they can be complementary.

First of all, before starting out on a link-building path, it is very important that the site is built in the right (search engine-friendly) way. When search engines do not understand what the website is about, because the technology, internal link structure or textual content are not accessible and clear, it's likely that the website will not score highly - regardless of how many good links you generate for the site. So, fix the website before starting optimisation!

Make an analysis of the competition

Before approaching potential link partners, you must research your competition to determine your goals. Make an analysis of the link profile of competitive websites to find out which links are pointing to these websites. Also look at the relationship between quantity and quality of these links. Conduct this analysis for eg your top three competitors. This can be done with one of the tools that provide insight into a link profile. These are discussed in paragraph 6.3.6.

Once you know which links you need, you can estimate whether you can obtain these links. In addition you may have access to links that a competitor does not have, which allows you to differentiate yourself. You can create a link profile analysis according to the following steps:

- You use the link pyramid to identify the best type of partners.
- Then you identify the quality of the links you receive from other partners.
- Do this for your top competitors.
- Ask yourself the question: 'To what extent do I have access to the same links and to better ones?'

Link profile analysis

Identify your potential link partners

Link partners are websites; they exist for a reason. When you learn what this is, you will learn a lot about the person or organisation behind the website. This is the key to eventually obtaining links and building relationships with these link partners.

Link partners

6.3.5   Link-building strategies

In this paragraph we will discuss how to obtain links.

The six most common link-building strategies are described according to three driving forces: definition, scalability and quality. A strategy is scalable if it is easy to perform large-scale. The seven strategies are:

1 manually requesting links
2 competitive link acquisition
3 linkbait campaigns
4 content, technology and API license
5 partnerships, link exchange and swapping
6 buying links
7 recovering or reactivating links

1 Manually requesting links

Description: Link builders or marketers contact websites and ask them to place a link on their website. See figure 6.3.

FIGURE 6.3 Manual request

Scalability: very low
Linking requests are a long-term and labour-intensive process.
Link quality: very good
By being selective, the quality of the links can be exceptionally high.
This strategy can also help you to build long-term relationships with site partners.

2 Competitive link acquisition

Competitive link acquisition

Description: link builders or marketers analyse the link profiles of competitors and copy their strategies. See figure 6.4.

FIGURE 6.4 Competitive link acquisition

Scalability: very low
Investigating or copying link profiles from competitors is a labour-intensive process.
Link quality: sufficient
There is no 100% reliable way to determine in advance whether links and strategies are worthwhile.
Note: Past successes do not guarantee the success of future projects.

3 Linkbait campaigns

Linkbaits

Description: linkbaits (bait to receive third-party links) ensure that other sites place links autonomously. Relevant content that appeals to specific audiences or websites is most likely to succeed. The same result is pursued with content marketing (see section 5.5). See figure 6.5.

FIGURE 6.5 Linkbait campaign

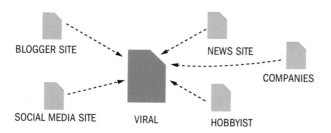

Scalability: very low
Developing linkbait strategies often takes a lot of time and money, but they can be very successful if the links are widely implemented on third-party sites.
Link quality: good
The quality of the links is then determined by the authority and diversity of the websites linking to your site.

4 Content, technology, and API license

Description: distributing licensed content or data that require the inclusion of links. Third-party sites should always mention the source of the links when using this kind of content. An example of this is www.flickr.com: when using photos from this source, they require you to reference them. See figure 6.6.

API license

FIGURE 6.6 Licensed content

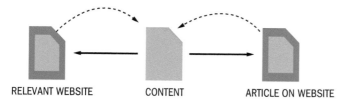

Scalability: very high
The development of licensed content or APIs is difficult (Application Programming Interface is a collection of definitions on the basis of which a computer programme can communicate with another programme or component).
When that is achieved, scalability is only limited by the inclusion of this content and APIs by third-party sites. A good example of this are the RSS article feeds from reputable news sites such as Huffingtonpost.com.
Link quality: good
Focus in link text can be controlled and strengthened by the relevance and power of the sites linking to your content.

Licensed content

API

5 Partnerships, link to exchange and swapping

Description: entering into long-term or short-term partnerships on the basis of exchange of reciprocal services that do not require direct financial compensation. See figure 6.7.

Link exchange

FIGURE 6.7 Link exchange

Scalability: average
Very dependent on the focus and tactics that are used to convince site partners to collaborate.
Link quality: sufficient
Very dependent on the exchanges and efforts of the link builders. As a rule, the easier the exchange, the lower the quality of the link obtained.

6 Buying links

Description: it is permitted to buy commercial links, but buying links is often used to manipulate results in search engines. As described in subsection 6.3.3, search engines prefer these links to be marked with a 'no-follow tag'. With this, a site indicates that the link does not contribute to the position in the organic search results. See figure 6.8.

FIGURE 6.8 Buying links

Scalability: good
Buying links is very scalable, but this can be limited by the available budget.
Quality of the link: very moderate
The quality can vary. The big disadvantage is, however, that the link will only remain as long as payment is made. In addition, paid links are prohibited by search engines from influencing the position within organic search results. See the earlier example of Interflora (example 6.1).

7 Recover or reactivate links

Links; - reclaim/ reactivate

Description: activating non-functioning/dead links and dated pages (404 reporting) on third-party websites. See figure 6.9.

FIGURE 6.9 Reactivating links

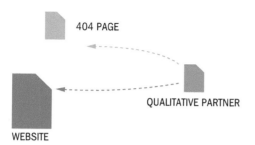

404 PAGE

QUALITATIVE PARTNER

WEBSITE

Scalability: moderate
Reactivating 'dead' links is a time-consuming and often manual process that requires different strategies in order to succeed. It is not possible to approach all sites in the same way.
Link quality: good
It is very dependent on which sources are used in order for the qualitative links to be activated. Reactivating links with authoritative and relevant partners can lead to impressive results.

Note: Everyone benefits from being linked to existing, relevant and current content.

6.3.6   Link-building tools
This section has so far dealt with what link-building is, how search engines view it, what strategies there are and what a link profile is. But how do you find link partners and how can you view such a link profile? The following tools can be helpful for this:
- Google
- Moz Open Site Explorer
- Majestic
- Linkbird
- Buzzsumo

Google
In Google Search Console you can view links that refer to your website. Google does not always show all the link partners, but what Google does show, is up to date.

Moz Open Site Explorer
In Moz's Open Site Explorer (https://moz.com/researchtools/ose/) you can analyse competitors' backlinks. To use this tool, however, a subscription is required.

Moz uses its own algorithm to assign value to link partners by using domain authority (DA) and page authority (PA). This helps you, as a link marketer, to more easily evaluate potential link partners.

Domain authority

Page authority

232

Finding links via Moz

Majestic
In Majestic's Site Explorer (www.majestic.com) the link partners can be requested in the Majestic index. The first results can be viewed free of charge. To view ten thousand results or more, a subscription is necessary. Majestic uses its own algorithm to assign value to link partners. This helps you, as a link marketer, to more easily evaluate potential link partners. Majestic has a very large index with historical data. Although this data is often not up-to-date, it can help a marketer to identify links and strategies used by competitors in the past.

Linkbird
Linkbird is a link management tool, with a fully-fledged CRM system for the link partners. With this online tool you can track the posted links, track the contact details of the link partners and the rankings of the keywords you are linking to.

Buzzsumo
With the Buzzsumo tool you can explore new possibilities for placing links based on relevant content. This can be done, for example, by means of a check on so-called 'brand mentions'. This feature allows for the possibility of examining the entire web to look for instances where the brand is mentioned. Besides brand mentions it is also possible to search for new topics and trending topics. This way you can discover new perspectives for finding potential link partners.

With Buzzsumo you can explore new possibilities for attracting inbound links based on relevant content

6.4 Mobile marketing communication

Mobile marketing is very important in the communication mix. About a quarter of the online shoppers use their smartphone to buy and search for products and services, for the latter, mobile is particularly important. A mobile device is direct, personal and most consumers always carry it on them. This makes it a different communication medium than the Internet on a PC or tablet. And the usage of smartphones continues to grow worldwide.

Mobile marketing

Mobile device

In this section we will first discuss the deployment of mobile marketing. Then we will describe basic channels and special techniques for mobile marketing. Next, we will cover the disadvantages of mobile marketing communication. We will conclude this section with a few important considerations regarding mobile marketing communications.

6.4.1 Deployment of mobile marketing

Mobile marketing communications makes it easier to achieve personal interactions with the target segment and to build a personal relationship. Because communication via a mobile device is tied to time and location, it can be used in a very well-considered and structured manner. This is possible at every stage of the digital marketing communication funnel: from creating awareness to encouraging loyalty.

An example is retail marketing: marketing used by retailers and directed at consumers. Until smartphones with Internet capability were developed about ten years ago, the retailer was dependent on the – spontaneous or otherwise - arrival of customers in their store. With the help of mobile marketing, they can now contact the consumer at any time. This makes it a very suitable medium for online shopping, but it can also be used as a complement to physical stores. One phenomenon that many retailers still have trouble with is the so-called 'show-rooming'. Customers search for products in the store and then compare these via their mobile device with other providers. Retailers assume that if they find the product is cheaper, they will order the product online or go to the other store. Research by Gensler, Neslin and Verhoef (2017) shows that the consumer is indeed often focussed on the price, but also about finding a product that better suits their needs and about waiting times before the store staff help them.

Retail marketing

Show-rooming

Retailers can use mobile marketing in the context of brand awareness and brand attitude, but also for sales promotions, for example to promote temporary offers or even for direct sales. Mobile marketing can be used on a very personal level: with permission, for example, loyal customers who are in the vicinity of a physical establishment can be invited to visit the store and make use of an individual offer.

Research shows that:
- Mobile marketing communication is more effective for branding and sales promotion than the traditional approach.
- Customer satisfaction increases if mobile marketing is used to offer streamlined, customised and enriched shopping experiences, as support for product use and communication after purchase.
- More interactivity within the various contact channels leads to better information processing by consumers and positive effects for the brand.

© Noordhoff Uitgevers bv

- The use of mobile marketing communications increases the return on investment for other marketing channels and leads to increased customer loyalty.
- When mobile marketing is structurally embedded in the organisation and in the cooperation with partners (eg manufacturers and retailers) this leads to a sustainable, positive effect on satisfaction, loyalty, brand perception and turnover (Ström, Vendel & Bredican, 2014).

6.4.2 Basic channels and special techniques for mobile marketing

In this subsection we will first discuss three basic channels for mobile marketing and then various special techniques.

Commercial communication forms

According to Otto (2015), the three basic channels of mobile marketing are:
1 messaging
2 mobile web
3 apps

1 Messaging

Messaging
Direct SMS

Using messaging, companies can communicate commercially in three ways:
- Direct SMS: this is the sending of advertising texts for direct marketing purposes in a text message to telephone numbers from a database.

Direct MMS

- Direct MMS: this is the sending of advertisements for direct marketing purposes in text, image or sound in an MMS to telephone numbers from a database.

Bluetooth marketing

- Bluetooth marketing: mobile devices can be connected to each other at a short distance via a Bluetooth connection. This can be used to distribute advertising in a specific location, for example a train or a shop. Beacons are a well-known Bluetooth application. These are transmitters that can send and receive signals, allowing users to receive push notifications at certain locations. Read more about beacons under the heading 'Special techniques' below.

SMS

Messaging via SMS is used more often than you might think, especially in the business market. For example, many service messages are sent via SMS. Examples are the confirmation messages sent by online retailers to confirm delivery times. Hairdressers, hospitals and dentists also often send out reminders for appointments via SMS. In addition, SMS is still the channel for all kinds of codes. Such as: codes for online banking. The big advantage of a text message is that it does not use the Internet: you can always reach people, provided they have a phone signal; even if they do not have Internet access. So arguably, it is not digital marketing communication!

Direct messaging

Private messaging

Smartphone users themselves mainly use direct messaging, for example via WhatsApp or (Facebook) Messenger. The result is that organisations also opt for private messaging where possible, exchanging private messages via messaging apps.

2 Mobile Web

Mobile website

Responsive website

Adaptive design

Organisations communicate via the mobile Web using a responsive website, that can adapt to the screen size of the laptop, tablet or smartphone, or a website with adaptive design that has separate, different content for display on a smartphone or even a separate website that is constructed entirely for mobile use (this last is diminishing in importance).

© Noordhoff Uitgevers bv

3 Apps

By an app, people usually mean a software application for mobile devices. Such a program does not necessarily require a mobile connection to function, but data is often exchanged via the mobile Internet. A web app is an application that can also be accessed from your regular PC (desktop or laptop) by entering a URL in your web browser. For example, programs for internet banking. To make things complicated, the term 'web app' is sometimes also used to describe a mobile version of a website. A native app is software that is written specifically for a smartphone operating system, such as Android or Apple iOS. These apps can be found in the Play Store or App Store. There are also hybrid apps, native apps that are filled with content from a website. As a result, an organisation does not have to release a new version of the app every time it is updated.

Apps are popular as a mobile marketing communication medium. Two possibilities are:

- Branded app: this is an application that deploys a brand for marketing purposes. An example is Zara's shopping app.

App

Web app

Native app

Hybrid apps

Branded app

Branded app: Zara

- Mobile game advertising: advertisers use mobile games to advertise. Recent examples of branded mobile games include Warner Bros, BBC and KPMG.

Mobile game advertising

The consumer is overloaded with so many communication messages every day, that it is impossible for them to see them all consciously, let alone to do something with them. Instead of limiting themselves to pure advertising, more and more companies offer a 'branded utility'. This is a form of marketing communication that is veritably useful to the user/customer. The focus is on functionality for the consumer. The application must therefore be usable as well as practical. Thanks to the interactive possibilities, a branded utility is an increasingly popular mobile marketing tool.

An example of a branded utility app is the L'Oréal Makeup Genius. This allows women to see what their new make-up looks like when applied (virtually) to their face.

Branded utility

Utility app

6

In the context of promoting loyalty, more and more brands are creating their own app that includes a customer loyalty 'card' where people can save up points. You do not even have to have the physical card with you anymore.

LEGO® Ninjago™ WU-CRU

LEGO® City: My City 2

LEGO® Ninjago™: Skybound

LEGO® Ninjago™: Possession

LEGO® Star Wars™ Ultimate Rebel

LEGO® Marvel™ Super Heroes: Team Up

LEGO has many mobile games advertising their brand

A branded utility from L'Oréal

EXAMPLE 6.2

Starbucks

Starbucks claims that about 27% of U.S. company-operated transactions pass through its mobile app. With one of the strongest loyalty programs in the industry, Starbucks enjoys a loyal following from its fans; most customers who purchased Starbuck's gift cards went on to use the cards themselves, seeking easier payment methods that simplified and enhanced their in-store experiences. Following this insight, Starbucks enhanced their existing mobile loyalty program to add in mobile ordering and payment, further improving the customer experience and consequently loyalty.

Starbucks mobile loyalty app

Source: Stablekernel, 2017

Also, the 'My environments' section for customers who are logged in, are increasingly being presented in app form, in addition to being able to access this content via the responsive website. An example is Airbnb.

Special techniques

In addition to the basic forms of mobile marketing communication, according to Otto (2015), there are various special techniques, such as:
- location-based advertising
- mobile coupons
- QR codes
- augmented reality

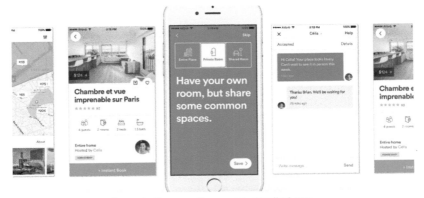

Airbnb has a responsive website as well as a very detailed app

- near-field communication (NFC)
- beacons

1 Location based advertising

Location-based advertising

Geolocation

Increasing numbers of companies are using location-based advertising as a tactic for marketing communication. Location based advertising uses location-based technologies eg geolocation, such as GPS or beacons. Almost every device these days has built-in GPS, and this allows the location of the user to be determined, but also, for example, that of the nearest grocery store. A digital marketer can send people messages that are relevant to them at that particular moment. For example, beer brand Corona showed mobile ads for their beer to people in places with a temperature of 20 degrees or higher and after 4:00 PM. Starbucks experimented with sending offers to customers who were physically close to a branch and now makes it possible to order online as soon as you are in the vicinity. Techniques for reaching people who are close-by are called proximity marketing tools.

Proximity marketing tools

Location based advertising from Starbucks app

2 Mobile coupons

Mobile coupons

Mobile coupons are digital vouchers that can be redeemed in the store. A consumer requests a coupon via their smartphone or tablet and a voucher is received in return. Mobile coupons are often distributed via apps but can also be sent to the user via MMS and mobile websites.

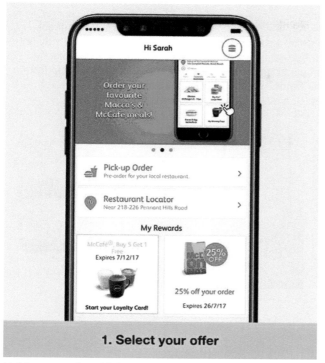

Mobile coupon from McDonald's

QR codes
A Quick Response code (QR code) is a two-dimensional barcode, which can **QR code** be scanned by smartphones with a QR-app and often redirect the user to a mobile site or app. QR codes are often applied cross-media by companies. L'Oréal Canada has included QR codes on all their Garnier products. They want to connect with all their Canadian consumers no matter which language they speak; English or French.

L'Oréal Canada uses QR codes on all their Garnier products

Augmented reality (AR)

4 Augmented reality

Augmented reality (AR) is a live representation of the direct or indirect physical world, in which virtual elements have been added in the mobile interface. Augmented reality is used by many companies for marketing purposes. An example is the Dulux Visualizer app. With this AR app from paint manufacturer Dulux, users can paint a space virtually and see the result immediately. Use of AR in marketing is expected to grow.

Dulux Visualizer app allows the mobile user to test virtual paint colours

NFC chip

5 Near-field communication

NFC (near-field communication) makes it possible to have a mobile phone that is equipped with an NFC chip, communicate with an NFC receiver. NFC is currently used as a tool for making mobile payments (see also section 9.2). However, there are also many marketing communication applications possible. An NFC chip works, as the name implies, only at very short distances (approximately 10 cm or less) and uses radio signals. You can include the chips for example in stickers, loyalty cards, books, magazines, posters, key rings, tags and wristbands. This allows you to make so-called 'smart posters', where you can hold your mobile phone near it for further information or a mobile coupon. Or you can open doors with it, like in the Disney hotels.

With an NFC chip in a mobile phone you can also open car doors

6 Beacons

Beacons are transmitters that can send and receive Bluetooth signals, allowing users to receive push notifications at specific locations. These beacons can also communicate with apps. This makes it possible for retailers to set up mobile loyalty programs, for example, where consumers are rewarded when they visit a store. Beacons are also used at airports to provide travellers with information relating to the time or their location.

Beacons

Travellers are provided information at airports via beacons

The diversity of communication applications is large, and the techniques are also expanding. For example, there is a relatively new technique that uses magnetic fields and the compass function on smartphones. This is especially suitable for indoor applications, where GPS does not work.

The marketing objectives determine whether you use mobile marketing and which channel you use for this. Table 6.2 shows which mobile marketing communication form you can best use for different types of objectives.

TABLE 6.2 Objectives matrix mobile marketing communication

Main objectives and mobile techniques	Brand awareness	Brand associations and attitude	Brand binding	Visit website or app	Sales	Visit physical store
Messaging						
Direct SMS	■					
Direct MMS	■					
Bluetooth	■					■
Branded mobile website			■		■	
Branded responsive website			■		■	
Mobile display advertising	■			■		
Mobile video advertising	■			■		
Mobile search advertising	■			■		
Branded app		■		■		
Mobile game advertising		■		■		
Location based advertising	■					■
Mobile coupons						
Augmented reality			■			
Near-Field Communication (NFC)				■		
QR codes				■		
Beacons	■			■		■

6.4.3 Disadvantages of mobile marketing communication

Mobile marketing communication offers many possibilities and often leads to higher response and engagement rates than marketing communication via the laptop or desktop PC. However, according to Otto (2015) there are certainly also disadvantages. He names the following disadvantages:

1 Fragmentation occurs due to the different operating systems on smartphones.
2 Mobile messages can be intrusive.
3 Many organisations still have insufficient experience with mobile marketing.
4 Most devices have a relatively small screen/limited space for the message.
5 The reach is relatively small.
6 Organisations receive a huge amount of data.
7 The content must be suitable for mobile use and mobile devices.

1 Fragmentation occurs as a result of the different operating systems on smartphones
The difficulty with an app is that it does not, as a rule, work on all mobile platforms. For each operating system, iOS (iPad, iPhone and iWatch), Android, Windows Phone and Blackberry, different software is needed. Fragmentation also occurs between the various Android versions. Due to limited budgets for mobile marketing, advertisers often have to make choices in terms of what platform to use.

2 Mobile messages can be intrusive
Making things personal can be an advantage, but also a disadvantage. After all, brands and companies intrude on the privacy of the user, which could be viewed negatively by some (potential) customers. In order to receive push notifications (mobile alerts), text messages or MMS messages, the user must give permission (double opt-in) in advance.

3 Many organisations still have insufficient experience with mobile marketing
Mobile marketing is a relatively recent channel and many organisations lack experience with it as well as demonstrably successful cases. This certainly applies to small and medium-sized businesses. In addition, the lack of knowledge about the return (ROI) is often a significant obstacle.

4 Most devices have a relatively small screen/limited space for the message
Mobile devices often have relatively small screens compared to other devices such as the PC or laptop, although there is a visible trend towards smartphone screens increasing in size. The small screen provides a different and sometimes lower quality user experience compared to the user experience on larger devices such as a PC. At the same time, choices must be made about which (visual) message a marketer can convey briefly and concisely. Responsive or adaptive communication messages offer a solution, but this requires thought, planning and effort.

Mobile devices

5 The reach is often relatively small
The reach is often smaller if you compare this to other forms of marketing communication, especially when it comes to apps. The app will be one of millions of other apps in the iOS App Store or Google Play and is often hard to find. Ensuring it can be found often requires a separate digital marketing communication campaign. In addition, the consumer must perform various actions before the app is actually on the mobile screen.

6 Organisations receive a huge amount of data
Collecting and applying data has enormous advantages (see also Chapter 12), but as a result of mobile marketing, the amount of date on usage and users is increasing rapidly. Organisations are not always equipped to deal with this effectively.

7 The content must be suitable for mobile use and mobile devices
Specific technology is not the only thing that mobile marketing demands of websites and apps. The content itself must also be suitable for consumption on relatively small screens and in different usage situations. For example, if you enter a store, the push message you receive only contains the discount code, not detailed information about the store. You

also have to impose different requirements on a video for mobile than on a video for a large screen (see section 5.4).

6.4.4 Points for consideration in mobile marketing communication

Mobile devices are interactive, practical and consumers always have their smartphone at hand. This sounds like the ideal marketing communication channel and that is indeed very often the case. However, mobile devices remain a means and should not become an end in themselves within a campaign. A campaign with a mobile component has many similarities with campaigns via other channels. The digital marketer must have detailed knowledge of their target segment, have SMART objectives in mind, ensure that the activities fit within the brand strategy, that the user experience is excellent and that the messages are relevant and personalised (Otto, 2015). We will explain the last three points below.

Excellent for user experience

User experience
(UX)

The *user experience (UX)* is especially important for mobile marketing tools, such as mobile websites and mobile applications. For other mobile marketing tools such as SMS, the user experience is largely determined by the handset manufacturer. A brand has virtually no influence on this user experience. A mobile website or app can be evaluated according to the following factors:
- *User-friendliness*: think of the extent to which consumer needs are fulfilled and the usefulness and user-friendliness of the application, in the eyes of the user.
- *Availability*: the application functions at the moment when the application is needed.
- *Performance*: the speed with which the application functions, meets the requirements of the brand and meets the expectations of the user.
- *Scalability*: the application continues to work well with a high demand on the (working) memory or data traffic.
- *Adaptability*: the application can function well in the interfaces of different sizes and types of devices.
- *Safety*: the application protects itself against hackers and thus guarantees the security of confidential information.
- *Cost efficiency*: the production costs and server costs are reduced without compromising the added value of the application.

Relevant messages

Research among the target segment is also an important first step in mobile marketing communication. When mobile devices are utilised properly, they add a lot of relevance to the entirety of a campaign. The brand is literally always at hand and the consumer can be approached in a very personal way. Relevance can be provided in several ways:

Physical
relevance

- physical relevance in two sub-forms:
  - *spatial relevance*: based on (GPS) location
  - *time relevance*: based on time

Personal
relevance

- personal relevance in three sub-forms:
  - *thematic relevance*: on the basis of the consumer's previously indicated favourites
  - *cognitive relevance*: based on the consumer's information needs
  - *activity relevance*: based on the activity of the consumer

An Esso logo appears in the maps of navigation company Navigon when you are near an Esso petrol station. This is an example of *spatial relevance*.

An example of *time relevance* is a mobile display campaign by the liquor brand Aperol, which was only shown (just before the weekend) on Friday afternoons (see image).

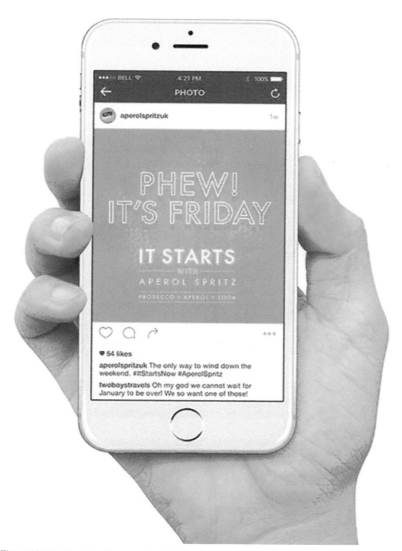

Time relevance: advertisement by the liquor brand Aperol

In some advertising services per SMS, the consumer only receives text messages from brands they find interesting. If the consumer indicates an interest in 'Sports' and 'Fashion', they only receive messages from brands such as Nike and Adidas. This is an example of *thematic relevance*.

An example of *cognitive relevance* is when consumers who have visited the TV guide on Nu.nl using their mobile on Friday are shown a mobile ad for the TV show The Voice of Holland.

When checking in via location-based services Foursquare and Swarm, consumers occasionally receive an award, such as a discount or a free cup of coffee. This is an example of *activity relevance*.

Personalising content

Personalising content is important for the relevance of the campaign. If the content is adapted based on the characteristics of individual consumers, this will increase its effectiveness. Context is one of the most important features in a campaign that contains a mobile component. However, a brand can of course ask a consumer about personal preferences within the mobile component or build a CRM database for this purpose.

A frequently occurring stumbling block for organisations is that campaigns on mobile devices provide insufficient reach. Using a mobile marketing campaign, a lot of scope can be achieved, but then there must be cross-media communication. The idea behind the cross-media approach is that the various communication tools reinforce one another. When mobile marketing communication is integrated with other channels, this ensures a better brand experience as well as results.

6.5 Use of social media channels

In Chapter 5 the digital marketing communication funnel was introduced: awareness, capture, conversion and loyalty. In this section you will read more about the role of owned and earned social media channels during the customer acquisition process, the steps towards a digital customer acquisition campaign and methods for stimulating sales on social media. You can read more about social media and advertising in section 7.4.

6.5.1 Role of social media channels in the customer acquisition process

Social media can play a role in all steps of the digital marketing communication funnel:
- *awareness*: create the awareness that it is interesting to visit the provider's online sales channel
- *capture*: 'catch' (engage) the visitor by convincing them of the attractiveness of a visit to the online sales channel
- *conversion*: motivate the visitor to buy the product
- *loyalty*: encourage the customer to make repeat purchases and to recommend the brand in a positive way

Awareness

Social media has become mass media. Facebook has 2.2 billion monthly active users globally (Statista, 2018). Young people spend on average more than 2 hours a day on communication via social media, mail or apps. This has made social media interesting channels for brands to become part of these activities. By paying for advertising, brands can use social media for awareness. Brands can also use social media free of charge at this stage of the buying process by setting up their own accounts/pages and attracting followers. In Chapter 5 you read the examples of Coca-Cola and McDonald's who have more than 100 and 70 million followers, respectively. Especially for brands who want to ensure a large amount of repeat purchases from existing customers and fans, building a page with followers is an interesting strategy.

Another way in which brands can use social media at this stage of the buying process is by relying on the creation of earned media and word of mouth. As a result of the open and transparent nature of social media, consumers can also ensure increased visibility for brands. In Chapter 5 we used 'Share a Coke' by Coca-Cola as an example of a campaign using this mechanism. Marketers must realise that it is very difficult to set up a successful word-of-mouth campaign.

In this phase brands generally use softer KPIs, such as brand awareness and reach.

Capture

In the 'capture' phase of the purchasing process, the influence of social media is strong. Many brands are continuously present on social media and post several messages per week on their channels. As a result, a brand creates much more room for communicating with customers than is traditionally possible with, for example, a TV campaign. Subsequently, brands can find more depth in their communication and convince consumers. A concrete example can be given on the basis of the digital marketing communication funnel for a new brand of detergent.

In the first step (awareness) you want people to become familiar with the new detergent brand. You do this for example by using a social media posts to introduce the new brand. Suppose there are several, perhaps five or ten, advantages of using this detergent? In a traditional TV campaign, you can never include all of these ten benefits in an advertisement. On social media you can try to convince customers by mentioning all these benefits in various social media posts. That way you can communicate for longer and more intensively about the same product.

During this step of the digital marketing communication funnel, it is advisable that marketers make an effort on social media to map out the benefits or background of a product or service and produce the content accordingly. In this phase, brands generally also use softer KPIs, such as brand consideration, reach, but also engagement.

Conversion

Social media offer various features that allow customers to buy directly from or within social media channels. Facebook, Instagram and YouTube make it possible to tell consumers a story in a fixed order. This is also called 'sequenced storytelling' (see section 6.5.3). For example, a shampoo brand that introduces a product in a first message can explain the benefits of that product in subsequent social media post and communicate a special offer from a supermarket in a final post.

Sequenced storytelling

Features that allow direct purchasing are also being integrated more often into social media channels (see KLM's example in the next image). Other options for buying directly via social media are 'offers', special prices within social platforms, location-based advertisements for sending direct traffic to physical stores and posts (messages) that generate leads, for example for requesting brochures.

At KLM you can book flights via social media

In this phase brands generally use soft KPIs, such as purchase intent, in addition to harder KPIs, ie direct (online) conversions. For example, Facebook tries to establish the relationship between Facebook campaigns and actual sales through links with store visits and sales data.

Loyalty

The part of the funnel where social media is traditionally strong, is the generation of loyalty and advocacy. This involves creating online 'word of mouth' (WOM) about a product that should lead others to consideration and action. Advocacy is a powerful way of boosting sales. Many well-known online retailers, eg LUVD (www.luvd.com) and designboom (www.designboom.com) offer you the possibility of sharing a purchase via a social media message. Sharing online reviews, product ratings and testimonials is also a common tactic for convincing other consumers.

Advocacy

Research by Econsultancy (Charlton, 2017) shows that 61% of consumers read online reviews before they make a purchase. Research from Salesforce (Salesforce Blog, 2016) showed that 92% of consumers trust online content from friends and family above all other forms of content, 50% of consumers find user generated content more 'memorable' than brand content and 53% of the consumers indicate that user generated content has influenced their purchasing decision.

In this phase, brands generally use softer KPIs, such as brand loyalty, sentiment of online conversation and share of voice. However, harder KPIs, such as repeat purchases, are also measured at this stage.

6.5.2 Steps towards a customer acquisition campaign on social media

Broadly speaking, a (buying) campaign can be set up by following these four steps:

Step 1   Find your target segment on social media.
Step 2   Connect with their behaviour and interests.
Step 3   Design a campaign message and flow.
Step 4   Create content.

Step 1 Find your target segment on social media
First you must determine which social media channels your target segment uses and how you can best reach them. The obvious thing to do would be to look at the social networks with the most users, such as Facebook and YouTube. However, other social networks often have more specific applications or users and for this reason may lend themselves better to your objective. For example, Facebook is a generic platform for friends, family and news with no clear focus. Instagram focuses strongly on photos and you will find many active users in communities in the 'health & beauty' field there. On Twitter you will find an influential audience, the medium is characterised by the fact that it is live, and for many users it is a place to discuss their passions and what they're doing right now. Snapchat is mainly used by a younger audience and Pinterest by a female audience. The social networks themselves publish a lot of information about their users audience and external research is also available, so that brands can determine which networks are best for them.

Step 2 Connect with their behaviour and interests
Brands want to tell their own story and communicate their own message. On social media however, we find that the brands that are most successful do not 'send' (or 'sell'), but are able to connect with the behaviour and interests of their target segment. What occupies them? What do they do when they are online? What do they interact with on social media? The social networks also map their users' behaviour and interests. For example, Facebook provides an 'Audience Insights' tool, that allows you to find out what the audience that is interested in your brand or another subject looks like. On Instagram there are also very specific behaviours (such as the frequent use of hashtags), that your brand can respond to.

Audience Insights

Step 3 Design a campaign message and flow
The third step is to generate a campaign message and flow based on the previous insight (see example in figure 6.10). This is no different than if you were to develop a traditional (offline) marketing campaign.

6

FIGURE 6.10 Part of the campaign flow of a social media campaign

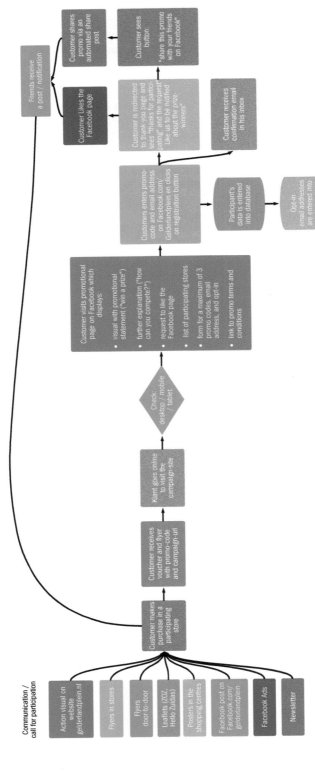

Source: Socialfabriek, 2017

Step 4 Create content
One of the benefits of social media is the variety of formats that you can use to bring your campaign to the attention of your target audience. A good transformation of a concept into the right tools makes the execution stronger. Usually that will be a combination of posts via owned social media channels and social media advertisements. In the next subsection we will delve deeper into formats and tools for generating sales via social media.

6.5.3   Methods for stimulating sales via social media
In this subsection we will discuss the following six formats that a brand can use to generate sales via social media:
1 sequenced storytelling/content marketing
2 shoppable ad formats
3 influencers
4 user generated content (on owned websites)
5 social referrals
6 social selling (filtering purchase signals)

We will conclude by mentioning a few concerns about the use of social media in the customer acquisition process.

Sequenced storytelling
In Chapter 5 we discussed the possibilities of giving some depth to social media in terms of the stories you want to communicate to customers. This can be done by sending people that are interested in your content follow-up messages on the basis of 'target by context'. Two techniques can be used: sequenced storytelling and content marketing.

Sequenced storytelling is a technique where you lead people through successive messages within a campaign in order to generate awareness, consideration and action. Each time, you tell a small part of the whole story. In funnel-based storytelling, the digital marketing professional uses

Sequenced storytelling

Funnel-based storytelling

A priming and reminding campaign by a clothing store. Throughout the week, the banner is shown on the left. At the weekend, the banner with a call to action to the store is shown on the right

a series of messages and multiple stages to entice potential customers to make a purchase. First, the consumer becomes acquainted with the brand. Next, they will be shown a message containing one of the brand's products. Then they are shown a message with a call to action. A priming and reminding campaign alternately displays different types of messages (text, photo, video). The first message is quite general but striking. It clearly shows the relevance of the brand. In the second 'sequence' of the story, the posts remind the recipients of the message from the first phase.

Priming & reminding campaign

You can read more about content marketing in section 5.5.

Shoppable content formats

Social media networks are becoming increasingly 'shoppable'. This means that the large networks are launching more different formats that enable the direct purchase or promotion of products and services. Facebook Collections, for example, make it possible to combine a brand message with a product offer. YouTube makes it possible to add shopping results to a video.

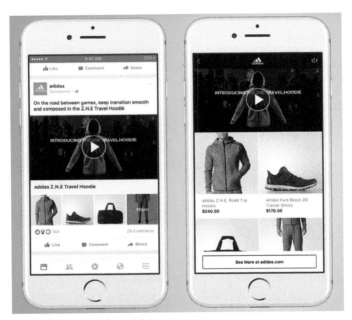

Shoppable content from Adidas

Influencers

Influencers
Influentials

A common technique on social media is the use of influencers (also called influentials). Influencers are people who excel at a particular skill or who have a lot of knowledge about a subject and who have the capacity to influence the opinion or behaviour of others. Many brands use influencers to promote products and services. Influencers are often thought to be more reliable than brands, so the effectiveness of such influencer campaigns on brands and sales is considerable. For example, the sale of UGG boots increased exponentially after Madonna was seen wearing them.

© Noordhoff Uitgevers bv

EXAMPLE 6.3

Neil Patel

For anything about online marketing and running a business online, Neil Patel has become the 'go-to guy'. He is one of the most famous people in the internet marketing and online business niches. He is an expert in various fields, as well as the co-founder of Hello Bar, Crazy Egg, and many other ventures. Neil is often used as an influencer by Viacom, GM, HP, Amazon and many other companies. Neil's Facebook follower count approx. one million and he has over 250,000 followers on Twitter.

Neil Patel's website allows you to quickly analyse your own website

---

User generated content

User generated content (UGC) literally means content that is created by users. This is information that is provided by users of a certain medium. Companies are adding social features to their own websites with increasing frequency. Publishing valuations of products or services in the form of numbers or stars is a common method for expressing the quality of a product in a credible way. Many companies also use online reviews to show consumers' opinion or experience regarding online products. Research by BrightLocal (2016) showed that as many as 84% of consumers trust online reviews equally as much as a personal recommendation.

User generated content

The famous luxury bag maker Michael Kors ran an innovative campaign: #WhatsInYourKors.
Michael Kors started this campaign in 2013 and it turned into a long-term social campaign. The fashion brand started the hashtag #WhatsInYourKors

and simply asked their customers to upload images of the various things they carry in their Michael Kors handbag every day. Some results:

- The campaign created positive engagement and conversation between brands and existing customers. Customers shared style tips and advice plus pictures. This generated a strong bond with Michael Kors.
- With this sharing of images of things that are very human and personal from a customer's daily life, Michael Kors built its brand and engaged its audience.

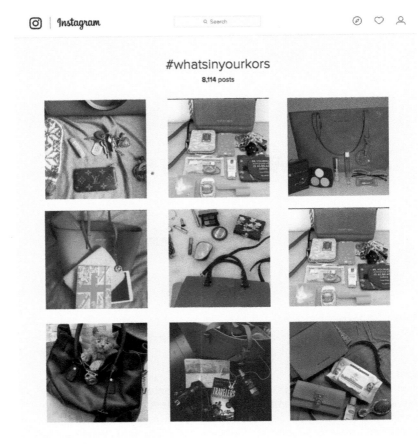

#whatsinyourkors

Social referral

Using recommendations is a commonly used sales strategy. (Traditionally known as member-get-member=MGM and recommend-a-friend=RAF). Traditionally, for example, many organisations give customers a discount if they introduce new customers. This mechanism is also called referral and can be applied within social media. Thanks to the effects of word of mouth, social referral can be a powerful mechanism to generate sales. Below is an example of a social referral campaign on a website that gives customers a discount if they share a message on social media.

Social referral

A call to social referral

Social selling

Another way that sales can be stimulated via social media is social selling: filtering purchase signals on social media and reacting in person or with an automated reply. Sometimes the sales process within organisations is highly dependent on relationships and personal contact, especially in business-to-business environments. For example, by training sales employees in the use of social media, organisations can maintain relationships and identify and follow-up sales opportunities. A large Dutch financial institution has trained its account managers in this way. Digital networks thus become an extension of physical networks. In the case of the financial service provider that we mentioned, the contact that account managers have with their business relations has increased considerably and new sales opportunities are being created. An important aspect of such programmes is that training courses are tailored to an employee's job title and the work they do. How does the programme make daily operations more efficient and effective? An approach to developing social selling programmes for employees:

1 Find out on which social media platforms the customers and prospects are active. On which platforms and on what pages and groups is there a lot of discussion about the relevant topics?
2 Identify the daily activities of employees.
3 Identify in which way social selling can facilitate and strengthen the daily activities of employees.
4 Develop a training program based on these insights.
5 Train, coach and mentor employees for a longer period of time, to ensure that an actual behavioural change occurs.
6 Ensure the correct preconditions are in place for employees to make use of social selling, such as support by management, tooling, help with the production, curation and distribution of content and making the results transparent.

Social selling

6

For business-to-customer organisations, social selling can also be highly effective. In such organisations, social-selling activities are assigned to a specific department. For example, employees monitor Twitter and Instagram and proactively answer questions about products and services. In this way they hope to add value and to entice consumers to purchase their own product. The new field of social selling has attracted some big-name B2B players including IBM, SAP, Thomson Reuters and Pitney Bowes. It equips salespeople with powerful new tools which help them find and engage customers.

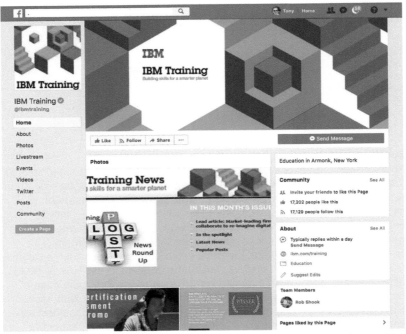

Besides third-party content, marketers at IBM have created a range of of shareable assets, including video, podcasts and infographics. This allows IBM's sales reps to draw their prospects' attention to more disruptive content than the 'old' whitepapers.

Comments on the use of social media in the customer acquisition process

There are many methods to successfully use your owned or earned social media channels in the customer acquisition process. However, there are some reservations. As the researchers Batra and Keller (2016) describe, the use of social media can support the customer acquisition process, but must be used in conjunction with other marketing communication channels, for the following reasons:

- When it comes to attracting new users of products and promoting brand penetration, social media is not always as effective as more traditional forms of communication.

© Noordhoff Uitgevers bv

- Research shows that there are differences depending on the brand and product in how successfully social media can be used. Media, charities and fashion score well, but consumer goods generate less interaction.
- Although consumers use social media to obtain useful information and to look for discounts, promotions and interesting or entertaining content, there is only a small percentage of consumers who really want to have a *conversation* with a brand.

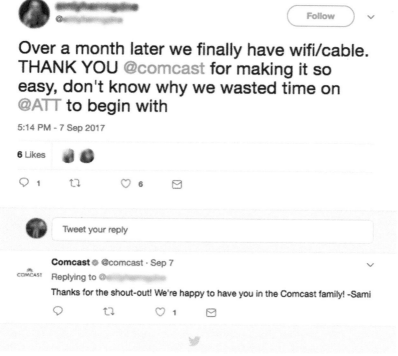

Social selling isn't easy; it may be difficult to distinguish a positive remark from a negative one

In this section you can read about how owned and earned social media can be used in the sales process. How paid social media can play a role in the sales process, can be found in section 7.4.

6.6 Email marketing

Email is an 'owned' channel. The organisation has full control over it. In this section we will first look at the background and objectives of email marketing. Next, we will shed light on what effective emailing looks like. The last two sub-paragraphs deal with the much-discussed topics of spam and mobile marketing.

6.6.1   Background and objectives of email marketing

We will discuss in depth the concept of email marketing and discuss the main objectives of email marketing. Then we will look at the role of email marketing in the digital marketing communication funnel. Following that, we will touch on the acquisition of email addresses. Finally, we will examine the opportunities email marketing can bring to an organisation.

The concept of email marketing

Email marketing

Email marketing is a form of direct marketing where the channel (email) and the email address are used by organisations for the purpose of interacting with their target segments. In principle, this is applicable to all target segments, such as customers, prospects, employees, press and companies. In email marketing it is important that the recipient gives permission in advance to the organisation that is doing the sending in order for them to be allowed to email them. In many countries this is determined in a Telecommunications Act or similar legislation (see also section 13.4). These kind of legislation is created to combat spam (unwanted messages, see section 6.6.3). As a result of this regulation, email marketing is also known as 'permission-based marketing'.

Permission-based marketing

Email marketing is one of the most direct ways of communicating with your target audience. It is fast, effective, personal and gives you the opportunity to generate a wide reach, response and digital conversion. The results of email marketing are also very measurable. This way you can see who has received the email, who opens an email and who clicks on which link. The actual sending of an email and the viewing of the results can be done using special software, offered by an Email Service Provider (ESP). When you integrate the software with digital analytics (see chapter 12), you can also see who ultimately purchased something.

Email Service Provider (ESP)

Email marketing lends itself particularly well to segmentation and personalisation. The content of emails can be determined based on customer data so that the message becomes relevant, resulting in more 'opens' and clicks and ultimately higher conversion. A good database with the right profile data that is well maintained is a requirement. We refer to this profile data, such as first name and place of residence, as 'static profile data'. Even more interesting is 'dynamic profile data'. This is profile data based on the behaviour that customers have previously shown in emails. For instance, the open and click behaviour of customers over a longer period. One person might click on a different link in the email from another person. This depends on the interests of the person in question. This gives you the opportunity to make the next emails more personal for each individual customer with varying interests (see also section 10.4). An example would be:

Opens

Static profile data

Dynamic profile data

1 An insurance company sends an email in which various insurance policies are promoted. For example, household insurance and home insurance.
2 You receive this email from the insurance company and you are interested in the insurance. That is why you click on a link in the email referring to the insurance policy.
3 The insurance company records this dynamic data (your click) and therefore knows that you are interested in a home insurance policy.

© Noordhoff Uitgevers bv

4 The insurance company can then choose to send you a follow-up email with specific information about home insurance only.

If you can make emails more personal in this way, it is possible to build a profitable relationship with your target segments by using email for acquisition, retention, loyalty and branding.

The average office worker receives 121 emails per day and 269 billion emails are sent each day (Expandedramblings.com, 2017). These can be personal emails, newsletters and invoices. Many people consult their email first-thing in the morning, although this varies widely between individuals.

Main objectives of email marketing

Before an organisation decides to begin an email marketing campaign, it is important to define the objectives. The following four main objectives (or combinations of them) can be pursued by email marketing:

1 *Sales*: emails are intended to attract customers or to sell more to existing customers. A good example is Amazon's email programme; targeted at both customers and prospects and driven by Amazon's deep and rich data on both groups.

2 *Retention*: email lends itself perfectly to the retention of existing customers by keeping them informed of developments, new products and the status of any deliveries. In addition, existing customers can be rewarded by giving them an extra discount via email marketing for a future order.

Retention

3 *Cost reduction*: by replacing traditional post with email significant savings can be made. Money is saved mainly in the reduction of envelopes, printing and postage. Particularly for companies that have large number of customers or stock, the savings can be considerable. One example is UK clothing retailer Next. Whereas in the past a huge number of bulky and expensive paper catalogues were sent by post, this has for the most part been replaced by email and the Internet.

4 *Encourage website visit*: email is perfect for encouraging website visits. By placing hyperlinks in your emails, the recipient is only one click away from (specific) parts of your website. For example, the recipient, who wants to buy the product that is promoted in the email, can purchase directly online via the website.

Email marketing and the digital marketing communication funnel

You might be forgiven for thinking that email marketing cannot play a major role in the awareness phase, because the addressee must have given permission to be sent emails. In practice however, it might be that someone receives an email with an offer for a brand that they do not know. Permission doesn't always have to be given directly to the organisation that ultimately sends the email. A brand can also be introduced by a different organisation using a 'partner mail'. People give permission to receive emails from partners for various reasons. For example, they may be genuinely interested in offers from an organisation's partners because they expect them to be in line with their interests. When someone subscribes to a hobby magazine, they can expect that the offers they receive from the magazine's email match their interests. Of course, great care needs to be taken to comply with relevant data protection and privacy laws.

Partner mail

6

On the other hand, the choice can also be less conscious. When participating in, for example, online contests, permission can be requested for the ability to send emails on behalf of partners. Motivated by the desire to win the competition, people give permission for partner mailings.

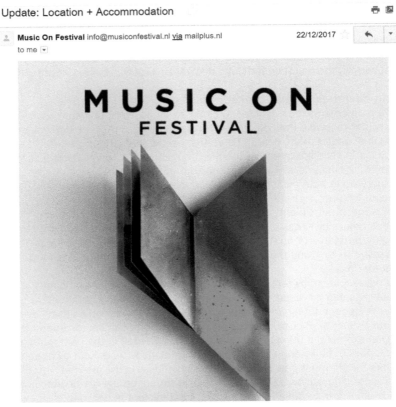

Update: Location + Accommodation

Music On Festival info@musiconfestival.nl via mailplus.nl   22/12/2017
to me

Partner mail

EXAMPLE 6.4

'Nuisance marketing'

In the UK, four companies that disrupted people with so-called 'nuisance marketing' were together fined a total of £600,000 by the UK Information Commissioner's Office (ICO).
Hundreds of complaints from the UK public about the firms prompted ICO investigations, and resulted in the following fines:

- Barrington Claims Limited, fined £250,000 for over 15 million automated calls.
- Newday Limited fined £230,000 for over 44 million spam emails.
- Limited, fined £40,000 for 111,367 spam texts.
- TFLI Limited fined £80,000 for over 1.19 million spam texts.

Crucially, all four of the businesses broke the law by not having people's agreement to be contacted by them. The key take-out is that marketers should always ensure the language used to signify consent is clear, easy to understand and not hard to find eg hidden away in a privacy policy or 'small print'. Rules are strict in most countries. If you don't know the law, check with a lawyer!

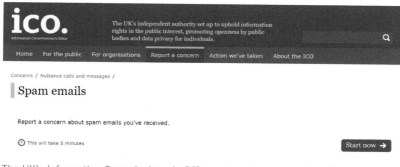

The UK's Information Commissioner's Office makes it very easy for citizens to report Spam

In the digital marketing communication funnel, email marketing can play a role in each of the following four phases. It is therefore a widely applicable communication method:

1 *Awareness*: via email, an organisation can introduce unknown brands of their own or belonging to partners easily and quickly. This can be done by sending emails consisting entirely of information about the unknown brand or by subtly bringing the brand to the attention in an email about a related successful product.

2 *Capture*: an email can generate interest among recipients, so that they can click through to the landing page or website. In an email, this can be achieved by personalising it.

3 *Conversion*: an email can lead directly to a shopping basket or order form. In practice, this can convert extremely well.

4 *Loyalty*: an email can strengthen the bond with existing customers. This is possible by, for example, the ease of use that is facilitated by the direct action that people can take from an email. Email is also used frequently to reward customer loyalty with special offers and discounts. Mainly through the use of data, for example the recipient's areas of interests, email allows you to build a relationship with the recipient. You can ask about their interests and then personalise the subsequent emails based on these interests.

Recruiting email addresses
The consumer is, by legislation, increasingly protected against the illegal collection and use of email addresses. There are strict rules that companies must adhere to, so that consumers do not receive unsolicited emails. That being said, it is not impossible for companies to collect new email addresses. It is important that permission is always requested (except for existing customers) when sending commercial emails. Only once the recipient has given permission, can a commercial email be sent. Furthermore, it must always be clear to the recipient in advance that it concerns commercial emails and/or provision of the email address to third parties.

Here are some examples of how you can obtain new email addresses:

1 Requesting during incoming/outgoing telephone calls: when customers make or receive calls, they can also be asked for their email address immediately. That is an inexpensive way, because customers are already being spoken to. However, the employee must explain what is involved, so that the customer knows exactly what the email address will be used for. Account must be taken of the fact that there is no written record of the fact that someone has given permission.
2 Enrolment for newsletter on your own website: this is a simple, easy way. If you make a clear call to action anywhere on the website, you increase the likelihood that people will actually do this.
3 Subscription via advertisement: in addition to mentioning the message you want to convey in the advertisement, you can also provide the opportunity to subscribe to the newsletter.
4 Registration via a prize competition: if people leave their details for the chance of winning a prize, an option for registering for the newsletter can also be included.
5 Renting email addresses: Some organisations, such as trade magazines with subscribers, ask their customers if they want to receive newsletters from other parties. This is done with the help of a checkbox (checkmark). These email addresses can be rented via a so-called 'list broker' (an organisation that sells consumer and/or company data to third parties). You can also do business directly with another party. In all cases, it must be perfectly clear to the person who signs up what they are consenting to.

List broker

Once you have the email addresses, maintaining and cleaning data is very important. The emails that the recipients receive must be relevant, otherwise the recipient can experience the emails as irritating. Therefore, make sure that people can easily unsubscribe (ideally one-click) if they feel that the emails are not interesting after all. Some people might report the email as spam, even though they have given permission for its receipt (see section 6.6.3). In addition, email addresses age quite quickly. Emails that are no longer deliverable, are called 'bounces'. A hard bounce is when an address really cannot be reached. These addresses have to be removed from the mailing list, because they do not yield good results when looking at the number of delivered emails (delivery rate), opens and clicks. Soft bounces occur, for example, when the recipient's mailbox is full.

Bounces
Hard bounce

Delivery rate
Soft bounces

Email marketing opportunities
Email marketing provides organisations with various possibilities. The most important ones are:

1 newsletter
2 product updates
3 store offers
4 support for letters
5 invitations
6 research
7 service emails
8 invoicing
9 internal communication
10 event emails

© Noordhoff Uitgevers bv

1 Newsletter

A newsletter usually has a fixed frequency (eg weekly), often looks the same in terms of structure and contains multiple items in one email. The newsletter is often used to generate website visits and to inform the recipient. An example of an newsletter is that of Econsultancy, part of Centaur Group. After much testing, they settled on a frequency of three days per week. The newsletter, named Digital Pulse, is delivered to inboxes every Monday, Wednesday and Friday. The target audience is English-speaking digital marketers anywhere in the world.

Newsletter

Econsultancy newsletter

2 Product updates

A product update aims to stimulate the use of products. Such an update is focussed on the provision of service and increases the loyalty of your customers.

Product update

3 Store offers

Store offers

Emails can encourage shop visits. The online store is the simplest, but it is also possible to attract visitors to physical stores. An example of this is emails from Suit Supply containing information about a promotional campaign or the new collection that can be viewed in the shops.

4 Support for other channels

Emails can be used to announce a letter, for example. This increases the attention value of a letter by announcing it via the email. Optionally, email can also be used after a letter has been sent. Then the email is more like a reminder for the letter.

Furthermore, the support of an SMS can also be considered. When you have purchased a product, you often receive an SMS when the order is ready. Prior to this, you often receive an email with the confirmation of your product and the announcement of the SMS.

5 Invitations

Invitations can be sent via email for, for example, seminars, fairs, congresses but also store openings.

6 Research

Email is regularly used to stimulate participation in a customer survey. The email is the channel linking to an online survey. For example, to ask how they like the purchased products and whether the customer might want to write a review about it.

7 Service emails

Service email

A service email aims to provide customers with service. Consider, for example, an alert that is sent to indicate that the invoice is online. Or the confirmation by email that the customer has provided a change of address. A special kind of service email is one that organisations send after a product has been purchased. It often requests an evaluation of the product and the associated services, with or without a transfer to social media or review sites.

8 Invoicing

Invoicing by email

Using email to send invoices is rapidly gaining popularity, partly due to the increase in the use of internet banking. Companies that increasingly make use of this are ones that frequently send deliveries, such as publishers, telecom providers and energy suppliers. Their most important motive is to save on expenditure.

9 Internal communication

Less well-known, but no less effective are emails from, for example, the marketing department to (all) employees in which they are informed about new campaigns, television commercials or sales developments.

10 Event emails

With increasing regularity people receive emails from companies with, for example, congratulations or a thank-you message. Important to this kind of personal email is that there is no reciprocation involved, so the recipient is not asked to respond by, for example, buying a product.

Email can therefore be aimed at things such as brand experience, or the provision of information to strengthen the bond or relationship.

6.6.2 An effective email campaign

For email marketing, the same rules and principles apply as for direct marketing communications in general. Effective emails are short and personal, they contain a clear call to action and they are always focused on what is beneficial to the target segment. The following are specific email marketing guidelines:

Email marketing guidelines

- First of all, there is the question of the *sender's address* (sender name= 'from' field). This address largely determines whether or not the recipient will open an email. It must be recognisable, consistent and reliable. The most important thing is to use the name of the organisation in this address at all times.
- Secondly, the email's *subject* is of importance. Try to indicate clearly in 40–50 characters what recipients can expect from the email, personalised where possible, avoid spam-sensitive words and use active language. Spam-sensitive words are 'loud' words, such as free, cheap and download. Symbols such as € signs, exclamation marks and the unnecessary use of capital letters are also detected by spam filters. If there are too many spam-sensitive elements in your email, it is likely that the email will not be delivered. The way spam filters and internet providers deal with spam is also called email reputation. Be aware that a very creative subject line can generate a high number of 'opens', but if the content is disappointing or worse, about something completely unrelated, then future emails will be less effective. You can try out different subject lines and test which subject line scores best. You could look at the results one week after sending and assess which subject line got the best results, for example, by looking at how often the emails were opened. Ideally, continue to work on this and progressively improve results.

  Spam filters

  Email reputation

- The use of a *headline* promotes reading. This title at the top of your email must serve as a complement to the subject line and should not be identical.
- If you know them, *address the recipient by his or her first name*. This increases the personal nature of the email. Cultural issues and B2C/B2B differences should be respected here.
- The actual message is placed in the *body copy*. Here it is important to be short and powerful in conveying the message. Emails are often scanned within 7 seconds (DDMA, 2013), so it is important that you quickly make apparent what your message is.
- A clear *call to action* aims to stimulate click behaviour. A call to action can be displayed in text, but visuals are also used regularly for this purpose. Be clear in the call to action about what you want from the recipient. For example, 'Calculate your premium' clearly states a goal. Mainly use a combination of different click options, so both visuals (images and buttons) and text links (words that can be clicked) to increase the number of opens, or the clickthrough rate. Also make sure that recipients have the opportunity to click for more information right at the beginning of an email. Of course, you can also do a so-called A/B test where you will test what works best in terms of recording click-ability (version A and version B). Please note, however, that it is advisable to apply only one change per test to keep the test clean.

  Call to action

6

- In some emails it can be important to mention *who the sender is*. This increases the sense of personal attention. It is important to mention someone who is recognisable (for example your account manager) or who holds a high position (eg the Director).
- The use of *visuals* in emails can improve clickthrough rates. Because visuals in emails could be too large, given the heaviness of the email and the loading time in your mailbox and the fact that they are not always shown automatically when opening the email, it is important to only use visuals if they add gravity to the message. This factor needs to be considered when planning your email campaigns.

The following image clarifies the aforementioned items using the example of an email from Jet Airways.

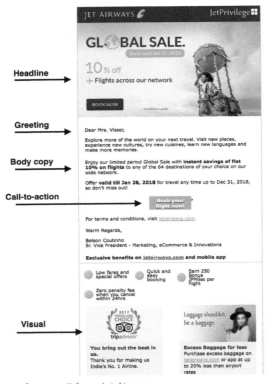

Elements of an email from Jet Airways

6.6.3   Spam

As already indicated in subsection 6.6.1, it is necessary to receive prior permission from the potential recipients of your email marketing messages before sending commercial messages via email. If this permission is not available, such messages are also called spam, or (some have suggested!) 'Sending People Annoying Messages'. Characteristics of spam are:

- spam is unsolicited email (without prior permission)
- spam is irrelevant/inappropriate
- spam is often commercial in nature
- spam does not include the option to unsubscribe

Spam

Furthermore, the following things are forbidden:
• reselling/renting out of addresses without prior knowledge
• charging customers money for making a complaint
• concealing your identity
• pretending your mail is not an advertisement

Because the recipient generally sees spam as being a very harmful burden on their email inbox, legislation has been made to regulate this and protect the recipient. Legal aspects of digital marketing are described in chapter 13, but because legal requirements for email marketing are very important, we will also discuss them here.
Under the new EU General Data Protection Regulation (GDPR) the maximum fine for data protection violation is either €20 million or 4% of annual turnover (whichever is the larger). This is giving many companies operating in Europe something to think about! The most important thing about this legislation is: prior permission.

There are five definable permission levels (see figure 6.11):
1 double opt-in
2 confirmed opt-in
3 single opt-in
4 opt-out
5 spam

Permission levels

FIGURE 6.11 Permission levels

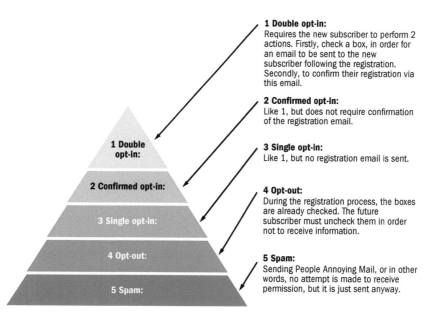

1 Double opt-in:
Requires the new subscriber to perform 2 actions. Firstly, check a box, in order for an email to be sent to the new subscriber following the registration. Secondly, to confirm their registration via this email.

2 Confirmed opt-in:
Like 1, but does not require confirmation of the registration email.

3 Single opt-in:
Like 1, but no registration email is sent.

4 Opt-out:
During the registration process, the boxes are already checked. The future subscriber must uncheck them in order not to receive information.

5 Spam:
Sending People Annoying Mail, or in other words, no attempt is made to receive permission, but it is just sent anyway.

The following two exceptions exist where prior permission is not directly relevant:
1 if it concerns the organisation's own and existing customers
2 if the messages are not commercial in nature

In the recipient's perception, a legitimate email (for example, an email from the customer's energy company) can be seen as spam. It is always important to indicate to recipients which emails they will receive, what the frequency of those emails will be and to indicate that they are able to opt-out of emails. If you do not do this properly, the emails can be regarded as spam even though it is not legally the case. How and when emails are perceived as spam is shown in the graph in figure 6.12.

FIGURE 6.12 What is spam?

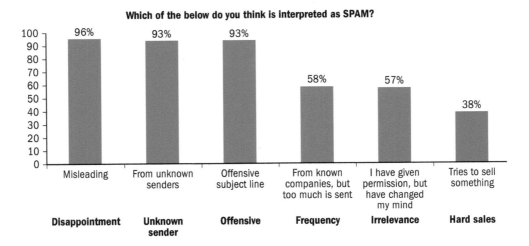

An unfamiliar sender, a frequency that is too high and irrelevant content are some characteristics of legitimate emails that are still perceived as spam. This is an important pitfall and requires a lot of attention and adequate policy from the sending organisation.

Data protection enforcement and advice to companies varies by country. However, the overall trend in both developed and developing economies is toward tighter restrictions, limiting the ability of marketers to use data and erring on the side of protecting consumers from any unwanted marketing activity.

6.6.4 Mobile email marketing

The use of mobile devices, such as a smartphone and tablets, has had a major impact on Digital Marketing and also specifically on email marketing. People are increasingly accessing their emails on a mobile device and doing this several times a day. That is why the display of an email on various devices is a much-discussed topic. Research by the DDMA in 2016 revealed that more than 40% of emails are opened on a mobile device. This number is still rising. This also highlights the importance of displaying ('rendering') an email adequately on mobile devices (DDMA, 2016). We will now briefly discuss mobile-friendly email and marketing automation.

Mobile-friendly email

An email must be legible on a smaller screen. It should not be made unnecessarily difficult for the recipient to be able to read an email properly and, if necessary, to take action, otherwise a recipient will drop out. There are therefore several technical solutions that you can apply to an email, so that the email can be read on mobile devices by the appropriate target segment.

Making sure an email adjusts to the size of the screen is called making it 'responsive'. Using a responsive design, the layout and displayed parts of an email are adapted to fit the screen. Scaling (reducing) the content and even not displaying certain elements in the email are examples of this.

Responsive design

Desktop (left) and mobile version (right) of an email from JUSTEAT

Marketing automation

A current hot topic within organisations is marketing automation. In fact, marketing automation is nothing more than automating your marketing activities. This applies to email marketing, but also to other channels. Within an automated campaign you can, for example, also use SMS and traditional direct mail in addition to email. You can set this up completely automatically. In this way, channels complement each other well and, because you do not have to send anything manually, you can work efficiently and effectively.

Marketing automation

Abandoned cart campaign

An example is an 'abandoned shopping cart campaign', a campaign that focuses on people who put products in their shopping cart but do not actually order anything:

1 You order clothing online and place a selected item in the online shopping cart.
2 You then leave the website before you pay. So, you did not (yet) purchase the item.
3 Naturally, the online retailer wants to entice you to complete the purchase process. This Organisations do this, for instance, by sending automated follow-up emails.
4 And this can be successful. Some of the potential buyers will return to finish the order process, following the automated emails.

6

Questions and assignments

NOW CHECK YOUR UNDERSTANDING:

6.1   Zappos.com is an online footwear retailer owned by Amazon.com.
   a Which owned and earned digital marketing communication channels does Zappos use to recruit visitors for their ecommerce website? Conduct a systematic audit based on the theory from this chapter.
   b What additional suggestions do you have?

6.2   You have been hired as a digital marketer for FedEx Office (www.fedex.com/us/office). Write a short note for your manager stating:
   a Why is it important to use search engine marketing?
   b What is the role of link-building and content in obtaining a high position in search engines?
   c What concrete suggestions do you have for short-term improvements?

6.3   Parisinfo.com is the official site of the Paris Convention and Visitors Bureau.
   a View the website and find out to what extent Paris Convention and Visitors Bureau uses mobile marketing communication techniques to better inform visitors.
   b Which (additional) mobile techniques do you advise Paris Convention and Visitors Bureau to use?

6.4   WE Fashion is an international fashion corporation.
   a Find out how WE Fashion uses its owned and earned social media channels for customer acquisition.
   b Which points for improvement do you see?

6.5   You want to sell good summaries of books to your fellow students. You decide to generate visitors for your website via email marketing.
   a How could you obtain the email addresses of your website's users?
   b Which requirements do you have to meet for email marketing to be successful?

6

6.6

Samsung UK targets SMEs
By Mike Berry

Samsung is a global technology company which follows a simple business philosophy: to devote its talent and technology to creating superior products and services that contribute to a better global society. To achieve this, Samsung sets a high value on its people and technologies. Samsung aims to create the products and services that give customers the best satisfaction.

Samsung UK wanted to drive B2B sales and, very simply, to make Samsung the first technology choice for SMEs. They decided to focus on key cities across the North of England, UK. They chose population centres with the highest density of SMEs in sectors which have a greater need for Samsung technology at work. The campaign was all about celebrating small businesses and the people who own and run them – those who don't get much sleep, who don't take enough time off but who love what they do.

Samsung UK targeted the owners and staff of these small businesses with tailored local promotional activity in each of the target cities, including a mix of: online content, social media and live events. Samsung UK used an emotional creative strategy, based on genuine human truths, to communicate a strong message to this busy and rather sceptical target audience. The campaign was called 'More Good Days at Work', which struck a chord with this hard-pressed entrepreneurial group. It also generated significant word-of-mouth campaign of this type.

Although this was a B2B campaign, the Samsung approach was more typical of B2C marketing, which made it unusual and attention-grabbing.

The campaign achieved immediate success in the launch city, Bristol in south-west England. Next, Samsung targeted 78,000 SMEs in the northern English city of Manchester. Here too, More Good Days at Work proved very successful in reaching and engaging the small businesses and getting them talking and thinking about Samsung products. In Manchester, Samsung reported an increase in sales of over 30%, positive ROI and a significant increase in those SMEs in who said 'Samsung would be their 1st choice for workplace technology' – a key metric identified by Samsung.

For the creative treatment, Samsung decided to focus on a real human (emotional) story but still it was important for them to relate the campaign to basic business reality. The central creative idea was that we are all today increasingly reliant on technology in our personal and working lives; so much so that we can get really stressed out when our technology doesn't work! The solution was positioned as Samsung who, through its superior technology solutions, can make sure we all have *more good days at work.*

Samsung UK placed Social Media at the centre of their strategy. They targeted small business decision-makers and their people through: advertising in targeted environments, out-of-home (billboards) media, sponsorship, online content, experiential and PR. The whole campaign was tied together on Samsung's key social media channels with the hashtag #MoreGoodDaysAtWork.

To extend the reach of the campaign even further, Samsung promoted 'More Good Days' through various events, blogs and extensive social media activity. Samsung incentivised the owners and staff of target SMEs with coffee, cupcakes, VIP events, free media space, and product discounts and deals

Those local businesses who tweeted about their 'Good Day at Work' using the hashtag '#MoreGoodDaysAtWork', were entered into a prize draw to win free billboard ad space. Three businesses won free media space and help with design to create their own business-specific ads. The ads were displayed on Manchester's largest full-motion digital screen, worth a total of over £4,500 per business, helping promote their business to over 140,000 adults in Manchester each day.

A collage of the #MoreGoodDaysAtWork campaign by Samsung

Samsung added a promotion: win a Barista visit: SMEs in Manchester were encouraged to connect with Samsung via social media, for the chance to win their own barista visit to their office so that their people could enjoy coffee and cupcakes. Activity was based around Manchester public transit stations with free chocolates and promotional handouts. Twitter was included (via Promoted tweets) as well as LinkedIn activity. 14 lucky businesses received free coffee and cupcakes from Samsung!

Another part of the campaign was the Samsung Apprentice challenge: Samsung worked with Manchester Metropolitan University (MMU), reaching out to entrepreneurially-minded students.

The participating MMU students were provided with free Samsung devices. Next, they were challenged to launch and build a business from scratch. The winning team placed tech at the heart of their idea by offering content as a service to other Manchester small businesses, using social media to promote themselves; they were judged by Samsung to be worthy winners.

Next, 'SME VIPs' were invited by Samsung to a special event in Manchester, designed to get businesses excited about the roles of technology and marketing in modern business. Samsung involved their famous brand ambassador, 5-time

Olympic gold medallist Sir Steve Redgrave, to share the viewpoint of a world-class athlete of what it means to have a 'good day at work' and amplify the effect of the campaign.

Most important of all, Samsung put their Social Media channels at the heart of this campaign. Samsung used social media to tie all activities together, to reach their key targets in SMEs and amplify the effect of all the activity, online and offline, under the hashtag #MoreGoodDaysAtWork.

Overall the results were extremely impressive. Samsung reported a total ROI of more than 500% within the campaign period, a 20% improvement in Samsung's brand preference' ie SMEs making Samsung their first choice for tech at work. Crucially, there was a 34% local sales increase after 2 months.

Sally Wright, Enterprise Marketing Director, Samsung UK:

'We wanted to have a bold approach to help us better connect with owners and employees of small businesses to jointly celebrate their achievements and efforts. Our 'More Good Days' message allowed us to really engage with these organisations on an emotional level and have more relevant conversations across various channels, resulting in some fantastic feedback and results.'

Source: www.b2bmarketing.net/en-gb/resources/b2b-case-studies
/awards-case-study-how-samsung-encouraged-smes-manchester-have-more-good

NOW CHECK YOUR UNDERSTANDING:

a Analyse how easily 'More Good Days' can be found via Google. Is the discoverability good? Has Samsung optimised around this keyword? Support your answer based on the theory from this chapter.

b Content is very important for Samsung in its efforts to reach SMEs. Explain the role of content for a business-to-business organisation based on the theory.

c Does link-building also play a role for a campaign of this sort? If so, what role and if not, why not?

d Sally Wright does not discuss the role of mobile marketing communication techniques in online customer acquisition. Amongst companies targeting SMEs, the use of mobile marketing is commonplace. Which mobile marketing communication techniques could Samsung implement and for what purpose?

e What was the role of Social Media in this campaign? Which channels/ platforms would you have recommended to Samsung?

f Do you believe Samsung could use email marketing within online customer acquisition for this audience? Base this on the list of possibilities from sub-section 6.6.1. Which requirements must Samsung's email marketing meet?

g Identify two ways that Samsung could acquire leads from SMEs. Design an effective campaign flow for each of these.

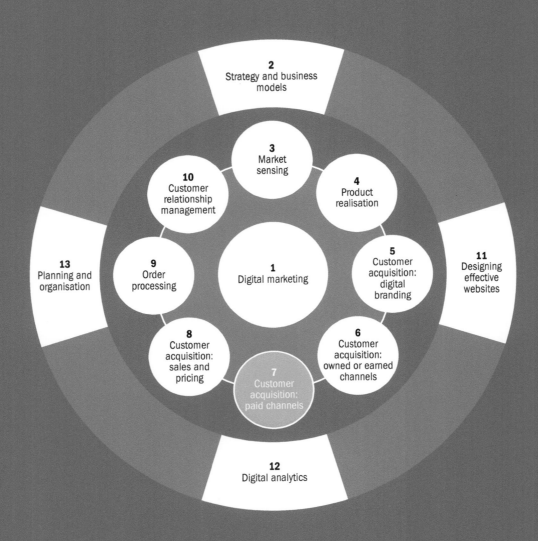

7

Customer acquisition: recruiting visitors through paid channels

Authors: Marjolein Visser (7.1), Martijn Hoving (7.2), Dennis Koops (7.3), Bart van der Kooi (7.4) and Ruben van Brug (7.5)

Previous chapters describe how the marketer can establish a clear idea of the market's wants and desires (the market analysis process) and how the Internet can be used to further product development and improvement as well as the creation of processes for the facilitation of the product or service (the realisation process). Once everything is customer-ready, it is time for the market approach. The customer acquisition process is comprised of defining target markets and acquiring new customers. Customer acquisition consists of four steps: marketing communications to draw attention to the brand and connect to the customer, the sales process for convincing those customers to actually buy the product and finally agreeing on the price of the product. The previous two chapters described the role of digital marketing communication in brand management and the use of paid marketing communication channels. This chapter illustrates how you can use paid channels·for the purpose of connecting to customers. The sales process and price determination will be covered in Chapter 8.

This chapter covers:
- digital marketing communication through paid channels
- search engine advertising
- display advertising
- social media advertising
- affiliate marketing

After reading this chapter you will know how to:
- explain how the digital marketer can optimise the results of search engine advertising.
- indicate how the digital marketer can optimise the results of display advertising, the roles of the different players within display advertising and the pros and cons of the currently applied pricing models.

- exemplify how the digital marketer can optimise the results of social media advertising.
- formulate how the digital marketer can optimise the results of affiliate marketing, the roles of the different players within affiliate marketing and how the digital marketer can motivate affiliates.

7.1 Digital marketing communication through paid channels

Previously, you've read that the final aim of marketing communications is to sell products, services or ideas to customers of the organisation. For every marketing activity the marketing managers, product managers and communication managers develop a detailed communications plan in which every step of the acquisition process is addressed. In doing so, they always try to find the tactics and channels that involve the lowest costs per sale. If they can motivate the target group to visit their (online) sales or communication channels through an 'owned' or 'earned' communication channel at relatively low cost in terms of creating content, they will do so. You read more about this in Chapter 6. In practice, it appears that for most organisations, online advertising is indispensable for attracting sufficient new visitors (the first step in the marketing funnel, see figure 7.1).

FIGURE 7.1 'Visit' is the first step of the digital marketing funnel

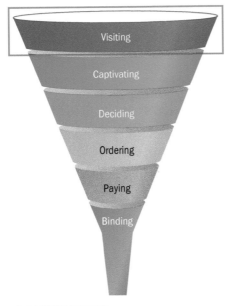

Source: © Marjolein Visser RM

Paid channels are applied to the digital marketing communications funnel, primarily aimed at creating 'awareness' and 'capture' (see figure 5.1), but they can also play a supporting role in 'conversion' and 'loyalty'.

Paid recruitment of visitors for online sales and communication channels can be done using search engine advertising, display advertising, social media advertising and affiliate marketing. These possibilities are further elaborated on in this chapter.

7.2 Paid Search (=Pay-Per-Click=PPC)

Section 6.2 describes how search engine marketing works. This section describes one of the paid marketing communication channels, namely paid search advertising. This entails placing advertisements (ads) that are displayed when someone types in a specifically purchased keyword. These ads are available in multiple search engines, but Google is the most used search engine in most of the world. Google's PPC advertising programme is called 'Google AdWords'.

Paid search advertising

PPC
Google AdWords

In scientific research we see more and more studies focussing on search engine advertising. Some striking results from these studies:
- Search engine ads have a significant impact on the brand awareness for the advertiser, and for the consumer, on the understanding that they have viewed an advertisement (Zenetti et al., 2014).
- Brand awareness has a positive effect on the clickthrough rate (the number of clicks versus the number of impressions) of search engine ads (Atkinson et al., 2014).
- As consumers who use less popular search phrases tend to put more effort into finding information and are closer to making a purchase, they can be targeted with search engine ads. Ads with a higher position in the search engine results achieve higher clickthrough ratios and more conversions (Batra and Keller, 2017).

Clickthrough rate

Before you put AdWords into practice it is useful to follow Google's most recent online tutorials: https://support.google.com/adwords. In this chapter, we will describe the basic principles.
In this section we will first discuss search engine advertising and the funnel process. Then we will elaborate on creating successful text ads. Then we will look at the landing pages that are linked to ads. Finally, we will cover some specific applications of search engine advertising.

7.2.1   Paid Search (PPC) and the funnelling process
In this subsection we will focus on keywords, but first we will refer briefly to the AIDA model, the foundation of search engine advertising.

The AIDA model as a basis
A frequently used model for search engine advertising is the AIDA model: a consumer starts off with attention (Awareness) for a particular product or offer, then they become interested (Interest), they long to buy it (Desire)

AIDA model

© Noordhoff Uitgevers bv

and then they take action (Action). In search engine advertising the corresponding elements in the funnelling process are (figure 7.2):

- keywords (attention)
- advertisements (interest)
- landing pages (desire)
- call to action/CTA (action)

FIGURE 7.2 Search engine marketing funnel

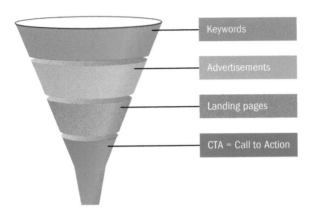

You might, of course, also work with the digital marketing communication funnel from subsection 5.1.2. You would then follow the steps awareness (keywords), capture (advertisements) and conversion (landing pages).

In the following images the way a consumer looks for a loft bed on ihttp://www.ikea.com/ is shown and how they then, through an advertisement and a landing page, end up in the ordering process. You can read more about landing pages in subsection 7.2.3.

Key word 'loft bed' leads to attention

In the previous image you can see that a search engine user has entered the keywords 'loft bed'. The user is taken to a page (The Search Engine Results Page or SERPS) on which search results are displayed (next image), that raises the user's awareness of the various suppliers (attention). Their interest in one or more suppliers is being piqued.

Loft Beds & Loft Bed Frames - IKEA
www.ikea.com/gb/en/products/beds/loft-beds-bunk-beds/loft-beds/ ▾
Visit IKEA online to browse our range of **loft beds**, and find plenty of home furnishing ideas and inspiration.
Loft bed frame STORÅ £239 · Loft beds & bunk beds · Loft bed frame SVÄRTA £130

Children's Loft Beds | Room to Grow
https://www.roomtogrow.co.uk/category/childrens-beds/childrens-loft-beds/ ▾
Products 1 - 12 of 75 - **Loft beds** are great for getting the most out of small spaces. Thanks to their clever design, they free up room underneath the bed. This can be turned into a work area with the addition of a children's desk, a cosy sitting space, or can even be used for additional storage. If you're looking for flexible space, ...

FLEXA Loft Beds - Platform beds and high sleeper beds for kids - FLEXA
www.flexaworld.com/products/beds/high-beds.html ▾
Casa high **bed** 80-17513-40, FLEXA White See product. ... 140 cm high **bed** 90-10623-1-01, FLEXA Classic See product. ... 140 cm high **bed** 90-10623-11-01, FLEXA Classic See product.

Loft Beds | eBay
www.ebay.co.uk/bhp/loft-bed ▾
Find great deals on eBay for **Loft Bed** in Bed Frames and Divan Bases. Shop with confidence.

The search result 'Loft bed' arouses interest

Suppose the search engine user clicks on one of the advertisements and views the advertiser's offer on their screen. The landing page they are taken to answers their need (if it's been well built and the traffic well targeted).

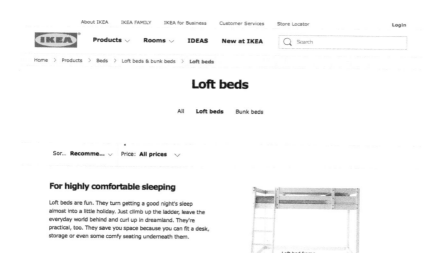

The landing page creates desire

Every product that is offered is accompanied by a 'call to action', the possibility to order, request more information, etc. By clicking on the ordering button, the product is placed in the shopping basket. Then the purchase can actually be made (action).

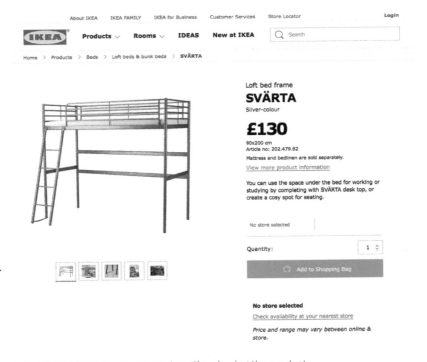

The ordering button encourages to action: buying the product

When we consider the role of search engine advertising within the digital marketing communication funnel (figure 5.1), we notice that the ad mostly plays a part in the 'awareness' phase: raising awareness of the organisation and its offer. The landing page is important for holding on to the customer (capture). After one or more intermediate steps, this will eventually result in conversion (which in the case of ecommerce generally means 'purchase').

As pointed out in subsection 6.2.1, search engine advertising offers the possibility to quickly test what variables result in a purchase or a reaction among the target segment. Important information is that, in the funnelling process, keywords and ads determine only 40% of the success. The landing page and the call to action together determine 60% of the success. Before we elaborate on this process, we'll now first discuss keywords and ads.

Since more than half of all searches take place on a smartphone, it is important to include this in a customer journey as mentioned before. Most orientation searches (such as 'loft bed') are already done on a smartphone. This means that the advertiser needs to take this into account with regard to creating landing pages.

© Noordhoff Uitgevers bv

Keywords

A keyword is the word (or phrase) that an Internet user enters into the
search engine (ie the search term or search query). If there's a match
between a user's search query and the advertiser's selected keyword, an
ad is presented. There are many possibilities for tailoring keywords to what
is searched for specifically. For instance, it is possible to present an ad for
the search query 'online accounting', but for the ad NOT to be displayed if
it is 'free online accounting' which is searched for. In this case, 'free' is
set as a negative keyword in AdWords.

Keyword

Views, clicks and conversion

Three essential 'metrics' (indicators for measuring results) of search
engine advertising are:

Metrics

1 *Clickthrough rate (CTR)*: this is the average number of times a PPC ad is
   clicked on as a percentage of the total numbers of impressions. For
   example, a click through of 1% means that out of one hundred views,
   one visit (clickthrough) took place.

Clickthrough rate (CTR)

2 *Number of conversions*: this is the % of site visitors, in this case from an
   ad, that display specific desirable behaviour, eg a purchase on the site.

Conversions

3 *Conversion %*: this involves the amount of obtained conversions, divided
   by the number of clicks on the advertisement, that was needed for this.

Conversion %

These indicators are essential to evaluating and fine-tuning the digital
marketing communications, and thus also for a search engine advertising
campaign. In AdWords, Google provides software to monitor these
indicators.

Keyword relevance

Relevance, ie finding whatever you are searching for, is the raison d'etre
for every search engine. After all, search engine users will only come back
if they can (quickly) find the information they need and if this information
proves to be relevant to them. Keyword relevance is the extent to which
the presented keyword-based advertisement is relevant to the search
engine user. In Paid Search, the clickthrough rate (CTR) is an important
indicator for relevance. The higher the CTR, the more relevant and
interesting the advertisement is to the search engine user in regard to a
particular keyword.

Relevance

Keyword relevance

Google AdWords rewards relevant advertisements greatly with a higher listing
at a lower cost per visitor. Less relevant or irrelevant advertisements are
'punished' by turning them off or by (significantly) increasing the price per
click. Google grades each ad with a 'Quality Score' (a number between 0 and
10) depending on the expected CTR, the relevance, the landing page, the
expected impact of the advertisement (whether extensions have been added)
and the bid. This score, together with the 'bid' ie maximum willingness to pay
PER CLICK in Euros, Dollars, GBP, etc determines the Ad Rank.

Ad Rank

Relevance is in the interest of all parties involved: search engine users can
easily find whatever they are searching for, advertisers can address only
the target segment and Google maintains their market position.

How does an advertiser remain relevant? By bidding only on specific
keywords that are directly related to a product or service. For example, if a
student is looking for a job, 'student job' is a relevant keyword. Do not use

7

broad keywords that only have a parallel relationship with student jobs. In this case the phrase 'earn money' would be far too general.

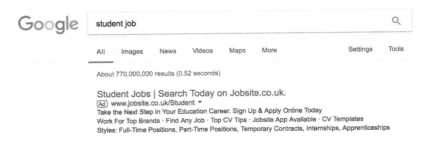

Student job is a relevant keyword

From target segment to keywords

Keyword research is important for incorporating the right words into the campaign. Experience has shown that thorough keyword research is seldom performed, so that advertisers bid on only a very limited set of keywords. By performing thorough keyword research, you can improve the effectiveness of campaigns significantly.

In search engines, the determination of the target segment is based on themes. Direct marketers used to use a description that looked like the following: 'Every small and medium business in Frankfurt (say) with, on average, 10 to 50 employees that use an obsolete accounting package'. This is not a suitable target segment for search engine advertising, but 'companies that are expecting issues with their electronic tax returns' is. For this you can find specific keywords that are related to the target segment's issue.

Look for themes ie the target segment's issues and 'pain points'. Examine keywords from the issue's point of view rather than from a solution's or product's point of view.

For example, 'VPN router' is a solution/product related keyword. 'Work safely from home' is a customer-issue keyword. 'Problem keywords' are often used earlier on in the sales cycle. This provides the opportunity to reach the potential customer sooner.

Keyword research

Keyword research consists of three steps:

Step 1   conduct an ideation session
Step 2   extend the list
Step 3   determine the value of the keywords found

Step 1 Conduct an ideation session
Get together with a number of people and write down all the words that are directly related to your product or service. Preferably, also include an outsider.

Step 2 Extend the list
You can extend the list of all the words you have written down in the following ways:
• Make sure that all the brand names, product names and product codes are on the list.

© Noordhoff Uitgevers bv

- Include all the plurals and diminutives of the keywords.
- Find synonyms for the previously found words.
- Check the current website, catalogues and folders for missed words.
- Look at the keywords that are currently being used to find you.
- Analyse the content of the competition's publications.
- Listen to the customer during a sales talk.
- Use Excel to keep an overview of keywords.
- Use tools.

Search engine users have an issue and are looking for a solution. Put yourself in their position and try to think like they do as much as possible.

Step 3 Determine the value of keywords found
Determine which keywords are most relevant. These can be focussed upon.

Don't try to think of all the keywords at once. Start a campaign with a limited set and stick with 'good' words. A good campaign will generate new words, whilst words that do not generate conversions, will be abandoned.

7.2.2 Making good textual advertisements
Of importance for a good textual advertisement is: the number of words used, the sites on which advertisements are shown, the position of the advertisement, the costs per click and the available budget and the proposition of the advertisement call to action. These subjects are focussed upon in this subsection.

Convincing with few words
When search engine users have searched for a specific keyword, they are presented with textual advertisements. Advertisements consist of three lines: a title of 25 characters and two text lines of 35 characters. Below is the site's URL. The limited space available therefore needs to be utilised as effectively as possible.

Vodafone UK Official Site - View Our Range Of Deals Online
Ad www.vodafone.co.uk/ ▾
Choose From The Latest Range Of Phones, SIMs & More. See What's New & Buy Online

Vodafone doesn't need many words

Limiting advertisements to a region
Textual advertisements are not only presented on www.google.com, but also on partner sites. For each campaign, the digital marketer can indicate where the advertisements should be shown. For advertising on Google itself (ie the Google Search Results Page or SERP), the country and the browser's language settings can be selected.

Within a particular country, AdWords also offers the option of presenting ads in a particular region only.

Google Display Network (GDN)

In addition to the Google site itself (SERP) there is also the Google Display Network (GDN). These are sites on which Google buys space in which advertisements can be displayed that are related to the contents of that particular site or app.

More information about online display advertising can be found in section 7.3.

Ad positions

Ad positions

Highly commercial

Auction pressure

AdWords advertisements are usually displayed at the top of the screen (just below the search query) and at the bottom. This advertising space is auctioned by Google. When the search query is 'highly commercial', a maximum of four results are displayed at the top of the page. Highly commercial means those keywords with a lot of competition. The degree of competition is also called auction pressure. This concerns a maximum of 5-10% of the searches in the search engine. When there are four ads at the top of the page, there will be another maximum of three ads at the bottom of the first page. This differs from one search query to another and depends on the level of competition. Usually, for searches that are less commercial, there will be three results and there may be more ads at the bottom of the page. In general, the higher an advertisement is on the page, the higher the CTR and number of clicks. A lot of visits however do not necessarily mean that the results (the conversions into sales or leads) will also improve. In a lot of cases the top listings attract a lot of visits from non-'buying' customers. For the lower listings, the results are often better due to the fact that the search engine user has by then already seen multiple advertisements before they click on that particular advertisement. We can therefore conclude that they are genuinely interested. For the lower listings, there is less traffic and therefore it becomes a matter of finding the right balance between visits and results. The position is determined by:

- the price the advertiser is willing to pay for a word
- the clickthrough rate
- the advertisement's quality score

This will be explained next.

Budgets and cost per click

Large insurance companies often spend tens of thousands of euros per month in order to sell insurance policies directly. As a result, it is almost impossible for small insurance brokers with a budget of €1,000 say, to sell their insurance policies using Google AdWords. However, using AdWords, a taxi company from Copenhagen say with a €1,000 budget can easily sell its services. In this case there is less competition from large companies and the taxi company can advertise locally. So before you decide whether AdWords is a good channel for your brand, it is important to find out how competitive the market is for your best keywords and what prices are typically paid per click. Google provides a good estimate of the costs per click, even before you start a campaign.

Quality score

Google only makes money once an advertisement is clicked on. The position of the advertisement is therefore not only dependent on the maximum price the advertiser is willing to pay per click, but also on the quality score of a keyword (0–10). Amongst other things, the quality score

7

is determined by the following factors: the advertisement's click through rate, the relevance of the landing page, the relevance of the advertisement itself in combination with the keyword that is used and its history within the AdWords account. The combination of the keyword and the advertisement results in a certain quality score for the keyword (0-10). Google uses Quality Score to 'manipulate' the AdWords auction; rewarding 'good' ads with high quality scores and punishing 'bad' ads with low ones.

For the digital marketer, the AdWords system is non-transparent, because the quality score of competitors and the competitive bids per click are unknown. What the advertiser can do is determine the effect of their actions based on the average position of their own advertisements.

The maximum bid per click can be set for both the ad group level and individual keyword level. An ad group is a number of advertisements that are focussed on the same keywords. It is advisable to start with a maximum bid per click on ad group level and then, after having measured the clicks and conversion rate, to set the maximum bid for each keyword. Consequently, a maximum daily campaign budget can be set. AdWords then makes sure that no more than the maximum daily budget is spent on any given day.

Ad group

AdWords will discontinue displaying the advertisements as soon as the maximum daily budget has been reached. Google can also 'spread' the frequency of advertisements showing up across the day. A bespoke method can be configured for each campaign. It is wise to check the maximum daily budget and the other settings regularly as search traffic on the Internet is still increasing and is subject to seasonal influences. It is vitally important to monitor conversion rates and compare with the actual costs paid per click.

One way of determining whether a campaign, advertising group or keyword is generating a satisfactory return, is by looking at the so-called ROAS: return on advertising spending.
The formula is:

ROAS

$$ROAS = \frac{(\text{Total conversion value} - \text{Total costs})}{\text{Total costs}}$$

An example: 10 conversions have been achieved with a total value of €50 per conversion. The total conversion value then is €500. 100 clicks have been registered, at, on average, a cost of €1 per click. Therefore, the total cost of the AdWords Campaign equals €100. So ROAS will be: (€500 - €100)/€100 = €4. For every €1 invested, €4 is generated.

Proposition of the advertisement
A good advertisement starts with a good proposition. A good proposition is:
- clear
- distinct
- specific
- concise
- highly customer-orientated

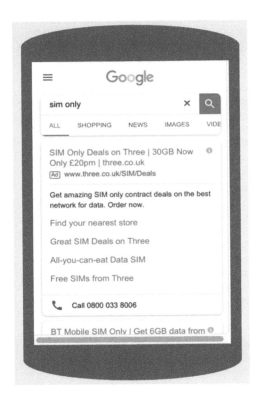

On mobile devices, search result ads are displayed in full-screen

The trick is to offer the customer an advantage that is not offered by competitors. As there isn't much space in search engines for advertisements, it is essential to concisely illustrate the core of the proposition. Using AdWords, a variety of propositions and their wording can be tested side by side.

The AIDA-concept can be used as a tool for creating good advertisements. In short this means that a good advertisement should attract attention first, interest and desire next, followed by a call to action that encourages the next step:

- *Attention:* is primarily drawn by the title using attractive words ideally including the keyword.

Compare Top 10 Life Insurance | Only Takes 2 Minutes | reassured.co.uk
[Ad] compare.reassured.co.uk/ ▾
Compare The UK's Top Insurers To Find Your Cheapest Quote. Get In Touch Today!
Highlights: Large Life Insurance Brokers, No Obligation Personalised Quotation
Compare Life Insurance - from £5.00 - From Just £5 Per Month · More ▾

Drawing attention using the title

- *Interest:* responding to the needs of the search engine user by mentioning a clear advantage.

Habito™ Online Mortgage Broker | Save £1,000s On Your Mortgage
[Ad] www.habito.com/Online/Mortgages ▾
★★★★★ Rating for habito.com: 4.9 - 376 reviews
Applying Is Quick & Seamless With Habito. Get A Quote Online Within Minutes Now!
Types: Mortgages, Remortgages, First Time Buyers, Self Employed, Buy To Let

Advantage arouses interest

- *Desire*: indicating how the search engine user can acquire what is of interest to them by the means of, for example, a (special) offer such as a free download, discount or sign-up gift.

HubSpot.com | HubSpot® Official | Schedule a Free Demo
[Ad] offers.hubspot.com/Marketing/Demo ▾
HubSpot® Makes It Easier to Manage Your Online Marketing. Schedule Demo Today!
Works With Any Website · Inbound Marketing · All-in-One Software · No-Hassle Integrations
Types: Marketing Automation Tool, Lead Capture Forms, Real Time Analytics

Perks create desire

- *Action:* activate customers to, for example, sign up for a newsletter, buy or request information or view a demo.

Ecommerce Store Solution | Start a 14 Day Free Trial Now | shopify.com
[Ad] www.shopify.com/ ▾
Everything You Need To Start Selling Online Today.
See Plans & Pricing · Find Products To Sell · Shopify Plus® Enterprise · Shopify® POS System

Encourage taking action

When the search engine user clicks on the advertisement they are directed to the landing page, where a confirmation of the proposition can be found.

Starting point for approaching customers

One of the most commonly made mistakes in the creation of Search ads is composing text that is too 'internally' focussed. Many advertisements are constructed 'inside-out'. The focus is on the presentation of the company itself to the outside world and includes phrases such as 'we are', 'we can' and 'we do'.

A potential customer is seeking a solution to a problem and therefore can best be approached with this problem (the theme) too. Put yourself in the customer's position when creating advertisements and consider problems/situations and advantages rather than products or services. Avoid professional jargon, unless your target audience is familiar with it, and run the advertisements by people from the target audience.

Laser Eye Surgery - LASEK & LASIK Treatment | Free Consultation
https://advancedvisioncare.co.uk/treatments/laser-eye-surgery/ ▼
AVC in Harley Street, London is a leading specialist in laser eye surgery - LASIK and LASEK treatments. Call 0800 652 4878 to book your FREE consultation today.

Laser eye surgery Prices: The 5 most important factors
https://www.londonvisionclinic.com/how-our-laser-eye-surgery-is-different/fees/ ▼
★★★★★ Rating: 9.8/10 · 948 reviews
We strive for excellence in everything we do, and that includes taking much more time and care over the testing and screening of your eyes, at no extra charge. Often, 2 to 3 times as long as other clinics, ensuring you get every test and treatment you need . The only way to keep the cost of Laser Eye Surgery low is to treat a ...

Inside-out

Outside-in

The ultimate goal of these advertisements is that they stimulate potential customers to make contact with the organisation and ultimately pay a visit to their website.

Extensions in advertisements

AdWords extensions

Google continues to expand its advertising possibilities within Google AdWords. Several types of 'AdWords Extensions' have become available in recent years. These are additions to a normal AdWords ad. The most commonly used extensions are the seller ratings extensions, the call extensions, the site-link extensions and the highlight extensions. Google encourages these, as it believes they give the user a better experience ie a better answer to their search query.

Guardian Weekly | Try 6 Issues for €6 | theguardian.com
[Ad] subscribe.theguardian.com/ ▼
★★★★★ Rating for theguardian.com: 4.8 - 331 reviews
Every week. The world in perspective. **Subscribe and save on your first 6 issues.**
Year-round savings · Free Worldwide Delivery · 6 for $6 · Weekly News

Insight and Analysis
Weekly analytical, insightful
commentary on world news.

Guardian Subscriptions
Discover All Guardian Subscriptions
And Find The Right Package For You

The highlight extensions (green frame) emphasise the advertiser's USPs

Seller ratings extension

Call extension

Site-link extension

The seller ratings extension shows a number on a scale of 1-5 alongside 5 stars, that the advertiser uses to show the organisation's or product's average rating. The call extension allows the viewer to phone the advertiser immediately with just one click within an advertisement. The site-link extension provides space for multiple 'deep links' (see subsection 7.2.3) under an advertisement, that the advertiser uses to draw attention to subtopics. The links under an advertisement that refer to deeper pages are called site links. These deep links also exist within organic search results, if someone searches for a brand name. Lastly, the highlight extension allows you to add an extra line to the advertisement in which the advertiser's USPs (unique selling points) can be 'highlighted'. Remember that an increasing number of Google searches now happen on a mobile device, and Google is progressively optimising the experience for mobile searchers.

Site links

Highlight extension

Car Insurance | We can save you over £300 | confused.com
[Ad] www.confused.com/insurance ▼
★★★★★ Rating for confused.com: 4.6 - 4,626 reviews
We check hundreds of insurers and give you instant quotes
UK Landlord Insurance · Confused.com UK · UK Life Insurance · Compare UK Energy
Buy A Car · Car Finance & Loans · Motor Insurance

In the frames: the site link extensions (red) and the seller ratings extension (green)

7.2.3   Landing pages

We will now discuss landing pages that are linked to Adwords advertisements as well as the advantages of landing pages. Also, in this subsection, we will cover the AIDA concept and how it is used for landing pages. Finally, we will discuss the way in which search engine marketing is more effective with landing pages and how this can also be measured. In section 11.6 you can read how to build a landing page that converts well.

Landing pages linked to advertisements

Every day, Google processes approximately 4.5 billion search queries (SmartInsights.com, 2017). Somewhere in the midst of all these searchers are many who belong to the target audiences that organisations are aiming at. When these users search for a product or service and then click an advertisement, they land on the website of a supplier. In principle, the visitors become potential buyers or leads from that moment on.

The landing page is a webpage that follows up on a direct marketing activity. It is the first page a search engine user lands on after clicking on an advertisement. The landing page can only be reached through your advertisement. If it consists of multiple pages, it is called a microsite. A landing page is designed to be an extension of a specific direct-marketing activity and is in fact an integral part of it. The aim of the landing page is to increase response and to convert as many of these visitors as possible into an actual customer or lead. This requires the website's visitors to turn to action: to buy something or leave their details.

Landing page

Microsite

The advantages of landing pages

A lot of marketers simply direct their advertisement traffic to the homepage of their website. A consequence of this can be disappointing results; the homepage consists of too many distracting elements that divert the reader's attention away from the desired call to action. The guiding principle is that 50% of traffic navigates away after landing on the homepage. In addition, the leads are then expected to find the correct link on the website by themselves. If they don't succeed at once, they are likely to give up and your investment will have been fruitless. A landing page ensures that the lead will be directed immediately to the page that includes the relevant information.

Some advantages of having a good landing page are:
- On an isolated page you can engage in dialogue with the searcher and discuss the offer.
- The page does not have any links to other products and/or services so the focus remains on the offer.
- The interest that is piqued by the advertisement will be taken to the next level on the landing page. The reader can be persuaded and be tempted into action.
- The landing page registers the reader's clicking behaviour. This way you'll get to know more about the lead's interests and desires, so that the PPC campaign and the website can be optimised for even better conversion.

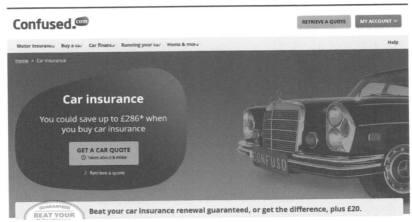

On Confused.com's landing page, the possible savings on car insurances communicated in the search ad can easily be found.

Split-run

Working with various landing pages provides you with the possibility to test-run different propositions regarding a product or service. In a so-called split-run you can link multiple landing pages to a single advertisement and rotate them in the search engine. This allows you to measure which page yields the best return in terms of conversions.

AIDA and the landing page

Following the AIDA-concept on a landing page, you can steer the searcher towards the desired action. Their attention is attracted by the advertisement. If the proposition as stated in the advertisement is interesting enough, it is likely that they will click on it. At that moment the search engine user enters your website and becomes a lead. The landing page then has to reaffirm that they are in the right place by repeating the advertisement's text and proposition. By responding to the visitor's need or problem, interest will be stirred much faster. Then the landing page needs to make clear how the user can acquire the thing they want (desire). Eventually, they must be encouraged to take action. This is the moment the visitor can be converted from a lead into a valuable lead or customer. It is very important to make as simple and transparent as possible, what it is precisely that the customer needs to do in order to buy a product or to request more information.

If someone does not buy something immediately, you still would like to have their details. There are various methods for collecting details. In exchange for personal or company details you can offer the customer something, a newsletter for example, an online demo, a document involving specific business knowledge (whitepaper) or a free consultation. The option of buying or requesting something must be clearly visible on the landing page, possibly in multiple locations.

Whitepaper

© Noordhoff Uitgevers bv

Call to action on the landing page

Search engine marketing is more effective when you optimise your landing pages

Bespoke (tailored) landing pages should really always be used in Search Engine Advertising campaigns. The results that are achieved when using a separate landing page that describes the specific issue are notably better than when the traffic is directed to the homepage. Preferably, landing pages should be used when the offer in products and services is variable. By using an advertisement and a landing page, as well as a combination of keywords that are as specific as possible, the searcher can then be directed to the solution (product or service) that most closely matches this on the website. If someone is looking for a cruise in the Caribbean, then they will respond better to a landing page with specific information than to the homepage of a generic travel agency that also happens to offer cruises.

Another variety of landing pages are so-called theme sites. These are microsites consisting of a smaller number of pages, on which the content is tailored to one particular theme. One example could be a microsite belonging to a large travel agency that focuses specifically on hiking holidays.

Theme sites

Measuring results

If landing pages can only be reached through the advertisement, it is easier to measure conversions and the ROI of the campaign than when the landing page is eg the homepage of the website. The URLs of the landing pages are specified as the destination URL of the search engine advertisements. Because every advertisement contains a personalised proposition, you would ideally have a different landing page for every advertisement. In practice, one landing page per advertisement group usually suffices.

If there are multiple propositions, landing pages can be used to test which one produces the highest return. By rotating the same advertisements with different URLs, the landing page and therefore the proposition that generates the most customers or leads can be identified.

7.2.4   Specific applications

In this subsection, we will cover two specific applications of search engine advertising: Google Shopping and re-marketing. Then we will provide some information about automating search engine advertising.

Google shopping

Google Shopping

Google Shopping is a search engine that has been custom designed by Google to enable the user to find products in Google. These products, offered by all kinds of online retailers, are uploaded to Google AdWords campaigns. As of February 2013 Google Shopping became a paid service, which means that the retailers pay for every click on a product (in accordance with the Pay-Per-Click model, just like in Google AdWords).

Pay-Per-Click

Google Shopping is seen as a serious competitor to online comparison sites such as moneysupermarket.com and moneysavingexpert.com. Important in Google Shopping is the uploading of products into the 'Google Merchant Centre'. A data feed that is as comprehensive as

Data feed

possible (a file which consists of the products and its variables) is desirable. This improves the chance of acquiring a better position amongst all the Google Shopping-products.

Shopping results are only displayed on searches involving a buying intention. In contrast, in general search queries, no images will be displayed in the search engine results, at the top or on the right.

Google Shopping has grown rapidly. In 2016, retailers spent nearly half of their Google AdWords budget on Google Shopping (Twinkle Magazine, 2016).

In June 2017, Google was hit with a huge fine by the European Commission, because the company favours their own price comparison service Google Shopping in the search engine that is used by more than 90% of Europeans. Google has filed an appeal, but at the time of writing this book, the exact consequences are not yet known.

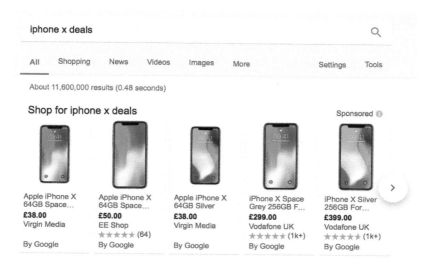

Google Shopping results for the iPhone X

Re-marketing List for Search Ads

RLSA, also called Remarketing List for Search Ads, is a technique that advertisers can use to target previous website visitors within the search engine. When people visit the advertiser's website, they will be included in an 'audience list'. The advertiser decides how these target segments are formed. An example is an online retailer of sport shoes. Target audience lists are for example: website visitors, viewed product, visited shopping cart, purchased product (became a customer). When someone has looked at a product and next time searches for 'Adidas running shoes' in the search engine, the advertiser can opt for a higher bid to get a better position. The reason for doing this is because the visitor will be more likely to convert on a website that they know already. Another possibility is to show another advertisement and/or landing page, including a discount for example. The chances of this visitor buying something are now greater, since we could already tell from previous information that this customer was interested in, in this case, Adidas sneakers and visited the site.

The same technique can be used by advertisers to exclude existing customers from paid search to preserve budget.

RLSA
Remarketing List for Search Ads

Audience list

Automate

There are, as you have seen before, many ways to advertise in Google, with a variety of different targeting options (such as keywords, ads, extensions, target audiences/RLSA, locations and devices). That means that it can be very difficult for large advertisers to manage. This is why there are many tools available to facilitate the management of campaigns. Examples include Genius and DoubleClick for search. These tools enable the advertiser to advertise based on rules. There are also ways to do this using 'AdWords scripts': these are JavaScript codes that are added to the AdWords account. These AdWords scripts automate an account with a number of rules. Bid Management tools enable automation of many elements of management of a large AdWords account.

7.3 Online Display advertising

When did you last see an MPU, skyscraper or leader board? Most people will not be able to answer this question. However, almost every web user will encounter them multiple times every day as they are part of one of the most common forms of advertising on the web: display advertising. Hated by some, praised by others. In any case, banners will continue to play an important role on the Internet. Even with the rise of adblockers (software that makes it possible to prevent banners from being displayed), display ads can increase visits to a website in most phases of the purchase process (Batra & Keller, 2017).

Display advertising

Adblockers

With the advent of new possibilities relating to targeting, technology and purchasing models for the deployment of banners, results have increased (as have insights and added value). Reaching the right person, at the right time, with the right message; that is the challenge of online display advertising.
In this chapter the various shapes, types, formats and the functioning of Display Advertising will be covered. Also, we'll give you an overview of the display-advertising landscape based on the sourcing possibilities. Finally, we will explain how, where and for what purpose you should set up a campaign. First, we will begin by telling you a little of history.

7.3.1 History of display advertising

The commercial advancement of the Internet began in the mid 1990s with the development of the world wide web (www). Just as in, for example, newspapers and magazines, website space was reserved for image advertisements. These advertisements were also known as online 'banners'. The owners of the websites that displayed the banners received a financial compensation from the advertiser.
In October 1994, the first real banner on the Internet was put on Hotwired's website in America by AT&T (see image).

Banner

The first banner by AT&T on Hotwired's website

This milestone in online advertising unleashed a true revolution. Not only did it become possible for website owners to (more easily) make money from their websites, but a completely new kind of advertisement was born: the interactive advertisement.
When a website visitor clicks on the banner, they will be directed to the advertiser's website. Due to this interaction, the level of engagement is much larger than in a static, non-interactive presentation. Instead of passively viewing an advertisement, the internet user is (potentially) actively involved in the advertisement's message. Online Display Advertising has developed into one of the largest and most important types of online advertising.

Interactive advertisement

A billboard and half-page ad from Google on ESPN's website

In recent years, the total spending on online display advertising has increased rapidly. IAB Europe's study (2017) reveals that approximately half of the total spend on online advertising is on display advertising (including advertising on Google Display Network, Facebook and other social media platforms). The biggest growth is found in mobile and video advertising.

7.3.2   Banner shapes, types and sizes

Over the years a lot of different banner shapes, types, sorts and formats have been created for the purpose of display advertising. The width and height are measured according to the number of pixels. In this subsection the most and least common shapes are further explained using visual examples.

After this we will first discuss the standard banner formats, the techniques that can be used to create banners and the guidelines and requirements that banners must comply with.

Standard banner sizes

The most frequently used banner sizes will be discussed next. For a regular banner campaign several of these types of banners should be created, in order to have an appropriate banner available for all relevant publisher sites. We will discuss the following banner formats:

- *Skyscraper*: 120 x 600 pixels – this is a popular format as this type of banner can have a relatively high clickthrough-rate.

Banner sizes

Skyscraper

Wide skyscraper	• *Wide skyscraper*: 160 x 600 pixels – this one is rarely used.
Medium rectangle	• *Medium rectangle*: 300 x 250 pixels – this one is seen as a very effective advertising tool, because it can usually be integrated within the content and is suitable for 'rich media content', combinations of text, images, video, etc.
Half-page ad	• *Half-page ad*: 300 x 600 pixels – this format is booming and ensures high visibility and impact.
Large rectangle	• *Large rectangle*: 336 x 280 pixels – this is a bigger version of the medium rectangle.
Full banner	• *Full banner*: 468 x 60 pixels – this was formerly a much-used format but has been decreasing in popularity in recent years.
Leader board	• *Leader board*: 728 x 90 pixels – this is a wide-screen heading banner.
Billboard	• *Billboard*: 970 x 250 pixels – a full-width webpage banner.

For an overview of the latest new formats, have a look on www.iab.net/risingstars. For mobile advertising, agreements have also been made about sizes and techniques. An example of this is MRAID: Mobile Rich Media Ad Interface Definitions. In addition to these sizes, we see a heavy increase in native advertising. This is a kind of advertising in which the advertisement is part of the environment in which it is displayed.

There are various techniques and guidelines in place for building banners. It is beyond the scope of this book to go into all the technical details. However, it is important for marketers to be aware of the principles and concepts.

Banner-building techniques
A banner can simply be a text along with an image, but many online advertisers invest in, for example, video banners and interactive advertisements. These are often more effective than old-fashioned formats.

The following techniques can be used to develop a banner:

Static banner	• *Static banner*: the simplest banner is a plain, static image. This could be, for example, a JPEG (.JPEG) or a GIF (.GIF) file.
Animated GIF	• *Animated GIF*: following the static GIF, animated GIFs have often been used in the past. These animated GIFs usually involved a 'mini presentation' consisting of three to four frames including a variety of texts and/or images.
Flash	• *Flash*: in the past a lot of banners were built using the Flash (.SWF) technique. Flash makes it possible to add better-looking and smoother animations.
HTML5	• *HTML5*: today, almost every banner is created using the HTML5 technique. HTML5's advantage is that is has the same good-looking and smooth animations as Flash but is also suitable for use on tablets and smartphones. This is not possible with Flash.
Backup GIF	• *Backup GIF*: Often, Backup GIFs are developed for the campaign alongside the HTML5 banners. These Backup GIFs are marked as 'backup banners' for the campaign, in case the HTML5 banner doesn't work properly.
Rich media	• *Rich media*: thanks to so-called rich media applications it has become possible to produce increasingly good-looking and complex banners. Video banners are a good example of this. Other forms of rich media communications are discussed in more detail in subsection 7.3.3.

Ford uses a 3D effect to present a new truck model

Not every network supports standard rich media expressions and sometimes there are issues displaying them. Among other things, this has to with heavier banner requirements (also see subsection 7.3.3). That is why displaying rich media needs to be organised differently from standard banners. This can be done, for example, in unison with specialised parties that are able to display rich media banners.

A pre-roll video banner by Heineken on Youtube

Guidelines and requirements that banners must comply with

Advertising network operators apply several (technical) rules that banners must comply with. They want to safeguard the uniformity and avoid unnecessary burdening/annoying the visitors to their websites. There are also technical requirements that advertisers have to comply with in order to enable placing and displaying on the websites. This is also known as an 'ad serving system'. In general, network operators' requirements are very similar. However, there are certainly differences. Before a banner campaign is deployed, you must always inquire with the network operator about their guidelines and requirements. Usually these are to be found on the operator's website. Requirements are:

- *Sizes*: this regulates the height and width of the banner, often expressed in the number of pixels.
- *Kilobytes* (kB): this is the 'weight' of the banner. Most operators accept standard banners up to a maximum of 149kB.
- *Loops*: the number of loops is the amount of times a banner may 'play'. There is often a limit set of three times, in order not to disturb the website visitor too much.
- *Duration*: this the total duration of the animation. This is usually about thirty seconds, three loops of ten seconds each. After this the banner must 'stop'.
- *Click tag*: this is a parameter that is used in banners. The parameter is the variable that defines the banner's destination URL or destination page. As a result of the click tag, data such as clicks and banner views can be ignored. As there is no industry standard for click tags, operators and banner developers use several variants of click tags.

Different requirements often apply to high impact communications or rich media communications, due to the content being tailor-made.

7.3.3 High impact communications and rich media communications

New banner shapes and sizes are continually being created. We will discuss a few of them. Then we will briefly explain more about the development of a banner.

Margin notes:
Ad serving system

Loops

Click tag

High impact communications

7

© Noordhoff Uitgevers bv

Commonly used types of advertisements

Organisations try to attract more attention in order to obtain higher visibility and more interaction. Frequently seen high impact communications and media communications are:

- Takeovers: as the term itself already implies, a takeover means, as it were, taking over a webpage with a banner. During a takeover, the whole page is dominated by the advertiser's communication.

Takeovers

A takeover by Columbia Pictures presenting their movie 'The Amazing Spider-Man 2' on IMDB.com

Usually, the page content is left intact (see previous image) so the website visitor can still read it. More radical takeovers also take place. For instance, Shazam has developed Mobile Home page takeovers which have already attracted brands such as Apple, Coca-Cola, McDonald's, HBO, Deezer and Netflix. The site's content becomes part of the display communication (see the next image). The advantage is that the website visitor has no choice but to see the banner, although there is a risk of annoying the visitor by doing this. The least radical type of takeover is when all of a website's standard banner positions are 'filled' by one advertiser.

A very radical homepage takeover on Adworld. Every element of the homepage changes and has a role in the story.

Homepage take-over

The takeover is often implemented on the homepage, as this is the most frequently visited page. This is also known as a HTO, short for homepage take-over.

Pre-rolls

- *Pre-rolls*: a pre-roll banner is a commercial that is shown before an Internet user starts watching an online video on, for example, YouTube. Often this kind of communication is created in a video format, in order to let the pre-roll and the video that will play afterwards flow into each other as smoothly as possible. Often the pre-roll can be closed or skipped by the user after a few seconds. A pre-roll video banner is similar to a 'normal' television commercial, though greatly differs by being interactive and 'clickable'.

Expandable

- *Expandable*: an expandable banner is a banner that expands when you hover the mouse over it. The retracted banner must attract the attention of the internet user. If they show an interest by hovering the mouse over it, the banner expands so more information can be given to the website visitor. In some expandable banners a full interactive mini-site is displayed. Other expandables are less extensive and 'only' have to be tempting enough to click on to go to the advertiser's underlying website.

Floor ads

- *Floor ads*: floor ads are elongated banner communications that are often displayed across the entire width at the bottom of the page. Floor ads usually move along with the page whilst scrolling. This way the website visitor can keep reading the content whilst the floor ad remains on the screen. Many floor ads are also expandables (see the image from Dell).

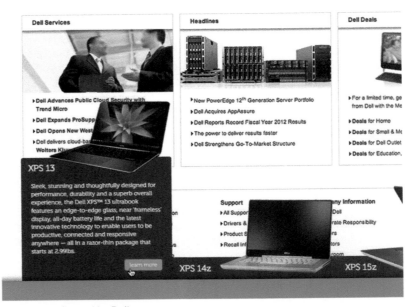

Expandable floorad by Dell

- *New sizes*: new sizes with flashy names are regularly introduced, Pushdown, Sidekick, Slider, Portrait, and Filmstrip to name but a few.

These larger, interactive communications are mainly focused on brand advertisers who can create a larger impact with their communications. Some new formats, such as the Half-Page Ad and the Billboard are becoming so popular that they are considered to be one of the standard formats. This is how display advertising continues to develop. Examples can be found on the website of the IAB (www.iab.net/risingstars).

Banner development
Developing banners is a job for specialists. In addition to the fact that one should have good design and technical skills, knowledge of and experience with of online 'user behaviour' are essential.
A banner should be in line with the advertiser's brand and the brand's style. This includes the use of colours, images/pictures, language and fonts. A good banner also contains a powerful message: clear, short and attractive texts and attractive, appropriate animations. Finally, the banner should contain a strong and concise call to action so that it's clear to the website's visitor what the expectation is after clicking on it. For example: 'Book now', 'Buy here', 'Yes, I want to become a customer', 'See how it works' or 'Request information'. A good banner developer not only takes the content of the banner into account, but also then location where the banners are to be placed and ensures alignment with any ongoing offline media advertising campaigns on for instance radio, TV or in print ads. All of this needs to be translated into brief expressions complying with strict technical requirements.
The banner campaign's success largely depends on its quality and developing that is an art in itself.

7.3.4 Purchasing and serving display advertising
A good banner does not equal an effective campaign. The banner space must be purchased and, at the right time and in the right place, it must be 'served up': presented to the target audience. This subsection provides more detail on these subjects.

Parties
At least two parties are needed to establish a banner campaign: the advertiser and the website owner (also called the website operator or publisher). The advertiser wishes to draw attention to their brand or product, the publisher wants to earn some (extra) money with their website. In reality there are many more parties that play a role within the display advertising landscape. These vary from parties who deliver the technology and systems for serving up banners to (media) agencies that use their expertise to support advertisers in deploying display advertising campaigns as effectively as possible.

Publisher

If you want to place a banner on a particular website, you can contact the website owner directly to ask if they are interested. This is quite labour-intensive and time-consuming. Especially because, in a banner campaign, various websites of the advertiser are being used. That is why nowadays there are networks that regulate display advertising for groups of websites. This could involve network's own websites, but also websites of third parties. The network controls the entire process from sales and invoicing to actual placement of the banners and measuring their performance. The network is also called a media operator because the network exploits its

Media operator

© Noordhoff Uitgevers bv

available online media space by making it available to advertisers. Besides a lot of small ones, there are a number of very large media operators.

We will now discuss what possibilities there are for purchasing banner space from the perspective of an advertiser and/or publisher. In subsection 7.3.7, that covers set-up and campaign management, we will elaborate on this subject.

From direct selling to self-service

There are several parties, options and ways of purchasing banner advertising space on a website. The most common ones are discussed below and will be illustrated using examples, namely:
1 direct selling
2 sales agencies
3 advertising networks
4 supply side platforms
5 demand side platforms
6 real-time bidding
7 open marketplaces
8 private marketplaces
9 deal ID

1 Direct selling

Direct selling

The simplest and clearest way is to directly purchase advertising space from the website owner. These can be small hobby websites, but also well-known cross medial publishers who own large and popular websites.

2 Sales houses

Sales agencies

A website owner will regularly outsource the sale of advertising space to sales agencies. Examples of these are Webads, Adfab and Adfactor. These sales agencies don't have websites themselves, but purely facilitate the commercial exploitation of third-party sites. Sales agencies often work exclusively for a certain publisher.

3 Advertising networks

Advertising networks

Online advertising networks provide a platform for publishers to sell and fill their advertising space. These advertising networks allow advertisers to centrally purchase publishing space for their banners on multiple websites and with multiple publishers.

The advertising networks often offer the publisher and/or advertiser specific technical services, such as targeting options, optimisation techniques and/or the creation of the banners. In addition to technology, an advertising network distinguishes itself in ways such as the quality of their affiliated publishers/websites or the advertisers who advertise via the network. Well-known examples of advertising networks are Widespace and Google AdSense. Unlike sales agencies, advertising networks usually don't work exclusively for one publisher.

4 Supply side platform (SSP)

Supply side platform

A supply side platform (SSP) bundles everything relevant for the supply side of the market. These systems provide access to a network of websites and allow automated trading of advertising space.

5 Demand side platform (DSP)

Using a demand side platform (DSP), advertisers can purchase advertising space on a large number of different websites, the demand side of the market. A DSP is often connected to a large number of SSPs where impressions can be purchased.

Demand side platform

Impressions

6 Real-time bidding

New technology and the use of so-called ad exchanges make it possible for advertisers to bid in real time on available advertising space. Ad exchanges are platforms that facilitate 'automated buying and selling' of online media in real time. This means both the advertiser and the publisher can make use of an ad exchange. Bidding on that advertising space is referred to as real-time bidding (RTB). This creates a sort of 'trading floor' where you can bid on positions that are relevant to the advertiser, continuously and in real time, using an online auction model.

Ad exchanges

Real-time bidding

7 Open marketplace

An open marketplace is a market place where all advertisers have access to the advertising space. Purchasing this space is usually done by way of real-time bidding.

Open market place

8 Private market place

A private market place (PMP) is a market place where publishers offer advertising space to one or a select and closed group of advertisers by way of real-time bidding.

Private market place

9 Deal ID

Publishers and advertisers can make special arrangements concerning, for example, the volume, price and targeting of the display advertisements (see subsection 7.3.5). In order to keep track of this, a Deal ID is used: a unique piece of code that enables the advertiser's system, the DSP, to recognise specific advertising space and to focus the campaign on it. This way of purchasing provides the advertiser more certainty about the effectiveness of their campaign.

Deal ID

To place banners on a website, a so-called ad serving system is needed. This system is often facilitated and managed by the publisher or the advertising network that is selling the banner space. It is also possible for an advertiser to purchase a licence for an ad serving system independently or via a digital marketing/media agency. This has a number of major benefits. The advertiser's banner campaign can then be centrally served (not per network) and measured. Also, setting up and managing a banner campaign takes less time and effort because everything can be done using one single system. There are also fewer restrictions regarding, for example, the use of campaign material. It is beyond the scope of this book to outline the exact functioning of ad serving systems. However, an upward trend can be seen in advertisers who often use an ad serving system themselves or via their agency, instead of doing everything via a network. This way the advertiser profits from more flexibility, increased targeting possibilities and a better understanding of the campaign's results. Lastly, it also provides the advertiser direct access to ad exchanges.

Ad serving system

7.3.5   Targeting

The aim of display advertising is to reach the right person at the right time using the right message. This is called targeting. The effects of digital marketing channels are measurable, meaning it is possible to 'target' specific variables. This is often the factor behind an online campaign's success. Below we will discuss the most common and most up-to-date targeting possibilities.

Targeting

Basic targeting options

Basic targeting options for display advertising are:

Fixed

- *Fixed*: if a 'fixed' banner position is purchased; it concerns a specific position that is purchased for a certain amount of time or for a particular volume of displays. The advertisement is only shown at that particular location.

ROS (run of site)

- *ROS (run of site)*: if the banner campaign runs on ROS, then the advertisement is displayed in multiple locations, but only on one specific site.

RON (run of network)

- *RON (run of network)*: if RON is used for the banner campaign, then the advertisement appears on all the websites connected to the publisher or operator's network. An example is the BBC, which offers advertisers online display advertising opportunities to target users who are outside the UK.

ROC (run of channel or run of category)

- *ROC (run of channel or run of category)*: if ROC is used in a banner campaign, then advertisements will be shown within a certain category, for example, the category 'automotive'. The various car-related (automotive) sites are good examples of this.

If one of the above options is selected, this does not guarantee that the target audience will be reached. Publishers provide solid research data concerning target audience information, but these are average values and won't tell you anything about an individual person who visits a specific page at a given point in time.

Latest targeting possibilities

To enable even better targeting, various additional targeting possibilities have been developed for online (banner) campaigns. The latest market trend shows that the number of ad placements based on specific websites is declining, with increasing focus on the basis of demography, context and internet user behaviour. We will discuss the following targeting possibilities:

1 socio-demographical and geographical targeting
2 contextual targeting
3 behavioural targeting
4 audience targeting
5 lookalike targeting

1 Socio-demographical and geographical targeting

Geographical targeting

A relatively simple method for displaying targeted online advertisements is by making use of socio-demographical and/or geographical targeting. During their activities on the Internet, internet users regularly leave behind interesting data. If someone registers with a social media network for instance, they are asked for their gender, age and location.

7

Publishers and advertisers can use this information to present targeted advertisements to a specific target segment. For example: men between the age of 25 and 45 who live in Lyon, France.

2 Contextual targeting

Contextual targeting involves tailoring the banner content to the content on the web page in question. For instance, a provider of flights to Italy would be appropriate on a website page that hosts an informative article about Rome.

Contextual targeting

3 Behavioural targeting

In behavioural targeting, the visitor's previous behaviour is used for showing him or her more relevant banners in future. This way an advertiser such as Norwegian (Norwegian Air Shuttle ASA) can 'follow' a visitor who, from the wide range of available destinations, has shown specific interest in a flight to New York (but didn't purchase a ticket) by placing a cookie in their computer. As soon as this specific person with an interest in New York is spotted on www.cntraveller.com for example, then Norwegian can display a banner including an offer on plane tickets to New York. The advertisement is adapted to be in line with previously observed behaviour on the website. This is also known as re-targeting or re-marketing.

Behavioural targeting

Re-targeting

The publisher can also apply behavioural targeting. For example, based on the actions of a certain internet user within a network of sites, a behavioural profile can be drawn up.

Behavioural targeting, provided it is properly used, greatly increases the relevance of the advertisement's content to the internet user. This will cause a substantial increase in the campaign's effectiveness. This behavioural data can also be combined with, for example, socio-demographical and/or geographical targeting.

4 Audience targeting

The basic principle of audience targeting is the purchasing of data profiles on the basis of pre-defined target segment variables. These variables can be combinations of socio-demographic and geographical, as well as behavioural, interest or intention variables. The data profiles are assembled online and consist of input from a variety of different kinds of websites. An example is that of an energy supplier that purchases data profiles for men with an above average income, an interest in environmental issues and that have shown an intent to purchase an energy contract. In this case the data has been collated by combining online searching and browsing behaviour and a visit to a comparison website that supplies energy contracts. Subsequently, these data profiles are associated with the purchased banner space. The banners are presented within the purchased advertising space to people who fall within this select profile. The data profiles can be purchased externally via data companies and/or networks. It is of course also possible for the advertiser to collect these profiles independently.

Audience targeting

The better the quality of the composition of these data profiles, the more concisely this specific target segment can be reached, regardless of the site that is used.

5 Lookalike targeting

Lookalike targeting

Lookalike targeting is used by the advertiser to target people who show similarities to the visitors on the advertisers' website, the customer database or the fan base. You can compose a database of website visitors based on an action such as completing a purchase or visiting a specific page. So-called lookalikes are sometimes referred to as 'similar audiences'.

Exclusion pixel
Ad server

It is also possible to prevent display ads from being displayed in places that are not suitable or from showing them to specific people, such as existing customers. This is done with the help of an exclusion pixel, a variable that the ad server, the computer system of the advertising platform, can recognise.

7.3.6 Pricing models for bannering

The first applied pricing models for bannering were created with an offline mind-set. Offline, the advertiser pays a fixed fee to place an advertisement for a certain period of time. So, if the advertiser paid for example €500, they were allowed to place their banner on the website for one month, regardless of the number of times that the banner was displayed or clicked on.

Later, the billing process became more focused on the actual impact of the banner.

Cost per Mille (CPM)

We will now first discuss the cost per Mille (CPM), paying per 1,000 banner impressions. After, we will take a closer look at cost per click (CPC) and cost per action (CPA).

Cost per Mille is a traditional way of thinking
If the CPM is €20 and the banner is displayed 100,000 times, the advertiser will pay (100 x €20 =) € 2,000 per 100,000 views.
Determining the CPM is dependent on several variables. The most important ones are:

- *Banner size*: larger (and therefore more prominent) banner sizes are more expensive than smaller formats.
- *Banner position*: the more prominent the banner's position on the website, the higher the price. Banners that are immediately displayed **Above the fold** without having scrolled first (this is called 'above the fold') are more expensive. Furthermore, banners positioned between the regular (non-paid for) website content (eg a news report) are more expensive than, for example separate banners at the top of a web page.
- Generic or specific to a target group: the more specific to a target group the website is, the higher the banner prices are. On a very generic website, the CPM is relatively low. On a very specific website, aimed at eg business-to-business, banner prices can be as high as €80 CPM. Depending on the aim of the banner campaign, the advertiser needs to assess whether the banner is worth paying that much money for in that position.
- *Market forces*: market forces are also important in determining banner prices. On a very popular website, one that many companies want to advertise on, the price is higher than on a less popular site that advertisers have little interest in. Thus, the scarcer the space, the higher

the price. The Latin proverb 'everything is worth what its purchaser will pay for it' applies here.
- *Targeting*: targeting techniques can also be used on (more) generic websites to address the target audience. The more targeted a banner is, the higher the price will be.

In practice, CPM prices can vary between less than €1 up to €80 per thousand views. The price that a website or media operator charges for their banner positions are often to be found on the website itself. The 'price list' including the applicable fees is usually included in the 'Advertising' section. In practice, prices are often negotiable. The amount of discount that can be given may depend on the size of the media budget.

Cost per click or cost per action
For some years now, advertising networks have been tasked with selling unsold inventory space on websites using the cost per click (CPC) principle. They run non-targeted banners across the entire site/networks (ROS/RON) and advertisers are only charged once the banner is actually clicked on (or even only once a conversion has taken place, ie cost per action, CPA). This is also called direct-response display advertising. In recent years, this type of display advertising has grown in popularity with advertisers. For publishers, it's a way of capitalising on unsold banner space without compromising the traditional and direct CPM ad income.

Cost per click (CPC)

Cost per action (CPA)

Direct-response bannering

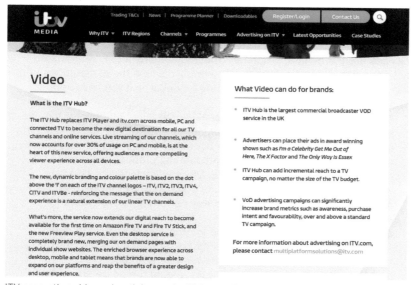

ITV promoting video advertising on its Video on Demand product

7.3.7   Set-up and campaign management
Now that we know what display advertising entails it is useful to see how the process of actually launching a banner campaign 'live', works. This process and that of setting up other online campaigns have a great many similarities (eg PPC advertising in search engines).
It all starts with a solid plan, which also applies to a banner campaign. To determine where and how you want to use your banners, the advertiser

must first have a clear set of guiding principles and prerequisites. The entire process of setting up and publicising a banner campaign online, as well as determining what the guiding principles and prerequisites should be, will be discussed below. In closing, we will explain the concept of conversion attribution.

Target audience

Before you begin, it is important to determine whom it is that you want to reach online. In other words: what is your target audience? The target audience can be described using socio-demographic variables (m/f, age, income group, etc.), but also in terms of behaviour or interests (eg people who are interested in a holiday to Italy).

Message/proposition

What message do you wish your banners to convey? What brand, what product or what service do you want to highlight? What's the proposition? It is important to pre-formulate a competitive proposition in order to attract the interest of the potential customer. The better the offer, the more response. It should also take into account what competitors are doing. It is important to get the proposition across clearly and concisely. As a search engine advertisement, you have limited space for pictures and text within a banner.

Objectives and key performance indicators

Everything starts with an objective. Therefore, the most important question above all is always: what is the objective of the campaign? What exactly do you want to achieve with the campaign (display or video)? When will you determine the campaign as having been a success? Which device or devices are the most appropriate? These questions must be answered both qualitatively and quantitatively. We will discuss these questions from the perspective of the digital marketing funnel, which you have learned about in subsection 5.1.2:

1 *Awareness:* This is traditionally speaking the initial purpose of the use of banners or video. Reaching the target audience online and bringing the advertiser's brand/product to the consumers' attention. In line with this, brand awareness, engagement and creating product and brand preference are the desired results. Obviously relevant is on which websites the ad will be displayed. In addition, they may be examined and optimised in accordance with Key Performance Indicators (KPIs) such as:

a *Unique reach*: how many unique internet users should be reached? This is often measured using IP-addresses and, possibly, by taking into account factors such as the browser settings.

b *Contact frequency*: how many times should the ad be shown to a particular internet user? The frequency cap (also simply called 'cap') determines how often one unique visitor can see a particular advert. For example, if the cap is set at 3, the internet user gets to see the ad a maximum of three times. If the cap is 5, it will be five times. Frequency caps can be set per period (eg 24 hours, per week, or for the duration of the campaign) and are always linked to a unique visitor. At what contact frequency is the banner most effective, for example in terms of clickthrough rate (CTR)?

Unique reach

Contact frequency

Frequency cap

7

c *Above/below the fold*: how many times should the ad be displayed above or below the 'fold' (the bottom of the screen without scrolling)?

Below the fold

d *View time*: for how long will the ad be displayed?

View time

e *Banner interaction*: what is the duration and frequency of the interaction (moving the mouse over the banner, watching the video)?

Banner interaction

2 *Capture:* how many people click on the ad and are directed to the landing page? For how long do they stay there? How many people click through to go to the main website?

3 *Conversion:* recently, banners are increasingly used for activation: to ensure that the people you reach online will actually do something. This is usually online activation, for example:

Activation

a purchasing a product

b requesting information

c joining the advertiser's Facebook group, or

d participating in a contest

4 *Loyalty*: this is not the primary aim of display advertising, although viewing banners or videos can stimulate brand recall and brand preference.

The desired activity can also occur offline, such as the purchase of a new product in a physical store. As an advertiser, it is important to realise that an activation banner usually has a positive effect when it comes to branding and awareness. In practice it appears to be complex to measure this positive effect, however, there are recent developments that make this data more transparent.

Sometimes an extra incentive is added to the proposition in order to persuade people. This is done using an incentive, often a gift, a discount or another perk. In the psychology of motivation, it is commonly accepted that the use of incentives stimulates desired behaviour due to the additional reward and the associated recognition. Of course, the marketer will determine what realistic KPIs are according to their research. If this result does not correspond with the desired results, the plans can be adjusted.

Incentive

Media plan and budget

When the objective, the target audience, the media budget and the message that will be communicated have all been decided, a media plan will be drawn up. This is a detailed plan containing the networks/websites on which you want to place your banners, together with a budget allocation, the purchasing model and the purchase price (eg CPM or CPC).

Media plan

Key figures for the costs of online advertising

- cost per Mille (CPM): cost per 1,000 ad views
- cost per click (CPC) or pay per click (PPC): cost per click on the advertisement

PPC

- cost per action (CPA): cost per fixed activity, such as conversion
- cost per lead (CPL): cost per generated lead
- cost per sale (CPS) or cost per order (CPO): cost per generated sale

A good media plan will also have formulated what the expected outcome of the campaign will be. Additionally, the campaign purchasing is put into a timeline. In other words: What networks and adverts be launched, and when? For example, a campaign can consist of several 'flights', ie the first two weeks of March and the last two weeks of April.

Flights

Therefore, the advertiser decides to advertise with a lot of views at specific moments during the year. This is called a burst strategy. A third option is to use a drip strategy. In this strategy, the advertiser decides to advertise more during specific predetermined moments or after certain promotional offers. There are also organisations that opt for continuous (always-on) use of online advertising, as you may have read in Chapter 5.

Burst strategy
Dripping strategy

When drawing up an online media plan, it is important to ask yourself where the defined target audience are to be found and how you can reach those people. What sites they visit, what they do online and how you can purchase banner space there. Media plans are often developed in an Excel sheet. This plan and the decisions that have been made are then further elucidated in a presentation and/or a supplementary document.

Media budget

For the advertiser to then proceed with running the campaign, they will need a budget. As well as the media budget, an additional budget is needed for developing the campaign concept (usually done by an advertising agency) and for preparing campaign materials. Often the advertiser turns to a media agency or a specialist online agency for purchasing the campaign, setting it up and managing it. This is a logical decision to make because digital marketing in general and display advertising in particular, are specialised professions, and are subject to rapid developments.

In addition, these agencies are usually able to attain favourable media contracts, because they have multiple advertisers as their clients. There is also more knowledge, expertise and experience on hand in order to make the campaign a success in practice.

Once the media plan has been definitively approved, the advertising space can be purchased from the media operators. Often purchasing and invoicing are done by the advertiser's (media) agency, but sometimes this occurs between the network and the advertiser directly. Once the contractual matters and conditions are completed and signed, the campaign material can be 'trafficked'.

Traffic of campaign material

Traffic campaign material

Once the banners or videos are developed and the contracts have been signed, the campaign can be 'booked in'. This is called 'traffic': the campaign materials will be shared, the pixels generated and positioned in order to run diagnostics on the campaign and everything will be tested to see if it works. This is an important and precise process requiring coordination between the advertiser and the publisher, which is often outsourced to a specialised media agency. Matters that must be tested in a structured manner before 'going live' with the campaign are:

Going live

- Do the banners and videos animate well?
- Do they direct to the right website?
- Is the measured data received by the ad serving system?
- Are conversions measured in the right way?

Once these questions are all answered positively, the campaign can go live. Because a campaign is often part of a larger cross-media campaign with a specific start and end date and because there is a strong sense of dependency amongst the various parties, the time pressure for trafficking is often tremendous. For advertisers this is another reason to bring in a specialised external party to manage this for them.

Campaign management

Purchasing and managing display advertising campaigns is a completely different challenge from purchasing for traditional media such as print, radio and TV. For these offline channels it is often the case that most of the work is done once the campaign is live. For online campaigns, including display advertising, this is when the work really begins. Digital marketing is a continuous process of monitoring, analysing, testing and optimising. Because online channels are easily measurable, adjustments can made based on actual results. This could include shifting media budgets between the various networks/websites, increasing or decreasing CPMs and/or CPCs, testing different adverts, disabling low-scoring ads and adjusting the frequency caps. Therefore, besides competitive purchasing, matters such as flexibility, speed and decisiveness are essential. This method guarantees the advertiser optimal results. It is therefore not only about how purchases are made, but also much more about the result that will be achieved. An example of a banner campaign is described in example 7.1.

The primary objective of an online display ad campaign is generally creating awareness and positive attitudes, with a secondary objective being to generate clickthroughs. The idea is to place banners in a prominent position on the page (eg a strip along the bottom or down the right-hand-side) where they will grab the user's attention, engage them and in some cases motivate a click.

7

EXAMPLE 7.1

Airbnb online display campaigns

Airbnb's goal was to build its brand globally and generate bookings from guests and enquiries from hosts. Airbnb started a partnership with Google and they were able not only to expand their reach, but also to target their audiences geographically. One of the main goals was to change the audience's perception from appearing as a 'budget' travel option. So they used target Google Paid Search and also display ads on the GDN (Google Display Network).

Results: They became an international brand, listings grew from 1 to 80,000 and today the brand is a major success. Watch this video about their use of display ads https://www.thinkwithgoogle.com/marketing-resources/airbnbs-success-with-google-display/.

Airbnb display banner on YouTube

In this way, online display advertising helps Airbnb to reach potential hosts and guests and drives them to the website where they can engage with the brand, sign-up and transact.

Conversion attribution

As a standalone channel, display advertising is an excellent tool that can be used for different purposes (branding, sales, traffic). There is a side effect though, aside from the immediate result of the banners, which often is even stronger than other online channels. Display advertising is a so-called push channel: the website's visitor didn't ask for a banner, the initiative for this comes from the advertiser. The use of display advertising has an impact on other (online) channels too. Whilst surfing, internet users are being alerted to something they previously might not have been paying conscious attention to. The banner is very important in the awareness phase of the digital marketing communication funnel. The banner can attract the interest and 'trigger' the internet user to look into the product being promoted in the banner. Of course, you could click on the banner itself and find out what the offer is. However, as a result, caused by the banner-induced trigger, you could go online to inquire about the product. You search in Google, take a look on comparison sites and then decide to buy the product. In the process, people often switch medium: they start off on a mobile device and end up on a laptop. Even though it was the visit to the comparison site that caused the proverbial straw to break the camel's back and lead to purchasing the product, without the initial display of the banner the deal would have never been made. Providing insight into the various online 'touchpoints' leading up to the final conversion is called conversion attribution. These are described in subsection 12.3.4. A pull channel such as search engine marketing will always score better than display advertising in terms of conversion rate. Nonetheless, display advertising can certainly be used to boost the search engine marketing and/or other channels.

Push channel

Conversion attribution

The added value of display advertising within digital marketing and communications is more than just the result that is recorded directly from the channel. For the marketer, this is an important fact to keep in mind. What the added value is exactly; varies per advertiser, product, service and campaign. Measuring of conversion and attribution are a way for advertisers to gain insight into this. Whilst in the past the effects of digital marketing were often evaluated per channel, we now see an increasing number of advertisers that are starting to use conversion attribution to calculate the real value of display advertising.

7.4 Advertising on social networks

Social media can be used for advertising, just like on search engine pages (search engine advertising) and on third party websites (display advertising). Due to the large number of users (their reach), social media can compete with traditional media such as radio or television. Ads can be tailored very specifically to the target segment, as a result of the large amount of data that social media users share, consciously or unconsciously.

In this section we will first discuss reach on social media. We will cover advertising tools very briefly. Subsequently, different types of advertisements will be addressed. We will also discuss targeting for social media. Lastly, we will look at privacy and legislation.

7.4.1 Reach on social media

Three types of reach on social media can be distinguished:

1 *Organic reach*: the number of unique individuals who saw your message in their news feed, ticker (an overview with real-time updates of what your friends like, comment on and 'update') or on your page.

2 *Paid reach*: the number of unique individuals who have seen a message in an advertisement.

3 *Viral reach*: the number of unique individuals who saw a message in friend's post. This can also be through the means of an interaction with content.

Organic reach

Ticker

Paid reach

Viral reach

In recent years we see that the so-called *organic reach* (reach you do not pay for) continues to decrease. This is explained by the fact that brands are becoming increasingly more active on social media and that they are filtering networks on user relevance. Advertisements are also a necessary revenue model for many social networks. In the past, on average, 20% of the fans were reached by companies when they posted a message on their page. In 2017, their reach had already dropped to less than 5% of the fan base. In order to generate the desired reach anyway, paid reach using advertisements has almost become a necessity.

There are different reasons for, and ways to, advertise on social networks. If we look at the platforms that are offering advertising possibilities, Facebook is by far the largest globally and now also owns Instagram, WhatsApp and the self-developed Messenger. It is almost impossible to imagine a desktop computer, smartphone or tablet device without Facebook and its reach within every target segment is large.

7

The value of Twitter's shares has been decreasing lately which has made advertising less attractive. Twitter is rapidly being outpaced by the Facebook platforms and Snapchat in terms of user numbers and popularity. Pinterest is also contributing with a permanent support base and rapidly developing advertising possibilities. To reach a specific audience, such as TV viewers (TV ad targeting) or event visitors, Twitter can still be a good option.

TV ad targeting

For business, LinkedIn is a *no-brainer*. Although it is still an expensive channel in terms of advertising, the reach amongst business professionals is large. As a video platform, YouTube also certainly participates.

7.4.2   Advertising tools

Social networks usually offer an online tool which can be used to publish advertisements. By using such a (self-service) tool, an advertiser can buy advertising space on the social media channel in an auction. On Facebook and Instagram this can be done in the Ads Manager or the Power Editor and also Twitter, Pinterest and LinkedIn offer a similar solution. Therefore, advertising on social networks is very accessible even without a media agency.

What's your marketing objective? Help: Choosing an Objective		
Awareness	**Consideration**	**Conversion**
Brand awareness	Traffic	Conversions
Reach	Engagement	Catalog sales
	App installs	Store visits
	Video views	
	Lead generation	
	Messages	

Facebook helps you with the objective of your ad campaign

7.4.3   Types of advertisements

There are different types of advertisements. For example, Facebook uses *like* ads. These advertisements consist of a title, a text and a visual and are located in the news feeds for both mobile devices and desktop devices. This advertisement is purely aimed at generating new page likes, so that they can be connected to the brand through the means of (sponsored) content. To keep the advertising costs in the campaigns as low as possible, A/B testing will be done with different combinations in titles, texts and visuals for segmented target audiences. Suppose the target audience is 18-50 years old, then you can divide these into segments of 18-30 years, 31-40 years and 41-50 years. Next, we will examine, for each target segment, which ads score best, and the budget is shifted to those ads. This is also known as campaign optimisation.

Like ads

A/B testing

In addition to the like ad, Facebook offers more formats:

- Link ad: This is an image ad which aims at generating clicks to an external website.

  Link ad

- Video ad: this promotes a video to generate a lot of reach or even follow-up actions.

  Video ad

- Carousel ad: this is an ad in which multiple photos can be browsed through and which are then linked to an activity, such as a click to the website.

  Carousel ad

- Canvas advertisement: this is a multi-format advertisement, in which photos, video, carousels, text and links are used to attract attention and to generate interaction (engagement) and link clicks.

  Canvas advertisement

Facebook can also be used to advertise on Instagram. In addition, in 2017 Facebook was also testing advertisements on their other platforms, Messenger and WhatsApp.

On Twitter, promoted tweets, trends and accounts can be used to gather more followers (promoted account), more visibility for a topic (promoted trend) and more interaction or website clicks (promoted tweet). With Twitter Cards you can enhance a tweet with, for example, an image or video that makes it more striking.

Promoted account
Promoted trend
Promoted tweet

On LinkedIn, image ads, link ads and video ads can be published to gather more reach, interaction, or website clicks. If you want to spread the word about a job opening to the appropriate target audience, LinkedIn offers a job posting. This is a paid position to get your job opening to the attention of potential candidates.

Job posting

7

OnBrand Magazine
Promoted

Have you bought your Super Early Bird ticket for OnBrand '17 yet? Join 2,000 international marketing professionals and learn from leading speakers from KLM, The New York Times and Ben & Jerry's. ...see more

ONBRAND

Beyond

13 Likes · 3 Comments

An advertisement in LinkedIn's newsfeed with the ultimate goal of selling tickets on an external website

Pinterest is offering the possibility to use various types of promoted pins as an advertisement among the target audience. Visual attractiveness of such an advertisement is of great importance to be clearly visible.

Promoted pins

On YouTube, for example, you can publish pre-roll banners that precede videos (see section 7.3) or advertise in the list of recommended videos or accounts. Advertising on Snapchat can be done in several ways, including the special lenses that are, amongst other things, based on location. For example, Quaker has developed Snapchat-sponsored filters were targeted with specific messages depending on the time of day.

Quaker's sponsored filter promotes their new product on Snapchat

7.4.4 Targeting

It is important to set specific good objectives in order to reach the right target audiences. In the previous section you have read that each channel has its own ecosystem and thus also offers different ways of targeting. With Facebook and Instagram, you can, for example, select on the basis of interests, age categories, place of residence and gender. LinkedIn uses industries and jobs and in Twitter you can select followers of specific accounts and interests.

Affinity audiences

In-market audiences

As a subsidiary of Google, video platform YouTube offers many of the features that apply to other Google products, such as interests, age, gender and specific audience targeting, the so-called affinity audiences and in-market audiences. At Pinterest, interests and keywords are the basis for reaching the right target group. Demographical and geographical characteristics such as gender, location and language can also be selected here.

By taking the time to select the right target group, an advertisement and the associated message becomes relevant and chances are that the desired action will be taken. If you do not use specific audience targeting, the ad campaign will end up resembling a scattergun approach, in a setting where many other organisations do the same. Very accurate targeting is important for achieving good results and you are also rewarded by the social channels themselves in terms of lower costs if your ad performs well. We will now discuss a few types of targeting.

External targeting

Various parties (including Facebook) set up an advertising network that goes beyond the social media channels themselves. Facebook knows when users are logged in and are able to link this user data to websites in order to display retargeting messages outside the platform. Due to the link with Instagram, Facebook users can also be targeted with advertising on their Instagram account. It's evident that that the use of and link with WhatsApp and Messenger will create many more possibilities.

Custom audiences targeting

A 'custom audience' is a file with user data (often email addresses) that can be used in Facebook, Twitter and YouTube to target existing customers. This is especially useful when communicating a message to existing clients, which differs from the message to prospects. These custom lists can also be used for creating a similar audience; a target audience that, based on characteristics, is very much the same as the current customers or relations.

Custom audience

Similar audience

Retargeting

Just as in display advertising, you can also apply re-targeting on social media. Instead of using demographical or geographical features for selecting a target audience, re-targeting uses website behaviour. Social media channels such as Facebook, Twitter and LinkedIn use a pixel that is placed on a website or specific web pages. This way it is possible to identify which individuals have been on the website, so that this group will see a specially targeted advertisement. This form of targeting is effective because of the 'warm' nature of the target audience. After all, the target group has already come into contact with the brand or company, which means that chances of a positive result from the advertising campaign are greater than 'cold' targeting.

7.4.5   Privacy and legislation

As with any form of online advertising, it is necessary to comply with legislation and privacy rules. There are no specific rules for social media channels, such as exist for email marketing and telemarketing.

The EU General Data Protection Regulation (GDPR) legislation indicates that there are two important considerations for any form of commercial communication, namely offering an opt-out possibility and informing your audience about this.

When advertising on social media, a user must be informed about the personal data used for advertising purposes. This applies to the targeting options regarding custom audience lists in particular, for which the customer must be informed that the organisation may use email addresses or telephone numbers. This can be implicitly communicated in, eg a privacy statement on the organisation's website. An option to unsubscribe (the 'right to object') can also be offered implicitly on the website via, for example, an email address or form. People who indicate that they no longer wish to be included in targeting methods that use email addresses or telephone numbers, must be excluded.

In the case of retargeting (website custom audiences), the codes (pixels) used for this must be described in detail using a cookie notification on the organisation's own website. Users need to agree to this before the pixel is activated and the re-targeting cookie is stored on their computers. You can read more about legislation in section 13.4. The main point about GDPR is to strengthen protections for individuals and the privacy and to make marketers seek informed consent at every stage where data is being collected and stored. It is expected that other Regions, including the Americas and Asia will move to a framework very close to GDPR ie there will effectively be Data/Privacy harmony across the globe.

7.5 **Affiliate marketing**

Affiliate marketing

The principle of affiliate marketing is centuries old. Someone sells someone else's product or service and receives a reward for it. You may have heard stories about the vendors who used to go from door to door to peddle vacuum cleaners. For each vacuum cleaner they sold, they were allowed to keep a part of the money for themselves. Or maybe you have been an 'affiliate' yourself when you had a side job as a face-to-face salesperson on the street. You tried to sell subscriptions to unsuspecting passers-by and you received an (extra) fee for every new customer.

In this section we will discuss the most important aspects of digital affiliate marketing: the aim, the stakeholders that are involved, what the market forces are, how to set up an affiliate marketing campaign, what the fees and the rewards are, how the marketing campaign is measured, in which way the affiliate marketing process take place in practice and how affiliate marketing can be integrated with the digital marketing mix.

7.5.1   Affiliate marketing on the Internet

Affiliate marketing is a performance-based digital marketing channel that is an integral part of today's marketing mix. A definition for digital affiliate marketing is (Wikipedia, 2017):

Digital affiliate marketing

Digital affiliate marketing is a form of digital marketing that involves the web shop (advertiser or merchant) paying the affiliate (publisher/webmaster) for every visitor, lead or sale that he or she generates via his/her website(s), newsletters or search engine campaign.

Performance marketing

Affiliate marketing (also referred to in some countries as performance marketing) revolves around the establishing of certain activities, such as a visit or information request, and/or the sale of services and products from advertisers on partner sites. Affiliates are also called publishers. Affiliate marketing is characterised by the outright 'no cure no pay' principle and is the ultimate 'performance based' form of digital marketing. The advertiser only has to pay the resellers (affiliates/publishers) if the results have actually been achieved. The result is determined and settled on the basis of a predefined activity: a conversion. More about conversion objectives can be found in subsection 7.5.2.

The advertiser is at low risk regarding their marketing and sales budget because of the no-cure-no-pay principle. That is why an increasingly number of advertisers are discovering this form of online advertising.

7.5.2   The aim of affiliate marketing

For the advertiser, the aim of affiliate marketing is always to achieve a direct result. The most common conversion objectives are:
- *sales*: purchases, reservations
- *leads*: information request, call for tender, newsletter registration
- *traffic*: visiting a website

Looking at these conversion objectives, advertisers often decide to focus on sales or leads. The leads can then be followed up, for example by having a call centre phone them and convert them into a sale after all. The purpose can also be to collect email addresses or other personal data from a specific target segment. This can enrich the advertiser's customer database. This data can be used at a later stage, for example to send mailings including a special offer. A combination of previously mentioned conversion objectives is also possible.

7.5.3   Stakeholders

The model in figure 7.3 maps which parties are involved in affiliate marketing.

FIGURE 7.3 Affiliate marketing stakeholders

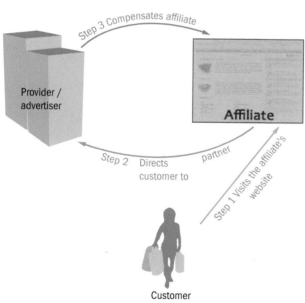

Source: http://en.wikipedia.org/wiki/Affiliate_marketing

On their website, the affiliate (publisher) sells the provider's (advertiser's) products or services. If a potential customer goes to the affiliate site (step 1) and then buys a product from the advertiser (step 2), the affiliate receives a (financial) compensation from the provider (step 3).

Separating the affiliates and the provider, is often an affiliate network. This is not depicted in figure 7.3. The affiliate network connects supply and demand from affiliates and providers and operates as an intermediary. Advertisers offer the products they want to promote via the affiliate network. In turn, affiliates can select the providers that are most interesting to them for inclusion and promotion on their website. Measuring the affiliate's activities and the financial settlement are often also done by an affiliate network. This is explained in more detail in subsections 7.5.6 and 7.5.7.

Affiliate marketing is characterised by intensive collaboration between the relevant stakeholders (affiliate, advertiser and the affiliate network). The advertiser facilitates their stakeholders to the best of their ability by making agreements and providing the necessary materials. This increases the reach within the appropriate target audiences, resulting in better online results.

Now, the various stakeholders and their interests will be discussed in further detail.

Provider

The provider or advertiser is at the basis of affiliate marketing. Their aim is to sell their product or service and they are willing to pay a certain amount for this from the marketing and sales budget. From this budget, the other stakeholders must be paid: the affiliate and the affiliate network.

The most popular industries within affiliate marketing are:
- *retail*, such as clothing, white goods, books, games and gadgets
- *travel*, such as trips, holidays, plane tickets and weekend getaways
- *finance*, such as mortgages, loans and insurance
- *telecom*, such as mobile phones, subscriptions and SIM only deals

The final type and amount of compensation that an advertiser pays depends on several factors, such as:
1 the objectives of the provider: sales, leads, traffic, branding/visibility or a combination of these.
2 margin on their product or service
3 competition within the affiliate networks
4 cost per lead/sale in other channels

Affiliates

Publishers

Affiliates are also called publishers or partners. In principle, anyone who owns a website can become an affiliate. All you have to do is register with an affiliate network and make (advertising) space available on your website. The use of affiliate marketing can be a great way for the affiliates to make money with their website.

Of course, the website must be attractive to the advertiser. Their products must fit into the context of the website and they should feel comfortable to be associated with the publisher. That's why in the past it was very usual that advertisers' friends and family were operating as affiliates. Nowadays, there are increasingly more 'genuine' companies that operate professionally and use affiliate marketing on a large scale.

Registering with an affiliate network is very simple

There are different types of affiliates. The most common ones are:
1 generic websites
2 niche websites
3 comparison websites
4 mailing parties
5 saving schemes/cashback websites

1 Generic websites
In principle you can use affiliate marketing with any website. The only thing you have to do is make (advertising) space available. So even if you write a blog about your life or if you are the administrator for the local football club's website, you can register as an affiliate.

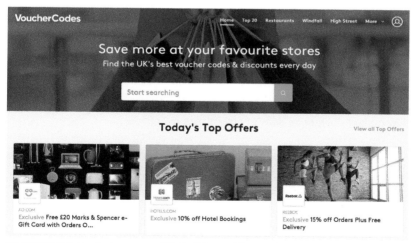

Vouchercodes.co.uk also uses affiliate links and is very interesting in terms of reach for advertisers

Many cashback sites including voucher codes.co.uk are in fact full of affiliate links; the site owner is effectively sharing part of the affiliate commission with the user.

2 Niche websites
Niche websites are sites that focus on specific target audiences or topics, also called interest sites. Examples are websites regarding specific information about mortgages, insurance, cars and so on. There are also sites that focus on specific target audiences, for example websites aimed at Mothers, eg mumsnet.com or dating (Match.com) As a rule, the more relevant a campaign is for a website, the better the results of the campaign will be.

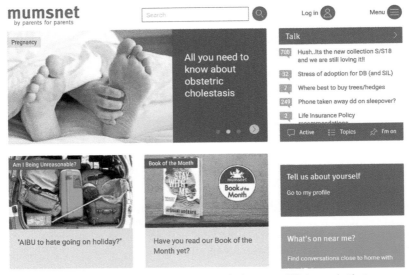

Niche website aimed at young parents that actively uses affiliate marketing

3 Comparison websites
On comparison sites different providers of certain products or services can be compared. A distinction can be made between general comparison websites and (industry) specific comparison websites (The largest comparison websites are often not registered with affiliate networks, but they make (affiliate) deals with advertisers directly.

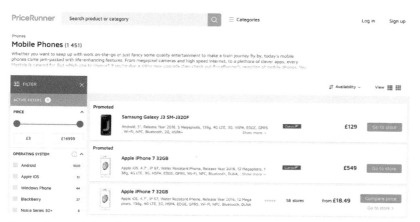

Comparison website with product information from various online providers

4 Mailing parties

Mailing parties have a huge database with consumer information and (sometimes millions!) of consumer email addresses. These consumers are registered with them and are regularly contacted with special offers and sales promotions from advertisers. Many mailing parties use so-called saving schemes (see 5). In addition to saving schemes, there are also non-incentivised mail parties operating within affiliate marketing that do not use a saving programme. There are considerably fewer clicks resulting from these mailings, because only the people that are interested in the product or service will click. For the advertiser this can be attractive nonetheless: the quality of the leads is greater.

Mailing parties

5 Saving schemes/cashback websites

Some affiliates, often mailing parties, try to provide their supporters with an extra incentive to respond to the promotions and offers that they send. They do this by using saving schemes or cashback discounts. Consumers who are registered with these affiliates receive a reward (points or money) when they open one of the affiliate's emails, click on an advertisement, complete a lead form or buy something.

The saving schemes use a credit award system. For example, you can collect 'pearls' and redeem them later for money, discount codes or a donation to charity.

Cashback websites are websites that link to various online providers. When a visitor buys something from a web store using one of these links, part of the purchase amount is stored as a cashback discount on the cashback website. When this stored amount has reached a certain minimum, it will be paid to the visitor in the form of a discount or money. Cashback websites often achieve their results using other online channels, such as search engine marketing and social media. Well-known cashback websites include Vouchercodes.co.uk, Quidco.com and Topcashback.co.uk

Cashback websites

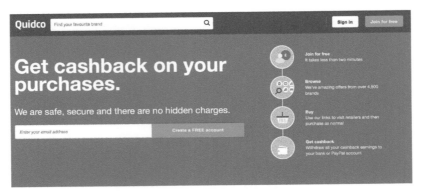

We partner with over 4,500 top brands to offer you cashback every time you shop

O₂   EE   Expedia   trainline   +4500 more

Cashback website Quidco.com

Affiliate networks

Affiliate networks bridge the gap between supply and demand amongst advertisers and affiliates. They are, as it were, a market place for both affiliates and advertisers and provide the campaign management system, the measuring system and the administrative processing. In addition, and often at extra cost, the networks can support the improvement of campaigns. Also, due to the fact that they oversee many different campaigns for various advertisers on a multitude of affiliate websites, they develop intimate knowledge of what is effective and what isn't.
It is also possible that the affiliate does business with the advertiser directly. If hundreds of different affiliates work for the advertisers, administrative processing is very complex and time-consuming. Furthermore, it is complicated to get the attention of all affiliates. These kinds of things are what an affiliate network is useful for. We will now briefly discuss the various possibilities for connecting affiliates and advertisers.

Open and closed networks
A distinction can be made between so-called open networks and closed networks. In their systems, open networks report exactly which affiliates are connected and generate sales for you. Closed networks do not present this information. In this case there is a 'black box', so to speak. You do generate sales, but do not know exactly where they originate.
Well-known and large open affiliate networks include:
- Zanox (Awin)
- Affiliate Window (Awin)
- Affilinet
- Tradedoubler
- Rakuten.com

Specialist networks
Some networks specialise in certain niches and focus on a specific target audience. Many affiliate networks have a powerful reach of the chosen

Margin notes:
Affiliate networks

7

Open networks
Closed networks

target segment and hence much in demand by advertisers. Examples would include Gealthtrader.com and Mainlinemenswear.co.uk.

Direct partner programmes
In order to use affiliate marketing as an advertiser, you do not necessarily have to join an affiliate network. You can also make deals directly with affiliate partners or even start your own affiliate partner programme, like amazon.com did. The principle is the same, but there is no involvement by networks. It is mainly large advertisers that sell a lot online that set up their own partner programme. The advantages of doing so are that the advertiser has more insight into the process and remains in control and can often collaborate even more intensively with affiliates. In addition, there is a considerable cost advantage, because the networks do not have to be paid.

Partner programme Amazon.co.uk

Advertisers that want to start their own partner programme should ask themselves in advance whether they have sufficient knowledge and resources to do this successfully and professionally in the long term. Besides that, it is a challenge to have a sufficient number of good affiliates registering to the partner programme directly. For smaller, lesser known parties, a self-developed partner programme is often less interesting. Due to the fact that it is a challenge to connect with sufficient and suitable affiliates directly, but also because of the efforts and costs involved, it is wiser for smaller advertisers to join a network.

Specialist agencies
As knowledge and continuous attention are essential elements for ensuring the success of an affiliate marketing campaign, a specialist

digital marketing or media agency is often called in, who, based on their expertise, help the advertiser to steer their campaign in the right direction. In terms of communication, the agency is in control (see figure 7.4): coordinating the various stakeholders and maintaining contact with all parties involved. The goal is of course, to ensure the affiliate marketing becomes more profitable. Sometimes, these agencies offer 'performance based' service, where they receive a percentage of turnover/profit. Another possibility is that the agencies get paid by the hour for the work they do for the advertiser on the affiliate campaign.

FIGURE 7.4 The agency is often central to affiliate marketing

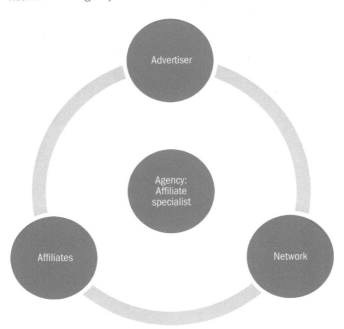

7.5.4   Market forces: the affiliates hold the power

Payment on the basis of an actual lead or sale is the dream of every marketer. Isn't this too good to be true? Could this dream really be just that? With the increasing demand from advertisers for affiliates to market their products or services, a market has been created. This means that the affiliates hold the power.

After all, they decide which advertiser and which affiliate network they want to work for. Especially the larger affiliates often enjoy easy pickings. Advertisers do their very best to build relationships with these affiliates. Examples of publishers whose sites feature affiliate ads include Allthesales.com.au, Vouchercodes.co.uk and Lucieslist.com.

Return on investment

The advertiser is not the only one who must take the income and the return on investment (return on investment, ROI) into account. Affiliates are also doing just that. If an advertiser's campaign has insufficient potential, affiliates will think twice before taking the plunge. The affiliates know that time and money will have to be invested in order to get a campaign 'off the ground'. In addition, affiliates also have limited advertising space available and will opt for a campaign with the highest ROI potential. The bottom line is that the advertiser will have to make the campaign attractive to *all* stakeholders.

This also means that affiliate marketing is not suitable for every advertiser. For example, it is difficult to carry out very specific campaigns for unknown advertisers and/or for a low fee. Business-to-business campaigns are also often less suitable for affiliate marketing.

The volume is often very limited. Some networks and affiliates even refuse campaigns with limited (volume) potential. On the basis of their knowledge and experience, networks and specialist agencies are often able to reasonably assess whether a campaign has potential or not.

7.5.5   Setting up an affiliate marketing campaign

It is important for a successful affiliate campaign to meet a number of preconditions. The important points for consideration here are:

- choice of networks
- affiliate offer
- consumer offer
- advertiser's reputation
- advertising material
- active campaign management
- administrative processing

We will now briefly discuss these points for consideration.

Choice of network(s)

Networks can differ from one another in, eg specialisms in specific branches, size, support and measurement and reporting systems. An advertiser must assess how many and which networks they ultimately want to collaborate with. Often, working with two or three affiliate networks is sufficient to ensure adequate coverage and to receive sufficient attention from all affiliates.

Affiliate offer

How much does the affiliate receive in return for displaying a banner, generating a click, a lead or sales? Adequate compensation ensures that affiliates will more easily take on the campaign. This compensation is a matter of weighing up the different factors and calculating the outcomes. On the one hand, the advertiser must be able to earn a healthy margin on sales. On the other hand, it must be attractive enough for the affiliate in order to make it worth their while to promote the affiliate program. In addition to the absolute amount of the fee, turnover potential also plays a major role. An affiliate would rather sell a hundred products for a fee of €30 than ten products for a fee of €50 (see figure 7.5).

FIGURE 7.5 Key factors for an affiliate to promote a program

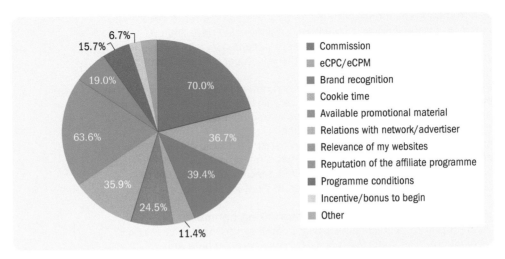

Source: Yonego, 2014

Consumer offer

Naturally, the offer for the consumer is also of great importance. They must purchase the product or make the information request. What added value does the product have for the consumer? Why should they buy the product? This information must be clearly presented to the consumer.

Advertiser's reputation

An advertiser's name and brand have a distinct influence on the success of an affiliate campaign. A strong brand's campaign often scores better and is more often taken on by affiliates than that of an unknown party.

Advertising materials

The advertiser is responsible for placing the advertising materials in the networks. Affiliates prefer appealing expressions; from which they expect a high conversion. It is also important that the banners and other expressions do not detract from their website. Of course, it is equally imperative to them that their visitors end up on a good website or landing page, on which information can be found and that instructs them to leave their information or directly make a purchase. More about effective websites and landing pages can be found in Chapter 11.

Examples of campaign material are:
1 banners and buttons
2 textual links
3 data feeds
4 landing pages
5 email templates

1 Banners and buttons

Banners and buttons are visual expressions that you can place on a website. The banners and buttons are often animated and are built in Flash or GIF. When you click on a banner or button, it will take you to the underlying website (see also section 5.3 on display advertising).

2 Textual links

Textual links are small pieces of text that link to a website. The text often describes the offer and includes an incentive (call to action) to click and/or buy.

Textual links

BEST PLASTIC BIB – BABYBJORN

Pros: Suitable from 4 months, spill pocket, waterproof, adjustable, comfortable
Cons: can be folded, no sleeve coverage

OUR VERDICT

The Babybjorn soft bib is made from plastic which is soft and flexible. The material makes the bib waterproof, easy to clean and comfortable for baby. It's designed with a deep pocket, to catch any spills before they fall onto your babies lap, saving any mess on their trousers.

This bib is super easy to clean by either wiping down, or even dishwasher safe which saves you a lot of extra laundry each day. We love that it doesn't satin or discolour easily, unlike fabric bibs. We recommend these bib for using at home, however they are not the best for taking out and about. They are quite large which is great for coverage, but they don't fold easily and can take up a lot of room in a carry bag, so check out our other bib suggestions.

BEST FABRIC BIB – BIBETTA ULTRABIB

Pros: soft, washing machine and drier safe, cute patterns, easy fold
Cons: baby can pull off, bobbling

OUR VERDICT

The Bibetta Ultrabib is a fantastic compromise between fabric and plastic bibs. The neoprene fabric is the same used for wet suits and stops water leaking through whilst remaining soft for babies comfort. This bib has a hand catcher pocket for any crumbs or spillage. Unlike plastic bibs the Ultrabib can fold away and won't take up space in your change bag.

Textual link for bibs on Mamaunion.co.uk

3 Data feeds

Using data feeds can be very useful for achieving good results. A data feed contains all or part of the advertiser's product range and is therefore also called a product feed.

Data feed

Product feed

If an affiliate includes a feed, they are better able to attend to the visitors within the website. This way, the visitor can easily search within the advertiser's product range on the affiliate's website.

An affiliate must have the necessary technical knowledge to be able to implement product feeds on their website.

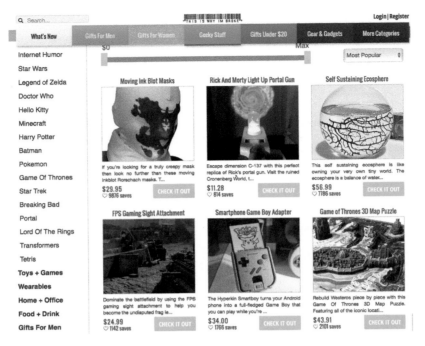

Product feed on an affiliate site from Amazon.com

4 Landing page

To increase the conversion, landing pages are often used. These are simple and targeted web pages that are fully geared for encouraging a certain activity. If using a special landing page is not an option, then it is advisable to 'deep link' the advertising material to the most relevant page on that subject. Deep linking is creating a link to a page 'deeper' within the website. Suppose there is a financial advertiser that provides both mortgages and insurance. In that case, it is useful to link the affiliate campaign for mortgages to the page about mortgages.barclays.co.uk/mortgages and the campaign for the home insurance policies to the insurance page barclays.co.uk/insurance/home-insurance.

Deep linking

5 Email templates

An email template is the design of an email in the way that the recipient will finally receive the email (including text, images and call-to-action buttons directing to the advertiser's website). Email templates are often used as advertising material by mailing parties to reach a large group of people via email (see subsection 7.5.3). Using an email template, the publisher can apply the campaign expressions as provided by the advertiser. In some cases, the publisher can also develop an email template autonomously. In this case, the advertiser must approve the expression before it is sent. This inspection takes place in order to safeguard the advertiser's brand image and the house style.

Email template

Active campaign management

Campaign management is essential. It is a continuous process of analysis, control and optimisation. This could include, among other things, the assessment of leads, establishing contact with affiliates and networks and

© Noordhoff Uitgevers bv

the further development and testing of the advertising materials. As with other online channels, an affiliate marketing campaign needs focus, expertise, time and attention. Only then can success be achieved. This is the reason that advertisers often hire a specialised agency to set up and manage their affiliate activities.

Administrative processing

Correct and smooth financial processing is indispensable for an affiliate campaign. Affiliates do not want to be kept waiting for their money. They have made investments in advance for the promotion of the advertiser's campaign. Accurate measurement, quick inspection and timely payment of the invoice is very important. For many large advertisers, who often use long payment periods, this sometimes causes problems. As mentioned in the introduction to section 7.5.3, the affiliate network is often an intermediary in measuring sales and financial processes.

7.5.6   Compensation and remuneration

From the compensation that an advertiser provides for a lead or sale, a percentage goes to the affiliate and to the networks. The affiliate makes efforts to generate conversions and the affiliate network makes its system available and arranges the financial settlement. This distribution varies from 60 to 80% commission for the affiliate and 20 to 40% for the affiliate network.

An example of such a calculation: suppose a financial institution provides a fee of €50 for a completed mortgage application. Based on a commission structure of 75% -25%, an affiliate earns €37.50 and the network earns €12.50 per lead.

The previous calculation is a simple example of the commission structure based on a fixed amount (per lead). However, there are various other options for filling in the commission structure.

There may be a fixed amount per 1,000 impressions, per conversion (click, lead/action or sale) or a percentage of the turnover or profit or a combination thereof. Figure 7.6 illustrates the advantages and disadvantages of each of these reimbursement systems. An amount per

FIGURE 7.6 Advantages and disadvantages of the settlement models

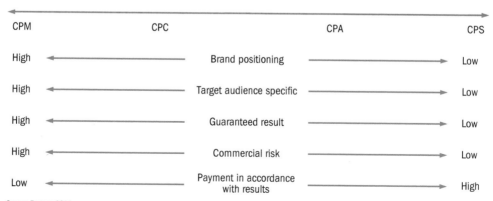

Source: Testnet, 2011

1,000 impressions is indicated with the initials CPM (cost per Mille), an amount per click with CPC (cost per click), an amount per action with CPA (cost per action) and an amount or percentage per sale with CPS (cost per sale). A combination of two or more of these settlement models is also possible. This is called a hybrid model. To be able to compare the different models, the costs are often converted to a result per click; this is called effective cost per click (eCPC).

Hybrid model

Effective cost per click (eCPC)

It is important that the advertiser tries to align their own goals with those of the affiliate and the affiliate network. See example 7.2.

EXAMPLE 7.2

Which reimbursement model?

Suppose American Airlines has an affiliate campaign running. The goal is to generate sales by selling tickets online. However, starting from New York, there is quite a difference in turnover for a ticket to Chicago of less than $200 compared to a ticket to London, which costs almost $1,000. Suppose the affiliates receive a fixed fee of $20 per sale, regardless of the destination and turnover, then it does not matter to the affiliate whether they sell a ticket to Chicago or London. Of course, American Airlines would prefer to sell a ticket to London because the revenue is greater. In this case, if a remuneration model of a percentage of the turnover is used, the affiliate is also encouraged and rewarded if they sell a ticket to a more expensive destination. Then there is a clear win-win situation.

It is also possible that the affiliates receive an extra bonus if they perform well. For example, if they acquire a lot of volume or if the quality of the conversions is very good. Advertisers regularly use these kinds of bonuses and (financial) incentives to encourage affiliates and networks to achieve even more and better conversions. Sometimes, non-financial incentives are given to affiliates as a reward (for example a telephone, a netbook or a trip). Nevertheless, the affiliates would prefer to receive monetary compensation (see figure 7.7).

It is important that the different stakeholders are all on the same page: the goal should be achieving an optimal result in terms of quantity and quality. Often, quantity is most important for the affiliate and the network. After all, the more sales, the higher the compensation. For the advertiser, however, quality is also important. If a consumer only makes a request for a quotation because they receive a nice key ring, the request is not very qualitative. In order to remedy this problem, it is often necessary to set up graduations that take quantity as well as quality into account and extra rewards are received for both. The fewer leads or sales that are rejected, the better the quality for the advertiser.

FIGURE 7.7 Affiliates prefer to receive financial incentives

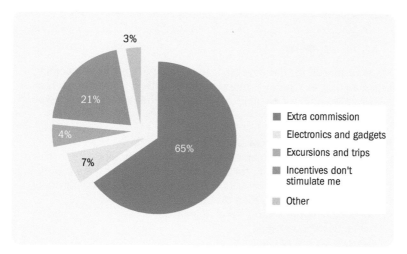

Source: Yonego, 2014

7.5.7 Measuring and inspecting

More than for other online channels, it is essential for affiliate marketing that the campaign is measured correctly. After all, the income of the various stakeholders depends on this.

Affiliate networks ensure the measurement of the campaigns and on that basis the administrative and financial settlement of the fees. The networks' measurement system consists of software that often operates on the basis of 'cookies', combined with IP- and fingerprint tracking. The system 'logs' the visitors and can see where they have originated from. Often, the system remembers the visitor for a period of 30 days. If the visitor returns to the website within 30 days and still commits the conversion, this is recorded by the network's measurement system. The different stakeholders receive a login for the network's system, in this way they can see the status and results of the campaigns at any time.

Fingerprint tracking

It is very important for the advertiser to carefully measure the campaign so that the affiliates and networks are paid fairly and not unnecessarily. Otherwise, if different networks (and measurement systems) are used side by side, overlapping and double counting can occur. See example 7.3.

- -

EXAMPLE 7.3

Avoid double counting

John wants to buy a new car. While reading an article on a weblog he is directed to network A on the BMW website via a banner. He looks around a bit, but he wants to orient himself a little further. Two weeks later, John returns to the same BMW website via an expression on network B and decides, after further investigation, to complete an application for a test drive. Both network A and network B's systems (using the cookie) count towards John's lead at that moment. However, advertiser BMW has only received one application for a test drive. By accurately applying measurements, the advertiser can 'un-duplicate' and find out which network John ultimately used to make the lead request. This is the network that is then rewarded. The other network receives a lower reimbursement, or none at all.

It is always a matter for the advertiser to approve or reject the incoming conversions before payment is made to the affiliates. Conversions have to be un-duplicated and, for example, checked for whether the data has been entered correctly.

7.5.8   The process: how does it work?

We now know what affiliate marketing is, which stakeholders are involved and what important matters to take into account. But how does it work in practice? What does the process look like? The process can be divided into four steps, which we will then discuss:

Step 1   determining the strategy and objectives
Step 2   selecting the network
Step 3   setting up the affiliate system
Step 4   managing the campaign

Step 1 Determining the strategy and objectives

The first step is to determine which products/services will be used for the affiliate marketing campaign and what the campaign objectives are. According to this selection, you must determine what the exact offer will be. Questions that need to be answered are:

• What is the maximum cost of a sale/lead?
• Which incentive strategy will we use?

Next, the advertiser must determine the communication strategy. How will they launch the product and what is the focus on? Here, the advertiser takes into account materials that must be developed; such as banner sets, links and/or landing pages. This strategy is linked to set goals (eg sales/ lead volumes and number of active affiliates) for the affiliate marketing campaign.

Step 2 Selecting the network

After step 1, the network selection procedure starts. The advertiser assesses, among other things, specialisations in specific branches, the size, the support, the measurement and the reporting system of the affiliate networks. For practical reasons, it is often useful to start with one network. The best-known networks have enough affiliates backing them to be able to run a campaign successfully. Once the first campaign has been successfully completed and both the management and the results are satisfactory, additional networks can always be added. After contractual agreements with the networks have been put in place regarding the amount of the fees, the duration of the agreement and the other conditions for cooperation, the affiliate system can be set up.

Step 3 Setting up an affiliate system

The relevant campaign network will be set up on the basis of the chosen network and the offer. Among other things, the campaign material is loaded, the campaigns are made measurable and affiliates are informed

© Noordhoff Uitgevers bv

about the campaign. After correct design, the campaign will go live and affiliates can include the campaign on their website.

Step 4 Managing the campaign

Campaign management starts as soon as the campaign is online. This is, as with other online channels, a continuous process of monitoring, analysing, managing and further optimising. This can be done at both operational and strategic level. Operationally, the campaign will be directed on the basis of tasks such as testing leads/sales, contacts with network(s) and affiliates, ensuring correct campaign measurement, selection and monitoring of websites, promoting the campaign within the network(s) and monthly preparation of reports. At a strategic level, consideration can be given to the current strategy, and looking forward, at how affiliate marketing for the advertiser can be further expanded in the future. For example, the advertiser looks at the development of the campaign proposition, tests different types of campaigns and fees (for example, paying per lead instead of per sale) and adds extra networks. In addition, it is advisable to maintain regular contact and plan (telephone) appointments with all stakeholders to review the progress and results of the campaign.

7.5.9   Affiliate marketing in the digital marketing communications mix

In the digital marketing communications mix, affiliate marketing is a bit of an odd one out. Factually, it comes down to the fact that the affiliates use various digital marketing forms to achieve results for the advertiser. Affiliate marketing is therefore not a defined online channel, but a collection of online channels that distinguishes itself by form (via resellers) and the settlement model (performance based). In this sense it is important for the advertiser to take this into account in their digital marketing strategy.

Sometimes, for example, it's useful to exclude affiliates from Google AdWords so that they do not compete and bid on the same keywords. On the other hand, the affiliate marketing campaign can sometimes take advantage of the other channels. Consistency in the message and coordination with other (online) media channels is often a reinforcing factor. In any case, it is useful to extrapolate the 'learnings' and positive results from the other online channels to affiliate marketing and vice versa. For instance, campaign statements and landing pages that will score well.

7

Questions and assignments

NOW CHECK YOUR UNDERSTANDING:

7.1 An increasing number of people aged 55 and upwards are signing up to dating sites, hoping to find a new partner in their later years. A new dating site wants to focus all their attention on this target segment.
  a What are the four basic steps of search engine marketing that the dating site must take to encourage someone to visit the website?
  b Provide recommendations for each basic step. Be as specific as possible.

7.2 National Zoo Canberra wants to attract families with young children to visit the zoo in the autumn holiday.
  a Create a plan to attract visitors to National Zoo Canberra website via online advertising in an effective and efficient way in order to encourage parents to order their tickets online.
  b Which external parties do you need in order to help you to carry out your plan?
  c Which price model do you prefer for this display advertising campaign?

7.3 Just-eat.co.uk is an online food delivery service. For them, social media is an important marketing channel. A key objective of social media advertising is to motivate potential customers to install and use the Just Eat app for placing orders.
  a Formulate a defined communication target segment for Just-eat.co.uk.
  b Which social media channels are suitable for approaching this target segment? Motivate your answer based on the theory.
  c Which tactics do you recommend applying for targeting? Motivate your answer.

7.4 Leading Academic Publisher Routledge wants to sell high-quality textbooks to students and universities using affiliate marketing.
  a What are the decisions that Routledge's marketing department must make regarding the design of the affiliate campaign?
  b Which steps, in terms of processes, should Routledge take to ensure the success of the affiliate marketing?

7.5

CASE

Under Armour Ecommerce (Google Shopping)
By Mike Berry

Under Armour, Inc. is an American company which manufactures footwear, sports and casual apparel. Under Armour's global headquarters are located in Baltimore, Maryland. The company was founded in 1996.

The European operation of Under Armour wanted to improve cost-effectiveness of its Google AdWords (Pay-Per-Click) campaigns via Google Shopping. They wanted to focus on getting higher quality clicks (ie clicks that converted at a higher rate) while minimising the cost per click. This meant taking a close look at the keywords (search terms) Under Amour was bidding on.

In all the countries in which it operates, ecommerce is a major (and growing) source of sales for Under Armour. Currently, over 16,000 items are advertised on Google Shopping and most of these products are available in 12 European countries via the Under Armour online shop. Although Under Armour had previously invested in campaign optimisation for Google Shopping, Under Armour wanted to optimise further and they devised a unique campaign structure that divided search traffic according to branded and generic keywords.

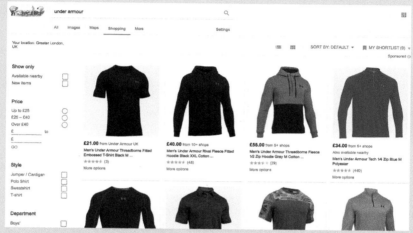

Using branded keywords allows Under Armour to reach athletes searching for Under Armour sports performance apparel and footwear

The objectives were to Increase visibility, improve insights and, most of all, to maximise the value of the clicks obtained.

The activity comprised 3 stages:
1 restructured PPC campaigns
2 divided traffic by branded and generic terms
3 established sophisticated bid management for different categories

The results of the campaign were impressive:
- branded terms: 99.5% impression share
- costs: 20% reduction
- sales: 20% increase
- return on ad spend: increase of 88%

'Through our improved funnelling, we achieved an almost complete share of possible impressions for our branded search terms, ensuring that we reach athletes searching for Under Armour sports performance apparel and footwear in an efficient way.'
                                    - Lauren Geenen, Search Marketing Specialist, Under Armour EU

© Noordhoff Uitgevers bv

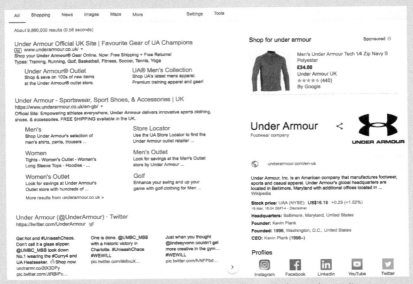

Searching for 'Under Armour' results in a very well branded search result page

Having launched in 1996, sports performance brand Under Armour had achieved an annual turnover of $5 billion, making them the third largest brand in its market globally. Ecommerce plays a central role in product sales. *'Over 16,000 items are advertised on Google Shopping alone'*, says Lauren Geenen, the brand's Search Marketing Specialist for Europe. Currently, almost all of the products are available in 12 European countries via the manufacturer's online shop.

But there were some serious challenges for Under Armour. Although they had invested in campaign optimisation for Google Shopping, they believed the effectiveness could be improved. 'The biggest challenge was that a large part of the traffic and sales were achieved by branded search terms within our campaigns', explained Lauren Geenen. 'This performance differed greatly from that of our generic search terms but were grouped in the same campaigns and ad groups.'

The problem was that the set-up of the PPC account on Google Shopping hindered effective bid management and limited the usable insights amiable to Under Armour.

So, to address these concerns, Under Armour worked with Google to run a 'Shopping Lab' to improve the campaign structure. They wanted to understand the 'search intent' of the consumer. They re-examined the overall menu structure of their ecommerce websites.

The decision was made to separate branded (ie 'Under Armour') from generic traffic (eg Sports Clothing') in Google Shopping through intelligent use of campaign priorities and funnelling of search terms. The result was that Under Armour could optimise separately for these two groups of search terms.

But Under Armour didn't stop there. They decided to split out best-sellers per category, based on information and forecasts from the Under-Armour demand planning team and then they did the same with price 'outliers' (high and low).

This represented a major change from a more normal Google Shopping optimisation strategy, in which bids on top-selling products are based only on their past performance. Now the bestsellers were identified by predictive insights from Under Armour using historical data.

Next, Under Armour EU used their Dutch website to test these improvements. The insights gained about funnelling search terms and improving the bidding strategy were tested. After just one-month, positive results clearly emerged.

'Through our improved funnelling, we achieved an almost complete share of possible impressions – 99.5% – for our branded search terms, ensuring that we reach all athletes searching for Under Armour sports performance apparel and footwear', Lauren observes. 'This wasn't possible with the previous structure.'

Even better, costs fell by 20%, sales rose 20% and return on ad spend increased by 88%. As a direct result of these improved numbers and the improved insights generated, Under Armour decided to implement a similar strategy for its UK and German ecommerce websites.

Source: http://www.digitaltrainingacademy.com/casestudies/2017/11/ecommerce_case_study_under_armour_revamps_shopping_with_google_insights.php

NOW CHECK YOUR UNDERSTANDING:

a Define the target audience and objectives for Under Armour, using the digital marketing funnel. (see figure 5.1).

b This campaign used Shopping Campaigns in Google AdWords (Pay-per-click) What significant changes did Under Armour make to their Shopping campaigns?

c In what way did results improve? What suggestions would you make to Under Armour regarding the targeting of their online display ads? Would it be better for them to adopt a Pay-Per-Click (PPC) or pay per thousand impressions (CPM) model? Explain the advantages and disadvantages of each. Which partners should Under Armour work with on the display ads?

d How would you suggest Under Armour optimises its social media activity (both organic and paid)?

e Do you believe Under Armour could benefit from affiliate (performance) marketing? How? Please explain your answer.

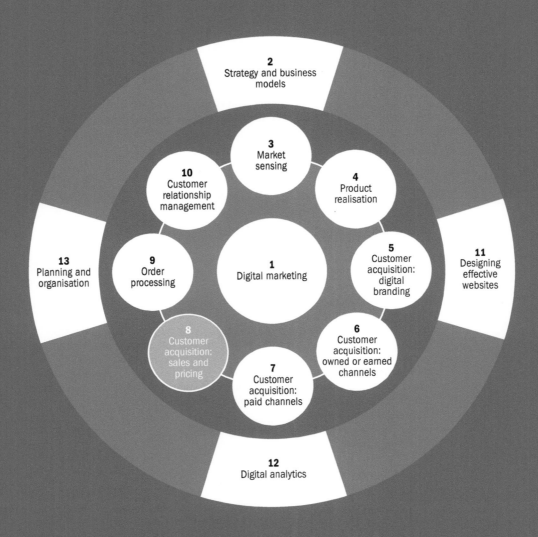

1 Digital marketing
2 Strategy and business models
3 Market sensing
4 Product realisation
5 Customer acquisition: digital branding
6 Customer acquisition: owned or earned channels
7 Customer acquisition: paid channels
8 Customer acquisition: sales and pricing
9 Order processing
10 Customer relationship management
11 Designing effective websites
12 Digital analytics
13 Planning and organisation

8

Customer acquisition: sales and pricing

Authors: Stephan Schroeders (8.1 and 8.2) and Marjolein Visser (8.3)

The previous chapters described how the marketer can acquire a good idea of the market's wants and needs (the market sensing process) and how they can use the Internet for the development and improvement of products as well as for the setting up of processes surrounding the product or the service (the product realisation process). When everything is ready for receiving customers, you enter the customer acquisition process: defining target markets and recruiting new customers. This process starts with marketing communication in order to get in touch with the customer. This was discussed in Chapters 5, 6 and 7. The provider then convinces the prospects via the online sales channels to buy the product. Then prospect and provider come to an agreement about the price of the product. This chapter details the sales process and the determination of the price.

This chapter will cover:
- online sales
- online sales advice
- online price determination

After studying this chapter, you will be able to:
- distinguish the different types of conversion and name methods for increasing the conversion of an ecommerce website
- indicate what methods there are for dispensing online sales advice
- indicate which decisions are relevant to the construction of the elements that make up an ecommerce website and, on that basis, describe a simple concept for an ecommerce website
- describe the three basic methods and the specific forms of online price determination as well as common temporary pricing tactics
- explain what dynamic pricing means and how it can be used

8.1 Online sales

Not all customer acquisition processes result in online sales.
Many organisations use digital marketing as a marketing communication
tool but then complete the acquisition process in a personal meeting
and/or a written contract. However, this chapter relates to the completion
of the agreement between customer and supplier online. The ecommerce
website also plays a central role in this. We will go into this in detail in this
section. We will also discuss in detail selling via mobile apps.

Amazon
The history of ecommerce websites dates back to 1995. In that year
Amazon, still a leading ecommerce website today, was launched. The
name Amazon is derived from the Amazon River, one of the largest rivers in
the world. Jeff Bezos, Amazon's founder, wanted to start one of the largest
ecommerce websites in the world. Starting as an online bookstore,
Amazon has grown into an international multi-billion-dollar company that
also sells DVDs, clothing, toys, food and most recently also films and
series via Amazon Prime video. Today, Amazon is still praised for its
innovative applications and advanced technology. Examples of this that
were copied many times after are '1-Click® Shopping' (also known as
one-click or one-click buying), a way to order a product with just one mouse
click as well as Amazon's 'wishlist', an option where customers can store
products and buy them later.

8.1.1 Ecommerce website

Ecommerce website

An ecommerce website is a virtual store on the Internet. An ecommerce
website can focus on both the consumer and the business market. An
ecommerce website provides visitors with the possibility of viewing articles
and/or services online, make their decision and then to order and pay. The
price, the quality and the characteristics of each item are shown, and the
visitor can put one or more articles and/or services in a virtual shopping
basket and buy them. A transaction is then established via a secure
connection, whereby the visitor can pay for the desired item and/or service.
The ecommerce website owner then sends the purchased article or proof
of purchase to the buyer. This order handling process is described in
Chapter 9.
Professional ecommerce websites often offer visitors extra features with
the aim of providing an optimal online shopping experience. Examples
include the ability to search for a specific product, reading product reviews
written by other buyers and an overview of the most popular items. Usually,
ecommerce websites aim to facilitate the largest possible number of
transactions.
After this we will examine the concept of conversion, one of the
characteristics of a successful ecommerce website. Then we will discuss
the various elements that make up an ecommerce website. We will then
look briefly at the staffing structure of ecommerce websites. Finally, the
latest developments for ecommerce websites and personalisation will be
discussed.

Conversion

One of the characteristics of a successful ecommerce website is that it can encourage a certain percentage of its visitors to make a purchase. Chaffey & Smith (2017) describe this conversion ratio as follows:

> Conversion is the percentage of website visitors that perform a specific action, such as buying something.

Conversion

In the previous definition, a purchase is used as an example, but there are more types of conversions:

1. Overall conversion, expressed as a percentage. In addition to a purchase, this could be, for example, a job application or registering for a newsletter.

   Overall conversion

2. Shopping basket conversion. This concerns the number of visitors who placed an article and/or service in the shopping basket, divided by the number of visitors that actually made the purchase.

   Shopping basket conversion

3. Visitor conversion. This can be calculated by dividing the number of conversion goals that are achieved by the number of unique visitors in a given period.

   Visitor conversion

4. Traffic source conversion. This concerns the number of visitors from a traffic source (such as Google), divided by the number of conversion goals that are achieved.

   Traffic source conversion

It goes without saying that the various conversions can be further segmented to gain insight into the quality of the ecommerce website visit. Examples include subdivision into new and returning visitors or according to different products.

Measuring the defined conversion goals is done using web analytics software, such as Google Analytics. You can find more about web analytics (digital analytics) in Chapter 12. We will now provide the overall conversion percentages and a number of methods for increasing conversion.

Overall conversion percentages

In general, an average conversion rate for an ecommerce website can be assumed to be between 0.5% and 2%. Such an average percentage is of limited value. The conversion rate depends heavily on things such as the type of customer, the type of product and brand awareness. A low conversion percentage means that the majority of visitors to an ecommerce website drop out earlier in the online purchase process and do not buy anything. It is therefore very important to study and analyse at which point the visitors drop out. The digital marketing funnel is a useful tool for this (see figure 8.1). Does the website succeed in captivating the visitor, does the visitor receive enough information to help them decide on the purchase, can they order easily and pay easily?

8

FIGURE 8.1 The Digital Marketing funnel

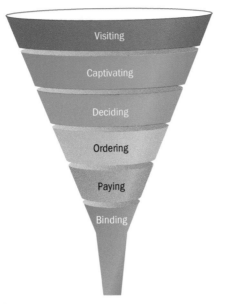

Source: © Marjolein Visser RM

Methods for increasing the conversion
Some methods for increasing the conversion are:
- a checkout bargain in the shopping cart/shopping basket
- several delivery or pick-up options

In addition, there are other, indirect ways to increase the conversion rate. An example is a feature such as the ability to add articles to a 'wishlist'. Often a visitor must first register in order to do this. Marketers gratefully use the data that such a feature provides; this data can be used for retargeting or email marketing programs, for example, where visitors are approached and tempted to complete the purchase after all.

Elements that make up an ecommerce website
An ecommerce website consists of various elements that are constructed with the aid of software modules. We will discuss the following elements:
1. ecommerce website software
2. homepage
3. catalogue management
4. search module
5. product pages
6. shopping basket/shopping cart
7. cross and upsell
8. payment modules
9. creating an account and buying without an account
10. programs for resellers

1 Ecommerce website software

The core of the ecommerce website is the software that it runs on and on which it has been constructed for desktop and mobile use. The costs of an ecommerce website range from several hundred to hundreds of thousands of euros for 'high-end' providers. Usually, ecommerce websites that consist of standard software are cheaper, but they are also less flexible than the custom-made variety. Customisation can be necessary if the ecommerce website needs to be multi-lingual, for example, or if complex price rules apply. An example of a complex price rule is a discount when purchasing multiple items that may not apply in combination with another offer. Customisation may also be necessary to manage links with underlying systems, for example with a planning system, an administration system or a purchasing system. An organisation sets up a list of requirements for setting up an ecommerce website and divides these into 'must have' and 'nice to have'. It is also important to determine what the range of products will look like. What does the target segment want and expect? Which products provide the desired return for online sales? Once the requirements are clear, the organisation can determine which provider will best meet these requirements.

Roughly, a distinction can be made between providers of web hosting and of ecommerce website software. There are numerous providers who 'host' ecommerce websites. The provider is then, as it were, the host for an ecommerce website and ensures that the ecommerce website continues to 'run'. An example of a provider of web hosting is Myshop.com. Providers of ecommerce website software, such as Magento, provide software that the organisation itself can use to create an ecommerce website and determine the design according to their own wishes.

Ecommerce website software

2 Homepage

An important factor for arousing the visitor's curiosity and for enticing *them* to click on an article is the design of the homepage. Navigating on the homepage of the (mobile) ecommerce website can be done in different ways. You can display the items on offer horizontally or vertically, ie centrally next to each other at the top of the page (horizontal) or to the left aligned below each other (vertical). As a result of the increased use of smartphones, the 'hamburger menu' is often used: an icon with three horizontal stripes that the user can click on open the mobile website's menu.

Homepage

Hamburger menu

How the hamburger menu is derived from a hamburger (source: Demac Media)

3 Catalogue management

One of the most important aspects of an ecommerce website is maintaining the catalogue, also called catalogue management. The catalogue contains all products that the ecommerce website wants to display. With the help of software for catalogue management, a structure can be applied and the range of products on offer can be presented in the ecommerce website. The way these products are presented is very

Catalogue management

important. In order to arouse the visitor's curiosity and encourage them to make a *decision*, the products on offer must be displayed as attractively as possible.

The ecommerce website is a kind of shop window. In such a shop window it helps if (one or more) images of the article are shown and if detailed product descriptions are available.

PIM systems

Larger ecommerce websites built by high-end providers and selling tens of thousands of items often use integrated PIM systems (Product Information Management systems). For such organisations, the product information is often divided over several departments or locations. By using a PIM, information such as photographic material and product characteristics are centrally and consistently stored in a database. Data can easily be integrated or imported from various sources, such as a stock information system. Data can also be exported to and published via an ecommerce website or physical product catalogue. The management of the catalogue can be done from a PIM or a standard catalogue system.

An example of a catalogue structure is the division into one or more main categories that are subdivided into subcategories (see figure 8.2). Subcategories then consist of products and possibly product items. The depth of the product hierarchy depends on the number of articles on offer. Ideally, you limit yourself to three to four layers, because the deeper a product is tucked away within such a structure, the more the visitor will have to navigate to view the desired item.

FIGURE 8.2 Example of a catalogue structure

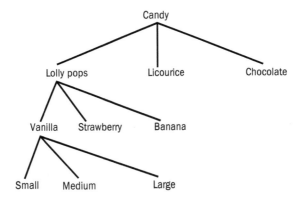

4 Search module

Search module

Searching within an ecommerce website is done via so-called 'navigated search', ie finding the desired article via the ecommerce website's navigation. By browsing in a certain product category, a filter can be applied to the search for the desired item.

Search function

Another possibility visitors can use to search for items is the ecommerce website's search function. In general, features for searching consist of the following elements:

Intelligent search

• Intelligent search. A search function that includes predictive text recognises misspelled words and makes suggestions for improvement,

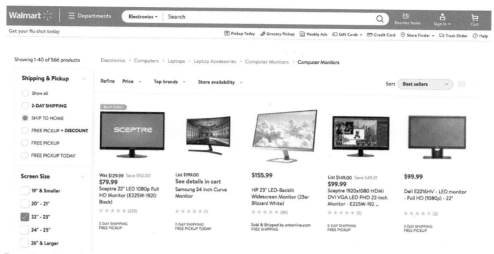

Browsing through product categories and applying filters

so that the visitor is directed to the correct article. In addition, synonyms of the search phrases that are used can be shown. The search results can also be manipulated, for example by showing articles in the order of the highest gross margin, best assessed or most frequently displayed. It is also often possible to display a banner based on a certain search phrase, indicating that there is a promotional offer or that can direct the visitor to related products.

Intelligent predictive text

- **Reporting.** Insight into visitor's actions provides valuable information for optimising the range of products on offer. If ecommerce website visitors often search for an item that you do stock, you can respond to this. A dashboard provides the ecommerce website manager with real-time insight into products that visitors are looking for.

  Reporting

- **Merchandise.** An integrated cross- and upsell application often makes it possible to display the most sought-after articles prominently on the homepage of the ecommerce website, for example on the basis of the highest gross margin, the best rated or most frequently displayed. The applications often also provide the option of A/B testing. Finally, options for space management are provided: the most popular products receive the biggest share of 'shelf space' in the ecommerce website.

  Merchandise

  Space management

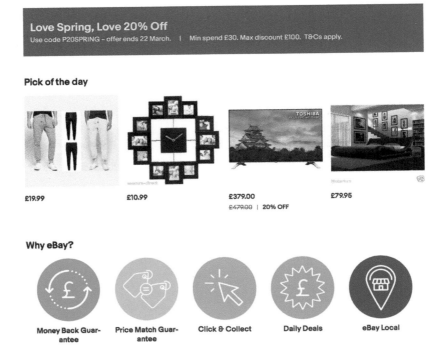

'Pick of the day' on eBay's homepage

Nykaa.com is a premier online beauty and wellness destination based in India. It offers branded beauty and wellness products for men and women at competitive prices. Its website promises 'a hassle-free shopping experience, the virtual makeover tool, beauty advice and assistance on the phone, free expert advice and articles on beauty trends and tutorials and celebrity looks as well as free home delivery for many brands. Nykaa is an example of merchandising. It makes recommendations based on individual user behaviour and/or the products they particularly wish to promote at that particular time, using data in smart ways to target customers with relevant offers.

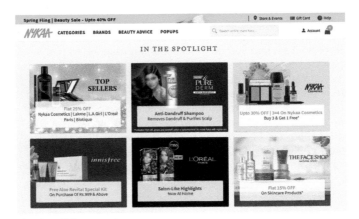

Merchandising on nykaa.com

5 Product page

The product page must entice the customer to *make the decision* to put the item in the shopping cart/shopping basket. It is therefore necessary that a detailed description of the product is given. The benefits of the product must also be clearly communicated, while the opportunity to compare the article and other people's reviews should not be missed. In addition, the conversion can be optimised, and returns can be reduced (because the customer makes a better choice to begin with) by using multiple photos, video and detailed photography. Proper management of images requires a digital asset management system (DAM system) linked to the PIM system mentioned under 3 Catalogue management.

An additional feature that is mainly used in the clothing industry, is the possibility to zoom in on the article, to share the article via social networks and cross- and upsell (related articles, customers also bought, recommended).

Product page

Digital asset management system

The website of H&M in Hong Kong is an example of several relevant features.

OTHERS ALSO BOUGHT

| Printed T-shirt | 3-pack T-shirts Regular fit | 3-pack T-shirts Regular fit | Skinny Low Jeans |
| HK$99.90 | HK$199.00 | HK$199.00 | HK$249.00 |

Website H&M Hong Kong showing products bought by others and making it possible to immediately favourite these items

6 Shopping basket/shopping cart

The shopping basket is the cash register of an ecommerce website. The visitor has found the desired item, decided that they want it and clicked on a button that places the item in the shopping basket/shopping cart. There are many variations in how the visitor is enticed into doing this.

Every ecommerce website makes a different choice with regard to shape, colour and text. This choice is the result of testing, testing and testing once again. There is no rule about whether a button should be green, orange or red; you simply try out a number of varieties and look at which variety the visitors click most often and lead to the most sales.

Once the visitor has placed the item in the shopping basket/shopping cart, he or she can still decide *not to order and pay* for the article. Final purchase and payment is called the checkout process.

Shopping basket

Shopping cart

Checkout process

8

Sometimes the checkout process does not succeed, for example for the following reasons:
- You will be charged for costs that were not mentioned before, such as delivery costs.
- The visitor had to register before they could make the payment.
- The delivery costs were too high.
- The customer did not know how to add/remove items and how to complete the purchase.
- The customer could not find all the information needed to complete the purchase.
- The customer was window shopping and used the shopping basket as a wish list or was using it to compare several different stores.

There is no clear answer to the question of what the checkout process should look like. It is a complex process and includes a number of fundamental conflicts between the interests of the customer and those of the ecommerce website owner. For example, the organisation wants to know as much as possible about the customer, while the customer wants to be finished with the process as quickly as possible. It is clear that the process must be organised as briefly and simply as possible and that testing various forms of communication, navigation and content must provide insight into an optimal checkout.

Abandoned basket email

Abandoned basket

An application that ecommerce websites often use is the so-called abandoned basket email. This means that an email is sent when a customer adds an item to his/her shopping basket but does not complete the order (abandoned basket). In the email the product from the shopping cart is offered to them again. The purpose of the email is to lure the user back into the buying process and complete the purchase after all. The result is that the conversion will eventually rise. A variant of this is done by retargeting, displaying articles or products that the visitor has previously put in their shopping basket the next time they visit.

7 Cross- and up-sell

Another very useful feature is the possibility of cross- or up-sell. The goal of cross- or upsell is to improve the user-friendliness of the ecommerce website and to increase the average order value conversion. A possibility for cross- or up-sell is one of the standard features of web hosting providers and ecommerce website software. Examples of this are attempting to sell you a more expensive item than the chosen item on the product page, for example a computer with more memory or an extra item entirely. An example of this could be offering you an earpiece to go with a mobile phone you are purchasing, or pairing articles together: a DVD of a feature film with the accompanying book in one package.

8 Payment module

Payment module

All ecommerce websites include, depending on the chosen solution or the subscription, a payment option. This must be user-friendly so that the visitor can not only order a product, but also actually *pay for* it. Should the visitor fail to do so, a reminder in the form of an email will often be sent. Online payments are discussed in more detail in Chapter 9.

9 Creating an account and buying without an account

Account

When a visitor orders in an ecommerce website for the first time, they often create a new account. The advantage of this is that the buyer does

© Noordhoff Uitgevers bv

not have to enter their information again in the event of a repeat purchase. Often, they are also asked whether they want this information to be remembered. The advantage of this is that the customer will be automatically logged in during any repeat visits to the website and that web retailers can start to personalise the content that they are then shown. In many cases it is also possible to place an order without creating a new account or to log in using your social media account. The advantage of this is that the customer doesn't have to spend time creating a profile (either by skipping this altogether or logging in via their social media account) and is therefore less likely to abandon the purchase.

The screenshot below from johnlewis.com shows the checkout process. Ecommerce retailers need to decide whether to insist on customers creating a profile before they can purchase, or egallowing them to login via a social media account (eg Facebook or Twitter)

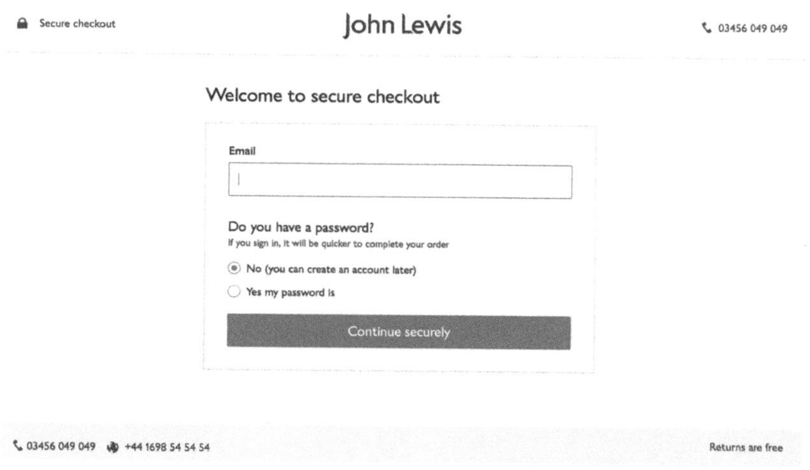

Paying on johnlewis.com with and without an account

Incidentally, it is wise not to subject a new customer to a barrage of questions. You can simply use progressive profiling. The first time the user visits the ecommerce website, they only have to supply a few basic details. Additional information is then requested at a later date. So instead of asking them to complete a form with a multitude of questions, you only ask them a limited amount of questions the first time and use follow-up forms later to collect all the data you need.

Progressive profiling

What motivates consumers to give permission for personal communication?

Krafft, Arden and Verhoef investigated which economic and psychological factors motivate consumers to give permission for personalised communication. They discovered that consumers are more likely to give permission if they receive relevant and/or entertaining information and retain a sense of control over the personal information that they choose to share. Consumers also appear to be less willing to give permission if the registration process is very demanding, if the personalisation comes across as intrusive or if they are concerned about their privacy. Financial incentives or give-aways turned out to have no influence (Krafft, Arden & Verhoef, 2017). It is therefore important that ecommerce websites ensure that the registration system is as customer-friendly as possible, that the customer can view and change their information, can easily enter and adapt their communication preferences and are able to read about what the ecommerce website intends to do with their information.

10 Programs for resellers

Reseller

Ecommerce websites often advertise the possibility of becoming a reseller of the products or services they have on offer. This can be done in the form of a reseller (partner) or affiliate program. Large players especially, such as Amazon offer partner programs (developed by the companies themselves) as an alternative to affiliate marketing partners such as Zanox (Awin) or Tradedoubler. The reseller (partner) is enabled to sell the products on their own website. Links and banners van be used for this purpose. The reseller receives a fee in compensation. You can read more about affiliate marketing in section 7.5.

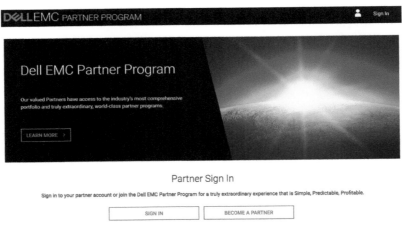

Dell promotes its reseller program

Staffing structure

Online shop manager

Ecommerce website manager

Usually, when an ecommerce website is just starting out, necessary activities such as purchasing, sales and marketing are done by just one person. For large organisations however, professional departments are created for dealing with the online activities. In the online world, roles such as online shop manager or ecommerce website manager are used. Typical tasks and responsibilities of an ecommerce website manager are, for example, ensuring and improving the conversion, margins and order sizes within the ecommerce website, creating cross- and up-selling opportunities and optimum convenience for visitors. The ecommerce website manager also coordinates the development and design of all graphical components on the website and analyses, evaluates and reports on any promotional activities.

Often, the ecommerce website manager works closely with the web analyst who collects and analyses web statistics. They will also work closely with the online acquisition manager who ensures that the ecommerce website draws in visitors. The ecommerce website manager is a true collaborator, working together with the marketing, sales, product management and marketing intelligence departments.

More about the structure of digital marketing can be found in Chapter 13.

Latest developments for ecommerce websites

Over the years, ecommerce websites have become increasingly professional. Let's take Amazon as an example again. The developments that Amazon's homepage has undergone over the years is the result of sophisticated insights into what customers do and want when they are online.

There are countless improvements to be seen when comparing the Amazon homepage from 1998 and its counterpart in 2018 (see the illustrations). The search bar is central in the 2018 version. Many visitors do not just want to browse for an article via the navigation links on the page; they prefer the ease of using the search bar feature.

What is more striking is the use of buttons such as the 'Cart' and 'Account & lists' that encourage visitors to add the product to their shopping cart or wish list.

In 2018, articles and services are also promoted prominently on the homepage to give an extra sales boost. Amazon's newest service Prime, a subscription service for video, e-books and music, is included in the navigation.

Another important observation is that the version from 2018 displays articles on the homepage that the visitor has previously viewed.

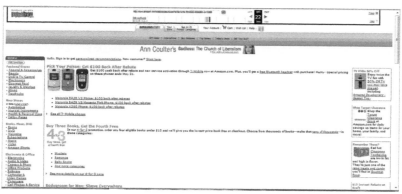

Amazon.com in 1998

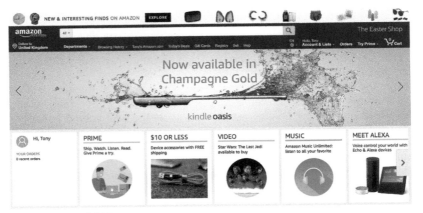

Amazon.com in 2018

Responsive design

Another trend is the use of responsive design. Given the explosive increase in the use of tablets and smartphones when visiting ecommerce websites, so-called responsive design where - simply put - the websites adapt to the visitor's screen resolution, is a development that no ecommerce website owner should let pass them by.

Social shopping

Social shopping is a trend that we can see ecommerce websites adopting with increasing frequency. On the one hand we see social shopping websites, where visitors assess and describe purchased or desired products. These ratings can then be saved and are public to others. On the other hand, ecommerce websites are using social networks such as Facebook as a new sales channel. Encouraging purchases, spending and

Social commerce

conversion via social media is called social commerce. Specific to

F-Commerce

Facebook, it is called F-Commerce. With over a billion of members

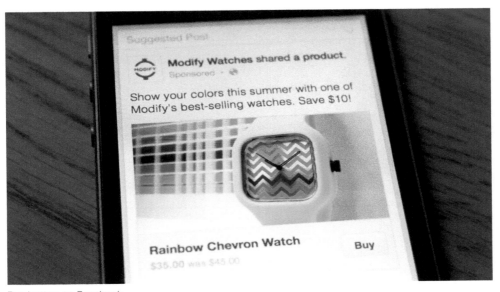

Buy button on Facebook

worldwide, ecommerce websites see Facebook as an attractive channel, the idea being that visitors no longer have to leave Facebook in order to buy products. For example, you can display products on Facebook including the price and a link to the order page (a so-called 'buy button').

Buy button

Personalisation

A major challenge for ecommerce websites is tailoring the offer to a specific customer need. As a result of the fact that information is collected about visitors and buyers, the offer that is made can become much more relevant and customers can receive bespoke service. It is essential that web analytics, transaction data, login data (on the various devices) and labelling of products are stored and can be opened up to personalisation tools such as RichRelevance. An example of this is an ecommerce site that makes product recommendations within a personal profile page based on, among other things, the purchase and browsing history.

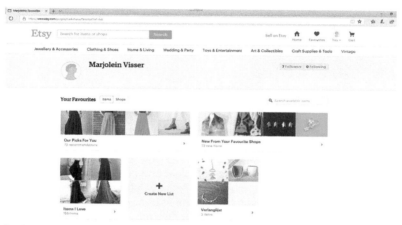

Product recommendations on personal profile

8.1.2   Selling via apps

An increasing number of consumers are using native apps on their mobile phones to make purchases. A native app is software that is created specifically for operating systems on smartphones, such as Android or Apple. The advantage of a native app compared to a web app (mobile version of the online store) is that it can make use of the available features of a mobile phone or tablet such as the camera, speaker, GPS, 3D touch and push messages. In order to send push messages, permission must first be given by the user. An example of how you could use this feature, is to promote an offer for a temporary discount.

Native app

With the help of the speaker feature, the app can allow users to perform a voice activated search. Native apps are usually much faster than a mobile website. All in all, a native app provides users with a positive shopping experience.

One of the drawbacks of a native app is that a separate version has to be developed for each app store (ie Apple iOS, Android, Windows mobile), this means that there are additional development costs. Which app stores an

Zara requests permission to send notifications (push messages)

app is developed for, is determined to a large extent by how many smartphone users from the target segment can be reached via that platform. To encourage the target segment to download the app from the app store, it is important to provide sufficient and positive reviews. Potential users who see that an app that has five stars are more likely to download it than when an app has only one star. Always look carefully at your target segment and realise that the native app must have something extra to offer compared to the mobile version of the online store.

Promoting a native app can be done, for example, by advertising in other apps, via social media or via your own website. For instance, Yoox.com, an online fashion provider, encourages the use of their native app by giving a discount to customers who buy something via the app.

Mobile commerce

Retailers especially tend to make use of apps for sales, so-called mobile commerce. Zara uses the push notification feature on mobile devices to send inventory notifications to users, to announce special events and to follow-up orders. The nearest store can also be located by using the phone's GPS. What many consumers do not realise, is that the apps they use provide companies with insight into their (location) behaviour (with the help of location services). Incidentally, not all retailers mention that cookies are being used in their app. Domino's Pizza for example, does notify users of this.

The product pages in Zara's app have a striking layout with a huge range of images that can be swiped. The process of adding an item to the shopping cart is very intuitive. Zara's checkout section has fields large enough to make purchases with even with the broadest of thumbs, making the purchase process very simple and enjoyable.

The Zara app is very easy to use for anyone

Amazon has a mobile app in the Apple store. Amazon uses the camera for the option of scanning an article's barcode or QR code using the app to immediately check its price and availability on Amazon. Showrooming is thus strongly encouraged.

The Amazon app allows you to scan any product and order it from their online shop

8.2 Online sales advice

Online sales advice

The absence of physical contact between the customer and the retailer in an ecommerce website is one of the differences between a physical store and an online ecommerce website. In a physical store you are welcomed by a sales employee who tries to persuade you to purchase a specific article. The absence of this physical contact has led ecommerce websites to organise the online customer experience in such a way that the visitor is still tempted to make a purchase. In addition to, for example, online video, cross and upsell, using specific techniques helps visitors make the right choice from the range of products on offer.

In this section we will discuss a number of techniques for enticing the customer into making an order and/or for helping the customer with their decision. But first we will get to grips with a theme that is very important for ecommerce websites: authority, professionalism and reliability.

8.2.1 Authority, professionalism and reliability
Especially for an ecommerce website that is just starting out, it is important to give off a sense of authority, professionalism and reliability. To achieve this, a number of techniques are available.

Verisign

Depending on which country you are doing business in and where you are shipping to, various trade organisations/quality marks exist which should be obtained and added wherever possible. As a result, consumers are secure in the knowledge that their money and information will be handled safely and privately, and a secure payment process, general terms and conditions, a reconsideration period and independent complaints mediation will be in place. After all, consumers know what kind of company they are doing business with and how to get in touch with them easily. Other symbols that are often used are, for example, those by Verisign. Verisign is a supplier of online security. The ecommerce websites are aided in establishing a secure connection (also called Secure Sockets Layer or SSL) to the consumer's computer.
Another way of exuding authority is by taking on the role of the expert. One example is the financial advice site Money Saving Expert (www.moneysavingexpert.com).

8.2.2 Techniques for enticing customers
There are different ways or techniques to entice people into making a purchase (see also the six principles of Cialdini for this). We will discuss social proofing and sympathy, scarcity, consumer reviews, online advice modules or systems, profile building, live chat, 'call me now/back', chatbots and the virtual fitting room.

Social proofing and sympathy

Social proofing

One of the techniques used for enticing customers is social proofing. For example, an ecommerce website will display its most popular items or show you which products buyers of similar items to those bought by you have also purchased, as well as showing testimonials. Booking.com

Social proofing

applies social proofing by creating a sense of urgency for hotel rooms with statements like 'Now very popular!', 'Only 2 more rooms available' or 'Booked 120 times in the past 24 hours'. In this way the visitor is tempted

© Noordhoff Uitgevers bv

to make a purchase soon, which in turn has a positive effect on the conversion. This technique is used by hotel booking services such as hotels.com. Positive feelings can be created after the purchase by, for example, congratulating the buyer on their purchase, showing reassuring reviews by satisfied customers and by mentioning again the positive characteristics of the product they have purchased.

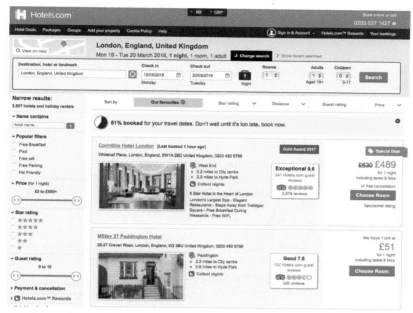

Hotels.com shows how other customers have rated the hotels that the customer is able to book via this website

Temporarily available products

Another frequently used, (well-known psychological) technique for enticing customers, is to display temporarily available products or articles. Evidence of this effect can be provided by testing the conversion of two similar articles in an ecommerce website where one item is listed as only being available 'while supplies last'.

Consumer reviews (user generated content, UGC)

Displaying reviews for the articles in the ecommerce website is another technique for enticing visitors to make a purchase. These reviews are now almost a standard component of an ecommerce website's features. Consumers want to see these ratings and if you do not show them, they will look for them elsewhere. For example, an ecommerce website like Booking.com sends people who have booked a hotel an invitation afterwards to give their opinion about the stay. An additional advantage is that Google also shows these ratings in its search results.

User generated content (UGC)

Hotels in Paris, France | Best Price Guarantee | booking.com
[Ad] www.booking.com/Paris/Hotels ▾
★★★★★ Rating for booking.com: 4.6 - 263 reviews
Book your **Hotel** in **Paris** online. No reservation costs. Great rates.
Read Real Guest Reviews · Secure Booking · We speak your language · Get Instant Confirmation
Book Now · Book for Tonight · Book for Tomorrow · No Booking Fees · Rent out your property

Airbnb - Official Site | Free Cancellation Up To 48 Hrs | airbnb.co.uk
[Ad] www.airbnb.co.uk/Paris/Hotels ▾
★★★★★ Rating for airbnb.co.uk: 4.3 - 248 reviews
Stunning **Hotels** in **Paris**. Book Now on Airbnb for a Great Price!
Best prices · Superb locations · 24/7 Customer Service

Hotels in Paris | Compare and Save up to 50% | hotels.com
[Ad] www.hotels.com/Paris/Hotels ▾
★★★★★ Rating for hotels.com: 4.4 - 151,769 reviews
Book your Cheap **Hotel** in **Paris** Online. Price Guarantee, No Booking Fee

Google search results containing consumer ratings

Online advice modules or systems

Online advice modules

Product selector

For products that require more advice, you can make use of so-called online advice modules or systems. The principle being, that by collecting information you are better able to link the right product to the appropriate buyer. One of the ways this can be done, is by using a product selector in which the most relevant article is presented on the basis of a number of questions. It goes without saying that a suitable product will always come out of this selector.

Relevance is the key word here: always make sure that this condition is met when the results are presented.

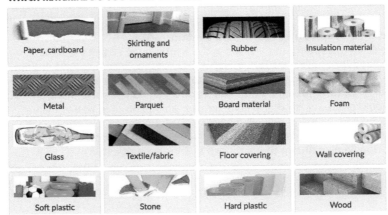

Product selector adhesive & sealant advice Bison.net

Building profiles

Another way of giving online advice can be done by building profiles, using online surfing behaviour and existing customer data. The idea behind this is that when visitors of an ecommerce website view certain articles, they are in a purchase or orientation mode. If this data is combined with customer data, specific segments can be created. To each segment, relevant promotions, information or images can be displayed dynamically during navigation within the ecommerce website. This way, the ecommerce website manager tries to get customers to form attachments to relevant articles. Almost every action a visitor takes in an ecommerce website can be recorded. Often the profile information is also used during a repeat visit to promote products and show relevant, personal information. This is called behavioural targeting. Various online retailers uses this technique.

Behavioural targeting

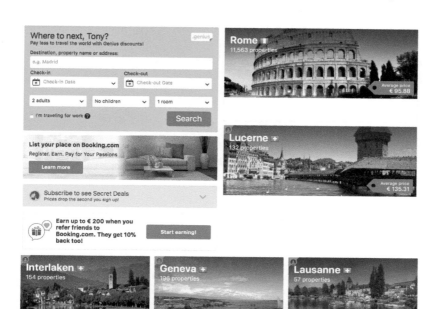

An example of behavioural targeting: this Booking.com customer once booked a hotel in Switzerland and also showed some interest in Rome. When the customer is logged in, Booking.com decides to show relevant places to visit in order to increase chances of conversion (repeat purchase).

Live chat and 'call me now/back'

Providing a chat option can also help give visitors to an ecommerce website that extra bit of advice that ensures the online purchase goes ahead after all. This option is often presented in a critical part of the online purchasing process, such as the shopping cart. The moment it is determined that the customer is about to drop out – for example because the checkout button is not clicked – a chat option can be offered. Such features increase the conversion. The same applies to the option of leaving a telephone number so that the ecommerce website can call back at a later time, at the visitor's convenience.

Live chat
Call me now

Chatbots

Chatbots

Chatbots or virtual employees, can also play a role in providing advice online. For the most part, they are used for customer service, but commercial use is also very feasible.

Starbucks lets you order your favourite drink or snack, by voice commands or SMS. The chatbot tells you when your order will be ready and the total cost. The chatbot is located inside the Starbucks app (for iPhone and Android).

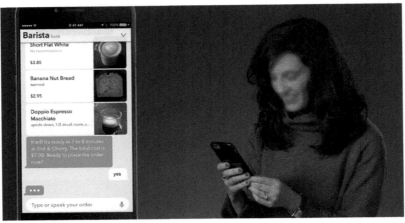

A screenshot of Starbucks' promotional video for its My Starbucks® barista app. It allows you to order your favourite drink by voice commands

Virtual fitting room

Virtual fitting room

A feature for attracting online shoppers that is mainly used in the online fashion industry is a virtual fitting room. A virtual fitting room gives visitors the opportunity to improve the online shopping experience and to ensure that the correct article or complete set is purchased. The advantage of this is that the conversion is increased, but also that the number of returns is reduced.

H&M's fashion studio

It seems that physical stores will always continue to exist. However most large chain stores that have physical stores have already opened their own ecommerce website. Even the smaller retailers have started. In summary, you could say that since the creation of ecommerce websites, online retailers have become increasingly better able to recreate the buying experience and influence that takes place in the physical world.

Cialdini's six principles
Robert Cialdini (2016) created six principles that are used by marketers. They can also be applied for motivating ecommerce website visitors to make a decision and place an order. The six principles are:
1 *Social proofing*: what other people think about a product or service can help others to make a decision.
2 *Sympathy:* no one likes to order something from an unsympathetic company.
3 *Reciprocity*: when someone receives a discount or gets help, they have a tendency to do something in return.
4 *Authority:* when you exude authority you are seen as competent and reliable.
5 *Scarcity:* when something is in short supply, it is more sought after. An exclusive product, at a low price and only temporarily available? Ecommerce website visitors will be extra motivated to order it.
6 *Consistency*: once someone has said 'yes' a few times, they are likely to continue down that path. If customers are led, step by step, through a 'yes process', the chance that they ultimately decide positively, order and pay is greatly increased.

8.3 Online price determination

One of the most important criteria that consumers and companies use when evaluating a product range is the price. In traditional marketing, the marketing manager fixed the price periodically. In this section we will first discuss the differences between an ecommerce website and a traditional store. Then we will look at the fundamentals of pricing and at the customer. Then we will discuss the relationship between pricing and the revenue model. After which you will read more about temporary pricing tactics and dynamic pricing. This section ends with the pricing procedure.

8.3.1   The ecommerce website versus the traditional store
Pricing for products that are sold online is theoretically no different than setting prices for products and services that are for sale in physical stores. But in practice however, there are big differences. This is because:
- buyers can easily compare prices online
- buyers react directly to prices, either by clicking or not going further

Because buyers can quickly compare the price levels of different providers, they make a more conscious decision between the expected quality of the delivery and the price. Price comparison tools aid in this. Large price differences for the same product hardly ever occur online, with the exception

Price comparison tools

of promotional campaigns. The offline and online prices are also moving closer together. See something you like in a store? Then why don't you quickly find out what it costs online?

Price comparison websites promote transparency of prices

Channel integration

An increasing number of providers are applying channel integration, meaning the prices are identical everywhere and the customer can seek out customer service online as well as offline, regardless of where the product was purchased initially.

The fact that customers can respond directly to the price online means all kinds of new business models have been created. Online auctions, models based on group purchases and websites where assignments can be bid on, are all examples of concepts that respond to the customer's desire to pay the lowest possible price. An example of a company that brokers in group discounts is Groupon: see example 8.1.

EXAMPLE 8.1

Groupon

Groupon is a company that offers products and services to members for a limited period of time, and at a greatly reduced rate. These include products such as beauty treatments, dinners, courses and trips. Participating businesses can indicate the minimum and maximum number of registrations in order for the activity or offer to go ahead.

This is attractive for the business, who receive a whole series of new customers all at once at very little cost in terms of communications, but also for the consumer who receives a significant reduction. However, experience teaches us that there are many 'bargain hunters' to be found among the users of this type of offer. The number of regular customers that the provider retains is often relatively small.

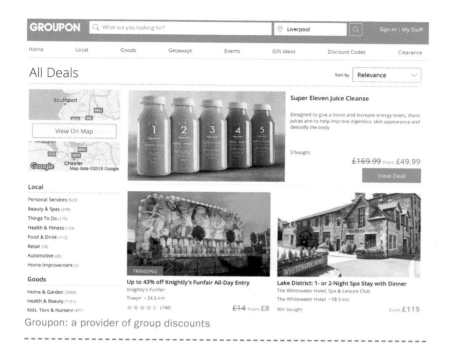

Groupon: a provider of group discounts

- -

8.3.2   Fundamentals of price determination

In order to determine the optimal price, the marketer looks at both the market and the internal situation. Insight must be acquired into the demand's price elasticity, awareness of the value that potential customers attribute to the product in comparison with competing products and knowledge of the prices of competing products and substitutes. In addition, it is of course important that the revenue of the product covers at least the variable costs of production and sales.

Fundamentally, there are three ways to set prices:

1 *Cost-oriented pricing*: the price is based on the costs incurred by the supplier to produce and provide the product.

2 *Competitive-oriented pricing*: the price is determined in accordance with the prices of the competition.

3 *Value-oriented pricing*: the price is determined by the value that the customers attribute to the product, the amount of money customers are willing to pay for the product. Of course, in this case you must also look at the prices of the competitors.

Cost oriented

Competitive oriented

Value oriented

From a marketing perspective, the last way of pricing is preferable. In practice, organisations often use multiple orientation points side by side: they look at the costs, at the competition, at the perceived value by the customer and at the marketing objectives. In business markets, the economic value for the customer is also taken into account. When the goal is to quickly gain a large market share, a low price will be chosen. If the organisation wants to maximise profits, the difference between the value that customers give to the product and the costs of production and sales is maximised.

8.3.3 What is the customer willing to pay?

As described in Chapter 3, when choosing a provider or sales channel, the customer not only looks at the price, but also at the product range, the

Perceived risk

perceived risk and the after-sales service. Reliability, ease of ordering and customer service also play a big role. The customer makes a trade-off between these elements and the total price to be paid, the time investment and the risks that they expect to run. As a result, the price that the customer is willing to pay for the same product, differs per provider (see figure 8.3).

FIGURE 8.3 The customer decides per provider whether they are willing to pay the requested price

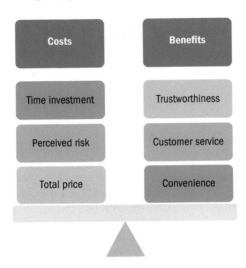

It is wise to test what the optimal price should be. At what price is the turnover or profit the highest? This can be done, for example, by performing an A/B test. Different prices are shown on two identical pages. Sometimes one price is shown, then the other. Then a comparison is done of which page scores best. Sometimes it might occur that the page which the higher price didn't sell as much, but that the provider still made more of a profit. In other cases, a lower price turns out to be better. It can even occur that more is sold at the higher price, because the customer then estimates the value of the product to be greater. For many products and services, the price serves as an indicator for quality. In addition, there is a minimum price threshold for each product. If the price is lower than this threshold, then the customer will find the product 'too cheap' and conclude that it might be a risky purchase.

8.3.4 Price determination and earnings model

An online provider will first have to determine the exact contours of the

Revenue model

revenue model before determining prices (see also Chapter 2). The earnings model is the description of how profit is generated. The organisation can opt for a direct or an indirect model. In a direct model, the visitor/user pays a fee to the owner of the website or application for the provided services or the purchased product. The indirect model generates revenue from third parties, for example from the manufacturers of the products that are on offer.

An example of the indirect earnings model is Moneysupermarket.com which is a UK price comparison website-based business specialising in financial services. The website enables consumers to compare prices on a range of products, including mortgages, credit cards and loans. The service is free to consumers but contains online display advertising and affiliate links.

TravelSuperMarket.com uses an indirect revenue model

Direct earnings models that are very common online are:
- direct sales of products
- a fee per unit sold (eg buying a song on iTunes)
- a subscription per user, per computer, per website, per hour, per amount of data or for unlimited access (eg listening to music on Spotify.com)

Direct earnings model

Within these general models there are specific forms of pricing. Sometimes it is a combination of forms:
- Individual price: every user in an organisation or household pays a certain amount of money based on the use of the product. An example would be software such as Microsoft Office.
- Layered price: the price per user depends on the amount of use, this can fall into different categories. An example is the pricing model that many agencies for stock photography use. Stock photographs are ready-to-use photos that can be used for brochures, for example. For up to five photos the price is low, but per photo it is relatively high. For 25 photos the price per unit is already more attractive. For unlimited use, the basic price is high, but the price per photo is low.

Individual price

Layered price

Hybrid price

- Hybrid price: this is a combination of a fixed subscription or admission price and a variable price for the use of the product. An example is a subscription for mobile internet.

Simultaneous user price

- Simultaneous user price: the price is based on the actual number of users at a specific time. An example could be a provider of research data for companies, who maximise the number of users logging into the system simultaneously.

Bundle price

- Bundle price: this is a lower price for a collection of products. An example is a combination of travel and cancellation insurance: together they are a lot cheaper than separately.

Upgrade price

- Upgrade price: this is a price for moving from one version of a product to the next. For instance, a new version of antivirus software or a more comfortable seat in an airplane.

In a number of industries, a direct earnings model has become virtually infeasible as visitors have become accustomed to free products or services. This is especially true for products based on information or data transfer, such as travel information, photo sharing, search engines and social networking sites. Some providers give away their entire product for free, others set limits, such as a time limit or a capacity limit for downloading. Often, a simple version of a product is offered free of charge and additional modules have to be paid for. This has made the pricing more reminiscent of a 'sample', a free preview, than of a real revenue model. This is also called a freemium. In this way, the provider builds on its brand awareness and its relationship database.

Freemium

For information-based products especially, it has become very difficult to come up with a profitable business model, even more so in highly competitive markets. As a result, indirect revenue models are often chosen, such as:

Advertising models

- Advertising models: revenue is generated from advertisements.

Click models

- Click models: income is generated by linking to manufacturers or suppliers.

Offer or discount models

- Offer or discount models: the manufacturers or suppliers pay a compensation fee for the products or services that are sold on offer or for the publication of the offer.

Auction models

- Auction models: the manufacturer/supplier pays a fee per auctioned product.

To ensure that this type of model is attractive for manufacturers of products and service providers, large numbers of visitors are necessary. In addition, those visitors must have sufficient willingness to make purchase, otherwise they will not click on banners and products. This makes it very difficult for start-ups to make sites or applications with an indirect earnings model profitable.

8.3.5 Temporary pricing tactics

Three commonly used temporary pricing tactics are:
- offering products at a discount
- bundle prices
- auctions

Offering products at a discount

Research shows that nearly half of all ecommerce websites offer products at a discount. It is possible that all products are offered at an extra low price, a number of products are sold at a discount or only the products that have to make room for new products quickly. Popular low-priced products attract visitors to the website and influence the provider's image in terms of value for money. Temporary price reductions are particularly suitable for making quick sales in order to make room in the warehouse or get rid of products that are about to be released in a new version.

Bundle prices

An alternative to temporary discounts is bundle pricing. For example, game consoles are often sold temporarily in combination with a matching game or with accompanying accessories. By doing this, the provider aims to save on the acquisition and transaction costs and to generate a higher turnover. There are different forms of bundle prices:

- Pure bundling: the customer can only buy the bundle as a whole, not the individual products.
- Mixed bundling: the customer has a choice whether to buy the bundle or the separate parts. Examples are telecom companies that sell bundles of telephony, Internet and TV subscriptions or the price of downloading music per song versus downloading the entire album at once.
- Add-on bundling: here there is a main product and a by-product. The by-product is not sold without the main product. An example is a maintenance contract for a new car.
- Tie-in bundling: this means that the buyer is obliged to purchase the by-product when purchasing the main product. For instance, compensation that has to be paid for the use of the airport when booking a plane ticket.

Bundle pricing

Pure bundling

Mixed bundling

Add-on bundling

Tie-in bundling

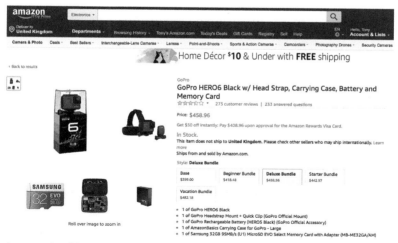

An example of bundling on Amazon.com

Price bundling is a mechanism to get more value out of the market. It also leaves room for temporarily making the offer more attractive by adding an extra product at a low price.

Auctions

Auctions are used if the product is unique and must be sold to the highest bidder. However, online auctions are also used by service providers who cannot keep products in stock, such as hotels and travel agencies. This way, they sell their overcapacity. At auction, there is a fixed set of rules that determine the price and the how the product is awarded to the bidder.

Real-time pricing

There is real-time pricing: the price is determined at the time of trading. The most important forms are:

English auction model

- The English model: there is a starting bid, increasingly higher bids are then made. The highest bidder may buy the item. An example of websites that use this model is Catawiki.com.

Dutch auction model

- The Dutch model: this starts with a high price and then the price drops steadily per bid. The first person to say that they want to purchase the product is awarded the item. Bidson.com uses this model.

Closed auction

Second price closed bid auction

- A closed auction: here the bidders cannot see each other's bids. The highest bidder may buy the item. Usually the amount of the highest bid is paid, sometimes the second highest. This is called a 'second price closed bid auction' or Vickrey auction. eBay uses this model for its 'Proxy Auction'. This is seen as a fair model, where it makes little sense to bid lower than what you are willing to pay for the product. If you did you might end up losing out. You also do not run the risk of paying much more than what others are willing to part with for the product.

Reverse auction

- A *reverse auction*: there are several providers and there is only one bidder. This is common in business-to-business environments. An auction can make a website more attractive, reduce the inventory costs of slow-moving goods, provide insight into the price elasticity and preferences of consumers as well as attract more visitors to the site.

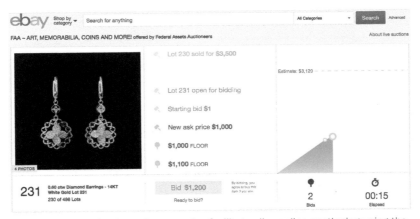

Besides its Proxy Auction, eBay now also facilitates live online auctioning using the English auction model

An auction can make a website more attractive, reduce the inventory costs of slow-moving goods, provide insight into the price elasticity and preferences of consumers as well as attract more visitors to the site.

As an example of a Dutch auction, The United States Department of the Treasury, through the Federal Reserve Bank of New York (FRBNY), raises funds for the U.S. Government. The FRBNY interacts with primary dealers, including both banks and broker-dealers who submit bids on behalf of themselves and their clients using the Trading Room Automated Processing System. The winning bids are announced within fifteen minutes.

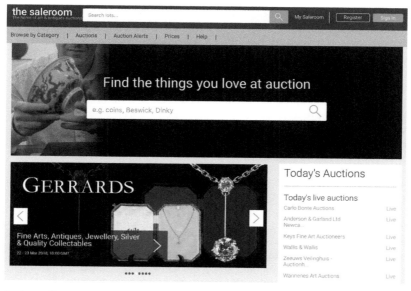

As for an English auction, The Saleroom (www.the-saleroom.com) is a major online auction site for art and antiques

Other temporary price tactics

Other temporary price tactics are:
- free give-aways along with the product
- free financing of the purchased product
- free shipping

Some ecommerce websites permanently offer their products or services in conjunction with one of these methods. It then ceases being a temporary price tactic, but a permanent form of pricing. This strategy is particularly attractive if more sales result in lower costs for the provider. A sustainable competitive advantage can then be created.

8.3.6 Dynamic pricing

A form of pricing that has only blossomed in recent years is 'dynamic pricing': the use of changeable prices. As the Internet allows for plentiful opportunities for interaction, as well as measurability, setting prices that lead to optimal results under specific circumstances or with specific target segments is relatively easily done. Dynamic pricing is used as an instrument for capacity management, but also as a price instrument to encourage groups of customers to make (additional) purchases. The use of dynamic prices to match supply and demand and optimise the return of an organisation is also called yield management or revenue management.

Dynamic pricing

Revenue management

Capacity management

Dynamic pricing as a tool for capacity management

Many companies struggle with under-capacity in certain periods and overcapacity at other times. Flights are fully booked in the summer period, seats are often impossible to find during rush hours, restaurants are overrun during festive holidays and most people want to go to the gym in the evening. One of the ways of creating a better spread in demand is to charge low prices when it is quiet and higher prices when it is busy. Before the introduction of the Internet, this usually occurred more or less on 'feeling'. Various solutions have been devised, such as last-minute offers, happy hour and off-peak subscriptions. The height of the prices and the timing of the offers were based on experience.

Large providers that have up-to-date sales data, such as airlines, use more advanced methods to determine at any given time which price leads to the best result. They rely on previously collected data and use mathematical models (algorithms) to predict demand. The dynamic pricing system combines these forecasts with the current demand, as shown by the number of sales or reservations. If a lot of demand is expected in a certain period, the base price will be high. If the current demand is higher than expected, the price rises further. As a result, it can occur that someone books a ticket for €500, while a friend pays €550 only an hour later. If the current demand is lower than expected, the organisation will lower the price accordingly.

In principle, the price can decrease until it is equal to the marginal costs of an extra customer. An example: the marginal costs for an airline are the costs that the organisation incurs in order to transport an extra passenger. As the plane will have to take off regardless and the staff are ready to go, these costs are relatively low. As a result, you can occasionally find flights with low-cost carriers for a few dozen euros. This is shown in figure 8.4. Incidentally, most airlines raise their prices closer to the departure date: anyone booking the flight will often be willing to pay the increased price anyway.

FIGURE 8.4 The price can drop until it is equal to the marginal costs that an extra customer will incur

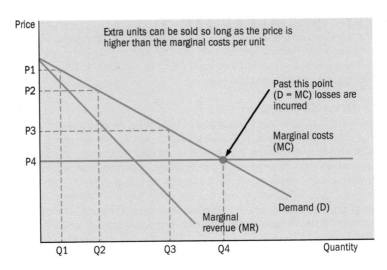

Without price discrimination, the organisation will choose the price that leads to maximum profit. This is the point where the marginal revenues (MR) are equal to the marginal costs (MC). When using price discrimination, you must determine, per customer or customer segment, what they are willing to pay. Customer group 1 is willing to pay P1, which leads to Q1 in quantity of products sold.

Customer group 2 is willing to pay P2 with Q2 on sales as a result and so on. The organisation sells for the price that customers are willing to pay up until the point where the price is lower than the marginal costs. There, the marginal yield is zero. If the provider sells at an even lower price, they will lose money. To prevent customers from speculating on a price reduction, websites can use cookies. This can be done, for instance, on websites that sell airline tickets. The cookies signal the price that the ticket was previously offered for. If the system ascertains that the customer has a high willingness to buy, then the website responds by offering the customer the ticket for the same or even a higher price.

Using dynamic pricing to influence demand over time is particularly interesting when the production of a product or service is expensive, or the product cannot be kept in stock (see figure 8.5).

FIGURE 8.5 Dynamic pricing is particularly interesting for fleeting products whose production is expensive

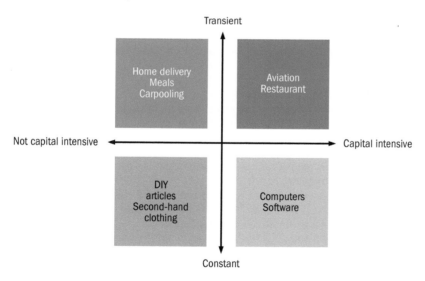

If the fixed costs are high and the variable costs are relatively low, the product can be offered for a more attractive price the moment that the fixed costs have been 'covered'. In addition, there must be a reasonably high price elasticity: a lower price must motivate people to buy the product or to use it at a different time than perhaps their ideal moment.

Dynamic pricing can also be used if the provider is confronted with cost differences in certain periods, for example because labour or shipping costs are more expensive. Services may be more expensive in the evening than during the day.

Dynamic pricing at customer segment levels

Another objective of dynamic pricing can be to encourage a group of customers to purchase the product and promote cross-selling, upselling or customer loyalty. For example, an ecommerce website that sells clothing can start a campaign to entice customers who have not ordered anything for a while to make a purchase. The ecommerce website recognises customers using cookies and determines how often the shop is still visited and when the last purchase was made. On the basis of their previous buying behaviour, the ecommerce website determines, for example, that the customer regularly looks for a specific brand of jeans. The ecommerce website can then make the customer an individual offer for a pair of jeans from their favourite brand at a reduced price. This way a double effect is achieved: additional sales and motivating the customer to visit the ecommerce website again.

It is important to consider whether customers will accept the differences in price. They only do so if there is a reasonable explanation for the price difference, such as a reward for customer loyalty. When Amazon.com experimented with price discrimination a few years ago, it turned out that customers would not accept that some customers were able to buy a DVD at a lower price, while others paid the full whack.

Dynamic price discrimination

There are a number of conditions for price discrimination at customer segment level:

- Differences in the value perception between segments of customers: one segment must be prepared to pay a higher price than the other.
- There must be obstacles to prevent customers from purchasing the product for one another or selling it on.
- Segmenting customers must be feasible on a technical and financial level.

8.3.7 Pricing procedure

Pricing

Before the marketer determines prices they must try to obtain as accurate a picture as possible of the following elements:

- The business and revenue model and the marketing strategy.
- The type of product: what are the risks that the customer expects to run when making a purchase, what is the product life cycle, is the product tangible or intangible, is it fleeting?
- The cost structure: different types of costs, fixed costs, variable costs, acquisition costs, changeability of the marginal costs, spread of costs according to, for example, time and location.
- Price levels and elasticity: response from potential customers to different price levels of each of the price elements (see below).
- The competition: the price levels and price systems of competitors.

On the basis of this analysis, the marketer determines the pricing method and the provisional prices. They must then test the potential customers' reactions in practice by, for example, a split-run test. In doing so, different price elements can be varied:

- the base price
- discounts
- shipping costs
- bundling of products and services
- returns and cancellations policy
- guarantees

When the marketer has found the right pricing method and the appropriate prices, continuous monitoring of the varying demand is necessary. Should there be a decline in the growth of the number of sales, it is important to try and determine the cause, and if necessary correct the prices (see figure 8.6). In order to do this, larger organisations are constructing a system that determines the ideal price with the help of mathematical rules (algorithms).

FIGURE 8.6 Pricing procedure

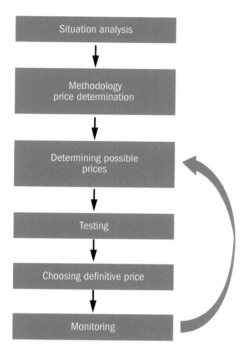

Questions and assignments

NOW CHECK YOUR UNDERSTANDING:

8.1   Go to www.hm.com, choose your country and study the website.
  a What elements does the H&M ecommerce website consist of?
  b What measures do you see in place to increase the conversion of the ecommerce website?
  c How does H&M dispense sales advice online?

8.2   As a digital marketing consultant you are approached by a wine merchant. She has conceived a plan to create a website that her customers can use to order online.
  Give her advice, in two to three A4 pages, covering the following topics:
  a What should the wine merchant consider before she employs an agency to develop the ecommerce website?
  b What elements should the ecommerce website consist of?
  c What methods can she use for dispensing sales advice online?
  d Should she choose a mobile ecommerce website or build a native app?

8.3   Go to the following websites:
  - www.notonthehighstreet.com
  - www.ryanair.com
  - www.comparethemarket.com

  For each website, indicate the following:
  a Is the chosen method of pricing cost-oriented, competitive-oriented or value-oriented? Give arguments.
  b What specific form of online pricing is used? Is it direct or indirect, and within that, what form?

8.4   For the following products, indicate whether dynamic pricing could lead to more profit for the supplier. Please substantiate your answer with the aid of the theory from subsection 8.3.6.
  a Hotel rooms
  b Digital books
  c Food

8.5

A critical review of ASOS.com
By Mike Berry

ASOS is a UK-based global fashion online retailer targeting twentysomethings. Its online platform selects the best fashion items from a variety of brands and presents these items on its website alongside the company's own products.

This strategy has not only helped ASOS sell their own-label products, but it has also led them to become a leading online fashion destination. Today, the company offers over 85,000 branded and own-brand products.

ASAO was founded in 1999 when founders Quentin Griffith and Nick Robertson envisioned a company that sold the outfits worn by celebrities. The name came from 'As Seen on Screen'.

The campaign was an immediate success, probably because most people in the target audience love to talk about celebrity style and celebrities are always a hot topic. ASOS won the Best Trendsetter Award from The Sunday Times. ASOS became an online fashion 'editor', with an emphasis on diversity. The business expanded from celebrity styles and soon included all forms of fashion.

Today, ASOS is a global success story and is still growing. It is known for its millennial-focused fast-fashion, selling own-brand products alongside brands like Adidas and Polo Ralph Lauren. 40% of sales are own-brand and the company launches 5,000 new products on its site each week.

ASOS grew rapidly to become a successful global fashion empire in just a few years, in part, through marketing strategies that focused on brand awareness. Another key factor was a deep understanding of its target audience; it knew how to source and display clothes that people wanted!

The company now sells 85,000 products with 3,000 new lines each week. Individual designers can even set up their own boutiques on the site and sell their products.

One thing that ASOS got 100% right was to sell products that include something for everyone; people have different styles and ASOS made all these styles available in one platform. By sharing their platform with hundreds of brands and designers, ASOS became an all-in-one fashion empire. They were curating the best in fashion for this Millennial audience.

A key communication tool is the ASOS Brand Magazine which includes High-Quality content; It is filled with glossy images, but it also has strong editorial content including celebrity style, shopping tips, outfit ideas and how-to articles. ASOS publishes both a print version of the magazine and a clickable e-magazine that allows customers to shop directly from the page. The magazine has over 480,000 readers and 820,000 online subscribers.

8

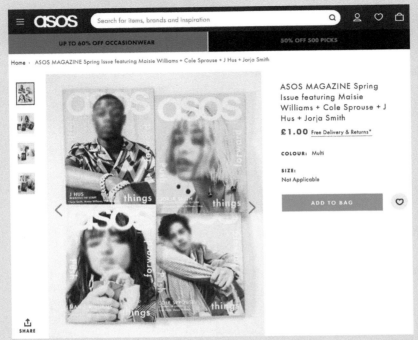

ASOS also sells hard-copy versions of their magazine online

ASOS didn't want to run another 'boring' fashion marketing campaign, instead they show to develop an Influencer Marketing Initiative: They knew that influencers were powerful allies in communicating their ideal messages, so they launched the 'ASOS Insiders Community'.

This is a group of 20+-year-olds who post their fashionable outfits on social media. These influential individuals curate OOTDs (Outfit of the Day) for ASOS, each influencer having his/her own unique style, from tomboy to '90s looks, street style to maternity wear, these ASOS insiders provide fashion inspiration to every type of ASOS customer and, importantly, interested customers can buy the featured outfits *straight from their social media accounts.*

As an example, on Instagram, users can see the relevant code for the product in the image caption. They can also visit the influencers curated page on the ASOS website through a tracked link. On Pinterest, images are directly linked to the product's page. At all times ASOS makes the experience as smooth and convenient as possible for its users by providing all the links and codes necessary to purchase. By making it so easy and indeed enjoyable to buy, ASOS turns interest into actual purchases.

In the description of ASOS' Instagram photos, users can see the relevant code for the products that are displayed

'We have always been committed to creating opportunities for young people to fulfil their potential.'

Nick Robertson, ASOS Co-founder

CSR (corporate social responsibility) is managed by The ASOS Foundation: which is responsible for educational initiatives with a focus on disadvantaged youth. ASOS has implemented training programs that aimed to provide opportunities for youngsters who are interested in technology and fashion. They also partner with charity organisations including The Prince's Trust. Overall ASOS is generally regarded as a responsible employer and 'a good company'.

Turning now to the all-important ASOS website, the key conversion goal is sales directly from the website and everything is geared towards this successful outcome.

So, what are the secrets of the success of ASOS?
- it offers a wide and diverse range of products
- it makes it easy for customers to make a purchase via an excellent customer experience (CX)
- the range of products are presented attractively and clearly with great photography and technology which shows the clothes to best advantage
- the navigation is intuitive and transparent
- at all times the user knows where they are, what they are buying, and what they could buy next
- the checkout process is fast and user-friendly
- ASOS makes it easy to browse, easy to shop and easy to pay
- it publishes high-quality content

- it leverages social media influencers to promote certain products
- it has built (and maintains) a strong brand image, and pays attention to its corporate responsibilities

This has proved to be a highly successful mix of activities, centred on a state-of-the-art ecommerce website; ASOS's full year turnover now exceeds £1.9 billion with pre-tax profit now exceeding £80 million.

Source: www.referralcandy.com/blog/asos-marketing-strategy

NOW CHECK YOUR UNDERSTANDING:

a What are the essential elements of a successful ecommerce business?
b What is ASOS's most important conversion goal?
c Make an overview of the key elements of the ASOS site and place them in order of importance for reaching that conversion goal.
d Make a list of the methods that can be used for giving sales advice online. Does ASOS do a good job here? Please substantiate your answer.
e Which revenue model does ASOS use? Could ASOS use temporary/pricing tactics? Which additional tactics could lead to more conversions?
f To what extent would it be beneficial for ASOS to use dynamic (=variable) pricing?
g Write a brief for ASOS's website builder (design and build agency), in which you clearly indicate which changes/ improvements need to be made and how they will improve performance.

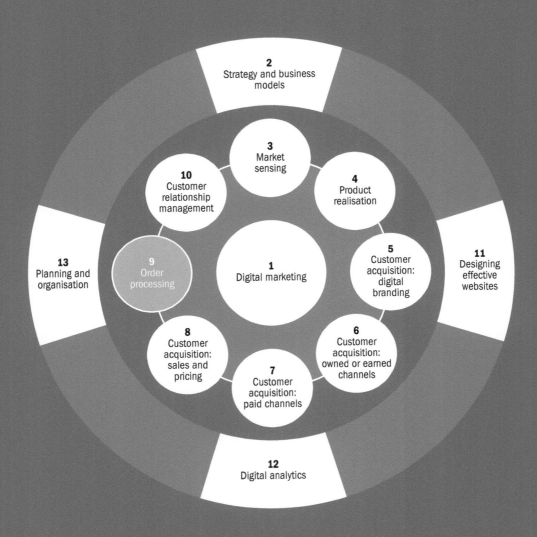

9
Order processing

Marjolein Visser (9.1), Patricia Ouwendijk (9.2), Stephan Schroeders (9.3) and Ernst-Jan Kruize (9.4)

Previous chapters describe how the marketer can establish a clear idea of what the market's wants and desires are (the market sensing process) and how the Internet can be used to further product development and improvement as well as for setting up processes surrounding the product or the service (product realisation). Once everything is customer-ready, the customer acquisition process commences: defining target audiences and recruiting new customers. All these activities lead to the ultimate goal of digital marketing: sold products. This chapter describes the order processes: how does an organisation manage the financial settlement and how does the customer get (access to) their product or service?

This chapter will cover:
- the selection of distribution channels
- payments
- order processing
- online service

After studying this chapter you will be able to:
- assess the effectiveness of distribution models and channels in different situations
- reflect the benefits of multichannel and omnichannel distribution
- express the importance of each sub-process concerning the handling of an order and indicate how these processes can be structured.
- distinguish the steps within the online payment process
- weigh the pros and cons regarding different methods
- indicate which parties are involved in an online payment
- explain the role of security in the online payment process
- illustrate the conditions for a successful online service and make a reasoned decision regarding contact channels

9.1 Selection of distribution channels

If the customer has completed the first four steps of the digital marketing funnel and has ordered a product, two more things must be done. They must be motivated to actually pay for it and the product must be delivered. The decision of how a product or service will be delivered to the customer is very important to customer satisfaction. The most common distribution channels are:

- your own physical store
- a physical third-party store
- home delivery
- delivery at a collection point
- online, if it concerns digital services (downloading or printing tickets)
- a service point (theatre, hair salon, restaurant, etc.)

Before we elaborate on selecting the distribution channel, we will first discuss the basic models for distribution. Finally, we will see that the selection is not limited to a single distribution channel. Most organisations decide to use multiple channels: multichannel or omnichannel distribution.

9.1.1 Basic models for distribution

There are two basic models: the product coming to the customer (delivery) or the customer coming to the product (pick up). For delivery, there are again two variations: personal and non-personal (see figure 9.1).

FIGURE 9.1 Basic models for distribution

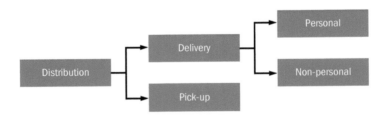

Personal delivery

Non-personal delivery

In the event of personal delivery the product is received by the customer, whereas in the case of non-personal delivery it can, for example, be put in the mailbox, picked up in a physical store or at a collection point of a logistical organisation. In the event of personal delivery, it is possible that the customer may select a day and time for delivery. An example of this is installation of a purchased modem by a telephone company.

Delivery options

The various delivery methods are called delivery options. Studies show that consumers find it important to be able to opt for a delivery option that best fits their lifestyle, as not everyone is home during the day. The period between the order and the delivery, the delivery period, is of great importance to customer satisfaction. Pick up is sometimes done in a shop, other times at a collection point of a logistical service provider (for example a FedEx or UPS Depot). Pick-ups in a store (the international term

Pick up

for this is Click & Collect) has its advantages over other delivery options, such as:

- The customer is sometimes given the opportunity to reassess the ordered product in the store (do the shoes fit for example?).
- In addition to the purchased product, the customer may buy other products from the store too.
- Sometimes the customer may postpone the payment until the moment he or she collects it.
- Usually, the retailer does not charge the customer shipping costs when the product is picked up at the store.
- Shop staff are available to provide support on how to use the purchased item.

Click & Collect

Convenience and costs are of major importance to the customer's choice of distribution channel. Customers like to shop with as little effort as possible and make as little investment as possible. For some people this means that they would like to have the ordered products delivered to their homes, for others it's easier to stop at a store. The risk perception also has a role in this. If the customer thinks it's likely that they will return the product, they will also take this into account in their decision.

Therefore, a consumer considers their decision very differently when buying clothes than when ordering a cable to connect electronic equipment. In addition, it is important whether the customer wants to buy something specific or is just looking for a shopping experience. Also, some customers do not like to pay up front when online.

For manufacturers who have the distribution of their products taken care of by retailers, it is sometimes a difficult and strategic decision to open an online store. After all, as soon as they decide to sell their articles to the consumer directly, the physical shopkeeper is passed by. This phenomenon is called channel conflict. Channel conflicts can be limited by generating leads in a web store for a physical store and by having the physical store deliver the articles that were ordered in the ecommerce website as well as using uniform prices.

Channel conflicts

What you need to be aware of is that customers perceive the distribution problems very differently than companies. Some companies still consider their physical stores to be a different channel than their online store, while consumers see it as a whole. Example 9.1 illustrates this.

EXAMPLE 9.1

The shop and ecommerce website are different companies

In December, my daughter Stacy wanted to buy a Just Dance video game for her little girl. She found it on the website of a large retail chain for $29.97. Just to be safe – Christmas was just around the corner – she decided to go to a local store to get it. But there, it cost $47.97, 60% more expensive. She was surprised, but she remembered the store's price guarantee, so she asked for the online price. No chance, said the cashier, that guarantee only applies to the prices of competitors.

'Wait,' Stacy said. 'I can buy this game online and have it delivered to the store for free, right?' The cashier agreed but warned that this would take a few days. 'But it's right here on the shelf. Can't I pay for it online and then take it from here?' Of course not, was the answer. The store and the ecommerce website were different companies. Stacy ordered the item on her phone and a few days later she came back to pick it up.

Source: Rigby, 2014

9.1.2   Selection of distribution channels

The question of which distribution channels the provider of products or services will use to make their products available to the customer, is one of all ages. However, the increasing role of the Internet has had major consequences for the distribution relationships in many industries. An example is the insurance industry. Previously, it was almost a given that the sale of insurance was done by an intermediary, the insurance agent. This intermediary maintained all customer contact: changes, claims, everything was done by the intermediary. Now there are only a few insurance companies left that work exclusively with intermediaries. In the next section we'll learn that an increasing amount of organisations are taking on distribution themselves and we will elaborate briefly on the effectiveness of distribution channels.

In-house distribution

The exchange of information and the logistical handling of goods is so much easier than it used to be, that it has become increasingly simpler for a producer to take the operations regarding the distribution channels into their own hands. Large transport companies such as UPS and FedEx are fully equipped to deliver single orders. For a company, there are a number of important advantages when taking over distribution:

- In-house distribution can lead to higher profit margins.
- More control is gained over the product range offered to customers.
- The company can better control in which environment the customer can get to know and/or use the product or service, as well as the provided support: better in line with the brand values.
- Direct contact with the end user leads to more customer knowledge and a better relationship.
- Less time and energy have to be put into keeping the intermediary traders happy.

Dis-intermediation

Direct distribution

Vertical integration

In many industries, the rise of the Internet has led to 'disintermediation' or shortening of the value chain, ie 'cutting out' one or more layers of intermediate channels in the distribution network. When an organisation doesn't use any intermediate channels (anymore), this is called direct distribution. This is referred to as vertical integration.
Eliminating intermediate channels also has its disadvantages. For example, the distribution channels' responsibilities include:

- creating demand: marketing
- collecting market information and customer knowledge
- advising customers
- ensuring sufficient market coverage: making the products available to as many people as possible
- keeping stock
- dealing with problems and complaints

© Noordhoff Uitgevers bv

These tasks must be taken on by the organisation. Failure to perform these tasks properly, may result in damage to the brand image, declining market shares and decreasing profits.

Many organisations opt for multiple distribution channels side by side: ecommerce websites that offer delivery and also have physical stores. Both the physical and the virtual stores can be self-managed but can also be managed by third parties. A combination of different distribution channels is called 'multichannel distribution'.

Multichannel distribution

Effectiveness of distribution channels

A company's choice of distribution channel influences the price of the products and the profit. Selecting a distribution channel requires much deliberation. A number of things can be analysed:
- Which channels are preferred by the organisation's various target segments?
- What price are they willing to pay for each channel?
- What will the potential customers do in case one of the distribution channels is not available? Do they switch to another channel or to the competitor?
- What are the estimated costs of operating each distribution channel?

By combining this data with different scenarios for the number of products sold, approximate calculations can be made of the financial consequences of the decisions. In addition, there are also a number of qualitative considerations:
- the acceptance of the elimination of a distribution channel by customers and society: the consequences for the brand image
- the consequences for the employees and the internal organisation
- the brand visibility

Another important aspect is handling returns. These are relatively common for online purchases, because customers cannot see or try out the product on beforehand. The costs of handling returns can be so high that they can make the online channel an unattractive option. The presence of a physical store that can be visited with goods that they wish to return or with questions and/or problems, can provide customers with an extra sense of security. This appears to be much appreciated.

Returns

9

Physical stores and ecommerce websites

Whilst more and more retail chains are going out of business, ecommerce giants like Amazon.com and Alibaba continue to grow rapidly.
Interestingly, Amazon Inc acquired the retailer Whole Foods Market, giving it access to over 400 physical stores in the US and UK. Possible models include 'order online collect in store (click and collect)', 'shop in store' or 'shop online and have items delivered'.

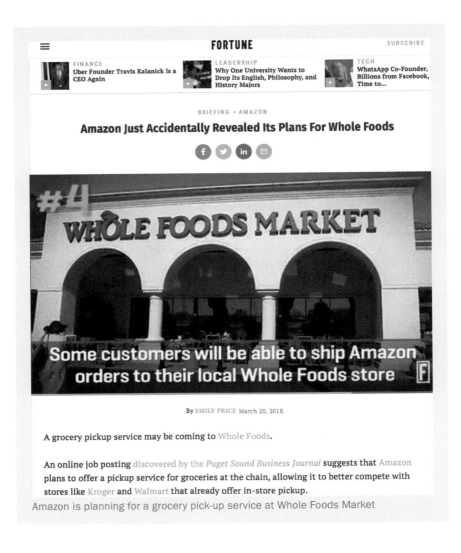

© Noordhoff Uitgevers bv

9.1.3 Multichannel distribution

As a result of the reasons mentioned in the previous sub-section, many organisations combine different distribution channels. One of the first questions that arises when using a new distribution channel, is whether it **Synergy** results in synergy or cannibalisation. When there is synergy, the channels reinforce each other. Research shows that among channels within the consumer market, synergy happens on a regular basis. For example, sending a catalogue appears to have a favourable effect on both catalogue sales as well as online sales and store sales. Online sales together with a call centre and self-owned stores also prove to reinforce each other, an effect that many banks use to their advantage. But cannibalisation also **Cannibalisation** occurs on a regular basis. It often turns out that when a new distribution channel is used, the original channel's turnover drops, but that it will pick itself up again after some time.

It is not possible to draw a meaningful conclusion: every decision regarding this, will have to be researched.

It is clear that customers select distribution channels in accordance with their own preferences. People who use multiple channels side by side do so because the channels are effective in fulfilling their shopping needs in different ways. If they can find their ideal channel under all circumstances, this leads to greater customer satisfaction and loyalty. A customer who uses multiple channels appears to spend more than a customer who only uses one channel. This can be due to the fact that other services are offered through the various distribution channels, which the customer uses at their leisure. One time they would like to try on a T-shirt, making a physical store more appealing, another time they might want to purchase the same T-shirt in a different colour, for which the online store is the easiest option. This freedom of choice leads to more satisfaction and a more intense bond.

Physical stores are particularly excellent at assessing the product's characteristics, acquiring the product quickly, their delivery times and exchanging and returning products without any hassle. Online is especially preferred when it comes to secure payments, customer service, price level and breadth of the product range.
By combining channels, providers are better able to respond to the needs of their customers. One channel's disadvantages can compensate for those of another channel. Ultimately, it's all about a seamless customer experience.

An important decision that organisations who opt for multichannel distribution must make, is the extent to which the different channels must offer the same range of products. Do the prices have to be the same? So far, prices have been lower in ecommerce websites than in physical stores, but the price differences are decreasing. Do the channels offer the same product range? How is the stock managed: jointly for all channels or for each channel individually? Are the terms of sale the same, is there an identical return policy? Can online purchases be returned to the store and vice versa? Does the customer immediately get their money back or do they have to wait for it to be transferred? Which channels are referred to in the advertisements? Some organisations try to apply complete uniformity throughout their channels, while others consciously opt for separate marketing policies per channel. One thing is agreed upon however: an integrated customer database is necessary. There must be one single record of the customer, throughout the entire organisation. The strategic final aim is omnichannel distribution: distribution by a sales organisation throughout multiple channels, in which all the channels are seamlessly connected.

Omnichannel distribution

In the following sections we will first discuss the payment of a product ordered online and subsequently order processing and support.

9.2 Payments

Once the customer is tempted to order a product, the digital marketer wants to motivate them to actually pay for it. Only then has an actual sale taken place.
The most important aspects for online payments are convenience, speed and security. From a marketing perspective, within the online ordering

process, the customer must be given as little opportunity as possible to have second thoughts. On the Internet, it's easy to decide to change your mind and order elsewhere.

Convenience Therefore, convenience (as few different pages as possible) and speed of continuity between the different pages are very important. In addition, the consumer who is going to pay not only needs to feel that the company where they order something is reliable, but also that the page where payment details are requested meets the highest security standards. All the more reason to not only look at the ordering process with a critical eye, but also at the payment process.

In this section we will first explain the process of online purchases. After that we will discuss the available payment methods and their pros and cons. Additionally, we will also cover mobile payments. Then we will examine some developments in online payments. Furthermore, the various service providers within the payment industry are pointed out. Lastly, we will elaborate on the security of the payment process.

9.2.1   Process of online purchases

The moment the customer has found the desired product or service, they will proceed to purchase. The steps involved in this are as follows:

- The consumer adds the desired product to the shopping cart.
- The consumer indicates that the order is complete.
- The consumer provides their address (and possibly invoice details).
- The consumer decides to pay for the order and is asked for the preferred payment method.
- When a payment method is selected, the customer is referred to the correct page (depending on the selected payment method) to finalise or initiate the payment.
- After completing the payment or after starting up a payment method, the consumer is redirected back to the online retailer's website, often accompanied by a message saying something along the lines of 'thank you for your payment/order'.
- Additionally, the customer can choose to receive an invoice, by post or in an email, or to have the invoice included together with the ordered product(s).

The way in which the completion of the process is followed up, is partly determined by the payment method that the consumer selected. For example, there are payment methods that allow the customer to immediately complete the payment (Visa, MasterCard, PayPal) and those that require the online retailer or payment service provider to take action before the consumer's payment is processed (Direct Debit, transfer or postpay).

9.2.2   Payment methods

Payment methods are available in many different forms. The diversity of payment methods makes it easy for consumers to make a decision that meets their payment preferences, but at the same time very complex for the online retailer. Some important payment methods are briefly outlined below, and their pros and cons will be mentioned. Note that these payment methods vary between countries.

Direct Debit

A frequently used payment method is Direct Debit. This payment method is mainly used because it is a fairly simple way of paying. The customer can pay by providing their bank account details. At a later date, the online retailer will then directly deduct the owed amount from the customer's bank account.

Pros of Direct Debit:
- The costs for processing the payment are low.
- The availability of this payment method is not dependent on which bank someone uses, so all payments are made accessible via a single route.
- The payment process is easily settled.
- The customer may reclaim the amount from the bank without the need to provide a reason.

Cons for Direct Debit:
- The customer can reclaim the amount from the bank without providing any reason (for the retailer, that is obviously a problem if the products have been shipped already).
- It is highly susceptible to fraud because no signature is required (yet).
- The online retailer (or payment partner) must keep a system for mandate management.
- An offline activity is required to collect the payment.
- Processing takes a relatively long time, partly because the Direct Debit method requires the pre-announcement of the direct debit to the consumer.

In addition to the regular acceptance of the Direct Debit by the consumer, as it has been done for years by means of the 'check mark', banks have been working on a 'digital signature'. By means of a so-called e-mandate, **E-mandate** the consumer can grant a company permission to collect an amount, once or multiple times, via a Direct Debit. The consumer 'signs' by identifying themselves, which is done in their own banking environment. With every (repeat) payment, the e-mandate is provided for approval. It is also possible to withdraw this e-mandate at any time.

The great advantage of issuing an e-mandate is that it is no longer possible to use just anyone's account number to start a Direct Debit. After all, identification is obligatory.

Note that these payment methods vary between countries.

Visa and MasterCard

In addition to the so-called debit payments, payments that are directly deducted from the account (similar to cash card payments), there is also the possibility to pay using credit. For this purpose, credit cards such as Visa and MasterCard are used. Because highly fraud-sensitive information is distributed over the Internet, these authorities have strict policies that web stores must comply with before being allowed to process the payment.

Pros for Visa and MasterCard:
- You can safely pay using credit.
- The payment is approved or rejected immediately after completion.

9

Cons for Visa and MasterCard:
- The costs for the online retailer are relatively high.
- It is possible to reclaim the deducted sum if goods are not delivered or in the event of fraud (this is a risk for the retailer).
- The pay-out from the credit card company usually takes an average of a few business days.

Visa and MasterCard have developed means of verification in the form of MasterCard Secure Code and Verified By Visa, which ensure that a consumer must complete the payment using a PIN or password. Amongst other things, this form of protection has made it impossible to make an online payment using only a credit card number. It also ensures that, in case of fraud, the risk is shifted from the (web) retailer to the issuer of the credit card. Of course, this doesn't absolve the (web) retailers from the responsibility of preventing fraud themselves, but it does provide a certain amount of security after having shipped the product(s).

PayPal
In addition to regular credit cards, PayPal is also often used. PayPal is a kind of virtual wallet, which can be topped up using various payment methods. Topping up can be achieved by, for example, transferring money from a bank account to the PayPal account or by crediting the balance using a credit card. When paying on a website or in an ecommerce website, two combination codes are used to complete the payment, meaning you don't have to provide your bank details on every website.

Pros for PayPal:
- You can easily transfer money worldwide.
- PayPal credit can easily be topped up with a credit card or via a bank account.
- No fraud-sensitive data is left behind on any website.

Cons for PayPal:
- When using PayPal, relatively high costs are involved for the receiver of the money.
- There is a possibility of chargebacks or assets being frozen when suspicious activities are being investigated.

PayPal has also added a certain 'insurance policy' regarding the risks for the (web) retailer. Traditionally, the so-called 'buyer protection' exists which ensures that the consumer has the right to reclaim the paid amount if the order delivery is not satisfactory or even fails. Online retailers can also reduce the risk of fraud by allowing only verified accounts and/or using AVS. (Address Verification System). By doing so, the online retailer also sends the consumer's address details, which PayPal then uses to perform an additional check. By using these methods, the risk of potential fraud shifts from the online retailer to PayPal.

9

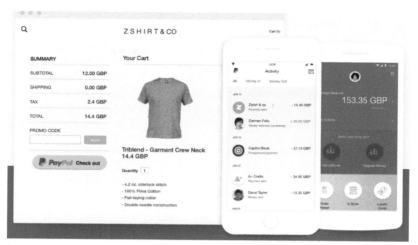

Paypal explained on its website

Postpay and bank transfer

Another payment method that is still often used, is the bank transfer.
Using this method, you don't have to leave fraud-sensitive information on
the web but can simply process the payment via your own bank.
Nowadays, this payment method is also used to complete the payment
online using your own banking application. For this purpose, the online
retailer's bank details are provided by email and used to transfer the
money from your own banking environment.

Pros for bank transfer:
• You can transfer the payment at any time.

Cons of bank transfer:
• The consumer could postpone the payment or not pay at all.
• The period of time between completing the order and receiving the
  payment is quite long.
• The risk of errors and delays in processing is relatively large.

This payment method (bank transfer) involves an additional problem for
online retailers. Online purchases are often impulse purchases, or they are
very focused on looking for a product and find it on the website. If the
payment process is then not immediately completed, chances are that
people will no longer pay or, whilst they were surfing, have found another
website and order the product or service from there. An alternative is:
deliver before the payment is completed. But then again, chances are that
after having shipped the products, the payment will never be received
which may cause the costs of a full debtor and collection management
system to increase very rapidly.

9.2.3   Mobile payment

Another development that is continually expanding is paying with or via the
mobile phone. The huge increase in the sale of smartphones with Internet
access, such as the iPhone, HTC and Samsung Galaxy has also ensured
that Internet purchases are increasingly being made via the mobile phone.

Mobile payment

© Noordhoff Uitgevers bv

For example, almost all organisations are promoting themselves on the web, with the focus on the different devices that the consumer can use. On every device the ease of use must be tailored as much as possible to the possibilities and screen size of the device.

In the case of a payment menu, consideration can be given to optimising the payment page by displaying the payment methods as compactly as possible and minimising the input fields.

A common solution for this is, for example, that the customer makes the payment via the bank's own app. This app often already has a simple verification module, in which the consumer no longer has to approve cumbersome codes or external devices.

The optimisation of the existing payment methods is one form of change. In addition, opportunities to develop payment methods that can be used both in the physical store and in the web store are being examined with increasing frequency. So the focus is, on the 'omnichannel' or 'multichannel' integration. With one integration, the same payment portfolio can be provided within the different ways of shopping. And with that, one complete integrated chain up to and including the stock systems and accounting systems.

Partly due to the increase in the use of smartphones, almost everyone has one at their disposal these days, companies are looking into the possibility of not only being able to pay on a mobile phone, but being able to pay with the mobile phone itself. An example of this is contactless payment, paying via an NFC chip, that has already been introduced.

Screenshot of Apple's website: how to pay with a mobile phone using Apple pay

Mobile payment methods can be divided into different categories:

1 The phone as a contactless wallet (NFC chip): mobile devices can be equipped with SIM cards that include an NFC chip, this chip can communicate with NFC terminals in stores. This makes contactless payments possible in stores, especially for smaller amounts.

NFC chip

2 Paying on the mobile web (mobile browser based): the payment menu used in the regular browser is automatically adjusted to the consumer's device. The payment menu is not only reduced, but the design is different, and the input fields are adjusted, so that legibility on a mobile device is maintained.

Mobile browser based

3 Paying with an application (iPhone and Android): the consumer installs an app on their smartphone that makes it possible to pay for the selected products or services.

4 The mobile phone as authorisation and authentication device: there are various internet payment methods that use mobile phones for authentication and/or authorisation on the Internet, in some cases linked to a wallet.

Authorisation and authentication device

5 SMS the consumer pays via an SMS message or calls an IVR system and pays per unit of time. This method is suitable for smaller amounts.

A last, but not certainly not least, new development that is currently taking place is the emergence of the so-called 'wallets'. Wallets are topped up with a (prepaid) balance. After doing so, they can be used in-app, for example, for playing games. It is not only the existing payment institutions that are involved with these developments, such as PayPal and now also MasterCard with the introduction of MasterPass, but also, Apple Pay and Google Pay for Android ie paying via a wallet in an increasing number of countries. A wallet makes it much easier for the consumer to pay, for example by storing the address data in it so that it does not have to be filled in again each time it is needed, along with all your different payment cards that are standardly included. You can pay with a verification directly from the wallet, without filling in all your financial information such as the bank account number or credit card number.

Wallets

9.2.4   Developments in online payments

Online payment is changing enormously. Some of these developments will be briefly reviewed below:

1 social payments
2 repeat payments
3 bitcoin and blockchain

1 Social payments

As the mobile phone plays an increasingly prominent role in the searching and purchasing behaviour of the consumer, payment solutions are increasingly being used within social media channels. Examples of this are payments that take place via WhatsApp, using a payment request from the banking app or with an app developed specifically for this purpose by the bank itself.

Social payments

For social payments, the most important goal is to make the payment process as simple as possible. Payments via social media are increasing in both business-to-consumer traffic and peer-to-peer, in other words, from one consumer to another.

Peer-to-peer

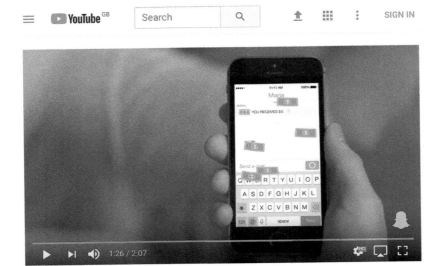

Introducing Snapcash!
An example of social payments is Snapcash, by which Snapchat users can send each other payments, easily and securely

2 Repeat payments
Repeat payments are used to facilitate repeat purchases. This not only fulfils the needs of online retailers but has also come to pass as a response to consumer's wishes. Increasingly, the consumer seems to want to opt for a pay-per-use model instead of purchasing the product. Good examples are media products, where people no longer buy DVDs or take out a subscription to the newspaper but pay per movie they have watched or per article they have read. In cases such as these, the account can be settled at the end of every fixed period of time.

3 Bitcoin and blockchain

Bitcoin

At the start of 2010, the first bitcoin market was opened, where people could buy and sell bitcoins with money. This created a network of users who agreed to pay each other in bitcoins. The participants within this network use the bitcoin software on their PC or mobile to perform transactions among themselves. All transactions are registered and can be paid quickly, easily, cheaply and securely to one another. Bitcoin was one of the forerunners in the field of paying outside of the regular system, but it is not the only cryptocurrency. Another example is Ethereum. Based on

Cryptocurrency

research performed in 38 countries, the University of Cambridge estimated the market in 2017 to be between 2.9 and 5.8 million users with between 5.8 and 11.5 million active digital wallets (University of Cambridge Judge Business School, 2017).

Blockchain technology is the foundation for this method of payment. You were able to read more about this in section 3.4. Blockchain technology means that no intermediaries (such as banks) are needed that provide financial control. This technology is expected to have a significant impact on the way online orders will be handled administratively in the future, especially where money, but also property rights are transferred.

9.2.5   Different service providers within the payment environment

In the world of online payment, there is a diversity of service providers and payment institutions. In order to get an idea of the various parties within the online payment cycle, the various links within the online payment process are shown schematically in figure 9.2.

FIGURE 9.2 Parties in the payment process

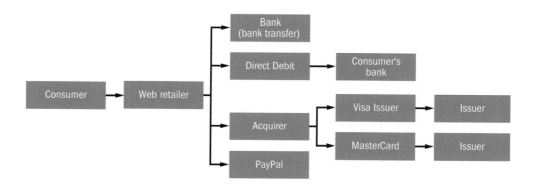

The following is an explanation of some of the parties mentioned in figure 9.2:

- Acquirer: this is the party that intercedes on behalf of online retailers with Visa and MasterCard. These authorities always work with intermediaries (acquirers) who each operate in their own region (Europe, the United States, Asia, etc.).   **Acquirer**
- Issuer: this concerns the organisation that issues consumer's cards: the party from whom the consumer has obtained the credit card. This can be a credit card from a bank, such as a MasterCard from HSBC or a branded credit/charge card eg the British Airways American Express Card.   **Issuer**

Over the years, the diversity of payment methods has only increased. For this reason, an increasing number of online retailers are opting for the use of a so-called payment service provider (PSP). A PSP is a company that takes care of the processing of online and offline payments for entrepreneurs. This means that they ensure the security of the payment process and continuous updates of both technical and procedural standards. In fact, they are the link between the online retailer and the various financial institutions and their payment products. This includes Visa, MasterCard, postpay and Direct Debits.   **Payment service provider**

PSP

Partly as a result of very strict requirements that are in place for processing credit card data and the ever-changing legislation regarding online payment processes, an increasing number of online retailers are choosing to use a PSP (see figure 9.3).

FIGURE 9.3 Payment service provider

The following are some important advantages of using a PSP as an intermediary:
- On a technical level, only one link is required for the various payment methods.
- The responsibility, in technical terms, for links to financial institutions is at the risk of the PSP.
- Enforcement of legislation and regulations and the associated system adjustments are at the risk of the PSP.
- The requirements regarding security, certifications and the safeguarding of personal data are at the expense of the PSP.

Particularly as purchasing via the internet also ensures that online retailers are no longer limited to one sales market and because they want to be able to increase their market to include countries outside of their own borders, a link with a PSP is extremely valuable. After all, they will then take care of the technical contacts and (supervision of) contracts with payment providers, so that the expansion of the portfolio of payment methods can take place quickly.

There are two different types of PSPs, namely the collecting PSP (figure 9.4) and the distributing PSP (figure 9.5). The big difference between the two PSPs lies in the way in which the financial institutions take care of the payment to the online retailer. For a distributing PSP, the money from the various financial institutions is paid directly to the online retailer, whereas a collecting PSP collects all funds on behalf of the online retailer and also connects all money to the recorded orders. In doing so, a large part of the debtor management and financial administration is taken out of the hands of the online retailer.

In addition to offering a variety of payment solutions, PSPs are increasingly focusing on related services as well. This could be the development of loyalty concepts, the follow-up of unpaid invoices, the so-called Credit Management, and the expansion of reporting options.

FIGURE 9.4 Collecting PSP

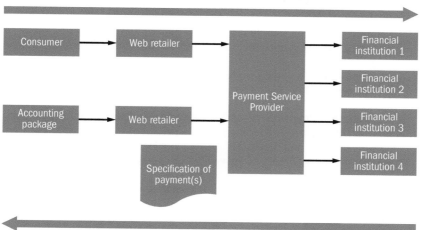

Data stream of payment and customer information

Payment of received transactions

FIGURE 9.5 Distributing PSP

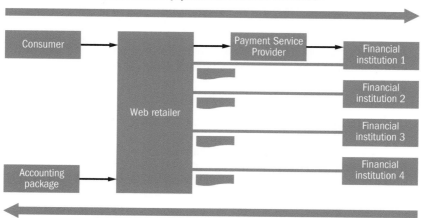

Data stream of payment and customer information

Payment of received transactions

9.2.6   Safety: what should a consumer be aware of?

The payment processing is not the only thing that can be risky. It is also of great importance that the consumer checks the reliability of the ecommerce website in advance, in so far as possible. An important element of this is checking whether the retailer in question is affiliated with a reputable organisation ie to confirm that they provide a complete screening before they issue an ecommerce website owner with a home shopping certificate. An example is the European Trustmark from Ecommerce Europe (www.ecommercetrustmark.eu).

The moment a consumer decides to proceed with making a payment, there are some characteristics to look out for that are a good indication of whether the location where the data is to be entered into, is secure. These characteristics include:

- an https://connection that is displayed in the browser URL on the page where the payment details are entered
- the image of the 'green lock' (and label 'secure') that is displayed in the address bar
- the presence of a Verisign logo After clicking on this logo, information can be obtained about the security applied to the website concerned.

If these characteristics are not visible, for example as a result of the integration of an iFrame, it is still possible to look at the page in the source code with the right mouse button. The original URL is always mentioned there. For most consumers however, that is a bridge too far.

Phishing

Another important point of attention, a phenomenon people are increasingly confronted with, are so-called 'phishing' emails. In such an email, the recipient is asked to perform a certain action via a link. In order to create a false sense of security, these emails often make use of an institution that is familiar to the recipient. This could be a fake email address, where the name of the company is used as the sender or an email that is completely drawn up in an identical format to that of the institution. A request is then made, asking to transfer money directly via a link or a report is made of potential abuse, whereby the login details must be checked and/or corrected.

In case of payment this will have been immediately transferred and the recipient can consider the money to be lost. If the login information for a bank is given, this data can be used for making purchases from third parties after receipt. From the online retailer's point of view, the payment then appears to be legitimate but ultimately turns out to have been made using 'stolen' account data.

9.3 Sub-processes of order processing

Order handling

E-fulfilment

Order handling is the process that is initiated after an order has been placed in an online store, in other words, the actual delivery of the goods or services. For the handling of online orders, the term 'e-fulfilment' is often used. This includes all activities that ensure that the buyer who has ordered products online, actually acquires access to those products.

Order handling consists of the following sub-processes:

1 order confirmation
2 readying the order for shipment
3 shipment of the order
4 billing
5 after-sales and returns

We will now discuss these sub-processes in more detail. The payment process has already been covered in section 9.2.

Dear Mrs. Visser,

Thank you for choosing **ibis Styles Nivelles** for your next stay in **NIVELLES**.

Please see below for details of your reservation.

We hope you enjoy your stay!

Kind regards,
Le Service Clients Accorhotels

Your reservation is confirmed.

Reservation made in the name of:	**Mrs. Visser Marjolein**
Reservation number:	FKKDDNCQ
Transaction number:	**FKKDDNCQ_0100000064104988PP2**

Date of stay:	From 02/06/2017 to 03/06/2017
Your stay:	1 room, 1 night
	3 adults , 0 child

"Please keep this reservation number safe; you will be asked to provide it for any information related to your stay."

ONLINE CHECK-IN

View
Cancel
Book

Example order confirmation Accor Hotels

9.3.1   Order Confirmation

Once a customer has completed an order, they will receive a confirmation of that order. Often this is done with an email, but it is also possible that an SMS is sent. The purpose of this confirmation is to provide the customer with the certainty that the order has been received correctly, the confirmation of the agreements that have been made and/or the option to be able to correct any errors that may have been made. An order confirmation usually contains details such as the order number, the payment method, the status of the payment, the purchased products or services and possibly a deviating type of delivery. The latter can occur if an order cannot be delivered in one go, for example if an item of clothing as well as a sofa are ordered.

Order
confirmation

The physical shipment of products is often carried out by a third party, such UPS or FedEx that event, a link is placed in the order confirmation to the sender's website that references the status of the order. In this way, the status of the order can be viewed in real time (track & trace) and the shipment process can be tracked in the event that the order does not fit through the letterbox and a barcode has been attached.

Track & trace

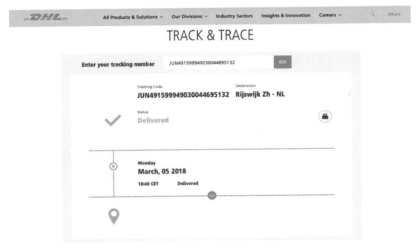

Track & trace at DHL

9.3.2   Readying the order for shipment

Preparation for shipping

Order picking

Once the order has been placed in the ecommerce website, the item must be shipped to the customer. The preparation for shipping of an order usually takes place in a distribution centre. This is where the products are received and stored. After the order has been placed in the ecommerce website, the ordered goods are collected (this activity is called 'order picking'), the order is packed and provided with a shipping label. Most ecommerce websites and multichannel retailers have their own distribution centres. Others outsource the storage, order picking and packaging activities to specialised logistical service providers. Distribution centres that handle web orders should primarily focus on two aspects:

Capacity planning

- Capacity planning: sufficient staff must be available to process the strongly fluctuating flow of web orders in a timely manner. On a Monday, for example, there are many web orders, as a result of consumers having made online purchases all weekend. There must also be sufficient space available to handle the fluctuating volume flows.

Stock management

- Stock management: keeping products in stock costs money. It is therefore important, on the one hand, to keep the stock as low as possible. On the other hand, the customer must receive deliveries in a timely manner. This can result in some tension. A stock management system is therefore of the utmost importance. Such a system can often be linked to the web store. This means adequate administration processes for incoming and outgoing items must be in place. Make good agreements with suppliers and keep them to this. Also determine which items you always want to keep in stock, such as top selling products. Customers also want to know if an item is in stock (see example 9.2).

EXAMPLE 9.2

Desired delivery options of the online buyer

DeliveryMatch investigated the 'desired delivery options of the online buyer'. In this survey, the question was asked: 'How much importance do you place on the ability to see if a product is in stock?' The reaction was: 90 percent responded with 'important' to 'very important'.

The most important findings in short:
- More than 80% of all consumers want to be able to choose a delivery day and delivery time during online checkout.
- The majority of online consumers think it is (very) important to have the option to chooser a delivery on Saturday or in the evening, while a third has a preference for evening delivery.
- A third of consumers want to be able to choose a delivery window of up to 2 hours.
- Most online consumers prefer to receive the ordered item at their home address.
- If an item is not in stock, more than three-quarters of all consumers will still buy it from the web store if the waiting time is no longer than a week.

They concluded that a better logistical supply, tailored to the wishes of the consumer, generates an average of 17% extra turnover, with peaks of up to 40%.

Source: DeliveryMatch, 2016

9.3.3 Shipment of the order

After the web order has been packaged and provided with a shipping label, the ordered article must be delivered to the customer. Ecommerce websites almost always outsource this delivery to the customer (often referred to as the 'last mile') to specialised logistical service providers eg UPS, FedEx and others. People who shop online can have the products delivered (possibly for a fee) to their home. There is also the possibility to have them delivered to another delivery address, for example at work or at an official pick-up point (eg FedEx). An increasing number of online retailers who also have a network of physical stores, designate some of these stores as so-called pick-up points of their own. Sometimes the consumer is not at home at the time of delivery. The web order can then be delivered to the neighbours or delivery can be attempted again on the following day. Another possibility is direct delivery. A direct delivery is when delivery and shipping is not organised by the ecommerce website online retailer itself, but by the supplier of the product. The online retailer transfers the order to the supplier, who then takes care of the direct delivery to the consumer.

Shipment

Pick-up points

Direct delivery

Walmart Pick-up point

9.3.4 Invoicing

Invoicing

The invoice that is sent to the customer after the order, ideally contains information from the retailer, such as the name, and the address of the company Sometimes the web merchant uses the invoice to communicate about alternative payment methods. In the picture you can see that the invoice from Amazon also serves as a contact moment for the promotion of the 'Amazon.com Visa Card'.

9

amazon.com   VIEW CART | WISH LIST | YOUR ACCOUNT | HELP

Thanks for your order,

Want to manage your order online?
If you need to check the status of your order or make changes, please visit our home page at Amazon.com and click on Your Account at the top of any page.

Purchasing Information:

E-mail Address:

Billing Address: **Shipping Address:**

Netherlands   Netherlands

Order Grand Total: EUR 19,70

Get the Amazon.com Visa Card and **get $30 back** after your first purchase. Plus get up to **3%** rewards.

Order Summary:

Shipping Details : (order will arrive in 1 shipment)

Order #:   104-6126249-1334655
Shipping Method: Standard International Shipping
Shipping Preference: Group my items into as few shipments as possible
Subtotal of Items: EUR 14.04
Shipping & Handling: EUR 5.66

Total for this Order: EUR 19,70

Delivery estimate: January 13, 2010 - February 3, 2010
Shipping estimate for these items: December 16, 2009
1 **"Enterprise 2.0: New Collaborative Tools for Your Organization's Toughest Challenges"**
  Andrew McAfee; Hardcover; $19.77

Amazon invoice with offer for a credit card

Also, take into account the fact that articles can be returned. Depending on the type of articles, the percentage of returned items can be substantial. This can particularly be the case with clothing.

9.3.5   After-sales and returns

Good accessibility via telephone, email or social channels is critical for an online store. Inaccessibility of a web store, for example if an incorrect item is delivered, leads to dissatisfied customers and a bad reputation. Especially if you do not have a physical visiting address, this is important. You can answer phone calls, emails, tweets or Facebook messages yourself, but if the volume becomes substantial, there are also alternatives such as outsourcing to external parties, however there are of course costs involved. Consumers have 14 working days (in many countries) to return an ordered item for a full refund. Often, a return form attached to the order can be used for this purpose. A retailer then has 14 days after receipt of the return form to reimburse the customer for the paid amount and – in the event that the entire order is returned – also credit the shipping costs. Returning an online purchase happens more often than returning a product to the store where it was purchased.

After-sales

A good returns policy and effective handling is of great importance to customer satisfaction as well as profit.

Returning purchases
Scientific research carried out by Minnema, Bijmolt and Gensler (2017) reveals the following causes and consequences of the return of purchases.

Causes of returning purchases
- A returns policy where the ecommerce website does not charge any return costs and doesn't have additional conditions, leads to more purchases, while a longer trial period leads to a lower incidence of returns.
- The information available at the time of purchase affects the incidence of returns. Information that leads to higher expectations increases the incidence of returns, while information that eliminates that uncertainty lowers the probability of returns.
- Viewing photos can increase or decrease the likelihood of returns. Photos that provide details and thereby remove uncertainty, reduce the risk of returns, while for example, model photography leads to higher expectations and therefore an increase in likelihood of returns.
- Reviews that are unrealistically positive, increase the probability of returns, as expectations are heightened.
- The likelihood of returns is higher for experience products (wine, holidays or other products that you can only rate after having experienced them) than for search products (products that you can reasonably make a judgement about 'on sight'). Customers experience more uncertainty regarding experience products.
- The likelihood of returns is higher for more expensive products and lower for products purchased at a discount, as customers are more critical of more expensive products.

Consequences of returning purchases
- Customers who are satisfied with the return process will be more likely to purchase something from that store in future, as they perceive the risks to be lower.
- Returning purchases can be done out of habit, some customers often send purchases back, while others almost never actually return products.
- Returning purchases also affects non-transactional customer behaviour. When a customer is satisfied with the return process, they are more likely to recommend the store to friends and acquaintances, thus creating value for the store.
- The inclusion of return behaviour in the determination of the customer value, allows for better allocation of marketing resources and increases the profit for the store.

9.4 Online service

Service

By service, we mean everything that a company does for a customer after the purchase of a product or service. This includes, for example:
- offering assistance with the implementation of the service or the product
- solving problems related to the service or the product
- information provision
- providing insight into all the benefits of the service provision

Service differentiation

Service is a subjective concept and is experienced by a consumer in different ways. This depends on the target audience and also on the product or service that is offered. It is therefore important for an organisation to apply service differentiation and to adapt the service to the target audience, or even better to the individual, as well as to the product or service that is provided.

Service is provided by companies through various contact channels, such as a contact centre, a store, a website or an app. In this section we will find out why service is so important. The emphasis will be on online service where the contact between the customer and the company takes place via the Internet. We will examine which developments are affected by this. We will also discuss the (use of) contact channels. Finally, we will discuss the conditions for successful online service.

9.4.1 Why is service important?

Chapter 3 talks about the digital marketing funnel the phases that a customer goes through and the way in which a marketer can successfully tap into this. For many of the choices that a customer makes during the customer journey, the service that is offered plays an important role. Enticing a customer to buy a product or service from you can be a challenge, but to bind and retain a customer for your organisation is even more difficult. This is not only closely related to the quality of the product or service, but also to the service that a company offers. In certain markets, competitors' products or services increasingly resemble each other and prices do not differ much either. This makes it hard for customers to make a choice and so a company has to distinguish itself in a different way. One way to do that is to offer good service. Good service is of course a subjective concept and always subject to change. What today is perceived as good service, may only be considered basic service tomorrow. With basic service it is impossible to distinguish yourself, basic service is simply expected. In order to exceed customer expectations, it is important to continually adapt the service that is provided to the expectations of the customer and to keep trying to continue to deliver added value.

9.4.2   Main developments affecting online service

By developments that affect online service, we mean the amount of information, the customer's control over the customer process, social media and the transparency of companies.

Quantity of information

A large amount of information is provided on the Internet and on organisations' websites. It is not always easy for consumers to find the information that is relevant to them amongst the excess of available information. Experience shows us that about 30% of visitors to a website are unable to find the information they are looking for. Often, the information on a website reveals that companies are unable to connect to the customer's perspective. They often operate mostly from the perspective of their own goals.

Particularly in large organisations, the communication, sales, marketing and service departments have their own section on the website where they post information relevant to them. This division of responsibility for the online channel does not contribute to the effectiveness of a website and has a negative effect on customer satisfaction when it comes to service

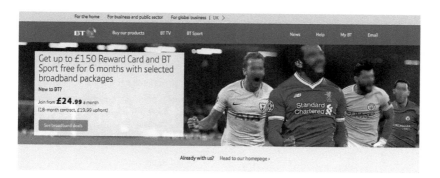

BT homepage needs to welcome a variety of different users

provision. Organisations also have a tendency to overestimate the importance of the homepage. Many customers arrive on the website via other pages and never even see the homepage.

Customer control of the customer process

The customer has an increasing amount of control over the customer process. The customer makes their own decisions regarding how and when they wish to receive their service. This also applies to the use of the Internet. A company may tempt the consumer to visit their website and make use of the 'My environment' section, but in the end the consumer determines whether or not they choose to do this. A company must try to guide the customer through the online customer journey to prevent the customers from becoming frustrated by completely closing off certain communication channels. This could be done by displaying the customer service phone number at the bottom of each page on the website.

Assisted service

Several forms of service are possible, either via the analogue channels (for example a store) or via the digital channels (eg the website or app). Figure 9.6 provides an overview of the different forms of service, the section within the dotted line comprising the digital forms of service. 'assisted service', where a person helps the customer, can be done for the digital as well as analogue channels. Aided digital service for example, is contact with an employee via chat or when a customer helps another customer via a forum. Digital self-service can be done via various channels, such as a website or app. These offer multiple possibilities. Organisations try to make the channel transition from digital self-service to aided service (where a person takes over) as seamless as possible.

FIGURE 9.6 Forms of service

Analogue channels		Digital channels		
Aided analogue service		Aided digital service	Digital self-service	
			Sub-channels	**Possibilities**
Store Counter Contact centre		Contact form Call-me-now Chat button Web care Customer helps Customer forum	Website Apps Text message Email	Content Tutorials Video Search tool FAQ Virtual employee My environment/Customer portal

Channel transition to aided service

Machine-to-Machine (M2M)

As more devices are connected to the Internet (Internet of Things), a larger amount of service is also provided. This is because devices communicate with each other and with systems of providers. This is also called Machine-to-Machine (M2M).

Social service

Social service (customer service via social media) has come of age and has now become an indispensable part of digital customer service in the space of only a few years. With social service, brands and organisations improve accessibility for their customers and consequently improve customer satisfaction. Customers share experiences on forums and weblogs and questions are answered without an organisation having to actively take part. Consumers often check information obtained from a company with other consumers. Research has shown that consumers have greater confidence in answers from other consumer than they have in the company that sells the product. Nevertheless, companies can play a role in this interaction and learn from customer information in order to continue to work on ever better service. On Twitter, 20% of all messages are about a brand or a product.

There are three distinguishable forms of social service (figure 9.7):

1 organisation helps customer
2 customer helps customer
3 customer helps organisation

Social service

FIGURE 9.7 Forms of social service

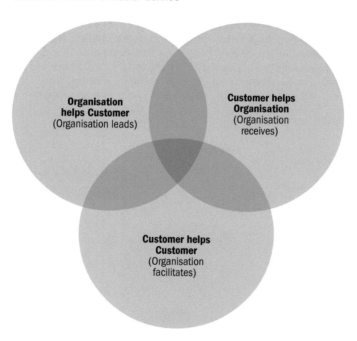

1 *Organisation helps customer*

Webcare or social customer service/social care is where organisations help the customer by actively examining where on Twitter, Facebook and forums they are being discussed and subsequently responding promptly to questions or problems that a customer has. Whereas webcare teams were often part of the marketing or communication department at first, we now find that most companies integrate webcare into the service department.

Webcare

Social customer service

Social care

Another remarkable development is the fragmentation of the number of social media platforms on which organisations are active. In addition to Twitter and Facebook; Instagram, Snapchat and (in some countries) Pinterest are now established 'channels'. In China, we could substitute WeChat, Toudou Youku and Weibo in this list. Appcare is also becoming more commonplace. Appcare is customer contact specifically via apps such as WhatsApp, Messenger from Facebook or within apps belonging to an organisation.

Appcare

2 Customer helps customer

When customer interaction via social media was only in its early stages, the focus was mainly on online customer service. In the meantime, attention has shifted somewhat to communities, partly because of the potential for self-service. Consider, for example, the 'customer helps customer' forum by T-Mobile or the UK telecom company GiffGaff that is entirely based on this concept.

Customer helps customer

3 Customer helps organisation

There is also a third form of social service: one in which customer feedback is central. The customer provides the organisation with relevant opinions, knowledge and information (customer helps organisation).

The model in figure 9.7 shows that there is an overlap between these three dimensions of social service. In this overlap the customer fulfils a central role within an organisation and the dividing lines between internal and external and between employee and customer are faded. Customers are much more involved in service processes. They answer questions from other customers, produce supporting content and share tips and ideas for improvement.

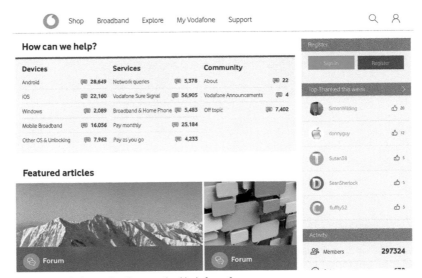

Customers help each other on the Vodafone forum

Transparency

In order to provide added value to consumers on the internet, it is important that companies disclose all relevant customer information to their customers. In the past, companies were used to making so-called back office information available only to a limited group of employees. This information is always at the front of the organisation (facing the customer) and clients can access a 'my environment' section on a website that contains all their data. Content information about products and services is also more often shared directly. As a company, if you really want to be successful in online service provision, you will have to relinquish some of the control and strive to be completely transparent. Open online platforms, such as communities where customers can discuss products and services, further contribute to transparency.

Transparency

9.4.3   Use of contact channels

There are many different ways the companies can offer service. The use of contact channels depends on the type of product or service, the customer need, but also on how much money a company can and wants to spend on service provision. Naturally, it must be possible for a company to earn back the costs associated with service provision (cost to serve). It is also becoming more attractive for companies to seek out contact channels that contribute to saving on expenses, whilst at the same time ensuring high customer satisfaction. In order for a company to choose wisely, it is important to make a business case and to compare the various options. We will discuss a few contact channels below.

Contact channels

Store and service counter

We still see the most traditional and personal way of servicing in stores and at service counters. By a service counter, we mean the possibility to visit your insurance company, your energy supplier or the municipality where you live. For an organisation, there are several reasons to maintain these channels, but one of the main reasons for continuing to provide this service is that these channels are sometimes necessary to solve the most complex issues or problems that occur. Especially when there are language barriers, face-to-face contact is sometimes required. The fact that consumers appreciate personal contact when the situation demands it is something that spans all generations.

Service counter

Contact centre

In a contact centre, all phone calls, emails, (web) chat sessions and webcare/social care requests from customers are handled. There are many companies that answer thousands of questions per day in their contact centre. It is a contact channel that is still widely used, as in general it is fast, simple and still personal. However, in comparison with most online self-service contact channels, it is expensive; an employee of the company must always be involved in the response. The expectation is that with the continuous improvement of online services, customers will make less and less use of the telephone. The telephone contacts that ultimately remain for call centres, will be for handling the most complex issues and that is why the employees of the future will probably need a different set of qualities than the current contact centre employees. As an example, think of helping a customer via Facebook; everyone is able to see this interaction, so it is even more important to formulate the correct answer as carefully as possible.

Contact centre

Website and app

Of course, a lot of service is provided on websites and in (service) apps. The challenge on a website or app is to enable the customer to find relevant information as easily as possible as well as be able to use it, in the excess of information that can often be found there, as mentioned in subsection 9.4.2. The possibilities for helping the customer are numerous and almost never dependent on technology anymore, but much more on the creativity of a company. The most common ones are:

- *Content*: information on the public areas of a site provides important online service support. Knowledge articles are easy to find via site navigation and (external) search engines. It is important to develop content from a user's perspective.

Guided tutorials

- *Tutorials*: step-by-step plans, problem solvers or guided tutorials contain additional information that can be clicked on to explain more complex content or processes. The user can be led through tricky material step by step. This form of online customer service is often used for technical issues,

- *Video*: the most visual form of online service is the use of instructional or how-to videos. They are ideal for explaining processes but are relatively expensive to develop compared to content or tutorials.

- *Search function*: of course, it should be possible to get to the requested content via the navigation structure of a website. Many users are accustomed to Google and readily set about using internal search features. However, they expect the same speed and possibilities (eg 'autosuggest') that Google offers.

- *FAQ*: a summary in the form of a list of frequently asked questions (and answers) still exists but is being overtaken by richer content forms such as tutorials and video.

Virtual assistant

Chatbot

- *Virtual assistant*: in order to return the personal nature of service, companies often opt for the use of a virtual assistant (also called a chatbot) who can take over the role of a customer advisor. The virtual employee accompanies the customer throughout their customer journey. Technology allows this employee to answer questions and have a conversation with the customer. Such an employee can also display questions and answers that are applicable to that specific visitor's context and web behaviour, but they can also help with instructions. Setting up a database with questions and answers costs a lot of time and money. The same applies to programming. However, once that has been done, it is a relatively low-cost option.

- *My environment* or *customer portal*: the service requirement extends beyond generic content. An increasing number of customers want to be able to view and alter personal data. As a result, an increasing number of organisations provide a secure personal environment where customers can log in. The most common form of 'My environment' is seen in internet banking, both via the websites and specifically developed apps.

Also, organisations often include so-called call-me-now and chat buttons in the online environment, to redirect customers directly to an employee if necessary. This may be because the question cannot be answered on the Internet, or because, in addition to a service request, there is also a sales opportunity. As mentioned in subsection 9.4.2, when providing services, it is not acceptable that visitors hit a 'dead-end' and become frustrated during their search for relevant information.

9

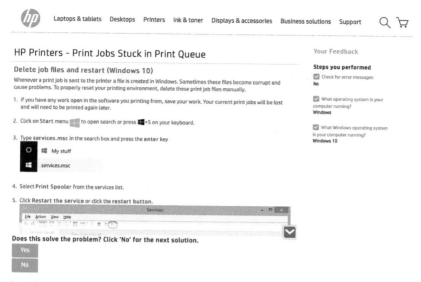

Step-by-step plan or guided tutorial 'Print jobs stuck in Print queue' on hp.com

Integration of contact channels

For service, just as with any other type of communication, it is important that companies provide their services via various available media. Experience shows that many consumers begin their search for answers on the Internet. If the relevant information is not available on the Internet, it is advisable that the company provides a different contact channel. Depending on the target audience and the subject, customers differ in the way they want to be helped. The complexity of some questions also sometimes means that a particular channel no longer suffices and an alternative opportunity for contact must be offered. Often, people then switch from the Internet to channels that are operated by people, such as web chat or a call centre. During the changing of channels, it is important that organisations ensure that the information from previous instances of contact is passed on to the next channel (seamless channel transfer). For a customer, it can be annoying if you have to repeat what your question or complaint was.

Contact channels

9.4.4   Conditions for successful online service

Many people will have experienced that it is not always easy for organisations to provide good service to customers. When looking for the cause, organisations sometimes only look at the service process and its improvement. However, most of the time, a bad experience with service has to do with the fact that companies' primary processes are not functioning properly. Companies are often not able to deliver their product and/or service without error straight away. The process of ordering, delivery and payment is and remains a big challenge for many companies. In addition, many large organisations have to deal with an outdated IT environment and a trove of different systems. Complex technical environments can slow companies down in their development and make it difficult to manage their service properly.

The correct management of knowledge within an organisation is essential for providing quality service. For service, this pertains to all information that has to do with customers and/or products. This knowledge must be available and specific to the various contact channels (multichannel). In order to achieve this, companies must set up a continuous process, in which available knowledge is always improved, added to and removed (only 40% of the questions and answers available in knowledge systems are actually used). Especially in organisations that are running several marketing campaigns, it is essential that everyone who communicates with the customer always has access to the most up-to-date information.

We will now sum up the conditions to the success of online service once again:
- Operate from the customer's point of view and not that of your organisation.
- Ensure optimal cooperation between the marketing, sales and service departments.
- Prevent an excess of information and consider what information is relevant to your customer.
- Be transparent as an organisation and unlock relevant information for your customer.
- Provide added value that exceeds basic expectations.
- Use several contact channels and make sure they are integrated with one another.

Voice of the customer

Finally, the role of the customer in keeping knowledge up-to-date and improving processes is increasing (client helps organisation). This is also called the 'voice of the customer'. Through the development, sharing and distribution of relevant information, customers can help organisations to build up relevant knowledge. Progressive organisations recognise this potential, for example by opening up knowledge systems to customers (often via their own forums). As a result, more so than before, knowledge systems are built up on an outside-in basis, which benefits practical usability.

9

© Noordhoff Uitgevers bv

Questions and assignments

© Noordhoff Uitgevers bv

NOW CHECK YOUR UNDERSTANDING:

9.1 Most suppliers of fresh food products have physical stores. In most cases, they also provide the option of ordering online. Examples include Tesco.co.uk, Asda.com and Carrefouruae.com.
a Explain what the most important considerations are for customers when choosing a distribution channel.
b Based on these considerations, weigh up the pros and cons of choosing a physical store, an ecommerce website for fresh food products or multichannel distribution. What would you recommend to small shop owners?

9.2 You have just started working as a digital marketer at online retailer ASOS.com. You are asked to critically review order processing.
a Which sub-processes can be distinguished within order processing? Apply this classification to ASOS?
b What criteria would you use for each sub-process to assess the extent to which the processes are effective and efficient?

9.3 A friend of yours starts a website where software can be downloaded. He asks you for advice about the payment options he should offer his customers.
a List the advantages and disadvantages of the various payment options.
b What should your friend look for when it comes to safety?
c Make a step-by-step plan for putting in place an effective payment system.

9.4 French Hotel chain IBIS wants to offer its guests more online service during the search for and reservation of a hotel room.
a What are the requirements for successful online service?
b Which contact channels does IBIS have and what are they used for?
c What ideas do you have for improving the online service? Support your proposal.

CASE

IKEA focuses on customer experience and self-service
By Marleen Bontekoe and Mike Berry

Global furniture store IKEA has a mission to help create a better daily existence for as many people as possible. The company does this by offering the widest possible range of well-designed, functional home furnishings at low prices, so that as many people as possible can buy these items. IKEA offers these low prices by investing in customer experience and allowing the customer to do more for themselves. The Swedish furniture brand sells a wide range of home furnishing products. Its affordably-priced but good quality products have grown popular globally. The entire range can be found in the famous IKEA blue stores. Here, customers are guided along, past all the home furnishings in a smart, convenient way. On the labels, the customer is able to read information about the product and the place where they can go to retrieve it. Small items can go directly into the cart or blue IKEA bag, big items, such as most furniture, can be picked up later by the customer in the self-service warehouse. Once the customer has collected all their items, they can go to the checkout. Then all items are brought home and assembled there by the customer. If it doesn't all fit in their car, IKEA provides other options to transport a purchase home. For example, everything can be delivered via IKEA's Transport Service. For this the customer pays approximately the same as the delivery costs for an online order. OR the customer can rent a trailer on site. And once the product is home, if the assembly of the furniture, kitchen or bathroom turns out to be too complicated, they can hire someone to come and do it for them; indeed specialist 'IKEA assemblers' have set up in business in many countries!

Building a global brand is not an easy task. While excellent product quality and affordable prices are necessary for penetrating new markets, how effectively a brand is marketed will, to a large extent, decide its fortune in the long term. IKEA has not achieved its success without some challenges in foreign markets. Cultural sensitivity has grown important in the 21st century. The 'one size fits all' approach doesn't work anymore. IKEA has faced various cultural hurdles while trying to penetrate new markets. Today, it is a highly recognized brand powered by marketing. IKEA has localised its approach where necessary. In its original (developed) markets, IKEA is positioned as a low-priced mass-market brand, but in emerging markets where low prices are already the norm, it targets a growing middle class that aspires to international lifestyle products. For these customers, design and a wide range under one roof are the attraction. This means that price is a less important part of the marketing mix for IKEA in China than it is, for example, in the UK or the USA.

When IKEA first started expanding to overseas markets, it did not at first achieve the kind of success it expected. IKEA came to realise that people's taste, style and preferences varied from market to market and culture to culture. So, IKEA decided to change both its products and its marketing techniques and adapt them to the local markets. From then on, IKEA took the time to understand local cultures and their preferences before introducing products in new markets, following which its products started growing popular in these new countries. Today, from product designs to catalogues everything is developed keeping local culture and tastes front of mind. This brand localization has helped IKEA achieve faster success in overseas markets.

In total, IKEA sells over 9,500 products from its stores. With such a large range of products, a brand needs excellent store design. This not only increases shopping convenience for the customers but provides a pleasant experience and helps create a strong brand image. If shopping from a store is a good experience in itself, then more and more customers will visit and revisit. Traditionally, the IKEA stores have been like warehouses located outside the town where customers can shop in peace and quiet. Recently however, IKEA has experimented with new formats. It has introduced pick-up points, smaller stores and even town-centre stores. The pick-up points are for online customers to pick up the products they ordered online. The smaller stores are built in towns where a full-size store may not be practical or necessary. These stores showcase a limited range of products. The third type, full size inside the town stores are being

9

opened at city centres in large towns. Overall IKEA has been flexible in designing its stores to provide its customers with the best possible experience.

The IKEA store design is a big attraction and in addition to customer convenience it helps customer engagement. Both these factors have been important in marketing a retail brand successfully in the 21st century. IKEA uses lots of clever techniques to turn browsers into buyers. Inside the stores there are tiny model homes, so the customers can borrow ideas for interior decoration. There is also space for customers to drop the kids or have lunch. The IKEA cafeteria serves cheap yet good quality food. IKEA has designed an entire experience inside its stores that maximizes shopping pleasure. The purpose is to engage the customers and attract and retain them in larger numbers.

IKEA's target audience is effectively the global middle class. It sells good quality and durable but affordable home furnishing products. These middle-class consumers generally look for products that are good in terms of design and quality but also low-priced. However, IKEA sells contemporary and stylish designs that are a big favourite among its millennial customers. It complements its products with a great customer friendly shopping experience.

IKEA uses a variety of promotional techniques. The most unique and most success-ful among the tools used by IKEA to promote its brand are the promotional cata-logues. These catalogues of IKEA products are printed in several languages and different catalogues are served in different markets. Apart from unique home furnishing ideas, there are real life stories and a wide range of products showcased through the hundreds of pages of the catalogue. The catalogue is available both in print (for now at least) and online. Apart from that an extended version of the catalogue is available in the IKEA app. The IKEA websites, publications, brochure, advertising and PR campaigns all play their part in the promotion of the brand.

IKEA uses social media to attract and engage customers. Individual IKEA country pages are used to engage customers on Facebook. Pinterest, Twitter, and other social media channels. Another key area where IKEA has focused to build a better reputation is sustainability. People and environment are an important focus area for IKEA. This has helped it build a stronger brand image.

Needless to say, digital media are important for IKEA in communicating with its target audience. IKEA has responded to changing customer media habits/behaviours by building digital and mobile experiences which match the branding and customer experience of the in-store environment.

Ikea's augmented reality app gives you an impression of how their furniture would fit in your home

IKEA's catalogues are its main channel of marketing communication. Print and now digital channels also play an important role in the marketing of its products and promotion of its brand. IKEA has also released an app and is ahead of other retailers in using Augmented Reality (AR) to provide customers with engaging experiences *outside* the stores.

Watch this video: http://bit.ly/2HIzYeP. IKEA's story shows that global marketing requires intense focus and in addition to localising advertising, brands must understand cultural differences and above all strive to maximise customer engagement using both traditional and digital channels.

Sources: www.cheshnotes.com/2017/04/ikea-marketing-strategy-and-practices-a-case-study and www.ikea.com

NOW CHECK YOUR UNDERSTANDING:

a Which basic distribution model does IKEA use?

b Which distribution channels has IKEA chosen? What are the advantages and disadvantages of each of the chosen channels as well as using a combination of those channels? Consider the experience from the customer's perspective, but also the effectiveness of the distribution channels from IKEA's point of view.

c Which processes does IKEA use for the processing of orders? What is your advice for improving these processes?

d How are customers able to pay online at IKEA? What are the advantages and disadvantages of choosing IKEA for online shopping and what could improve the experience?

e What can IKEA do to optimise the safety/ security of ordering and paying online?

f What is needed to deliver successful online customer service? How do you rate IKEA's online service in your country?

g Evaluate IKEA's online service channels as regards their effectiveness. Would you recommend that they add other contact channels? Please substantiate your answer.

9

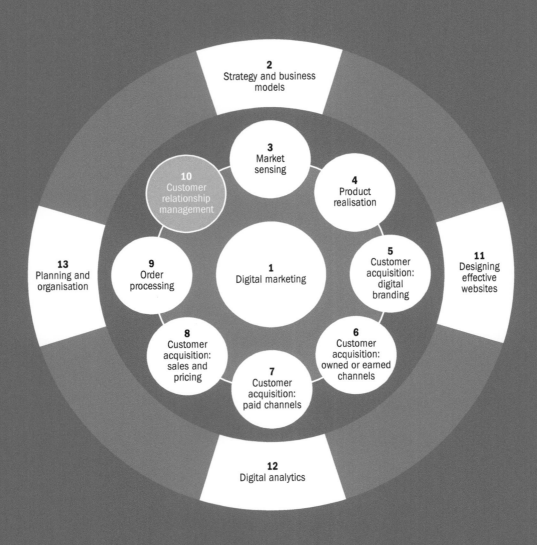

10
Customer relationship management

Authors: Marjolein Visser and Marcel Fokkema

Previous chapters describe how the marketer can establish a clear idea of what the market's wants and desires are (the market sensing process) and how the Internet can be used to further product development and improvement as well as for setting up processes surrounding the product or the service (the product realisation process). Once everything is customer-ready, the customer acquisition process commences: defining target audiences and recruiting new customers. After the order processing has been completed successfully, the customer relationship management process starts: the organisation tries to strengthen their relationship with the customer. On the one hand the aim of this process is to ensure that the customer is satisfied with the relationship and turns into a loyal customer, whilst on the other hand the customer's return for the organisation increases. This chapter describes how digital marketing can support this process.

This chapter will cover:
- digital customer relationship management
- working with customer segments
- increasing customer value
- individual value propositions
- social CRM

After studying this chapter, you will be able to:
- indicate what digital CRM entails and how it can be used
- explain how a digital marketer can compile customer segments and build customer personas
- indicate how customer value can be increased by using digital tools
- indicate what individual value propositions entail and how a digital marketer can use different forms of customisation and personalisation
- clarify how social CRM can be used

10

10.1 Digital customer relationship management

Product, price and quality are becoming less and less distinctive in the battle for the customer. That is why increasingly more companies and institutions are deciding to use a customer-oriented business strategy. This strategy is called customer relationship management (CRM). Using CRM, companies do not compete on price or product, but on customer orientation and customised service provision. CRM is about building more understanding, a relationship with and a personalised offer for individual customers.

Customer
relationship
management

In this section we will first discuss the concept of (digital) CRM. Then we will explain the digital CRM process. After, we will focus on customer value and customer share. Finally, the topics customer satisfaction and loyalty are covered.

10.1.1 The concept of digital CRM
The definition of CRM used in this book is (source: PKO):

CRM

> CRM is a strategy that a company or institution uses with the intention of optimising (customer) relationships in terms of customer satisfaction and customer return. CRM is a continuous and systematic, organisation-wide activity in which IT has a supporting role.

When introducing CRM, four objectives are focused upon:
1 attracting customers who meet the desired customer profile
2 retaining customers by strengthening customer bonds and customer loyalty
3 increasing customer value by creating personalised offers (customisation)

Customisation

4 reducing the number of loss-generating customers by using a differentiated service

Digital CRM

Social CRM

CRM is an organisation-wide strategy in which the online and offline environment as well as old and new media are used in a targeted and integrated manner. This goal-oriented and integrated approach are critical success factors. The Internet, mobile applications and social media are increasingly shifting the emphasis from traditional CRM to digital and social CRM. These developments have made it possible to approach potential customers in a more targeted manner. Organisations also recognise the importance of an offline environment supplementing online ordering and customer service; consider the example of Alibaba. which has partnered with FedEx and Maersk for logistics. Meanwhile Alibaba has been building its Hema grocery store concept for several years. It now has 13 locations, the bulk of which are located in Shanghai and Beijing. These large supermarkets combine online and offline shopping, where customers who have downloaded the Hema app can scan bar codes on the products and pay with their Alipay digital wallet.

E-CRM

'Digital CRM' or 'e-CRM' involves the creation of a CRM strategy using digital tools such as a (mobile) website or an *app*. 'Social CRM' means the creation of a CRM strategy using social media. This is discussed in more detail in section 10.5.

10

© Noordhoff Uitgevers bv

Although CRM is an activity that includes both the online and offline environment, in this chapter we will study CRM from a digital perspective.

EXAMPLE 10.1

Booking.com rewards loyal customers

Booking.com uses digital CRM in order to increase customer satisfaction, customer loyalty and customer efficiency. Booking.com has developed the loyalty program Genius. A loyal customer will receive the Genius guest status after five bookings in a year's time. The benefits:
- customer service on a free phone number
- extras such as late check-out and discounts on room upgrades
- 10% discount on a large number of accommodations. As a result, Genius guests are likely to choose a different hotel booking website. According to Booking.com, the chance that they will make a reservation is twice as high (Booking.com, 2017). In addition, Booking.com can track the searching behaviour of these regular customers even more efficiently: they have to log in to see the discounts.

Booking.com rewards loyal customers using the loyalty program Genius

---

10.1.2   The digital CRM process

CRM is based on entering into a long-term relationship with individual customers. This long-term relationship only works if the organisation responds adequately to the wishes and needs of that individual customer. To be able to do that, a lot of customer knowledge is needed. Knowledge that is built up step by step over an extensive period of time.

The organisation then focuses on continuously adapting the supply to the wishes and needs of the individual customer. Key to this, is to invest in customer loyalty, to focus on customer value (customer lifetime value) and to present a differentiated and personalised offer (customisation and personalisation).

The introduction of digital CRM represents the introduction of a continuous process and a 'learning organisation'. A learning organisation comes to pass when there is intensive contact with customers, whereby the organisation continuously asks for feedback and immediately processes this feedback into the way customers are being treated. The digital CRM process consists of five steps (see figure 10.1).

CRM process

Customer value

Customer lifetime value

Personalisation

10

FIGURE 10.1 'On going' process of digital CRM

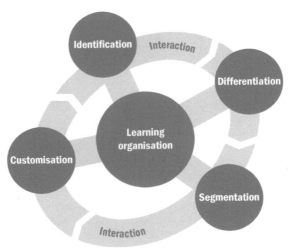

Identify

First of all, the organisation must get to know its customers (identify). After that, the organisation must distinguish its customers from each other on the basis of their wishes and needs, surfing behaviour, shopping behaviour, customer value or willingness to enter into a relationship (differentiate). By doing so, the organisation can determine its customer segments and customer profiles (segment). During contact with the customer (interaction), the organisation must then acquire additional data or otherwise gather, register and analyse it in order to be able to adapt the products and services in such a way that customer's desires are met (customisation). Every new moment of contact with the customer continues where the previous one left off. The organisation continues to learn how to better adapt themselves to the customer's wishes. Various topics play a role in all these steps of the process. Such as the importance of:

Differentiate
Segment
Interaction

Customisation

- recording and updating customer data
- identifying customer interests and preferences
- analysing surfing and shopping behaviour (see example 10.2)
- recognising different customer segments
- steering towards customer value and customer share
- the importance of very satisfied customers
- responding to the changing media behaviour of consumers
- delivering bespoke products or services and customer experiences by employing co-creation and personalisation of products and services

----

EXAMPLE 10.2

McDonald's App

The McDonald's App, which was downloaded more than a million times within a short period of time after its introduction, uses a smart CRM system. The app generates discount coupons based on previous purchasing behaviour, the weather, the time of day and the frequency of visits. In addition, customers can, for example, share coupons as gifts with their friends and receive a small surprise on their birthday.

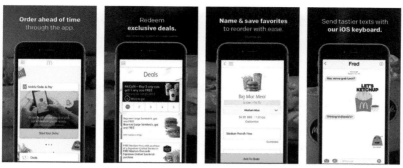

By providing practical features in its mobile app, McDonalds receives valuable customer data in return

----

A good digital CRM strategy without relevant customer data is an illusion. That is why gathering, registering, analysing and applying customer data in a smart way, are important success factors. Three main types of customer data can be distinguished:

1 basic data
2 profile data
3 behavioural data

1 Basic data

Basic data involves identification data that is essential to being able to recognise the customer for administrative, marketing and communication purposes.

Basic data

Consider data such as:
- IP address
- cookie ID
- customer (and card) number
- login data
- email address
- opt-in
- name
- gender
- address and postal code
- phone number
- place of residence
- payment details

2 Profile data

Profile data involves additional (usually static) data and is used for compiling customer profiles (customer profiling) and segmenting customer. Consider data such as:

Profile data

Customer profiling

- date of birth
- interests (such as sports, cooking or traveling)
- preferences (such as favourite newspaper, music or holiday destination)
- belongings (such as make of car, computers or electronic equipment)
- education
- job title and profession
- family income

- family composition
- number of children
- digital preferences

3 Behavioural data

Behavioural data

Behavioural data involves dynamic data that changes continuously as a result of the interaction between the digital provider and their customer. Consider data such as:
- purchased products
- products that have dropped in price
- product use
- purchasing times
- channels used for each of the phases during the purchasing process (website, mobile website, app)
- switching channels
- existing customer or new customer
- content used (how often, when, what pages, where 'bounced')
- source of traffic
- promotional offers received (email, re-targeting ads, suggestions on website, etcetera)
- response to promotional offers
- opening and clicking behaviour in emails
- contents of previous shopping basket
- contents of wish list
- downloads
- information requests
- use of online service modules, for example logging into the 'My account' section
- moments of contact with the customer service department
- offered prices
- price sensitivity
- payment methods used
- shares and likes
- social media data

Digital data sources

This customer data can be drawn from different data sources. Table 10.1 lists a number of frequently used digital data sources. In addition, companies can also collect customer data by developing special campaigns or methods. Disney for example, collects customer data using the MagicBand: bracelets that are equipped with RFID chips. They keep track of the wearer's location, what activities they perform and what they buy.

TABLE 10.1 Sources of digital data

Type of customer data	Sources of digital data
Basic data	Application form and registration form Connection with postal code and address file Connection with social media (such as Facebook, LinkedIn, Instagram and Pinterest) Cookies

© Noordhoff Uitgevers bv

TABLE 10.1 Sources of digital data (continued)

Type of customer data	Sources of digital data
Profile data	Explicitly via web forms
	Explicitly via online customer surveys
	Implicitly via measurable hyperlinks in the email
	Implicitly via standard and self-owned server log files
	Connection with social media
	Connection with other websites
	Connection with digital consumer or business databases
Behavioural data	Implicitly via measurable hyperlinks in the email
	Implicitly via standard and self-owned server log files
	Counters
	Web analytics tools (such as Google Analytics)
	Connection with transaction systems
	Connection with social media
	Connection with other websites
	Connection with digital consumer or business databases
	Connection with wearables

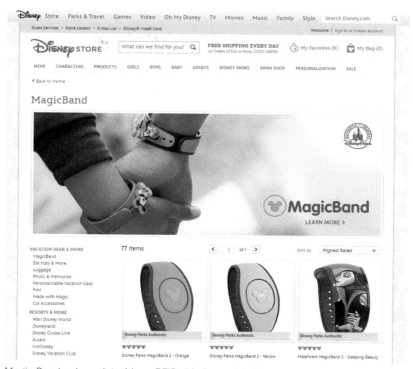

Magic Band, a bracelet with an RFID chip is used in Disney's theme parks

Customer data can be analysed using analytics tools. You were able to read more about this in section 3.8.

These database analyses can be used for different purposes, such as:
- determining customer segments by distinguishing them based on customer value, interests, preferences or willingness to enter into relationships (customer segmentation)

Customer segmentation

Target segment selection	• identifying target segments for specific marketing activities and predicting response (target segment selection)
Sales profile analysis	• determining the characteristics of buyers of a certain product (sales profile analysis)
Response analysis	• identifying variables that predict the response to a marketing activity (response analysis)
Predictive analytics	• predicting customer behaviour, such as purchasing behaviour, future customer revenues and opportunities for customer retention (predictive analytics, also see sub-section 3.8.3)
	• analysing purchasing behaviour for the development of targeted marketing campaigns (cross-selling, deep-selling, up-selling, see sub-section 10.1.3)
Acquisition profiles	• detecting promising prospects and predicting responses to promotional offers (acquisition profiles)
Retention profiles	• detecting potential 'run-aways' and predicting responses to churn reduction activities (retention profiles, see sub-section 3.8.3)
	• determining the chance of success for sales promotions and predicting response to promotional offers (cross-selling, deep-selling, up-selling)

Ubiquitous CRM

Another new concept when it comes to customer data processing is 'ubiquitous CRM'. A synonym for ubiquitous is 'omnipresent'. Using ubiquitous CRM, contextual customer data; such as the time, their location and their identity are automatically gathered. An example of this is storing data when someone checks in with a personal public transport card, storing transactions made with a debit card or registering when someone checks in at a specific location with a mobile phone. Techniques such as RFID and Bluetooth are used to find out who is in which place at what time. Organisations can use the collected data to proactively offer personalised services.

As you can read in sections 3.8 and 6.6, organisations can approach large numbers of customers with relevant information and offers using marketing automation. The number of investments that are being made in marketing automation systems is increasing all the time and there any many providers to choose from; ranging from only a few euros per month to hundreds of thousands of euros. Companies use this to build databases for storing customer data and continuously update them with relevant information from websites, apps, emails or social media. Examples are: visited pages, clicked links, interesting articles, completed forms and so on.
In these systems, triggers can be built in that automatically alert if (potential) customers perform a certain activity or in case a certain event occurs. A few examples:

• Taxi app Uber sends an automated welcome email to everyone who registers. This email is straightforward, welcoming new users and thanking them for signing up. To assist new users and to encourage them to actually start using Uber, the welcome email also explains how Uber works and includes helpful tips on getting started.
• Cloud storage platform Dropbox sends an email to re-engage people who signed up for Dropbox but have not yet installed the software on their computer.
• Dropbox uses personalization to address the recipient directly, using their first name The email is very brief and suggests a few specific ways Dropbox can assist you. It's short, to the point and very helpful.

- A few weeks before your trip, Booking.com will send an email to ask if you want to extend the stay and whether you want to visit other locations that people like you have visited.

10.1.3 Customer value (Customer Lifetime Value) and customer share

An important part of digital CRM is managing the customer's value for the company. You have been able to read more about the concept of customer value in section 4.1. Investing in a stronger customer relationship only makes sense if future revenues are greater than the costs for attracting, developing and retaining that customer. Therefore, it is not only important to consider the short term, but the entire duration of the relationship. This is because short-term investments may lead to higher revenues in future. After all, the costs precede the results. In order to be able to manage the customer's value, the expression 'customer lifetime value' has been introduced. We define this as follows:

> Customer lifetime value (CLV) is the total of all future profits (revenues minus costs) resulting from a customer. In other words: what a customer is worth money-wise during the period that he or she is a customer or could be a customer of the company.

Customer lifetime value (CLV)

What is a customer actually worth?
A credit card customer costs €102 in the first year and returns €520 profit after five years. Recruitment of a newspaper subscriber costs between €100 and €250, but the potential lifetime value is approximately €4,000. Car manufacturer Nissan has calculated that an average buyer spends about $250,000 on cars in their life. Nissan also discovered that if a customer is satisfied driving a Nissan, they will probably bring in five additional customers. For a single customer, this results in a total turnover of 1.5 million dollars and that doesn't yet include the turnover of the five customers that bring in new customers also. Therefore, the amount of 1.5 million dollars potentially costs the same as the loss of a single customer. So, the question arises: how much should be invested in that single customer?

Source: CRM in de praktijk, *Van Leeuwen, 2015*

10

The customer value can be influenced by the organisation. On the basis of customer knowledge, targeted promotional offers can be made for other or more expensive products (cross-selling, up-selling and deep-selling). This increases the customer revenue.

Cross-selling is selling other products or services to existing customers than they have already purchased, while deep-selling aims to increase sales with existing customers, for example by offering premiums or incentives. In this case the promotional offer is aimed at a product or service that was already purchased by these customers. Up-selling is a form of deep selling in which is attempted to sell a more expensive version of the product.

Cross-selling
Deep-selling

Up-selling

For their own benefit, companies can also aim for greater customer loyalty so that customers limit their spending at competitors. This achieves a higher 'customer share' (share of wallet). For example, research shows that an average of 5% to 30% of a company's customers are not at the highest level of possible turnover. Therefore, companies can still gain a lot of customer share at the expense of competitors. We define customer share as follows:

Customer share

> Customer share (share of wallet) is the percentage of total spending in a given product category at a certain company and not at its competitors.

We will clarify this definition in example 10.3.

EXAMPLE 10.3

Customer share

Suppose a customer spends $200 on their weekly shopping. Once a week they go online to do their big weekly shopping at grocery.walmart.com for $160. Aside from this, a couple times a week the same customer goes out to the neighbourhood store to do a small shop for some missing items for a total of $40. In this example, the customer share of Walmart is 80% (160/200) and that of the neighbourhood store equals 20% (40/200). Based on the number of repeat purchases, the customer seems most loyal to the neighbourhood store, but the online store grocery.walmart.com still has a larger customer share.

Order fresh groceries online at Wallmart Grocery

Customer value formula

In order to calculate the customer value (CV), this simple customer value formula is often used (Harvard Business School, 2000):

$$CV = ((T \times N \times P) - C)$$

© Noordhoff Uitgevers bv

in which:

T = the estimated number of transactions during the entire relationship
N = the number of purchases per transaction
P = the average price per purchase
C = customer acquisition costs

For digital marketers, it is relevant to compare the customer value that is generated via the various online and offline channels.

There are different methods for calculating customer value. You have already been able to read about the concept of customer lifetime value in section 4.1. The definition for the customer lifetime value calculation is as follows:

> Customer lifetime value is the net present value of the expected flow of future net costumer contributions to the company's operating profit.

If you add up all the customer lifetime values of every customer of an organisation, this results in the customer equity.

Customer equity

The simple transaction-oriented customer value calculation by Harvard Business School (2000) does not take into account the time value of money and part of the costs of the customer. This makes the calculation inaccurate. That is why organisations nowadays often use a more complicated formula for the customer lifetime value (CLV). In this formula, the CLV is calculated on the basis of the average turnover of a customer per given period (N × P), the average cost of that customer per period (AC), the retention probability (r) and a discount rate (d). By using a discount rate, you bring future cash flows back to the present or, to state it more simply, you decide how much the money that you will be paid by a customer in a later stage is worth to the organisation now. For example, the discount rate takes inflation into account. The margin per period m is the turnover minus the costs per period (N × P - AC). The formula for the CLV is:

CLV

$$CLV = \sum_{t=0}^{T} m \frac{r^t}{(1 + d)^t}$$

In words: the CLV equals the sum of the periodic margins multiplied by the retention probability divided by 1 + the discount rate. The small t represents a period (one year for example). For each period, a customer value is calculated, and all those periods together add up to the CLV. By raising the retention probability to the power of t, you take into account that a relationship with a customer does not last forever. For digital CRM it is relevant to compare the CLV of different customer segments. For example, do customers who buy from the web shop, have a different average CLV than customers who buy from the app? And how does that compare to the physical store? On the basis of their profile or behaviour, are you able to distinguish customers with a high CLV from other segments? If so, what digital CRM activities can you use to further increase the customer value? And at the end of a period you can check whether the CLV actually increased for that customer segment.

EXAMPLE 10.4

EasyJet tells a personalized story

For its 20th anniversary, budget airline easyJet ran a campaign which was highly creative and innovative in the way it used personalisation. EasyJet used dynamic content, links, and images to tell a personal and unique story for each easyJet customer. Each customer received a personalised email that highlighted everywhere they had travelled with easyJet in the past 20 years.

Even more personalisation by easyJet: your photo on its 20th birthday plane

Source: Campaignlive.co.uk, 2017

Digital marketers look at the current and potential customer value. The current customer value is calculated on the basis of the customer's current purchasing behaviour. The current customer value indicates how much the customer is currently worth if their current purchasing behaviour continues.

In addition, ways of positively influencing the individual customer value by performing certain activities are examined. In that case, you can determine how much the customer is worth if their purchasing behaviour develops optimally. Based on this, the potential customer value is calculated. Based on the current and potential customer value, the digital marketer can determine whether a customer is attractive to retain, whether there is a need for further development, or whether the customer is (and remains) loss-generating and that the relationship should be phased out.

In his book *How Brands Grow*, published in 2010, Byron Sharp illustrates how usually only a small part of the customer base consists of 'heavy buyers' and therefore have little impact in terms of turnover. Therefore, merely focussing on this segment is not a wise thing to do. In addition, Sharp explains that there is more success to be achieved by continuously persuading much larger 'light buyer' segments to buy your product.

When attracting new customers, organisations especially target potential customers who are very similar to the profile of 'best customer'. Potential customers who match the loss-generating profile 'bad customer', are preferably not targeted.

On an aggregated level, the total customer lifetime value indicates the company's current value, given the expected future revenues. The potential value of the customer database portrays the company's growth potential. The success of digital CRM is mainly determined by the extent to which a company can exploit these growth opportunities.

10.1.4 Stimulating customer satisfaction and loyalty

The essence of digital CRM is generating more profitable customers by achieving satisfaction and loyalty. Loyalty is a complex concept because many factors are involved and they all influence each other to a greater or lesser extent. These relationships are depicted in figure 10.2.

Loyalty

FIGURE 10.2 Stimulating customer loyalty

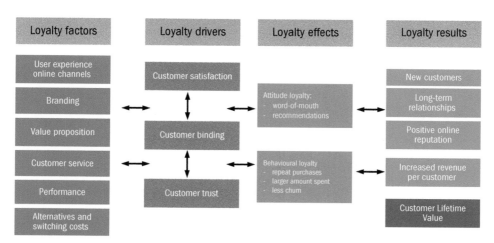

Source: based on Van Leeuwen, 2015

Some important concepts lined up:
- Customer satisfaction: this is the extent to which the online provider has met the customer's expectations or the extent to which the online provider's solution to problems and complaints has met the customer's expectations. In customer satisfaction, the main focus is on past experiences.
- Customer bonding: this is the extent to which a customer feels an emotional and psychological connection with an online provider (emotional bonding) and / or the extent to which a customer wants to continue the relationship in the belief that they will benefit more by retaining the relationship than by ending it(rational bonding).

Customer satisfaction

Customer bonding

Emotional bonding

Rational bonding

10

Customer trust
- Customer trust: this is the extent to which a customer is confident that (also) in future, an online provider will stick to their agreements and promises and will act in the customer's best interest. It is the confidence that the online provider will act reliably, transparently and with integrity, also with regard to the protection and use of customer data (privacy and security). In customer confidence, the focus is on expectations regarding the future.

Customer loyalty
- Customer loyalty: this is the extent to which a customer, in terms of attitude (*attitudinal loyalty*) and / or behaviour (*behavioural loyalty*) remains loyal to an online provider, even if there are other, better or cheaper alternatives.

In general terms, the following factors influence customer satisfaction, customer bonding, customer confidence and customer loyalty:

User experience
- User experience for online channels: think of aspects such as speed, design, usability, personalised websites, content, search options, shopping opportunities, choice of language, privacy and security and technical stability. You can read more about this in Chapter 11.

Branding
- Branding: this concerns building brand recognition and a positive image, creating customer engagement, setting up online communities and social media activities for building a good brand reputation. You were able to read more about this in Chapters 5, 6 and 7. Online communities are covered in section 10.5.

Value proposition
- Value proposition (*value proposition*): this concerns the quality of the offer in a general sense, a good price-quality ratio, the composition of the product range, selection of choices, customised products, guarantees and so on. This also applies to the degree of personalisation of the offer via, for example, online advertising, email and in the online sales channel itself.

Customer service
- Customer service: this refers to being easily accessible via online channels, but also offline if necessary, responding quickly and accurately to questions and complaints, self-service options and multiple payment and delivery options. You were able to read more about this in Chapters 8 and 9.

Achievements
- Achievements: this concerns the previous achievements by the online provider and the extent to which promises are fulfilled. Think of accurate and timely delivery (fulfilment) and the correct handling of payments, questions and complaints.

Switch costs
- Alternatives and switch costs: this is the ease with which a customer can switch to another provider. The less alternatives there are or the higher the costs related to switching, the greater the chance that the customer remains loyal to their online provider.

Online retailer ASOS is proud of its Price Promise: If a customer finds a branded (non-ASOS) item cheaper on another site, ASOS will match that price. Here ASOS reinforces its value proposition, offers customer service and cements loyalty with this single policy.

Home > Customer Care> How does the ASOS Price Promise policy work?

🔍 Search help

HOW DOES THE ASOS PRICE PROMISE POLICY WORK?

Last updated 11/01/2018 02.52 PM

Contact us to let us know which item you've seen selling for less, and which site it is on.

Select the 'Price Promise – I've seen a branded item cheaper on another website' category in the 'Subject of your query' field. Tell us as much about the item as you can and the price you saw it at.

Once we've checked it out, we'll send you a discount/promo code for the difference. You can then buy the item you want from ASOS at the lower price.

If you've already bought your item from ASOS and then seen it cheaper on another website, just let us know within 28 days and we'll send you a discount/promo code for the difference. You'll be able to use this on your next ASOS purchase.

RELATED QUESTIONS

Can you tell me more about your Price Promise policy?

Can I get a refund if the price has changed since I ordered it?

Can I use more than one promo code on my order?

DID THIS ANSWER YOUR QUESTION?

☹️ 🙁 😐 🙂 😀

The ASOS price promise

Online providers can influence customers' sense of attachment (customer bonding) on three levels:

- The first level is the creation of a financial bond. This comes about because customers have a financial advantage by being a customer. Think of price discounts and rewards using, for example, loyalty programs.
- The second level is the creation of a social bond. This is a form of emotional bonding that has to do with how the organisation and its brands communicate with customers. Online communities and fan programs are increasingly being used for this purpose. Companies such as Apple, Nike, Heineken and Ducati (see example 10.5) are very successful in this.
- The third level is the structural bond. This is a form of bonding that directly has to do with the delivery of products and services. Tools for this are subscriptions, contracts, customised products or tedious or expensive switching procedures. For example, Amazon has the Prime subscription, which entitles you to free shipping (with a purchase threshold) and services such as video-on-demand. Subscribers to this service order more than non-subscribers.

In order to establish customer loyalty, there must be a win-win situation for the company and the customer. If one of the parties sees insufficient advantage to be gained from a close relationship, sustainable customer loyalty will be difficult to achieve.

Customer bonding

Financial bond

Social bond
Emotional bonding

Structural bond

10

EXAMPLE 10.5

Join the Ducati fan club

Ducati is a classic motorbike brand. The company was founded in 1926 by Antonio Cavalieri Ducati and his three sons, Adriano, Marcello, and Bruno.

Ducati riders are fans who ride a Ducati in their free time and keep themselves busy maintaining and personalising their bike. Ducati drivers were already able to vote via web polls for prototypes that then had to be produced and were then able to provide feedback for further product development. You can also join one of the eighty worldwide Ducati fan clubs. Recently, Ducati fans have been working in virtual teams with professional designers and product managers from the manufacturer.

Together, they are defining the characteristics and technical features of the 'new engine'. Motorcyclists post more than 150 messages a day on Ducati forums and chats. Popular are the discussions about 'motor experience'. Community managers for Ducati actively participate in the discussion via websites, online magazines and niche portals for motorcyclists. They also try to identify 'influentials' that are able to sway the choice behaviour of motorcyclists. Ducati calls its new business model 'virtual community management' and 'customer collaboration management'.

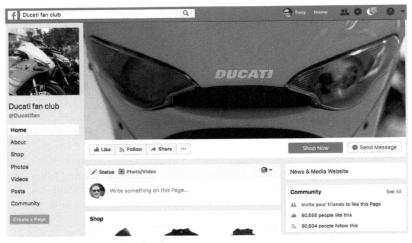

Ducati fan club also on Facebook

Source: Customer in the driver's seat, *Van Leeuwen, 2012*

Loyalty programs

Companies often use loyalty programs to strengthen customer loyalty. Examples are programs such as Singapore Airlines Krisflyer Programme and their Krisflyer miles, the previously described Genius discount from Booking.com or (see example 10.6). Starbucks reward program Most loyalty programs generally have a positive effect on loyalty, especially in terms of repeat purchases and / or customer retention (relationship expansion). Loyalty programs where customers are immediately rewarded for their purchase are the most effective. These are, for example, the so-called direct benefit and savings programs.

Programs that do not have a direct relationship with the purchase, such as competition and event programs, turn out to be a lot less effective. Customers prefer to get straight to the point. Loyalty programs are not always successful because they sometimes cost more than they bring in and because companies cannot easily end them.

EXAMPLE 10.6

My Starbucks Rewards

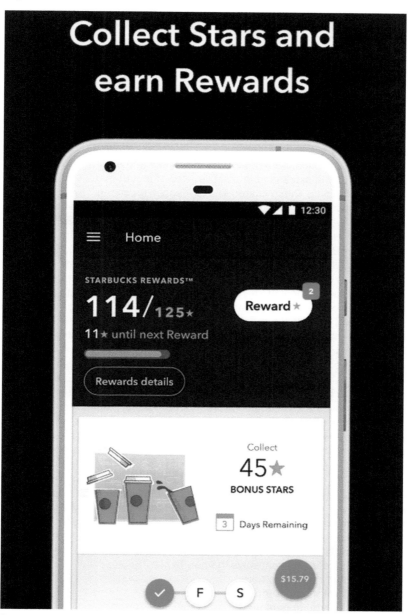

Collect stars to earn rewards with the Starbucks reward program

My Starbucks Rewards is a simple loyalty program to reward customers every time they purchase any food or drink at a Starbucks outlet, or via the mobile app.

For each purchase, customers earn a Star. These stars add up to earn them exclusive Starbucks rewards, eg free drinks. The more stars they collect, the more rewards they earn.

To join, customers just set up an account using their Starbucks card. They can track how many Stars they have collected on Starbucks website or mobile app. When a customer collects enough stars to earn a reward, they are sent an email.

- free drinks
- special offers on customer's favourite items
- exclusive early access to new products
- quick and easy payment with our mobile app

Source: Starbucks.com, 2017

Customer loyalty

Attitude loyalty

Customer reviews

Customer satisfaction, customer bonding and customer trust ultimately lead to customer loyalty. Loyalty can express itself in two ways, both of which increase sales, namely via attitude loyalty and behavioural loyalty. Attitude loyalty is expressed in positive word-of-mouth and recommendations. These customer experiences (customer reviews) are becoming increasingly important, social media is full of it, websites such as TripAdvisor and restaurant review sites use them and even Google displays an organisations' ratings by clients in the search results. Research by Purnawirawan, De Pelsmacker and Dens (2012) shows that people strongly value the opinion of the majority. A single deviating opinion isn't given very much gravitas, even if it is the opinion of an expert. Moreover, it appears that an adequate response from management (consisting of at least an apology and an explanation) to negative comments, lead to positive reactions and word-of-mouth from those who read the review.

Companies that respond to this in a clever way, can create veritable ambassadors who provide positive word-of-mouth advertising. Think of promoting the use of the 'like button' on Facebook or LinkedIn. Negative assessments can be corrected, and criticism can be used to improve products and services. Why do expensive market research if customers let us know what their wishes and expectations are for free? Holidaywatchdog.com is a website that is entirely based on user-generated content (UGC) in the form of customer reviews. On this review site, a few million holidaymakers have reviewed their vacations. These reviews have a large influence on the future choices of holidaymakers.

Behavioural loyalty

Churn

Behavioural loyalty can be expressed in two ways. On the one hand, customers can make a larger amount as well as more frequent purchases (repeat purchases, higher average amount spent). On the other, customers can decide not to leave, so there is less departure of customers churn. Attitude loyalty and behavioural loyalty together, can influence the customer value in different ways, namely by:

- accretion of new customers
- extension of the duration of the relationship
- a higher customer revenue

The right 'customer experience' plays an increasingly important role when it comes to cultivating loyalty.

Would you recommend our company to others?

A prevalent way of measuring customer loyalty is the Net Promoter Score (NPS). The NPS method is based on asking one central question to customers: 'How likely is it (on a scale of 0 to 10) that you would recommend our company to a friend or colleague'? The NPS method distinguishes three groups of respondents: 'Promoters' (9-10), 'Passive satisfaction' (7-8) and 'Detractors' (0-6). The Detractor's score is then subtracted from the Promoter's. The result is the NPS, a score that gives an indication of the level customer loyalty of a company (Reichheld, 2011).

Net Promoter Score (NPS)

The goal is therefore to create as many Promoters and as few Detractors as possible. An important point of criticism of the NPS is that this KPI only measures the intended behaviour (Would you recommend us?) And not the actual behaviour (Did the customer indeed make a recommendation? And will they actually remain a customer themselves?). Moreover, it proves difficult to demonstrate a direct relationship between NPS and turnover. Of course, focussing on customer satisfaction and loyalty, remains in itself a good way of ensuring growth.

AO.com (formerly Appliances Online) is an online retailer specialising in electrical goods. AO.com has a Net Promoter Score (NPS) of 80 (npsbenchmark.com, 2018). The NPS is a primary indication of customer satisfaction. Customers who would recommend AO.com are usually customers who will re-order. Especially those people who give a company a 9 or 10 are the ones who enable growth.

Loyalty can also be accomplished by paying customers more attention and involving them in product development with, for example, co-creation, crowdsourcing and user generated content (see section 4.2). As a result, trust and satisfaction are automatically increased. Starbucks' crowdsourcing platform MyStarbucksIdea.com is very successful (see picture). In the first year, customers had already contributed more than 70,000 ideas and points for improvement. Ranging from new coffee flavours to suggestions for new store locations. Consumers can vote on these ideas, and the proposals with the most votes are taken on by Starbucks. However, it is important to remember that true loyalty is not created from one day to the next but is built up over a longer period.

10

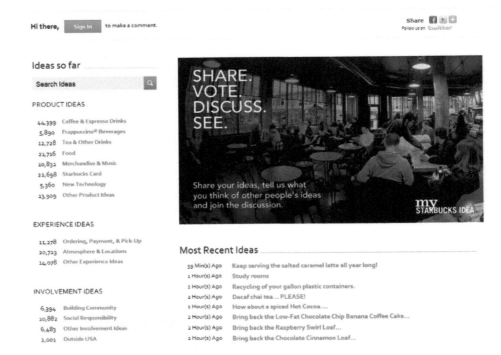

Crowdsourcing among customers of Starbucks

10.2 Working with customer groups

Although there are an increasing number of opportunities for approaching clients individually and in a personalised way, working with customer groups is still an important part of CRM. In this way, organisations can approach customers in a targeted manner and thus receive a greater profit from their digital marketing efforts.

Customer groups

Customer groups arise by first looking for differences (differentiation) and only then bringing the customers that are alike together (segment). Customers can be segmented from four angles:

1 the value they represent to the organisation (customer value)
2 the wishes, needs, interests and preferences they want to see fulfilled (customer needs)
3 the extent to which they are willing to enter into a long-term relationship with the organisation (willingness to form a relationship)
4 a combination of these three: customer value, customer needs and/or willingness to form a relationship

From target segment to customer group

You will undoubtedly live in the same postal code area as your neighbour and you most likely also belong to the same income class, but ... do you also have the same wishes and needs as your neighbour and do you also represent the same (current and potential) value for the company?

Source: CRM in de praktijk, *Van Leeuwen, 2015*

A customer profile is created for each customer group. This is also called *customer profiling*. A customer profile describes the characteristics that a customer must have in order to belong to a particular customer group. Depending on what customer group the customer belongs to (and the customer profile that they fit into), the organisation will adapt their approach accordingly.

These customer groups can be further divided into sub-groups based on, for example, internet use (goals), media use (online, offline) and shopping behaviour (channels). Chapter 3 contains more about the market sensing process.

Customer profile

Customer profiling

To make customer groups workable, the concept of the customer *persona* has been defined. A customer persona is no more than 'an archetype of a user'. In other words: a customer persona gives a customer group a 'face' and thus acts as 'gauge'. In practice, a customer group can be divided into three to eight concrete customer personas that are characteristic of the relevant customer group. Various data is collected for determining and describing customer personas, for example regarding personal wishes, needs and preferences, media and consumer behaviour, lifestyle, network and relationships, health, and so on. The use of customer personas provides the opportunity to more accurately describe the behaviour of groups of customers, to understand them better and to be able to respond to them more effectively in, for example, communication and the development of products, services or extra service.

Customer persona

Many organisations already know who their target audiences (or segments) are. Such a target segment forms the basis of a persona, supplemented with further customer information from existing systems. This basic persona can then be further expanded by the relevant people in the organisation. Insofar as possible, this is done on the basis of data analysis, supplemented with knowledge that employees have of markets, customers and products. The persona can then be further developed using deeper customer research. This can be done with surveys, panel discussions or interviews. Naturally, online customer behaviour will be discussed in depth. As a final step, the persona really acquires a personality: a name, age, family situation, job, hobbies and so on. You then use this persona to develop new products. The persona makes it easier to empathise with your customers and figure out how to solve a problem for this specific user using online marketing.

Of course, personas are also very useful in the development of the online tools, such as websites and apps. The input for the target segments can

10

be derived from web analytics and user research. For example, on a website for coffee machines you were able to define two personas: Gerald and Rose. Gerald likes to find out all of a machine's specifications in order to compare it with other machines. Rose, on the other hand, finds it important that the coffee machine has designer appeal and matches her interior. On your website, you would like to sell to both customer groups, and therefore have to ensure that both their needs are met.

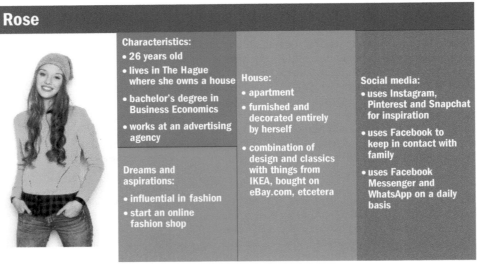

Rose

Characteristics:
- 26 years old
- lives in The Hague where she owns a house
- bachelor's degree in Business Economics
- works at an advertising agency

Dreams and aspirations:
- influential in fashion
- start an online fashion shop

House:
- apartment
- furnished and decorated entirely by herself
- combination of design and classics with things from IKEA, bought on eBay.com, etcetera

Social media:
- uses Instagram, Pinterest and Snapchat for inspiration
- uses Facebook to keep in contact with family
- uses Facebook Messenger and WhatsApp on a daily basis

Customer Persona Rose

The use of personas can be very successful for approaching your client in a more focused manner. Subsequently, it is important to understand what your customer needs your product for, or better yet, what problem it needs to solve. This approach is also described as 'Job To Be Done' (JTBD). Clayton Christensen describes it in his book *Competing Against Luck* (2016) as follows: 'We hire products to do jobs for us. His theory comes down to the fact that customers are looking for solutions to certain 'jobs'. Their circumstances, or the context the customer finds themselves in, determine their choice.

For organisations, this means that the same customer, depending on their situation, can have different needs. For example, a visitor on a travel site may be known as someone who takes an expensive family holiday twice a year. Offers and advice can be tailored accordingly. However, if this same person is now responsible for organising a bachelor weekend with ten friends, different rules apply. For example, a lower budget, different location or distance to the entertainment in the town centre. It is important to be able to respond to this in the customer journey.

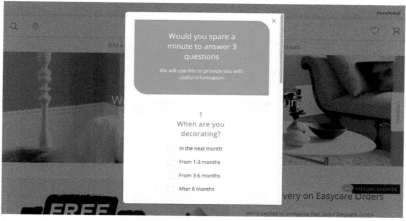

A brand like Dulux asks customers who are registering on their website, whether they are about to carry out a paint job and what kind of job it is. On the basis of this information, the customer receives pointers and advice via email regarding starting and finishing the job successfully

Four levels of adaptation of digital marketing communications

When you develop digital marketing communications, you have to determine in advance to what extent you want to tailor them to the devices your customer uses and to the customer group to which they belong. For example, for websites, emails and advertisements there are four options, which are illustrated in table 10.2.

TABLE 10.2 Overview of possibilities for increasing customer value

Static content and layout	The layout and content remain the same, regardless of the customer group and the equipment used.
Responsive design	The layout of the advertisement adapts to the device that the customer uses, but the content remains the same.
Adaptive content	The content of the expression adapts to the circumstances: the target segment, the behaviour of the person or the situation in which they find themselves. This content can be presented within an expression with responsive design.
Dynamic contextual personalisation	Both the content of the advertisement as well as the layout are fully tailored to the customer's goals and the devices they use.

Adaptive content

Dynamic contextual personalisation

10

If customer segmentation is carried out to the maximum, each customer group would consist of exactly one customer. After all, every customer is unique in their wishes, needs and current and potential value for the company. We have now reached the much debated 'one-to-one approach', where all marketing, sales, production and service processes are geared to the wishes and needs of that individual customer. This is the purest form of CRM as Peppers and Rogers (1993) described in their classic *The One To One Future*. See example 10.7 South by Southwest on their one-to-one approach.

One-to-one approach

EXAMPLE 10.7

South by Southwest Interactive

SXSW is an annual event in Austin, Texas which brings together the latest innovations in new technology, the independent music scene, and movies. It started as a meet-up of just 700 creatives in Texas and is now a global event. Today, over 400,000 people attend SXSW every year, and email marketing a key tool for the event's marketing team.

SXSW has an extensive database of customers (subscribers) many of whom have attended in previous years. But how do they structure and implement a CRM program to send the right customer the right message at the right time? The objective of course, is engage visitors and exhibitors to drive attendance; this is an annual challenge.

Using segmentation, SXSW can target subscribers with the most relevant information according to the previous behaviour. Suppose a subscriber only wants information about the SXSW Music, Film & Interactive event, then they will only get emails about that particular conference/festival. There are multiple opportunities for users to indicate exactly what they want and opt out of content they're not interested in.

SXSW deliberately spaces out the emails to make sure they do not bombard their subscribers When people sign up, they get a stream of relevant content which they have effectively agreed to receive (permission marketing). Segmentation has resulted in greatly improved open rates, a higher click-through rates, and many more shares. Adopting this strategy, SXSW has reported a 140% growth in subscribers.

Clearly the campaign is working and uses are sharing it with their friends.

Source: Campaign Monitor, 2015

For many companies, a true one-to-one approach for all customers is not realistic. The enormous investments in employees, knowledge, systems and databases required in order to do so would never yield the desired return. For most companies, a customer group approach is therefore the best approach from a business economics point of view. The trick here is to give every customer the idea that he or she is the middle point of the organisation. As a result of aiming their approach at individual customers or customer groups, the number of marketing campaigns that companies are involved in is increasing explosively. From a handful mass marketing campaigns per year, companies are now carrying out dozens if not hundreds of customer group-oriented marketing campaigns. This requires excellent campaign management.

10.3 Increasing customer value

Another important part of CRM is the targeted increase of the customer value of individual customers. Improvements in customer growth (new customers), profit per customer and customer retention can result in a spectacular increase in a company's turnover and profits (see figure 10.3).

FIGURE 10.3 Value optimisation model of digital CRM

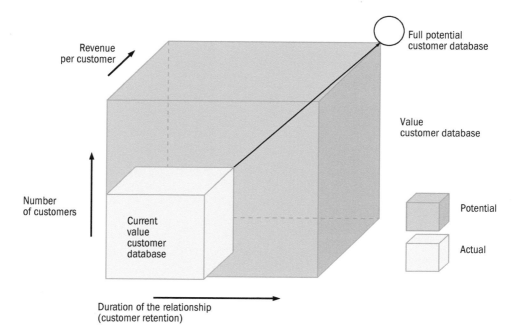

Important questions in this regard are:
- How many new customers does the company attract? What is there to gain when the amount of new (profitable) customers increases?
- How much of their budget do customers spend on the company and how much on competitors? What is there to gain if customers would spend a larger part of their budget with the company?
- How long on average do customers stay with the company? What is there to gain if customers stay with the company for longer?

The possibilities for lowering customer costs at an individual customer level and increasing customer revenues are countless. An overview of options for increasing customer value at an individual customer level is included in table 10.3.

10

TABLE 10.3 Overview of possibilities for increasing customer value

Increase customer value by ...	Example
Increasing customer revenue	
• cross-selling: stimulating the customer to purchase other products and/or services	• selling insurance in addition to booking a holiday
• deep selling: increasing the purchase of more products or services from the selection	• not only sell clothing and shoes in your web shop, but also bicycles and travel bags
• upselling: encouraging the customer to purchase a more expensive version of the product	• selling a more expensive 'special edition PC' instead of an ordinary standard version
Increasing customer growth	
• references: encouraging customers to recruit other customers	• member-get-member offers in online bookstores, sharing and promotion via social media
• word-of-mouth advertising: encouraging customers to make recommendations	• customer reviews, tell-a-friend options and the use of the like button
• social shopping: encouraging customers to involve others in the purchase	• social shopping at Etsy.com and social group purchasing at Groupdeal.nl
• win-back actions: reacquiring customers who have left	• approaching former customers with an offer to come back, for example used by energy companies
Increasing customer retention	
• customised products and services	• customised cars, clothing and bicycles
• increased customer engagement	• co-creation and crowdsourcing like LEGO
• retention and loyalty programs	• British Airways Avios, Genius discount from Booking.com, My Starbucks Rewards
• outstanding service	• Zappos' 365-day exchange guarantee
• customer-friendly 'lock-in' situations	• subscriptions, contracts spanning multiple years
Increasing customer yield	
• reduce amount of 'loss-inducing' customers	• implement price increases or let customers go
Decreasing customer costs	
• lower acquisition costs by engaging customers	• member-get-member programs at online bookstores
• lower promotion costs by engaging customers	• customer reviews, tell-a-friend options and the use of the like button
• lower communication costs by applying a targeted approach to customer groups	• 'event-driven communication' aimed at specific groups of customers
• lower transaction costs by shifting activities to the customer	• self-service, for example at petrol stations or internet banking
• lower quality costs by automating business processes	• automated ordering procedures with 'ingrained' checks
• lower operating costs by more efficient use of products and resources	• website with 'frequently asked questions' and virtual service (chatbot)
• lower service costs by using tools and engaging customers (crowd)	• webcare/social care teams (social media search) and user communities that answer questions from customers about products
• reducing price sensitivity	• bolster customer loyalty with loyalty programs

The following possibilities for increasing customer value are explained below:
1 cross-selling, up-selling and deep-selling
2 social shopping and social group buying
3 event driven marketing

1 Cross-selling, up-selling and deep-selling
Cross-selling, up-selling and deep-selling are all about selling a greater amount of more expensive products. Tour operators, airlines and fashion stores are increasingly displaying combinations of products in their online stores, this results in customers simultaneously buying insurance, a car or a jacket in addition to booking a hotel, flight or buying a pair of trousers.

© Noordhoff Uitgevers bv

Companies such as Dell and American Express are masters at getting online shoppers to purchase a more expensive version of the product, in combination with all kinds of other products that they had not originally intended to buy. Web shops such as Amazon and bol.com use many instruments such as 'recently visited', 'lovers of this article also ordered', 'more related articles' and 'best rated' to entice customers. Online music service Spotify applies a smart up-selling strategy by offering a family plan. This not only tries to sell the customer a subscription, but also their family. In the travel industry, 'dynamic packaging' is being applied with increasing frequency. Expedia.com offers customers a seamless combination of flight, hotel, car and travel insurance. Tailored to the wishes of the customer regarding departure date, destination and number of people. All the results that the customer sees are available and can be booked directly as a 'package'. An effective way to significantly increase the amount of sales Personal shopper site Stylelyrical.com invites women to sign up for a personalised service. Customers fill out their Style Profile and then consult with their stylist on the phone to discuss their needs and preferences. Finally, the selected wardrobe items are delivered straight to the customer's door. This service is targeted at busy professional women who may have money to spend but are 'time poor'.

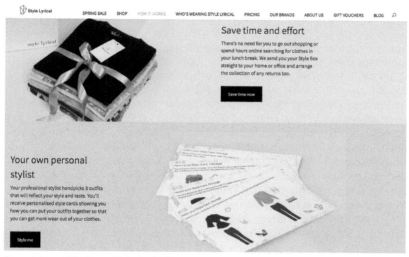

Complete outfits from Style Lyrical

2 Social shopping and social group buying
Another development is 'social shopping' where customers can have people from their social network such as Facebook and Twitter look on and advise them whilst buying products online. Users can create a profile on social shopping sites and display their favourite products. An example is Etsy, a platform where people from all over the world can make contact for the purpose of buying and selling products. This mainly concerns artwork and handicrafts, such as clothing and art, but also homemade chocolate bars, cakes and the like. You can indicate what your favourite products are, and if others like what you have chosen, they can then follow you.

Social shopping

Social shopping lends itself well to products such as fashion, travel, furniture and electronics. Other well-known social shopping sites are Wanelo.com (Want, need, love) and ModCloth (modcloth.com).

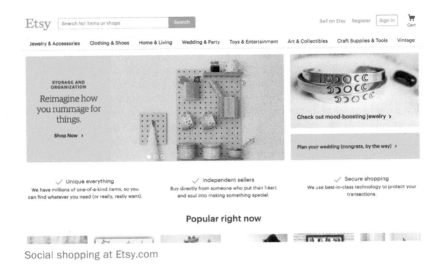

Social shopping at Etsy.com

Social group buying

Another form of social shopping is 'social group buying' via online providers such as LivingSocial and Groupon.com. The formula is simple. Every day there is an exclusive deal with a very high discount on offer. This could be anything such as products, food, drinks, activities, day trips, wellness or shopping. Every deal is only on offer temporarily, so people have to sign up quickly. The deal will only continue if there are enough buyers. That is why participants are encouraged to get friends, family and acquaintances interested in this deal through social media such as Facebook and Twitter. By closing time, of there are enough applicants, the deal will be final, and the participants will be charged. Participants will receive a voucher by email that remains valid for a certain amount of time. Social group buying is an effective way for local businesses to be able to offer their products to large groups of customers without risk. There are countless advantages. Their customer base increases, more traffic is generated to the store or website and sales are upped. The only drawback is that the participating companies have to give very large discounts on their products that benefit the operator and the consumer.

10

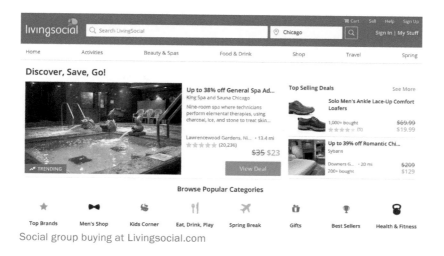

Social group buying at Livingsocial.com

3 Event-driven marketing

The question is at which moments and at what events your offer is most relevant to your customers. This is also called 'event-driven marketing'. This is a marketing method based on identifying changes in the situation or needs of customers, and responding to them with predefined marketing campaigns as soon as these changes occur. Examples include events such as moving house, marriage, birthday, birth of children, first job or retirement, but also things like holidays, seasonal changes, staff expansion, company expansion, periodic maintenance, inspections or the expiration of a subscription, contract or guarantee. In short, these kinds of events are all related to:

- changes in the personal situation of the customer (consumer or company)
- changes related to the purchased product (product lifecycle)
- general social and national, regional or local events

Event-driven marketing

For example, many companies use their customers' birthday to bring their brand to the customers' attention again. By improving the timing of the offer, it becomes more relevant to the customer. This increases the response to marketing campaigns by 10% to 20% in comparison to the traditional approach.

The better the timing, the more relevant your message and the more chance of success. For example, DIY stores have discovered that people do the most work on a new house in the first three months after moving in. It is precisely during this period that you become relevant as a construction market, removals company, contractor, painter, kitchen and bathroom supplier, furniture store and garden company. To this end, these types of companies purchase address changes from specialist providers. They are subsequently able to make an appropriate offer to the new residents at the correct time. Using a discount voucher or special offer, they try to attract these potential customers to their businesses.

With the help of customer data analyses, you can anticipate these types of events sooner. People who suddenly do a series of searches on new kitchens, household items and curtains appear to have bought a house

10

The restaurant Red Lobster gives you a discount by email when it's your birthday

and want to move in. clearly companies selling products would wish to approach these people. In this way you are able to pinpoint people who are planning to move house, become parents, get a new job, start up a new business or buy a new car and so on in the near future. Using the 'clues' that people leave on the Internet, you can predict what drives someone and what they are planning to do. The question is, at which moments and at what events your offer is most relevant to your customers. Note however data protection issues are relevant here (including GDPR within Europe).

During the application of all these variables, it is necessary to find the right balance. For example, a marketing campaign aimed at retaining customers for longer periods of time, can lead to an increase in customer costs.
On the other hand, aggressive cross-selling actions could lead to shortening of the duration of the relationship because customers might not appreciate such an approach. At the customer (group) level, an optimal combination of coordinated measures must therefore be put together.

10.4 Individual value propositions

CRM means responding to customers' individual wishes and needs. An important question that arises with the introduction of CRM is therefore the extent to which a company is able to provide tailor-made solutions. In practice, two main forms of customisation are recognised: mass customisation (*mass* customisation) and individual customisation (*mass individualisation*).

Mass customisation

For mass customisation, a company chooses its customers from an X number of product variations based on the use of standard components (mass customisation). In addition, 'true customisation' goes even further. Customers can choose from an unlimited number of product variations (mass individualisation). Delivering truly customised work, is a bridge too far for most companies. The production capacity needed for such a thing is simply not in place, or the economic benefits in terms of scalability and efficiency are simply not enough for them to be able to produce such highly customised products at an affordable price.

Mass individualisation

As a result of new developments such as the Internet, customer intelligence, social media, mobile telephony and fast and wireless data communication connections, new types of mass customisation have become possible, such as:
- personalisation
- behavioural targeting
- location-based services (LBS)
- product configuration
- community-based creation

We will now discuss these types in further detail.

10.4.1   Personalisation

There are roughly two varieties of personalisation, namely the personalisation of websites and apps and the personalisation of products and services.

Personalisation

Personalisation of websites and apps

When personalising websites and apps, users are offered information that is tailored to them. The best-known personalisation techniques are rule based (based on a set of fixed rules), content based (based on the history of the user's interests) and Collaborative filtering (based on the preferences of many different users) where information from other users with a similar interest profile is provided ('buyers of this book also bought'). Online retailer Amazon was the first ecommerce site that applied personalisation on a large scale. Every visitor sees a website where products, offers and advertising messages are tailored to their personal profile. This is also increasingly being done via personal pages. The Amazon.com homepage is an example; once the user has logged in, they will see a personalised display based on previous browsing behaviour and products purchased.

Rule based personalisation

Content based personalisation

Collaborative filtering

Personalisation of products and services

Another form is the personalisation of products and services. At mymuesli.com, consumers can create their own muesli and Barclays Bank allows customers to personalise the debit card with the favourite image – see picture. With the help of these kinds of personalisation techniques,

10

customers are offered a unique product. Customers are more than happy to pay for it!

Personalisation at Barclays Bank

10.4.2 Behavioural targeting

Geo-targeting
Profile targeting
Behavioural targeting

There are roughly three kinds of targeting that are often used in combination with one another. Based on geographical origin (geo-targeting via IP address or mobile), based on a customer profile (profile targeting) or based on click behaviour (behavioural targeting). A form of geo-targeting is applied by Walmart, a big spender on online display and targets using various information derived from users' location and previous online behaviour.

Indeed, Behavioural targeting goes even further. The focus is on the click behaviour in combination with other data such as the location and the

Geo-targeting by Gourmet Burger Kitchen. The discount offered depends on the customer's location.

© Noordhoff Uitgevers bv

customer profile. Websites and pages that are visited, time, length and frequency of visits are all analysed. This behaviour is combined with other data such as gender, age, place of residence and purchased products. Based on these analyses, images, text, sound, news, offers and / or advertisements are displayed that are fully tailored to the individual website visitor. The Vodafone homepage contains a number of special offers or texts that vary depending on the profile of the visits. If the visitor has already been recognised (for example by logging into the 'My environment') an advertisement for the use of the Vodafone app will be shown upon return. An unrecognised customer (read: potential prospect) will be told the benefits of a subscription.

By applying behavioural targeting, customers experience a more personal and improved service with higher click-through ratios as a result. Software for behavioural targeting is self-learning, meaning that it continuously responds to changes in areas of interest and the online behaviour that is shown.

10.4.3 Location based services

Location based services are used to tailor the service to the specific location of the customer. A central role in this is the continuous determination of the consumer's location using GPS chips (such as with TomTom) or the GSM network (Global System for Mobile communications, the nearest signalling mast).

Location based services

Starbucks App with location-based services

10

Location based services

Location based services are used for; tracking and tracing (people, vehicles and possessions), paying for something (per location and per event), the delivery of information (lifestyle, Yellow Pages, traffic, route, object- and location information), safety purposes (police, ambulance, roadside assistance and security), marketing (advertising and special offers), entertainment (games and lotteries) and social networks (where are my friends and what are they doing?).

For example, Clothing store American Eagle sends Foursquare users the message: 'Check in at one of our stores and receive a 15% discount on your next purchase. Limited to one per customer'.
Starbucks has an app with all kinds of features that allow customers to receive bespoke service (see the picture). For example, Starbucks sends mobile customers who are in the vicinity of one of their branches a digital discount voucher in the Starbucks app that they can use at the nearest coffee shop.

10.4.4 Product configuration

Product configuration

Using product configuration, you are able to assemble products on Internet entirely to your own preferences. In an increasing number of cases, the website is directly linked to the production process so that you are able to receive custom-made production on order. At Yahoo! Music you are able to create a profile for yourself based on a radio station's playlist. You can then customise it by adding your favourite artists, DJs and bands. Once you have done this, you receive your own online radio station where you are able to rate every song on a scale of 1 – 10 or indicate that you don't wish to hear a particular song again. After a few weeks you will have your own radio station that exactly matches your personal preferences.
At Bivolino.com, the customer can create and order a tailor-made shirt according to their own taste via an online product configurator (see the illustration).

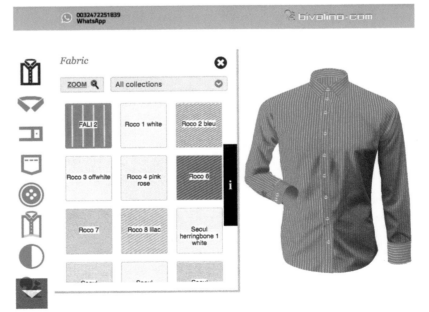

Bivolino's product configurator

The tailored shirts that Bivolino sells online, are based on four simple personal characteristics: size, length, age and weight. Using the online product configurator, the visitor can compose a tailor-made shirt to their own taste, selecting from a choice of different fabrics, colours, fits and fashionable accents. The customer's choices and measurements are saved so that they are able to use them for repeat purchases.

10.4.5   Community based creation

An increasing number of companies are combining mass customisation with social media, crowdsourcing, co-creation and viral marketing. One example is the community-based company Threadless.com (see the picture). Anyone can design their own T-shirt and submit the design online. The Threadless community then has seven days to review the design and comment on it. If Threadless decides to produce the design, the designer will receive two thousand dollars, as well as five hundred dollars each time the design is re-used for production. This mixture of personalisation, co-creation and community shopping is becoming increasingly common.

Community based creation

Community based creation at Threadless.com

10.5 Social CRM

Social CRM is the collective name given to methods for using social media in the context of CRM. On social media, the initiative lies with the customers, the role of the organisation is to offer added value by facilitating and activating a dialogue between and with customers. Social CRM aims to focus on individual customers by converting online content into conversations, to expand conversations into 'collaborative experiences', and to turn those experiences into meaningful relationships (Van Looy, 2015). It is a good idea to enrich the customer database with data from social media. This starts with collecting and recording the data from customer's social media accounts.

Social CRM

Collaborative experiences

Social media accounts

Although many consumers view social media, there are relatively few who actively participate. For most consumers, social media is about keeping in touch with friends and family. Companies that are present on social media

10

are not always viewed in a positive light by all consumers. Their motivation for communicating with companies often depends on concrete rewards and sometimes brand loyalty. In exchange for their personal data, time and energy they like to receive something tangible in return.

Customer engagement

Besides the personal attitudes people have regarding social media, the degree of customer engagement is also important. For example, someone with a low involvement will only click on a like button. Someone with a high level of involvement will actually think about the brand or product and, for example, take the trouble to post a review. If consumers judge an organisation positively, they are already loyal. Loyalty does not arise through interaction via social media, it is the basis of it.

Social CRM activities can have the following goals:
1 acquiring customers (see Chapters 5 and 6)
2 building up knowledge about customers
3 finding influencers
4 increasing the customer value by having customers buy more
5 stimulating customer satisfaction and customer retention
6 reducing costs of maintaining the customer relationship
7 developing customer engagement, a sense of commitment from the customer to the brand, to promote social loyalty and ambassadorship
8 motivating customers to co-create, co-innovate and participate in online communities

1 Acquiring customers
As you were able to read in Chapters 5 and 6, social media plays an increasingly important role in the consumer's decision to buy products and when choosing a sales channel. Social CRM can be used to motivate customers to express themselves positively about an organisation and thus stimulate others to become customers. This can be done, for example, by 'share-and-win' campaigns or by calling on customers to leave positive reviews on social media. Organisations can also use their brand communities to spread messages and strengthen brand awareness. They can create a buzz or 'rumour around the brand' (see figure 10.4).

FIGURE 10.4 Creating a buzz by the targeted approaching of influencers

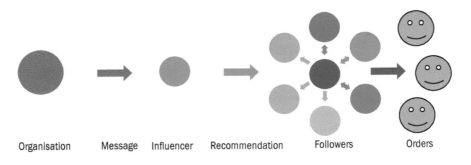

| Organisation | Message | Influencer | Recommendation | Followers | Orders |

2 Building up customer knowledge

Organisations can use social media monitoring to find out, for example, what keeps their customers occupied as well as what they are satisfied and less satisfied about. In this way, they can also find out if customers are looking to replace a product that they own and then actively respond with an offer. Digital marketers can also use customer communities to build up common knowledge and solve problems.

By linking the CRM database to social media monitoring tools, you can see what your customers are doing on social media, who they are, what they like and what they care about (see the example in figure 10.5). You can also see which of your customers are social influencers. As a result, you can personalise your messages, but also advertisements, so that they are increasingly more in line with your customers' needs. A disadvantage is that some customers may find it off-putting if they notice how much an organisation knows about them. Customers can also feel disadvantaged if others receive specific offers or information and they do not. You must also diligently stick to the letter of the law (see Chapter 13).

FIGURE 10.5 If you link social media monitoring to a CRM database, you can see in real-time what customers are saying about your brand or products on social media

3 Finding influencers

Organisations can analyse social conversations to discover trends and important influencers for their type of products or services. Once organisations know who the most important influencers are, they can communicate with them and thus influence their (potential) customers. Important influencers can be 'ambassadors', loyal customers, but also negative customers. In this way, it is also possible to identify customers who, from a business point of view, it would be better to part ways with, but who maintain special social contacts with other clients (Malthouse et al., 2013). For example, a 'fashion blogger' could be known for having bad credit in a store, but at the same time be someone who ensures clothing from that same store gets a lot of publicity.

| *Instagram*

Search

zoella ✔ Follow ▼ ⋯

1,501 posts   **11m followers**   **531 following**

Zoella
cordially-invited.co.uk

Zoella is a fashion and beauty vlogger, YouTuber, and author with more than 11.1 million followers on Instagram

4 Increasing customer value
As you are aware, there are three ways that customer value can be increased: by attracting more customers, by making customers stay longer and by allowing them to buy more. We will mainly focus on the last possibility. Organisations can actively monitor social media for customer buying signals and respond to them. This can be done via the medium that the purchase signal was picked up on, but also via email or via a direct message. Digital marketers can also post messages on social media, highlighting products and innovations. To make purchases easy, they can even include buy buttons on social media. Organisations can also target (re)target customers who have clearly indicated their interest in a new product with a new offer via social media advertising.

Direct message

Buy button

Twitter

Facebook

Google

Buy buttons on social media

10

5 Stimulating customer satisfaction and customer retention
Organisations can actively monitor social media for complaints and cancellation signals and respond to them. This is done by the webcare team. By distributing customer cases, reviews and testimonials via social media, digital marketers ensure customers see that their choices are continuously confirmed. This can also be done by re-targeting customers with social media advertisements. Organisations can also ask their customers to participate in crowdsourcing and co-creation via social media and in this way increase involvement and loyalty (see section 4.2).

6 Reducing costs of maintaining customer relations
Via social media, organisations can, in a way, make customers do part of their work (crowdsourcing). Some examples are; promotional activities, creating content and answering questions. This can lead to a decrease in costs. For example, a website like Weebly.com, where you can build websites, does not provide customer service to customers with a free account, but refers them to the online community.

7 Developing customer engagement and promoting social loyalty
Via social media, organisations can enter into a dialogue with their customers, inform them and influence them. Customers who feel a sense of involvement with a brand often become loyal customers. Creating social loyalty plays a role in this: rewarding loyal customers, fans and followers. This can be done by giving them a stage online, for example by using customers' content, by giving away prizes during campaigns and special offers, but also using loyalty programs. Consider, for example, opportunities for customers to save up for discounts or groups of friends who, together, can make use of special offers. This means that the organisation has multiple goals: motivating customers to brand loyalty, allowing customers to actively participate in online conversations and to create and share content.

Social loyalty

Customers who are satisfied and feel appreciated can become the advocate for a brand or organisation. A brand advocate is more than an influencer. They are very satisfied customers, who recommend a brand or products to others, without asking for anything in return. Research by Nielsen (2015) shows that no less than 66% of people trust recommendations from 'brand advocates'.

Brand advocate

8 Motivating customers to participate in co-creation, co-innovation and online communities
In sections 4.2, 4.3 and 9.4 you were able to read how customers can be used in the product realisation process and in the context of webcare (social care). Consumers and business customers alike often have an economic motive for working together with organisations. The hope is, that co-creation will lead to better products or services on the market, and that they will benefit from this themselves (Roberts, Hughes & Kertbo, 2014). They are also regularly rewarded for their efforts with discounts or a financial compensation. Other motives that you can respond to as a digital marketer are:
- people enjoy helping others and each other
- people like meeting new people with shared interests
- it gives people a sense of recognition when a company actually records and uses their input

10

As a digital marketer, you must answer the following questions when coming up with a plan for social CRM:

- At what events do we want to communicate with our customers via social media? What are our objectives?
- What information do customers need at that moment?
- What needs can we anticipate at that moment?
- What do we want to highlight at that moment?
- Why should customers believe us?
- At what moments do we want to connect with customers and when will they allow us to do so?
- What do we want to do in those moments: inspire, inform, support, encourage buying, let them help us or encourage them to become advocates?

Social media technology

Research by Trainor shows that investments in social media technology can lead to considerable benefits when it comes to customer relationship management, especially if this technology is compatible with the existing CRM systems. Using this enriched customer data, customer satisfaction and customer loyalty can be significantly increased. This is particularly true in business-to-business markets (Trainor, Andzulis, Rapp & Agnihotri, 2014).

Because social CRM involves individual employees communicating with customers in public visibility, it is very important that not only a good system is set up, but also that there is a clear strategy in place. In addition, it is important for the organisation to consider how social CRM will be controlled and managed, how the organisation will maintain an overview and that all employees are properly trained in what they do and do not publish online. You can read more about the organisation of digital marketing activities in Chapter 13.

10

Questions and assignments

NOW CHECK YOUR UNDERSTANDING:

10.1 Explain why organisations with an online business model often apply customer relationship management more intensively than organisations that mainly operate offline.

10.2 Go to Amazon.com and indicate how this organisation tries to increase the customer lifetime value of its customers. Divide the activities into the three theoretical ways for increasing customer value. For each activity, indicate what customer data Amazon should have at their disposition in order to make this possible.

10.3 To what extent do you think customers' satisfaction is present for online booking sites such as Skyscanner.com or Ticketmaster.com? To what extent do you think customer loyalty is present? What type(s) of loyalty is/ are involved? Support your answer.

10.4 Check out www.vodafone.com (or the official Vodafone site for your country). Which customer groups does Vodafone distinguish on their website? What approach has Vodafone chosen for the creation of customer groups? Support your answer based on the theory from this chapter. Following that, create a concept for two customer personas that Vodafone's digital marketers can use for digital CRM.

10.5 What is an individual value proposition? Which online forms of customisation can you distinguish? For each form, find an example online that is not mentioned in the text.

10.6 In section 10.5 you will find eight goals that social CRM can be used for. Using these goals, find out how German airline Lufthansa uses social CRM. Try to find an example for each of the eight goals.

10.7

CASE

Blue Water Mortgage uses marketing automation to retain customers and improve lifetime value
By Mike Berry

Blue Water Mortgage is a successful Mortgage broker based in Hampton, New Hampshire, USA. Blue Water had a challenge. And an opportunity. Their market was changing. Their customers trusted them to provide loans for house/apartment

10

purchase at competitive rates of interest, but with the rise of email marketing, it had become easier for their competitors to target Blue Water's loan customers directly, using email to send them regular offers for refinancing, sometimes at lower rates, plus a range of other mortgage and banking products.

The priority for Blue Water was retention - to lock their customers in – ie to build customer loyalty. To achieve this, Blue Water adopted a new secret weapon: marketing automation.
Marketing automation has become something of a buzzword recently, in effect it's a combination of channels/techniques marketers have been deploying effectively for some time. It can include any or all of: direct mail, personal selling, telephone marketing and importantly, email marketing.

Marketing automation helps email marketers stay out of the spam folder and to improve both engagement and open rates. Automated campaigns can be a powerful tool, yet brands sometimes hesitate. Maybe they're worried about sending out spam, or it all just seems too much like hard work to set up and manage.

The good news for marketers is that marketing automation does most of the 'heavy lifting' of CRM and if you don't have a big marketing team, automation is a great way to get better results with minimal use of human resources.

Blue Water's free Home Buying Guide. All you have to do for it is to leave some personal details which drive their marketing automation activities

Marketing automation never forgets - it ensures you don't forget to keep in touch with the people who drive your business. Marketing automation also gives you useful analytics; so that you can measure, improve and continue to test and refine what you're doing. Of course, one of the great advantages of email marketing is measurability; if you can measure something, you can improve it. Blue Water approaches marketing automation as an iterative process, with the goal of constantly improving return on investment (ROI).

Hi Tony,

I see that you recently downloaded our eBook, *10 Questions To Ask Before Buying a Home*, and I hope that you've found it helpful as you begin your home buying process.

One of the most frequent questions we receive from homebuyers is—**How much can I afford?** Knowing your mortgage amount is key when starting to look at homes. It can keep you from getting in over your head and can help you get into something you can afford without changing your quality of life.

Wondering how much you can afford? I recommend having a chat with one of our loan officers. They will give you an idea of how much you can afford and what your monthly payments will be.

Step 1: Complete this form

Step 2: A loan officer will reach out to schedule a non-committal meeting. After your meeting you'll have a clear understanding of how much you can afford.

Step 3: Enjoy your search for your new home!

Sincerely,
Mary Ruth
Your Blue Water Mortgage Concierge

Blue Water Mortgage, NMLS #1291
Website I Blog I p. 603-926-9695

Follow-up email (believed to be automated) from Blue Water

Blue Water implemented a 2-year-long email 'nurture' campaign – comprising five separate email blasts. They emailed more than 7,500 people in total, with an impressive open rate of 35.4%.

For the first email, customers received a survey that not only gained customer information, but also helped Blue Water improve its online reviews.

Email 1 was sent to customers 2 days after they purchased. If they left a 4- or 5-star review, Blue Water followed up asking them to post on Google or Facebook as well.

Three months later, the second email informed the customer how their new mortgage would improve their lives. This email reminded the customer what kind of documents they needed for their tax return and suggested they begin thinking about things like investments and life insurance of course Blue Water was available to help whenever they're ready to talk.

The next email (#3) landed in customers' inboxes another 90 days later. This third email was more of a 'check-in', to make sure customers understood credit

10

reports, to see if they have questions and generally just to keep Blue Water's brand front-of-mind.

After the first year, customers received a fourth email asking if they were ready to refinance their loan.

If they didn't take up this offer, then one more year after that, customers received the campaign's last email, which achieved a very high 28% open rate. This time they were asked whether they had any questions about refinancing and reminded that Blue Water could help.

This was a carefully planned programme of actions by Blue Water. By making regular contact at those key moments in time, Blue Water significantly improved their customer retention rates.

Blue Water's web analysts were able to identify both when customers would most want to hear from Blue Water and importantly what messages they would be open to at that point in the mortgage cycle.

Blue Water identified when customers were most vulnerable to approach by competitive vendors, so they could create an automated campaign geared toward retention which combined perfectly with Blue Water's other marketing channels.

Throughout the campaign, Blue Water studied the sales funnel and considered how automation could improve customer retention. They (rightly) see marketing automation as an iterative, ongoing process of continuous improvement in which testing is continuous, in order to increase return on investment (ROI).

Source: Medium.com/mailchimp, 2017

NOW CHECK YOUR UNDERSTANDING:

a Which of the four objectives of CRM did Blue Water pursue in their marketing automation campaign?
b Explain how this campaign could increase the Customer Lifetime Value for Blue Water.
c Could the campaign also lead to a larger market share (ie boost acquisition)? Please substantiate your answer.
d What customer data did Blue Water need to carry out this campaign?
e Did the campaign involve customisation and/or personalisation?
f How did Blue Water improve the customer journey with this campaign'?
g What could Blue Water Mortgage do within social CRM to bind customers even more?

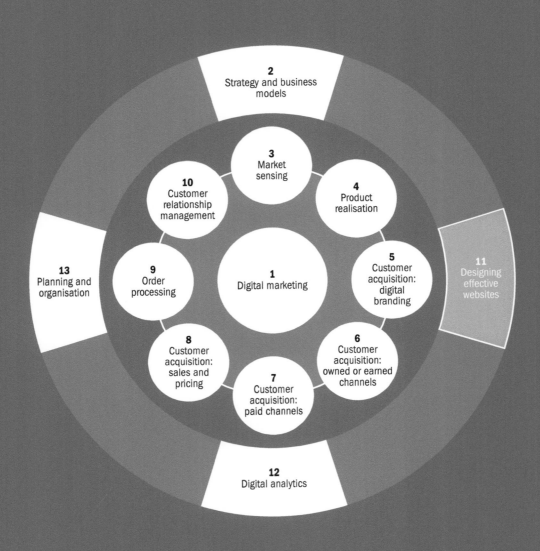

1 Digital marketing

2 Strategy and business models

3 Market sensing

4 Product realisation

5 Customer acquisition: digital branding

6 Customer acquisition: owned or earned channels

7 Customer acquisition: paid channels

8 Customer acquisition: sales and pricing

9 Order processing

10 Customer relationship management

11 Designing effective websites

12 Digital analytics

13 Planning and organisation

11

Designing effective websites

Authors: Marjolein Visser (11.1), Wim van der Mark (11.2 - 11.7) and Martijn Hoving (11.8)

Previous chapters describe how the marketer can establish a clear idea of what the market's wants and desires are (the market sensing process) and how the Internet can be used to further product development and improvement as well as for setting up processes surrounding the product or the service (the product realisation process). Once everything is customer-ready, the customer acquisition process commences: defining target segments and recruiting new customers. Then their orders are processed. During the customer relationship management process, the relationship is further developed and deepened. To achieve this, it is important to design websites, landing pages and apps in such a way that they lead to the largest possible number of conversions: as many visitors as possible must actually buy a product or service. In this chapter you will be able to learn what you, as a digital marketer, need to pay attention to if you want to create an effective website.

This chapter will cover:
- effectiveness of a website or an app
- influencing visitors
- website usability
- web content and web texts
- interaction and conversion
- effective landing pages
- the content management system (CMS)
- search engine optimisation (SEO)

After studying this chapter, you will be able to:
- indicate which elements of a website or app determine the quality from the user's perspective and how to measure the user experience
- list methods for analysing and influencing the behaviour of visitors on a website
- give advice on how the usability of websites can be improved
- review web texts and optimise web content
- formulate proposals for increasing the interaction and conversion on a website

- assess landing pages for effectiveness
- indicate what the quality requirements are that must be set for a content management system from the perspective of the organisation and safety
- explain how digital marketers can use search engine optimisation (SEO) to increase the effectiveness of their websites

11.1 Effectiveness of a website and app

In this section we will explain how an effective website contributes positively to an organisation's objectives. These may be objectives related to sales, but also to communications and production. You will learn why it is important to make a depiction of the 'customer journey' before you start building a website. We will then look at what determines a website's quality in the eyes of the visitor.
A website does not stand alone, but fulfils a specific role in the marketing, production and service processes of an organisation. In Chapter 3 you learned that digital marketers want a website's visitors to follow the steps of the digital marketing funnel as quickly as possible (see figure 11.1): they need to *visit* the website, be intrigued, *choose* a product, *order*, *pay* and finally be sufficiently satisfied so as to experience a *bond* to the website and return for a future purchase. To achieve this, the website must be useful, accessible and attractive to the visitor.

FIGURE 11.1 Digital marketing funnel

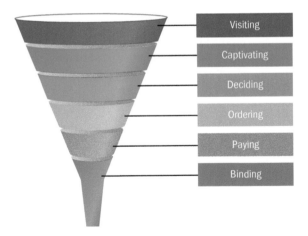

| Visiting |
| Captivating |
| Deciding |
| Ordering |
| Paying |
| Binding |

11.1.1 Customer experience

The visit to the website should lead to a positive customer experience. The 'customer experience' is the sum of what a customer experiences during their interaction with an organisation and the feeling that this experience evokes. It is something very personal: one customer experiences contact with an organisation very differently from another person. The more

Customer experience

© Noordhoff Uitgevers bv

pleasant the customer finds using the site, the greater the effect will be on the sales results and the brand experience.

Customer experience management systematically influences the customer's experience. The aim is to achieve a 'triple bottom line': a tripling of profit. This involves organising the processes in such a way that the customer comes away with an experience that is as positive as possible (1), that the organisation's employees are happy with them (2) and that the organisation earns more profit as a result of cheaper and more efficient processes (3). In reality, you are trying to keep all parties happy.

Triple bottom line

In order to positively influence the customer's experience, it is important to clearly understand the 'journey' that the customer makes, from the search for information, choosing of a product or service, selection of a sales channel to the final purchase. Which channels do they use? What are the contact moments? This is called the customer journey. You have read more about this in subsection 4.4.1. Based on the customer journey map you can determine which role the website or app should have in the process of the organisation and which features should be included. Then you will be able to determine how to offer the user the best possible experience.

11.1.2   Quality in the eyes of the visitor

A website is effective when it has high conversion rates and supports an organisation's brand objectives. But what makes a website effective from the customer's perspective? Hasan and Abuelrub (2011) found out that, from the visitor's perspective, the quality of a website is related to the quality of the content, the design of the website, the structure of the website and a website's usability (see figure 11.2).

Quality of websites

Usability

FIGURE 11.2 A framework for the quality of websites

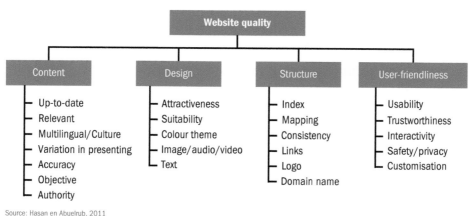

Source: Hasan en Abuelrub, 2011

But of course, you not only want to know what to pay attention to, but also how to measure the user experience. Jeff Sauro (2016) surveyed thousands of website users and concluded that in order to measure the user experience, you must examine three factors: user-friendliness, trust in the website and the appearance of the website (see figure 11.3).

11

FIGURE 11.3 A framework for measuring websites' userexperience

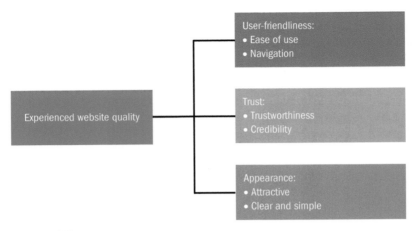

Source: Sauro, 2016

Based on his research, Sauro formulated the 'Standardised User Experience Percentile Rank Questionnaire' (SUPR-Q). This questionnaire has a difficult name, but is actually very simple (see box). By using a pop-up, you can submit it to people who have just used a website, or you can send them an email with a link to the survey. Sauro also published a checklist for professionals for testing the quality of websites in advance. This CEG list has no less than 105 check points (see http://bit.ly/2qE5UZK).

SUPR-Q
Sauro's SUPR-Q (2016) has eight items: seven statements and a question. The seven statements are measured on a 5-point scale from 'fully agree' to 'completely disagree'.

There are two statements regarding the usability:
1 This website is easy to use.
2 It is easy to navigate the website.

There are two statements regarding the level of trust in the website:
1 The information on this website is reliable.
2 The information on this website is credible.

There are two statements regarding the appearance of the website:
1 I find the website attractive.
2 The website looks clear and simple.

There is a statement and a question about the perceived quality of the website:
1 I will most likely visit this website again in the future.
2 How likely is it that you would recommend this website to a friend or colleague?

The question is measured on a scale from 0 to 10, where 0 is very unlikely and 10 very likely. Asking questions in this way is in line with the Net Promoter Score (NPS), a research method used by many organisations for measuring customer satisfaction.

To maximise the conversion within a website, the content, design, structure and usability must be optimised. Comparable requirements apply to mobile websites, but the smaller screen must be explicitly considered. This influences the legibility and ease of navigation. Apps also have their own success factors. Table 11.1 illustrates the requirements users impose on apps (Hussain & Kutar, 2009). People who complain about an app, mostly do so regarding functional errors, crashes and features that are missing. However, complaints regarding privacy, ethics and hidden costs of the app, affect the user experience most negatively (Khalid et al., 2015).

TABLE 11.1 Requirements that users set for apps

Effectiveness	Simplicity	Convenience of: • entering data • using the output • the installation process • learning to use it
	Accuracy	• reliable results • no errors
Efficiency	Speed	• reactions • results
	Features	• support/help • touchscreen • voice support • system requirements • automatic updates
Satisfaction	Safety	• when using the application • in the user environment, for example whilst driving
	Attractiveness	• user interface

Before you start the construction of a website or app, you always have to ask yourself the question 'Under which circumstances it will be used the most'? Is that for example on a tablet? Then you must choose a 'tablet-first design'. Are the users usually on the road? Then you must choose a 'mobile-first design'. From the perspective of search engine optimisation, mobile-first design is preferred (see section 11.8).

Tablet-first design

Mobile-first design

11.2 Influencing the visitor

Knowledge of your visitors' behaviour is an essential condition to be able to influence them. In this section we will first discuss how to gain insight into the behaviour of a website's visitors. Then we will discuss the viewing, reading and click behaviour. Finally, we will examine the influence of sight words on viewing behaviour and viewing order.

11

11.2.1 Understanding the behaviour of website's visitors

Insight into the behaviour of visitors can be obtained by:

1 eyetracking and mousetracking
2 facial scanning
3 neurological examination
4 web analytics
5 user tests
6 optimisation team

The structural monitoring of important industry partners, competitors and other prominent websites is also an important source of knowledge.

1 Eyetracking and mousetracking

Eyetracking

Eyetracking uses special techniques that monitor what someone sees, in which order and how long someone looks at something. This allows us to deduce what encourages the visitor to read (amplifiers) and what makes visitors stop reading (filters). Eyetracking research requires specific knowledge to convert the data into usable improvements. The position that someone is looking at is portrayed as a moving dot. On a heatmap, it is then clear which parts of a screen have, and which have not been looked at.

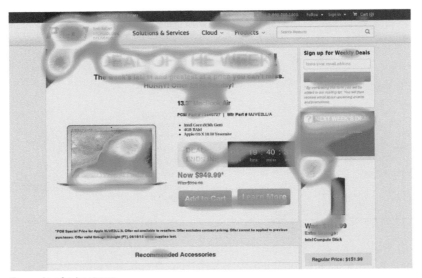

Example of a heatmap
Source: Eyetracking by Heat-map.com

11

Mousetracking

Mousetracking does not follow the eyes, but the mouse movements of visitors and gives a more superficial insight into the strengths and weaknesses of a web page. It is very accessible and easy to implement.

2 and 3 Facial scanning and neurological examination

Facial scanning

There are several techniques available for investigating how the brain responds to stimuli. Facial scanning or facial coding is a research method where the facial expressions of panellists who are viewing something are interpreted and translated into emotions such as: anger, aversion, fear, sadness, desire and so on. This research can be combined with speech, where the panel members are asked to express into words what they are feeling. These methods are used more often for assessing (concepts for) TV commercials and advertisements than for assessing websites.

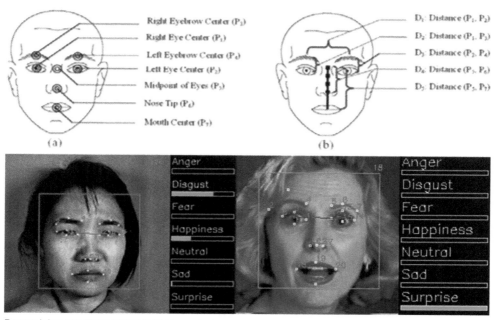

Recognising emotions using facial scanning

Facial scanning can be supplemented with the ZMET method, whereby the facial expressions and associations of each subject are determined by taking a series of photographs of the subject's face beforehand and using this to make a folder containing a collection of each individual's different facial expressions.

Neurological research is also possible via functional MRI scans. The researcher uses brain scans to check which parts of the brain light up and with which emotion that then corresponds. This method is not widely used, it is difficult to test this in a natural environment (the person being examined has to be stationary) and the costs are relatively high.

Neurological research

4 Web analytics

Using data from web analytics or digital analytics is essential for the structural detection of elements of web pages that could potentially perform better. Chapter 12 covers digital analytics in detail.

Web analytics

5 User tests

User tests, or usability research, conducted among users from the target audience by specialised research agencies, provides useful, directly applicable information. In addition, it is also possible to conduct user tests on a small scale during the development and optimisation of a website or a web page. Only three or four users are needed to make this possible. They can be recruited from neighbours, friends, or family of colleagues.

User tests

11

These tests can take place in your own office and can be supervised by a willing and patient employee. They give simple assignments and ask the test subject to think aloud. Of course, nothing is explained or clarified beforehand. Via a video camera aimed at the screen, people from the Development team and from Marketing can observe the process from another room. The results can be discussed immediately afterwards, and action points can be agreed. This step-by-step approach ensures that any bottlenecks will become clear relatively quickly.

6 Optimisation team
With increasing frequency, beta versions of websites are being launched first, which are then used by only a limited number of visitors. Based on the data analysis and feedback by these users, the first version of the 'final' website is then launched. A website is never finished. Once the website is live, the real work starts.

Optimisation team

Each organisation should have a digital optimisation team. Depending on the size of the organisation, the team may consist of a data analyst, a content manager, a web marketer and someone from IT for the technical implementation. An optimisation team periodically identifies areas for improvement based on web analysis and information from the helpdesk or the service department. The team uses resources such as eyetracking, mousetracking, user research and feedback from colleagues to identify points for improvement and subsequently prioritises these. The team tests improvements where necessary and reports widely in the organisation about the improvements and results that have been achieved in order to ensure optimal involvement and support. See Chapter 13 for more about the organisation of digital marketing.

One of the most important objectives for optimisation is optimising the conversion rate (see section 11.5). To describe this, many organisations use the phrase conversion rate optimisation (CRO).

Conversion rate optimisation (CRO)

The conversion rate or conversion ratio, is the percentage of all website visitors who successfully perform the desired action.

11.2.2 Watching, reading and clicking behaviour

For more insight into viewing, reading and clicking behaviour, it is important to know how the brain works. In this subsection we will make a distinction between the left and right hemispheres of the brain. But first we will see that less is being read and more is being scanned.

Less reading and more scanning

Viewing, reading and clicking behaviour

Research into viewing, reading and clicking behaviour has made it clear that the consumer spends an increasing amount of time scanning pages, rather than actually reading what they say. The fastest half of people searching for something via a search engine on the Internet, make their choice within four seconds. It is impossible to read all the results that quickly. We therefore rely on our judgment, based on a few separate fragments in a certain shape.

Before a person reads something, they first look at the whole. Viewing therefore comes before reading. Furthermore, it has been scientifically proven that viewing behaviour has an effect on reading behaviour. The impression that a person gets from viewing, is decisive in what they subsequently choose to read. The content is thus distorted by the feeling that the reader, before actually knowing what that content is, has about it. The feeling that content evokes, is therefore very important.

Left and right hemispheres
The differences between the left and right hemispheres of the cerebral cortex have become evident in the past forty years, although more questions than answers still remain. The way the brain functions is very complex. What has become increasingly clear, is how people react to certain stimuli. We are increasingly better able to explain that behaviour.

When influencing people through communication, both the differences as well as the connections between the brain halves play an important role. For web communication, it is essential that messages for both hemispheres are given equal importance. The differences are:
• shape, image and layout for the right hemisphere
• text and content for the left hemisphere

The right side is dominant in the instinctive processes and for getting an impression of a website. The left side is dominant in rational processes such as reading, understanding and comparing. Decisions are taken together, on the basis of feeling as well as reasoning. The picture is not black and white; many processes take place both halves. It's about dominance. The primary differences are set side by side in table 11.2.

TABLE 11.2 Differences between right and left hemispheres

Right brain	Left brain
Emotion	Reasoning
Scanning	Reading
Overview	Details
Speed	Slow
Multifunctional	One thing at a time
Pictures and headers	Texts
Shape	Contents

The right hemisphere is extremely fast and multifunctional. This half is of the utmost importance for scanning all possible information at lightning speed and then making a choice. Most of the text is not read, without the feeling of missing something. Only a small part of the information on offer receives attention from the left hemisphere. Without attention from the left hemisphere, little more is achieved than a vague memory of an image or brand. This is insufficient to satisfy most marketers.

11.2.3 Sight words and viewing order
There are important indications that we are able to recognise a few hundred 'sight words' as images with our right hemisphere. Sight words are the most recognisable to us in the form that we are most used to seeing them in: in black on white.

What a sight word is, can best be explained by comparing it to the way a child of 4 or 5 years old, who cannot yet read, tries to read. The child

Sight word

11

recognises the words dad, mum, granddad, grandma and their own first name by the way they look. The child can also 'write' these words (in reality, draw them). To recognise sight words is therefore a separate skill to reading or writing. In the same fashion, an adult person can recognise hundreds of words without actually reading them and is able to get a quick impression of a piece of text, provided there are enough words in a prominent place that are also present in their vocabulary of sight words. These are mainly simple words.

Places where these words will be most noticeable, include:
- headers
- the top words in a piece of text
- the first words of a line
- words that have been made conspicuous (eg coloured or bold)

Eyetracking shows that people view things in a predictable way. Next, we will elaborate on viewing orders and we will find out which topics influence the viewing order.

Understanding the viewing order
People see images first, then headers, then the body of text. Large images are seen before smaller images. Warm colours (orange and red) are seen before colder colours (blue and green). Images of people are seen before images containing objects. The eyes of people who are making eye contact are, in a business sense, the strongest visual magnet. There are even stronger images: images of naked people and pictures of a sexual nature are seen earlier. All the way at the top, are moving images.

Of course, not everything that attracts attention is also functional. A moving image on a website diverts so much attention from the message that although it can sometimes be functional, it is more often a disadvantage than an advantage. The same applies in most cases to images of naked people.

Viewing order

Understanding the viewing order makes it possible to give a message a much better timing. So, you can present your arguments in exactly the right order, just as you would do in a face-to-face conversation. The power of the message increases exponentially when the best arguments are seen in the correct light as well as in the right order. It is therefore important when creating web pages to ensure you are presenting your arguments and answers to questions from visitors in the right order. In reality, people don't actually look or read from top to bottom or from left to right.

Viewing order by subject
Basic motivators

In addition to images and layout, subjects are also a motivator for reading on. Most attention is paid to what are called the basic motivators. These are subjects that encourage people to act: continue reading, clicking, responding. Analysis of viewing behaviour provides insight into people's basic motives. These motives are almost entirely in line with Maslow's hierarchy of needs. The three basic motivators are:
1 greed
2 fear
3 status

11

The direction in which the model in the photograph looks towards influences the direction that the visitor looks towards

1 Greed
Responding to the visitors' greed' can be done in the following ways:
- offer more results
- give them opportunities to save money or offer discounts
- give away something for free
- offer them the opportunity to win something

2 Fear
People are uncertain about many things. Society is changing rapidly, and as a result, uncertainty is even increasing. Knowledge of your visitors'

uncertainties and subsequently responding to them, means you are more likely to succeed.

Responding to fear can be done positively as well as negatively. Phrases such as 'satisfaction guaranteed' and 'money-back guarantee' play a positive role in fear. Texts (or questions) such as 'poor vision costs lives' and '80% of emails go unopened' are examples of negative responses to fear.

3 Status

People are very concerned about how others see them. In fact, this stems from the second basic motivator: uncertainty. For this reason, we spend fortunes on branded goods, cosmetics, clothing, jewellery and cars, to express who we are and what we stand for. Profiles on social media are also an expression of the human need to be seen in a certain way.

A website that pays attention to visitors' basic motivators will receive more attention in return, and a higher rating.

Very important

Slightly less important

By far not as important

Control the web visitor's eyes with images, text formatting and basic motivators

When looking at a web page, visitors quickly scan from top to bottom and from left to right, with striking elements and basic motivators having the greatest chance of being noticed.

11.3 Website usability

Website usability

Website usability is about the ease with which a visitor reaches their goal. In this section we will first look at how the layout of the website plays an important role in this. We will then discuss which components on a site can ensure its usability. Then we will go over the display of websites on tablets and smartphones. Finally, we will briefly discuss user research.

11.3.1 Layout of a user-friendly website

To make it easy for its users, almost every website has a main page that acts as a base for the visitor. For example, a visitor can navigate from one section to another via the homepage.

Websites are often logically arranged in a hierarchy. The site is divided into topics and sub-topics, each with its own page. To make it even easier for the visitor, this path can be made visible. This is called bread crumb navigation.

Bread crumb navigation

A hierarchical layout, in which all subjects can be found neatly and logically arranged, does not guarantee that the visitor will be able find all subjects quickly and easily. Visitors are in a hurry, read badly and only have eyes for what they are looking for. Visitors are clicking faster and faster and on the basis of less information, often as a result of habitual behaviour.

To respond to this habitual behaviour, we will provide you with the following rules of thumb:
- Preferably, place navigation buttons at the top.
- Place the company logo on the top left and give the logo a link to the homepage.
- To indicate that a piece of text is clickable, give it a colour or underline it.
- Place call-to-action and other buttons on the right.

Before a visitor clicks through, there is an expectation about the follow-up page. As the expectation is confirmed by the content of the follow-up page, the visitor remains satisfied. Usability is about responding to the expectations of the visitor. Usability is the collective word for ease of use. If a visitor can easily find what they are looking for, then usability is good, if not, then usability is not good.

Usability

A website can be visited with the sole purpose of finding the telephone number or address of the company in question. If that phone number can be found directly on the homepage, then the usability for this visitor is satisfactory. There are hardly any rules or pointers for good usability, as websites are often visited with totally different search queries. Empathising with questions that visitors might have provides the most useful information for the design of the website.

11.3.2   Components of a user-friendly website
Hyperlinks and control of the screen are important items for website visitors. Also, a search box, reviews and feedback and videos contribute to optimal usability.

Hyperlinks: living up to expectations
Hyperlinks in a web text are important for smooth clicking behaviour. Hyperlinks bring the visitor a step further. For this reason, visitors are also alert to hyperlinks.
Due to the fact that hyperlinks are often coloured and/or underlined, they also receive extra attention. Optimal usability demands that the visitor gets exactly what they were expecting after clicking. This is only possible by informing the visitor to the best of your ability about the content on the follow-up page. Simply using the words 'Click' or 'Click here' do not raise any expectations at all. A good hyperlink informs visitors and creates expectations that are then met. Example 11.1 gives examples of clear hyperlinks.

Hyperlinks

11

EXAMPLE 11.1

Hyperlinks on a site for washable wallpaper

A website about washable wallpaper could, for example, contain the following hyperlinks:

- Read more about washable wallpaper
  A link to a web page with html text about washable wallpaper.
- Download a pdf brochure about washable wallpaper
  A link to a pdf document about washable wallpaper.
- Request a brochure about washable wallpaper
  A link to a form, that can be filled in to request a brochure.
- Request a quotation for washable wallpaper
  A link to a form in which questions about surface, quality or extra services are asked.
- Calculate your price for washable wallpaper
  A link to a calculation module, where the visitor can play around with prices, surface, quality and services.

Search box

Search box

On websites with a lot of content, a lot of products or many different services, the search box is the most important navigation tool. As the number of pages increases, the role of the search box for 'site search' becomes more important. As the search box becomes more visible, the more white space there is around the search box. For Google, the search box is so important that the entire website consists of a search box.

Google's search box is the central feature

Reviews and feedback

During their orientation, web visitors are increasingly seeking out reviews. Posting reviews and feedback on your own website is becoming more and more important. Google Plus makes it very easy to write reviews about all local businesses on the Google Plus page in the local search results.

Furthermore, there are an increasing number of tools for actively asking customers for feedback, automatically publishing this feedback and integrating star ratings into the search engine results. A great many companies are actively asking customers for reviews when they have bought a product, stayed in a hotel, used an app, and so on. Some companies offer services for collecting customer feedback and integrating it directly into the web content.

Video
Video gives an extra dimension to a website. Short video impressions offer the web visitor the opportunity to intensively become aware of your added value.
Examples are instruction videos; customer cases and videos where customers talk about their experiences.

Do not let a video start automatically. Visitors like to decide for themselves what they do and don't watch, for how long and in what order. You can influence the viewing order, but you cannot force visitors. A self-starting video is no more than a form of push. The probability of the visitor immediately stopping or clicking away the video is very large. That was most certainly not the video's intention.

11.3.3   Display on a tablet or smartphone
Broadly speaking, there are two possibilities for display on a tablet or smartphone:
1 responsive design (scalable website)
2 adaptive design

1 Responsive design (scalable website)
With responsive web design the website adapts to the screen size of the device it is being used on. Parts move or slide among under each other, depending on the device being used. Images scale and adjust to the available space on the screen. A responsive website has the same features as the display on a desktop. To make it easier to scale up and down, the screen format of a tablet is often used as a starting point in the design process. This is also called tablet-first design.

Responsive web design

Tablet-first design

Responsive design: The Boston Globe website adapts to the screen size of the device being used

11

2 Adaptive design

Adaptive design

The alternative to responsive design is adaptive design or AWD (Adaptive Web Design). This goes a step further than responsive design and means separate, different content for display on a smartphone. An adaptive design responds to the fact that someone behind a desktop or tablet can have different information needs than someone who is out and about. The smartphone recognises this and displays custom content. The content is written separately and designed to display different content on mobile devices (fewer images, shorter texts). Route descriptions, address details, telephone numbers and such are much more important on a smartphone than on a desktop. Navigation is done via 'thumb-friendly' buttons and you often see a 'hamburger icon' in the top right-hand corner that represents the menu.

Apps are often used as a replacement for mobile websites. As you have read in section 11.1, apps have slightly different quality requirements.

11.3.4 User research

Usability research

Usability research among users from the target segment can provide useful, directly applicable information.

Specialist research agencies observe how visitors on your website behave from behind their screens. In addition, it is also possible to conduct user tests on a small scale during the development and optimisation of a website or a web page. Only three or four internet users are needed to make this possible. They can be recruited among neighbours, friends, or your colleagues' family members.

An employee gives simple assignments to one subject and asks the subject to think aloud. The screen on which the test subject clicks is recorded on video, together with what the test subject says. The employee must not say or explain anything!

If there are three or four test subjects, you will be able to discuss the results directly as well as name the action points. This way of working ensures that the most important usability bottlenecks of a new site are quickly visible.

11.4 Web content and web text

Content

Websites exist by the grace of their content (content). Interesting content results in many visitors and referrals. By being referenced, the content is better rated by search engines. This will result in even more visitors and more referrals. For uninteresting content, the exact opposite applies: it is not searched for and not referred to, so search engines do not rate it. In this section we will show you how you can tailor web content to the website visitor. Then we will discuss the writing of web texts. Finally, we will cover the optimisation of web texts.

11.4.1 Web content, tailored to the website visitor

Rules of thumb for creating good web content are:
- Use an appropriate content style.
- Apply the methodology of 'from inside out to outside in'.
- Tailor the web text to the visitor.
- Use arguments to encourage a visitor to perform desired behaviour.
- Use confrontation text in addition to reading text.

Content styles

A web visitor could be in differing phases of the customer journey. The web visitor's information requirements differ per phase. As a marketer, you have a different goal that you want to achieve for each phase.
The content style that you use depends on the purpose and phase of the customer journey that the web visitor finds themselves in. Content styles are the different communication styles that are used to meet the different information needs per phase in the customer journey.

Content style

We can distinguish four content styles:
1 *Informative*. Informative content consists of blogs, vlogs, informative articles, news items and the like. The aim is to provide the reader with information that helps them to make choices. Furthermore, with good informative content the authority and expertise of the writer is increased.
2 *Motivational*. Motivational content is meant to spur the reader on. This could be diverse activities such as comparing, calculating and looking up more information.
3 *Sales oriented*. Sales oriented content aims to encourage the reader choose a product, service or concept. Think of making an appointment, an invitation to come to a showroom or to put something in the shopping cart.
4 *Service oriented*. Service-oriented content is content for web visitors who have already purchased something. Often, these are assembly instructions, guarantees, instructions for use and the like.

From inside out to outside in

A lot of the time, web content comes into existence as the result of an internal workgroup who have thought long and hard about what should be on the website. All aspects of the organisation, the departments, the products and the news bulletins have been collected, classified, described and placed on the website in a logical order. This principle is called *inside out*. Literally thinking of what the outside world wants to see from the inside out. This method rarely delivers content that is also appreciated by visitors.

Inside out

Many third and fourth generation websites are now filled with content that is tailored to search queries: *outside in*. On the basis of reports from AdWords campaigns, the first thing to be determined is which keywords and combinations of keywords (search phrases) are most likely to deliver profitable visitors.

Outside in

Search phrases

These search phrases are then grouped, and based on these groups, the written content is then tailored to the search query. It is even possible to tailor the product and service range to search requests.

11

Customising web texts

Adapting web texts to the visitor (see figure 11.4) requires a certain amount of empathy. An important portion of all visitors to companies' websites are only looking for an address or a telephone number. These visitors want to send, deliver or request something.

FIGURE 11.4 Write about what the visitor wants to know

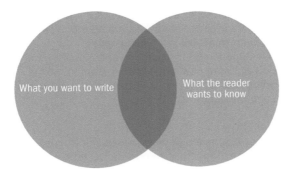

What you want to write

What the reader wants to know

Tailoring web texts to the visitor, in those cases, means that the most basic contact information should not be hidden under a contact button, but in a prominent place on every web page. Customising content also means using the exact same words that the visitor has used in their search. If these are many different words, you can also use landing pages tailored to the search query.

Arguments

Web content contains arguments that encourage a visitor to exhibit the desired behaviour. The homepage usually contains what is called the core arguments. It is essential for a company to distinguish itself on the basis of arguments. The competition is huge, and the main competitors are only one mouse click away in the list of search results. It is therefore essential to come up with arguments directly, this is what the visitor will be looking for when they decide to remain on a website.

Core arguments

Many companies and organisations think they can distinguish themselves with words such as customer-oriented, reliable or flexible. These words however appear millions of times all over the web and are therefore far from distinctive. Arguments that everyone uses are not arguments. Companies that call themselves trustworthy often evoke suspicion rather than trust.

In a highly competitive environment, it is essential to make the added value clear and specific in a few words or sentences.

Confrontation text and reading text

Someone who is looking for something and is directly confronted with an enormous piece of text, often immediately clicks away immediately. Someone who is looking for something specific will scan and search on the Internet. The content is filtered as described in section 11.2. Only the most necessary information is taken in. The person who is searching can be most quickly informed by using short pieces of text. It is no coincidence that advertisements should contain no more than a header and two lines of text of 35 characters each. More advertising space is not for sale. And that is a good thing: more text does not increase the chance of clicks, but rather decreases it. Twitter also limits the size of its messages. It is precisely in that limitation that their strength lies. For this reason, many web shops and news sites that analyse clicking and reading behaviour work with short confrontation texts during the time that the visitor is still searching and scanning, and only offer reading texts once the visitor has found what they are looking for.

Confrontation texts are short. They consist of one to five lines, contain the essence of the advantages, respond to motivators and consist of short sentences averaging less than nine words per sentence. Confrontation texts end with a hyperlink that invites you to read on. This hyperlink leads to the real reading text. The reading text can start off with the confrontation text as its first paragraph.

Confrontation texts

Reading texts

11.4.2   Writing web texts

Writing texts for a website requires a specific set of skills, both in terms of content and layout. Here are a few pointers for increasing the legibility of a website:

Web text

- Make the text collapsible.
- Write in short sentences.
- Ensure an optimal layout of the web text.

Make text collapsible

Text becomes collapsible by making a summary of a piece of text, consisting of a few sentences. This summary is summarised once more in an *intriguing* header. The basic principle is that the visitor is first confronted with the header, then with the essence of the text (this is often the confrontation text) and only then with the total content.

Collapsible

Short sentences

Because reading texts from a screen is much more tiring than reading texts on paper, sentences in web text must be much shorter than for example in letters or brochures. An average length of between 12 and 15 words per sentence is considered optimal. For screen texts, the optimal average is 9 words per sentence.

The average sentence in this book has 11 words. That is perfect for paper, but too long for web text.

SUGGESTION
When you are using the spell checker in Word, you can go to 'preferences' and select 'show readability statistics' by default. For each piece of text, you will then be able to find out the average number of words per sentence, the amount of characters per word as well as the number of verbs in a passive voice. Easily readable content has an average of 5.5 characters per word and as few verbs in a passive voice as possible.

11

Layout of the web text

To increase the readability of online texts, the following are essential:

1 text width
2 length of the text blocks
3 use of sub-headings and bullet points
4 font and font size
5 colour use
6 printable version

1 Text width

The width of a block of text plays an important role in the readability of a web text. A block of text across the full width of the screen is very difficult to read. A narrower block of text reads much more pleasantly. For an informative web text, a width of between 60 and 80 characters including spaces is optimal.

2 Length of the text blocks

When reading a piece of text, the reader makes a subconscious estimate of the amount of energy and time that reading will cost them. A long block of text requires more reading energy than a short text block. Reading texts from a screen is already more tiring, so blocks of web text should not be as long as text blocks in magazines. The optimal length of longer pieces of web text is between 7 and 12 lines per text block.

When scanning a piece of text, the brain forms a sort of image of the text block that looks like a word cloud

3 Using sub-headings and bullet points

By placing an intermediate header above each piece of text, you give the reader the opportunity to scan the text. Short, petitioning sub-headings make for a considerably more readable text than paragraphs without sub-headings.
A summary using bullet points also reads much easier than consecutive sentences.

11

4 Font and font size
Consistently use the same font throughout your website and the same size on each page. Research has shown that the Calibri, Arial, Verdana and Tahoma fonts are the most easily read fonts on screens. For web text, choose font size 10 or 11.

5 Colour use
Text blocks are easiest to read if the background is light and the text itself is dark (black, dark grey or dark blue). Colours may be used for headings. Any colour that stands out is good. On your website, always stick to one colour for the headlines and another colour for the (underlined) hyperlinks.

6 Printable version
Reading text on a website is often about one specific topic and sometimes contains a lot of information and details. A lot of people prefer to read this information from paper. Text on paper is easier and faster to read. For this reason, make sure you have a printable version of the reading text available, that can be printed without navigation buttons and without missing a portion on the right.

11.4.3   Optimising web text
Optimising web text is mainly a matter of empathising and eliminating. Empathising is the most difficult, eliminating often meets with internal resistance.
If web text begins with a promise, an offer or an advantage, it immediately raises questions from the reader. A good web text is limited to the answers to questions raised in the reader's mind.
The fact of the matter is, if you don't know what your readers' questions are, you cannot write.

Here are a few suggestions on how to optimise web texts:
1 Get rid of anything that is not an answer to questions that your readers may ask.
2 Add enumerations.
3 Use slick, modern language.
4 Limit the use of passive voice verbs and auxiliary verbs for expressing the tense.
5 Avoid weak words and expressions.
6 Add strong words.
7 Use the imperative tense.
8 For every piece of text, don't forget to factor in mobile users.
9 Ensure a good final editing.

Get rid of anything that is not an answer to questions that your riders may ask
Omitting anything that is not an answer to questions that your readers may ask, is our most rigorous suggestion. You will discover that most information about your organisation is not something that visitors would ever ask about and can therefore be deleted. Questions about the organisation only come to light *after* the reader has become interested in the first place. Information about the goals, work processes, structure and employees of an organisation are some of the most uninteresting texts. You can delete these texts almost entirely.

11

Add enumerations

The eyes of web visitors are drawn very quickly to enumerations, as they provide them with the essence of the content. Use enumerations and stick to the following suggestions:

- An enumeration draws extra attention.
- They look like a compact summary.
- Draw attention to the points.
- Limit the list to three, or a maximum of five points.
- Stick to one line per sentence.

Use slick, modern language

When people write, they often use a curiously old-fashioned form of written language that has not been used for decades. Change the text so it consists of more engaging expressions. The text will become more readable. Table 11.3 shows which words could be used to replace the old-fashioned language.

TABLE 11.3 From old-fashioned language to modern language

Old-fashioned	More modern
On the basis of	From
Due to the fact that	As
Nevertheless	Still
Consequently	As a result
Accordingly	Such as
With the help of	Using
With regard to	Concerning
Considering	Seeing
In order to	For
By way of	By
With a view to	So that
Yet	Although
As well as	Also
Provided that	If
With pleasure	Gladly
Per	By

Limit the use of passive voice verbs and auxiliary verbs for expressing the tense

'You discover' is more effective than 'You will discover'. A wording like 'We would like to inform you about this ...' is much more vivid when written: 'I would like to inform you about this ...' Many websites state that the sender 'will get in touch' if they receive a message It is much more active to simply say that you will contact them. Also, limit the use of auxiliary verbs (will, become and can) and conjugations of those verbs.

Avoid weak words and expressions

Examples of weak words and phrases that you should avoid are:

- actually and in principle
- hope, try, do your best, soon
- generalisations
- denials

© Noordhoff Uitgevers bv

Actually and basically
The words 'actually' and 'in principle' raise doubts in the minds of readers. If someone says that you are actually right, then you are in fact not. If in principle there is no negotiating a price, then usually a discount can be given.

Hope, try, do your best, soon
'Hope', 'try', 'do your best' and 'soon' are excuse words. They make the user of those words appear less reliable. Someone who says he is trying, in fact says that there is a chance that it will not work. Someone who says that he hopes, in fact says that he is doing nothing at all.

Excuse words

Generalisations
'All', 'everyone', 'everywhere', 'always', 'nobody', 'nowhere' and 'never' are generalisations. The use of these words gives the impression of exaggeration. 'Everyone' involves a whole lot of people, billions of people in fact. Who could possibly make a statement like that?

Generalisations

Denials
The denial of a denial is equivalent to a confirmation. 'Not expensive' can be better put as 'attractively priced'. The fact that something is 'not difficult' is in many cases better illustrated by using 'fairly easily' or 'simple'. Also, be careful with the word 'not'. Sometimes a reader's brain will accidentally skip that word. Many negations are meant to stop the reader from thinking a certain thing. However, you can't not think something, only think it. If I ask you not to think of a white elephant, your brain has only one option: it thinks of a white elephant. What is someone about to do when they tell you: 'I don't want to nag, ...' Exactly, guaranteed they are about to nag you about something.
More or less the same applies to the word 'no'. Suppose you are on an aeroplane and the sound system is switched on: 'Ladies and gentlemen, this is your captain speaking. There is no reason for panic, there is nothing wrong with the left engine.' Is that reassuring?

Negations

Add strong words
Here are a number of strong words. Adding a few of these words usually makes web texts more effective. The following are all strong words:

Strong words

- synonyms of the reader
- free
- you, your, and so on
- new
- personal
- confidential
- now
- today
- temporarily
- quickly
- only for ...
- exclusively for ...
- save
- for the first time
- finally
- unique

11

- how you …
- win

'Free' and 'new' are striking words

Use the imperative tense

Imperative tense

The imperative tense is a quick, short way of writing something and directly asking for interaction. The imperative tense is fully accepted on websites and in other media such as radio and TV. Examples of this are:

- profit from …
- go to …
- do it today …
- come to …
- play and win
- order now

For every piece of text, don't forget to factor in mobile users

Each piece of web text could be read on a smartphone. Keep that in mind. Mobile readers use their thumb to easily scroll through texts. Pay a great deal of attention to scalability via sub-headings. Make sentences and paragraphs even shorter.

Mobile first

The term 'mobile first' means that you write your text primarily for people who are going to be reading it on a smartphone and assumes that the desktop reader will only benefit from this.

Text blocks, sentences and paragraphs can almost never be too short!

Ensure a good final editing

Read your text aloud again and listen critically to the way you have written it. If the text does not sound convincing or doesn't read smoothly, the text is not ready yet. Afterwards, you must divide the attention of the reader by emphasising some pieces of text with headers or making some passages bold or italic. Finally, for a commercial website, it is important that you ask yourself for each article whether or not you can ask the visitor to interact.

11.5 Interaction and conversion

The success of websites is ultimately determined by the impact that the web visit has on the behaviour of the visitors. That behaviour is preferably expressed in interactions or responses. Possibilities for response include:

Response

- downloading an article, white paper or checklist
- signing up for a newsletter
- requesting information

11

- call up
- visit the store or showroom
- make an appointment with an advisor or account manager
- become a donor
- become a member or subscribe
- buy something

In this section we will explain how you can promote interaction. Then we will discuss thresholds to response and finally we will give some suggestions for response forms.

11.5.1   Promoting interaction

A lot is known currently about ways to promote interaction. The use of specially designed landing pages has provided a lot of knowledge. The presence of a contact button on each page is far from sufficient for prompting the visitor to respond. Directly, and more frequently asking for reactions increases the number of reactions that will be given. This can be done under every article and on every page. The structure and content of a page can even be arranged in such a way that it stimulates response behaviour. The person building those pages needs to know what errors are being made and how to avoid them in future.

Interaction

Common mistakes

If there is something that has the capability to be interactive, it is the Internet. Nevertheless, at the moment a lot of websites are not equipped for receiving reactions. Three common mistakes are:

1 *Only relying on the presence of a contact button*
Each text can be ended with a request for follow-up action in the form of a hyperlink.
2 *Referring to an email address*
More than 90% of the visitors who want to respond and then end up in an email program, end up not responding. The visitor hesitates about the subject line, the introduction, which data is required, and so on. A missed opportunity!
3 *Having to scroll down to respond*
Scrolling is in decline. Increasingly often, the visitor assumes that the most important information is at the top of the screen. Asking for comments at the bottom of pages that are only visible after scrolling, will cost you a response.

Suggestions for increasing the response

In order to increase the response, the previous mistakes must not be made. Here are four practical suggestions that promote interaction:

1 *Create special pages that match the search query*
Using special landing pages per query is a very effective and important promoter of interaction. Many companies achieve very good results by using landing pages that are designed for interaction. In the last part of this chapter we will come back to this in detail.
2 *Use eye-catching action buttons*
Using eye-catching action buttons with texts such as 'become a member', 'order', and 'call me back', is very effective. They are usually displayed on the right-hand side of the screen, immediately visible without having to scroll down.

11

3 *Create a specific response form*
Creating a specific form on which the offer is repeated once again for each respondent also appears to have a positive effect on the response. There are a number of suggestions for creating response forms in subsection 11.5.3.

4 *Designed for the next step*
On some web pages, it is crystal clear what the visitor has to do in order to move ahead. One of the clearest examples is the Booking.com website.
As soon as you land on the website, you know what is expected of you.

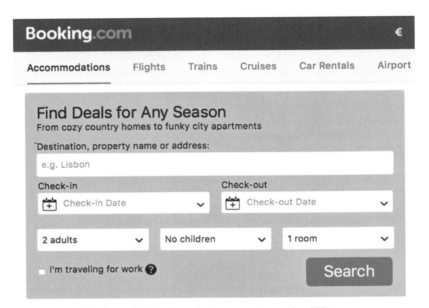

Booking.com: it is immediately clear what your next step should be

If at a glance it is not clear what action is the be undertaken, the homepage or web page is not 'designed for the next step'.

Distractions in the form of things we want to hastily tell our visitor before they move on are the greatest barrier to interaction. Many websites are very similar to a babbling salesman, who does not pay any attention to his customer's questions.

11.5.2 Thresholds to response

Thresholds to response

People who respond to an offer on a website are taking the first step towards something that could become a relationship in the future. The decision to take this step depends on the balance between what the visitor hopes to receive and any possible obligations. In other words, what the visitor will have to spend or give up in order to receive something in return. If the visitor expects to have to 'pay' a lot, this is a *high threshold to response*. If the visitor doesn't have to relinquish a lot, this is a *low threshold to response*.

© Noordhoff Uitgevers bv

There are many forms of response. These types of response can roughly be divided into two categories:

- Category 1 is response where only address data (*leads*) are collected.   Leads
- Category 2 is response in which a transaction is also made.

Response category 1: generating leads

The following are examples of address data collection in ascending order from a low response threshold to a high response threshold:

- downloadable white paper with objective information in exchange for an email address
- a newsletter in exchange for an email address
- a checklist in exchange for an address
- a company brochure in exchange for an address and telephone number
- a quote in exchange for address details and information regarding specific needs
- an appointment with an account manager in exchange for time

Each aforementioned offer is a form of lead generation. The kind with the   Lead generation
lowest response threshold will in all probability yield 20 to 50 times more response than the kind with the highest response threshold. Responses to offers with a higher response threshold are of better quality. In many cases however, an offer with a low response threshold will, after telephone screening, still lead to better quality leads than an offer with a high response threshold. Offers with a low response threshold provide an opportunity for building a relationship gradually and as a result represent an investment in the future. Offers with a high response threshold sometimes yield better results in the short term.

Response category 2: closing transactions

Below are some examples of closing transactions. Again, in ascending order from a low response threshold to a high response threshold:

- receiving the first two weeks for free with a subscription
- the first shipment with free ...
- no shipping costs for the first shipment
- two weeks to try it out and then make a decision
- buying with a satisfaction guarantee and return options
- buy and pay afterwards with an invoice included
- buy and pay immediately
- buy with a future obligation (membership or a subscription)

Whether a low response threshold will yield more than a high response threshold is a matter of calculation and weighing up the risks. Calculate and compare the total value over time based on possible follow-up orders (lifetime value from a customer). Base your decision as much as possible   Lifetime value
on objective criteria and whether an offer with a high or low response threshold will be the most profitable.

11

BBC

Register with the BBC

What's your date of birth?

Day _____   Month _____   Year _____

What's this for? **∨**

Continue

Low response threshold when signing up on BBC website

11.5.3   Suggestions for response forms

Whatever a web visitor is expected to do, the easiest way of reacting is via a response form. You will receive a considerably larger amount of completed forms if you refer to the form in various places and on a lot of pages and directly ask for a response.

Response forms

Some suggestions for *response forms*:
- Keep the form short.
- Give the respondent an overview of the total process of filling in the form.
- Limit the number of required fields.
- Place asterisk (*) next to any required fields.
- Enable the active input field.
- Choose a logical sequence.
- Enter any previously known details automatically.
- Provide sufficient input space.
- Give a concrete indication of what has been entered incorrectly.
- Let the user decide on the format that they use to fill in telephone numbers etcetera.

Order forms

The following suggestions apply specifically to *order forms*:
- Save the completed data.
- Give feedback on orders (repeat).
- Display a thank you page after they have sent it off.
- Send an email automatically to confirm the receipt of the form.

A short response form can also be placed on the landing page. This sometimes results in enormous conversion in combination with a low response threshold.

© Noordhoff Uitgevers bv

Example of a form on the landing page

11.6 Effective landing pages

One of the most important ways of improving a visitor's user experience is to directly connect content to the visitor's origin.
Compare it with a conversation. As a digital marketer, you are having a conversation with a potential customer via Google, Facebook, a newsletter or a banner, and with just one click, that conversation continues on your website. That click to your website must be a logical continuation of the conversation. If this is not a logical transition, you risk putting the visitor off and the probability that they will leave again increases. This kind of behaviour is called a '*bounce*' in Google Analytics.

In order to optimise this conversation, you can set up different landing pages per source of origin, because it is virtually impossible to respond optimally to all different visitor flows, each with their own search queries, with only one website.

As we previously described in subsection 7.2.3, the landing page is the page that the visitor ends up on after a clicking on an (AdWords) advertisement or a link in an email. The landing page seamlessly matches the previous link and contains specific information that aims to encourage the visitor to perform the desired action. Landing pages are generally intended to create higher conversions than are possible using the regular website.
Next to conversion-oriented landing pages, there are also landing pages that are intended to be more easily found in the organic search results of search engines.
In this section we will discuss what experience has taught us regarding landing pages and we will find out which factors contribute to a successful landing page.

Conversion-oriented landing pages

11

11.6.1 What experience has taught us regarding landing pages

There are companies in existence where several people manage hundreds of landing pages full-time, continuously optimising them in order to achieve the highest possible conversion. These companies have a huge amount of knowledge about searching, viewing, reading and response behaviour.

Experience has taught us the following about landing pages:
- *Visitors hardly scroll.* Landing pages that fit on one screen perform better.
- *Visitors read less and less.* Information from pictures, headings and pieces of text are sufficient for encouraging visitors to respond.
- *People like to look at other people.* Landing pages that include an image, preferably of a person, perform better on average than landing pages without images.
- *Draw people's attention to an action button.* Visitors tend to follow the same viewing direction that the people in the image are looking in.
- *Noticeable and clear action button.* The 'call to action' button must be prominent and immediately clear. On a landing page, you may be asked to perform the same action several times. The following picture shows that clear, noticeable action buttons perform better.

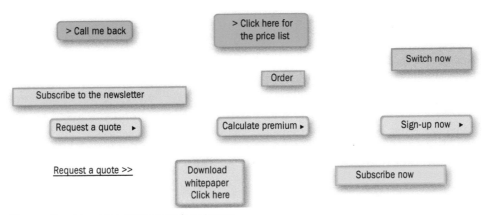

Clear, noticeable action buttons perform better

- *Preferably only use one proposition per landing page.* Landing pages where the visitor has only one choice perform better than landing pages that contain multiple propositions.
- *(In 'frame') of the regular website.* Use the same layout as the regular website. This is reinforced as a result of many companies adapting their website to match successful landing pages.
- *Regular website easily accessible.* Visitors appreciate a 'home' button and want to remain under the impression that they are staying on the same website.
- *Headline* (same as advertisement). A headline that is almost identical to the ad that was clicked, usually scores better than a different headline. A separate landing page for each advertisement is therefore optimal.
- *Few distractions or exits.* Landing pages exclusively fitted with top navigation that is limited to a few buttons do better than landing pages

11

with navigation on the left. Any information that is not directly related to the proposition will distract from it and could cost you the conversion. As an example, the navigation on the landing pages of certain health insurance companies only consist of 'home', 'calculate premium' and 'transfer'. In these cases, it has been decided that 'less is more'.

- *Short text with a clear offer.* Landing pages with a lot of text don't score as well on average as landing pages with less text. As an example, UK insurance comparison site Compare the Market uses a landing page which immediately segments serious insurance enquirers from those interested mainly in promotional deals on movie tickets and plush 'Meerkat' Toys.

Compare the Market landing page

11.6.2   Successful landing pages

Factors that contribute to successful landing pages are: sticking to a good basic layout, cultivating trust, preventing common mistakes and testing.

Basic layout

If you were to study the results of thousands of landing pages, you would find that there is a kind of basic layout for successful landing pages. This basic format is approximately as follows:

- top navigation with four or five buttons
- on the left, a photograph that is related to the problem or the needs of the visitor
- in addition, a noticeable headline that complements the image
- underneath that, a sub-header consisting of two lines
- a block of text consisting of four or five lines
- a list of benefits (maximum of five)
- on the bottom right, a noticeable action button

Trust

The more trustworthy a landing page appears, the higher the conversion. Visitors naturally derive most confidence from a well-known and safe brand.

11

In addition, the inclusion of reviews, quality marks and a privacy statement have a positive effect. Also, including a telephone number has a positive effect on the online conversion.

Specifically, for web shops, the provision of guarantees, a return option, low shipping costs, short delivery times and the ability to pay upon receipt of the order increase the trust and therefore the conversion.

Common mistakes on landing pages

The most common errors on landing pages are:

- one landing page for many advertisements, this affects the relevance
- use of the regular website layout with too many distractions
- too much text
- poorly legible text as a result of using a font size that is too small
- too many (intermediate) steps to the conversion page
- lengthy response forms
- inappropriately high response threshold
- photos and text that are not relevant to the offer

Testing

Testing is of the utmost importance for the success of a landing page. Landing pages are ideal for experimenting with. For example, via A / B testing (see the box in section 12.3.3).

11.7 Content Management System

Wireframes

A website consists of a structure, in which the elements and the layout of different types of pages are recorded in wireframes. You fill this structure with content.

Content management

Content management is the storage, management and distribution of the various types of data, such as text, images, sound clips, video images and graphs.

Content management system

Customers are communicated with via the website, but also via email, virtual employees, apps and the like. All communication channels must communicate in the same way. Product descriptions, conditions, procedures and prices must be identical, whether they are on the website or in a brochure. To achieve this, organisations use a content management system (CMS). Within the content management system, information is entered in fields and the information from those fields is then used for the various communications. This way, a change only needs to be entered once to ensure that identical data is seen everywhere. The challenges within content management increase as the organisation uses more communication channels. For example, how does it ensure that the texts in a corporate blog or on a Facebook page consistently convey the same brand values? How does it ensure that the video of the old commercial is replaced by the new one everywhere? And how does it ensure that a customer who complains via Twitter gets the same answer as they did an hour earlier from a virtual service employee?

There are also content management systems that are only intended to manage the content of a website.

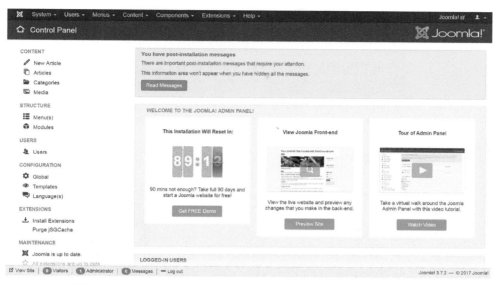

Joomla is a well-known open source content management system for websites

This section briefly discusses the requirements for a CMS, web security and the domain name.

11.7.1   Requirements for a content management system

Not every content management system (CMS) that is used to maintain websites, is equally flexible. For example, you want to be able to quickly create new landing pages as well as be able to create them outside of the navigation. In addition, you want to be able to test them. Many content management systems have no flexibility regarding the lay-out and the location of the navigation buttons. Another necessity is that that the user must be able to create their own forms.

CMS

A CMS that is optimally suited for creating many different 'new pages' has an online 'image bank' often containing hundreds of photos that can be tested. In order to measure the test results, measurement scripts (eg JavaScript) must be able to be placed. Furthermore, it is ideal if there are links with other systems (CRM, ERP).

11.7.2   Web security

Websites can be hacked, so it is essential to be well aware of the risks. Web security is a dynamic phenomenon. Methods for circumventing this security are developing rapidly. Installing updates of content management systems in a timely manner should be a primary concern for every company with a website.

Web security

11

Hackers don't remain idle (Independent.co.uk, 2017)

A website that has been hacked could be provided with any conceivable information and it could be impossible to log in. This can cause enormous (reputation) damage. Additionally, companies increasingly have customer data at their disposal. Customer data is covered by privacy legislation. It is therefore a legal requirement to protect this data optimally.

In June 2017, news channel Al Jazeera reported on Twitter that it had been the target of a digital attack. 'The websites and digital platforms of Al Jazeera Media Network systematically endure hacking attempts. These attempts are becoming increasingly severe and are taking on several different forms', according to the Al Jazeera website. Hacks are not always the work of hobbyists. It can also be the work of criminal, political or terrorist groups from anywhere in the world.

11

Al Jazeera under cyber-attack

Nu.nl, 2017

The digital marketer can do the following to safeguard their website:
- They must be constantly aware of the risks and appeal to suppliers.
- They must ensure that updates from the latest versions of site builder software are installed.
- They must ensure that customer data is stored securely and that this process complies with the laws of the relevant country/jurisdiction.
- They must constantly place the subject of security on the agenda during discussions with IT, the hosting provider and the software or (CMS) supplier.

11.7.3 Domain name

Every website can be accessed via a domain name. The top-level domain name (TLD) is the right-hand part of an internet domain name example .co.uk, eu, .tv, .org, .edu or .com. Among other things, the ICANN grants this to independent nations.

Domain name
Top-level domain name (TLD)

If a website's target audience consists solely of people in one country, it is advisable to choose the relevant country code as a TLD to ensure it can be easily found (more about this is covered in section 11.8). Alternatively, if the world is your target audience, you should use .com and for Europe, .eu. If your .com or .eu website is available in more than one language, organising it clearly for Google can be done in the following way:

- www.domainname.eu/fr/ for the French version
- www.domainname.eu/de/ for the German version
- www.domainname.eu/nl/ for the Dutch version etc.

These websites can be registered separately for each language and target region using Google Search Console.
The TLDs .org, .net and .info are recommended for international use. Using these TLDs for a website that is intended for the national market only, might get in the way of how easily your website can be found. It is more difficult for a search engine to segment on the basis of content than from clear domains or directories (groups of files).

⬤11.8 Search Engine Optimisation (SEO)

You want your website to be able to be found as easily as possible. In section 6.2, you were able to read about how important that is. The higher you are in a search engine's organic results list, the better. Search engines such as Google, see it as their task to ensure that the best web page ends up as high in the list as possible. But what constitutes the best web page? These are pages with relevant and popular information. This is determined with the aid of an algorithm. Those algorithms are constantly evolving and becoming increasingly sophisticated. In order to improve the effectiveness of your website, you have to check whether it is sufficiently **Internal** optimised for search engines. This is called internal optimisation. That is **optimisation** work for specialists, but we will give you a short impression in this section. External optimisation means that the contextual relationships with other **External** websites are improved. Link building is one way of achieving this (see **optimisation** section 6.3).

Crawlers The search engine robots, so-called crawlers or spiders, are constantly **Spiders** searching through the billions of documents on the web. They find the pages via links, try to decipher them and divide them into parts that logically match a search query and store the results in a massive **Search engine** database. An important starting point for search engine optimisation (SEO) **optimisation** is realising that your website should not only be understandable to visitors, but also to the robots that search through your website. For example, search engine robots cannot read forms and sometimes have difficulty with rich content, such as certain types of videos. Search engine robots search for websites with unique content, with as high a valuation as possible. If you have virtually identical content on a page for customers as you do on a page for employees, a search engine robot will conclude that this information is 'not unique'. This will result in 'negatives': the pages are seen as less relevant. Some of these types of problems can be dealt with if you have sufficient knowledge, while others cannot.
For example, Google recommends the following:

11

'Make pages primarily for users, not for search engines. Do not fool your users and don't present different content to search engines than you show to users, a practice often called 'cloaking'. Create a site with a clear hierarchy and text links. Each page should be accessible from at least one fixed text link. Create a useful, information-rich site and write pages that clearly and accurately reflect your content.'

Cloaking

The difficulty is that search engines keep their algorithms a secret, to prevent the results from being manipulated or the algorithm from being copied. Nevertheless, Google, but also organisations like Moz, have great tutorials to help you on your way. You have previously already been able to read many suggestions related to search engine optimisation, such as placing the right 'keywords' or search phrases in your text. We will now give you some more. These suggestions include: keywords, indicators of good content, enrichment of search results, Google Search Console (Webmaster Tools), mobile SEO and voice search.

11.8.1 Keywords

Search phrases or keywords are the foundation of search engine optimisation. As you have read in sections 6.2 and 7.2, you must choose them with care. If you have found out that people who want to travel to Paris by coach mainly search for the combination of 'bus' and 'Paris', it is useful to ensure that these words appear in the content on your website that is accessible to search engine robots. The more specific your chosen keywords are, the less pages you will be competing against. 'Budget bus' to 'Disneyland Paris' is much more specific than 'bus' and 'Paris'.

Search phrases
Keywords

Keywords should be used in your headlines, text and in the metadata. This is information about the 'real' data, for example a short description of the content of the page. You can read more about this later on.

Metadata

One thing search engines do not like, is using keywords without any associated content. If, for example, you slip in the word 'Disneyland' in various places, while there is no information about a bus to Disneyland at all, this will result in 'negatives'.

The headline, or 'title tag' is incredibly important because it is shown in the search results. However, the crawlers and spiders only search the first 65 letters or so, meaning you will have to put your keywords at the beginning and keep it short and powerful.

Title tag

Metadata is information about a document. Metadata is entered in the content management system when you create a page. An important element is the meta description, a short description of the content of the page. Search engines do not use this section for the ranking, but for 'snippets', text fragments that are shown in combination with the search results.

Meta description
Snippets

URLs, the addresses of pages on the web, are very important. Search engines show the URL in their results and they are also used in the ranking. For this reason, it is advisable to include the keywords in the URL. This way, you ensure that people as well as search engine robots can see that your page is relevant. You can also see the URL in the browser and sometimes also on social media. It's is nice if it contains a logical set of words and in doing so becomes recognisable and attractive.

URLs

Choosing good keywords to describe images is also relevant for a better result in search engines. If there is a picture of 'Budget bus at Disneyland Paris' on a page with the keywords 'budget bus' and 'Disneyland Paris', the two reinforce each other. In this way, optimised images also influence the

11

accessibility of the images themselves in Google Image Search. When Google sees a resemblance between searches that are often performed in Google Image Search and searches in the 'regular' search engine, Google will also display these images together with the regular search results. This also applies to video (via YouTube) and locations from Google Maps.

About 2,720,000 results (0.55 seconds)

Including results for *birthday* cards
Search only for bday cards

Moonpig Birthday Cards | Create Your Own Unique Card | moonpig.com
[Ad] www.moonpig.com/Personalised/BirthdayCards ▾
Personalise A Unique **Birthday Card** That's One Of A Kind. Shop Our Selection Now!

Buy & Send Birthday Cards | Personalised from £1.79 - Funky Pigeon
https://www.funkypigeon.com/cards/birthday-cards ▾
★★★★★ Rating: 8.7/10 - 109,235 reviews
Send a **happy birthday** greeting with a special touch from our personalised birthday card selection at **Funky Pigeon**, with cards for all ages. Customise cards until your heart's content! You can add photos and/or text to all of our card designs to make your birthday greeting **stand** out from the rest.
Birthday Cards for Her · Sport Cards · Birthday Cards from Son · Spoof Cards

Birthday Cards | Rude Birthday Cards | Funny Birthday Cards - Scribbler
https://www.scribbler.com/birthday-cards ▾
Whether it's for a dog lover, cat lover or general animal lover our birthday cards will always a delight. Getting older. Their old age reminds you of how young and youthful you are. Family Birthday Cards. Find that special **happy birthday** card for your mum, dad, brother or sister. Children's Birthday Card. Age cards.

Images in the search results (outlined in green)

11.8.2 Indicators of good content
Search engines want to refer to sites with good content. They use at least three indicators:

1 The behaviour of the users of the search engine: do they click on a link, but then almost immediately return to the search results and click on the next link? In that case, then the first site they ended up on was apparently irrelevant.
2 If many other websites link to a site, it would seem to be popular and relevant (see link building in section 6.3). We call these links from other websites to your own website 'back links'. The robots also look at the text that is used behind which the URL is hidden, the anchor text. Are

11

the right keywords present there? A link must also be somewhat 'fresh'. You can read more about link building in section 6.3.

3 The content of the page itself: how much relevant content does it contain, is this content unique, is there a lot of overlap between pages, is the content itself written or, for example, collated via affiliate marketing?

They also look at social shares, how often a link to a webpage is shared, is an indication of its popularity.

Social shares

11.8.3   Enriching search results

Another way of optimising a website is to ensure that the search results are enriched. Search engines show horizontal and vertical search results. Vertical search results come from a search engine that is designated for special types of information (think for example YouTube for videos and Google Image Search for images). By horizontal search results we mean all composite search results in eg Google. Recently, Google often combines local (from Google Maps), social (from Google+) and other vertical search results in the horizontal search results. The combination of vertical and horizontal search results in Google is called Universal Search.

Vertical search results

Horizontal search results

Universal Search

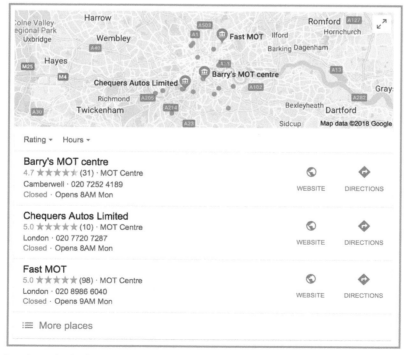

Local results in the 'horizontal search results' (outlined in green)

In addition to the combinations that Google makes by using vertical search results in the horizontal search results, there are also ways of enriching search results yourself. These enriched search results are called 'rich snippets'. These rich snippets are shown because Google recognises that these websites provide additional information (such as reviews, ratings or, for example, touring dates of musicians). This information needs to be put into the website by the builders in the correct way, in accordance with search engine standards. On http://schema.org/, you can find the standard, an agreement that all the major search options made with one another. Another form of enrichment involves site links: the links under organic search results (when searching for a brand name) that refer to deeper pages. These deep links also exist within search engine advertisements.

Rich snippets

Deep links

London Concert Tickets - Viagogo
https://www.viagogo.co.uk/London/Concert-Tickets ▾
Buy & sell **Concert** Tickets in **London** at viagogo. Tickets for **Concerts**, Sport, Theatre at viagogo, the ticket marketplace. Buy and Sell Tickets 100% safe and guaranteed.

Sun 18 Mar	Knocked Loose	Teragram Ballroom, Los ...
Sun 18 Mar	Sepultura	KOKO Camden, London ...
Sun 18 Mar	Cannibal Corpse	O2 Forum Kentish Town ...

Dates of events processed in the search result

Ratings

The most eye-catching rich snippets are search results that include ratings. These stars in the search results give a positive signal to the user, because they stand out and inspire confidence. A user is therefore more likely to click on a search result that contains a lot of stars and a good evaluation.

Rose Beauty Salon at James & Peter First Floor | Beauty Salon in ...
https://www.treatwell.co.uk › ... › Manchester City Centre › Central Retail District ▾
★★★★★ Rating: 4.7 - 307 reviews
Located at the Royal Exchange, Rose **Beauty Salon** is an exclusive boutique providing luxurious treatments to help glamourise your look. Situated inside James and Peter **Hair salon,...**

Ratings processed in the search result

These reviews are often given by customers of web shops that have purchased products or services. The web store allows the customer to give a rating and/or write a review. Online retailers stimulate this by, for example, sending the customer an email asking them to write a review two weeks after a purchase. These ratings and reviews are then placed on the site itself.

11.8.4   Google Search Console (formerly Google Webmaster Tools)

Search engines help you to optimise your website. Google, for instance, has Google Search Insights. It contains important information about, for example, the traffic to your website and any problems Google encounters in crawling your site.

Google Search Insights

Traffic

Google Search Console offer you statistics that come directly from the Google search engine. Search Console provides insight into the number of impressions and number of clicks to your website. An important part of this overview is the enumeration of terms your visitors use in Google.

Traffic in Google Search Console

Website health

If Google runs into many problems within a website, this is detrimental to the visibility of this website in Google's search results. Examples of this are pages that Google cannot find (a so-called 404 page), technical problems with web servers or duplicate content. This is page content that is exactly the same as on other pages. Google prefers unique content. Google Webmaster Tools provides insight into these types of errors, so that you, as a website owner, can respond quickly.

404 Page

Duplicate content

Not provided

Since 2012, Google has been blocking an increasing number of searches in Google Analytics, due to 'privacy considerations'. Users who are logged in with a Google account and users who use Chrome and Firefox (two popular web browsers) have their search phrases blocked. In concrete terms, this means that a certain amount of the keywords in Google Analytics' keyword list show up as '(not provided)'. This only applies to traffic from Google's organic results. This makes it difficult to measure SEO success in the right way, because you are missing a piece of information about your visitors.

(Not provided)

As of today, no working solution has yet been found to counter this phenomenon.

11.8.5   Mobile SEO

People have become accustomed and addicted to smartphones. The device is easy to use and handy for quickly finding something. Since 2015, this has meant that more searches are being performed on smartphones than on desktops. This also means that website owners must take the user experience on smartphones into account.

11

As you have already read, a mobile-friendly website is very important. Technically speaking, there are a number of ways to do this:

- *responsive design*: the web page adjusts to the screen format of the device
- *dynamic serving*: the same URL, after which the appropriate content is sent to the user once the device has been recognised
- *mobile website*: a separate mobile website with a separate URL

In the past, Google has indicated to prefer responsive design, but provided the implementation is done properly, any of these options will work on smartphones. The same goes for SEO.

App Store Optimisation

Not all websites are suitable for smartphone search results. Apps are also listed in the search results on a smartphone. This applies to the app as a whole, but also to deep links in the app. Making these deep links possible requires a technical implementation, it does not happen automatically. Apps are usually located in the App Store (iOS) or in Google Play (Android). Making an app discoverable in these places is called App Store Optimisation.

Mobile first index

At the moment, the desktop is the primary input for Google's index. However, they have announced that the smartphone websites and 'mobile index' will become the primary input in the near future. If a website is not suitable for smartphones, this could have adverse consequences after this switch. The expectation is that Google will have already implemented this at the time this book appears.

11.8.6 Voice search

Voice search

Voice commands are gaining popularity: Google announced in mid-2016 that 20% of all mobile searches are performed by 'voice search' (Searchengineland, 2016). This changes the style of the search. Voice-controlled searches are longer and do not contain concrete keywords as we have come to know them in Google. A query such as 'What is a tasty Italian restaurant in Midtown Manhattan?' seems more natural than 'Italian Restaurant'. That means a new challenge for SEO specialists. Increasingly the search engines are becoming adept at understanding intent (ie not 'what did they **type**?' nor 'what did they **say**? 'but rather 'What do they **want**?'

© Noordhoff Uitgevers bv

Questions and assignments

NOW CHECK YOUR UNDERSTANDING:

11.1   According to Hasan and Abuelrub, the quality of a website, from the user's point of view, is determined by four elements. Sauro distinguishes three factors that you need to investigate in order to measure the user experience.
  a Go to the websites: home.bt.com and o2.co.uk. Assess both websites on Sauro's three factors based on his SUPR-Q questionnaire.
  b To what extent do the elements that Hasan and Abuelrub defined differ from Sauro's three factors? Support your answer.
  c What can both organisations do to gain a better understanding of the behaviour of visitors to their websites?

11.2   Hussain and Kutar list six requirements that users set for apps.
  a What are these six requirements?
  b Download the Ocado app: groceries made easy (for Android or iOS) To what extent can you explain the success of this app using Hussain and Kutar's six requirements?

11.3   Search YouTube for a few recent videos on eyetracking and facetracking for testing the usability of websites.
  a What do you consider to be the most important pros and cons of both methods?
  b What other ways, that you consider to be useful, have you come across for testing the usability of websites? Copy the addresses of the videos and indicate why you think these are useful methods.

11.4   In the UK, The BSI Kitemark™ is a quality mark and one of the most recognised symbols of quality and safety indicating providers of products and services offering true value to consumers. If a site displays the Kitemark the visitor knows that the website has been legally and financially checked and that the website adheres to a number of agreements about safety and consumer protection.
  a Indicate why a guarantee such as the BSI Kitemark is important for the effectiveness of a website.
  b Indicate the consequences of insufficient security for a website.

11.5   On the Dutch website Geboortekaartjes,nl, people can order birth announcements. In the introductory phase, people were able to order a sample copy online before they completed their order. On the advice of an agency, the request button was given a more prominent position as well as a larger size and the short indication on the button was changed into an

11

appealing message. After a week, the A/B test showed that already twice as many visitors had applied for a sample copy on the new page.

a Why do you think the position and format of the request button are so important?

b Why does a short, appealing sentence like 'Request a free sample copy' work better than a simple indication such as 'request' on the request button?

11.6 Go to the ecommerce website www.beatsbydre.com.

a Make a list of the requirements for website usability that you can find in section 11.3 and rate www.beatsbydre.com on the basis of those criteria. What is your conclusion?

b Make a list of the requirements for web content and web text in section 11.4 and see to what extent www.beatsbydre.com adheres to them. What is your conclusion?

c Would this website also have received a prize from you? Please substantiate your answer.

11.7 Search online for the keyword 'round trip to Machu Picchu'. Check whether Trailfinders.com is listed in the paid results and/or in the organic results.

a What is your first conclusion about Trailfinders.com search engine marketing?

b Which requirements must a landing page meet? Does Trailfinders.com landing page comply with this?

c Make an inventory of the organisational consequences if Trailfinders.com didn't have a content management system.

11.8 Choose a random website and see if it is optimised for SEO. Also look at what you see when you perform the following tests.

a Find a free 'spider test' or 'web crawler tool' (like the SEO Spider by Screaming Frog) and determine what Google thinks about the website you've chosen.

b Use a free tool, for example from Moz.com, to check the search engine optimisation. What are your results?

c What can you say about the internal and external optimisation of the chosen website?

11.9

CASE

A Webby for the Smithsonian National Museum of African American History and Culture
By Marjolein Visser

The Smithsonian National Museum of African American History and Culture (NMAAHC) opened its doors in Washington, DC at the end of 2016. The museum makes African-American history tangible for its visitors using permanent exhibitions as well as periodical exhibitions, with subjects such as 'Slavery and Freedom', 'Through the African American Lens' and 'Musical Crossroads'.

According to the museum's management, it befits a new museum to have a modern, attractive and user-friendly website. The online experience must reflect, complement and add to the museum's striking physical shape. The management called in the help of Forum One, an agency specialising in digitisation for non-profit organisations. The design and composition of the website was an intensive project, that was rewarded with two Webby Awards. Both the professional jury and the international public rated the NMAAHC website as the best website for a cultural institute in 2017.

The Smithsonian National Museum of African American History and Culture's website

The design of the website started with a comprehensive discovery phase. Forum One held interviews with the 'content owners', such as the communications specialists and curators of the museum. In addition, the agency organised a series of workshops with a team from the museum to identify the most important needs and goals of both the future users and the museum itself. Based on this, user journeys were mapped.

The ultimate goal was to build a website with an impressive visual design, an intuitive user experience and a smart mobile implementation, according to Forum One. Of course, the design had to be a reflection of the museum itself: the architectural lines, the colours and spaces were the starting point for the design of the website. The characteristic pieces from the collection had to be presented in such a way that their meaning and context was clear and coherent. To ensure user-friendliness, someone was explicitly responsible for the user experience in all phases of the project. Forum One says: 'This approach resulted in a digital home for the NMAAHC that tells personal stories, is a tribute to the museum's historical importance and allows all Americans to experience their shared history and this iconic national monument (the museum itself – ed.)'

Obviously, the user experience on all devices had to be good. That is why Forum One designed a fully responsive website that uses the entire width of the screen. 'A sharp and intuitive mobile menu and well-considered interactions streamline the user experience, while a floating action button at the bottom of the screen subtly follows the users as they scroll and jump back to the top with a single tap', Forum One says about the mobile version.
In addition to the mobile website, visitors to the museum can also choose the app, developed by Clearly Innovative. In addition to general information about the museum, the app contains the stories behind the exhibitions, the building, places in

11

the vicinity of the building, additional media such as video clips and special stories for children. The stories can be responded to and they can also be shared via social media. The app scores 4.7 out of 5 points in the Google Play Store.

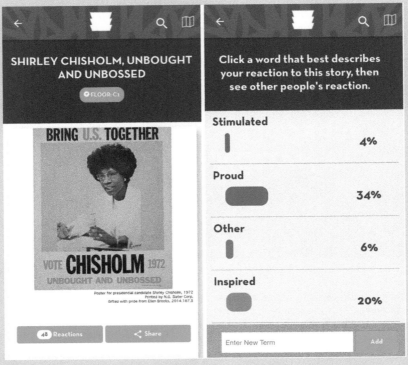

In the app, you can respond to stories about the exhibitions

Sources: www.nmaahc.si.edu, www.forumone.com, www.clearlyinnovative.com and https://play.google.com

a Which of the four elements that determine the quality of a website in the eyes of the user has the Smithsonian National Museum of African American History and Culture (NMAAHC) focused on?

b What do you think about the content, design, structure and ease of use of the NMAAHC's website? Also look explicitly at the content, the text, the use of images and the interaction with the visitor. Prepare a list of criteria based on the theory beforehand. What points for improvement do you see?

c Draw a simple customer journey map for:
1 people who want to find out what they can experience in the museum
2 people who want to buy a ticket for the museum
Compare both customer journeys with your user experience when you use the NMAAHC website yourself (see https://nmaahc.si.edu/). What conclusions do you come to?

11

d Users impose different requirements on apps than on websites (see table 11.1). Why do you think people are so enthusiastic about the NMAAHC app?

e What arguments do you think NMAAHC has for creating a mobile responsive website as well as an app? Do you think that is a sensible decision?

f Which methods could Forum One use to gain more insight into the behaviour of the visitors to the site they built for the NMAAHC?

g What requirements should the NMAAHC impose on the content management system from the perspective of the organisation?

h What requirements does NMAAHC have to impose regarding safety on the site?

i Write a short advice to Forum One how they can make the websites more effective through Search Engine Optimisation?

11

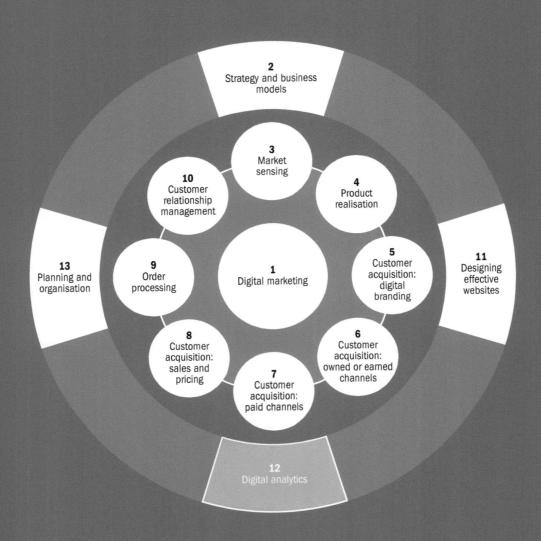

12
Digital analytics

Authors: Tom van den Berg and Marjolein Visser

The first eight chapters of this book describe how the marketer can establish a clear idea of what the market's wants and desires are (the market sensing process) and how the Internet can be used to further product development and improvement as well as for setting up processes surrounding the product or the service (the product realisation process). Once everything is customer-ready, the customer acquisition process commences: defining target segments and recruiting new customers. When the order processing has been executed as smoothly as possible, the relationship can be further expanded and deepened during the customer relationship management process. You have also been able to read what requirements are imposed on effective websites and apps. This chapter addresses the question of what needs to be measured in order to monitor and improve the digital marketing process. In addition, it provides you with insight regarding the basic concepts of web analytics and the most important indicators that are used by web analysts.

This chapter will cover:
- digital analytics: definition and starting points
- performance indicators
- traffic sources
- the ABC model
- recognising the phase that the visitor is in
- social media metrics
- web analytics within the organisation

After studying this chapter, you will be able to:
- describe in your own words what digital analytics entails, what the most important performance indicators are and what the role of digital analytics is within digital marketing
- explain the most important basic values in web analytics, interpret statistics of these basic values and indicate what additional information you need for a good interpretation
- indicate how, in web analytics, the various digital marketing communication tools are included in the traffic sources

12

- identify the relationship between the phase of the digital marketing funnel that the visitor is in and the key performance indicators
- explain how the ABC model works and how you can use it to structure digital analyses
- identify the most important social media metrics that should be included in a social media monitoring program, explain why these are important and translate them into recommendations regarding improvements to communications via social media
- indicate which six factors determine the maturity of an organisation in terms of digital marketing analytics and why these factors must be balanced

12.1 Digital analytics: definition and starting points

Web analytics

In the past, we referred to web analytics. According to the Web Analytics Association (WAA), the definition of web analytics is 'the measurement, collection, analysis and reporting of internet data for the purposes of understanding and optimising web usage' The definition is broad enough to remain applicable. The terms 'web' and 'website' are somewhat old-fashioned due to the popularity of apps, tablet devices and mobile phones. The focus is shifting towards 'digital' or 'omnichannel analytics'. Omnichannel means 'all' channels, both offline (physical stores and print media such as leaflets) and online (digital media such as websites and apps).

Digital analytics

Digital analytics provide market insight, show how target segments respond to campaigns, what visitors are doing on the website and help to evaluate and improve digital marketing decisions.

The digital world is constantly evolving: website visits from a desktop or laptop have become less important. Brands are also increasingly present on channels that are not self-owned, such as Facebook, Pinterest or Twitter. This means that content is often viewed via apps or mobile browsers on tablet devices or mobile phones. Where the majority of people used to go to websites' homepages first, now content on specific pages is often what they are looking for when they have been shared by people from apps or on social channels such as Facebook, Twitter or Pinterest. Some of the comments and visits 'remain' on that channel as a discussion or thread. Others refer directly to the specific page on the website with a 'short link'.

You not only want to know what the visitors are doing on their desktop or laptop, but also what interactions they have via apps and mobile pages, and on social channels such as Facebook or Twitter. Ideally, you would like to link all those separate interactions to one customer or prospect, but this isn't always easy to do. However, new tools are becoming available to map the complex and personal customer journeys: for example, staying logged in on Gmail, Facebook or Twitter ensures that you remain recognisable on all your devices. This way, a web analysis program detects that the evening visit from a tablet device was done by the same account as the short visit earlier that day that came from the mobile newsletter (Kremer, 2012).

This is one of the most important developments: analysis is shifting from 'device' level to user level, which allows you to observe a real customer journey.

Tracking code and Google Tag Manager

Before you can see how visitors behave on the website, it is essential that you implement the tracking code for the analytics package. This is a piece of JavaScript code that forwards data. You can implement this in two ways:

1 Directly into the code: the *tracking code* can be added straight into the website's code. The downside of this is that every change that you'd like to make to a measurement, must be done by someone with sufficient IT knowledge. However, it may be beneficial to add certain tracking codes as high up as possible in the website's code in order for them to be loaded faster.

2 *Tag manager*: An increasing amount of companies are using a tag manager. A tag manager is a tool that allows you to manage all your tags (analytics, digital marketing, etcetera). Previously, all these tags were added straight into the website's code, one at a time. The problem with this is that IT departments often only deploy a new release once or twice a month. This would mean that if you want to adjust one of your tags, you may have to wait for a month. To tackle this problem, a tag manager was developed. You only have to add a script once: that of the tag manager. After this is done, you can implement and modify as many tags as you'd like using the tag manager.

Market insights are not simply gained by solely conducting digital measurements. Avinash Kaushik (2007) depicted this very well in figure 12.1. He states that by measuring clicks, you only find out what happens online (What) and that by combining the results of digital measurements, you discover the extent of the impact (How much). By experimenting and testing, in combination with listening to the customer, you are able to find out what the reasons are for digital consumer behaviour (Why). In order to listen to the customer, you need more than just measurements, you also need market research for example (see Chapter 3). In order to make good marketing decisions however, you will also need to know what your customers' alternatives are (What else). For this, you will have to take stock of the competition and continue to monitor them. Only once you have combined all this information, can you actually gain market insight. Kaushik refers to this as Web Analytics 2.0 (see figure 12.1). In this chapter you will find more information about the first two steps of this model. To get a full understanding of the market, you can combine this chapter with the research and analysis methods from Chapters 2 and 3.

Web Analytics 2.0

There is an important precondition for starting an analysis: ask yourself what you hope to gain from the analysis. What will you ultimately be able to do with the results of the analysis? Will these results lead to actions, or is it just nice-to-know? In that case: save your efforts and look for analyses that will lead to action. You are looking for 'actionable insights'.

Actionable insights

12

FIGURE 12.1 Web Analytics 2.0

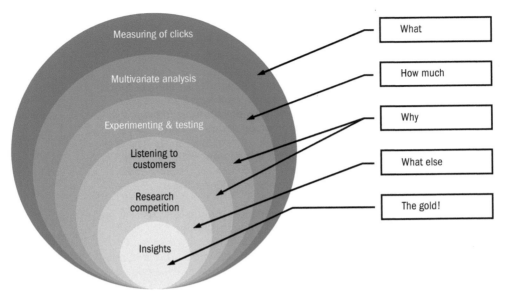

Source: Kaushik, 2007

Analytics experts Online Dialogue and Webanalisten.nl have compiled a list of the top 10 analysis questions:

1 Which *channels* generate the most traffic to the website? What is the aim and the conversion rate for each of the different channels/media? What is the ratio between paid and unpaid traffic?
2 What *keywords* lead to people *visiting the website*? And what is the conversion rate of those keywords?
3 On which *days* and at what *time* is the website visited most often? And on which days and at what time are people most likely to convert?
4 What *browsers* and *devices* are used most often and is there a difference in the number of conversions between these browsers?
5 What are the top 10 *landing pages* in terms of visitor counts and conversions? What does the clicking behaviour look like on these pages for the most important segments?
6 What are the *most visited pages* on the website in general? On which pages do a lot of visitors leave the website?
7 How do people *navigate* on the website? Use main navigation, filters and so on.
8 What *keywords* do people *use on the website*? And how successful are those keywords?
9 What does the *funnel* look like and where in this funnel do the largest group of *exits* appear to be.
10 Which *channels* are responsible for the *final conversion*? Which channels are responsible for orientation visits (*conversion attribution*)?

12.2 The digital marketing funnel translated into performance indicators

One of digital marketing's greatest charms is that the process is measurable from beginning to end. However, in order to properly monitor and fine-tune the digital marketing activities, organisations must determine in advance what the key performance indicators (KPIs) are. These are the indicators that they use to assess whether their digital marketing activities are successful. For example, a KPI could be the number of visitors per day or the monthly turnover of the web shop. These KPIs vary per industry and per organisation and are highly dependent on the website's purpose. You can imagine that an online newspaper uses very different KPIs than a website that sells mobile phones.

Key performance indicators

KPI

In Chapter 3 you have read about the digital marketing funnel (see figure 12.2). KPIs can be defined for every level of this funnel. For the sake of convenience, from this point onwards we will refer to 'the website', but it may also be a mobile site, a landing page or an app.

FIGURE 12.2 The digital marketing funnel

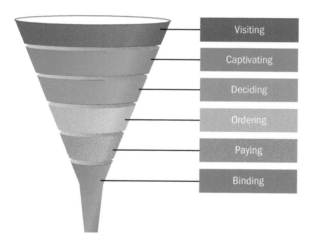

In the following sub-sections, you will be able to read about the KPIs that are used in each phase. Then, from section 12.3 onwards, we will talk about how to use digital analytics in practice.

12.2.1 Visits

Sometimes, companies will comment on visits in the press, for example: 'We have 100,000 visitors per month.' What does this mean? A visitor is someone (or actually a new cookie) who goes onto your website. If this visitor returns within thirty days, then they are one visitor who visits twice. A visit means that someone enters a website and performs activities on the website within 1,800 seconds (= half an hour). Suppose someone returns to the website after half an hour has expired, then this is registered

Visitor

Visit

12

Page views

as a new visit, but still as one visitor. If someone goes to a website, receives a phone call after five minutes, has a ten-minute conversation and then continues with their website visit, this is still considered one visit. In addition to visitors and visits, there is also a third concept that is often mentioned in web analytics: page views (*page views*). During one visit by one visitor, multiple pages are often viewed.

Within two days, one visitor may visit three times and view a total of 18 pages.

EXAMPLE 12.1

One or two visitors, one or two visits?

Suppose you are busy looking for a holiday on a website. You have found a holiday that you want to book. Your partner also agrees. Suddenly the doorbell rings and you leave your computer to open the door. When you return, your partner has already booked the trip. In web analytics, this is regarded to as one visitor and one visit, but in fact this should be two visitors with two visits.

The same problem may arise the other way around. If you visit a website on your mobile phone today and on your laptop tomorrow, web analytics records this as two visits by two visitors. Whilst in fact, it involves two visits from a single visitor. You are, of course, the same person. The reason this happens is because you are not identified as a person, but on the basis of cookies. You use a different browser on your mobile phone, in which a new, unique cookie is installed. You can however be identified anyway if you are logged into an account or in Gmail/Facebook.

Example 12.1 illustrates that there is not always one truth in web analytics. It is a matter of interpreting the data the right way and not just making assumptions indiscriminately. A hundred thousand visitors per month are basically 100,000 individual people who have visited the website at least once. However, if people use each other's devices, then those figures are no longer completely accurate. The same applies to visitors that are not logged in and visit the website on multiple devices.

Important KPIs for the 'visits' phase are the reach, the click rate, the percentage of new visitors and the acquisition costs.

Reach

The reach of a website is the percentage of the target segment that uses the website. For example, 'The reach of Huffingtonpost.com on the Internet further decreased in the past year' means that of all people who read an online newspaper, there is a smaller percentage reading Huffingtonpost.com than the year before.

$$\text{Reach} = \frac{\text{Number of unique users of the website in period T}}{\text{Total number of unique users in the target segment}}$$

12

A visit occurs when users actually end up on the website.

The definition of reach however, depends on the circumstances that it is used in. For ads, for example, Google considers the unique reach to be the total number of people to whom an ad is displayed. However, the term reach is also used by Google in a very different context, namely the level that a statistic from Google Analytics relates to: user level, session level, product level or hit level. A hit occurs when the Google tracking code is triggered by a visitor interacting with the website. In short: always properly check the definition used for reach before you draw your conclusions based on these figures.

Another important KPI in this phase is the click rate or click-through rate: the number of clicks on an email, advertisement or other expression in relation to the number of impressions of this expression. 'The click rate of the banner was 2%' means that two out of one hundred people that could have seen the banner, clicked on it. This has nothing to do with whether people actually saw the banner: it's about the banner being displayed on a page that they opened.

Click rate

$$\text{Click rate} = \frac{\text{Number of clicks}}{\text{Number of impressions}}$$

The percentage of new visitors to a website is also an important indicator for the effectiveness of digital marketing communications. A visitor is 'new' if they are visiting the website for the first time in thirty days. Of course, what the ratio should be between the number of new visitors and existing visitors depends on the type of website. Web shops want to engage their visitors. Whilst orientating or during their decision-making process, people who are looking to buy something will usually view the website multiple times before they make their final purchase. In that case, a high percentage of new visitors can be unfavourable. That's because this means that many people only visit once. But if the web shop has just started a campaign to attract more visitors to their website, the percentage of new visitors will be relatively high and that is a positive thing.

Percentage of new visitors

I essence, a news website wants visitors to come back daily to read the latest news but will also want an increasing number of new visitors. So, should such a website have a high or low percentage of new visitors? That is, of course, completely dependent on the objectives (Kremer, 2012).

The acquisition costs are the cost per click or cost per impression. The costs of an individual expression, such as a banner, are expressed in CPM (cost per Mille) or CPC (cost per click).

Acquisition costs

$$\text{CPM} = \frac{\text{Costs of the expression}}{(0.001 \times \text{the number of impressions})}$$

CPM

$$\text{CPC} = \frac{\text{Costs of the expression}}{\text{Number of clicks}}$$

CPC

12

In figure 12.3, the CPM for all expressions together is €15.19 / (0.001 × 12,122) = €1.25. In other words: it costs 1.25 euros to show your banner to 1,000 people.
The CPC is €15.19 / 92 = €0.17. In other words: it costs 0.17 euros to receive one click on an advertisement.

FIGURE 12.3 Core results indicators CTR en CPC

Ad group	Status ⓘ	Standard max. CPC	Max. CPC for self-chosen placements	Max. CPC for the Display Network ⓘ	Amount clicks ⓘ	Impressions	CTR ⓘ	Average. CPC ⓘ	Cost ⓘ
Excursions for the elderly	Suitable	€ 0.20 🗹	€ 0.20	€ 0.20	78	11,861	0.66%	€ 0.17	€ 13.24
Excursions for the elderly	Suitable	€ 0.20 🗹	€ 0.20	€ 0.20	14	261	5.36%	€ 0.14	€ 1.95
Total - all, excluding removed ad groups					92	12,122	0.76%	€ 0.17	€ 15.19
Total - search ⓘ					67	4,156	1.61%	€ 0.16	€ 10.83
Total - Display Network ⓘ					25	7,966	0.31%	€ 0.17	€ 4.36
Total - all ad groups					92	12,122	0.76%	€ 0.17	€ 15.19

An overall indicator of the acquisition costs is made according to the costs per contact: the marketing expenses in a period per obtained visitor.

Costs per contact

$$\text{Costs per contact} = \frac{\text{Marketing expenses in period T}}{\text{Visitors in period T}}$$

Suppose that, during the week depicted in the previous example, €200 was spent on general advertising costs and this led to 108 extra visitors, then the costs per contact for this period are (€15.19 + €200 / (108 + 92) = €1.08.

Connect rate

In addition, many digital marketers measure the connect rate: the actual number of people who visited a page, as opposed to the number of people who clicked but did not visit the page. This could be because, for example, it took too long for the page to load or because an error occurred. A visitor on a forum wrote:

'I have a rather peculiar problem. I want to visit a certain website (belonging to a travel agency), but I only get to see half a page, showing the message 'Ready with errors'. The links on that page also not doing what they're supposed to. When I asked around in my neighbourhood, I found out that all my neighbours are able to access the website without any problems. I, on the other hand, am unable to.'

App analytics

The number of people that visit your website on their mobile phone continues to increase. Analysing the results of mobile marketing is also known as mobile analytics. People do not only use mobile websites, but also apps. Many apps, such as Spotify or Facebook, require visitors to be logged in. Within app analytics, the metrics that are reviewed differ slightly from the ones used for web analytics. Important metrics are, for example, the amount of app-installs (the number of times an app is installed), the number of log-ins, the number of pages viewed, the session duration, the number of advertising clicks and how often the app has been used in a week. The Apple and Android store statistics, for example, are also important, such as the number of downloads, installations and searches.

App-installs

Ultimately, your aim is to get a unified picture of the visitor whether it is via the app, mobile website or desktop website. This can be done using universal analytics, this is the version of Google Analytics that revolves around the visitor.

12.2.2   Captivate

When someone visits the website, it is important to captivate them so that they can begin to take the first steps towards a purchase. Retention is the extent to which the site holds onto the visitors.

Retention

Two simple indicators are:

- *Depth of the visit*: how many pages did the user visit?
- *Average duration of the visit*: how much time did the user spend on the website?

The objectives must be taken into account for both indicators, in order to interpret them properly. For example, a news website benefits from many pages per visit as this will increase the value of the advertisements. A web shop will also benefit from many pages per visit, provided this is a visitor who is still in the orientation phase. After all, the purchase process must be smooth, otherwise potential buyers will pull out. Someone who already knows what they want to buy, will want to place their order in as few steps as possible, ie via as few pages as possible.

The value 'average duration of a visit', reflects the amount of time a visitor spends on the website on average. If this is extremely short, then the challenge is to make the website more interesting for your visitors. A very long stay however, isn't always indicative of anything good. Visitors may have difficulty finding information.

12

A long visit?

The relationship between the duration of a visit and the pages per visit is important. By comparing these two values, you are able to deduce a visitor's average time spent per page. The average time someone stays on a page says something about their behaviour, but precisely what that is depends on what can be found on the page. If a customer stays on the contact page for a short amount of time, that's a good thing. If they remain on a product page for only a short amount of time, it may mean that they are not interested (Kremer, 2012).

Bounce rate

The bounce rate is the percentage of visitors who leave the website almost immediately. If this percentage is large, then the website is not interesting and probably not relevant or not trustworthy enough for the visitor. In practice, this also appears to be more nuanced. For example, if someone is looking for a phone number and finds it immediately, they will leave quickly, but still be satisfied.
A significant reason for a high bounce rate may be the mismatch between a banner and the website. It is relevant for example, that the layout and content in the banner matches the website. Otherwise, visitors may wonder if they are on the right website after they have clicked through. You were able to read more about effective advertising in Chapter 7.
Sometimes, a high bounce rate is inherent to the type of website or web page. If there are many outbound links on a page, such as on a home page like Kadaza.nl, then a high bounce rate is a good sign.

12.2.3 Decide

It is extremely difficult to see whether a visitor has finally decided that they want to purchase a product or service via the website but have not yet put in an order. An indicator of the number of people who have decided to purchase, but for whatever reason fail to follow through, is the abandonment ratio. This is the percentage of visitors who fail to complete a certain step in the ordering process.

Abandonment ratio

An example of such a ratio is the 'cart abandonment rate': the percentage of visitors who fill their shopping cart, but then do not complete the order. Some causes of a high abandonment ratio could be: an overly lengthy checkout process, a disappointing number of options for paying, sudden display of shipping costs or a long delivery time. For some products, the visitor might return later, after they have consulted someone else about their decision.

Cart abandonment rate =

$$\frac{\text{Number of visitors who fill their shopping cart but do not order}}{\text{Total number of visitors that have filled their shopping cart in period T}}$$

Cart abandonment rate

Cart abandonment

In order to get an impression of the decision-making process, organisations will sometimes measure the *velocity*: the speed at which the average buyer moves from one step in the digital marketing funnel to the next.

12.2.4 Order

For websites that sell products or services, the order (and the subsequent payment) is the most important goal. In addition to the usual KPIs such as turnover and sales per period, the conversion rate and conversion costs are particularly important at this stage. At this stage, the conversion rate expresses what percentage of the visitors places an order. If the website in question is not a web shop, the conversion rate can be, for example, the percentage of visitors who apply for a job, request a leaflet or a quote, or who register for a newsletter.

$$\text{Conversion rate} = \frac{\text{Number of visits resulting in a goal in period T}}{\text{Total number of visitors in period T}}$$

Conversion rate

12

Visitors	E-commerce Conversion Rate	Target value per visit
72.273	**1.59%**	**€ 1,91**
% of site total: 100,00%		Siteav: € 1,91 (0,00%)

Conversion rate of 1.59%

The previous web statistics show the number of visitors (72,273), the conversion rate (1.59% of the visitors made a purchase) and the target value per visit (€1.91). The target value per visit is the sum that the average visitor brings in.

Web shops also look at the conversion costs in this phase: the cost per sales (CPS) or cost per order (CPO).

CPO

CPC

$$CPC = \frac{\text{Costs of the expression}}{\text{Number of items sold}}$$

The CPS must of course always be lower than the profit made on the product, otherwise the result is negative. By comparing the CPS of different instruments and websites, the most effective digital marketing communication method can be chosen.

12.2.5 Paying

If the order is placed but the visitor does not pay, then this is also a form of abandonment. On most websites the order will not be processed in such a case. Discontinuation in the very last phase of the ordering process is also called 'check-out abandonment', this ratio can also be determined.

Check-out abandonment rate

$$\text{Check-out abandonment rate} =$$
$$\frac{\text{Number of visitors who do not fully complete an order}}{\text{Total number of visitors who have ordered a product in period T}}$$

There are often many discontinuations in this part of the process. There are various reasons this could happen. Examples could be: 'I still have to consult with my partner', 'I am now on my mobile, I will finish it at home on my laptop' or 'I suddenly see there are delivery costs, I had not seen that before'. Visitors in this phase probably are willing to buy from you because they have found their product or service and have clicked through to pay. Yet, something has prevented them from completing the order. To find out, you could, for instance, ask them to complete a survey.

An organisation that rents out holiday homes discovered that a significant percentage of the people who indicated that they wanted to rent a house via the reservation page did not complete this reservation with a final confirmation and payment. By contacting these people, they discovered that there were additional questions and wishes that customers felt unable to voice properly online. By solving this, the check-out abandonment rate went down considerably. In this example you can clearly see the combination of number analysis on the one hand, and knowledge of your

© Noordhoff Uitgevers bv

customer, by contacting the customer personally or using an online survey or feedback tool (feedback button on the site), on the other.

12.2.6 Bonding

Once a visitor has ordered something once, the digital marketer would like them to come back. In order to establish loyalty, you must look at four indicators: frequency, recency, period of use and monetary value. Frequency measures how often a user has visited the site. Recency is the time between visits to the website and how long ago the visitor was active on the site. The period of use is the number of hours a visitor spends on the website per visit. The monetary value refers to the amount that a visitor spends within a period.

Frequency
Recency
Period of use
Monetary value

$$\text{Frequency} = \frac{\text{Number of visits in period T}}{\text{Number of unique visitors in T}}$$

$$\text{Recency} = \text{Time that has elapsed since the last visit}$$

$$\text{Period of use} = \frac{\text{Total amount of time spent on the website}}{\text{Number of visits in period T}}$$

$$\text{Monetary value} = \frac{(\text{Number of orders} \times \text{average price of orders})}{\text{Per period}}$$

In Universal Analytics, the web analytics system introduced by Google in 2013, it is possible to determine the customer value of visitors from this basic data.

Universal Analytics

An indicator of the extent to which visitors are bound to a website is the stickiness. You can calculate this by looking at how often visitors use the website on average, how much time they spend on the website and how many visitors the website counts in a given period.

Stickiness

$$\text{Stickiness} = \text{frequency} \times \text{period if use} \times \text{total reach of the site in period T}$$

Attrition occurs if after a fixed period of time a customer is no longer active, whereas they were before. Churn is an indicator of the number of departed website users in a given period. It is the opposite of retention.

Attrition
Churn

$$\text{Churn} = \frac{\text{Total number of departed website users in period T}}{\text{Total number of users in period T}}$$

12

Data quality

Something that is regularly underestimated by companies is the data quality. In this case, we mean the quality of the data within the analytics package (eg Google Analytics). All kinds of decisions are taken on the basis of this data. If, for example, it turns out that a certain advertisement within Google performs better than another, it may be worth using more of that type of advertisement. You do then have to be sure that the data is correct and not that some of the ads have been clicked on by colleagues, lowering the conversion rate. You want to exclude colleagues' visits as this data is not representative.

In addition, a lot of what is called 'referral spam' occurs these days. These are bots that send hits to analytics, purely to pollute your data. You want to exclude this from your data, for example by setting up filters on certain IP addresses that these bots use to send their traffic from.

12.3 Different traffic sources within digital analytics

Traffic sources are the sources of origin for visitors to the organisation's website: places where click-through options are available on the website. Within web analytics, there are usually three groups of traffic sources: direct traffic, referred traffic and search engines. In addition, there are 'other' sources. Below, you will be able to read how to handle the web analytics for every traffic source and what the most important pitfalls are.

12.3.1 Direct traffic

Direct traffic

Direct traffic are visitors who enter the web address of a website directly into the address bar of the browser. Another form of direct traffic are favourites. A visitor who is seen as direct traffic is a visitor who is already familiar with a website or at least made a conscious choice to come to the website.

Default Channel Grouping ⑦	Sessions ⑦	Pages/sessions ⑦	Av. session time ⑦	New sessions ⑦	Bouncerate ⑦
Direct	323,557 % of total: 35.26% (917,631)	5.74 Siteav: 5.60 (2.58%)	00:03:53 Siteav: 00:03:50 (1.42%)	49.04% Siteav: 36.87% (33.02%)	29.25% Siteav: 34.38% (-14.91%)

Direct traffic in Google Analytics

In the example above, you can see data regarding direct traffic. The bounce percentage is rather high, because 29.25% for direct traffic is a little unusual. This requires further investigation: for example, the URL of the website may be very similar to that of another website. An example of this is: www.vouchercodes.co.uk and www.myvouchercodes.co.uk. This can cause user (and even customer) confusion.

What also stands out here is the high number of new visitors relative to returning visitors (49.04%). That is special, you would expect a low number of new visitors for direct traffic. The organisation may have implemented an offline media campaign, which includes the web address. Digital analytics is more than viewing statistics. You learn very little if you are not aware of the backgrounds. In general, conversions via direct traffic are always higher than via the other traffic sources, because someone who consciously chooses a site is already further along in their decision-making process.

Pitfall
Nowadays many visitors type the name of the website in the search bar of a search engine, but that is not counted as direct traffic. They then click on a search result or a paid search engine ad. The actual number of direct visitors can be a lot higher than the statistics show (Kremer, 2012).

12.3.2 Referred traffic

Visits via a link on another website fall under referred traffic. It is interesting to find out from which source a visitor came on the website and what this visitor subsequently did on the website. Referred traffic can sometimes be very diverse in terms of bounce rate and the number of pages being visited. The following figure shows that the bounce rate is relatively low, and the quality is better than that of direct traffic (more pages per session and longer average session duration).

Referred traffic

Default Channel Grouping ⑦	Sessions ⑦	Pages/sessions ⑦	Av. session time ⑦	New sessions ⑦	Bouncerate ⑦
Referral	2,455 % of total: 0.27% (917,631)	11.20 Siteav: 5.60 (100.02%)	00:14:30 Siteav: 00:03:50 (277.84%)	2.12% Siteav: 36.87% (-94.25%)	17.84% Siteav: 34.38% (-48.10%)

Referred traffic in Google Analytics

This also illustrates how a digital marketer can control quality if they keep an eye on such traffic. The marketer can use the analytics program, for example, to see where the visit comes from, on which page the visit lands and what is then done there. A targeted approach can then be used for directing traffic to the website and turning the visits into conversions. Suppose, for example, that many visitors enter a website about indoor plants via women's magazines' websites. This could be a reason to try to get more links or to place content in other women's magazines, or more generally: on websites for women. You can also use referred traffic to find websites that are interesting to advertise on (Kremer, 2012).

12.3.3 Search engines

The search engine as a traffic source is divided into sub-groups in almost all web analysis programs. For example, you have the traffic from organic results (SEO) and the paid results (SEA). We will now discuss some sub-groups of traffic sources.

Traffic from organic results
In the results of organic traffic, you often you see that more or less direct traffic is also included. Visitors use the search window on Google and enter part of the domain name there. This is seen as organic traffic, while this is actually direct traffic.

Companies that do not do a lot of SEO will score better from this traffic source than companies that do a lot of SEO. That sounds strange, but it is a consequence of 'disturbed' direct traffic. If a website does not do a lot of SEO, they will usually be found using the company name or a variant of it.

12

Longtail

Visitors using this search term genuinely have the intention of visiting the website and will therefore generally stay longer and have a lower bounce rate. If you do a lot of SEO, then you will generate more visitors in what is called the 'longtail'. These are visitors who search on specific search terms instead of on general search terms. For example, they have searched for 'car sleeper train in winter to Innsbruck' as opposed to 'train to Austria'. Visitors that perform a very specific search, are often critical of the information and inclined to leave quickly (read: bounce rate). They view the page they need and with that, your website has met their information needs. A low number of pages per visit and a short average visit duration is not unusual for this group.

Pitfall
Visitors who search in a very targeted manner, as well as visitors who orient themselves extensively on the website, enter via the SEO traffic source. It is important not to see these visitors as a uniform group (Kremer, 2012).

Paid search engine traffic
The image below shows an example of paid search engine traffic. It is an optimised SEA campaign. You can tell because it has a low bounce rate and an average time on the website that is reasonably proportional to the number of pages per visit (5:09 = 309 seconds / 8.30 = 37.2 seconds). If an SEA campaign is not optimised, the collected data won't be quite as good.

Default Channel Grouping ?	Sessions ?	Pages/sessions ?	Av. session time ?	New sessions ?	Bouncerate ?
Paid Search	85,497 % of total: 2.20% (3,888,763)	8.30 Siteav: 5.84 (42.07%)	00:05:09 Siteav: 00:03:54 (32.03%)	23.79% Siteav: 37.03% (-35.75%)	17.31% Siteav: 33.49% (-48.30%)

SEA traffic (search network) in Google Analytics

Pitfall
You often see that digital marketers spend a relatively high amount of money on AdWords, unnecessarily so. Low cost per click, or a high CTR (click-through rate = the ratio between impressions and clicks) are then the only indicators for continuing a campaign. The marketer increases the daily budget or the cost per click on the assumption that more turnover will be generated on the site. Spending more money on advertising is often easier than analysing the behaviour on the site or implementing a content strategy on social media. That 'more AdWords' will attract more visitors is certainly the case, but are these extra visitors of good quality? Could not you have attracted people to your site in a cheaper way?

Advertising for your customers?
One of the special things about Google AdWords is that these results appear in Google 'above' organic (unpaid) results. Many people who have been your customers for a long time already, use your expensive Paid AdWords as a sort of bookmark; a quick way to get to your site without typing the URL. The search engine benefits from this more than if a visitor

types the URL in the address bar. That is why the cursor is already 'ready' in the search bar. You then spend a lot on advertisements that are clicked on by visitors who are already your customer or are a regular visitor. By looking closely at the behaviour of people who arrived on your website via paid ads, you will see that they do not convert, but for example log into the 'My environment' or have come to your site many times before. A good technical analyst can fit the advertisements with a piece of code where people who have ever logged in before or have visited the website more than 10 times are not targeted. For some companies, the percentage of customers who click on ads is 85%. So they only use 15% of their advertising budget for recruiting new customers or visitors.

Display network

The display network is a paid form of advertising that includes everything outside of the search engines (see also section 7.3). For example, ads on ITV.com or YouTube are display ads. In the following picture you can see an example of a traffic source that consists of so-called display visits. This kind of visit is often characterised by a high bounce rate, a short time spent on the website and few pages per visit. This is logical because visitors in the display network were actually busy doing something else, before they were tempted by the advertisement to visit the website. There more care that is taken when selecting the websites that the ads are placed on, the more favourable the results will be (Kremer, 2012). It is important to mark or tag the ads in the Analytics program separately with what is called a UTM code. This allows you to measure which variant of the banner or which location works best on any given site.

Display network

UTM code

Default Channel Grouping ⑦	Sessions ⑦	Pages/sessions ⑦	Av. session time ⑦	New sessions ⑦	Bouncerate ⑦
Display	45,896 % of total: 5.00% (917,631)	2.64 Siteav: 5.60 (-52.87%)	00:01:23 Siteav: 00:03:50 (-64.11%)	40.34% Siteav: 36.87% (9.43%)	74.10% Siteav: 34.38% (115.55%)

CPC or CPM traffic (display network) in Google Analytics

Pitfall
If a digital marketer is running a campaign with a high bounce rate, there could be several causes. It does not necessarily mean that the wrong websites have been chosen for the campaign. For example, the banner can be misleading or even 'too nice'. If a banner is very exciting or appeals to the imagination, visitors will also come to your website without any intention of purchasing anything. It is also possible that a landing page does not match an advertisement. Also, very few pages per visit combined with a high average time on the site, can be a sign that something is wrong. For example, it may be that the page is not clear or that the visitor is stuck. So your visitor does want to make a conversion, but simply cannot figure it out. Analysis, visitor research or A/B testing of banners and landing pages could provide a solution in this situation (Kremer, 2012).

12

A/B tests, multivariate tests and experiments. What are they?
Which images, texts and buttons influence the conversion on websites?
Using *A/B testing* and *multivariate testing* web pages can be optimised for
the best possible result.

When conducting an *experiment*, different elements of a web page are
compared. Think of headlines and headers, images, text, call-to-actions
and page layout (Jansen, Klaassen & Visser, 2015). It is important to have
a clear idea beforehand about the factors that influence the conversion
based on the objective of that specific web page and the pre-analysis that
has been done. Interesting insights into the data, such as a high drop-out
rate, a lot of clicks between product and category pages or a short time
spent on the page, can be input for a hypothesis that is then validated
using an A/B test.

In principle, only one element is tested at a time in A/B testing. More than
two variants of an element can also be tested, such a test is also called an
A/B/n test. In practice, digital marketers often change multiple elements
within an A/B test. This has the advantage that there are bigger
differences between A and B. The possible impact might also then be
bigger. The disadvantage is that if a positive or negative result comes out
of the A/B test, you do not know exactly which element caused it.

In multivariate tests, multiple variants are tested simultaneously, for
example A/B/C/D. In such a case, you test which combination of elements
yields the highest conversion. In multivariate tests, for example, the
header and a picture can be tested simultaneously. It is also possible to
determine which element has the greatest influence on the conversion.

If multiple variants are tested (for example four), this means that the
number of visitors per variant will be lower than with an A/B test (two
variants). This means that this a type of test needs a longer running time
or a higher *uplift*, a greater positive effect, in order to be able to recognise
a significant difference.

These tests usually use specific software such as Visual Website Optimizer,
Optimizely, AB Tasty or Google Optimize. Google Optimize is also available
in a free version (in addition to the paid version). The software sends
visitors to different versions of the page and calculates which elements
yield the highest conversion. Seasonal or temporal influences are excluded
because different versions of a web page are tested simultaneously.

Here is an example in the case of a luxury hotel website:
- On the page containing the form, it was found that approximately 50%
  of the visitors dropped out (ie exited the site).
- To understand why visitors drop out here, a survey was conducted
  among visitors who appeared to be about to leave the page (mouse
  outside the active browser screen). This is also called an exit survey.

- The question was: 'Would you like to help us by indicating why you are about to leave the website?' Perhaps surprisingly, 100 visitors answered this and about 30% of them complained about the fact that check-in and check-out times were not mentioned anywhere.
- These times were then simply added to the page quoting the price for the room.

This optimisation resulted in 5.5% conversion increase. This means that on the B variant, 5.5% more visitors eventually booked a room compared to the A variant. 5.5% more conversion means 5.5% more turnover: a considerable sum!

Before you start optimising and A/B testing, it is important to do good research. The combination of quantitative and qualitative research is ideal in this situation. Data shows you visitors' behaviour (in the example, the 50% drop-out percentage), but this does not tell you why that is the case. By carrying out qualitative research you can get to the bottom of the visitors' motives (in the example, an exit survey).

12.3.4   Other traffic sources
The other traffic sources are usually categorised in campaigns and are also viewed using the so-called UTM codes. If you do not use UTM codes, this traffic will be seen as referred traffic. We will use newsletters and affiliate marketing as an example. Then we will discuss conversion attribution.

Newsletters
The traffic source 'newsletters' is a tricky one. You have read more about email marketing in section 6.6. Several factors depend on the success of the newsletter and influence the statistics.

Default Channel Grouping ⑦	Sessions ⑦	Pages/sessions ⑦	Av. session time ⑦	New sessions ⑦	Bouncerate ⑦
Email	10,823 % of total: 10.89% (99,363)	1.75 Siteav: 3.60 (-51.32%)	00:00:46 Siteav: 00:03:46 (-79.78%)	46.49% Siteav: 41.80% (11.24%)	52.58% Siteav: 30.36% (73.19%)

Newsletter as a source in Google Analytics

In a qualitatively good newsletter system an analysis feature will always be included. The digital marketer can check whether the mail has been opened, which article of the newsletter is clicked on most often and sometimes you can even see who has clicked on a particular article. You can also see what email the client uses. Data such as this will help you to use the knowledge of such a newsletter system and optimise it for frequently used devices. If your email is opened on an iPhone in 60% of cases, you can advise the marketing department to optimise the length of the header. The site can then also be optimised for navigation on a mobile with a mobile template or a site can be built that is 'responsive' and adjusts the content to the screen size.

12

How well a newsletter performs, depends entirely on the content of the newsletter and what the organisation's connection to the recipients is. If the newsletter is strongly focused on the needs of the recipient and the target audience finds the newsletter interesting, then the quality will be significantly higher than if the digital marketer approaches large numbers of people in an unfocused way. The example above shows that on average this newsletter performs much worse than the rest of the traffic sources (Kremer, 2012). Compared to the costs of advertising, the low costs of creating and sending a newsletter mean that this is a frequently used method. As a result, people are receiving an increasingly greater amount of emails and they don't pay as much attention to them.

Pitfall

You can conclude that the organisation mentioned should not send newsletters or at least change its approach. But, the recipient's behaviour can be explained logically. In principle, the marketer determines the moment the newsletter is sent. Often a subject line or the attractive layout acts as a trigger to click through but having to read the landing page comes at an inconvenient moment, or the recipient actually has no intention of making a purchase at that time. Often, those who click through are curious visitors. However, these visitors can contribute to a longer-term conversion (Kremer, 2012). This is called conversion attribution (see later in this sub-section).

Affiliate networks

Affiliates are websites that receive a commission for, for example, a purchase or a registration. You have read more about this in section 7.5. An affiliate visit can best be compared to referred traffic, with one significant difference. Referred traffic often has link building as a primary goal, so that a better score is achieved in the search results. Affiliate marketing is primarily concerned with conversion, such as a notification or a purchase. Affiliate sites often present themselves as a 'friend' of the visitor, as a critical comparison site, but actually earn their money from a commission from the sites to which they refer visitors, eg moneysavingexpert.com and moneysupermarket.com.

Default Channel Grouping ⑦	Sessions ⑦	Pages/sessions ⑦	Av. session time ⑦	New sessions ⑦	Bouncerate ⑦
Affiliates	86,342 % of total: 9.41% (917,631)	5.31 Siteav: 5.60 (-5.16%)	00:04:04 Siteav: 00:03:50 (5.91%)	11.40% Siteav: 36.87% (-69.08%)	31.65% Siteav: 34.38% (-7.92%)

Affiliate networks as a source in Google Analytics

In principle, the affiliates should score well, both in the number of new visitors they deliver and on the depth of the visit (Kremer, 2012). Using analytics, digital marketers remove badly scoring affiliates from their network and determine the price per lead.

© Noordhoff Uitgevers bv

Online advertising, what should you pay attention to?

As a web analyst or digital marketer, you will often be asked for your opinion on online advertising. You will also be approached by sellers who promise you mountains of gold if you advertise on their website. What should you pay attention to in these situations?

Advertising on other websites has been made very transparent by web analytics. As a rule, you can find this traffic at the 'referred traffic' source, but you can also attach tracking codes, such as UTM codes. You can then view what kind of traffic an advertiser forwards, what exactly this has yielded and what exactly it cost. You can also compare various banners and banner positions to achieve maximum return on investment.

An advertising salesperson wants the most revenue with as little effort as possible. This means that an advertising salesman prefers to sell a banner at a fixed price. As a web analyst or digital marketer, you want to pay as little as possible for a guaranteed success. That means that you actually prefer to pay on a CPS (cost per sale) basis, in that case you only have to pay if you have actually sold something. In between are all kinds of variants such as paying per click (CPC = cost per click), paying per 1,000 impressions of a banner (CPM = cost per mille), or paying per registration, application or registration (CPL = cost per lead).

It's common knowledge that advertising salespersons are inclined to make things appear more favourable than they actually are. As a web analyst or digital marketer, you obviously mustn't fall for this. What to look out for:

- The advertising salesperson: 'We have 100,000 visitors on our website!' Visits and visitors are great, but is it the right target audience in terms of age, willingness to buy, phase of orientation process?
- The advertising salesperson: 'We have a lot of unique visitors!' You often hear this, but you already know that many unique visitors are not necessarily a good thing.
- The advertising salesperson, after an initial analysis of the results: 'We deliver 1,000 people a month to you!' Are they the 'right' visitors? Advertisers tend to focus on delivering people to your doorstep, whereas you are focused on those people who help you to meet your KPIs. As an analyst or marketer, you will therefore have to 'follow' visitors on your site to determine whether an advertiser provides you with the right 'type' of visitors.

Prices of ads do not say very much, other than that you have to be able to pay them of course. More important is the cost per conversion, this must be relatively low compared to the expected revenue and compared to other channels, marketing or sites where you could just as easily place your banners. Finally, always request a probationary period. If the advertising salesperson is so convinced of their own product, then this advertising salesperson will have no objection to testing an ad for a month. You can then look at your web analysis to examine the ad's effect and provide management with valuable advice (based on Kremer, 2012).

12

Conversion attribution

Conversion attribution

Conversion attribution simply means that you do not assign a conversion to one traffic source, but to multiple. Suppose someone makes a purchase in response to an ad via Google AdWords, you would normally be able to attribute this conversion to this ad. This would also make you more inclined to spend extra money on Google AdWords and less on other ads or marketing. But a visitor comes to a website in different phases and often needs several visits to eventually come to a conversion. The visitor may have entered via a newsletter during the first visit, then via a referred link **Referral** (referral) and finally via the Google AdWords campaign. This conversion can therefore be attributed to three traffic sources, namely newsletter, referred traffic and Google AdWords. Google Analytics also shows so-called **Assisted conversions** assisted conversions: key figures that show which online channels have played a role in the preliminary stage of the conversion. As a result, a digital marketer is better able to estimate how conversions come about and might find that they do not have to spend all their budget on Google AdWords, because newsletters are a very important source of conversions. The image below shows an example of a conversion attribution summary from Google Analytics.

Conversion attribution in Google Analytics

Universal Analytics

In Universal Analytics from Google, a user ID is used to measure the behaviour of users across various browsers, devices and channels. In the older versions of Google Analytics, a visitor's visits were measured separately, and you were not able to fully establish the complete 'customer journey' that precedes the conversion.

There are a number of different conversion attribution models:

Last click model

1 *Last click model*: this is the traditional payment model. 100% of the conversion value is assigned to the last click. This model is easy to calculate but is less than optimal for basing your budget distribution on. All other clicks are given no value at all, while they have contributed to the conversion. If consumers type your company name in Google and click on your ad as a result of a radio commercial, the source of traffic

12

in the 'last click' model would be a paid search machine. A specific form of the last click model is the last-non-direct-click model. Sometimes a visitor has been in contact with the website or another digital communication expression several times but goes directly to the website at the time of purchase. Using the last-non-direct click model, direct traffic is disregarded, and the conversion is fully allocated to the last channel the customer clicked through from, prior to the conversion. Google also uses the last AdWords click model, where 100 percent of the conversion value is attributed to the most recent AdWords ad that the customer clicked on prior to the conversion.

Last-non-direct-click model

Last AdWords click model

2 *First click model*: 100% of the conversion value is assigned to the first click. This is the opposite of the last click model. In this case, the model is also fairly simple, but again sub-optimal. A lot of touchpoints are ignored in the allocation of conversion value. Someone clicks on a banner and comes to your site. By placing a cookie, you will recognise them the next time they come via a comparison site. But the 'click' then goes to the banner.

First click model

3 *Linear model*: in this model the total conversion value is evenly distributed over all clicks in a conversion path. In this model, you could wonder whether all clicks deserve the same value. Isn't a direct visit worth more than a visit from a banner? For example, someone clicks on a banner and comes in again later via a comparison site and finally via a search engine. The attribution is then 33.3%, 33.3%, 33.3%.

Linear model

4 *Time decay model*: this factor takes into account the factor of time. Clicks that took place on the same day of the conversion will receive more value than the clicks that took place more than 7 days ago. If the banner click was 10 days ago and the comparison site, search and purchase were all on one day, then the attribution is 10% for the banner, 40% for the comparison site and 40% for the search engine.

Time decay model

5 *Position based model*: the first and last click of a conversion path get more value than the intervening clicks. The attribution would then be 40% for the banner, 20% for the comparison site and 40% for the search engine.

Position based model

6 Own attribution model: in many analytical packages it is also possible to define your own conversion attribution model, so that it suits your company.

Example 12.2 describes how Google uses the different attribution models.

Attribution models

EXAMPLE 12.2

Google's attribution models

A customer finds your site by clicking on one of your AdWords ads. She comes back to your site a week later via a social network. That same day she comes back a third time via one of your email campaigns. A few hours later she comes back again, this time directly, and she makes a purchase.

According to the attribution model *'Last interaction'*, the last point of contact, in this case the 'Direct' channel, would get 100 percent of the value points for the sale.

Using the attribution model *'Last non-direct click'*, the direct traffic is completely disregarded and 100 percent of the value points for the sale go

12

to the last channel the customer clicked through from prior to the conversion, in this case the channel 'Email'.

According to the attribution model 'Last AdWords click', the last AdWords click (in this case the first and only click to the 'Paid search results' channel) would get 100 percent of the value points for the sale.

In the attribution model 'First interaction', the first point of contact (in this case the channel 'Paid search results') would receive 100 percent of the value points for the sale.

According to the attribution model 'Linear', every point of contact in the conversion path (in this case the channels 'Paid Search Results', 'Social Network', 'Email' and 'Direct') would receive the same number of value points (25 percent each) for the sale.

According to the attribution model 'Time Decay', the contact points that are closest to the time of the sale or conversion, receives the most value points. In this specific sale, the channels 'Direct' and 'Email' would receive the most value points, because the customer interacted with these two channels a few hours before the conversion. The 'Social Network' channel would receive fewer value points than the 'Direct' or 'Email' channel. Since the interaction with 'Paid search results' took place a week earlier, this channel receives considerably fewer value points.

According to the attribution model 'Position based', 40 percent of the value points are attributed to both the first and the last interaction, and the remaining 20 percent are evenly distributed over the intermediate interactions. In this example, the 'Paid search results' and 'Direct' channels would each receive 40 percent of the value points, while the 'Social Network' and 'Email' channels would each receive 10 percent of the value points.

Source: https://support.google.com/analytics/answer/1662518

A nuanced view is required
It is important to know that there is no uniform truth! You will have to experiment to find out which model best suits your customers' customer journeys. If the customer requires only an average of two contact moments, then a linear model is probably sufficient. However, if a customer takes an average of 60 days to make a purchase and there are many more touchpoints, then a time decay model is probably better. People also tend to use different devices, meaning they often do not fit into the model. There are also consumers who discard their cookies in the meantime. Many corporate networks even do this daily.

12.4 The ABC Model: the digital marketing funnel

In the previous sections, we introduced the concept of digital analytics and discussed the most common metrics in relation to the digital marketing

© Noordhoff Uitgevers bv

funnel. In this section you will learn about a different model that is often used in digital analytics: the ABC model (see figure 12.4).

In this section, we will now take an in depth look at the use and application of the ABC model.

FIGURE 12.4 The ABC model

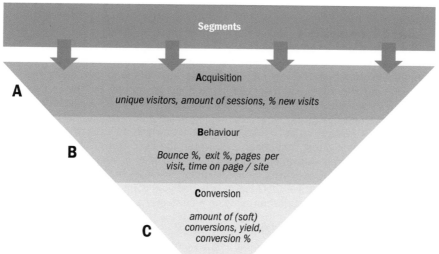

12.4.1   Use of the ABC model

Using the ABC model, you look at the marketing funnel from the bottom to the top. You start at the bottom of the funnel, at the conversion (C) and then move up to the behaviour (B) and the channels and segments (A) (Jansen, Klaassen & Visser, 2015).

Analyses for a website only become meaningful when you make a distinction in segments. So, ask yourself which important visitor segments can be distinguished:

- prospects versus customers
- desktop versus mobile visitors
- one-time buyers versus loyal customers
- browsing versus focused visitors
- visitors from a comparison site versus from a newsletter
- visitors coming in via different landing pages
- segmentation based on geography, day of the week, time of day and the like
- origin; channel: direct traffic, referred traffic, other

Then make an analysis for each of these important segments, keeping your knowledge about the company in mind. Only then can you acquire real insights!

Level C in relation to B

You look at which visitors successfully convert (C) and then see if you can find out where they differ in behaviour on the site (B) in comparison to people who do not convert. Do they look at more, different or less pages and what are the top 10 pages of those who convert? Have they visited before? These questions give you hints that you can use to check if there is a way to bring the 'success factors' to the attention of the people who aren't converting.

Level C in relation to A

When you are finished with level B, you must look at level A. From which channel did the visitors who bought something come? (C). Did they arrive relatively often from a Google AdWords advertisement (and if so using which search phrase), did they type in the address directly, did they arrive from a Facebook advertisement or did they just click in the newsletter? These are all ways for not only determining which ad or channel delivers the highest ROI (return on investment), but also which advertisement, keyword or blog within that channel delivered the best return. Ultimately, it's not so much about which banner delivers as much traffic as possible to your site, it's about having a banner that delivers as many people as possible that do whatever corresponds to the goal you set (C). For example, becoming a customer, staying a customer or reading articles.

ROI

12.4.2 Application of the ABC model

In this sub-section, we will discuss some points for consideration in the application of the ABC model.

The ABC model per channel

The ABC model can be applied to the totality of the traffic, but also per traffic source. In this way you can put the (average!) importance of the traffic sources or segments into perspective and find out which channel or combination of channels delivers the best bang for your marketing buck (or dollar, pound or the euro). You must look 'up' through the model; from the conversion all the way through the model up to the channel that delivers the visit. This allows you to assess the conversion per channel, revenue per channel or lifetime value per channel. Be aware: visitors nowadays often use multiple channels, so you shouldn't only look at the channel that they came in through when they bought something. You must look at which different channels they passed through on the way to making the purchase and analyse what the importance was of each channel: the conversion attribution (see section 12.3).

Averages are the enemy of truth

When using the model, pay attention to the details and don't fixate on the averages. If, for example, advertisements on a search engine *average* less than a banner campaign, this does not mean that advertising on search engines can't be favourable. Suppose you advertise with ten banners and they don't deliver much on average. So, the 'banners' channel has a negative ROI? Does this mean you are going to stop using banners? No, you look for those five banners that do have a positive ROI.

Soft and hard conversions

The KPIs that you as an organisation set, will determine to a large extent what you consider to be a 'conversion', the C in the ABC model. If you sell wind turbines costing 16 million euros each, you will not assume that someone will simply 'put it their shopping basket and pay online'. In that case, you're looking for 'soft conversions' such as registration for an event or signing up for the newsletter.

Soft conversions

For many companies, conversion is the goal and the thing that they use to determine the success of 'everything else'. These conversions can be 'soft' or 'hard'. Examples of 'soft conversions' include downloading a white paper, liking something, or sharing an article. A 'hard conversion' is often the purchase of a product or service. Incidentally, it is not either/or but and/and. For more complex products you often see that a few 'soft conversions' will precede the 'hard conversion'. Using personal data (email or postal address, telephone number) that is left behind, the evolution from soft to hard conversions can be helped along.

Hard conversion

Looking at the visitor

Preferably, the conversion isn't related to the visit but to the visitor. If your visitor visits once and buys something, the conversion rate of that visit is 100%. You might be forgiven for thinking that it doesn't get any better than that, but do you want this visitor to return? That is actually what you are saying when you only look at the conversion rate. This is why a value such as customer lifetime value (see Chapter 10) is often a better indicator. It teaches you to go beyond the target of that visit and that month and not to be too short-sighted in your service and marketing. Many organisations use the Net Promoter Value as a KPI for that very reason. Are your customers fans of your brand? Would they recommend you? For that reason, many companies also regularly conduct research among a part of their visitors. They ask whether the customer is satisfied, whether it was easy to perform a certain task and whether the customer would 'recommend' the brand or organisation. These are all ways for determining whether the organisation and the online team are 'doing a good job' (Jansen, Klaassen & Visser, 2015).

12.5 Recognising the phase that the visitor is in

As described earlier (in Chapter 3), visitors to the website can be in one of six phases of the digital marketing funnel. This model is based on a purchase and for this reason it would look different for a news, corporate or comparison site.

In this section we will focus on the question of how to recognise and encourage a visitor to move on to the next stage. For this we will first look at the interpretation of the phases. Then we will discuss how to recognise the purchase phase in your visitor numbers. Finally, we will explain why online engagement the answer to the question of is how to connect visitors to your online goals.

12.5.1   Interpretation of the phases

For the interpretation of the digital marketing funnel, we will repeat the six phases once again:

1 visit
2 captivate

12

3 decide
4 order
5 pay
6 bind

Keep in mind that much of the orientation and decision process takes place outside of 'your' site. Consumers read reviews, use product and price comparisons and products are recommended to them via social media. For example, visitors to a website such as Laptopsdirect.co.uk may have done extensive 'homework' before they arrive at the site and they already have a good idea of the manufacturer and model they wish to purchase. This means that actual time on site may be relatively short with users' attention focused on specific pages rather than general browsing.

1 Visit

People who visit a website for the first time often aren't inclined to make a purchase immediately. Usually these kinds of visitors have a high bounce rate and stay on the website for a relatively short time. At first glance they don't look like interesting visitors, but that is not correct. You create awareness among these visitors and ensure that they can move on to the next step.

2 Captivate

The next step is captivating them; the visitors already know your website. The bounce rate for these visitors will still be high, but they are willing to stay longer on your website and thus view more pages.

3 Decide

Visitors who are in the decision phase, consider using the website for a conversion, but are not completely there yet. This kind of visit can sometimes be recognised by the fact that it includes many pages per visit and a longer than average time is spent on the website. Also, look at where they come from: it is possible that the decision process has taken place on a review or comparison site. If they make the decision on 'your site', then these are visitors who view a lot of pages because they are looking for confirmation that they would do well to, for example, make a purchase on your website. These visitors return more often within thirty days and will contribute to a high return visit ratio.

4 and 5 Order and Pay

FTCs

Visitors in the ordering and payment phases make a purchase or other form of conversion for the first time. These FTCs (*first time customers*) are reasonably similar in terms of behaviour to the visitors in the decision phase.

6 Bind

Visitors in the bonding phase are customers who regularly make a purchase on the website. These visitors are of good quality and spend an above average time on the website. When actual bonding takes place, these visitors become ambassadors of the website. You can recognise this type of visitor by the fact that they make a (repeat) purchase and spend a lot of time on your website. It does matter what kind of product you sell. An online clothing site or mail order company will have more repeat customers than an online bed store.

© Noordhoff Uitgevers bv

12.5.2 How to recognise the purchase phase by your visitor numbers

Sometimes, the origin of your visitors can give you an indication of which purchase phase the visitors are in. In your ABC model (see section 12.4) you will see that visits coming from price comparison websites (A for Acquisition) behave very differently (B for Behaviour) and convert quickly (C for Conversion). The keywords they search for or the ads they respond to are also an indication.

If someone searches for 'safe family car', then the person is early in the orientation process. A little further along is the person who enters the keywords 'Station wagon with 14% tax addition'. A visitor searching for 'Volvo v60 plug-in hybrid in stock' is ready to buy. You have to provide good content on your site for each of these stages of orientation and decision. These examples are an indication of the importance of these 'phase models'. An added difficulty however, is that search engines increasingly often hide the search terms. For this reason, marketers have to look for other ways to figure out what phase the visitor is in.

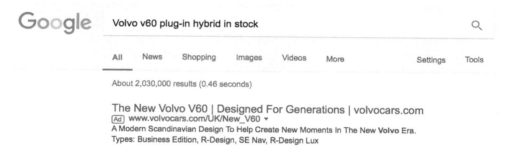

A visitor searching for 'Volvo v60 plug-in hybrid in stock' is ready to buy

12.5.3 Online engagement

How do you recognise all these different types of visitors and how do you connect them to your online goals? The answer to this question is Online engagement. Using online engagement, you can, as it were, assign points to the visitor. Each behaviour yields points. To subscribe to a newsletter, to visit a specific page, to visit a specific part of the website for a long time, to watch a video, to 'like' a product or to 'tweet' a message. Any activity that a visitor performs online and that you can assign points to. Of course, you still don't know who that visitor is, but by the placement of cookies you can identify the visitor using a unique number.

Online engagement

The moment the digital marketer is able to identify visitors from the different phases of the digital marketing funnel, they can respond to the wishes and needs of that particular visitor.

12.6 Social media metrics

Social media can make an important contribution to website visits, both in quantitative and qualitative terms. Trusov, Bucklin and Pauwels (2009) investigated the relationship between 'word-of-mouth' advertising via

Social analytics

12

social media and conversion. According to their research, the effect of such a recommendation via social networks was twenty times greater than the effect of marketing events and thirty times as large as publications in traditional media.

Referred traffic from social media is easy to measure: this is directly visible in the traffic sources. It is more difficult to measure how many people respond to a referral, but do not click on a link. The long-term effects of communication via social media are also difficult to quantify.

Kaushik (2011) states that the following five ratios must be measured:
1 reach
2 conversation
3 amplification
4 applause
5 economic value

To be able to put this in perspective, you will first have to have an idea of the reach of your message.

1 Reach

Reach

According to Kaushik, the reach is the number of times a message has been seen. The number of people who have seen your message is not equal to the number of followers on the social media channels. Many Twitter followers are not active every day, so they miss your message. A social network like Facebook does not necessarily show a message to all your followers. According to the Facebook algorithm, some messages are routed only to people who often respond, like or share your messages, photos or videos. If you are a 'brand' page owner on Facebook, you will see the number of people who have viewed your post in the bottom left-hand corner. If your message is shared or liked very often in a short space of time, the Facebook algorithm will ensure that your message is seen by many more people than only your 'followers'. If it is shared by influential people who in turn have many followers, a huge reinforcement of the audience is possible: your message will be 'viral'.

The ratios below can help you to get an idea of how well your brand is performing on social media. The following applies to all these quantities: if you follow these quantities over time, you will automatically get a feeling for how to respond.

2 Conversation

Conversation rate

The conversation rate is the number of responses to an organisation's message. This can be easily measured for each social network, but in order to get an overview, a good social media monitoring program is indispensable. The latest generation of programs provides insight into the authors, sources and content of what is said about a brand or organisation on social media. It is also possible to check whether the respondents are influential.

3 Amplification

Amplification rate

The amplification rate is the number of times a message is forwarded. On Twitter, that is the number of retweets per tweet, on Facebook and Google+ the number of 'shares' per message and on a blog or YouTube for example the number of 'share clicks' per message or video. The digital marketer can check, per message, how often it has been forwarded and to

12

how deep within the network of relations. Based on the reach of a message, you can see which messages really 'affect' the target audience.

4 Applause

The applause rate measures the number of times that people give a message a positive rating. This can be seen in the following ways:

- Twitter: number of 'Favourite' clicks per message
- Facebook, blogs, YouTube, etc.: number of 'Likes' per message
- Google Plus: number of '+1's' per message

In most cases, the individual numbers can be found in the social media tool itself. A social media monitoring tool is required for an overall picture.

Applause rate

5 Economic value

For the digital marketer, the final ratio is ultimately decisive: the economic value, usually simply translated into a conversion rate. Here too however, soft and hard conversions must be considered. In order to calculate the economic value, you have to add up the returns for the short and long term, add any cost savings and then deduct the costs of active social media marketing. Then you will know what the yield of the investment in social media will be. More advanced social media monitoring tools will allow you to calculate this easily.

Economic value

In addition to the power of social media in the recruitment of customers, it has perhaps an even more important role in ensuring that those customers remain satisfied. Fast and adequate responses by webcare employees ensure that customers are more satisfied, will recommend your organisation to others, stay on as customers for a longer time and buy from you more often. There isn't a 'standard' for demonstrating this, but it is possible. You will have to look carefully at your organisation's strategy, develop an appealing ratio and adhere to it.

Insight into your Facebook activities via Facebook Insights

In addition to Google Analytics, a digital marketer regularly uses *Facebook Insights*, the statistics package that every Facebook page owner has access to. The most important statistics that Facebook Insights will allow you to direct, are divided into three categories:
1 reach
2 engagement
3 fan data

1 Reach

In this category you can see how many people (unique users) you have reached with your posts, advertisements, via your *Timeline* and so on. The total each is split into organic reach and the paid (via advertising) reach. This reach is established by impressions: how often has your content been shown? A unique user can see multiple impressions. Similar to unique users versus page views in Google Analytics. The distinction between organic and paid is also visible for impressions.

12

2 Engagement

Once you know how many users you have reached, the question is how actively your fans are involved with your content. In other words, to what degree do they participate, or what is their *engagement*? There are various distinctions to be made:

- *Engaged users*: the number of unique users who have done something with your content, for example clicked, viewed a photo, played a video, liked, commented or shared.
- *Engagement rate*: the percentage of unique users who have done something with your content, divided by your reach in unique users. This will show you how involved your fan base is. A frequently used metric for this is IPM+ (interactions per Mille) : a formula that compares the number of interactions with the number of posts × 1000.
- *Talking about this*: the number of unique users who write a post themselves or create a story using your content or about your brand.

IPM+ (Interactions per Mille)

3 Fan data

It is also possible to find out a lot about your fans. How many unique users have 'liked' your page, how many 'likes' and 'un-likes' occurred in a certain period? Where do your fans come from? How old are your fans, etc. etc.

For further analysis or to compare Facebook statistics and users with other sources, an export option is available. You could export an overview of your fans to compare it with your customer data (is the average age of your fan base the same as for your customer base?), or to determine which post worked best.

Content Engagement Index

An unusual metric is the Content Engagement Index (CEI). The CEI was originally conceived by Shell and provides insight into the extent to which your content has reached your target audience and the level of engagement you have reached. Multiply the number of likes by 20, the number of comments by 50 and add them up to the number of visitors you have measured. Then you divide the result by the intended audience × 100. The intended audience is the number of people in the target audience that you wanted to reach. Factors 20 and 50 reflect the relative importance attached to likes and to comments.

Intended audience

$$\text{Content Engagement Index} = \frac{\text{Number of visits} + (\text{number of likes} \times 20) + (\text{number of comments} \times 50)}{\text{Intended audience} \times 100}$$

12.7 Web analytics in the organisation

Web analytics is accessible and has a low threshold, many marketers find it truly incredible what can be 'conjured up' using web analytics. For this reason, it is often seen as a kind of panacea. There are however a few pitfalls:

- The first and actually also the biggest pitfall is the fact that everyone casually asks to be sent a report, meaning the web analyst has to provide the management with stacks upon stacks of paper containing all kinds of wonderful reports. But what is someone intending to do with it and what does that person want to know? Often, there is a question behind the question and if the analyst knows what they want to find out, they can be of much better service to that person.

- Another pitfall is that people will see web analytics as a kind of panacea and think that everything can be measured. That is why it is also important to find out what the marketers intend to do with the collected data, so that you can determine whether the data collection will actually solve the problem (Kremer, 2012).

In this section, we will make room for a short commentary on dashboards within organisations. Then we will review the OTA model. We will conclude with an explanation of the OAMM model.

12.7.1   Dashboards within organisations

Almost every company has them, big and small: dashboards. A dashboard displays the core performance indicators of an organisation in a visual way. This allows you, at glance, to quickly assess whether a company is doing well in terms of their targets. It is essential to display this information in the correct way. Example 12.3 illustrates this.

Dashboard

EXAMPLE 12.3

Added value of a dashboard

Imagine that the dashboard shows that the number of online products sold in the last month was 10,000. This sounds like a lot, but in reality, you cannot make that conclusion on that basis alone. Suppose that the company sold 20,000 products in the same month last year, then it is only half the target amount and so it is actually a bad month. A KPI has to be compared with the objective or with another period of time in order to give context/meaning to it. For example, you could pair it with a traffic light system (green, orange, red) in order to interpret it. Red: bad score, orange: not bad but not great either and green: good score. Used like this, a dashboard has added value.

12.7.2   The OTA model

Web analytics is an indispensable part in the optimisation of a website and traffic to a website. The OTA model in figure 12.5 illustrates this. Traffic (T) comes to the website and is analysed. Which traffic source has ensured that visitors arrive on the website? What type of visitor is this and what phase are they in? After analysis (A), the digital marketer optimises the digital marketing activities (O). This optimisation will again lead to better traffic on your website. By re-analysing this visit, you can optimise again, ensuring even better traffic and so on. It is a permanent cycle of quality improvement. This optimisation towards ever better visits will lead to more conversions and ultimately to more sales.

OTA model

Up until now, this chapter has dealt with how the digital marketer or web analyst can use and incorporate web analytics. In the following section we will discuss in depth how this can be done with regard to an organisation.

12

FIGURE 12.5 The OTA model

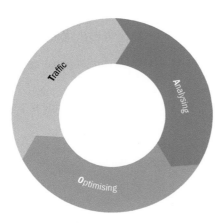

Source: Kremer, 2008

Online Analytics
Maturity Model
(OAMM)

12.7.3 The OAMM model

Stéphane Hamel (2014) laid the groundwork for the Online Analytics
Maturity Model (OAMM). This model (see figure 12.6) is a framework for
helping organisations to assess their current situation in terms of the
maturity of their online analytics and what they can do to optimise this. We
will briefly explain the principle of this model.

FIGURE 12.6 Online Analytics Maturity Model (OAMM)

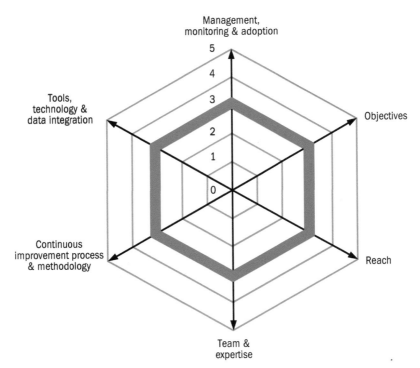

Source: www.cardinalpath.com

Put simply, the OAMM looks at six focus areas where, using five different levels, the balance is sought between these focus areas (see figure 12.6). Per focus area, an organisation can score between '0' ('impaired') and '5' ('addicted'). Determining these levels, also called maturity levels, is done on the basis of a survey.

Maturity levels

However, the focus areas are not all equally important. For example, 'Management, governance and adoption' is the most important. To be successful, Hamel says, the management of the organisation must understand that web analytics is more than a reporting system and is an effective way of identifying weak and improvement points. They need to see digital analytics as a means of improving the performance of all departments. In other words, there must be a solid foundation of support from within the organisation.

The other areas are 'Objectives', the question being what the company's objectives are and whether they have been drawn up in accordance with the SMART principle. This means:
- **S**pecific: the objective must be unambiguous.
- **M**easurable: it must be clear under what measurable or observable conditions the goal was achieved.
- **A**cceptable: the objective must be feasible and acceptable for the target audience and/or the management.
- **R**ealistic: the objective must be feasible. Sufficient knowledge, capacity and resources must be available in order to meet the objective.
- **T**ime-bound: it must be clear within what period of time the objective must be achieved.

The next focus area; 'Scope', is the so-called playing field of web analytics. What are you, and what aren't you going to analyse? Are you looking at one website or at all aspects of digital marketing? For example, are social media and mobile included?

'Analytics: team and expertise' is a focus area that looks at the composition of the team that will be working on the web analytics. Which departments are represented in this team and what knowledge and experience is there? The focus area; 'Continuous improvement, processes and methodology', examines whether the processes and methods used for digital marketing are continuously being improved in a structured manner. The final focus is on 'Tools, technology and data integration': how advanced are the tools and methods that the web analysts work with?

The OAMM is about finding a good balance between these focus areas. A good balance means that all focus areas are on the same level. The OAMM strives for steady growth, Stéphane Hamel states that one level per year is a very good starting point. Following the OAMM from start to finish would take around five years. As mentioned, maintaining the balance between the focus areas is very important. Suppose, for example, that the company is at the forefront of the 'Tools, technology and data integration' focus area and is therefore at level 5, but at the same time the 'Team and expertise' focus area is at level 1. In such an organisation, web analytics will never be able to undergo fully-fledged growth. If the team is not competent enough to use them, high level tools won't be of very much use. If the balance isn't right, it is important to make improvements first. Only then can web analytics be used successfully.

12

Questions and assignments

NOW CHECK YOUR UNDERSTANDING:

12.1 Your first job after completing your education is as a web analyst for a major fashion chain. In the elevator, you meet an old friend. He asks you what you get up to these days. How do you explain it to him in a few short sentences?

12.2 Pinpoint the difference between 'traditional' web analytics and web analytics 2.0 according to Kaushik.

12.3 You work at a bank. One of the managers calls you in to her office. She has seen the figures from the web page containing the product conditions for a new savings account. She wonders how it can be that the bounce rate for the page listing the product conditions is very high, but that the product is still selling well. What are you going to tell her?

12.4 Make a list of all KPIs and base values (performance indicators) that you have come across in this chapter.
  a What values should every organisation measure (need to know) and which do you think are useful to measure, but not necessary (nice to know)? Support your answer.
  b If you use the digital marketing funnel to examine, per phase, your answer to question 12.4a, what can you conclude?

12.5 The conversion of your website has risen considerably in the past month. Your manager gives you the following problem statement and asks you to use the ABC model to analyse the cause of the improvement, so that he has hard figures to present to the management.

> 'The conversion went from 1.5% to 2% last month. The target segment for young people aged 18-24 years scored a conversion of 4%, the segment 25-34-year olds scored 2% and the segments 35-44 and 45-54 years old scored 1% each. It would seem that the introduction of dynamic content, where younger visitors are shown something different to older ones, was a success. In addition, an adaptive site was chosen, so that the display on smartphones is now more attractive. It is unclear what the increased conversion should be attributed to: the improved display of the website on smartphones, the dynamic content or both.'

What does your step-by-step plan look like? Please substantiate your answer.

12.6 Look up the most important free social media monitoring programs online. Choose three and enter the name of your educational institution. What exactly do the programs measure? Do they measure the ratios that Kaushik mentions? What strikes you as the best program and for what reason?

12.7 Figure 12.7 shows the results of a measurement of the six factors that determine the maturity of an organisation with regard to digital marketing analytics. What are your conclusions based on this picture and what would your advice be for the organisation in question be?

FIGURE 12.7 Completed Online Marketing Maturity Model

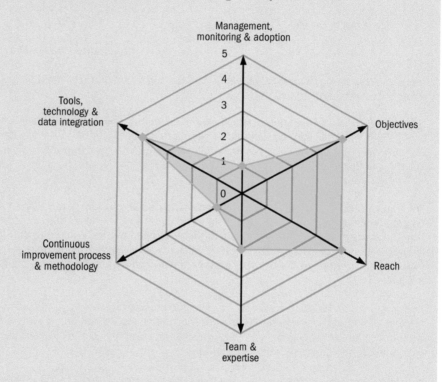

12.8

CASE

Digital Analytics in practice at Bonnington's Irish Moss (Australia)

By Mike Berry
This is the story of is a traditional Australian family cough and cold remedy, Bonnington's Irish Moss invented in the 1870s. In Ireland, the active ingredient is known as carrageen (chondrus crispus). Watch the video on Bonnington's Irish Moss Cough Syrup: http://bit.ly/2prp8CL.

12

Although some older Austrians remembered it, Bonnington's had not had much advertising support in recent years; it had been massively outspent by competitors with 'deeper pockets'. Unsurprisingly, sales were showing year-on-year declines of 20% for the last 2 years. Worryingly, there was a serious threat to Bonnington's pharmacy and supermarket listings; distribution was key for the brand.

In its new role of 'challenger brand' Bonnington's were trying to drive sales with a budget of just $100k. That represents just 0.42% Share of Voice (ie share of ad spend) in the $24million 'Cold and Flu' category. They needed to be sure that their targeting was completely focused on the audience who needed it the most ie Aussie people with the first symptoms of 'flu!

> 'It's not the strongest or the most intelligent of the species that survives, but those who can best adapt to change'.

> – attributed to Charles Darwin.

Since the 'flu season varies significantly by year and by market, Darwin's quote is appropriate in this case!

However: advertising spend analysis shows that the Australian 'Cold and Flu' category ad spend is very predictable. It seems that each year from April to August Bonnington's' competitors roll out multi-million-dollar TV campaigns with the same strategy, ie they spend big in winter and just hope that the Aussie 'flu season hits while their ads are on TV!

This didn't seem very smart to Bonnington's who decided to tackle the market's biggest challenge; a changing 'flu season, and use it to their advantage by becoming 'the most adaptive cold and 'flu brand in the Australian market', ensuring that their investment was targeting those sick Australians who needed Bonnington's at the exact time they needed it most. So: Bonnington's used a secret weapon – big data analytics!

Bonnington's decided to accurately monitor and predict the changing 'flu season, Australian region by region, and to ensure that Bonnington's marketing was delivered when most Australians would be receptive. From their analysis of what data was available, Bonnington's found 5 rich data sets:

First and foremost, they knew that Bonnington's own web analytics data provided valuable insights into interest in their products year on year – which correlated with the timing of the 'flu season historically and they supplemented this with external data sets:
- 8 years of Google Search data (AdWords)
- 1 season of brand search data
- historical weather information
- real time Facebook and Twitter buzz
- 10 years of GP claims from the Medical Benefits Schedule (Doctor appointments)

So firstly, Bonnington's analysed all of the historical data and they used correlation, regression and multi-linear-regression (MLR) analysis, to understand the relationship between behavioural indicators (search and social data) and actual behaviour (eg visit to the local GP) and also factored in environmental factors (eg weather data).

Then, having worked out the relationship between the above data sets, Bonnington's then built its 'patented' predictive Flu Tracker to guide Bonnington's spend.

By scrutinising both weather and 'flu trends, Bonnington's established that there was a statistical correlation between the weather conditions and the above 'flu behaviours. They then added real-time social and search data sets to long-range weather forecasts and were able to accurately forecast the peak of the 'flu season in each local market within Australia. This told them the absolute right time to run the precious (and expensive) brand advertising!

In other words, Bonnington's were ready and waiting for the 'flu season to hit!

Now, with the unique 'Flu Tracker' tool built and ready, Bonnington's added their online advertising 'Trading Desk' to make certain all the planned digital budget was invested as soon as (but not before) the 'flu season started to peak in each region.

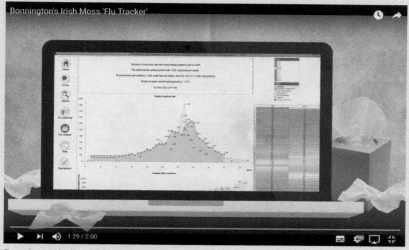

Bonnington's Flu Tracker explained on YouTube

With the use of 'Real-Time' programmatic buying, Bonnington's targeted those who were most likely to be suffering from 'flu at that time but also those that were 'at risk' of becoming sick (by understanding the upcoming 'flu peaks).

Bonnington's didn't even stop there - understanding that 'flu victims were most likely to be bored sitting around sick at home, Bonnington's built in an engagement mechanic to positively influence sales results via a branded promotion!

Using some funny messages and 'daypart targeting', Bonnington's invited their bored target audience to 'Discover the secret of Bonnington's Irish Moss'. Using this programmed learning plus a contest inviting sufferers to purchase the product and perhaps win a cash prize, Bonnington's targeted this key sick-and-bored-at-home audience!

12

An impression of a Bonnington's advertisement on social media

Looking to future activity, Bonnington's has since added a 'social scanner' that looks for relevant keywords across Twitter and highlights each individual user's Twitter name and location. The intention is to build a database so that Bonnington's can in future engage each sick Australian in a way that no other cold or 'flu medicine has ever attempted (subject to Australian Data Protection law, of course). This assumes that some poor Australians will get 'flu every winter!

As regards results, the Bonnington's Flu Tracker was a big success at predicting the peak influenza period in Australia and ensuring that 100% of Bonnington's limited budget was invested just when Aussies needed the product the most ie when demand for 'flu remedies was at its peak!

By ensuring that the budget was invested at the optimal time, Bonnington's was able to significantly improve Bonnington's marketing 'share of voice' and the relative 'cut-through' of its advertising with an 86% increase for each $1 invested, moving from $1 vs $240 competitive dollars to $1 vs $33 competitive dollars of spend. The improved Share of Voice helped drive a positive business return:
- During the key 'flu season, Bonnington's Irish Moss experienced a 23% uplift in sales vs the same period in the year before.
- With this increase Bonnington's began the new financial year with sales 149% greater than the first quarter the previous year. Sales were at a 3-year high!

In addition, Bonnington's retained all its crucial pharmacy and supermarket listings in an increasingly pressured and spend-driven market.

By targeting sick Australians with a combination of real-time data sets they succeeded in being 'the most adaptive cough and cold brand in Australia'; the clever investment in understanding big data gave Bonnington's a very healthy return!

Source: www.creamglobal.com/case-studies/latest/17798/35928/bonningtons-flu-tracker

NOW CHECK YOUR UNDERSTANDING:

a Considering the Bonnington's example above, please explain what is included in digital analytics, what are the most important performance indicators, and how digital analytics can be used to improve the effectiveness of digital marketing.

b List and explain the most important basic metrics in web analytics; how should web analysts interpret them?

c Bonnington's developed the Flu Tracker, drawing on a number of data sets. What key traffic and engagement metrics from its own web analytics could also guide its future decision-making?

d With reference to Bonnington's, what is the relationship between the point of the digital marketing funnel that the visitor is likely to be at, and which are the most relevant key performance indicators (KPIs)?

e See 12.3 above. Which specific channels would you expect would be the main sources of traffic for Bonnington's? How can an understanding of the relative importance of these various sources of web traffic help Bonnington's improve the return on its marketing investment (ROI)?

f What is the ABC model and how could Bonnington's use it to structure digital analyses and improve effectiveness?

g What social media ratios should Bonnington's monitor? Explain why these are important and how they can be used to improve the effectiveness of Bonnington's social media communications.

h Use the six factors (section 12.7) to determine the 'analytics maturity' of Bonnington's. How could Bonnington's improve this campaign for future 'flu seasons?

12

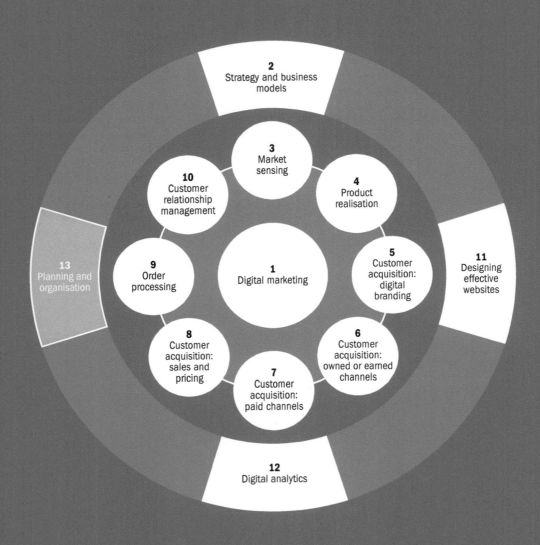

13

Planning and organisation

Authors: Shirley Klever (13.1 to 13.3) and Arnoud Engelfriet (13.4)

The first eight chapters describe how the marketer can establish a clear idea of the market's wants and desires (the market sensing process) and how the Internet can be used to further product development and improvement as well as for setting up processes surrounding the product or the service (the product realisation process). Once everything is customer-ready, the customer acquisition process commences: defining target segments and recruiting new customers. During the customer relationship management process, the relationship is further developed and deepened. Next, we looked at how digital marketing supports order processing, how you can develop an effective website and how you can improve the quality of digital marketing using digital analytics. In this chapter, you will be able to read how you can plan and organise digital marketing. The chapter ends with a section about the legal aspects of digital marketing.

This chapter will cover:
- organising digital marketing activities
- the digital marketing plan
- project management
- legal aspects

After studying this chapter, you will be able to:
- indicate the ways in which digital marketing activities can be incorporated in an organisation and how the required competencies can be included in team structures
- name the elements of a digital marketing plan and indicate how they are interrelated
- explain the basic principles of project management and indicate which of the three project management methods is the best fit for different kinds of situations
- indicate what digital marketers are required to know with respect to authorities and legislation regarding privacy, promotional activities, general conditions and ecommerce

13

13.1 Organising digital marketing activities

How a company incorporates the digital marketing activities in the organisation, depends on the selected business model. As a digital marketer, you can be placed in various parts within the organisation and may experience different kinds of structures.

The Internet is an essential part of the interaction between the customer and the organisation and is therefore intermixed with the business processes (Floor & Van Raaij, 2015).
Communicating with users of digital channels affects different parts of the organisation. For example, questions about products are directed from customer service to the product owner and the answers return to the customer via the same route. Besides affecting marketing specialists, the ordering process of a product also affects internet specialists, sales, logistics and customer service. For this reason, organising digital marketing activities is not easy. In this section, we will compare it to organising traditional marketing activities. Before we do this, we will first consider the Internet's role within business operations. Then we will explain which organisational forms are used most often, as well as the digital marketing team's structure. Finally, we will discuss the reasons for outsourcing digital marketing activities.

13.1.1 Organising digital marketing activities vs. traditional marketing activities

Organising and managing digital marketing activities requires a different approach from that of traditional marketing activities. This affects the organisation, and therefore also the digital marketer. The main differences relate to:
1 communication
2 competition
3 dynamic environment
4 customer data
5 costs

1 Communication
Online, it is possible for anyone to communicate anywhere and make use of services 7 days a week, 24 hours a day. Organisations determine in what places and at what times they are present. Banks, online retailers and travel planners want to be able to promise that they can be contacted 24/7. This is less important to companies with a corporate website (ie not ecommerce). If the website happens to go offline during the weekend, it can be resolved on Monday without an immediate loss of income.

The changes in purchasing behaviour and the fact that online retailers are 'always open' (24/7), creates a lot of discussion surrounding the opening hours of physical stores.
As Huib Lubbers, director of Retail Management Center observes

'... consumers get used to longer opening hours because, for example, supermarkets and hardware stores, have been open until nine or ten o'clock

© Noordhoff Uitgevers bv

for years. Furthermore, the number of households earning a double income and consequently have less time for shopping, continues to increase. If they do go out for shopping, then it better be as pleasant as possible. Add to that the fact that people are better informed by orienting online before they go out. In line with this, and as a result of this preceding orientation, consumers are more inclined to make a purchase and to spend more time in the shopping areas. For retailers, it's wise to capitalise on that extra time by making a visit to their stores as fun as possible.'

Source: www.retailwatching.nl

The ability to communicate via the web has been the catalyst for an increase in internationalisation. This has many organisational consequences. A greater number of markets can be tapped in to for sales and procurement. Multilingual communication is also involved, but outsourcing can also be considered, for example, call centres on the other side of the world that provide customer service 24 hours a day.

Online, a faster response time is expected by customers and the public than in an offline situation. Implementing a permission system won't work within a hierarchical structure. There are also higher standards for content: a website showing content that is over a month old is often not acceptable. Above all, transparency is expected. The omission of certain information can lead to higher conversion in the short term, but transparency ensures appropriate expectations and a better customer relationship in the long term. For example, in most countries, it is legally required to inform users of all additional costs before booking an airline ticket. However, airlines are sometimes unclear with what is, and what isn't included in the price, such as checked-in baggage. Sometimes this is only revealed in the (small) print, for example to keep the price down on comparison sites. From a legal point of view, transparency is often also required (see section 13.4). Consider, for example, privacy legislation and the use of cookies: companies must indicate exactly how they use the data and the user can decide whether or not they consent to it. In other words, organisations need to be more 'revealing' to build customer trust.

2 Competition
Using the web makes comparisons easier and faster, for both the consumer (comparison websites, quickly surfing from one website to another) and organisations (purchasing prices, suppliers). Comparison is based on price, but also on quality. User ratings have an important role in this, as do comments on social media. Being conscious about the competition and consumer opinions is necessary. For example, active management is required to adjust bid prices for positions within Google AdWords relative to what the competition is doing.

3 Dynamic environment
The digital environment and online consumer behaviour are changing continuously, so that the effectiveness of online activities lacks a typical pattern. KPIs should be geared to overarching business objectives and

13

results continuously monitored. The effectiveness of digital applications or campaigns can be tested in real time. Users' click behaviour can be analysed immediately via web analytics (see Chapter 12). Therefore, it is possible to take action more quickly in order to better meet the needs of (potential) customers: both in terms of product and communication, and in this way, to steer them in the direction of your KPIs.

Keeping up with technical developments is also a continuous process. Often, 'moving fast' provides a head start (first mover's advantage), but it also requires an investment and comes with potential risks. On the other hand, digital marketers do not want to wait too long either, because then the developments - and the competitors - will catch up with them. A digital marketer can never sit still and flexibility is a key requirement for success: managing based on data, conducting experiments and considering the ROI of each investment instead of fixed plans and budgets.

Development of voice search as a trend for the coming years

One of the most important trends is the continuing improvement of voice search. Increasingly often, people use their voice to run a search or to do other things. According to Google, voice searches make up 20% of all mobile searches and 55% of all teenagers' search for something using their voice every day. Up until two years ago, in most cases, devices were only able to recognise about 80% of the words. Nowadays, this %age has already gone up to around 92%, making its use increasingly user-friendly. With voice search, Google wants to enter a new phase, in which it has the ambition to develop the ultimate mobile assistant that can help you with anything in your daily life.

An important difference is that the way that we speak is different to how we write. As a result, voice search has a major impact on the type of search queries that are used and, for that reason, website content must be adapted to this new situation. It also affects Google's business model itself, which is currently based on clicks. As voice search is gaining popularity, Google could start to transform itself into an umbrella platform that accepts orders directly, eg should someone tell their phone to order a pizza.

Voice search via Alexa on the Amazon Echo device

13

The growth of voice search will not only be a result of mobile internet usage, but also a result of the increase in the number of devices such as Google Home and Amazon Echo (Alexa). The impact of these devices should not be underestimated. Today they are used by a still relatively limited group of enthusiasts, but considering how mobile internet usage has developed, we know how quickly a new revolution can be unleashed. This is an important lesson for marketers; it is important to be experimenting with these devices already and to consider how you, as an advertiser, can respond to these developments.

Source: Toonders (2017) on www.frankwatching.com

4 Customer data

Online, personal data can be collected more easily because of, eg contact forms, the emergence of social networks providing access to personal data and interests, but also because of (multi-device) surfing behaviour. This data can then be used to effectively target and personally appeal to potential consumers. In addition, digital marketing can also be applied on the basis of specific locations (see also 6.4.1). Using customer data, you can in many cases address customers online in a much more relevant way than by traditional marketing.

5 Costs

In digital marketing communication campaigns, it is not always possible to determine in advance exactly what the campaign will cost. The costs are often determined per click. Bid strategies are changing from a fixed CPA, CPL or CPS to KPIs that underpin the overarching business objectives. A CPA of €50 instead of €40 is acceptable if, for example, the volume increases in such a way that the absolute bottom line profits are growing. Obviously, a maximum limit can be set to monitor the maximum budget for project management reasons, but the focus usually remains on return on investment (ROI).

In short: the methods of working within digital marketing often differ considerably from those of traditional marketing and they are constantly changing.

13.1.2   The Internet's role within business operations

In Chapter 2 you were able to read about the different types of business models and revenue models that organisations use as the basis for formulating business objectives. All of an organisation's activities must serve these objectives. The way in which digital communications and services via the Internet contribute towards the commercial objectives, determines what part of the organisation the Internet activities are assigned to. The role of the Internet can vary from that of a marketing communications tool, to that of a channel for doing business entirely online. In this sub-section, four roles are explained, based on the ideas of Chaffey (2015):

1 online as a (brand) communications channel
2 online as a service-oriented extension of offline activities

13

3 online as a sales and purchasing channel
4 online as a core business
We will examine these roles in turn.

Role 1: online as a (brand) communications channel

If the Internet is used as a channel for marketing communications within companies, the website often revolves around the brand experience and relates to branding campaigns (brand recognition, brand image). Consider, for example, the campaigns in many countries for the global beer brand Heineken. Heineken uses traditional media such as TV and radio commercials and extends the campaign online via a campaign website and online advertising. Another example is governmental websites, on which you can mainly find generic information and contact details.

Companies in the fast-moving consumer goods (FMCG) industry, governments and foundations are increasingly choosing to use the Internet as a (brand) communications channel (as they have used offline advertising for years).

Role 2: online as service-oriented extension of offline activities

In many traditional organisations, the Internet is seen as an extension of the company. In these companies, core services are offered offline as well as online. The web is used as a tool for providing information, relationship management and generating leads and potential customers, but can also be used for actually offering the key activities.

The influence that the Internet can have on an entire business operation can be seen in the banking system. Where physical office buildings used to be the place for all kinds of cash transactions, they are now primarily a channel for new customers and financial reviews. The management of matters such as cash withdrawals and money transfers is now largely digitised.

Role 3: online as a sales and purchasing channel

An organisation can also offer their services or products direct to end-users online. Consider US department store Macy's for example, which owns both physical stores and an online store.
Types of organisations that use the Internet in this way include banks, energy companies, insurance companies, car brands and retailers.
A possible problem for organisations who use the Internet in this way, is

something called channel conflict. This means that friction can arise between the physical stores and the web channel. It may be that multiple departments are responsible for a single channel. Another type of friction arises when products are offered on the Internet at a lower price than in the physical store. It is very important that someone is ultimately responsible and has an overview in order for the channels to be used in the most effective manner. For example, an organisation may decide to offer a limited range of products online or to offer the full product range online and to limit what can be found in the physical stores or in the catalogue. The key thing is to make it easy for the shopper to buy whatever they want, in whatever way is most convenient for them. The organisation's offerings need to be 'joined-up'.

Role 4: online as core business

Companies that have their core business online have fully equipped the physical organisation (such as housing, logistics, resources and tools) to support their services on the Internet. Retail, financial services and travel agencies are examples of industries where many organisations choose to use the www for this purpose.

First Direct's core business is online

For example, consider Ocado.com and First Direct (firstdirect.com). These companies conduct all of their business activities online. The web is the only channel through which offer their product or service and not via any physical store. Physical premises are only used as office space for administrative purposes, customer service (call centres) or for logistics/deliveries.

Ocado explained on its homepage

13

13.1.3 Organisational forms

On the basis of the chosen business strategy, the business objective and the four roles of the Internet within business operations as described in the previous, it can be determined which organisational form is most effective. Next, we will discuss four ways of locating the digital activities within the organisation; ie where it fits into the overall structure.

Internet activities take place within:
1 the communications department, marketing department or sales department
2 a separate marketing channel
3 a separate department
4 other:
   a a mixed version of the above
   b outsourced to external agencies

The part of the organisation that you assign the online activities to, is mainly determined by the business objectives.

1 Digital marketing activities within the communications department, marketing department or sales department
For corporate communication objectives, such as corporate branding, reputation management and public relations, the activities can be located within the communications department. Consider, for example, government agencies, that focus on service provision. An increasing number of people within companies now communicate with the 'outside world'. This has become necessary due to the focus on digital service provision and social media. A satisfied customer is incredibly important for your online reputation.

If the business objective is marketing-related, the digital marketing activities are best located within the marketing department. This form applies, for example, to organisations in which the role of the Internet is limited to marketing communications (role 1 in 13.1.2). The execution of website and campaign development is usually assigned to another department (creative team) or external agencies. In this case, the marketing department is the (internal) client.

If the online objective is sales (role 3 in 13.1.2), it makes sense for activities to be assigned to the sales department. Then, within the relevant department, all sales or marketing activities are also adapted for the Internet. In this situation, the execution of website and campaign development is also often invested elsewhere.

2 Digital marketing activities within a separate marketing channel
Another way of organising online activities is to combine them in a single and separate marketing channel, parallel to the other channels that are used for sales or distribution of products and services. Other channels include, for example, offline advertising (such as TV, radio and print) and direct marketing (face-to-face sales, telemarketing). The digital team reports to the person responsible for all channels, for example the marketing director. This option is often selected in organisations where the Internet has the role of a service-oriented extension (role 2 in 13.1.2).

13

3 Digital marketing activities within a separate department
Within organisations where the Internet is at the centre of business operations (role 4 in 13.1.2), the decision is often made to combine all 'digital specialists' together in a single team. This often happens as a response to the increasing strategic importance of digital within the organisation. This team, like the marketing department, reports directly to senior management. All disciplines are represented in the team in order to manage, develop and execute the digital activities throughout the organisation. In addition to digital specialists, the team can also include staff positions, such as administration, purchasing and project management. The department can be regarded as an independent profit centre. Note that so-called 'channel-conflict' can occur in these kinds of organisations, because online and offline are effectively in competition with one another.

Figure 13.1 illustrates a schematic representation of the three ways of organising digital marketing activities that were discussed previously.

FIGURE 13.1 Ways of organising digital marketing activities

1. The communications, marketing or sales department   2. A separate marketing channel

3. A separate department

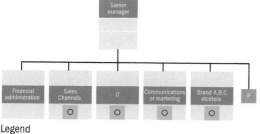

Legend

Organisational element

P   Primary responsibility online

O   Supporting digital competences

Source: Chaffey, 2015

13

4 Mixed forms or outsourcing to external agencies

Hybrid form

In practice, you often see that organisations use more than one of the organisational forms as described before, opting for a hybrid form. An example is an organisation where digital marketing is the marketing department's responsibility, but where the digital marketers use the services of a department that has digital experts within the IT department. In cases such as these, one of the three organisational forms (in this case the form 1) is used as a basis.

Sometimes there is an intermediate phase, in which the responsibilities gradually shift from one department to another:

- Around the year 2000, an organisation's digital activities were often assigned to the IT department. Within most organisations, the responsibility for digital activities is now at the front, in the vicinity of 'customer contact', such as communications or sales. In some cases, parts of the technical management and further development are still assigned to the IT department.
- Organisations where digital only has a small role often spread out the digital activities throughout the organisation.
- As the importance of digital increases, activities are centralised within a separate channel or department. Smaller teams can be set up as soon as the need for specific expertise arises (from a specific target segment or customer journey).

Many organisations also choose to outsource their digital marketing activities entirely or partially. In 13.1.5 you can read more about the pros and cons of outsourcing to external agencies.

13.1.4 Structure of the digital marketing team
In this sub-section, we will discuss the different roles within digital marketing. Then we will elaborate on the team structure.

Roles within digital marketing

Regardless of the chosen organisational form, at least 30 separate digital marketing roles can be defined. A distinction can be made between the initiation of the activity, the development (execution, such as design and programming) and the management and optimisation (see figure 13.2). Depending on the size of the organisation and the organisational form that is used, digital marketing managers can decide to combine roles or to invest them in one person or in a team. For example, a single digital marketer can take on the role of affiliate marketer, SEO marketer, email marketer and display marketer. In addition to managing content, a content manager may also be copywriting.

Team structure

Team structure

There are several ways for digital marketing specialists to work together in a team. Certainly, in the organisational form where digital marketing activities are invested in a separate department, team distribution is necessary. We will discuss the following team structures:

1 functional or competence (discipline)
2 customer life cycle
3 channel
4 combination

© Noordhoff Uitgevers bv

FIGURE 13.2 The 30 digital marketing roles

Roles digital marketing	Description	Initiation	Development	Management / optimisation
Interaction designer	Designer of the engagement (interaction) between people and applications		■	
Graphic designer	Designer responsible for the visual presentation of text, images and features		■	
Copywriter	Writer who is specialised in advertisements and other recruiting texts, specifically for online		■	
Content manager	Manager of content (text, images, video), within the Content Management System (CMS)		■	■
Functional designer	Bridge between customer and technology: describes the features of the application (in unison with the Interaction designer)		■	
Technical designer	Designer that describes how parts must be created on a technical level		■	
Front-end developer	Developer that presents data from the systems visually in the browser for the end user		■	
Back-end developer	Programmer that links the front-end and servers to the databases		■	
Web analyst / Data scientist	Analysing and optimising of online media, based on web statistics and usability			■
SEO specialist	Search engine optimisation for organic searh results (technical and key words) , link building			■
SEA marketer	Responsible for the optimal design and management of search engine campaigns			■
Affiliate marketer	Responsible for the placement of advertisements on partner sites (affiliates), for the generated sales or leads in exchange for a fee			■
Email marketer	Responsible for direct marketing in the form of emails in order to send commercial or service-aimed messages to the target audience			■
Internet marketer	Responsible for the conceptual and strategic interpretation of a brand online; the marketing sub-budgets, informing of management, coordination between departments	■		
Display marketer	Responsible for advertisements on websites, such as banners		■	■
Social media marketer	Responsible for the community management and advertisements on various social media platforms. Sets up the social media strategy and content and manages the channels	■	■	■
Community manager	Responsible for the launch, growth and retention of a forum or, for example, Facebook community	■		■
E-commerce manager	Leader of the e-commerce team and responsible for turnover and profit objectives for the e-commerce channel	■		
Functional manager	Responsible for maintenance and management of functional documentation and the correct use of the information systems			■
Technical manager	Responsible for the upkeep of the infrastructure of the information system			■
Project (/team) manager	Link between the internal customer (for example, a marketer) and the project team. Keeper of the budget, the planning, the scope and the quality of the projects	■	■	■
Scrum master	Organises and facilitates the scrum activities such as daily stand-ups, demos, refinement sessions, retrospectives and coaches the team in order to achieve maximum results	■	■	■
Product Owner	Responsible for maximising the value of both the product as well as the project team. Creates and exhudes a vision, manages expectations and coordinates between the business and the IT organisation	■	■	■
Digital strategist	Advisor regarding how best to present a brand online, combinations of cross-media possibilities between web, email, mobile, social media and offline channels	■	■	
Digital product manager	Responsible for actualising the product positioning, pricing, promotion, product portfolio and stance regarding the competition	■		
Business analyst	Link between automisation and operational management: meeting, recognising and translating the business' needs into practical solutions	■	■	
Compliance specialist	Responsible for testing the judicial system that creates and follows the laws of a company		■	■
Database marketer	Analyst of the database information in order to develop and facilitate the organisation in such a way that long-term and effective relationships with customers, partners and for example stakeholders are made possible	■		■
Growth hacker	Multi-skilled person responsible for rapid growth of the company (traffic, conversion) by experimenting, analysing and improving processes. Often a technically skilled marketer	■	■	■
CRO-specialist (Conversion Rate Optimisation)	Responsible for the management and execution of conversion optimisation in order to accomplish growth	■	■	■

13

1 Functional or competence

In a team structure that is organised functionally or according to competences, professional specialists are put together in a team. For example, there is a team consisting of content managers, a team with internet marketers and a team of web analysts. This team structure ensures optimal knowledge sharing and knowledge building within each discipline. The downside is that the different specialisms do not always have the same prime objective in mind. Consider a copywriter whose objective is conversions and a copywriter that is hired specifically for customer service purposes.

NETFLIX JOBS   WE ARE NETFLIX   TEAMS   LOCATIONS   INCLUSION

Social Marketing Manager, Netflix Originals - France

⚲ Amsterdam, Netherlands   ⚎ Marketing

Do you know how to get to the uʍop ǝpᴉsdn?
Do you know the difference between Plata and Plomo?
Do you often talk about Picasso in a shower ?

Netflix is looking for an experienced, passionate entertainment fan to join our team of social media marketing for France. The position is based in our EMEA HQ in Amsterdam.

Netflix is looking for a Social Marketing Manager in Amsterdam for the French market

2 Customer life cycle

Customer life cycle

Another team structure is based on the 'customer life cycle'. This involves responding to the different phases that a consumer goes through in the online orientation and purchasing process, for example searching, website visit, purchase and repeat purchase.
Responsibilities per phase:
- *Website traffic*: encouraging visits to the website (search engine, advertising).
- *Conversion on the website*: have the user convert on the website from landing to checkout process (purchase).
- *Customer service*: providing customer service after the purchase.
- *Retention*: retain customers and tempt them to purchase more products or services (cross- and up-sell).

13

Each phase has its own team that includes various professional specialists. Possible teams are, ie a traffic team, a conversion team, a customer service team and a retention team. Each team has a distinct objective that the specialists work towards together. An increasing number of companies put the customer at the heart of their business strategy. In order to implement improvements, a roadmap of the customer touchpoints is created (see 4.4.1).

3 Channel
Sometimes a large part of digital marketing takes place outside the company's own website. For this purpose, digital channels such as affiliate marketing or paid search marketing (PPC) are used. In this case, the brand's own website can be considered a separate channel. Teams are set up according to the channels that are used, and as a team, they are responsible for that channel's total activity, for example an affiliate team and a PPC team. All 'life phases' that a customer goes through within the relevant channel are represented by the channel team.

4 Combination
In practice, mixed forms of team structures are also used. Depending on the chosen solution, external agencies might also be brought in. They often work together in so-called multidisciplinary teams.

Multi-disciplinary teams

Horizontal organisational structures emerge that operate using a combination of team structures.

One approach to structuring marketing teams follows the lead of successful technology-driven companies such as Google, Netflix and Spotify. The idea is that employees are organised in a structure of 'tribes' and 'squads' (or small interdisciplinary teams) working together. Each team focuses on a customer goal that they try to achieve and after completion they start their next project. A group of squads working on a joint process together form a 'tribe'. There are also 'chapters' of squad members that perform the same kind of work (eg data analysis). Within these chapters the subject-specific skills of the respective squad members are developed. The objective is that employees don't feel like just a cog within a larger wheel, but rather they are made responsible for their own goals, which increases their job satisfaction and motivation levels.

With the digital transformation of existing companies and also the launch of brand-new companies in the digital age, new 'ways of working' (internal processes) have emerged. Companies including Spotify, Google and Netflix are have adopted an approach called 'Agile and Scrum'.

Spotify calls their development teams 'Squads' which gets away from the idea that a Development Team should only contain developers. Other names for these teams include Crew, Party, Unit, Faction, Troop and Line-up.

The squad concentrates on a single customer goal at any one time. It is possible to have a number of these squads working collaboratively on a

13

joint process and also to have 'chapters' of squad members who are doing similar tasks (eg data analysis). This ensures that all employees are empowered ie responsible for their own goals. The idea is that people are more motivated, more engaged and more efficient.

Spotify also introduces the terms 'Tribes', 'Chapters' and 'Guilds', Whatever language we use, the objective is to promote teamwork, collaboration and innovation, as well as giving team members ownership and a sense of enablement.New technologies and new customer behaviours sometimes require new corporate structures and ways of working.

13.1.5 Organising internally versus outsourcing to external agencies

What are the considerations for conducting digital marketing activities internally versus outsourcing them to external agencies?
Four considerations should be made when deciding whether or not to outsource digital marketing activities to external agencies:
1 expertise
2 business strategy
3 flexibility
4 costs versus benefits

Expertise
External agencies specialise in one or a limited number of activities (eg search engine marketing or web development). They do this for a wide range of customers. As a result, they have a great amount of expertise for this specific activity, which is reinforced by the fact that several people with the same competences work together (see section 13.1.4). Internally, it seems to be much more difficult to keep up with the developments in a specialist field with the same kind of intensity. The organisation decides to hire this specialist skill which provides them with the advantage of not having to expand on their own knowledge. Nowadays, internal digital marketing expertise is growing. Developing knowledge of what is effective and how to best experiment is becoming increasingly important. In addition, digital marketing also requires close collaboration with the IT department.

Business strategy
Some organisations decide to do a lot of things internally, while others outsource many things and focus on their core business. An organisation may pursue a certain strategy and consciously decide to outsource a certain %age of the work. The greater the Internet's role within business operations, the more activities must be performed. More capacity is needed, and the business strategy is decisive in deciding whether or not to outsource.

Flexibility
The required capacity is not always evenly distributed over the year. Campaigns and projects sometimes run parallel and there are peaks at a specific time, eg,alcoholic drinks and fragrance companies in many countries focus on the Christmas holiday season. Also, not everything can

be defined in advance. Consider, for example, new insights and possibilities as a result of technological developments.

The level of occupancy within internal organisations usually cannot be expanded in the short term only to be reduced again. After all, in order to do so, (new) colleagues need to be hired and then dismissed, which is not easily done nor is it desirable.

Expanding in size is more simply done by working with external agencies or external specialists. External agencies can spread their capacity across multiple clients and projects.

Deloitte can help on many fronts

Costs versus benefits

At first glance, the costs for outsourcing seem to be greater than hiring someone because of the higher hourly rates. However, due to internal costs for accommodation and fringe benefits, the expenditure does not differ much from the outsourcing tariff. If the required capacity for a specific specialism (for example web analysis) is less than one full-time employee (FTE), outsourcing is a logical decision. As soon as this specialism is needed on a full-time basis and spread out over the entire year, it is beneficial to hire someone. Due to the increasing role of digital within organisations, more budget is being allocated to internal digital marketing specialisms.

An example of a collaboration with an external agency

Email and Marketing Automation company MailChimp worked with agency Droga5 to create a highly creative campaign which was in effect a play on words around the company name. The 'Did you Mean Mailchimp' campaign won the prestigious Cannes Cyber Lions Grand Prix for Integrated Multi-Platform Campaign.

13

This quirky campaign featured three videos which deliberately misspelled in the company's name into 'MailShrimp', 'KaleLimp', and 'JailBlimp'.
This is an example of an external digital agency adding a 'left-field' creative idea which the client company would probably never have come up with on their own.

Award winning Mailchimp campaign featuring three videos

Adobo Magazine, 2017

13

(13.2) Digital marketing plan

A detailed digital marketing plan serves as a foundation for the organisation and for the execution of digital marketing activities. It is important to provide direction and focus to the activities. The advantages of a marketing plan include:

- Permanent focus on determining, measuring and optimising digital marketing, leads to maximising the results.
- It improves the effectiveness of the capacity and resources used. For example, it prevents that – due to a lack of coordination – activities are performed twice.
- It provides a clear idea of how the digital marketing department prioritises and where to adjust.
- It makes it easier to prioritise adjustments to IT systems.

Digital marketing is not an isolated thing. At the highest level, an organisational strategy is defined and a business plan, including a business model, is drawn up, as you can read in Chapter 2. On the basis of the organisational strategy, a long-term marketing strategy is established. The way in which digital activities relate to this, is described in a digital marketing plan. The selected organisational strategy and the role of digital activities are central to the development of the digital marketing plan (see figure 13.3).

The strategic direction of an organisation is determined for several years. Within the marketing strategy you determine the marketing objectives that you wish to achieve in the long term. This serves as input for the marketing tactics and operations, in which you determine how you can accomplish the marketing strategy in the medium and short term. A digital marketing plan is part of this and usually covers a period of one year, during which specific components are updated as often as necessary. Using the agile methodology, the components are reviewed during short iterations. See previous section 13.3.3.

Digital marketing plan

FIGURE 13.3 Consistency between organisational and digital marketing plan

Organisation plan

Marketing plan

Digital marketing plan

13

A digital marketing plan can be part of the marketing plan or a plan unto itself. For example, a separate plan is used in organisations where internet-specific roles and responsibilities are split from traditional marketing roles. The structure of a digital marketing plan is no different than that of any other (traditional) marketing plan. The customer is at the centre of both plans and the same components are discussed, see figure 13.4. Two things are taken into account when composing the digital marketing plan:

- The customer is at the centre: the plan is written on the basis of customer insights and needs, not products or tactics (outside view).
- The plan is set up flexibly, so that there is a possibility to easily update information and to adjust the planning on the basis of novel insights. For example, a vision for one year and a detailed elaboration per quarter.

To put together a good digital marketing plan, five steps are described (see also figure 13.4):

1 Analysis: inventory of the current and future situation, resulting in a SWOT analysis.
2 Objectives and KPIs.
3 Strategy: the way in which the objectives are achieved in the longer term.
4 Action plan: activities at tactical and/or operational level, costs and planning.
5 Evaluation and review.

In this section we will discuss these components whilst focussing on specific aspects relating to digital marketing.

FIGURE 13.4 The components of the digital marketing plan

13.2.1   Analysis

As you were able to read in Chapter 2, writing a marketing plan starts with performing a strategic analysis: considering the expected market developments, the opportunities and threats and the organisation's strengths and weaknesses. Based on this, a SWOT analysis is made.

The first part of the marketing plan, the analysis, can be divided as follows:
1. situation analysis: inventory of the current and future situation
2. SWOT analysis

Based on this, you are able to decide what digital marketing activities you need to perform in order to respond effectively and efficiently to the market situation. We will discuss both parts of the analysis below.

Situation analysis

In the situation analysis, the organisation's internal and external environment are described. This concerns the current and future situation.

Situation analysis

External environment

The analysis of the external environment involves an analysis of the developments, events and influences to which the organisation, the product or target segment is subjected. It contains conditions that the organisation cannot change or control. These consist of conditions on both macro and meso level:

1. Macro conditions are political, legal, demographic, social and technological developments. Consider, for example, a change in legislation that has an impact on the running of digital marketing campaigns. Technology has an important role in this: what are technological developments? Consider the launch of new devices, new mobile apps, new ways to analyse data and so on.

Macro conditions

2. Meso conditions: what are the trends in the specific industry/market that are relevant to digital marketing? Specifically, three groups of relations are considered:

Meso conditions

   a *Target segment*: segmentation of the target audience and how the target segment uses the Internet. What trends and developments exist within the target segment? Consider, for example, the daily use of tablet devices among the over-50s that increased by 15% compared to the previous year. What does their decision-making process look like and what does this mean for digital marketing? For example, gathering and comparing information, asking friends and family for advice and buying in physical stores. Chapter 3 provides various tools for conducting research among customers.

   b *Suppliers* and *stakeholders*: what trends and developments exist within the target segment? For example: increasing usage of seamlessly connected distribution systems. What does this mean for digital marketing?

   c *Competition*: what is your competitor's online market share and how do they use the Internet to achieve business objectives? What developments have they initiated? There are many tools available for assessing the competition's tactics, for example in the field of search engine optimisation. Consider an organisation that uses AdWords and is identical or similar to a certain campaign by a competitor that has invested a lot of media towards it. In this way, they benefit from the effects of the competitor's campaign.

13

For certain financial products such as 'loans', there is intense competition in Google AdWords

Internal environment

The role of the Internet in achieving the formulated business objectives within the organisation itself, is analysed as described in section 13.1. This is done for three components: the digital organisation itself, internet usage and partners:

1 *Digital organisation itself*: what is the digital mission and what are the digital objectives? The current communications, organisation, processes, administration, finances (costs and benefits of the internet activities), IT and people (how many full-time employees and what positions are there within the digital marketing organisation, as discussed in section 13.1) are described. Consider, for example, the logistical processing of online orders, the entire organisational structure and the digital activities within it.

2 *Internet usage*: analysis of the organisational performance online. Questions raised herein include:

- What is the current online market share, how and where is the organisation represented, what is offered digitally: products, services or information?
- How do you position the online offer, what activities is the Internet used for, how are these activities related to achieving the business objectives?
- How does the organisation use the Internet for market sensing, product realisation, customer acquisition, order processing and CRM?
- What parts of digital marketing is the organisation doing well and what could they improve on?
- Is the entire digital marketing funnel taken into account: do you recruit visitors effectively? Is the website's content and its product range relevant enough for the visitors? Are the tools to help them

decide in the right place? How does ordering and paying work? Are these processes up to date? Are enough customers sufficiently bonded to your website?

- What knowledge and resources are available to continue to optimise digital marketing? For example, if you are able to set up 'same day delivery' or 'Click & Collect' (ordering online and collecting it in a store), this is a logistical skill that you could (also) benefit from by using it in your online positioning and communication. If the customer would like it, and the competition is not able to do it as well as you are, your organisation has a competitive advantage. As an example, online retailer boohoo.com offers customer a choice of delivery options.

Multiple delivery options at Boohoo.com. Now offering free next day delivery, but you'll have to order quickly

3 *Partners*: which partners are currently contributing to achieving the business objectives and how do they use the Internet to do this? Consider distribution channels, affiliate channels or organisations that sell additional products. Are there online platforms that have a large part of the defined target segment registered with them?

The situation analysis is used as input for the SWOT analysis.

SWOT analysis

As described in Chapter 2, a SWOT analysis is a model that takes stock of the Strengths and Weaknesses of an organisation in relation to the Opportunities and Threats in the market. Based on the situation analysis, the strengths and weaknesses are displayed in a quadrant. Within the organisation, the greater the Internet's impact on achieving business objectives, the more aspects of digital developments and positioning will be reflected in the results of the analysis.

A simple example is table 13.1.

SWOT analysis

13

TABLE 13.1 Example of a SWOT matrix

Strengths (internal)	Weaknesses (internal)
• Digital market position: company has a strong digital market position, third place in relation to the market leader. • Top position in the social media monitor. • Market sensing: customers are well-informed and accessible using the database. • Product realisation: customer satisfaction regarding digital services scores a 7.6, product development strongly technology-oriented. • Customer acquisition: relatively high online conversion rates. • CRM: customers are well-informed and accessible using the database. • Order processing: delivery within 24 hours.	• The company's profit development is moderate. • Product realisation: product development is strongly technology-oriented. • Customer acquisition: low position in search engines for top products, online discoverability is poor. • Customer acquisition: relatively high costs for SEA, visitors leave during the 'pay' step. • CRM: digital communication less personalised than competitors. • No mobile website. • Low retention. • Limited digital service channels.
Opportunities (external)	**Threats (external)**
• Economic climate: disposable equity increases by 1.1%. • Demographic trends: more over-50s buy online. • Technology: new production techniques for devices result in lower costs. • Mobile internet usage surpasses desktop usage. • Target segment: increasing use of social media. • Partner has developed a mobile platform. • Customer engagement has an exponential influence on buying intention.	• More stringent privacy legislation. • Competition: the biggest competitor is starting an online loyalty program. • Channel conflict: margins are under pressure. • Successful affiliate programmes at competitors.

Confrontation matrix

It is possible to assess the situation based on the SWOT matrix in table 13.1. Which opportunities need to be addressed in a very serious way and against which threats must the digital marketer defend face off? This is illustrated using a confrontation matrix. In this confrontation matrix, the internal and external elements are placed opposite each other. These combinations generate issues. Only the most important issues are taken into account. Below is an example of such a combination:

Probability:
• Customer engagement has an exponential influence on buying intention.

Strengths and weaknesses:
• Customers are well-informed and accessible using the database.
• Product development is strongly technology-oriented.

Issue:
• Product development method does not match the market requirements. Question: how do we ensure that our product development method meets the market requirements?

13

Possible option:
- Contact customers to develop products using co-creation.

13.2.2 Digital marketing objectives and KPIs

In the second part of the digital marketing plan, the digital marketing goals and KPIs are described. The business objectives and the analysis (see previous sub-section) provide enough information to select the digital marketing goals. These goals will be pursued in the coming period and formulated into concrete objectives. This may concern, for example, objectives relating to the turnover that must be achieved with internet activities, the digital market share and brand awareness.

The objectives are set at three levels: from abstract to concrete and from long term to short term. Objectives for a period of longer than one year are included in the organisational strategy and/or overall marketing strategy, the digital marketing plan describes the medium-term vision and a period of one year in detail. Here is an example for a provider of slimming products:

1. The medium-term vision is described. For example: we aim to be the market leader for slimming products within two years.
2. The vision is exemplified into concrete SMART objectives. For example: during the next year, the digital market share for the product segment 'dietary supplements' should increase to 32%.
3. KPIs are the indicators for this performance. These are defined for shorter periods, for example per quarter, and help to monitor the SMART objectives. The KPIs can be adjusted over time. The KPIs are in line with the phases of the digital marketing funnel, but in practice, not all objectives are exemplified for all intermediate steps. Examples of KPIs for the period of a quarter are:
   - 100,000 unique visitors on the website per month:
     - a higher position within search engines for the product group 'dietary supplements': from an average position of 6 to an average position of 2
     - a click-through rate (CTR) of 5% for organic search results
     - an average CTR of 0.16% for advertising
   - a conversion rate of 10%:
     - 8,000 online sales of the 'protein shakes' product in the first quarter
     - 2,000 online sales of the 'fat burner' product in the first quarter
   - contract with three affiliate marketing partners
   - sell the product 'total diet' 50 times via affiliate marketing

Keeping track of statistics is necessary for measuring, monitoring and adjusting the KPIs. As you were able to read in 13.1.1 under ad 5, it is necessary to not only steer towards individual KPIs, but to keep an eye on the overall objectives.

It is important that the digital analytics are well organised and maintained. For this, see Chapter 12.

13.2.3 Digital marketing strategy

In broad terms, the digital marketing strategy describes *how* the previously mentioned digital marketing objectives and KPIs can be achieved. On the one hand this is done in an analytical way, on the basis of a minimum number of points resulting from the confrontation matrix, but it also

Digital
marketing
strategy

© Noordhoff Uitgevers bv

13

requires a creative process. The outcome of the rational and creative process is consolidated in the global tactic.

In section 2.2 you were able to read that the strategy is formed by answering a number of questions. In the digital marketing plan, the answers to these questions are divided into four sub-items:
1 *Target audiences* and *segmentation*: the characteristics, needs and behaviour of online customers.
2 *Brand* and *proposition*: brand description, core values and propositions and how the brand promises are kept. For example, if you say you are going to be transparent, you shouldn't wait until the end of the online ordering process before including additional costs.
3 *Positioning*: describes how the organisation is positioned in comparison to its competitors, but also the online offer in relation to its other channels.
4 *Marketing mix*: incorporating the main features of the positioning and objectives into the core processes for each marketing instrument accordingly.
   a *Market sensing*: how do you collect information about your markets?
   b *Product realisation*: what products do you sell online, how do you organise product development, digital product realisation and services?
   c *Customer acquisition*: what are your starting points for digital marketing communication? What tools do you use? For instance:
      • link building
      • search engine marketing
      • display advertising
      • email marketing
      • virals and games
      • social media marketing
      • affiliate marketing
      • content marketing
   In addition, the basic principles for online sales advice, online sales, affiliate marketing and online pricing are also described.
   d *Customer relationship management*: how important will customer relationship management be and how will it be used?
   e *Order processing*: how do you organise the order processing? Consider fulfilment, distribution channels, payment methods and online customer service, such as live chat and social media.

UK online/telephone bank First Direct has consistently won awards for its customer service it has regularly, been commended for its competitiveness, flexibility and helpful customer service (voice, live chat and email).

One voter says: 'Customer service is second to none and the rates are so competitive. When I had a gap between sale and purchase of new property, First Direct was able to keep my fantastic rate on hold for me. I couldn't recommend it highly enough.'

Source: www.moneywise.co.uk

13

f *Integration and tactics on the Internet*: specific to digital marketing, the following components are also discussed:

- Conversion and content: description of the method for continuously improving the website's conversion rate based on the statistics. Consider reports and optimisation, such as a re-design, the required content (texts, white papers, video, etcetera) or to influence the brand experience for target segments and to tempt them to purchase your products and services.
- Data tactic: developing and expanding a customer database, keeping the information up-to-date and personalising on the basis of the data.

  Data tactic

- Multichannel integration and communication: integration of the organisation's online and offline channels. What collaborations already exist or need to be set up in order to achieve the business objective? A customer encounters the organisation in different ways and via different channels. This section describes the intersections and the details. Consider a website visitor who wants to know more about a product and clicks on a 'call me back' button. Here, the intersection with the Internet is customer service. How is the follow-up by the customer service department for this type of messages organised and what agreements have been made about this, for instance in terms of time?

  Multichannel integration and communication

An example of multichannel integration: Amazon.co.uk has partnered with the UK postal service Royal Mail to allow shoppers to collect packages from their local Post Office, expanding the online retailer's click-and-collect locations across the UK to over 16,000 outlets.

Collect your Amazon package from you local Royal Mail Post Office

13

Social media tactic

- Social media tactic: social media is used for campaigns within the digital marketing activities, but in many cases, they are also part of the overall organisational strategy, for example customer service.

Digital marketing is developing so quickly, that the strategy will have to be recalibrated at least every year.

Now that we have described how an organisation's objectives must be achieved, these objectives can be set out in activities.

13.2.4 Action plan

The fourth step consists of creating a detailed plan of action, in accordance with the strategy. It specifies the implementation of the previously described sub-items (one by one). For example, the year is divided into quarters or campaigns, the next of which is elaborated on in detail. This provides the possibility to learn from previous periods and to anticipate what needs to be done in the periods that will follow.
This last step is to explain the actions by means of:
- a planning: an overview of all actions and when they are to take place
- a budget:
  - costs: investments in the digital marketing activities in order to achieve the preconceived goals, the required manpower, the media budget
  - expected returns and ROI (return on investment)

13.2.5 Evaluation and review

In the final part of the digital marketing plan you must describe how you will check whether all digital marketing activities are going according to plan and when and how you will evaluate the results. The aim is to learn from everything that is going well as well as from everything that isn't and to constantly improve the quality of your digital marketing.
Using a KPI Dashboard (see also Chapter 12) helps you to monitor the progress of these indicators in relation to the SMART objective. This is a real-time or periodic overview in which the results are compared with the objectives. At a glance you are able to see what is going well and what isn't. Often, a backlog is displayed in red, a lead in green.

Online Scorecard

The Online Scorecard is a concept by Geert-Jan Smits and Joost Steins Bisschop (2014). It involves a method for taking stock of whether digital marketing is being used successfully.
The scorecard is determined according to the following steps:
1 The strategic objectives for digital marketing are phrased in a measurable way.
2 On the basis of the objectives, success factors are determined for four perspectives (see example in figure 13.5):
  a Financial: how do we become financially successful?
  b Customer: how do we get into contact with visitors and how do we satisfy our visitors' and customers' needs?
  c Online: how are we present, active and accessible online, so that it contributes towards satisfied customers and financial success?
  d Organisation: what needs to happen in the organisation to implement our digital strategy?

© Noordhoff Uitgevers bv

FIGURE 13.5 Success factors for bol.com

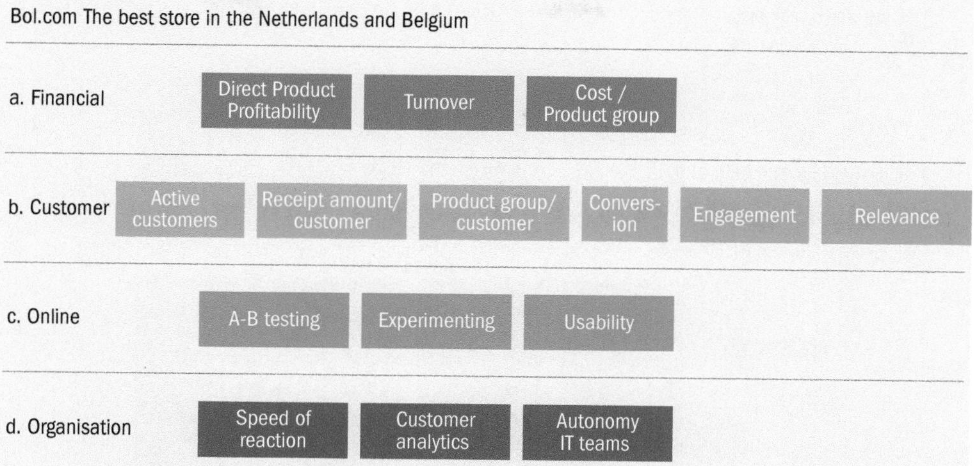

Bol.com The best store in the Netherlands and Belgium

| a. Financial | Direct Product Profitability | Turnover | Cost / Product group | | | |

| b. Customer | Active customers | Receipt amount/ customer | Product group/ customer | Convers-ion | Engagement | Relevance |

| c. Online | A-B testing | Experimenting | Usability | | | |

| d. Organisation | Speed of reaction | Customer analytics | Autonomy IT teams | | | |

Source: Jungle Minds, 2015

3 The digital mission, strategic objectives and success factors are combined into a Strategy Map (see figure 13.6).

FIGURE 13.6 Combine into a Strategy Map

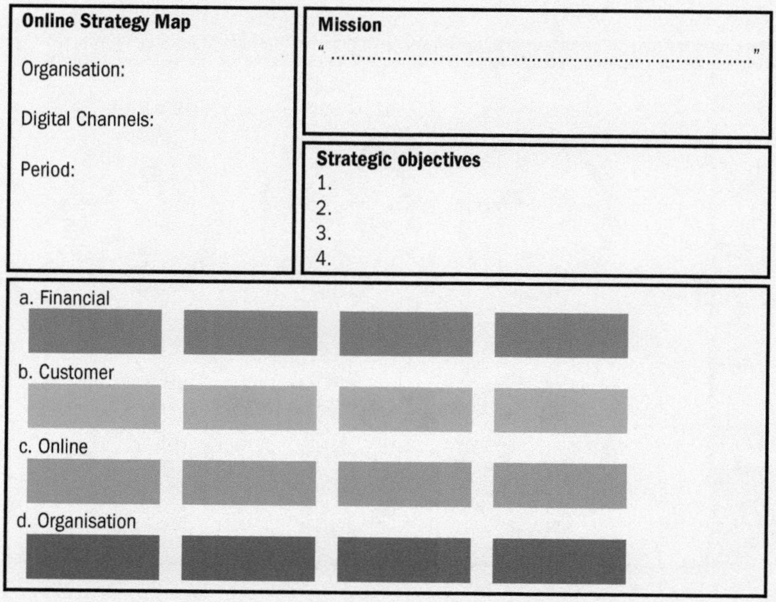

| **Online Strategy Map**

Organisation:

Digital Channels:

Period: | **Mission**
" .... "

Strategic objectives
1.
2.
3.
4. |

a. Financial

b. Customer

c. Online

d. Organisation

Source: Jungle Minds, 2015

4 The success factors are exemplified to create measurable indicators, objectives and the associated actions (see figure 13.7).

13

FIGURE 13.7 The digital Strategy Map is used to create the online scorecard

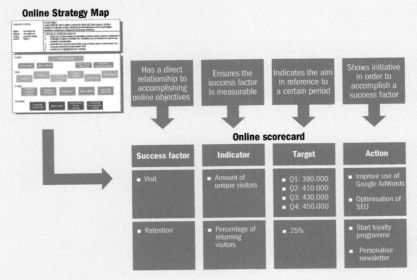

Source: Jungle Minds, 2015

5 The indicators are used to create a dashboard (see figure 13.8).

FIGURE 13.8 The indicators are used to create a dashboard

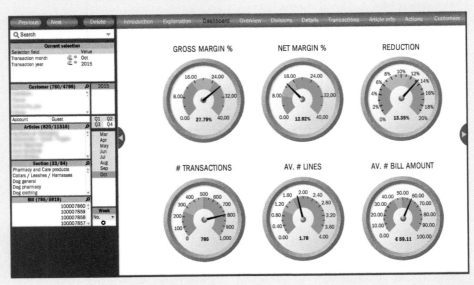

Source: Jungle Minds, 2015

At first, this model was called the *Internet Scorecard*. This concept is still widely used in business.

Source: Jungle Minds, 2015

It is important that the digital marketing plan distinguishes between activities that are part of the daily working routine and those that belong to projects. Activities that only have to be performed once and occur only once in a certain period, such as expanding a web shop or setting up an information system, are executed as a project. These require a different approach and organisation. This will be discussed in more detail in the next section.

13.3 Project management

In this section we will focus on project management and how project management methods can be used for the execution of digital marketing activities.

As an internet marketer, regardless of the organisational form, your team will fall under a hierarchical (line) manager, but you can also be part of a project team. In the latter case you report to the relevant project manager, next to your line manager.

In organisations, there is not always a clear separation between line activities (such as keeping track of statistics, managing content on websites and communications) and project work (such as redesigning a website or developing an online shop). As a result, these activities coalesce, and it is sometimes difficult to set priorities. Projects often aren't finished on time, because there is simply too little time available, or due to lack of planning everything has to be done at the same time.

In this section we will make a distinction between four different digital marketing activities and what is involved in their implementation. Then the role of project management will be described. We will discuss three methods of project management and the connection with the type of activity that you as an internet marketer can encounter within a project.

13.3.1 Digital marketing activities

Within digital marketing a distinction can be made of the following types of activities, each of which requires a different approach:

1 digital platform:
    a development (project)
    b management and further development (line activity)
2 campaign:
    a development (project)
    b management and optimisation (project)

1a Digital platform/application: development
The development of a new digital platform, such as a corporate website, an e-shop or a community site, has a long running time and a clearly defined scope and places considerable demands on capacity and financial resources.

Digital platform

The planned start and end date are known. The activities are carried out on a project basis by a project team, led by a project manager. The development of a digital platform can be partly or fully outsourced to an external agency and/or ICT party. As you were able to read in section 13.1.5, the choice whether or not to outsource depends, among other things, on the competencies and the capacity of the organisation. Figure 13.9 gives a schematic overview of the development of a digital platform.

13

FIGURE 13.9 Development of a digital platform/application

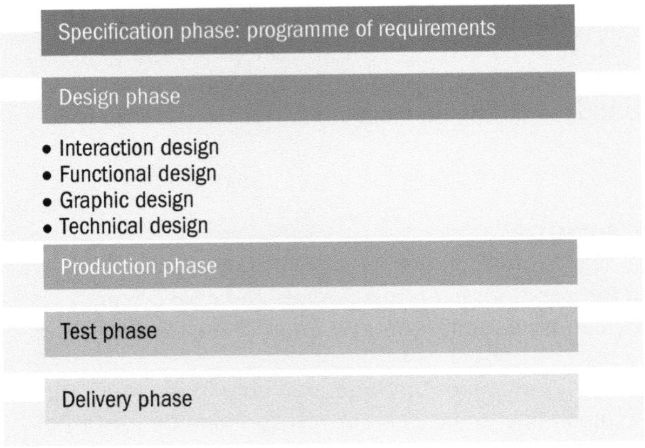

Specification phase: programme of requirements

Design phase

- Interaction design
- Functional design
- Graphic design
- Technical design

Production phase

Test phase

Delivery phase

The requirements set by the project's primary client form the starting point for the briefing and the project plan that is required before the implementation of the project can be started.

The interaction, functional, graphic and technical designs are developed and then serve as the basis for technical development. The interaction design describes how the user can interact with the website or the online application. It is, as it were, a blueprint of the pages of the platform, without texts or visual elements. The functional design describes which features the application or website offers, in other words: what should the website do on the basis of the interaction? The graphic design is the visual design of the platform. The technical design shows the 'building plan' of the system and serves as the basis for the programmers. Once the first version of the platform has been built and tested, the platform will be published. Improvements, such as the addition of the FAQs (frequently asked questions) or a payment module, are then often added step-by-step. The project ends when the digital platform, including the predefined features, is ready and has been approved by the (internal) customer and is published. With that, the platform has been delivered.

Parallel to the development of the digital platform, related digital marketing activities are carried out, such as determining keyword tags for the discoverability in search engines (see Chapter 5) and producing a sitemap of the content. The sitemap is an overview that contains all the links on a website, sorted according to importance. This is a useful tool for visitors and search engines to find pages on a site.

1b Digital platform: management and further development
After the publication of the digital platform, the project has ended, but the development is not over. The platform must be continuously maintained and further developed in order to continue to connect with the target audience and the defined objectives. This is a continuous process without a direct end date and is therefore considered a line activity. If the activities involve a major change, a new project can be defined, and a project manager and team appointed.

Any further development is often carried out step-by-step. For example, it may concern updates of errors in the platform, altered features or entirely

Margin notes:
Interaction design

Functional design

Graphic design

Technical design

Sitemap

13

© Noordhoff Uitgevers bv

new features. What needs to be done can be determined on the basis of new market and customer insights and statistics. A team reports on and analyses the statistics of the website. Should the results be disappointing, points for improvement are determined. Text changes, images and small graphic changes can often be implemented by the relevant permanent team, designers, content managers and sometimes front-end programmers themselves. Any larger or technical changes, take place in a so-called 'iteration' or 'release' within the IT department or a completely new project is defined.

Even though user surveys could be carried out during the further development, it is not easy to predict how a (new) change will catch on with the public. This is where A/B testing can be used. Some of the visitors will see version A and the other part version B. The version that scores the best will eventually be implemented. You have read about this in Chapter 12. An A/B test means that two versions (of images, text, and/or features) are published and tested for effectiveness.

A/B test

2a Campaign: development
Similar to the development of a digital platform, the development of a digital marketing communication campaign takes place within a project. The development of a campaign is often carried out by an external agency. The project ends upon completion of the development or after the end of the campaign. The start of the media deployment often counts as a deadline for the project.

Campaign

2b Campaign: management and optimisation
Since the development of the campaign and the optimisation during its running time require a different dynamic, their implementation is often relegated to (sub)projects.

Activities that are carried out for the management and maintenance are: measuring, analysing, reporting and optimising. The development pertaining to the content is therefore determined on the basis of the interim results of the campaign. Based on the number of visitors, drop-out moments and conversion, we measure which parts of the campaign are effective and what needs to be improved.

As these are often small changes that need to be implemented quickly, this is often done ad hoc or iteratively. The optimisations may concern changes in the campaign statements, but also in the media deployment, such as the target segment specification or where the ads appear. The development of platforms also means that this is done more and more frequently. See previous section 13.3.3.

13.3.2 Basic principles of project management
Project management involves overseeing projects. It is the way projects are organised, prepared, executed and completed. We will first introduce the basic principles before you read more about project management specific to digital marketing.

Variables
Projects are always executed according to the variables time, costs, scope and quality. These variables can be projected in the 'project management triangle' (see figure 13.10).

Project management triangle

13

FIGURE 13.10 Project management triangle

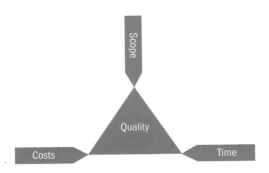

Scope

The quality of the end result of a project is directly related to the three variables time, costs and scope. An organisation decides what the requirements for this quality are. If one of the variables changes, the other variables will have to adapt accordingly in order to achieve the desired quality. If, for example, the scope is expanded in the development of a web shop by adding a number of new features, this means that more time is needed, and the costs will increase. At the start of a project, the project manager and the primary customer agree which of the variables must be fixed. Consider, for example, a campaign that is linked to an event, such as the Olympic Games. All connected activities must be ready in time for the event. In such a situation, a company might be prepared to pay extra money, limit the scope (less features on the campaign site) or set lower quality requirements. The factor 'time' is fixed.

Toyota rolls out 'Start Your Impossible' global campaign that reflects the Olympic and Paralympic spirit of encouragement, challenge and progress. The factor 'time' is fixed.

The work of the project team must be organised in such a way that all variables can be completed to the desired level. To achieve this, an approach with a number of standard phases is chosen.

13

Standard phases in project management

Regardless of the type of project, the following standard phases are completed (see figure 13.11):

- *Initiation*: In this, the nature of the project and the scope are determined by/with the primary customer, as well as the margins for error with regard to the variables. Input from specialists involved is very important at this stage. If the creation of a sitemap for a digital platform is based on a maximum number of menu items and a particular design, problems may arise if, for example, product categories are added at a later stage.
- *Schedule*: on the basis of the defined scope, the activities are planned in terms of time, costs and resources (knowledge, resources, capacity) and risks are identified. Careful consideration must be given to what could go wrong during the project or at the beginning of its implementation.
- *Production and execution*: a project manager coordinates the activities of all team members and the resources that are deployed during the project. The project manager monitors the integration of the activities and forms the link between the various specialists such as internet marketers, programmers and potential partners. They also communicate with the departments that are involved. For example, the customer service department must be aware of the content of digital marketing campaigns. They also manage any external agencies.
- *Monitor and control*: the project manager monitors and signals problems that arise during the execution of the project. These are often identified by the individual team members. If necessary, corrective measures are taken. Consider, for example, an email that goes out on a certain fixed date. If the development of the landing page is delayed, the email will have to be postponed.
- *Closing*: this concerns the formal acceptance of a project by the primary customer, also called 'discharge'. After this an evaluation is made and the documents belonging to the project are archived.

FIGURE 13.11 Standard phases in project management

SMART

The SMART principle (specific, measurable, acceptable, realistic, time-bound) is used not only to determine digital marketing objectives, but also as a way of monitoring project phases and outcomes.

SMART

Specific
The objective of the project must be unambiguous. If a project manager defines the result as 'a new digital platform that converts better', this is not concrete enough. To specify what needs to be done, the six W's are often used: **What** do we want to achieve, **Who** is involved, **Where** are we going to do it, **When, Why** and **What** parts of the objective are essential? The project manager and the digital marketer maintain close contact during this phase.

13

Measurable
It must be clear whether the goal has been achieved. For example: the new website must achieve a 3% increase in conversion within a year. In this case, a baseline measurement is needed first to determine the exact starting situation (the current conversion).

Acceptable
There is enough support from within the organisation. All parties involved must be in agreement about what has been decided in the previous phases (specific and measurable). This fosters motivation, a sense of responsibility and the feeling that it has been given sufficient priority by the various departments.

Realistic
The feasibility of the objective is estimated on the basis of previous experiences, current figures and competitors. For example: if the conversion rate is already 50%, doubling it is not realistic. That would mean that ten out of ten visitors to a website actually become customers.

Time-bound
A clear start and end date for the project's objectives must be defined. For example: the project starts on 1 January 2019 and the conversion must be 4% by 31 December 2019, an increase of 2% compared to 31 December 2018.

13.3.3 Commonly used methods for project management

In this sub-section you can read more about the three commonly used project management methods that you, as a marketer, might encounter in the course of your digital marketing activities:
1 waterfall method and sashimi model
2 iterative method (such as agile)
3 PRINCE2 method

The matrix in figure 13.12 shows which method corresponds to what kind of activity. For each method there is a description of how it can be used and how it slots in to the different types of digital marketing activities.

FIGURE 13.12 Matrix digital marketing activities versus appropriate project management

	Digital Platform	Campaigns
Development	PRINCE2 Waterfall	PRINCE2 Waterfall
Management/further development	Iterative Line activities	Iterative

13

Waterfall method and sashimi model

The most traditional method for project management is the waterfall method. For this method, the project is divided into five phases (see figure 13.13), with an online web shop as an example:

Waterfall method

1 *Analysis*: such as analysing the disappointing contribution of the online conversions towards achieving the business objectives.
2 *Design*: a new interaction, graphic, functional and technical design for an improved online ordering process.
3 *Implementation*: implementing the modified design in the web shop and the underlying processes, such as logistics.
4 *Testing*: functional and technical testing of the new online ordering process.
5 *Management*: managing the new ordering process, measuring whether it's a better fit and further developing it on the basis of the statistics.

Tests could be carried out using focus groups (a guided discussion about the opinions, perceptions and feelings of a group of users) and usability tests. This often takes place during the design phase.

FIGURE 13.13 Traditional waterfall method

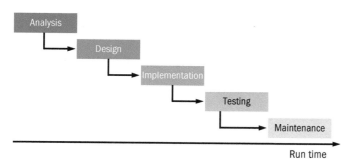

Run time

Each phase is fully completed before the next phase is started. For example, within the design phase, the interaction design will have to be agreed upon before starting the graphic and technical design.

Only once these have been given the green light, can programming be started. The waterfall method is a stage-gate process as described in Chapter 4: each time, a part has to be approved (gate), before the next phase can be started (stage).

The project team consists of people from different disciplines, but per phase, only people with similar competencies work together (see the overview of the various competences in section 13.1.4).
As the work is completed in series, it is very important that sufficient consultation takes place between the different competencies. In the design phase, graphic designers must, for example, take into account the technical limitations and possibilities.

13

Sashimi model A variant of the waterfall method is the sashimi model (see figure 13.14). There may be limited overlap of the phases. For example, programming is started, while the graphic design is in its final phase. This allows the design to be adjusted during programming if it appears that a certain animation is not technically feasible within the set variables (see section 13.3.2).

FIGURE 13.14 In the sashimi model, phases can overlap each other

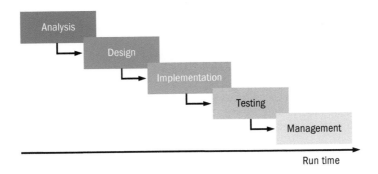

The waterfall method is suitable if:
- it is a large project
- the primary customer has a clear end result in mind
- many changes can be expected from different departments
- no changes with a major impact are expected

If it is unclear what the end result should look like or whether it is expected that the wishes might change, this approach is not suitable.
Digital marketing projects often involve various departments, such as operations, customer service, sales and marketing. This means different interests and opinions that, if not properly managed, can lead to continuous changes. The waterfall method can help to prevent the project from running over time. Everyone involved has to be on the same page before the next phase begins.

This method is well suited to development of the basis of a digital platform, such as a web shop or a completely new component such as a 'My Client Profile', that has an impact not only on the front but also on underlying processes and departments. It is also suitable for a large project that has evolved from further developments such as a re-design or the development of large campaigns where many resources are used, such as a campaign website, game, traffic resources and so on.

Iterative or agile method

Iterative method The iterative method is the opposite of the waterfall method. The project is a series of relatively small tasks whose content is constantly redefined, instead of a completely pre-planned process. Each iteration produces a working product: it provides value for the customer. Iterative also means step-by-step.
In advance, the organisation determines in broad strokes which features will be completed in each defined period. Think for example of an informative

website that is being developed into a web shop with an online payment system and keeping track of the order status using an individual customer account. In the first period, a feature is added for product information, in the next period a feature for current prices, then the possibility to order, next the possibility of online payment and finally the creation of a customer account including the ability to follow the order. After each iteration, the project priorities are re-assessed. This is determined, among other things, by test results. For example, it may be that a customer account is created in an earlier period than the possibility of online payment.

As with the waterfall method, the experts who contribute to the different phases are part of a project team. But unlike the waterfall method, they work simultaneously on the project. As a digital marketer you are part of this multidisciplinary team, that provides useful result per sub-period. It is only during the last delivery that all predefined requirements are met: an online shop with a customer account and order status. There is frequent communication with the final users and the customer, where satisfaction, new wishes and problems are discussed.

The iterative method is illustrated schematically in figure 13.15.

FIGURE 13.15 The iterative method

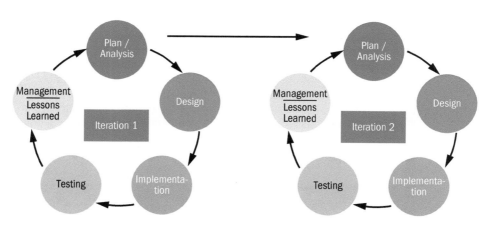

An example of the iterative method is the agile method (also called lean method). This is a method for projects with a short running time (weeks instead of months) and based on intensive collaboration. A specific form of the agile method is scrum. The same principles apply to the agile method as to the iterative method.

Agile method

Scrum

The iterative method is suitable for projects that:
- are difficult to predict
- where the application must and can be continuously optimised
- where close cooperation is possible in order to limit the risk

The close involvement of clients and users has two advantages:
1 users gradually get used to the (new) platform
2 optimisation is made possible by the connection with the target audience

13

For example, suppose that the goal of the digital marketer is to achieve a higher conversion. A means can be a new checkout process or generating more traffic, but the prices or the layout of the order page can also have an influence. Based on web statistics and qualitative user research, it is possible to choose which feature will be optimised or developed in the next iteration. The impact of false assumptions and evolving insights remains minimal. By correcting an error as early on as possible, the negative effects are limited.

From an organisational point of view, the suitability of iterative work can be measured in three dimensions:

- *culture*: being open to discussion, an organisation in which decisions can be taken quickly
- *people*: competent, smaller team (twenty to forty people)
- *communication*: personal, direct communication

The team members have to take the strong dynamic into account and they must keep in mind what the original objective is. The risk is, that as a result of the continuous adjustments, the basic objective disappears from view. For example, the online shop can become the objective instead of facilitating online purchases that contribute to the company profit. The online shop is a means. Perhaps better results can be achieved by setting up an affiliate program (see section 7.5).

The iterative method is often best suited for development work if there is a foundation on which to develop further. It is suitable for the management of a digital platform and campaigns, because they have a dynamic and fast nature: small steps that can be tested and adjusted where necessary. The management of the platform is a line activity and not a project, but the development is also often carried out iteratively, so that (parallel) optimisations can be implemented. If the activities become larger and more complex, they are carried on in a project with a project manager.

The agile method uses a 'scrum board' to keep track of how the project is progressing

PRINCE2 method

PRINCE2 (Projects IN Controlled Environments) is a process- and product-oriented method in contrast to linear methods such as the waterfall method.

PRINCE2
method

Just like in the waterfall method, a project is divided into manageable phases that first have to be completed before the next phase can begin. At the conclusion of each phase, the project manager provides the results or a document containing the results. These results are compared with the initial starting points to determine whether adjustments are necessary (see figure 13.16).

FIGURE 13.16 PRINCE2 method

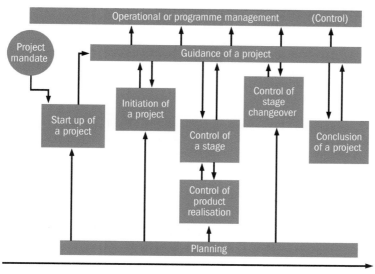

Think, for example, of transferring a banking system to a new online system. This is a long-term project and a lot can change during the running time. The chosen system is based on a number of starting points. Due to a new policy or new objectives other wishes may arise, as a result of which the system changes or features have to be added.

An important document within the PRINCE2 method is the business case. This document explains, among other things, why the project is necessary, what the business objectives of the project are, what the investments and risks are and what happens if the project does not go ahead. On the one hand this makes it possible for the organisation to be aware of how much priority a project should receive in relation to other projects, but it also ensures that the financial and practical consequences of changing circumstances and starting points are continually reassessed.

13

Within this method, everything can be adapted to the specific project, as long as the seven PRINCE2 principles are met:

1 Continuous justification using the business case: this is to ensure that a project does not lead a life of its own but continues to contribute to the business objectives.
2 Learning from experience: think of keeping track of best practices and new insights.
3 Defined roles and responsibilities: it is clear who is responsible so that no grey areas exist.
4 Management per phase: everything is aimed at providing the responsible management with sufficient directional information and instruments.
5 Managing by exception (*management by exception*): only if the margins for error at a certain level (such as time and money) are about to be exceeded, is the higher level of management activated.
6 Being product-oriented: the focus is on defining the products that have to be delivered, with the corresponding quality criteria.
7 Adapting to the project environment: customisation per project to meet the needs of that specific project in that specific environment; for the development of an online shop, for example, a different set-up is required than for a module for webcare.

PRINCE2 is applicable to all projects and has great flexibility. Aspects of the method that are not applicable or that are not useful for a particular project can be modified. The team members must be flexible and go along with any change in the project's circumstances or results. PRINCE2 provides clear stipulations on how to handle changes. This contributes to clear expectation management for the primary customer but is also useful for projects with several interested parties. This is often the case in digital marketing activities (customer service, sales, marketing, ICT, creative agencies).

This method is particularly suitable for complex projects, such as the development of new platforms and large-scale campaigns, where you cannot accurately assess in advance what you might encounter.

The methods combined

Within organisations, there is often a preference for a specific method (waterfall, iterative or PRINCE2), but it also occurs that they are used side by side or combined. When developing a digital platform, a combination of project management methods can work well: for example, setting up a base platform via PRINCE2 or waterfall and additional features using the iterative method. In figure 13.17 the methods are listed again, one after the other, for comparison using an identical running time.

FIGURE 13.17 Project management methods compared

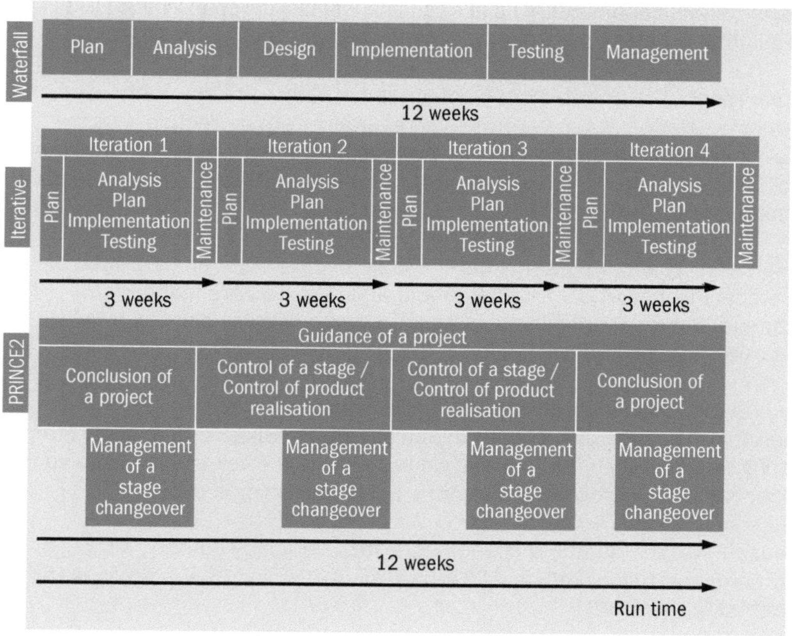

13.4 Legal aspects of digital marketing

In the previous sections you were able to read how digital marketing can be organised and how management must handle digital marketing projects. Whether you, as a digital marketer, are responsible for projects, campaigns or specific activities such as email marketing, or whether your customer assumes this responsibility, in all cases you will have to know within which legal frameworks you need to operate. In this section you can read more about:

- privacy legislation
- rules concerning promotional actions
- terms and conditions
- legislation on ecommerce
- domain squatting
- authorities that you, as a digital marketer, must take into account

13.4.1 Privacy

Privacy is a topic that has attracted increasing attention in recent years. On the one hand, it is very important for consumers, on the other hand it is something for digital marketers to keep a close eye on. For example, companies such as Google and Facebook know a lot about their users and use this information to display targeted advertisements. Both consumers and authorities are starting to wonder whether the privacy of the internet user is not at stake in this way. Below we will discuss privacy legislation in depth.

Privacy

13

Data Protection Laws

Processing (storing, publishing or using) personal data is only allowed under certain conditions. This is regulated in the European Privacy Regulation, formally the General Data Protection Regulation (GDPR),

Interestingly, the United States does not currently have any centralized, formal legislation at the federal level regarding data protection, but the USA does regulate the privacy and protection of data through various laws including the United States Privacy Act, the Privacy Shield and the Health Insurance Portability and Accountability Act.

When we talk about personal data, this is all data that can be traced back to a specific individual. Your name and address are personal data for example, but also an online account or a photo. We will discuss a few of the rules.

Requesting, informing and registering permission
Everything that you can do with personal data is called 'processing'. From letting people subscribe to a magazine to keeping track of who visits your Facebook page or following a visitor's behaviour using a cookie

Please note that data and privacy legislation varies by country, although the European Union with its GDPR has a single privacy law – which is the strictest in the world.

The general principle is one of *informed consent*; the customer must be fully aware of what data he or she is sharing and what the data user intends to do with it over what period of time. Whereas in the past marketers in some countries may have been allowed to adopt an opt-out regime (ie if you do nothing we will assume you are happy with us using your data in this way) the emphasis increasingly is on opt-in.

Additional complexity is added if you are involved in cross-border trading. Be sure to consult a legal expert before embarking on major projects.

Cookies

Personal data is not only collected via online forms but can also be collected using cookies. A *cookie* is a file that is placed on your computer by an advertiser, containing personal data such as an identifier that helps the advertiser recognise you on the Internet.
The cookies that Amazon.com uses to remember what you had in your cart the last time you visited the website are *first-party cookies*. Even when Amazon.com uses cookies for its web statistics, these are first-party cookies.
However, the cookies placed by advertisers on your computer when their banners are shown to you via websites for the purpose of behavioural targeting, are called *third-party cookies*.

13

Securing personal data
In most countries, Brand owners who collect data from users are legally obliged to strictly protect all personal data against misuse and theft In addition to fines, the theft of personal data can also result in considerable damage to a company's reputation. And beware: brand owners are still liable if they outsource data collection or management. So carefully consider what kind of companies you are working with.

Inspection, correction and deletion
In most countries (and certainly under GDPR) every individual whose data you process is entitled to inspect this data. This person may also demand that you correct or even delete the data if they so wish.

Exception for customers
In many countries, there is one group whose permission you are not legally required to obtain before you can send advertisements via email: paying customers. You must have clearly stated this beforehand and people must then immediately be given the opportunity to object. For this reason, the boxes in newsletters or order forms may be ticked by default; removal is objection. Note however that the law varies depending on what country you are doing business in so always check with local experts.

In many countries, in order to apply to this exception, advertising must be about your own products and services, which are also related to the product or service that the customer has purchased. If you have purchased a games console from amazon.com the company is allowed to send you an email with an offer for games or accessories to go along with this game console. An email with an offer for a new drill is not 'related' and is therefore only allowed if the marketer obtains a separate permission.

Cookie legislation
Personal data is not only collected via online forms but can also be placed in cookies. An cookie is a text file that an advertiser places on your computer, containing a unique code that helps the advertiser recognise you on the web. With each visit, it keeps track of which pages you visit (and what you will find interesting), and links it to that code. This way, overview of your interests is collated.

Cookie

For example, cookies are used to select ads that match your interests (behavioural targeting). Cookies can also be used to find out that you recently wanted to buy something from a web store, and you can subsequently be shown ads from that website whilst you are on a different website, in order to lure you back (re-targeting). Compiling website statistics (Web Analytics) also uses cookies.

For several years now, there has been a cookie law in Europe; indeed, Europe is comparatively strict on cookies. This legislation requires you to explain to users exactly what cookies are and request permission before you are able to use them. Because many visitors do not voluntarily give permission, websites often require people to give their permission in order to visit the site. Whether this is customer-friendly, you will have to decide for yourself.
No permission is required for cookies that only facilitate technical features (ie the actual functionality of the site). so, although the content

13

of your shopping cart is monitored using a cookie, no permission is required for this.

Cookie notice on bbc.co.uk

Several industry associations have meanwhile joined forces in developing a 'do-not-follow-me register' called Youronlinechoices (www.youronlinechoices.eu). For every advertisement that makes use of cookies, an icon appears that makes it possible for internet users to indicate that they no longer want to be followed (opt-out). Unfortunately, not all companies are connected to this initiative as of yet.

13.4.2   Promotional actions

We come across them regularly, online campaigns from brands where you have a chance to win a prize. However, if you cannot influence the result, such a result is considered to be a form of gambling, or a game of chance. Depending on the country, it may be an illegal lottery and that usually is a criminal offence.

Laws on gambling

In most countries, according to the laws on gambling it is forbidden to offer gambling activities without a license. Some countries, such as the Netherlands, make an exception for promotional games of chance, provided the company that organises it adheres to the relevant national Code of Conduct for promotional games of chance.

Code of Conduct for promotional games of chance

Typically, this code of conduct contains various conditions, such as:
- The primary objective of the game is to promote a product, service or organisation
- The game must be temporary
- The organisation cannot ask for money to participate
- There is a maximum to the total prize money that can be handed out annually
- As an organiser you are obliged to draw up general terms and conditions and to make these available to the participants

The Code of Conduct for promotional games of chance is mainly aimed at ensuring that it 'remains a game'. In this way, companies are able to organise a game of chance for their customers without a permit, but betting offices and casinos still require a license.

Games of chance are, for example lotteries, roulette or blackjack. In these games you cannot improve your chances of winning, no matter how hard you try. A slogan contest is not a game of chance because if you try hard enough, you might come up with the most beautiful slogan. Whether poker is considered a game of chance is unclear. On the one hand you are dependent on whether you are dealt a good hand, on the other, a good poker player will win more often than a bad one.

Once again, laws vary by country; always check with a local lawyer (in-house or external) who knows about marketing legislation.

13.4.3 General terms and conditions

As the owner of a website you may decide who is able to visit it. In the so-called general terms and conditions or terms of use, you can determine the rules that apply on your website. This may include how the ordering process is organised or what a social networking site may or may not do with the pictures and videos that you upload. Next, we will discuss a few rules and points of interest regarding general conditions.

General terms and conditions

Availability of terms and conditions

General terms and conditions must be displayed in a timely manner on the website visitor's screen. This means that the visitor must be able to read them before ordering or registering on your site. That is why, in the registration or ordering form, you are almost always asked to agree to the general terms and conditions. A hyperlink to the terms and conditions is added to the text in which you are asked to agree, in order for you to be able to read them (should you so choose). Legally speaking, a tick is not necessarily obligatory: if you mention something along the lines of: 'By clicking on 'Submit order' below, you also agree to our general terms and conditions,' just above the ordering button, then that's enough. Provided that you, of course, add the hyperlink.

Unreasonable terms

Not all general terms and conditions apply without exception. General terms and conditions may not be unreasonably onerous, otherwise they may be invalidated by the court.

How do you know whether the terms and conditions are unreasonably onerous? There are no general rules for this. It depends on whether these conditions are fair to the visitor or customer. Demanding that someone has to pay upfront, but that you do not have to deliver if you don't feel like it, is not fair. So, such a condition is typically not allowed.

Subject to printing and typing errors?

A frequently used phrase in the general terms and conditions of online retailers is subject to print and typing errors. This is to prevent customers from taking advantage of errors in prices or product descriptions. However, the law is clear in most countries: if the customer can reasonably assume that a price or description is correct, then you cannot simply cancel the purchase because of this condition. You are obliged to deliver what was on your website, even if that wasn't your intention.

Subject to print and typing errors

13.4.4 Ecommerce

Ecommerce relates to informing about goods and services on the Internet, as well as promoting, selling and distributing them. In the broadest sense, it covers all commercial activities on the Internet. Legally speaking, when you engage in ecommerce, two things are of importance: identification and the Distance Selling regulations. You may also be dealing with copyright and the right to quote, creative commons, trademark law and Google AdWords. We will now discuss these matters in more detail.

13

Identification

Identification
requirements

It may seem self-evident that you are who you say you are, but according to the law of most countries, as a company, when you communicate via the Internet, you are confronted with identification requirements. In all external communications, you are required to state your full company name, legal form, VAT number and place of establishment. This means on your website, but also in all business-related emails and newsletters that you send. Do you also sell things via the web? Then you must also clearly indicate the specifications and the price of each product – including the shipping costs if these are calculated per product. In addition, you are obliged to inform the customer of how the ordering process will proceed, what guarantees they have and how products can be returned.

Distance Selling Regulations

Distance Selling
Regulations

In most countries, when selling products to consumers on the Internet, you have to comply with the local Distance Selling Regulations. These describe the rights and obligations of both the buyer and the seller. For example, a consumer who buys something at a distance, is entitled to a minimum legal cancelation period of seven days, which starts one day after receiving the product. The consumer is entitled to a refund, including any shipping costs paid. These must be repaid by the seller within a fixed period of time, say 14 days. Did you fail to mention the minimum legal cancelation period? Then the customer is entitled to a cancelation period of no less than twelve months.

However, this does not apply to all products. For example, time-bound products such as magazines are not included, nor are holidays, custom-made products, perishable products and services that start immediately, such as a mobile phone subscription of which the contract begins the same day. Please note that you must inform the consumer in advance that this exception applies. In the case of services, you must even explicitly let them tick the box that states that they want the service to be provided immediately and renounce the right to cancel.

Again, please note that the law varies between countries and you should always consult a local lawyer.

Copyright and the right to quote

When building your website, writing texts or publishing other content, you must take copyright into account. This applies to, for example, texts, drawings, photographs, video and audio recordings.

Copyright

The copyright gives the creator of an 'own intellectual creation' the right to reproduce and publish. This also includes editing, downloading, translating or filming a work. The filming of the Harry Potter books is covered by reproduction. Publishing means the distribution of a work. This involves broadcasting on TV or on the radio, but also streaming music on Spotify is an example of publishing.

A work is an 'own creation' when it involves some kind of creativity. This doesn't take much to achieve; the standards aren't high. Therefore, virtually all texts and photos on the Internet are protected. You do not need to deposit a work; you will automatically receive copyright. You do not even have to add the copyright sign ©!

© Noordhoff Uitgevers bv

In the event of a violation of copyright, the rightful claimant can immediately file a claim for damages. He doesn't have to warn you first or demand that you immediately remove the text or photo.

A recent example is when Matt Furie, the creator of the meme Pepe the Frog, filed a lawsuit against the website InfoWars. The artist sued the conspiracy theory website for copyright infringement over an item for sale in the site's online store, a poster that features an image of Pepe the Frog. The poster's design was attributed to 'artist and patriot Jon Allen' and priced at $29.95.

An exception to the aforementioned protections is the right to quote, in the USA known as fair use. This regulation covers the right to quote a relevant part of a copyrighted work for certain purposes, provided that the source is cited. These purposes involve announcing, discussing and criticising the work. Simply using something as decoration is not allowed as a quote, even if you mention the source.

Right to quote
Fair use

A short fragment of Lady Gaga's new single could be added to a review of her album, but not as background music for your website. In an article about mills, using a picture of a beautiful windmill is also not a quote.

Creative Commons
In addition to regular copyright, there is also something known as Creative Commons. Where copyright is primarily focused on protecting your rights as a creator, Creative Commons licenses are aimed at sharing your work with the rest of the world.
If you decide to designate your work as a Creative Common (CC), everyone may do anything with it, except for the restrictions you have selected. You can select three restrictions:
1 no commercial use
2 no derivative works (modifications)
3 share equally (if your piece of music is used in a remix, this remix must be made available under the same Creative Commons license as your original piece of music)

Creative Commons

Creative Commons licenses are valid forever. As soon as someone has taken your work under a CC license, you can no longer adjust this. However, you can decide to publish your work again under a different license.

In addition to the restrictions that you choose as an author, legal exceptions such as the right to quote also remain applicable.

Trademark law
Just like anywhere, regulations apply to the Internet for protecting trademarks such as logos and company names. Over the course of years, companies such as Coca-Cola have invested in building a brand that evokes certain associations among consumers. But also, smaller entrepreneurs with a good reputation have an interest in protecting their name.

Trademark law

13

Another may not just use your brand for promoting their own products or services. This applies to both the same and similar products. The prohibition applies to a name that is exactly the same, but also to a name that can cause confusion, such as the brand name with 'dealer' added to it or a deviating spelling. This applies to using a brand name in an advertisement, but also in the URL of a website.

In advertising, it is permitted to use someone else's brand to indicate that you sell that product, or that your product is meant for it. For example, on a bag of coffee capsules it is OK to state that these are meant for the Nespresso machine. You may also mention a brand to compare your own product/service to it, as long as the comparison is objectively true.

Google AdWords

Google AdWords displays ads based on keywords entered by the user. This means that an advertiser can use the name of their competitor in two places. They may decide to advertise using their competitor's brand name as a keyword, but they may also decide to include their competitor's brand name in the text of their advertisement.

After a ruling by the highest European judge, Google decided that companies within AdWords are allowed to advertise using brand names of competitors. Both the use of a competitor's name as a keyword and using the name of a competitor in your advertisement, is now possible. However, when you apply for protection of your trademark in Google, no one can use your brand name in the text of Google ads without your explicit consent. You can still display your own advertisements using someone else's brand name as a keyword, but these ads may not explicitly mention the other brand's name.

13.4.5   Domain squatting

A domain name can be a valuable place on the Internet. A well-known brand name allows you to be easily found, and a general word can also result in a popular site: if you want to know more about football for example, you will soon be going to www.football.com (and asked to choose between American football and soccer!) Therefore, registering domain names with famous (or general) names, is a popular activity. So-called domain hijackers or domain squatters hope that interested parties will then buy the domains off them for a significant sum. Also, typos in a domain name are an attractive 'target' for these people.

Domain squatting

There is usually not much you can do to prevent domain hijacking. First come is first served, even when claiming a domain name. If you want to have a website about football, then you will have to come up with something different because football.com is already taken. However, if the domain name contains your registered trademark or company name, then you do have some legal options. A competitor using a domain name that has your brand name in it, is simply trademark infringement, and that allows you to claim the domain name in court, even if it is slightly different, eg featuring a spelling mistake.

Domain hijacking

Simply owning a domain name is not a trademark infringement. Only if it had turned out that the domain name owner was indiscriminately claiming domain names as a way of doing business, one might still be able to reclaim it. This is considered abuse.

In addition to the courts, you can also turn to the issuing authority of domain names in your country. They have so-called arbitration procedures that, on the basis of their own regulations, assess whether someone has to hand in a domain name. For this, the likelihood of confusion between brand name and domain name has an important role, as is the amount of domain names the other person is registering. From a business perspective, buying the domain name is often the best thing to do – and domain hijackers know this as well.

13.4.6   Authorities

If you violate the laws mentioned in this chapter, you can be sued in court. However, other authorities also exist that supervise or issue fines if you, as a digital marketer, do not sufficiently take laws and regulations into account. We will discuss this next. We will also elaborate on a few institutions that represent the interests of digital companies.

Consumer Authority

Many countries have a Consumer Authority: an independent administrative body with the responsibility of protecting consumers and their rights from unscrupulous businesses and individuals. An example is the FTC's Bureau of Consumer Protection in the US. This agency stops unfair, deceptive and fraudulent business practices by collecting complaints and conducting investigations, suing companies and people that break the law, developing rules to maintain a fair marketplace, and educating consumers and businesses about their rights and responsibilities. In the UK, The Consumer Rights Act 2015 consolidates previous consumer protection laws, giving consumers a range of rights and remedies, dealing with consumer contracts for goods, digital content and services and unfair terms.

National Data protection authorities

National data protection authorities are authorities guarding information privacy. In the UK, the body is called the Information Commissioner's Office (ICO). They describe themselves as: 'The UK's independent authority set up to uphold information rights in the public interest, promoting openness by public bodies and data privacy for individuals'. Similar organisations exist in other countries.

Advertising Standards Authority

Many countries have an advertising standards organisation which seeks to protect consumers from misleading or fraudulent advertising in any channel.

The Advertising Standards Authority or ASA is the UK's independent regulator of advertising across all media and applies the Advertising Codes, which are written by the Committee of Advertising Practice (CAP). It aims to promote responsible advertising. If a consumer finds that an advertisement does not comply with the rules of the Advertising Standards Authority (ASA), they can file a complaint. The CAP assesses these and may decide that the advertising must be adjusted. Although the CAP's rulings are technically not binding, the majority of advertisers will adjust their advertisements to comply with a CAP ruling.

Advertising Standards Authority or ASA

13

In 2014, the well-known hotel website Booking.com was reprimanded by the CAP. They mentioned things such as 'Only 1 room left' but did not make it clear whether or not this only referred to those rooms that could be booked on Booking.com. Booking.com then modified its website and now clearly states that it means the number of rooms that are still available on Booking.com itself: '1 room left on our website!'.

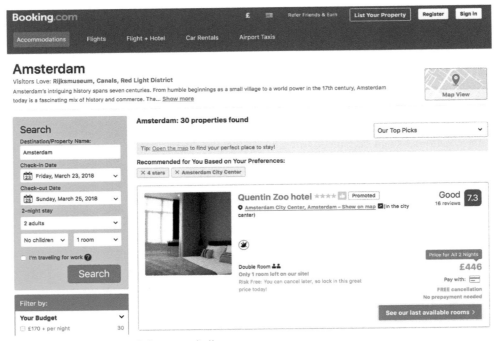

Booking.com 'Only 1 room left on our site!'

IAB

IAB

The Interactive Advertising Bureau (IAB) is an organisation that deals with the professionalisation of the digital advertising industry. They too try to promote the interests of digital advertisers by, among other things, influencing legislation. The IAB Europe has initiated the self-regulation code 'Youronlinechoices.eu' in response to the intention to introduce stringent cookie legislation in Europe.

© Noordhoff Uitgevers bv

Questions and assignments

© Noordhoff Uitgevers bv

NOW CHECK YOUR UNDERSTANDING:

13.1   For some years now, research has shown that marketers find structuring their own organisation to be one of their biggest challenges. Imagine being appointed as Digital Marketing Manager for a retail chain that, so far, has mainly sold products via physical stores. You will be asked for advice on how to embed digital marketing in the organisation.

   a What ways exist for a company to embed digital marketing in their organisation?
   b What is of importance to the decision to take on one of these organisational forms?
   c Many marketers consider the collaboration with the IT department to be a major stumbling block. For which organisational form do you expect the least problems?

13.2   In this chapter you have become acquainted with 30 digital marketing roles (figure 13.2). Just as in question 13.1, you were appointed as a Digital Marketing Manager at the same retail chain.

   a What type of projects do you think you will be managing? Put together a team for each project and include people with different roles.
   b If you have to create teams using a functional set-up based on competences (discipline), which roles will be joined together in a team?
   c Which roles are joined together in teams if you organise them on the basis of customer life cycle?

13.3   In this chapter, a distinction is made between the digital marketing strategy and action plans.

   a Indicate how a digital marketing strategy is created.
   b Why are the digital marketing strategy and action plans not one whole?
   c Name a few examples of things that will be included in an action plan but not in the digital marketing strategy.

13.4   In this chapter, three different project management methods have been discussed.

   a Explain the basic principles of project management and why these basic principles are important for the success of your digital marketing projects.
   b Identify the most important differences and similarities between the waterfall method, the iterative method and the PRINCE2 method for project management.

13

    c Think of a department store, eg Harrods or Selfridges. Which method do you think a large department store can best use to set up a campaign to promote its annual sale?

    d Which method is most suitable for improving their online customer service?

13.5 Imagine you are a digital marketer for an online retailer selling expensive audio equipment. You want to conduct a promotional campaign, in which people are offered the chance to win back the total amount of their purchase. To qualify, they must make the purchase, sign up, leave their personal details and give permission for sending a newsletter.

    a How can you best ask the participants for permission to send the newsletter? And what should you mention in the privacy statement?

    b Name a few attractive promotional offers that are permitted by legislation pertaining to games of chance, and at least one that is only allowed as a (promotional) game of chance.

13.6

CASE

Online food delivery service Deliveroo
By Mike Berry

Deliveroo (www.deliveroo.co.uk) started out in London back in 2013. It has rapidly grown into one of the UK's leading 'high-end' food delivery services and is beginning to expand internationally.

However, at the time of this case, awareness and market share were still fairly low and there was a significant opportunity to grow their presence, especially in key target Northern UK cities including Manchester, Leeds and Liverpool.

To build the Deliveroo brand and win new customers outside of London, Deliveroo planned a creative campaign to build their profile in Leeds, Manchester and Liverpool focusing on their local Twitter accounts, aiming to massively enhance their profile, social engagement (with both customers and restaurants) and ultimately drive an uplift in sales whilst always sticking to the national (UK) brand values of Deliveroo.

> *'Deliveroo began working on campaigns focused on raising the social media profile on Twitter, driving greater engagement and delivering an uplift in sales in key cities across North West England. The results have exceeded the expectations.'*
> - Charlotte Bailey, Commercial Manager, Deliveroo North West

To achieve Deliveroo's challenging business objectives, Deliveroo developed a strategy combining targeted paid advertising (in order to reach new audiences) with real-time social media management and specific contributions to conversations (to actively engage audiences and restaurants) focusing on Deliveroo's Manchester, Liverpool and Leeds Twitter accounts.

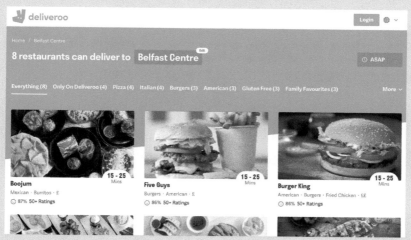

Deliveroo's homepage

Overall the goal was to improve brand awareness and crucially drive trial and repeat purchase; it was not enough to persuade consumers to participate in promotions. Indeed, Deliveroo was committed to building a base of loyal customers who would effectively act as unpaid salespeople, influencing friends and family.

Deliveroo combined engaging copy, brand-orientated creative and micro-targeting to ensure that the new visitors Deliveroo generated weren't just freebie hunters. Instead they sought to attract people who would regularly order in the future. The results of the campaign were extremely positive:

- 542% increase in average engagement across all accounts
- 1993% growth in Twitter follower growth rate on Leeds account
- 349% uplift in Twitter follower growth rate on Manchester account
- 244% growth in Twitter follower growth rate on Liverpool account
- 1075% increase in click rate on Leeds Twitter account
- 1333% uplift in average retweet rate on Manchester Twitter account

Deliveroo judged this to be their most successful social media campaign ever these results over a short time frame and with a very limited budget.

Although the activity focused on Twitter initially, it was expanded into other social channels and generated a significant increase in: engagement, shares and click through rates across all Social Media accounts. Engagement increased by almost 2000% in some areas, with clicks growing (on average across all three of the cities) by over 500%.

Deliveroo measured both follower interaction and follower growth trends during and following the activity to gauge brand awareness and engagement growth.

Overall, the campaign beat all its targets with ease; note these targets were all about long-term sales growth rather than short-term promotional volume.

13

Deliveroo ✔ @Deliveroo · Mar 13

Londoners, who said there was no such thing as a free lunch?! We'll be at the Old Truman Brewery (Brick Lane) today from 12pm until 7pm (or until stocks last) giving away burgers from our burger billboard 🍔👋 #EatMoreAmazing

💬 3   🔁 27   ♡ 58   ✉

No such thing as free lunch? Deliveroo begs to differ on Twitter

Most importantly, Deliveroo reported an uplift in sales across all three regions during the period of the campaign, in fact Deliveroo's marketing team presented the activity to their Board as a benchmark for all future social media campaigns.

The company has since centralised their Social Media profiles, to ensure this level of quality and service can be maintained and built upon in the future. Nationally, Deliveroo followed up this regional activity by tapping into the changing preferences that are part of the unpredictable British summer weather, with a campaign involving ultra-specific targeted audio ads, again supported by carefully-crafted Social Media activity through all its channels.

'Our new summer campaign has been developed to provide bespoke interactions between the public and Deliveroo, so our customers always receive the right message at the right time, in the right place.'

-Dan Warne, Managing Director, Deliveroo UK

As an example of how radio is evolving in the digital age, Deliveroo's audio campaign ran on Spotify and Digital Audio Exchange (DAX), with the potential to serve 46,000 different creative combinations, with specific content of the ads determined by location, time of day, weather, day of the week and local restaurant supply potential.

Delivery also-ran dynamic out-of-home (Billboard) ads, referencing relevant calendar events such as the Wimbledon tennis championships, festivals and TV show launches.

Source: After Digital, 2018

© Noordhoff Uitgevers bv

NOW CHECK YOUR UNDERSTANDING:

a Describe how you would organise digital marketing/social media activities within Deliveroo

b What are the core competences that Deliveroo needs for digital marketing/social media? What kind of teams would you put together?

c What elements should Deliveroo's digital marketing plan have? Consider the different target segments, such as end consumers in different regions of the UK and partners (= restaurants = meal suppliers).

d Which of the three project management methods is most suitable for furthering Deliveroo's development? Support your answer.

e If, in the future, Deliveroo decides to enter the French and German markets, what legislation regarding privacy, promotional campaigns, general terms and conditions and ecommerce would Deliveroo need to consider?

13

References

Abell, D. (1980). *Defining the business: The starting point of strategic planning.* Englewood Cliffs: Prentice Hall.

Adobo Magazine (2017, June 21). *Cannes Lions 2017: Cyber Lions winners announced, RBK Communications, Clemenger BBDO, Melbourne, Droga5 win Grand Prix Awards.* http://adobomagazine.com/global-news/cannes-lions-2017-cyber-lions-winners-announced-rbk-communication-clemenger-bbdo

After Digital (2018). *Deliveroo – Social media marketing.* http://afterdigital.co.uk/work/deliveroo-social-media-marketing IAB Europe (2017). *IAB Europe study: AdEx Benchmark 2016 preliminary results.* https://www.iabeurope.eu/research-thought-leadership/programmatic/adex-benchmark-2016-study

Amos, C., Holmes, G. & Keneson, W. (2014). A meta-analysis of consumer impulse buying. *Journal of Retailing and Consumer Services*, Vol. 21, Issue 2, pp. 86–97.

Anderson, R.E. & Srinivasan, S.C. (2003). E-Satisfaction and E-Loyalty: A Contingency Framework. *Psychology and Marketing,* 20 (2), pp. 123–38. www.booz.com/global/home/what_we_think/reports_and_white_papers/ic-display/49009342, opgeroepen op 16 augustus 2011.

Atkinson, G., Driesener, C. & Corkindale, D. (2014). Search Engine Advertisement Design Effects on Click-Through Rates. *Journal of Interactive Advertising*, 14(1), pp. 24–30.

Batra, R. & Keller, K. (2016). Integrating Marketing Communications: New Findings, New Lessons, and New Ideas. *Journal Of Marketing*, 80(6): pp. 122–145.Business Source Premier, Ipswich, MA.

Baye, M.R., De los Santos, B. & Wildenbeest, M.R. (2016). Search Engine Optimization: What Drives Organic Traffic to Retail Sites? *Journal of Economics & Management Strategy*, 25(1), pp. 6–31.

BBC Bitsize (2017). *Shopping online.* http://www.bbc.co.uk/schools/gcsebitesize/ict/implications/1lifestylerev5.shtml

Belleflamme, P., Lambert, T. & Schwienbacher, A. (2014). Crowdfunding: Tapping the right crowd. *Journal of Business Venturing*, 29 (5), pp. 585–609.

Booking.com (2017). *What's the Genius Program?* https://partnersupport.booking.com/hc/en-us/articles/207223309-What-s-the-Genius-Program

BrightLocal (2016). *Local Consumer Review Survey 2016 | The Impact Of Online Reviews.* https://www.brightlocal.com/learn/local-consumer-review-survey/#13

Bullas, J. (2014). *4 simple steps to content marketing success.* http://www.jeffbullas.com/2014/07/01/4-simple-steps-to-content-marketing-success

Campaign Monitor (2015, August 20). *How SXSW Used Email Segmentation to Increase Subscribers by 140%.* https://www.campaignmonitor.com/blog/customers/2015/08/how-sxsw-uses-email-segmentation

Campaignlive.co.uk (2017). *How easyJet transformed customer data into emotional anniversary stories.* https://www.campaignlive.co.uk/article/easyjet-transformed-customer-data-emotional-anniversary-stories/1414488

Chaffey, D. (2015). *Digital business and E-commerce management* (6th ed.). Harlow: Pearson.

Chaffey, D. & Smith, P.R. (2017). *Digital Marketing Excellence: Planning, Optimizing and Integrating Online Marketing.* Routledge.

© Noordhoff Uitgevers bv

Charlton, G. (2017). *Ecommerce consumer reviews: why you need them and how to use them*. https://econsultancy.com/blog/9366-ecommerce-consumer-reviews-why-you-need-them-and-how-to-use-them/

Christensen, C. (2016). *Competing Against Luck. The Story of Innovation and Customer Choice*. New York: HarperCollins Publishers Inc.

Cialdini, R.B. (2016). *Invloed. De zes geheimen van overtuigen*. Amsterdam: Uitgeverij Boom.

Cooper, R.G. New Products, What separates the winners from the losers and what drives success. In: Kahn, K.B. (2005). *The PDMA Handbook of New Product Development*, pp. 3–28. Hoboken: Wiley.

Dainton, M. & Zelley, E.D. (2005). *Applying Communication Theory for Professional Life, A Practical Introduction*. Thousand Oaks: Sage Publications.

Dalli, M.G. & Galvagno, M. (2014). Theory of value co-creation: a systematic literature review. *Managing Service Quality*, 10/2014, pp. 643–683.

DDMA (2013). *Meer met minder in je e-mails*. https://ddma.nl/emailblog/meer-met-minder

DDMA (2016). *DDMA Nationale E-mail Benchmark 2016*. https://ddma.nl/actueel/ddma-nationale-e-mail-benchmark-2016-dynamische-content-personalisatie-en-segmentatie-zorgen-voor-meest-succesvolle-mails/

DeliveryMatch (2016). *Wat wil uw klant als het gaat om verzending*. http://www.deliverymatch.nl/wp-content/uploads/2016/01/Wat-wil-uw-klant-als-het-gaat-om-verzending_-Een-onderzoek-door-DeliveryMatch.pdf

Delft, F. van & perre, m. van de (2015). *Customer Insight Management, Maximising Customer Value & Customer Experience*. Amsterdam/Antwerpen.

Deloitte (2017). *Digital marketing stijgt met 20% in de marketingmix*. Retrieved July 2, 2017, from https://www2.deloitte.com/nl/nl/pages/over-deloitte/articles/digital-marketing-stijgt-met-20-percent-in-de-marketingmix.html

Dev, C.S. & Schultz, D.E. (2005). In the Mix: A Customer-Focused Approach Can Bring the Current Marketing Mix into the 21th Century. *Marketing Management*, 14 (1), pp. 18–24.

Drucker, P. (1973). *Management: Tasks, Responsibilities, Practices*. Collins Business Essentials.

De Vries jr. & Dekker (2011). *Strategie voor dienstverleners*, Groningen: Noordhoff Uitgevers.

Engel, J.F., Blackwell, R.D. & Miniard, P.W. (1990). *Consumer Behavior*. Chicago: Dryden Press.

Expandedramblings.com (2017, November 12). *85 Interesting Email Statistics and Facts (2017) | By the Numbers*. https://expandedramblings.com/index.php/email-statistics/

Figarodigital.co.uk (2017, July 14). *Global Retailer Figleaves Chooses Adestra As Marketing Technology Provider To Make Campaigns More Customer-Centric*. https://www.figarodigital.co.uk/press-release/global-retailer-figleaves-chooses-adestra-marketing-technology-provider-make-campaigns-customer-centric

Floor, J., Raaij, W. van & Bouwman, M. (2015). *Marketingcommunicatiestrategie: reclame, public relations en voorlichting, sponsoring, promoties, direct marketing en dialoogmarketing, winkelcommunicatie, persoonlijke verkoop, evenementen, geïntegreerde communicatie*. Groningen: Noordhoff Uitgevers.

Forrester (2012). http://www.techjournal.org/2012/05/a-picture-is-worth-1000-words-an-online-video-is-worth-1-8-million

Forsythe, S. & Shi, B. (2003). Consumer patronage and risk perceptions in Internet shopping. *Journal of Business Research*, 56 (2003), pp. 867–875.

Frambach, R. & Nijssen, E. (2017). *Marketingstrategie*. Groningen: Noordhoff Uitgevers.

Frank.news (2017). *Carlijn Postma: waarde van merk zit in publiek*. http://www.frank.news/2017/04/05/carlijn-postma-waarde-van-merk-zit-in-publiek

Franzen, G. & Goessens, C. (1998). *Merken en Reclame*. Amsterdam: Kluwer.

Gensler, S., Neslin, S.A. & Verhoef, P.C. (2017). The Showrooming Phenomenon: It's More than Just About Price. *Journal Of Interactive Marketing*, nr. 38, pp. 29–43. doi:10.1016/j.intmar.2017.01.003

Hamel, S. (2014). *Online Analytics Maturity Model.* https://www.frankwatching.com/archive/2014/10/02/model-voor-volwassen-webanalytics-zo-houd-je-je-data-behapbaar

Harvard Business School (2000). *HBS Toolkit – Lifetime Customer Value Calculator.* http://hbswk.hbs.edu/archive/1436.html

Hasan, L. & Abuelrub, E. (2011). Assessing the quality of web sites. *Applied Computing and Informatics*, 9, Issue 1, pp. 11–29.

Hauser, J.R., Urban, G.L. & Weinberg, B.D. (1993). How consumers allocate their time when searching for information. *Journal of Marketing Research*, pp. 452–466.

Heitz-Spahn, S. (2013). Cross-channel free-riding consumer behavior in a multichannel environment: An investigation of shopping motives, sociodemographics and product categories. *Journal of Retailing and Consumer Services*, Volume 20, Issue 6, pp. 570–578.

Hippel, E. von (1986). Lead Users: A Source of Novel Product Concepts. *Management Science 32*, no. 7, pp. 791–805.

Houtgraaf, D. & Bekkers, M. (2013). *Businessmodellen.* Culemborg: Van Duuren Media.

Howe, J. (2006, juni 14). The Rise of Crowdsourcing. *Wired Magazine*, 14(6), pp. 1–4.

Hufen, B. (2015). Virals, video's en games. In M. Visser & B. Sikkenga, *Basisboek Online Marketing* (pp. 221–228). Groningen: Noordhoff Uitgevers.

Hulsebos, L. (2009). *Afstudeeronderzoek.* Amsterdam: Universiteit van Amsterdam.

Hussain, A. & Kutar, M. (2009). *Usability metric framework for mobile phone application.* ISBN, 978-1. Liverpool: PGNet.

Jansen, M., Klaassen, A. & Visser, M. (2015). Chapter 12 in Visser, M. & Sikkenga, B. (2015). *Basisboek Online Marketing.* Groningen: Noordhoff Uitgevers.

Jerath, K., Ma, L. & Park, Y. H. (2014). *Consumer click behavior at a search engine: The role of keyword popularity.* Journal of Marketing Research, 51(4), 480-486.

John, L.K., Emrich, O., Gupta, S. & Norton, M.I. (2017). Does 'Liking' Lead to Loving? The Impact of Joining a Brand's Social Network on Marketing Outcomes. *Journal Of Marketing Research (JMR)*, 54(1), pp. 144–155. doi:10.1509/jmr.14.0237

Jongsma, S. (2013). *Een weekje SEO: van Interflora tot Google Plus.* http://www.marketingfacts.nl/berichten/een-weekje-seo-van-interflora-tot-google-plus

Jungle Minds (2015). Presentatie gebaseerd op Smits, G.J. & Steins Bisschop, J. (2014). *De online scorecard 3.0. Meet en verbeter je online resultaten.* Amsterdam: Pearson Benelux B.V.

Kaushik, A. (2007). *Rethink Web Analytics: Introducing Web Analytics 2.0.* https://www.kaushik.net/avinash/rethink-web-analytics-introducing-web-analytics-20

Kaushik, A. (2011). *Best Social Media Metrics.* http://www.kaushik.net/avinash/best-social-media-metrics-conversation-amplification-applause-economic-value

Khalid, H., Shihab, E., Nagappan, M. & Hassan, A.E. (2015). What do mobile app users complain about? *IEEE Software*, 32(3), pp. 70–77.

Keller, K.L. (2013). *Strategic brand management: Building, measuring, and managing brand equity.* Upper Saddle River, NJ: Pearson/Prentice Hall.

Ketelaar, P.E., Janssen, L., Vergeer, M., Reijmersdal, E.A. van, Crutzen, R. & 't Riet, J. van (2016). The success of viral ads: Social and attitudinal predictors of consumer pass-on behavior on social network sites. *Journal of Business Research*, 69(7), pp. 2603–2613.

Kleiner Perkins (2017), *Internet Trends 2017.* http://www.kpcb.com/internet-trends

Koelewijn, R. (2017). *Zo ziet reclame er in 2017 dus uit.* https://www.nrc.nl/nieuws/2017/02/10/het-is-ook-reclame-6630113-a1545305

Kooiker et al. (2011). *Marktonderzoek.* Groningen: Noordhoff Uitgevers.

Kotler, P. & Keller, K.L., (2014). *Marketing Management.* Upper Saddle River: Prentice Hall.

Kotler, P., & Armstrong, G. (2013). *Principles of Marketing* (16th Global Edition). Essex: Pearson Education.

Krafft, M., Arden, C.M. & Verhoef, P.C. (2017). Permission Marketing and Privacy Concerns – Why Do Customers (Not) Grant Permissions? *Journal of Interactive Marketing*, 39, pp. 39–54.

© Noordhoff Uitgevers bv

Kremer, K. (2012). Section 12.4 in Visser, M. & Sikkenga, B. (2012). *Basisboek Online Marketing*. Groningen: Noordhoff Uitgevers.

Kukar-Kinney, M. & Close, A. (2010). The determinants of consumers' online shopping cart abandonment. *Journal of the Academy of Marketing Science*, 38 (2), pp. 240-250.

Lauterborn, R. (1990, 1 oktober). New Marketing Litany: 4P's Passe; C words take over. *Advertising Age*, 26.

Leeuwen, G.S.M. (2012). Chapter 10 in Visser, M. & Sikkenga, B. (2012). *Basisboek Online Marketing*. Groningen: Noordhoff Uitgevers.

Leeuwen, G.S.M. (2015). *CRM in de praktijk – Het succesvol invoeren van een klantgerichte bedrijfsstrategie*. The Hague: Academic Service.

Leeuwen, G.S.M. (2012). *Customer in the driver's seat – Klantgedreven innovatie met cocreatie, crowdsourcing en communities*. Culemborg: Van Duuren Management.

Lim, W.M. (2015). Antecedents and consequences of e-shopping: an integrated model. *Internet Research*, Vol. 25 Issue: 2, pp.184–217

Looy, A. van (2015). *Social Media Management. Technologies and Strategies for Creating Business Value*. Basel: Springer International Publishing Ag.

Malthouse, E.C., Haenlein, M., Skiera, B., Wege, E. & Zhang, M. (2013). Managing Customer Relationships in the Social Media Era: Introducing the Social CRM House. *Journal of Interactive Marketing*, Volume 27, Issue 4, November 2013, pp. 270–280.

Marco Derksen/Upstream (2011). Bewerkt door DVJ Insights. Figure 1.3: The development of marketing, brands and media.

Marvin, G. (2017). *5 key e-commerce & retail trends from Mary Meeker's Internet Trends report*. https://marketingland.com/5-key-ecommerce-retail-trends-mary-meekers-internet-trends-report-216447

McQuail, D. (1987). *Mass communication theory*. Londen: Sage Publications.

Meeker, M. (2017). *Internet Trends 2017-code conference*. Glokalde.

Medium.com/mailchimp (2017, August 22). *Customer Retention Through Automation: A Case Study – Issue 53*. https://medium.com/mailchimp-for-agencies/customer-retention-through-automation-a-case-study-8cf797769c6c

Merks-Benjaminsen, J. (2015). *Online brand identity*. Amsterdam: Adfo Books.

Minnema, Bijmolt en Gensler (2017) in: A.E. Bronner et al. (red.), *Ontwikkelingen in het marktonderzoek: Jaarboek MarktOnderzoekAssociatie*, dl. 42, 2017. Haarlem: Spaar en Hout.

Mittal, B. & Lee, M.S. (1989). A causal model of consumer involvement. *Journal of economic psychology*, 10(3), pp. 363–389.

Moth, D. (2013, October 23). *B2B social: five case studies from brands achieving great results*. https://econsultancy.com/blog/63646-b2b-social-five-case-studies-from-brands-achieving-great-results

Moz (2016). *How Voice Search Will Change Digital Marketing – For the Better*. https://moz.com/blog/how-voice-search-will-change-digital-marketing-for-the-better

Muntinga, D.G., Moorman, M. & Smit, E.G. (2011). Introducing COBRAs: Exploring motivations for Brand-Related social media use. *International Journal of Advertising*, 30(1), pp. 13–46.

Mycustomer.com (2017, March 15). *Customer journeymapping vs process design: Do you know the difference?* https://www.mycustomer.com/experience/engagement/customer-journey-mapping-vs-process-design-do-you-know-the-difference

Nicolay, A. & Arun, S. (2009). *Optimal Design of Crowdsourcing Contests. Proceedings International Conference on Information Systems*. http://aisel.aisnet.org/icis2009/200. New York: New York University.

Nielsen (2015). *Global Trust in Advertising. Winning strategies for an evolving media landscape. September 2015*. https://www.nielsen.com/content/dam/nielsenglobal/apac/docs/reports/2015/nielsen-global-trust-in-advertising-report-september-2015.pdf

Nu.nl (2017, June 8). *Al Jazeera slachtoffer van cyberaanval*. http://www.nu.nl/internet/4754745/al-jazeera-slachtoffer-van-cyberaanval.html

© Noordhoff Uitgevers bv

Oosterveer, D. (2017). Digital Analytics. In M. Visser and B. Sikkenga (Eds.), Basisboek Online Marketing (pages of chapter). Groningen: Noordhoff.

Osterwalder, A. & Pigneur, Y. (2009). *Business Model Generation.* Retrieved January 15, 2015, from http://www.businessmodelgeneration.com/downloads/businessmodelgeneration_preview.pdf

Otto, R. (2015). Chapter 10 in Visser, M. & Sikkenga, B. (2015). *Basisboek Online Marketing.* Groningen: Noordhoff Uitgevers.

Payne, J.W., Bettman, J.R. & Johnson, E.J. (1993). *The Adaptive Decision Maker.* Cambridge, UK: Cambridge University Press.

Pauwels, K., Demirci, C., Yildirim, G. & Srinivasan, S. (2017). The impact of brand familiarity on online and offline media synergy. *International Journal of Research in Marketing,* 33(4), pp. 739–753.

Peppers, D. & Rogers, M. (1993). *The One to One Future – Building relationships one customer at a time.* New York: Currency Doubleday.

Pousttchi, K., Selk, B. & Turowski, K. (2002). *Enabling mobile commerce through mass customization.* Retrieved January 8, 2015, from Munchen Universitat: mpra.ub.uni-muenchen.de

Prahalad, C. & Ramaswamy, V. (2004). *The Future of Competition.* Boston: Harvard Business School Publishing.

Purnawirawan, N., De Pelsmacker, P. & Dens, N. (2012). Balance and Sequence in Online Reviews: How Perceived Usefulness Affects Attitudes and Intentions. *Journal of Interactive Marketing,* Vol. 26, No. 4, pp. 244–255.

Reichheld, F. (2011). *The Ultimate Question 2.0.* Boston: Harvard Business School Press.

Rigby, D.K. (2014). Digital-physical mashups. *Harvard Business Review,* 92(9), p. 84.

Roberts, D., Hughes, M. & Kertbo, K. (2014). Exploring consumers' motivation to engage in innovation through co-creation activities. *European Journal of Marketing,* 48(1/2), pp. 147–169.

Salesforce Blog (2016). *User-Generated Content is Transforming B2C Marketing - Are You Ready?* https://www.salesforce.com/blog/2016/02/user-generated-content.html

Sauro, J. (2016). Measuring the Quality of the Website User Experience (Doctoral dissertation, University of Denver).

Searchengineland (2015). *It's Official: Google Says More Searches Now On Mobile Than On Desktop.* http://searchengineland.com/its-official-google-says-more-searches-now-on-mobile-than-on-desktop-220369

Searchengineland (2016). *Google says 20 percent of mobile queries are voice searches.* Retrieved July 4, 2017, from http://searchengineland.com/google-reveals-20-percent-queries-voice-queries-249917

Sharp, B. (2010). *How brands grow: What marketers don't know.* South Melbourne, Vic: Oxford University Press.

Sicilia, M. & Ruiz, S. (2007). The role of flow in web site effectiveness. *Journal of Interactive Advertising,* 8 (1), pp. 33–44.

SmartInsights.com (2017). *Search Engine Statistics 2017.* http://www.smartinsights.com/search-engine-marketing/search-engine-statistics

Socialfabriek (2017). *Activatie campagnes door Socialfabriek.* http://www.socialfabriek.nl/activatie-campagnes-door-socialfabriek

Solis, B. (2013). *The Ultimate Moment Of Truth And The Art Of Digital Engagement.* Briansolis.com: http://www.briansolis.com/2013/11/the-ultimate-moment-of-truth-and-the-art-of-engagement/

Srinivasan, S., Anderson, R. & Ponnavolu, K. (2002). Customer loyalty in e-commerce: an exploration of its antecedents and consequences. *Journal of retailing,* Volume 78, Number 1, Spring 2002, pp. 41–50.

Statcounter (2018). *Search Engine Market Share Worldwide 2017.* http://gs.statcounter.com/search-engine-market-share

Statista (2017). *Number of connected things/devices worldwide by vertical from 2015 to 2021.* https://www.statista.com/statistics/626256/connected-things-devices-worldwide-by-vertical

Statista (2018). *Number of monthly active Facebook users worldwide as of 4*th *quarter 2017 (in millions).* https://www.statista.com/statistics/264810/number-of-monthly-active-facebook-users-worldwide

Steins Bisschop, J., Smits, G. & Reijsen, M. van (2014). *De Online Scorecard 3.0.* Amsterdam: Pearson Education.

Stefan Maatman (2012, februari). Retrieved Januaru 15, 2015, from stefanmaatman.files.wordpress.com: http://stefanmaatman.files.wordpress.com/2012/02/business-model-generation.png

Ström, R., Vendel, M. & Bredican, J. (2014). Mobile marketing: A literature review on its value for consumers and retailers. *Journal of Retailing and Consumer Services*, pp. 1001–1012.

Surowiecki, J., & Silverman, M. P. (2004). The wisdom of crowds. *American Journal of Physics*, *75*(2), 190-192.

Tamaki, J. (2005). You be the judge; more consumers are going online to hunt for products and find good deals. *Los Angeles Times*, December 3, p. 6.

Teerling, M.L. (2007). *Determining the cross-channel effects of informational websites.* Groningen: Rijksuniversiteit Groningen.

Teo, S.T. & Yeong, D.Y. (2003). Assessing the consumer decision process in the digital marketplace, *Omega*, 31, pp. 349–363.

Toonders, J. (2017). *Online marketing: een terugblik & de trends voor 2017.* https://www.frankwatching.com/archive/2017/01/12/online-marketing-een-terugblik-de-trends-voor-2017

Trainor, K.J., Andzulis, J.M., Rapp, A. & Agnihotri, R. (2014). Social media technology usage and customer relationship performance: A capabilities-based examination of social CRM. *Journal of Business Research*, 67(6), pp. 1201–1208.

Trusov, M., Bucklin, R.E. & Pauwels, K. (2009). Effects of Word-of-Mouth Versus Traditional Marketing. *Journal of Marketing*, 73(5), pp. 90–102.

Tucker, C.E. (2014). The reach and persuasiveness of viral video ads. *Marketing Science*, 34(2), pp. 281–296.

Twinkle Magazine (2016). *Google Shopping: dit is pas het begin (deel 1).* http://twinklemagazine.nl/2016/07/google-shopping-dit-is-pas-het-begin-(deel-1)/index.xml

Ulwick, A. (2005). *What Customers Want: Using Outcome-Driven Innovation to Create Breakthrough Products and Services.* Columbus: McGraw-Hill.

University of Cambridge Judge Business School (2017). *Global Cryptocurrency Benchmarking Study.* Opgehaald op 21 juni 2017 van https://www.jbs.cam.ac.uk/faculty-research/centres/alternative-finance/publications/global-cryptocurrency/#.WUowA2iGOUk

UPS (2016). *Pulse of the Online Shopper. Executive summary.* https://pressroom.ups.com/assets/pdf/2016_UPS_Pulse%20of%20the%20Online%20Shopper_executive%20summary_final.pdf

UPS (2016). *Pulse of the Online Shopper. Tech-savvy shoppers transforming retail.* https://pressroom.ups.com/assets/pdf/pressroom/white%20paper/2016_UPS_Pulse%20of%20the%20Online%20Shopper_white%20paper%20final.pdf

Van Bel, E.J. & Sander, E. (2006). *Event-Driven Marketing.* Kluwer: Deventer.

Verhoef, P., Kooge, E., Walk, N. (2016). *Creating Value with Big Data Analyisis, making smarter marketing decisions.* Routledge.

Visser, M. & Sikkenga, B. (2015). *Basisboek Online Marketing.* Groningen: Noordhoff Uitgevers.

Visser, M. & Sikkenga, B. (2017). *Social Media Management vanuit een commercieel perspectief.* Groningen: Noordhoff Uitgevers.

Vlems, E. (2015). *Scoren met Content Marketing.* Amsterdam: Entopic.

Voorveld, H.A., Neijens, P.C. & Smit, E.G. (2009). Consumers' responses to brand websites: an interdisciplinary review. *Internet Research*, 19, Issue 5, pp. 535–565.

Vroomen, B. (2006). *The Effects of the Internet, Recommendation Quality and Decision Strategies on Consumer Choice.* Rotterdam: Rotterdam School of Management (RSM) Erasmus University, Erasmus Research Institute of Management (ERIM).

Vucovic, M. & Bartolini, C. (2010). Towards a Research Agenda for Enterprise Crowdsourcing. In: Tiziana, M. & Steffen, B. *Leveraging Applications of Formal Methods, Verification and Validation*, Part 1, pp. 425–34. Berlin Heidelberg: Springer Verlag.

Wang, H.C., Pallister, J. & Foxall, G. (2006). Innovativeness and involvement as determinants of website loyalty. *Technovation*, 12/2006, pp. 1357-1373.

Wang, X., Yu, C. & Wei, Y. (2012). Social Media Peer Communication and Impacts on Purchase Intentions: A Consumer Socialization Framework. *Journal of Interactive Marketing*, Issue 26, pp. 198–208.

Ward, E. (2008). *Reply to Link Building Best Practices Question: How do I determine good link targets?* http://www.ericward.com/bestpractices/2008/09/reply-to-link-building-bestpractices.html

We Are Social (2018, January 30). *Digital in 2018: World's internet users pass the 4 billion mark.* https://wearesocial.com/blog/2018/01/global-digital-report-2018

Whiting, A. & Williams, D. (2013). Why people use social media: a uses and gratifications approach. *Qualitative Market Research: An International Journal*, Vol. 16, Iss 4, pp. 362–369.

Wikipedia (2011), *Amazon.com.* Retrieved June 19, 2017, from http://en.wikipedia.org/wiki/Amazon.com

Wikipedia (2011). *Definition Onsite Behavioral targeting.* Retrieved June 19, 2017, from http://nl.wikipedia.org/wiki/Behavioral_targeting#Onsite-targeting

Wikipedia (2017). *Definition Affiliate marketing.* Retrieved June 17, 2017, from https://en.wikipedia.org/wiki/Affiliate_marketing

Yonego (2014). *Yonego Affiliate Onderzoek 2014.* http://www.yonego.nl/images/Resultaten_Affiliate_Enquete_Maart2014.pdf

Yoo, C.Y. (2014). Branding potentials of keyword search ads: The effects of ad rankings on brand recognition and evaluations. *Journal of Advertising*, 43(1), pp. 85–99.

Zain (2016). *Why A Backlink Exchange Program Is Bad For Your Website.* https://www.shoutmeloud.com/why-link-exchange-program-is-bad-for-your-blogs-health.html

Zenetti, G., Bijmolt, T.H.A., Leeflang, P.S.H. & Klapper, D. (2014). *Search Engine Advertising Effectiveness in a Multimedia Campaign.* International journal of electronic commerce.

Ziegele, M. & Weber, M. (2015). Example, please! Comparing the effects of single customer reviews and aggregate review scores on online shoppers' product evaluations. *Journal Of Consumer Behaviour*, 14(2), pp. 103–114.

Websites

http://computer.financialexpress.com/news/marriott-expands-mobile-check-in-and-checkout-services/2494/

http://customer-profile.com/apparel-and-fashion/athletic/athletic-apparel/patagonia-customer-profile.htm

http://epicprgroup.com/5-things-you-should-unlearn-about-marketing/

http://europe.autonews.com/article/20171124/ANE/171129861/bmw-expands-car-sharing-program-to-china

http://schema.org

http://mobileapp.marriott.com

http://nationalzoo.com.au/

https://asos.com

https://forumone.com/work/national-museum-african-american-history-and-culture

https://ico.org.uk

https://moz.com/researchtools/ose/

© Noordhoff Uitgevers bv

https://neilpatel.com
https://npsbenchmark.com/companies/ao-com
https://secure.booking.com/welcome_genius.en-gb.html
https://support.google.com/analytics/answer/1662518
https://support.google.com/webmasters/answer/66356?hl=en
www1.firstdirect.com/1/2/
www.alibaba.com
www.autoevolution.com
www.b2bmarketing.net/en-gb/resources/b2b-case-studies/awards-case-study-how-samsung-encouraged-smes-manchester-have-more-good
www.bbc.co.uk/privacy
www.cardinalpath.com
www.cheshnotes.com/2017/04/ikea-marketing-strategy-and-practices-a-case-study
www.clearlyinnovative.com/nmaahc-mobile-app
www.creamglobal.com/case-studies/latest/17798/35928/bonningtons-flu-tracker
www.demacmedia.com/wp-content/uploads/2014/07/top-header-image1.jpg
www.digitaltrainingacademy.com/casestudies/2017/11/ecommerce_case_study_under_armour_revamps_shopping_with_google_insights.php
www.drive-now.com
www.emarketer.com/corporate/clients/marriott
http://europe.autonews.com/article/20171124/ANE/171129861/bmw-expands-car-sharing-program-to-china
www.fedex.com/us/office
www.hm.com
www.just-eat.co.uk
www.iab.com/guidelines/mobile-rich-media-ad-interface-definitions-mraid/
www.iab.net/risingstars
www.ikea.com
www.investopedia.com/articles/personal-finance/070715/success-patagonias-marketing-strategy.asp#ixzz4n6OvoAly
www.majestic.com
www.marketingtribune.nl/design/nieuws/2017/05/[interview]-de-oermarketing-van-patagonia/index.xml
www.mckinsey.com/business-functions/digital-mckinsey/how-we-help-clients/digital-labs
www.moneywise.co.uk
www.npsbenchmark.com
www.opensiteexplorer.org
www.parisinfo.com
www.press.bmwgroup.com
www.pressroom.ups.com
www.referralcandy.com/blog/asos-marketing-strategy
www.ritzcarlton.com
www.starbucks.co.uk/card/rewards
www.sxsw.com
www.thinkwithgoogle.com.
www.wefashion.com
www.whizsky.com/2017/09/case-study-cleartrip-business-model-marketing-competition-indian-travel-sites-market
www.youronlinechoices.eu
www.youtube.com/channel/UCWRV5AVOIKJR1Flvgt310Cw
www.youtube.com/user/GoogleWebmasterHelp
www.zappos.com

Illustrations

© Noordhoff Uitgevers bv

Index

© Noordhoff Uitgevers bv

About the authors

Digital Marketing Fundamentals has been developed in collaboration with a large number of professionals, who have each provided insights into how to get the best returns from Digital Marketing, speaking from their own practical experience. Authors Marjolein Visser RM and Berend Sikkenga SMP have created a theoretical framework based on academic research and have supplemented the views of the co-authors with research results and their own vision. Mike Berry has added his insights in global digital marketing and turned the originally Dutch publication into a truly international book. Below you will find their biographies, followed by the list of original co-authors.

Marjolein Visser RM is an advisor and interim manager who helps to improve the marketing efficiency of service providing organisations and to develop innovative new business models. She is managing consultant of the consultancy firm MarketWise and founder of TourWise, who provide digital marketing solutions for tourism and recreation. In addition, she provides in-company training and is involved in various master's programmes and higher professional education programmes. Amongst other companies, Visser worked in (interim) marketing and executive positions for De Hypothekers Associatie, Achmea, Youri Group, Delta Lloyd, AEGON, SNS Bank, Randstad and various healthcare organisations, charities and other non-profit organisations. She has written six books and dozens of articles on various topics related to marketing. Ever since she took her first internet course in the Netherlands in 1994, she has been fascinated by the many possibilities that digitisation has to offer.

Berend Sikkenga SMP is a passionate digital manager with almost twenty years of experience from both an agency perspective and a corporate perspective. As head of ecommerce at LEGO, he is currently responsible for ecommerce and omnichannel in the Benelux. He also provides training and guest lectures and has been a contributing author in the Marketingfacts yearbook for several years. Sikkenga started his career at internet consultancy firm Red Hot Minute (formerly Booleanpark) and subsequently led marketing management, sales management and service management at Essent and Ziggo in a variety of roles.

Mike Berry FCIM, F IDM started his career at Procter & Gamble. He then went agency-side with roles at EHS Brann (Havas Helia), Wunderman (Y&R), Bozell/FCB (Senior VP) and Head of Digital for EMEA at Jack Morton (Interpublic). Today he's a Digital Marketing consultant, trainer and academic (Professor of Practice at Hult International Business School, Course Leader at Imperial College London and Visiting Lecturer at Cranfield University). He is the author/co-author of 4 books including The Best Of Global Digital

© Noordhoff Uitgevers bv

Marketing Storybook 1 and 2 (with Hando Sinisalu). Mike is a Fellow of the CIM (Course Director) and of the IDM (Course Tutor on PG and Professional Diplomas).

Co-authors

Guido van den Anker is web editor and final editor at Entopic. In this capacity he also provides training in web editing and writing for the Internet. His favourite topics are content marketing, social media and blogging. In addition, he is director sportif of www.italiaanseracefietsen. com. In a few years he has transformed this publication from a personal blog into the go-to website for enthusiasts. He trains on his Gios Torino weekly; the most beautiful blue bicycle in the world.

As an analytics & optimisation expert, **Tom van den Berg** is continuously working on the optimisation of digital environments for various companies. With a background as a web analyst (at T-Mobile and Rituals) he tries to bridge the gap between data and marketing. His aim is to stimulate companies in making their decisions based on data and to keep optimising continuously. Ultimately, this ensures that you get a better understanding of your customers and the visitors on your website. In addition to his work, Tom enjoys playing sports and he wants to see as much of the world as possible.

After his bachelor's degree in Marketing, **Ruben van Brug** continued to focus on the subject during his master's in Marketing Intelligence at the University of Groningen. His passion for online started during his degree and he has continued to develop this whilst working in various in-house marketing positions. At the agency Storm Digital, Ruben works as a consultant for the largest brands and companies. Here he was able to broaden his expertise for various digital marketing facets (e.g. SEO, SEA, affiliate, video and display).

Sandra Christiaansen works as an account director at Loyalty Lab. Loyalty Lab is a company specialised in designing, developing and implementing loyalty strategies for independent entrepreneurs (SME). Sandra's passion is monitoring and influencing consumer behaviour by studying data (customer files) and market developments and, in accordance with her findings, devising the most optimal marketing strategy for the entrepreneur. By using the right message, at the right time and via the right channel (online/offline), she is able to captivate, bind and enthuse existing but also potential customers in such a way that the entrepreneur will achieve better results.

Frank van Delft is an expert in data science and predictive marketing based on (big) data and its implementation in large (international) and medium-sized companies. His core competence is helping companies to effectively increase customer value and value for the customer, by combining data, analytics, customer insight and marketing activation into a structured process. Educated in quantitative business economics and higher informatics, he gained his working experience in marketing, data and communications. Since 2013 he is managing partner at CIM7, customer insight management.

Wout van den Dool has been working for Triodos Bank as manager online activities since 2010. He has been an online professional since 2004. Wout was, amongst other things, web shop manager for AEGON Bank and digital marketer at Spaarbeleg. He is currently responsible for the further development of the international internet strategy as well as the actual creation of it. Contact Wout on twitter.com/wout or via his blog www.lifestreamen.nl.

Arnoud Engelfriet is a lawyer specialised in ICT and partner at ICTRecht in Amsterdam. He specialises in internet law and has been doing so since 1993. His website is one of the most extensive sites about internet law, technology and intellectual property in the Netherlands. Since 2007 Arnoud blogs daily about internet law on blog.iusmentis.com.

Marcel Fokkema has been working on the cutting edge of customer service, technology and marketing for more than fifteen years. In the past five years he has done this as interim manager in the field of CRM, marketing and digital.

Martijn Hoving has a passion for search engines and the quick updates/major developments that are involved in search engine marketing today. As a freelance SEO consultant, he helps organisations to increase their exposure within search engines.

Lucas Hulsebos is co-owner of market research firm DVJ Insights. Lucas has over 20 years of experience in market research for branding and advertising research purposes. Lucas worked at GfK, Verify, Metrixlab and EffectiveBrands. He has extensive experience in conducting online research and the functioning of digital media. He is also involved in the Brand Boardroom, member of the Advisory Board of SWOCC as well as the marketing department of the University of Groningen and lecturer at EURIB. In 2008 and 2015, Lucas was chosen as researcher of the year by the MOA.

Matthijs Jansen has five years of experience in digital marketing and specialises mainly in search engine optimisation. As a former SEO consultant, he has specialised in setting up link building strategies in a variety of industries. At the moment he works on a daily basis at setting up the SEO strategy for the European websites of the sport brand Under Armor and optimising them.

Co van Kempen has over eight years of experience in digital marketing and specialises in SEO, link building and conversion optimisation in particular. In addition, he also has experience in analysing and setting up performance-driven marketing campaigns within various industries. Challenges in which owned media, earned media and paid media together form the ultimate consumer experience, are an everyday occurrence in his role as digital strategist at iProspect.dage

Shirley Klever's passion for online has seen her working in this field since the late nineties, at the interface between consumers and businesses. As a consultant with a European master's degree in Interactive Media, she works on projects both strategically and hands-on, for agencies as well as individual customers. Since 2010, she has helped companies in various sectors (DEMB, Rabobank, Essent, Achmea and T-Mobile) as a

© Noordhoff Uitgevers bv

self-employed expert under the name Interseccion, contributing fully towards the company's objectives. She also wrote about planning & organisation in *E-business* (2015).

Martin Kloos is head of strategy & consulting at Isobar Social Embassy. This is a digital creative agency with 'social DNA'. Kloos advises and guides brands in the field of digital and social media marketing, based on the vision that creativity and technical developments bring inspiration (branding) and transaction (performance) closer together. Before that, Kloos worked as a consultant at Deloitte. He is also an infrequent blogger at Marketingfacts.nl and a columnist at MarketingTribune.nl. He also made an important contribution towards *Social Media Management* (2017).

Bart van der Kooi is digital marketing strategist at digital marketing agency Storm Digital. He advises organisations on digital trends and developments and guides them on a strategic level. His interest in innovation and online developments form the basis of his daily (advisory) work. Van der Kooi is an avid blogger on various platforms and regularly provides training courses, for example at Frankwatching. He is also author of *The Social Media Model Book* (2014) and *Map the Customer Journey in 60 minutes (2017)* and he also made an important contribution towards *Social Media Management* (2017).

Dennis Koops has already started working in digital marketing during his education in Groningen and has been working at Storm Digital since 2013. There, he started working in display advertising and he has now looked to broaden his expertise within search and social advertising. He is also interested in the latest developments within these fields of work, such as the use of data within online advertising.

Ernst-Jan Kruize has been working in the field of customer contact and customer service since 1996. He has extensive experience in the field of customer contact centres as well as digital self-service concepts. Kruize worked for various trade associations, training institutes and consultancy firms. Currently he is working for the service providing organisation of the Municipality of Utrecht. He regularly speaks and publishes about the value and importance of customer service. Commissioned by the Customer Service Federation (KSF), Ernst-Jan runs a think tank that is developing a vision on customer service in 2027. He also made an important contribution towards *Social Media Management* (2017).

Wim van der Mark (Dialoogtrainers.nl) helps his customers to keep on top of the changes in the sales process of tailor-made training courses, presentations and advice. His training and presentations are practical and meant to achieve quick results. His first book *Improve your direct mail letters* reached a total amount of nine editions. Now, the third edition of *Convincing & Interactive Writing* has been published. In 2017, the fourth and completely renewed edition of his latest book *Marketing.com 4.0* (Noordhoff Uitgevers) was published.

Robin van Ommen had chosen the Marketing & Communication study program during her degree. Specialising in Customer Relationship Management, her interest in marketing had grown strongly, including in email marketing. That's why the decision to continue in marketing was very easily made. Robin works at Add to Favorites, the agency of choice for effective customer contact.

Patricia Ouwendijk has already had more than fifteen years of experience in the field of 'online payment & ecommerce' after her degree HEAO-CE. She has worked as operational manager, partner manager and eBusiness consultant at Triple Deal / Docdata Payments. At the moment she is responsible for the relationship management team as team leader and for the key accounts of Buckaroo, one of the leading payment service providers in the Netherlands.

Stephan Schroeders has been working in various management and consultancy positions within the online industry since the late nineties. Since 2015, Stephan has been working as Head of eCommerce at ABN AMRO Digital Banking. In this capacity he is part of the eCommerce management team and, together with his team, he focuses on ABN AMRO's strategic products: mortgages and loans.